Jane Stewart Smith

The Grange of Saint Giles

Jane Stewart Smith

The Grange of Saint Giles

ISBN/EAN: 9783337396046

Printed in Europe, USA, Canada, Australia, Japan

Cover: Foto ©Lupo / pixelio.de

More available books at **www.hansebooks.com**

THE
GRANGE OF ST. GILES
THE BASS : AND THE OTHER
BARONIAL HOMES OF THE
DICK-LAUDER FAMILY
WRITTEN AND ILLUSTRATED WITH
PEN, PENCIL, AND CAMERA, BY
MRS. J. STEWART SMITH

EDINBURGH
PRINTED FOR THE AUTHOR BY
T. AND A. CONSTABLE, PRINTERS TO HER MAJESTY
AND SOLD BY THOMSON BROTHERS
74 GEORGE STREET
1898

ERRATA

P. 18, line 14, for *Romish* read *Roman*.

P. 85, line 19, for *Brougham Hall* read *Brougham Castle*.

P. 88, line 16. The name of the little lady mentioned in the incident regarding Sir Walter Scott should have been *Miss Susan, the eldest* daughter of Sir Thomas Dick Lauder, and not *Miss Beatrice, the youngest*.

P. 135, foot of page. It was not the present Sir William Dick-Cunyngham, tenth Bart., that was appointed to the command of the 2nd Battalion Gordon Highlanders, but his uncle, Colonel William Henry Dick-Cunyngham, V.C. The Baronet is still Lieutenant in the Black Watch.

P. 253, 6th line from the bottom, should be: 'Here Thomas the Rhymer was born —and finally "feyed away,"—but he first met the Fairy Queen on "Huntlie bank" beside the Eildon Tree.'

P. 255, line 5, should be, 'In the reign of David I.,' instead of Malcolm IV.

P. 323, line 10, read *his* for *this*.

P. 345, line 5, *Charlotte* should be *Julia*—Mrs. Thomas Mitchell Innes.

P. 379, last line, should be: 'died two months *after* her father in 1848.'

P. 380, line 34, Charles *Duckell*, Esq., should be *Duckett*.

,, line 35, Sir Thomas North Dick Lauder, '10th' Rifles, should be '60th.'

This Record

IS RESPECTFULLY INSCRIBED TO THE MEMORY OF

SIR THOMAS DICK LAUDER

SEVENTH BARONET OF FOUNTAINHALL AND GRANGE,

AS A TRIBUTE OF UNFEIGNED ESTEEM FOR

HIS MANIFOLD VIRTUES AND ENDOWMENTS.

NOBLE SCION OF A NOBLE RACE.

PREFACE

THE end of the nineteenth century seems to be peculiarly notable for the opening up of charter-chests and family histories, and the present work partakes in a measure of this character, dealing, however, with places as well as people—barons and their baronies. As far as the author is aware, the history of the Lauder family as such has never been previously written, and the aim of the writer now is to present a faithful record of their connection with the popular events of historical interest between the years 1056 and 1848. The reason for attempting such a task has been already given. The historical and biographical statements made have been gathered from Scottish records, old chronicles, family papers, and direct personal information, only dipping into traditionary lore when the legend or story gives warrant for at least some possible measure of underlying truth. From these remarks the reader will readily perceive that the intention of the book is not history pure and simple, nor yet a herald's genealogical chart of mere succession only. The aim has been rather to present the successive generations of the knights and barons, churchmen and warriors, landowners and lawyers, provosts and merchants, of the family, in the midst of the historical episodes of their own period, in the events of which they mingled, thus helping to form the history transpiring around them. Not that these things have been portrayed with the freedom and picturesqueness of romance; dry facts have been sometimes unavoidable—charters being more indispensable to verity than the most romantic legends.

The author has simply endeavoured to trace the twofold family through seven centuries of good and ill fortune: the De Dycks from Orkney, whose forefathers were merchants and aldermen, and the Lauders of the Bass from their sea-girt nest on the Auld Crag and the ancient Tower of Lauder in the quaint mediæval burgh on the Leader. The verification of the information thus gathered has formed no inconsiderable part of the undertaking, the writer finding, like all others who search for truth, that historians, heralds, and authors in general, differ very much from one another with regard to names and dates, and that such mis-statements are most unheedingly handed on from one to another, causing a considerable amount of confusion, from which it is not always easy to extricate the verity. In searching for proofs from the Public Records, the author is indebted to the courtesy and kindly assistance of Matthew Livingstone, Esq., and the Rev. John Anderson, of the Historical Department at the Register House, and also to the efficient services of Mr. Henry Paton, M.A., a searcher of the Records, without whose skilful aid many of the original documents would have remained undeciphered, so tedious and almost insurmountable is such work to the uninitiated.

There was some little difficulty in making the family history appear to flow consecutively, owing to the twofold name necessitating the tracing up of the separate genealogies, each from their earliest records. The author has therefore divided the subject-matter into three parts, viz., the Dicks, the Lauders, and the Dick Lauders, bringing each individual line up to the point of union, and then continuing the double line up to 1848, ending with Sir Thomas Dick Lauder, seventh Baronet, not wishing in any way to intrude on the sacred privacy of the personal history of the living members of the family, to whom the writer is deeply indebted for the courteous assistance and sympathy rendered during the process of the work, special thanks being due to Lady Anne Dick Lauder, Miss Cornelia Dick Lauder, and Sir Thomas Dick Lauder, the present proprietor of the Grange Manor, not only for the valuable information obtained from the charter-chest, but also for the kind permission given to sketch the family mansions and family relics—by no means the least pleasurable part of the work having been the taking of the sketches

PREFACE

and photographs for the various illustrations, all of which have been carefully reproduced by the mechanical processes of Messrs. Scott Brothers, whose co-operation throughout has been most kindly, intelligent, and obliging.

It is a strange and noteworthy coincidence that the book entitled *Curiosities of a Scots Charter-Chest*, edited and arranged by the Honourable Mrs. Atholl Forbes, should also contain the portrait of Sir William Dick and the three old engravings relative to his chequered career, seeing that Mrs. Forbes and the author of the present volume are perfect strangers to each other, neither knowing that such was the intention of the other; but beyond thus illustrating the mutual ancestor of the Dicks and the Lauders, Mrs. Forbes' interesting volume of the private letters in the Prestonfield charter-chest makes no allusion whatever either to the Lauder family or the Grange of St. Giles.

The writer takes this opportunity of tendering her sincere thanks to those friends who have so kindly assisted her, by advice or otherwise, in gathering material for her work, which has been from first to last purely a labour of love.

J. S. S.

8 KILMAURS ROAD, *September* 1897.

INTRODUCTION

LETTER TO MISS CORNELIA DICK LAUDER OF LAUDER HOUSE

8 KILMAURS ROAD, EDINBURGH.

DEAR MISS DICK LAUDER,
 You ask me to tell you what first induced me to commence the History of the Grange House and its connection with the Lauder family. Strange as it may seem, I must frankly admit the impulse arose from a strong desire to find an elucidation or corroboration of a very curious dream, or rather dream-vision, which came to me so suddenly and so forcibly that I was impelled to take note of it; and as it happened upon my return from a visit to the Grange House, I naturally concluded the solution of it must also come from thence. Sometimes, in a casual way, a simple occurrence becomes quite by accident, as it were, the key to a chain of unexpected coincidences, and one is fain to acknowledge the unseen potency of even the most trivial event. Doubtless you will understand my meaning better when I tell you the dream.

As I said, I had just returned from the Grange House—which to me has always a peculiar charm of its own,—with its wealth of ivy, its quaintness, and its irregularity. The long, narrow corridors with deep recesses, stairs here and stairs there, leading to unexpected nooks and corners, all most suggestive—especially as the shadows of twilight deepen, and the solemnity of the effect is enhanced. Such may have been the thought of my mind that day, but still, to me, the Grange House was then simply a picturesque old mansion of whose history I knew nothing whatever, nor yet the life-story of its former inhabitants.

If there is such a thing as Geist-memories floating in the palpitating air surrounding these old historic buildings, then surely some such influence must have imperceptibly clung to me, for with startling rapidity a series of remarkable tableaux presented themselves before me—more like a panorama than a dream. Fortunately I had sufficient consciousness to bear each vision in my mind until the end, when I immediately noted down the whole experience for future elucidation.

INTRODUCTION

My notes are as follows, dated Monday, January 26th, 1891 :—On returning from the Grange House to-day I distinctly saw, or *dreamed* that I saw, a gentleman dressed in black velvet of the King Charles period, with lace and ruffles and a short cloak. He held a large plumed hat in his hand as he stepped into an oak-panelled room. His face was haggard and worried-looking, but his whole bearing had a noble appearance. He laid his hat upon the table, and I particularly remarked the position of the window. A lady then came hurriedly forward to meet him, and, throwing her arms round his neck, she laid her face on his shoulder and wept. I could see the convulsive movements, but heard no sound. She was dressed in a grey silken material fashioned of the same period. Her hair may have been fair, but to me it was decidedly grey. She was tall and stately in form, though elderly, but the man was much older-looking. The scene suddenly changed to another room, in which the same lady met a younger one, clad in lighter clothing, with an anxious frightened look on her face. I noticed this lady's hair was much darker and most picturesquely arranged. The two forms entered an upper room very hurriedly, and appeared to speak to a young man, who rose from a reclining position on a kind of settle or low couch. His costume was of the same period, but of a brownish-coloured cloth, and as he was in semi-deshabille, he had neither coat nor ruffles on. His clothes were of the finest texture, and his linen superlatively white. The three stood close together for an instant, evidently speaking in a whisper, then it seemed as if they were startled by some unwelcome sound, and were listening breathlessly. The younger lady leaned on the gentleman's arm as though she clung to him for protection. Suddenly the young man stooped down and drew a rapier from beneath a heap of clothing, and they all quickly disappeared through another door. Instantly another tableau presented itself. I felt as though it was still at the Grange House, but in an upper corridor, where a man suddenly appeared dressed in the Cromwell costume, with a large dark cloak wrapped about him, top-boots, and grey hat. His hand was on the hilt of his sword, and he moved stealthily along the passage on tiptoe, bending down and prying into every corner. He entered the long room which the other forms had just vacated, still peering round about him, with a sinister expression on his face, as though seeking some Royalist foe. After a fruitless search he also passed hurriedly out, disappearing in darkness, which remained for a few seconds, and then the figure of a blackamoor came into view—not a negro, for he had on a strange head-dress and Turkish-looking trousers, and a deep red vest. His face was grinning with satisfaction as he stood in the passage just outside a door on the landing. He

INTRODUCTION   xiii

clapped his breast, then laid his hand significantly on the wall, and looking straight at me, he instantly vanished through an opening in it. All was blank for a moment, then I seemed to be in the long upper room again, where I saw the same grey-haired lady, only this time she had on a peculiar black hat, and was wrapped in a fur travelling cloak, as if going on a journey. She had the same stately mien, but her eyes were red with weeping. She glanced furtively about her, and passing quickly out of the room, she descended a staircase, and emerged into the darkness by a postern door, the position of which I also specially noted.

After this I felt as though I were groping my way along a passage in the dark, when slowly rising out of the gloom near a turret stair I saw the form of a monk in a brown friar's dress. His face was terribly bruised, and his hands all bleeding. He was apparently groaning in deep distress, raising his eyes several times beseechingly, as though imploring aid. With this painful sight all vanished, leaving me dazed and astonished, but in no way able to account for these strange visions, knowing at that time absolutely nothing of the history of the Grange House; and as the whole panorama was purely pantomimic, not a clue could I gain from any sound or utterance of speech. But from the suddenness and the consecutiveness of the tableaux I distinctly felt there must be an underlying meaning somewhere, which it might be interesting to unravel. But what it all had to do with the Grange House puzzled me greatly to know, and that was exactly what I resolved to find out. A month later I was forcibly reminded that I had allowed the whole thing to lapse unheeded, for in the same sudden, unaccountable manner the tableaux recommenced, very like the moving pictures in a camera-obscura. First there appeared a rolling cloud of mist, out of which some distant forms began to emerge. As they increased in size and clearness I could distinguish a lady clothed in a long cloak, with a kind of hood over her head. She was making her way with difficulty through a storm of wind and snow, holding two children by the hand, a boy and a girl, also struggling with the storm, and pressing forward. The little faces were red with the piercing wind, and their hair all blowing about from beneath the quaint, Dutch-looking headgear. There was a look of deep anxiety on all the faces, with a strong determination to brave the storm and attain some all-important end. As I noted the leaden sky, the wintry hedges, and the snow-trodden road, my heart went forth to the struggling travellers, but in an instant they were gone, and, with the rapidity of limelight views, another picture was before me. It was a large building with a heavy doorway, standing in front of which, as though on guard, was a soldier of the Commonwealth; he was listening with an air of indifference to a youth in a civilian's dress, who had a pale, beseeching face. The soldier held a large, old-fashioned gun, into which he was ramming a rod, as though he were cleaning it. I heard nothing of the conversation, but the look of disappointment on the lad's face was most pathetic. This was the end of the pictorial panorama in 1891, and a whole year elapsed before I got the first clue to the unravelling of it, and that by accidentally seeing a unique folio volume in the Signet Library about the *Distressed Case of Sir William Dick*, which, with the special permission of the librarian, T. G. Law, Esq., I was kindly allowed to copy. I then commenced to search out the history of the Grange House in earnest, but, circumstances hindering the work, it was not until two years later that I really found how thoroughly the one corroborated the other, the dream-pictures being wonderfully true types or symbols of various states and conditions in the lives of the persons there represented, whom I found had absolutely been former inhabitants of the Grange Manor. It is not difficult to name them now that the facts lie before us; but that the solution should be forthcoming, even five or six years after the vision, only increased the feeling that for some reason the work was given me to do. Accepting it as such, I resolved to spare no pains in making it a faithful record of the noble family which claims Sir William Dick as one of its ancestors,—the same Sir William whom in my dream I saw bidding adieu to his affectionate spouse at the Grange House before his final journey to London, after he was denounced as a malignant, hunted by Cromwell's party, and fleeced of his enormous wealth.

That Lady Dick and her family found shelter at the Grange with their son William and his open-handed wife, Lady Janet, we know now; and also that Dame Elizabeth went to London to see her unfortunate husband in prison, and their daughter-in-law arrived in the depth of winter with the younger children in time to secure a proper burial for the aged grandfather, whose grandson and heir long petitioned in vain for redress from the Commonwealth. Each of these events had been panorama'd before me, even to the fact of Sir William's connection with the 'Dominion of the Turks,' and also the suppression of the whole monastic order at the Reformation, which arose out of the darkness and the gloom, the suffering and the bloodshed, of many imploring souls.

In trying to verify these simple statements my interest grew apace, not only in the old mansion itself, but in the early history of the family to whom it belonged, whose twofold family name, while it added to the historic interest, also widened the research, disclosing ties so closely interwoven that it was

INTRODUCTION

impossible to write of the one and ignore the others. Thus the matter grew beyond its first conception, and from the history of the Grange manor it has come to be the history of the Dick Lauder Family and their Baronial Homes.

Now that my labour of love is accomplished, I leave it in your hands, dear lady, to deal with it gently, for it is verified facts, not fiction, I have sought to lay before you as the record of your noble ancestors, a long line well worthy of being recorded by a much abler pen than that of your ever faithful scribe,

JANE STEWART SMITH.

September 1897.

CONTENTS

PART I

CHAP. | PAGE
I. SANCT GEILIE-GRANGE: ITS HISTORICAL AND ECCLESIASTICAL ASSOCIATIONS, 1
II. THE CHAPELS OF ST. ROQUE AND ST. JOHN, AND THE CONVENT OF ST. KATHERINE OF SIENA, 10
III. THE LANDS AND MANOR-PLACE OF GRANGE, 21
IV. THE DICKS OF ORKNEY, 31
V. SIR WILLIAM DICK OF BRAID, KNIGHT, 46
VI. THE HEIRS OF BRAID AND DICKS OF FRACAFIELD, 57
VII. THE BARONS OF GRANGE AND THE SETONS OF PITMEDDEN, 66
VIII. PRINCE CHARLES EDWARD AT THE GRANGE, 74
IX. SCOTTISH CELEBRITIES AT THE GRANGE, 83
X. SIR ANDREW DICK OF CRAIGHOUSE, 92
XI. ALEXANDER DICK, LAIRD OF HEUGH, AND THE BARONY OF PRIESTFIELD, 107
XII. SIR JAMES DICK OF PRESTONFIELD, THE WISE PROVOST, 115
XIII. PRESTONFIELD MANOR, 126
XIV. DR. JOHNSON'S VISIT TO EDINBURGH, 137

PART II

XV. THE LAUDERS OF LAUDER AND BASS: AS WARRIORS, 151
XVI. THE LAUDERS OF BASS: AS CHURCHMEN AND AMBASSADORS, 168
XVII. THE CASTLE OF BASS, 189
XVIII. LADY BASS AND THE LAUDERS OF TYNINGHAME, 203
XIX. THE LAUDERS OF HALTOUN AND BRUNTSFIELD, 222
XX. THE ANCIENT BURGH OF LAUDER, 253
XXI. THE LAUDERS OF LAUDERDALE, 271

PART III

XXII. SIR JOHN LAUDER, FIRST BARONET OF FOUNTAINHALL, 289
XXIII. THE BARONETS OF FOUNTAINHALL, 303
XXIV. RELUGAS, 316

CONTENTS

CHAP.		PAGE
XXV.	THE GRANGE HOUSE AS A BARONIAL RESIDENCE,	327
XXVI.	SIR THOMAS DICK LAUDER, ...	337
XXVII.	LITERARY WORK OF SIR THOMAS DICK LAUDER AND HUGH MILLER'S CORRESPONDENCE, ...	349
XXVIII.	OLD STONES, FAMILY RELICS, TRADITIONAL STORIES,	363
	CONCLUSION,	379

APPENDIX

NOTE I., ... 383
NOTE II., ... 384
NOTE III., ... 385
NOTE IV.—Will of Thomas Bannatyne, ... 385
NOTE V.—Copy Estimate of Sir William Dick's Estate as made out by his fourth son, Mr. Alexander Dick, ... 388
NOTE VI.—Copia of Scotland's Letter to the House of Commons, 1st May 1644, . 388
Copia of Scotland's Letter to Sir William Dick, 12th December 1645, . . 389
Recommendation by the Assembly of the Church of Scotland, to the Parliament and Committee of State in that Nation, concerning Sir William Dick, date the 15th June 1646, ... 389
Copia of Two Letters from the Scots Commissioners at London, to the Committee of Parliament at Edenburgh, and the Committee of State at Newcastle, date 12 Sept. 1646. Concerning Sir William Dick, ... 390
A Short State of the Debts due by England and Scotland to the deceased Sir William Dick, and of the securities he hath thereupon, ... 390
Copia of Scotland's Letter to the Parliament of England, concerning Sir William Dick. Date 21 Nov. 1648, ... 391
NOTE VII.—The Burial-place of Sir William Dick of Braid, Knight, Provost of Edinburgh, . 392
NOTE VIII.—Petitions to Parliament of Family, etc., of Sir William Dick, . . . 393
NOTE IX.—Kirk-Session Records anent the Corstorphine Communion Cups, . . 396
NOTE X.—Charter of the Entail of Priestfield, ... 397
NOTE XI.—Charter to George Lauder of Bass, ... 398
NOTE XII.—Extracts from 'The Loadstar, or Directory to the New World and Transformations,' Considerations to the Parliament, Sept. 1639, ... 399
NOTE XIII.—Memorandum for Sir John Lauder anent the Patent—and also for a libell agt., etc., 1690, ... 403
NOTE XIV.—Holograph Notes of Sir John Lauder, Lord Fountainhall, from the Charter-Chest of Sir Thomas Dick Lauder, ... 407
Notes from a MS. in the Advocates' Library, by Sir George Mackenzie, anent Lauder and Haltoun, ... 408
NOTE XV.—Catalogue of the Family Portraits at the Grange House, . . 409
NOTE XVI.—Catalogue of Sir Thomas Dick Lauder's Works, ... 410

LIST OF ILLUSTRATIONS xix

LIST OF FULL-PAGE ILLUSTRATIONS

BISHOP LAUDER, WITH LATIN INSCRIPTION,	*Frontispiece*
PORTRAIT OF SIR WILLIAM DICK OF BRAID, PROVOST,	*facing page* 45
SIR WILLIAM DICK WITH HIS BODYGUARD AT LEITH,	,, 50
SIR WILLIAM DICK IN PRISON,	,, 55
SIR WILLIAM DICK IN HIS COFFIN AT WESTMINSTER,	,, 56
GARDEN GATEWAY, PITMEDDEN,	,, 70
PORTRAITS OF SIR ANDREW LAUDER AND DAME ISOBEL DICK,	,, 72
OLD PILLAR OF THE ORIGINAL ENTRANCE TO PRESTONFIELD,	,, 115
YEW TREES, PRESTONFIELD MANOR,	,, 131
BIRTHPLACE OF SIR WALTER SCOTT, COLLEGE WYND,	,, 144
CHANCEL ARCH OF ST. BALDRED'S CHURCH, TYNINGHAME,	,, 217
THE SITE OF LAUDER TOWER,	,, 253
'WHEN THE KYE COMES HAME,'	,, 260
RELUGAS ON THE FINDHORN,	,, 326
THE GRANGE HOUSE FROM THE BOWLING-GREEN,	,, 327
PORTRAITS OF SIR THOMAS DICK LAUDER, SEVENTH BARONET OF FOUNTAINHALL, AND LADY LAUDER,	,, 329
THE AVENUE, GRANGE HOUSE,	,, 336
PORTRAIT OF SIR THOMAS DICK LAUDER, SEVENTH BARONET, WITH AUTOGRAPH,	,, 337
THE MONK'S SEAT, GRANGE GARDEN,	,, 364
'MEMENTO MORI' WATCH PRESENTED BY QUEEN MARY TO LADY MARY SETON,	,, 369
THE MONK'S WALK, GRANGE HOUSE,	,, 374
THE HAUNTED TOWER,	,, 378
PLAN OF THE LANDS OF GRANGE,	,, 380

LIST OF ILLUSTRATIONS IN TEXT

PAGE

HEADING—SANCT GEILIES' GRANGE,	1
ST. CUTHBERT'S CHURCH AND THE NOR' LOCH,	4
GRANGE HOUSE IN 1700,	5

LIST OF ILLUSTRATIONS

	PAGE
THE RUINS OF ST. ROQUE'S CHAPEL,	9
BLACK DEATH RECORD,	10
BELL AND INSCRIPTION,	13
OLD STONE, ST. ROQUE'S,	14
SETON CHAPEL,	16
DOORWAY, ST. GILES',	19
STEEPLE, ST. GILES',	20
OLD LINTEL STONE, GRANGE HOUSE,	24
CARVED STONE—MASTER JOHN CANT AND KATHERINE CREICH,	26
ROSYTHE CASTLE,	30
ST. MAGNUS' CATHEDRAL, KIRKWALL,	33
TOKEN, ST. MAGNUS' CATHEDRAL,	33
SIR WILLIAM DICK AND HIS FAMILY,	38
OLD WINDMILL, NORTH RONALDSHAY,	43
SCALLOWAY CASTLE,	44
COAT-OF-ARMS,	46
SIR WILLIAM DICK'S COIN,	56
DICK COAT-OF-ARMS,	65
SETON BOOK-PLATE,	66
JANET M'MATH'S TOMB, GREYFRIARS CHURCHYARD,	67
SUN-DIAL, PITMEDDEN,	70
DICK LAUDER ARMS,	73
PRINCE CHARLES' THISTLE,	74
PRINCE CHARLIE ROSEBUSH,	75
KING'S STABLES, CULLODEN MOOR,	77
CHARTER-CHEST,	79
CULLODEN HOUSE,	82
SIXTEENTH-CENTURY GARDEN AT THE GRANGE,	86
THE GRIFFIN GATEWAY AND OLD NORTH ENTRANCE AT THE GRANGE,	88
THE SCOTT MONUMENT,	91
ANCIENT PILLAR FROM ENTRANCE-GATE, CRAIGHOUSE,	92
OLD STONE OVER DOORWAY, CRAIGHOUSE,	102
CRAIGHOUSE,	104
OLD LINTEL STONE, CRAIGHOUSE,	106
DOVE-COT, HEUGH, NORTH BERWICK,	107

LIST OF ILLUSTRATIONS

	PAGE
RUINS OF THE PRIORY, NORTH BERWICK,	108
DUDDINGSTON LOCH AND CHURCH,	113
HIGH SCHOOL WYND AND CARDINAL BEATON'S HOUSE,	120
CHILD FEEDING SWANS,	123
COMMUNION CUP,	125
ROYSTON CASTLE,	128
GRANTON FROM SILVERKNOWES,	129
SUN-DIAL, PRESTONFIELD,	132
PRESTONFIELD HOUSE,	134
OLD STONE AT PRESTONFIELD, WITH THE DATE OF RECONSTRUCTION (SAME AS OVER THE DORMER WINDOWS OF THE OLD MANSION),	136
EDINBURGH CASTLE,	137
LAWNMARKET AND WEST BOW,	143
TABLET OVER BURIAL-PLACE OF JOHN KNOX,	148
COAT-OF-ARMS,	151
RUINS OF THE AULD KIRK ON THE SHORE AT NORTH BERWICK,	157
OLD PARISH CHURCH, NORTH BERWICK,	158
URQUHART CASTLE, LOCH NESS,	163
ARMS OF BISHOP LAUDER ON GLASGOW CATHEDRAL,	168
INSCRIPTION OVER DEAN'S SEAT, CHAPTER-HOUSE, GLASGOW CATHEDRAL,	170
RUINS OF THE CASTLE OF BERWICK-ON-TWEED,	175
ARMS, LAUDER (BASS),	181
THE BASS,	187
OLD WEAPONS—LAUDERS OF BASS,	188
CASTLE OF BASS,	194
PRISONS OF THE BASS,	199
TENANTS OF THE BASS,	201
WHITEKIRK,	206
ANCIENT TOMB IN THE RUINS OF ST. BALDRED'S CHURCH AT TYNINGHAME,	213
RUINS OF ST. BALDRED'S CHURCH, TYNINGHAME,	218
TEMPLAR'S TOMBSTONE, TYNINGHAME,	220
WHITEKIRK TOKEN AND BOSS FROM THE PORCH,	221
COAT-OF-ARMS—LAUDER OF HALTOUN,	222
HALTON HOUSE,	247
BRUNTSFIELD HOUSE,	250

LIST OF ILLUSTRATIONS

	PAGE
MUIRCLEUCH RUINS,	259
LAUDER PARISH CHURCH, AND SITE OF MARKET CROSS,	262
OLD TOLBOOTH, LAUDER,	276
TOMB OF THE LAST LAIRD OF LAUDER,	283
BURN GRANGE,	285
OLD STONE FROM LAUDER TOWER,	286
LORD FOUNTAINHALL'S BOOK-PLATE,	289
FOUNTAINHALL,	290
BARONETCY PATENT—LAUDER, 1688,	294
COAT-OF-ARMS, LAUDER OF FOUNTAINHALL,	303
THE PATH THROUGH THE WOODS,	308
WAITING FOR THE YOUNG LAIRD,	309
OLD CROSS AT ORMISTON VILLAGE,	310
OLD HALL AND ENTRANCE TOWER,	311
WISHING WELL IN THE GLEN,	313
THE JOUGS AT THE KIRK,	314
OLD TOMB, PENCAITLAND,	315
OLD GARDENER, DUNPHAIL,	317
OLD ROCK IN THE FLOOD,	325
OLD FAMILY CHAIR,	330
BELFRY TOWER, GRANGE HOUSE,	332
THE WARRICK VASE AVENUE,	333
DOGS' CEMETERY,	335
SUN-DIAL, GRANGE HOUSE,	336
DICK LAUDER COAT-OF-ARMS,	337
THE OLD TOLL AT THE CAUSEWAYSIDE,	348
OUTLINE SKETCH OF GRANGE HOUSE BY SIR THOMAS,	357
THE DICK LAUDER TOMB, GRANGE CEMETERY,	361
MONOGRAM—16 WD 74	363
OLD STONE—BURGH ARMS,	365
THE PENNY WELL,	366
THE GRANGE GATE TOLL,	367
CARVED SETTLE,	371
SIR WILLIAM DICK'S CABINET,	372

PART I

CHAPTER I

SANCT GEILIE-GRANGE: ITS HISTORICAL AND
ECCLESIASTICAL ASSOCIATIONS

LTHOUGH, strictly speaking, the old manor-house called the Grange is unable to lay claim to the historic interest of an ancient feudal tower, whose titled lords are enrolled in the earliest annals of our international wars, the picturesque mansion has a charm peculiarly its own, allied, as we find it ever to have been, with the ecclesiastical and literary men of the nation, such as have wielded the pen rather than the battle-axe and the spear, though many of these ancient warlike trophies do at present form a goodly share in its interior adornment. When and by whom it was originally built is enshrouded in the hazy mystery of the past. No document seems to be extant giving us any clue as to whether the foundation-stone was laid by Lord or by Abbot. There is, however, sufficient evidence of a certain amount of antiquity in the ecclesiastical record

of its name. About 1112 Alexander I. had erected a new Parish Kirk in Edinburgh, which he dedicated to St. Giles, a name so familiar in our day that it seems difficult to believe this tutelary saint was not a sturdy Pict or Scot, but of Grecian origin and of royal birth.

The fame of 'Sanct Geill and his Hynde' had been widely spread over the continent of Europe many years ere his name was a familiar by-word for sanctity in Scotland. It is believed by antiquarians versed in ancient ecclesiastical records that there had been a church in '*Edwinsburch* dedicated to St. Egidius, or Giles, as early as 854.'[1] That may be, but we shall certainly not attempt to tack our '*Sanct Geilie-Grange*' on to it. We do very well when we claim a connection of seven hundred and fifty years between the Kirk of St. Giles and its Grange—and this can be verified from the Burgh Records, which inform us that '*Sanct-Geill-Grange*,' with various adjacent lands, was conferred by David I., Alexander's successor, on the monks of 'Holme-Cultrane,'[2] an Abbey beautifully situated near the sea, in Cumberland, twelve miles from Carlisle. The Grange of St. Giles must therefore have been built about the same time as the new Parish Kirk of St. Giles, so as to have been a habitable dwelling worth presentation so early in the twelfth century as 1128; but it is very evident, whatever rental rights the monks thus obtained, the 'superiority' remained with the King—he being Suzerain or *supremus*, the monks of 'Holme-Cultrane' being *dominium directum*, and the vicars and prebendaries of the Kirk of St. Giles being *dominium utile*, or vassals, for Maidment affirms that in 1153 Sanct Geilie-Grange belonged to the perpetual vicar of St. Giles as *vassal*. This order shows itself most plainly in all the future enactments concerning the feu-farm of Grange under its ecclesiastical tenure. It may seem strange that these Midlothian church-lands should have been conferred upon an English Abbey, but at that time the whole county of Cumberland belonged to King David, having been bequeathed to him by his brother, King Edgar, in 1107, and he had erected this Abbey of 'Holme-Cultrane' upon his own estate; but it was only after his accession to the throne of Scotland that he endowed it with the lands of Priestfield, part of Liberton, called Spittleton, and the broad acres of 'Sanct Geilie-Grange'—this donation most probably taking place when a fresh distribution of the church-lands became necessary after the founding of the Abbey of Holyrood in 1128, the King as *superior* having them entirely at his disposal.

We can well understand how the heart of David, the youngest and most tenderly beloved son of the saintly Margaret of Scotland, should have yearned

---

[1] Maitland, p. 270.   [2] Also called Harehope.—Holinshed, p. 288.

HISTORICAL AND ECCLESIASTICAL ASSOCIATIONS

to promulgate the pious truths he had learned from his Saxon mother's missal, while his father, King Malcolm, and his two brothers were away fighting the English. When he first came to the throne the land was filled with the clamorous strife of civil war—despotic feudalism being everywhere rampant. 'Micht was richt,' and every baron in his castle-keep had full power of 'pit and gallows.' There rose in the King's peace-loving spirit the strong desire to promote learning and agriculture among his people as a counterfoil to the fierce proclivities and lawlessness of those feudal barons, for which reason he began to build Abbeys and Churches in all the principal centres; and so beneficial did he find the result that in the twenty-nine years of his reign he built no fewer than fifteen abbeys and two convents, besides erecting four bishoprics.[1] Each of them he endowed with fair lands and rich rents, besides sundry other commodious possessions, causing as complete a change in the land as that effected four centuries later by the Reformation itself. Before the year 1100 monasteries were almost unknown in Scotland, and churches, though at all times a dominant power, were few. We can readily comprehend the different aspect assumed by the little hamlet called 'Edin,' with its rock-built castle and immense forest, when Abbot Alwin and his 'Black Canons' took possession of the beautiful abbey built for them at Holyrood. Their royal charter of privileges granted them power to erect a burgh between the church and the town, which is styled by King David as '*Burgo meo de Edwinsburg*' (my own burgh of Edwin's burgh).

These Augustine monks therefore soon formed a settlement outside of the monastery, in the little village then called Hebergare, already in existence. It consisted merely of one straggling street, having no walls of defence, its inhabitants relying solely upon the holy protection of their monastic superiors, after whom it soon came to be called *the Canonsgaet*, or the Canons' Street—all residents and builders being vassals of 'the Monastery of the Holy Cross.' Ere long the village became a burgh of regality, bearing its own arms and official seal. Besides these lands and houses, the abbots, canons, and friars enjoyed immunity and freedom from all customs, toll, and duty whatever throughout the kingdom, and they had royal tithes of meal and malt, with salmon and herring from the royal fisheries, tallow and hides from the King's cattle, and ewes and lambs from his flocks. Can we wonder that the monks throve and grew fat and multiplied in the land? whereas the royal exchequer was yearly impoverished to the extent of sixty thousand pounds Scots.[2]

'A sair sanct,' indeed, for the Crown was St. David! as King James said when

[1] Holinshed, p. 288.　　　[2] *Ibid.* p. 289.

SANCT GEILIE-GRANGE

he stood beside his tomb at Dunfermline. None profited more from the truth of this fact than the Abbots of Holyrood, upon whom the King bestowed so largely, giving them not only the 'Church of St. Cuthbert and all that pertained to it,' but also the chapels of Corstorphine and Liberton, leaving a diminished portion for the new Parish Church of St. Giles, built by his brother, to which 'Sanct Geilie-Grange' belonged.

ST. CUTHBERT'S CHURCH AND THE NOR' LOCH.

About a hundred years after the first charter of 'the Holy Rood,' we find mention is made in its records of the Church of St. Giles and its perpetual vicar, he being one of the dignitaries who affixed their seals in attestation of a Papal Bull, given in 1214,[1] in the reign of Alexander II., great-grandson of David I. At that period every parish church had its arable lands and its orchards to cultivate, with a grange or farm-house, for the use of the superintending husbandman and the assistant secular brethren, who brewed and baked and attended to the housing of the cattle and the storing of the grain, while the serfs who tilled the land were fed by them, but slept elsewhere, the farm-dwelling being too small to locate all the out-door workers when the arable lands were extensive. These serfs, during the Middle Ages, were attached to the soil, and willingly surrendered their services either to the monasteries or to the ecclesiastical farms for the sake of the religious benefits they derived, thus forming a kind of servile secular brotherhood, completely under the dominion of their masters for perpetual service. In this respect a grange differed from a monastery. In course of time, as the people became enlightened, their condition improved, and these serfs, or labourers, became more independent.

According to the Chartularies of the eleventh and twelfth centuries, the better class of the rural population of Scotland was divided into husbandmen and cottars, and the land was subdivided into oxgates, husbandlands, and ploughgates.[2] The original number of the acres of 'Sanct Geilie-grange' is not definitely stated, but they must have been pretty extensive, judging from

[1] *Liber Cataruni Sancte Crucis*, p. 55.
[2] An oxgate was thirteen acres, a husbandland twenty-six acres, and a ploughgate one hundred and four acres.

the various grants of land given from time to time to the subsequently built chapels and convents. Under the appellation of 'Sanct Geilie-grange' the house itself was of simple structure, consisting of a strong well-built square keep, three stories high, as seen in Storer's view of it, and ornamented with two turrets and a battlemented roof. Its position was isolated, standing as it did at the eastern end of the Burghmuir, which at that time consisted of waste tracts of moorland and morass, stretching out southward as far as the Braid Hills, and eastward to St. Leonard's Crags. The moor had originally formed part of the dense forest of Drumsheugh, which must at the time of the building of the grange of St. Giles to a very large extent have still surrounded it. In this ancient forest the earliest kings of Scotland had followed the chase of the elk and the wild boar; and their royal successors from the eleventh to the sixteenth centuries still hunted the fox and the hind, with all the 'noise and

GRANGE HOUSE IN 1700.

din' of bugles and hounds. Here also, in the valley below Arthur's Seat, took place the incident recorded in the legend of the White Hart of King David, which resulted in the clearance of the primeval oaks, and the subsequent founding of the richly endowed Abbey of the Holy Rood.

In thus trying to imagine the position of the Grange at this early date, it is well to bear in mind all the features of its immediate neighbourhood; for the miles of land now covered by houses, churches, cemeteries, bridges, railways, etc., was then but partially cleared from the original forest, 'while deep pools and wide morasses, tangled wood and wild animals, made the rude diverging pathways to the east and westward extremely dangerous for long after; though lights were burned at the Hermitage of St. Anthony on the Crag, and the spire of St. John of Corstorphin, to guide the unfortunate wight who was foolhardy enough to travel after nightfall.' As landmarks above the expansive woods there ever rose the heights of Arthur's Seat and the Calton Hill—the '*Dhu Craig*,' or Black Craig, as it was then called,—a bare mass of rock, most fitting site for a Druidical altar, surrounded by Drumsheugh Forest, which stretched its stately branches uninterruptedly from thence to the extreme west end of the Burgh.

What we now call 'The Meadows' was at that time a loch, about three-quarters of a mile long and a quarter of a mile broad. It was known as the 'Burrow Loch,' and was coeval with Duddingston Loch, and a certain portion of it came within the boundary of Sanct Geilie-Grange lands, called '*waste*,' being on the east side of the Burghmuir. Even at that time the Tower of Brounisfelde stood on the moor, forming, with Merchiston Castle on the west, and the Grange Keep on the east, an almost equilateral triangle.

The little Parish Church of St. Giles was not quite a mile and a half distant from its grange, the roadway to it lying through the outskirts of the wood, while the King's garden, which lay below the Castle, stretched along the valley of what afterwards became the Nor' Loch. Edinburgh itself was but an assemblage of rude huts, and the 'Castle of the Maidens,' as it was then styled, was more like a prison-fort than a royal palace. In fact, like all King David's habitations, it had been converted into a monastery, '*Monasterium Sanctæ Crucis de Castello*.' A small hamlet constituted the whole burgh; just a few wooden houses promiscuously huddled together for protection, clinging limpet-like about the base of the Castle Rock.

All arable lands connected with dwelling-houses being too valuable for pasturage, the outlying portions of the royal woods were let for the feeding and herding of cattle and swine; this was called *pannage*, but when the woods in question belonged to any of the numerous fraternities of the monks or canons, it was called *canveth*, and much of the wealth of the first clerical communities consisted in the use thus made of these otherwise unremunerative tracts of land, a proportion of which belonged to the Kirk of St. Giles and its community at the Grange.

Sir Daniel Wilson gives us a very good idea of what this little parish kirk was like in the reign of David I.: 'Built in the massive style of the early Norman period, it would consist,' he says,[1] 'simply of a nave and chancel, united by a rich Norman chancel arch; altogether occupying only a portion of the centre aisle of the present nave. Small circular-headed windows, decorated with zigzag mouldings, would admit the light to its sombre interior, while its west front was in all probability surmounted by a simple belfry, from whence the bell would daily summon the natives of the hamlet to matins and vespers, and with slow measured sounds toll their knell as they were laid in the

[1] *Memorials of Edinburgh*, p. 379.

HISTORICAL AND ECCLESIASTICAL ASSOCIATIONS 7

neighbouring churchyard. This ancient church was never entirely demolished,' but no record preserves to us the names of those who designed the original building, which from 'the small parish church of a rude hamlet' gradually became a 'wealthy collegiate church, with its forty altars' and its ever increasing number of chaplains, priests, and canons.

Strange to say, the Midlothian lands, including the Grange of St. Giles, made over to the Abbey of Harehope or Holme-Cultrane by King David I., were two hundred years later withdrawn by David II., upon his return to Scotland in 1355, after his eleven years' captivity in England. They were resumed in consequence of the monks having forfeited his goodwill by their adherence to Edward III. during the struggle for the supremacy between these two Sovereigns ; but it was not until 1376, five years after King David's death, that Robert II., his nephew and successor, granted the superiority of them to his own son, John Stewart, Lord Kyle, Earl of Carrick,[1] whose ancestor, the father of King Robert Bruce, lay buried in Holme Abbey, which was under the jurisdiction of the Bishopric of Lindisfarne or Holy Isle.

When the Earl of Carrick succeeded his father on the throne of Scotland, he changed his name from John to that of Robert, on account of the weaknesses and the misfortunes of John King of France, John King of England, and John Baliol of Scotland—popular belief in omens holding sway,—but unfortunately it required more than a mere change in name to bring the 'lucky star' of Robert Bruce within the horoscope of John Stewart, Lord of Kyle and Carrick, even under the name of Robert III. However, the year after he ascended the throne, in 1390, we find him disposing his right over the lands at Priestfield and the Grange of St. Giles to one of the Wardlaw family ; which is evidenced by an entry in a roll in the time of King Robert III., proving there had been a charter [2] 'To Andrew Wardlaw of the lands of Priestfield and St. Gile Grange, in the sheriffdom of Edinburgh.' The charter itself being amissing, we cannot exactly say whether the grant was made to Sir Andrew Wardlaw, Knt., of Torrie, brother of the Cardinal (Walter Wardlaw, Bishop of Glasgow), or to *Andrew Wardlaw*, son of Mariota and Gilbert de Wardlaw, who obtained a charter the same year from King Robert of the lands of 'Warynstoun' and 'Ricardistoun,' in the barony of Currie, dated on the 20th October 1391 ;[3] but there is every reason to

---

[1] *Register of the Great Seal*, 1306-1424. 'Robert II. grants to John, Earl of Carric, Steward of Scotland, his eldest son, the lands of Prestisfield, *Grange of St. Giles*, and Spetelton, within the sheriffdom of Edinburgh, which had fallen in the King's hands by the forfeiture of the friars of Harehope, subjects of the King of England, and so at war with him. To be held of the King and his heirs until the said friars return to their obedience and allegiance. Dated at Perth, 16th June 1376.'—P. 132, No. 27.
[2] Robertson's *Index of Missing Charters*, p. 146, No. 41.
[3] *Register of the Great Seal*, 1306-1424, p. 209, No. 40.

8   SANCT GEILIE-GRANGE

believe it to have been the latter (who is said to be a nephew of the Cardinal's), seeing that the lands of 'Sanctgely-grange' were resigned into the hands of King James IV. by James Wardlaw of '*Ricardtoun*' one hundred and fifty years later. These Grange lands, with the houses, tenants, and part of the common moor, were then granted by the King to John Cant, burgess of Edinburgh, and 'Agnes Carkettill,' his spouse, on the 29th October 1506.[1]

During the century which elapsed while the ecclesiastical family of the Wardlaws held the lands of the Grange of St. Giles, great changes had taken place in its surroundings. The fine old forest-trees between Holyrood and the Castle were by that time completely cleared away, and stately residences for the nobles built along the high level ridge within the city walls. Some of these mansions remain to this day, so substantially were they built with stone from the quarries and oaks from the forest of Drumsheugh. As time wore on the space within the shelter of the walls became excessively cramped, and the nobles got tired of building up tier upon tier towards the sky, hoping to get more air and more light. So running the risk of conflagration from Southern invaders, they began to erect their noble mansions in the hollow at the foot of the steep brae, covered with prickly whins and tangled brushwood. Upon the southern slope outside the city wall, this low-lying land had until then been merely a rural roadway, along which undoubtedly the cattle must have been driven to and from the distant pasturage, giving rise to its popular but inelegant name of '*the Cowgaitt*.'[2] The whole of this district ere long became the most fashionable quarter of the city, wherein the highest dignitaries in Church and State, bishops, lords, and senators, vied with each other in the erection of palatial homes along either side of the King's highway, beautifying them with terraces and orchard gardens. This *Via Vaccarum* led directly into the Grassmarket below the Castle at the western end, and into the back of the Canongate on the east, and was as distinct from the High Street as any city suburb, having the high town-wall completely separating it. It was at this period also that timber grants were made by James III. to those who cleared the Burghmuir of its dense masses of trees; preparing the ground eventually for the small farms and malt-barns which again completely changed the whole aspect of the city within the next hundred years. During this time, and in fact throughout the whole of the Stuart dynasty, the people set earnestly to work erecting those quaint timber-fronted houses which have long formed one of the chief characteristics features of old Edinburgh.

[1] *Register of the Great Seal*, 1424-1513, Charter No. 2999.
[2] *Gaet* being the Saxon for *way* or street.

HISTORICAL AND ECCLESIASTICAL ASSOCIATIONS 9

In the meantime the district immediately surrounding the Grange of St. Giles seems to have been chosen as the spot best fitted for the founding of chapels and convents—most likely on account of the whole land from the farm-dwelling to the kirkyard of St. Giles being under the vassalage of the vicar and prebendaries—John Cant as mid-superior under the King.

The first chapel thus built upon the Burghmuir was dedicated to St. Roque the healer, and it cannot fail to be peculiarly interesting to us, seeing it was not only the nearest building to the Grange farm on the south-west, but one of its oldest neighbours on that part of the moor,[1] and as such its history forms an important link in the story of the Grange of St Giles.

[1] The Tower of 'Brounisfelde,' belonging to the brave knight Sir Alan de Lawdre, the venerable Tower of Merchiston Castle, and the Peel Tower of Wrychtis-houses, were all much older than the Chapel of St. Roque. 'Merchestoune' stood at the extreme west of the Burghmuir, and the latter midway between it and the city. Both were owned by different branches of the ancient family of Napier—one of whom, William Napier of Wrychtis-houses, was Constable of Edinburgh Castle in 1390, and others filled the office of Provost in the reigns of James II. and James III. (See Appendix No. I.)

THE RUINS OF ST. ROQUE'S CHAPEL.

CHAPTER II

THE CHAPELS OF ST. ROQUE AND ST. JOHN, AND THE CONVENT OF ST. KATHERINE OF SIENA

'The whilst the bell, with distant chime,
Merrily tolled the hour of prime,
And thus the Lindesay spoke:—
"Thus clamour still the war-notes when
The King to mass his way has ta'en,
Or to St. Catherine's of Sienne,
Or Chapel of Saint Roque.

To you they speak of **martial fame**,
But me remind of **peaceful game**
When blither was their cheer."

"Nor less," said he, "I moan
To think what woe mischance may bring;
And how these merry bells may ring
The death-dirge of our gallant king."'
                                                    Marmion.

N a lonely spot at the west end of the Burghmuir, within half a mile of the old Grange House, this ancient shrine of the 'Holy Confessour, Sanct Rok,' was erected. It is not known by whom it was founded, nor the exact date of the building; but from the Burgh Records it is evident that it was a well-frequented shrine early in the reign of James IV., who made a special offering in person to this chapel on St. Roque's Day, August 15th, 1507. In 1501 there had also been a donation; but it was in the month of September 1513 that the shrine of St. Roque won its lasting title to historic fame—the day on which King James, flushed with chivalrous expectation, knelt there in lowly devotion ere he marched with the ill-fated 'Flowers of the Forest' to the fatal field of Flodden.

THE CHAPEL OF ST. ROQUE

A rare sight indeed it must have been for those who witnessed the mustering of those 100,000 men upon the moor—with pennons and pipers, and all the pageantry and pomp of martial array,—men in the flower of youth, and the prime of life, all actuated by the same spirit, and fired with heroic zeal for Scottish chivalry and fame,—men who ere long,

> 'On Flodden's trampled sod,
> For their king and for their country
> Rendered up their souls to God.'

Only one such gathering had ever tramped the Burghmuir, and that was in 1482, when 50,000 men under James III. had marched from out the Drumsheugh oaks to face the Southron foe.

We cannot say whether the little Chapel of St. Roque was nestling beneath the shadow of Blackford Hill at that time; but we do know that seven years had barely passed from Flodden's dread disaster before the shrine of St. Roque became the most eagerly besought in all the land, for the plague had come to the city, and the protective efficacy of this Saint as a safeguard from the pestilence was firmly believed in by all classes in the Middle Ages. Yet how very few were ever healed of this scourge, called the 'Black Death,' though multitudes knelt in prayerful faith day by day at the shrine of the healer. Nor did they fail to find some self-devoted priest willing to stand as mediator between them and the most loathsome of all diseases. Be our creed what it may, we can never deny the fact that the monks of old who thus officiated among the plague-stricken people were truly imbued with the heroism of martyrs; men who had learned to face death unflinchingly for the good of others. Of such men in our day was Father Damien, the Apostle of the Lepers—a true disciple of his prototype St. Roque, of whose personal life we in Scotland seldom hear, though his fame in his native city exceeds that of St. Giles. He was born in Montpellier, of a noble family, and first came in contact with the plague during a pilgrimage to Rome, while passing through the town of Piacenza. Here he gave himself up so devotedly to the sick and the dying that ere long he also fell a victim to the pestilence; but notwithstanding all his noble deeds of mercy, he was immediately shunned by every living creature except his faithful dog, which persistently followed him into the woods, where he had crept away to hide himself and die. Such was not his fate, however; for his hour had not come, and his task lay unfinished; but, like Lazarus in the parable, he found the very dogs were more humane than the rich. His dumb companion brought him food, gave him warmth, and moreover

THE CHAPEL OF ST. ROQUE

licked his sores until they were healed. So miraculous was his recovery that on his return to Montpellier he discovered the fame of his self-sacrifice had reached the city before him ; but the ovation he received only strengthened his vow to devote the rest of his life to the healing of loathsome diseases. He died among the poor of Montpellier in 1327, and was canonised ere the close of the fourteenth century.

This was the patron saint of the little Chapel of St. Roque, built upon the Burghmuir, which presented a vastly different scene in 1520 from its martial array in 1513. Instead of the bannered tents of King James, there hastily arose the log huts erected for the pest-stricken people who were driven on to the moor by order of the Burgh Council. All around the 'Bore Stone,' the spot where the Royal Standard had been pitched the night before the solemn march to Flodden, the shanties and the huts were crowded, some even beneath the very walls of Merchiston Castle, while the shadow of death hung like a cloud above them.

Part of the thirty-three acres of ground belonging to St. Roque's Chapel was used as a burial-place for the victims of the plague, and as the Grange of St. Giles was at the nether end of it, the secular brethren must have also taken part with the clergy in the sad services of those gruesome days—

> 'When the angel of death spread his wings on the blast,
> And breathed in the face of the foe as he passed.'

Weird indeed must have been the sight, also, of that huge boiling caldron seething night and day upon the moor, for the purifying and cleansing of the clothes of the plague-stricken. This took place near the Burgh Loch, under the superintendence of two citizens, called *'Bailies of the Muir,'* who, together with the cleansers and the bearers of the dead, wore grey gowns, with white St. Andrew's crosses 'behind and before,' and carried a long staff with a white cloth at the end of it.[1]

As the number of the victims rapidly increased, their clothes were either burnt or buried with them ; indeed, ere long individual burial became an utter impossibility, and deep pits were dug in the kirkyard of the Greyfriars Monastery, and other places, into which the ghastly burden of the *'dead carts'* was flung, as men would empty a cart of city refuse at present. Even this accumulated gathering of the bodies was at length prohibited, and the dead were buried where they fell, which accounts for the number of human bones found from time to time in private gardens in the infected districts.

[1] *Council Register*, 1568 ; Maitland, p. 31.

THE CHAPEL OF ST. ROQUE 13

Such were some of the stern realities taking place just beyond the fields and orchards of 'Sanct Geilie-Grange' shortly before the Reformation—a living centre of constant work for priest and friar each time this deadly plague revisited the city, which it did thirteen times within two centuries. Can we wonder, therefore, that the little Chapel of St. Roque was so enthusiastically supported by its votaries at such a period? The mass had not then been prohibited, and as each stricken household gave up its dead, solemn re-quiems ascended from the altar of the healer's shrine, and the passing-bell tolled night and day from *every* chapel tower. Never since

**Defunctos Plango.
Vivos Voco.
Fulmina Frango.**

BELL AND INSCRIPTION.

the knell of King James after Flodden had the 'great bell of St. Giles' rung out such solemn sounds—true to its ancient inscription : ' I mourn the dead ; I summon the living ; I disperse the thunder.'

Not a vestige now remains of this ancient chapel, the ruins of which stood, until the beginning of the present century, within a short distance of the Grange House. The site is still called St. Roque, with a modern mansion built over it. Upon the demolition of the ruin many of the beautifully carved stones were removed, and built up into the walls of an adjacent property, and are still in excellent preservation.

Among the sacred altars erected by pious donation at this period we find the little Chapel of St. John the Baptist, at the eastern end of the Burghmuir.

This Chapel was even more closely allied to the Grange of St. Giles than the shrine of St. Roque, being built upon part of the farm-lands, eighteen acres of the lands of 'Sanct Gelegrange,' and the quarry-land, and an acre and a

THE CHAPEL OF ST. JOHN

quarter of the muir-land, having been made over to it by Sir John Crawford, a prebendary of St. Giles, on the 15th of February 1512. In the charter of confirmation of this 'mortification,' as these charitable donations were then called, the position of the land is clearly set forth as 'lying at the east side of the common muir, betwixt the lands of John Cant[1] on the west, and the common muir on the east and south parts, and the Mureburgh, recently built, on the north.'

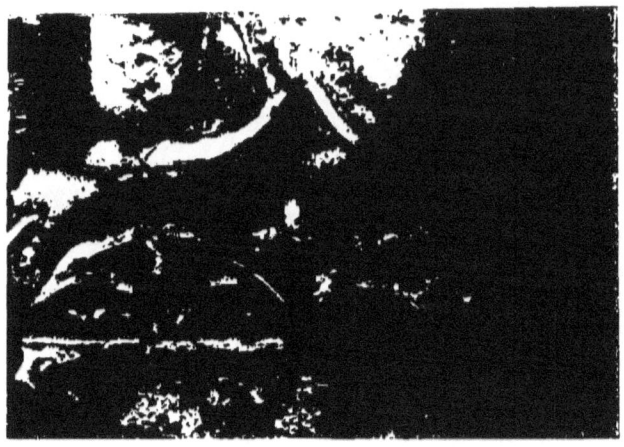

OLD STONE, ST. ROQUE'S.

Everything tends to show that this Chapel of St. John the Baptist was not built for a public place of worship, but rather as a hermitage chapel for some holy recluse, whose ministration was that of offering up perpetual prayers for the dead. Hence its perfect seclusion, away from the beaten city track, hedged in by trees on all sides, with only one officiating chaplain of advanced age, who lived like a hermit, clothed in a long white garment, bearing the representation of the patron saint on his breast, and for whose support an acre of ground was allotted, with a house and garden adjoining. The monks of this order were sometimes called *Studites*, and were supposed to live without sleep, being employed night and day chanting and praying for the dead, an office of no small emolument at that epoch in Scottish history. That such was the ex-

[1] At that time possessor of 'Sanct Geilie-Grange.'

THE CONVENT OF ST. KATHERINE OF SIENA 15

clusive purpose for which the Chapel of St. John was built is evidenced by the charter[1] itself, confirmed by James IV. on the 2nd March 1512-13, also by the conditions upon which, five years later, it was given over to the nuns of the newly erected Convent of Saint Katherine of Siena, which was built in 1517. In the deed of conveyance we find this clause or reddendo: 'Upon the day of the death of Sir John, and on the anniversary of it every year, the exequies for the dead shall be sung, with a mass for the repose of his soul, the bells being rung, and the wax-lights kindled upon the great altar with solemnity and decency.' In addition to this the Convent was to keep a lamp burning in the Chapel of St. John day and night, the cost of which was to be 'defrayed out of the oblations to be given on the Sacrament.'

This Convent also owed its foundation to Sir John Crawford, and it stood within a short distance of his little chapel. Some historians ascribe the erection of the Nunnery of St. Katherine of Siena to the piety and munificence of the Countess of Caithness, the wife of the opulent and powerful Sinclair of Roslyn, but Maidment says, 'this is altogether erroneous, for although the influence of the noble families of Seton, of Douglas, of Glenbervie, and of Lauder of the Bass was used to obtain the Papal authority for the endowment of the convent, it was to the venerable Sir John Crawford, and to the piety of a citizen of Edinburgh, called John Cant, and of his wife, Agnes Kerkettill, that the nuns were indebted for the *land* on which the building was erected, and from the produce of which a revenue for its support was to be derived.'[2] This fact is verified by their charter, which is dated 17th April 1517, and is confirmed by James V., with consent of the Duke of Albany, the Governor of the kingdom, on the 25th day of May following. By this charter of mortification or sacred donation, 'John Cant, burgess of Edinburgh, and lord of the lands mentioned, with consent of Agnes Kerkettill his spouse, and of Sir John Craufurd, chaplain, who held the lands from said John Cant, moved entirely by pious feelings, grants in pure alms to Josina Henrisoun and the rest of the sisterhood of the order of St. Dominic, commonly called St. Katherine of Sceinnes, in the place of Sheins, at the Church of St. John the Baptist (founded upon the lands of the said John Craufurd, there serving God), and to their successors, 18 acres of arable, built upon, and waste lands of the messuage of St. Giles, lying between the other lands of the blessed Giles, called Sanct Gelis Grange, and the lands of the Burrow-Muir of Edinburgh, with the right of

---

[1] *Register of the Great Seal*, 1306-1424, p. 132, No. 27.
[2] *Liber Conventus S. Katherine Senensis prope Edinburgum.* Printed for the Abbotsford Club. Abridged by James Maidment, Advocate.

THE CONVENT OF ST. KATHERINE OF SIENA

patronage of the aforesaid Church, which Sir John Craufurd resigns to them, with all profit or emolument arising therefrom.'[1]

But although the ground and endowment had been thus obtained, the building of the Convent itself was chiefly erected at the expense of Janet Hepburn, daughter of Patrick Hepburn, first Earl of Bothwell, wife of George, third Lord Seton, who was slain at Flodden. It was to this sacred retreat that the widowed Lady Janet Seton retired as soon as her eldest son George came of age. In the Nunnery of St. Katherine of Siena she died, in 1558, having survived her husband forty-five years. Her body was transported from the Convent by her grandson George, fifth Lord Seton, and interred in the Chapel of Seton, which she had partially taken down and rebuilt. The 'speciall actis and deidis of this ladye' are enumerated in the Chronicle of the Seton family,[2] who maintained at that time almost princely magnificence and state at their 'Palace of Seton'—so called in their Royal Charters. Lady Janet's granddaughter Katherine, second daughter of

SETON CHAPEL.

---

[1] *Register of the Great Seal*, 1513-1546, No. 701.
[2] *Cronicle of the Hous of Seytoun*. Printed for the Maitland and Bannatyne Clubs.

THE CONVENT OF ST. KATHERINE OF SIENA 17

the fourth Lord Seton, refusing every offer of marriage, took the veil and became a nun at the Sciennes, living there until its abolition. Her name appears as one of the sisters in the Letters of Reversion[1] granted by Dame Christian Bellenden, the prioress, in favour of Sir James Hamilton, at the time that they began to part with their lands. Katherine Seton shared the fortunes of the Sisterhood up to her death, in her seventy-eighth year, and she was buried in the Convent graveyard.

She was a very different person in every respect from the Catherine Seyton who figures so vivaciously in Sir Walter Scott's *Abbot*. The real Katherine Seton of the Sisterhood of the Sciennes was aunt to Mary Seton, the Queen's maid-of-honour, who had been chosen in her childhood as one of the four 'Maries' who went to the Court of France with the young Queen of Scotland. Mary Seton was the eldest daughter of George, sixth Lord Seton; and her half-brother, who was also George Seton, was Provost of Edinburgh in 1557. He was Queen Mary's most faithful adherent, both before and after her imprisonment in Loch Leven. These facts become extremely interesting as links in our history, when we remember that a branch of this Seton family shortly after this became possessors of the Manor House of the Grange by intermarriage with the Dicks and the Lauders.

It was at this period that the convents and monasteries throughout the British Isles had fallen into such bad repute, owing to the luxurious lives and scandalous habits of so many of the easy-going abbots and their jovial begging friars, unfortunately thus giving a warrantable pretext for the already grasping hand of those in power, whose palms were itching to possess the church-lands with their fair rents and revenues. What the country owed to the learning and the industry of these monasteries in earlier days, appeared of little weight when reformation was so sorely needed among them, possessing, as most of them did,

[1] Letters of Reversion by Dame Christian Bellenden, prioress of 'the place of the Sisteris of the Senes vpon the Borrowmure of Edinburght' (the Convent of the Sisters of St. Catherine of Sienna), in favour of James Hamilton of Crawford-John, Knight, for redemption of his lands of Manerstoun, in the sheriffdom of Linlithgow, mortgaged by him to the Convent for 1000 merks Scots. Upon the payment of which sum on the high altar of the church of said Convent, 'in gold & syluer efter following, that is to say, twenty sevin score gude crovnis of the Sone of gold price of the pece twenty-foure schillingis, nynetene gude vnicornis of gold price of the pece twenty-thre schillingis, ane rydare of gold price thareof thretty schillingis, ane crossat ducate of gold, ane abbay crovn price of it twenty-thre schillingis, and the rest of the said soume in gude & usuale money of Scotland haifand cours of payment for the tyme,' the prioress binds herself and the convent to renounce and resign the lands in favour of Sir James Hamilton. Dated 31st July 1555. The following are the sisters whose signatures are upon this document, written by themselves or a notary: 'Sister Christian Bellenden, prioress; Sister Elizabeth Napier, sub-prioress; Sister Katherine Seton; Sister Elizabeth Herries; Sister Margaret Napier; Sister Agnes Napier; Sister Marion Crawford; Sister Isabel Cant; Sister Agnes Maxwell; Sister Jean Douglas; Sister Elizabeth Napier; Sister Katherine Nisbet.'—*Historical Manuscripts Commission*, Duke of Hamilton's MSS., No. 167, p. 222.

C

more means than morals. Even into the secluded convents there had been gradually creeping a mundane spirit of frivolity, causing them no longer to be desirable seminaries for the daughters of the nobles, nor sacred sanctuaries for the pious recluse seeking safety from the foibles and fashions of society.

It was no doubt due to the beautifully consistent character of Lady Janet Seton, the first patroness of St. Katherine's Convent, that the nuns belonging to it excelled all others in the strict purity of their lives. Of this we have the testimony of Sir David Lindsay, a contemporary and a Protestant. Mr. James Muirhead also corroborates the fact in a letter to Mr. Charles Kirkpatrick Sharpe, in which he says: 'In duty bound, I have been charitable to the Sciennes ladies of the Scotch nunneries,' for 'those at Sciennes and Haddington were really respectable.' Strange indeed had it been otherwise, considering the virtuous example of the guardian saint of their order; for of all the patron saints of the Romish calendar, St. Katherine of Siena bore the sweetest likeness to the purity of the lily, the flower of her choice, even in her earliest maidenhood. We are told, 'Purity clothed her as with a garment,' the radiance of which was felt and acknowledged, not by austere monks alone, but by the nobles and the rustic youths whom her beauty and intelligence attracted to her parents' lowly home in the Contrada d'Oca, in the quaint old town of Siena. But even 'undoubted respectability' could not save the nuns of St. Katherine's Convent when the decree of destruction had gone forth. The first intimation that their sacred domicile was not destined to stand for generations came with the rude shock of the battering-rams of the English in 1544; and yet, for several years after this, the gentle sisters found shelter within the shattered walls of the Nunnery,—in fact, until they were driven out by force in 1567.

Part of their land had been feued to the Town Council several years previous to their expulsion; and now, on account of the destruction of their place—church, gardens, and houses,—the expelled nuns of the sisterhood were obliged to disperse themselves, in their absolute poverty, among their friends and relations.

In 1571 the rest of the ground, being eighteen acres of arable land, with the gardens and orchards of the ruined convent, lying between 'Sanct-Gely-grange,' and the lands of the Burghmuir, was feued for certain sums of money, by Lady Christina Bellenden, the 'Prioress of St. Katherine de Cenis,' to her nephew, 'Henry Kyncaid, second son of the deceased John Kyncaid of Warriestoun,' to descend to his brothers Alexander and John Kyncaid. They belonged to the Kyncades of Campsie, whose kinsman, David Kincaid of Coates, had been nominated first Constable of Edinburgh Castle in 1542, the

THE CONVENT OF ST. KATHERINE OF SIENA 19

year Queen Mary was born. This charter of Lady Christina Bellenden is dated at Warriestoun and Edinburgh, 5th July 1571.[1] That part of the convent lands which had been feued to the town in 1537 lay on the south bank of the Burghmuir loch, with a pathway leading directly to 'Sanct-Gely-grange,' past the Nunnery of the Sciennes. The Moor loch being at that time completely on the outskirts of the town, it was used, as such places usually are, by the rural population for the washing and drying of clothes—so much so that the Provost and Bailies, after taking possession of their portion, ordered 'that no persons should wash any clothes in this loch in future, under pains and penalties.'

From a loch, in course of time by sundry drainings it became a marsh; and eventually it was leased in varying portions to different tenants. But ere this the clerical community of St. Giles had shared the fate of the Sisters of the Sciennes—being all scattered or imprisoned, and their goods and chattels confiscated. The community had consisted of at least a hundred ecclesiastics, under a Provost, a Curate, and sixteen Prebendaries, supported by particular endowments and lands, with the oblations and donations to the various altars. These altars were now all taken down, and

DOORWAY, ST. GILES'.

[1] *Register of the Great Seal*, 1546-1580, No. 1980. It is strange that there should be so much dissimilarity in the ways of spelling the word Siena. In the various records of this period we find it written, Scheynnes, Schenes, Shiens, Siens, Cenis, Senis, Senys, Siena, Sienna, and Sciennes.

completely stripped, all the valuables cleared out, the gold and silver articles being carefully secured and catalogued,[1] and the mob winding up their proceedings by throwing the ancient relic, the arm-bone of St. Giles, into the churchyard to find its own grave. John Knox was installed as sole pastor in 1560; and henceforward the cathedral again became a simple parish kirk; but its old name still clung to it, notwithstanding all the efforts of an excited populace to banish 'Sanct Geil' from the city, first drowning his image in the Nor' Loch, and then erasing his effigy from the burgh seal and city banner, supplanting it with the old Scottish thistle.

STEEPLE, ST. GILES'.

In spite of all that, even in this protesting nineteenth century, there he still sits in his niche over the doorway as guardian saint of the old historic pile, called, as of yore, the Cathedral of St. Giles. The beautiful Gothic crown, however, did not pass altogether unscathed through that stormy period; but it was repaired 'without detriment to its original character' in 1648, and the Scottish metropolis is as proud of its commanding beauty to-day as in the days of Marmion, when

> 'High o'er it rose St. Giles' belfry crown
> Of curious fret-work, whence the moonlight stole
> In regal guise.'

---

[1] The inventory of the sacred utensils of the different altars, as taken by the Town Clerk, is given in the Appendix, Note II.

CHAPTER III

THE LANDS AND MANOR-PLACE OF GRANGE

'The honest heart that 's free frae a'
Intended fraud or guile,
However Fortune kick the ba',
Has aye some cause to smile.'

BURNS.

E now come to that portion of the history of the Grange of St. Giles in which it passed out of ecclesiastical hands entirely, and became the 'Manor-Place of Grange.' The 'superiority,' as we have already seen, had been transferred from the Wardlaw family into that of Cant, in 1506, a few years previous to the building of the Chapel of St. John and the Convent of St. Katherine of Siena, when John Cant and his spouse, Agnes Kirkettill, were empowered, in 1517, to grant to the nuns eighteen acres of its lands, as superiors, whereas Sir John Crawford consents as vassal and prebendary of St. Giles. There is every reason to believe the above-mentioned pious couple were then residing in the family mansion in Cant's Close—upon the gable-ends of which their initials I. C.—A. K. are still distinctly to be seen, cut on two shields, where, notwithstanding the narrowness of this ecclesiastical wynd, there are also two splendid pillars of ashlar-work, with huge stone balls on the top, the remains of a magnificent entrance to this once elegant place of residence, where Adam Cant lived, who was Dean of Guild in 1450, and mid-superior of the lands of Priestfield; for the Cants were a very ancient family, noted as merchants, burghers, and churchmen. There is also documentary evidence that the Cants retained the superiority or lordship of Sanct-geligrange for one hundred and thirty years; during which time several deeds and charters were granted in reference to it. From these we learn that John Cant and Agnes Kirkettill had two sons, Thomas and Walter. The elder heired his father in the Grange of St. Giles, and Walter is styled 'indweller in Leith.' Thomas Cant of Sanct Geligrange[1] had also two sons, John and

[1] In the *Register of Deeds* we find Thomas Cant of Sanctgillygrange standing surety to 'Mergret Levingstoune, Lady Yester,' in an obligation to her son William, Lord Hay of Yester, dated 13th September 1566.—Vol. vii. fol. 321.

James, and in 1572 he made a grant of the lands of the Grange, with the manor-place, houses, buildings, tenants, etc., to his eldest son and heir-apparent, at the same time reserving his own liferent therein. As no mention is made of his spouse, it would appear as though the deed were enacted in consequence of her death—for on the 7th January (1572) 'Sasine' of the lands was taken by the said John ; one of the witnesses of the transaction being Robert Fairlie of Braid, but it was not until 1st November 1577 that the charter was confirmed by King James VI. at Holyroodhouse.[1]

These family contracts between one member and another are sometimes rather complicated. Two years later we find that John Cant, now styled '*fiar* of Sanctgeligrange,' died, leaving a son and heir called Walter—whereas the grandfather, Thomas Cant, liferenter in the Grange, was still alive, also the grandfather's brother, Walter, the 'indweller in Leith,' and James Cant, uncle to Walter junior, in which case the lands of Sanctgeligrange did not fall to his inheritance, the position of 'fiar' being taken up by his uncle James. But Walter Cant the younger appears to have been left with means, and sufficiently independent to be enabled to lend his uncle 400 merks, which he binds himself to refund by an annual rent of 40 merks, payable out of the Grange lands. This contract was registered on the 5th October 1579,[2] and also another deed on the same day, whereby Walter Cant junior lends to his grandfather, Thomas Cant, and his uncle James, conjointly, 700 merks, as a mortgage or '*wadset*' on the same lands, for 70 merks annually—they being interdicted from selling the property, by Walter Cant, elder, at that time one of the Bailies of Leith, and heir of the liferenter.[3] Immediately after this we find young Walter Cant paying to his grandfather and his uncle James another sum of money (1750 merks), in order that they may redeem certain bonds which exist over the lands of Sanct-geligrange, and James Cant engages himself never to '*wadset*' them again, granting his nephew, Walter Cant, and his heirs, a Charter of Alienation —in security of the money lent—that he may uplift the annual rent or interest thereof without impediment, and Walter promises in return to give them a 'Letter of Reversion.'[4]

But James Cant was never called on to fulfil his share in the engagement anent the mortgage, for during the next year (1580) both he and his eldest son James passed away, leaving the second son, Alexander, to heir them both and fulfil their duties towards his great-grandfather Thomas, and his great-uncle Walter the bailie. In his first recorded deed, which is a contract with Sir

---

[1] *Register of the Great Seal*, 1546-1580, No. 2733. [2] *Register of Deeds*, vol. xvii. fol. 251.
[3] *Register of Deeds*, vol. xvii. fol. 252. [4] *Ibid.* fol. 254.

THE LANDS AND MANOR-PLACE OF GRANGE 23

Alexander Napier of Merchiston, Master of the Mint, dated 1580,[1] we find he is already married to Cristane Rae, and consequently of age to enter into the agreement made by his grandfather concerning the lands of Sanctgeligrange. This charter was not confirmed by the King until 1582, when Walter Cant, the Bailie of Leith, had retracted his interdict, and consented to the *bona fide* sale of the Grange property to his young relative Walter, who, in the interim, had become espoused to Margaret Prestoun, grand-daughter of Sir Simon Preston of Craigmillar, in whose town mansion, called the 'Black Turnpike,' Queen Mary was lodged as a prisoner after her surrender at Carberry—Sir Simon Preston being Provost of the city in that memorable year, 1567. In this Contract of Acquisition, besides the 'lands of Sanctgeligrange,' it distinctly states 'the manor, mills, coal tenants, etc.,' and also that the liferent of the old man, Thomas Cant of Sanctgeligrange, is still reserved. The confirmation of this charter by James VI. at Dalkeith is dated 8th May 1582,[2]—two years and six months after the contract had been signed. (It was five years in the case of the former charter between Thomas Cant and his eldest son, John, which often gives rise to considerable confusion in the matter of dates.) From subsequent deeds it appears evident that the Cants lived at the Grange house, leasing and letting various portions of the lands, with the farm-buildings and cottages upon the estate; and as this is the last charter in which Thomas Cant is mentioned, we may naturally conclude that, having exceeded his threescore years and ten, he was now gathered to his forefathers, leaving his great-grandson Walter Cant as lord of the manor.

The next transaction publicly recorded with regard to Sanctgeligrange is the reversion of the eighteen acres of the arable lands of Sciennes, formerly belonging to Sanctgeligrange, which Henrie Kincaid had feued from the Prioress of the Convent, and afterwards disponed to 'John Naper, fiar of Merchiestoun, Anna Chisholm his spouse, and John Naper their eldest son,' under reversion for payment of '2000 twentie-shilling pieces *of the fynnes of ellewin deneris.*' This sum being paid down by Walter Cant, they promised to release the lands, and *infeft* him and Margaret Prestoun his wife in them before Whitsunday 1593 at furthest. Six of these acres had been leased to John Rae in the Potterrow: most probably the father of Cristane Rae, whom young Alexander Cant, Walter's cousin, had married. There was a whole year's delay in the fulfilling of this contract on the part of the Kincaids, owing to the dishonesty of James Logan, the notary whom they had employed, and against

---
[1] *Record of Deeds*, vol. xviii. fol. 63.
[2] *Register of the Great Seal*, 1580-1593, No. 396. Appendix III.

whom Henry Kincaid of Auchinreoch lodged a complaint, stating that having intrusted him with the completing of the contract in 1592, he had for some reason put it out of the way, and fraudulently refused to deliver it for registration.

However, on being summoned, he produced it, and the parties being present, and agreeing to the registration, it was done on the 2nd August 1593.[1]

The sudden domestic changes which took place at Sanctgeligrange immediately after are rather startling. Within one short year we find that Walter Cant is dead, and his widow the affianced bride of Mr. Alexander Thomson of Duddingston, Advocate. There is no mistaking the fact, for the deed whereby he grants to 'his future spouse Margaret Prestoun, relict of Walter Cant in St Giles Grange, the land of Wester Duddingston and half the mill in liferent,' is signed and dated at Edinburgh, on the 18th July 1594. Among the witnesses are John Moresoun, burgess there, and Isaac Moresoun his son.[2]

It is as though we had arrived at a distinctly marked epoch in the history of Sanctgeligrange, and a complete veil was suddenly cast over this hitherto notable family, whose old manor-place now mourned its master in silence.

The quaint inscription in Old French,[3] carved on the lintel of the original doorway, not only commemorates to us the exodus of the family, but also the transition of its possessors from the Romish to the Reformed faith. It is almost like a seal above the portal, closing it for a time.

REPOSE A DIEVRS AN ANNO 1592

More than four hundred years had passed since Sanctgeligrange was handed over by King David to the 'friers of Harehope,' and during all that period its owners had been under the dominion of the Catholic religion, and in many instances in immediate connection with the Romish Cathedral of St. Giles.

In anno 1592 the Reformed Church of Scotland was *legally* established by James VI., and from thenceforth Protestantism held sway. It was a new era

---

[1] *Register of Deeds*, vol. xliv. fol. 310.
[2] *Calendar of the Laing Charters in the University of Edinburgh*. Edited and Abridged by the Rev. John Anderson, Assistant Curator of the Historical Department, Register House. 1594, No. 1276. [1077. Box 29.]
[3] This inscription is still perfectly legible, notwithstanding its many coats of paint. It is easily seen half-way down an inside stair leading from the butler's pantry to the servants' hall at the Grange House.

THE LANDS AND MANOR-PLACE OF GRANGE

for Scotland, and also for this particular manor as an ecclesiastical grange. Serfs, monks, abbots, canons, and vicars had all disappeared, and with them the whole brotherhood of St. Giles had gone to 'rest elsewhere.'

The next heir to Sanctgeligrange was John Cant, Walter's son, who could only have been a lad of eight or nine years of age.

The greater part of the lands were under lease at that time. John Dougall junior, son and heir of the late John Dougall, maltman, and burgess of Edinburgh, and his widowed mother, Janet Hutoun, had 'six acres and one rig' on lease, and John Rae had six acres as tenant. The eighteen acres of the Sciennes land, which had been redeemed by Walter Cant, with the proviso of a five years' lease after redemption, were still in the hands of the Napiers.

The lands of Ravensbee appear also to have belonged to the Cants, and the first public document signed by young John Cant is the disposition of this property to 'William Guthrie of Gogie,'[1] which is recorded in the Books of Council and Session 11th June 1605, which, as far as we can judge, would be the year of his coming of age. Then follows the unmistakable proof of his marriage seven years later, upon which he resigns his lands of Sanctgeligrange into the King's hands as 'Suzerain,' and they are again royally confirmed to him in conjunction with the name of his spouse; thus—'James VI., for himself and as administrator for Prince Henry, confirms to Mr. John Cant of Sanctgeliegrange, and Katherine Creech his spouse, the lands of Sanctgeliegrange, with the manor-place, mills, coal tenants, etc., which the said John resigned on the 14th May 1612, to be held by them and their children, whom failing, the heirs and assignees whomsoever of the said John, of Prince Henry, for payment of a pair of gloves at the feast of St. Giles in the Church of St. Giles, at Edinburgh, in name of *blench.*' Dated at Edinburgh 15th May 1612.[2]

We are delighted to find substantial evidence that the old manor-place of Grange again became the bridal home of another generation of the Cants— and there is little doubt that Mr. John Cant repaired and embellished it in a manner befitting his position, in token of which he placed above the PAX · VOBISCUM of the Past another sculptured stone proclaiming his marriage to posterity.[3] In the initials of Master John Cant and Katherine Creich there is no ambiguity whatever, nor in the nine martlets in tiers of three on the sinister half of the shield as borne by the family of Creich, the date

---
[1] Burke's *Commoners.*   [2] *Register of the Great Seal,* 1609-20, No. 651.
[3] This stone is at present over the archway leading into the courtyard of the Grange House, its position from the principal entrance having been changed in the later alterations, on its reconstruction as a baronial residence.

26   THE LANDS AND MANOR-PLACE OF GRANGE

1613 being also most legible below the shield, the dexter half of which, however, does not represent the heraldic bearing of Cant pure and simple as given by Sir David Lindsay—which was a bend engrailed between three crescents

CARVED STONE—MASTER JOHN CANT AND KATHERINE CREICH.

sable,—but this difficulty clears itself when we study the whole composition, as a compound coat of arms, according to the marshalling so prevalent at that period, in recording an alliance by marriage, combined with other heraldic insignia. In this case the dolphins and fleur-de-lys surrounding the shield might denote the protection of the Royal Suzerain of the lands, Prince Henry Stewart, the dexter half of the shield being a combination of the crescent of the Cants with the mullets of the Kincaids, with whom they were closely allied in the past. It would also appear as though the 'bend engrailed' had been changed to the bendlet sinister to denote some irregular alliance in the family. With its unmistakable initials, however, it is one of the most authentically interesting relics of that period of the history of the Grange of St. Giles.

Before going further it may be well to note the frequent recurrence of the word *coal* among the appurtenances of the Grange lands. The 'privilege of digging coal,' as mentioned in many old Scottish charters, dates as far back as 1291; but at first this privilege was confined to the abbots and monks of the different priories and monasteries, who, among the usual alms bestowed upon the beggars at the church doors, included lumps of coal. This fact is mentioned by Æneas Sylvius while travelling in Scotland early in the fifteenth century, before he became Pope under the title of Pius II., and by him coal is called a black stone. 'This species of stone,' he says, 'whether with sulphur, or whatever inflammable substance it may be impregnated, the people burn in place of wood, of which their country is destitute.'[1] But coal had by no means come into general use even in the sixteenth century, and there is no mention of any pits being opened on the Grange land—in fact, no nearer than Gilmerton, and these were not put into active operation until 1627, but the specification of it in the charters secured the right of ownership to any coal subsequently

[1] Ænei Sylvii *Opera*, p. 443.

found below the surface of the lands leased. There were two mills on the estate, and two quarries, but no coal-pits.

With regard to the Burghmuir lands adjoining Sanctgeligrange, there are some interesting documents about this period, which are very minute in some of their boundary specifications, giving us a good deal of insight as to the condition of the immediate outskirts of the city at the close of that century —for instance, the Charter of Feu-farm, in 1586, 'by William Little, Provost, Andrew Sclater, William Naper, William Fairlie, and another, bailies of Edinburgh, narrating the exhaustion of their treasury in former years by giving money to the King; by public works and the pressure of this *last pestilence*; relieving the poor, and saving the city, empty of citizens; and that, in the meantime, the Common Moor, though in various parts pastured and cultivated by those in its vicinity, yields little or nothing. They have therefore determined to lease it, and have appointed some prudent citizens, that, reserving the rough, hard, and stony places for masonry, *and the use of the pest*, they should measure the arable parts, and divide them in convenient portions: which labour over, they determined on a public auction, desiring intending buyers to appear on a certain day to that end:—which being done, Andrew Stevinson, merchant in Edinburgh, offered the annual rent understated, the other company holding themselves in silence. Therefore the granters dispone in feu-farm to the said Andrew in liferent, and John Stevinson his grandson and his heirs-male, whom failing to the eldest heir-female, without division, all and whole that part of the waste lands of the Wester Common Moor, containing eight acres of land, lying betwixt the old part of the Common Moor belonging to John Dougall, younger (of Sanctgeligrange), on the east, the Powburn on the south, the highway leading towards the said burgh, of eighteen ells in breadth on the west, and a path nine ells wide on the south, for the sum of 40 merks Scots paid down. To be held of the Burgh in fee, etc. Reddendo fourteen bolls of barley between Christmas and Candlemas, and £16 on entry of each heir. Dated at Edinburgh 3rd October 1586.'[1]

Six years later another portion of the moor is granted in feu-farm by Provost Little and the bailies 'to John Wall, ironsmith, and his heirs-male, whom failing, the elder heir-female, on that piece of *arable* land, along with the *east garden* of the late sisters, nuns of the Seynis (Sciennes), formerly occupied by Henry Kincaid, and recovered and evicted to the burgh by a decree of the Lords of Council; also that piece of waste land of the Common Moor, next

[1] No. 1122, *Calendar of the Laing Charters in the University of Edinburgh*. Edited and Abridged by Rev. John Anderson. [139. Box 4.]

adjoining the said piece of (arable) land, on the north side of the same, extending in all to two acres and three particates of land, measured, lying within the liberty of said burgh and shire of the same, betwixt the *Lone* leading towards the village of Libberton and fixed stones, and the piece of arable land called the "lane of the buttis," with the passage towards St. Giles Grange on the east; the church, houses, and yards of the said nuns and the stones there fixed on the west; the arable lands of Mr. Archibald Graham, the said Henry Kincaid, and the heirs of the late Mr. James Makgill on the south; and the said highway or common passage leading from the said burgh to the place of the said sisters, the Wester Moor of said burgh and stones there fixed, and the piece of waste land, etc., on the north. To be held of the Burgh. Reddendo yearly five bolls and a half of barley as feu-farm. Dated at Edinburgh 4th August 1592.'[1] Among the witnesses are Alexander Uddert, Dean of Guild, and George Heriott, younger, goldsmith.

Strange to say, the next great change at the manor-place of Grange comes down to us through the ancient game of golf, which for many centuries past has been the national sport of Scotland, every hill round Edinburgh being then, as now, famous for its golfing-ground.

It was during a game on the 'furzy hills of Braid' that Mr. John Cant and Mr. William Dick, the merchant prince of Edinburgh, arranged the disponing and purchase of the estate of Sanctgeligrange, which they ratified by written offer and acceptance on their return at the manor-house of the same. The Disposition[2] which was afterwards drawn up was dated 19th March 1631. As this Disposition contained a clause of registration and a Precept of *Sasine*, from it we gather the facts of the transaction, but we need only transcribe such portions of it as are serviceable to our purpose :—

'In nomine Dei, Amen. Be it known to all men, by the present public Instrument, that on the 29th day of September, in the year of our Lord 1631, and of the reign of Charles, by the grace of God King of Great Britain, *France*, and Ireland, Defender of the Faith, the 7th year . . . William Dick, merchant burgess of Edinburgh, and Elizabeth Moresoun his spouse, holding in their hands a certain Charter of Sale and Disposition containing in itself a Precept of Sasine, made and granted by Master John Cant of Sanct Gillie-Grange, heritable propertor of the said lands, with consent of Katherine Criech, his wife, in favour of William Dick and Elizabeth Moresoun, and the longer liver of them, in conjunct fee, and the heirs born and to be born, etc. etc.

'All and haill of the lands of Sanct Gillie-Grange, with the manor-place, houses, lands, dove-cot, mills, etc. etc. And containing 6 acres, and one acre *lie lig.*, of the

---

[1] *Calendar of the Laing Charters*, No. 1239. [140. Box 4.]
[2] The Disposition is in the charter-chest of Sir Thomas Dick Lauder, and the Instrument of 'Sasine' is in the Register House.

THE LANDS AND MANOR-PLACE OF GRANGE

lands of Sanct Gillie-Grange, which sometime belonged in property to John Dougall, son and heir of the deceased John Dougall, merchant burgess of Edinburgh, and was resigned by him into the hands of the said John Cant, as superior thereof. But excepting the 18 acres of the said lands of Sanct Gillie-Grange, and the house and gardens, which were feued (or leased) to the Sisters of Schennis, and which sometime pertained to the deceased Henry Kincaid, and by him were disponed to John Naper of Merchiestoun, Ann Chisholm his spouse, and John Naper their son (these 18 acres not being comprehended in the Disposition). Which Disposition William Dick and spouse presented to James Murray of Balberton, Master of Works to the King, as Bailie on the part of John Cant and spouse, and which Disposition the said Bailie received into his hands.

'The Deed is written by William Chalmeris, servitor to Robert Pringill, Writer to the Signet . . . Which Disposition, dated 19th day of March 1631, is signed in presence of Sir William Nisbet of Deane, Knt.; Thomas Thomesoune of Duddingstoun; James Murray of Balberton; Master Ludovic Stewart, Advocate; the said Robert Pringill, and William Chalmeris.

'After reading of which Disposition and Precept therein contained, the said Bailie gave Sasine to William Dick and Elizabeth Moresoun his spouse.

'Done on the ground of said lands, in the Manor-place of the same, at 11 o'clock A.M., or thereby. Present—Sir William Nisbit, Master Ludovic Stewart, Master John Dick, son and heir-apparent of the said William Dick, John Moresoune, John Smaill, and Archibald Hamilton, burgess of Edinburgh.'

The term sasine, or *seisin*, was of much greater import in the law of Scotland than of England, and at that period the ceremony of infeftment which it implied was also more literal in the transaction. No person was then considered to possess a legal right to any landed property unless he had been presented before two witnesses with some of the actual earth and stone of the very soil by the party selling the land, a legal outcome, no doubt, of the more ancient method, called

'the simple plan,
That they should take who have the power,
And they should keep who can.'

Sir John Napier mentioned in this Disposition as possessor of the eighteen acres of *Sanctgelegrange* land was the famous inventor of Logarithms, who was born in 1550, and 'Ann Chisholm his spouse' was his second wife, John Napier junior being their eldest son. Sir John Napier's only son by the first wife (Elizabeth Stirling of Keir) was Sir Archibald, heir to the barony of Merchistoun, who afterwards leased the earldom of Orkney. These 'eighteen acres' were inherited by the said John Napier junior upon the death of his father in 1617, but five years later they again changed hands, according to a registered charter,[1] dated 30th July 1622, granting to Alexander Napier of

[1] *Registrum Magni Sigilli Regum Scotorum*, Register House, 1620-1634, No. 342.

Lauriston ' 18 acres of the lands of Shiennes, called Sanct-Gelegrange, with the place of Shiennes (Seynes) in special warrandice, on the resignation of John Naper of Chambaudie,' whose sister Margaret married James Stewart of Rosythe, the family to which Sir William Dick's mother belonged, thus forming another connecting link with the new proprietor of Sanct-Gelegrange, who had however not been knighted at the time that he took possession of the old manor-place. These eighteen acres of 'Shiennes' land eventually came into the Dick family, as we shall see further on.

By the sale of Sanctgeligrange the last link was riven in the chain whereby for nearly one hundred and thirty years the Cant family had held possession of the lands and manor-house of Grange. Mr. John Cant soon after became laird of Colmestoun, and Sir William Dick knight of Braid; but before we narrate the subsequent events of his remarkable career, we will turn back and take a glance at the earlier records of his family.

ROSYTHE CASTLE.

CHAPTER IV

THE DICKS OF ORKNEY

'Where rise no groves, and where no gardens blow,
Where e'en the hardy heath scarce dares to grow,
But rocks on rocks in mist and storm arrayed
Stretch far to sea their giant colonnade.'

SCOTT.

THE primogenitors of William Dick, merchant burgess of Edinburgh, who purchased the Grange estate from Mr. John Cant, were of Danish extraction, having been Dyke-Graafs, *i.e.* eminent officers of trust in Holland, before they appeared in Scotland, but his immediate ancestors came from Orkney. The first of that name on Scottish record was William de Dyck, alderman, first magistrate of the city of Edinburgh, anno 1296,[1] which implies a family of distinction even at that early date, the bent of whose energies had evidently been towards commerce from their earliest commencement.

The greater part of the foreign trade in those days was with Holland and the Netherlands, and the principal trading city for nearly four centuries was Campvere, where the De Dycks helped to form a settlement which eventually became exclusively Scotch. The export trade consisted chiefly of 'wool, woollen and linen yarn; hides, tallow, butter, oil and barrelled flesh, salmon, and herrings; also plaiden stuffs and stockings,' in return for which every manufactured article conceivable was imported, from a 'pin' to a 'wheelbarrow,' besides every species of luxury in spices, fruits, wines, jewellery, and silk, each article being marked 'made in Flanders' as conspicuously as at present they are 'made in Germany.'

This corporation of Scottish merchants at Campvere dates back to the reign of James I. of Scotland, whose sister Mary married Wolfaard van Borssele, Lord of Vere, in 1444, from which year the Scotch staple-right was transferred from Bruges to Campvere; and they elected a chief of their own, called a

[1] Burke's *Baronage*.

'Conservator.' They formed an entirely separate community, with the right to be governed by the laws of Scotland, perfectly independent of the local authorities, and also of 'their High Mightinesses of the Netherlands.' They had a quay and a street to themselves; and their staple-right prevented any goods from Scotland entering the Netherlands by any other city; neither could they be transferred from Vere until they had been sold there, thus securing the full monopoly of the trade. As a religious body they were also quite separate, having the choice of a minister of their own after they had adopted the Reformed faith; and even then the mayor of the city had to pay him 'a salary of 900 guilders per annum.' 'The Conservator, with a council of six, or at least four, was entitled to adjudge in every case connected with Scottish merchants or merchandise.'

In this community at Campvere the De Dykes became men of wealth and importance. We find, therefore, that for many generations they were successfully employed in the foreign traffic of this country, adding in no small measure to its mercantile prosperity at home and abroad. Mere names are of little interest; but when we come to the reign of James V. we still find them men of note and judging from the various charters under the Great Seal which were granted from time to time to different branches of the Dick family, they must have been possessed of no inconsiderable amount of property. It is well for us to mention the dates of these royal grants of land, as it is only by this means we can at present trace the origin of family estates.

In January 1539 the King granted a charter to James Dick, merchant burgess of Arbroath, of certain lands in that port which he found most convenient for his extensive shipping trade with Holland. Sir Alexander Dick was at that time Archdeacon of Glasgow—a zealous churchman of the Romish faith,—and he also obtained a charter under the Great Seal, commencing 'Domino Alexandro, Archidecano Glasguen. terrarum de Dillerburn, Dogflatt, etc. etc., in the county of Peebles, etc.,' dated 29th September 1548. We cannot say whether the Archdeacon and the merchant were brothers; but travelling northward, we find the son of the latter settled in Kirkwall in the Orkneys, as a man of property and a man of letters, who seems to have taken part in the political and religious struggles in the latter end of Queen Mary's reign. He is styled Alexander Dick, 'Provost of the Cathedral Church of St. Magnus,' and being a man of learning, he had both influence and power in the North—the Provost position being next in dignity after the Bishop. From a Disposition dated 7th January 1571, it appears that he sold a land of houses in Kirkwall to William Gude, burgess merchant there, which deed was after-

THE DICKS OF ORKNEY 33

wards confirmed by royal charter on the 13th April 1576, with the consent of Regent Moray, King James VI. being a minor.

The fine old Cathedral of St. Magnus, of which Mr. Alexander Dick was 'Provost,' was founded in 1138 by Rognvald, Jarl of Orkney, as a thankoffering for the recovery of his rights, and in honour of his uncle, Jarl Magnus, who had been cruelly murdered in Egilshay by his own cousin, and afterwards canonised by the Pope. 'This Cathedral of St. Magnus, with its massive proportions forming a complete cross church, is still a noble monument of the power of these ancient Norsemen; and while its colossal pillars stand, and its walls of red sandstone—from the island cliffs—hold together, Orcadians are not likely to forget Saint Magnus, whose piety it was designed to commemorate, nor Saint Ronald, who, aided by the wisdom of his father Kol, built it, nor the days of the glory of the Viking jarls, when their forefathers were such men of war as few Southerners cared to face.'[1]

ST. MAGNUS' CATHEDRAL, KIRKWALL.

The Bishop's Palace, close beside the Cathedral, is now a complete ruin, even the round tower, which was added to it in 1540 by Bishop Reid—the same Robert Reid who bequeathed to the town of Edinburgh the sum of 8000 merks for the purpose of erecting a University within the city. His statue still occupies its niche on the wall of his ancient tower, though time and weather have done much to mar its primitive stateliness. The Earl's Palace is even more ruinous than the Bishop's, though the date of its erection is 1600; but few care to remember the name of the infamous earl, Patrick Stewart, who built it, and still fewer will regret that its halls and its dungeons are deserted. Fearsome were the horrors perpetrated within its now silent walls, where torture and bondage were then synonymous with pow'r.

TOKEN, ST. MAGNUS' CATHEDRAL.

Orkney being, as it were, the cradle of the Dicks, its history is in a great

[1] J. T. Reid, *Art Rambles in Orkney and Shetland.*

measure so interwoven with their commercial and judicial transactions in the north, that it will be well, for a better understanding of their position, to record a few of the leading facts of the government of these northern isles prior to their day.

For four centuries from the year 870 the Norwegian jarls had kept undisputed sway over the lands of Orkney and Zetland. The greatest of these jarls were St. Rognvald, St. Magnus, and St. Clair; but the last jarl of that name, William St. Clair, exchanged his earldom of Orkney for the lands and castle of Ravenscraig in Fife, A.D. 1471, to facilitate the marriage settlement of James III. of Scotland with Margaret, daughter of Christian I., King of Norway, Sweden, and Denmark. 'By charter under the Great Seal, dated 26th January 1531, the earldom lands were feued to James, Earl of Moray, but by Act of Parliament in 1540 they were re-annexed to the Crown.'[1]

Most unfortunate was the subsequent creation of the Dukedom of Orkney, which Queen Mary bestowed upon the notorious Earl of Bothwell in 1567, while the lands of the earldom had already been conferred on Sir Robert Stewart, a natural son of James V.; but it was not until 28th October 1581 that he was created Earl of Orkney and Lord of Zetland by James VI., Bothwell having died in his prison at Malmö on April 14, 1578.

Dark and dismal in the extreme became the life and bondage of the Orcadians under the oppression and tyranny of Earl Robert, who made his chief abode at Birsay, where, upon the ruins of an old Norse castle, he, by cruelly enforced labour, erected a splendid palace after the plan of Holyrood. Over the gateway he placed the following bombastic inscription:—

DOMINUS ROBERTUS STEUARTUS, FILIUS JACOBI QUINTI, REX SCOTORUM, HOC EDIFICIUM INSTRUXIT. SIC FUIT, EST, ET ERIT.

(Lord Robert Stewart, son of James V., King of Scots, built this house. 'So it was, is, and shall be.')

This is one of the Stuart mottoes; but the word *Rex* instead of *Regis* very nearly cost him his head, and added terrible weight to the charge of high treason in the trial of his even more infamous son, Earl Patrick, who succeeded him in 1592, and whose 'pomp was so great that he never went from his castle to the kirk, nor abroad otherwise, without the convoy of fifty musketeers, and other gentlemen of guard; three trumpeters always sounded as he sat at dinner and at supper.'[2]

[1] *County Families of the Zetland Islands.* By Francis J. Grant, W.S., Carrick Pursuivant of Arms.
[2] *History of James VI.*, p. 386.

THE DICKS OF ORKNEY 35

Besides the palace at Kirkwall, near the Cathedral of St. Magnus, Earl Patrick also built a castle for himself in the most picturesque part of Shetland, at the east end of the village of Scalloway. Mr. Gifford of Busta, writing of Scalloway, says, 'It has been a very handsome tower-house, with fine vaults, cellars, and kitchen, with a well in it, a beautiful, spacious entry, with a turret upon each corner, and large windows.' Considering the length of time it has been unroofed, the building is still in wonderful preservation. The walls are massive and well built; but the memories attached to every residence of this infamous earl are odious in the extreme. On one of the chimneys there is a huge iron ring, by means of which he is said to have hanged the victims of his vengeance—and they were many. Earl Patrick, like his father, Lord Robert Stewart, also placed a strange inscription over his doorway which seems to have been very prophetic of his own well-merited fate—

PATRICUS·STEVARDUS·ORCADIÆ ET ZELLANDIÆ COMES. I·V·R·S. *Cujus fundamen saxum est, Domus illa manebit stabilis; e contra, si sit arena, perit.* A.D. 1600.

(Patrick Stewart, Earl of Orkney and Zetland. James v., King of Scots. The house which is founded upon a rock will stand; but if, on the contrary, it is built on sand, it will perish.)

Earl Patrick being so little of a scholar that he could neither read nor write, he is indebted to the Bishop for the choice of this significant inscription, which was literally fulfilled in 1614, when he ignobly perished on the scaffold, paying the just penalty of his heartless oppression, his crimes, and his treason. With all his pomp and splendour, so ignorant was he, that it is said his execution had to be delayed until he could be taught decently to repeat the Lord's Prayer. Yet, such was the man whose power was paramount in Orkney—he not only made the laws, but his word was law. He chose the bailies and made the burgesses, uplifted all the customs, rents, and duties on houses, land, and property, and none dare come or go in his earldom without his permission. The sheriff was his deputy, and the bailies his tools. There was none to deplore his death, but many who could rejoicingly sing :—

> 'This dreaded prince no more
> Can harm us as of yore.
> Look grim as e'er he may,
> Doomed is his ancient sway,
> A word can overthrow him.'

But while this death-dooming pirate-earl had been so cruelly oppressing the

THE DICKS OF ORKNEY

Orcadians, the Dicks, descendants of Alexander, Provost of St. Magnus, were endeavouring to uphold and enrich the commercial prospects of those northern isles—not that there was sufficient financial scope for the whole family in Orkney, but they seem to have possessed chartered vessels for trading between the ports, and some of them we find wending their way southward, attaching themselves to royal burghs as bailies and burgesses; others again obtained grants of land, turning their attention to agriculture. Among these we find John Dick of Cartmore, who, with 'Elizabeth Kinnimonth his spouse' was granted a charter of the lands of Easter Cartmore in the county of Fife, dated 12th May 1587, and George Dick the lands of Meiklewood in Ayrshire. But John Dick, the eldest son of the Provost of St. Magnus, appears to have remained, for some time at least, in the Orkneys, possessing a considerable amount of property in the quaint old town of Kirkwall, besides the islands of North Ronaldshay and Oronsay—picturesque but low-lying rocky islands where the primitive Dutch-looking windmills are still in use owing to the flatness of the soil.

Mr. John Dick having imbibed the principles of the Reformed Faith from his father, it assisted him greatly in his commercial intercourse with Denmark, which country being at that time Lutheran, it specially favoured all Protestant traders. Finding it would be advantageous to his prospects, therefore, Mr. John Dick took command of one of his own ships, and went in person to prosecute his business over there.

Fortunately for him, it so happened that he chose the same year in which King James VI. went over to Norway to meet his bride, the Princess Anne of Denmark; and, in consequence, Mr. Dick not only became an eye-witness of the royal marriage which took place at Christiania, in the Cathedral of St. Halvard, on the 24th November 1589 (the ceremony being performed by the Rev. David Lindsay, who had gone over with the King), but was also invited to return with the royal squadron which conducted the Queen to Scotland in the following spring—the royal pair having remained in Denmark for the winter. This was the first step on the ladder to personal royal favour made by Mr. John Dick, the Orkney laird; and, being a man of learning and ability, he soon became a great favourite with King James, and a notable man at court.

His marriage about ten years before with Margaret Stewart, a descendant of the Stewarts of Rosythe, had also augmented the status of the family. The only son of this marriage was Sir William Dick, born in 1580, whose history we are about to relate.

THE DICKS OF ORKNEY

He commenced his public career very early in life, applying himself most assiduously to commerce. He began by farming the crown rents in the northern isles at £3000 sterling, and acquired so much wealth even in his father's lifetime that he was enabled personally to advance to King James VI. 'the sum of £6000 sterling, to defray his household expenses when he held a parliament in Scotland, anno 1618.'

With the Scottish King James as with all his predecessors of the Stuart race, ready money was ever a scarce commodity, even after his Majesty's accession to the English throne. From this time forth many and weighty were the pecuniary obligations of the royal family to Sir William Dick—which obligations King Charles a few years later acknowledges by royal precept in the first charter granted to Sir William, in these words: 'Our said Sovereign lord for the good and faithful services done and performed by the said Sir William Dick to his Majesty and his Highness' umqhile fayther of worthy memory, in time bygane and for several other good reasons and considerations mouving us,' etc.

This charter we shall mention in due course, and in the meantime we find Mr. William Dick increasing his responsibility in the Orkneys.

At that period the Islands of Orkney and Shetland again belonged to the Crown—and 'on the 19th May 1627 Charles I. leased the Earldom of Orkney and Lordship of Zetland for five years to Sir Archibald Napier of Merchiston,' who had been appointed Treasurer-Depute of Scotland in 1622. 'For an augmented rental of 7000 merks, Sir Archibald sublet his rights in these islands to Sir William Dick,' then styled merchant-burgess of Edinburgh, but two years later, 'Sir Archibald resigning his lease into the King's hands, together with his *subtack* to William Dick, the King conferred these rights upon John Murray, Earl of Annandale, for the period of eight years from Whitsunday 1629.' At the close of this lease in 1637, King Charles, having proved still further the loyal fidelity of Mr. William Dick, granted to him 'a direct tack from the Crown, for six years, at an annual rent of £35,733, 6s. 8d. Scots.'[1]

Besides this heavy rental Mr. Dick also farmed the customs on wine at £6222 sterling per annum, or, as it was then stated, one hundred and twelve thousand merks.[2] He next established a commercial intercourse with the Baltic and the Mediterranean through bills of exchange, eventually becoming

---
[1] *Zetland County Families.* By Francis J. Grant, W.S., Carrick Pursuivant of Arms.

[2] Act of Parliament, Charles I. 1633, whereby—'To William Dick, merchant-burgess of Edinburgh, the said impost of wynes ar sett for the space of fyve yeirs efter his entry quhilk was upon the 1st of November 1629 yeirs—for the yeirly payment of the soume of 112,000 merks.'—Vol. v. 1625-1641.

the most eminent banker that Scotland had yet produced, his bills extending even to 'the dominions of the Turks.' But it required all the tact and energy which the future Provost, Sir William Dick, possessed in a remarkable degree, to carry on these various commercial enterprises, in some of which he was greatly aided by his sons. Sir William had married very early in life, being espoused in 1601 to Dame Elizabeth Morrison, daughter of John Morrison of Prestongrange and Saughtonhall, whose son, Henry Morrison, merchant-burgess and bailie in Edinburgh, married Katherine Dick, Sir William's only sister.' The children begotten of Sir William and Dame Elizabeth were seven in number—five sons and two daughters. The two elder sons studied the law and attained the degree of advocates, the third and fourth sons became merchants, and the youngest entered the navy.

SIR WILLIAM DICK AND HIS FAMILY.

When Mr. John Dick, the eldest son, had been three years at the bar as an advocate, he was appointed Sheriff-Depute of Orkney in 1628, the year before his father obtained his new lease as 'tacksman' of the lands of the Earldom of Orkney. This sheriff appointment being for life, Sir William settled his son in their northern property, and directed his own steps southward again, where he became Provost of the city of Edinburgh. The family of Dick continued for many years in close connection with Zetland and the Orkney Isles, and by their foreign trading did much to improve the primitive ways of the people among whom their lot was cast. At that period these northern islands were in a much more peaceful and unanimous condition than in the previous century, when the inhabitants had been so cruelly oppressed and rack-rented by the unscrupulous noblemen upon whom the Earldom of Orkney had been conferred.

In 1630 Mr. John Dick, Sheriff-Depute, also called fiar of Braid, was granted a seat, or official pew, in the Cathedral of St. Magnus, of which his great-grand-

THE DICKS OF ORKNEY 39

father had been provost. At this time he could not have been more than twenty-eight years of age. He took for his bride the young widow of Sir John Morrison of Dairsie in Fife, Nicolas Bruce, the daughter of Sir George Bruce of Carnock. They had three sons—William, John, and Andrew—who must all have been very young when their father died in 1642. By his early death Mr. John Dick was spared not only the sorrows that befell his own family, but also the disastrous pillaging with which Cromwell's soldiers ravaged his sheriffdom after the death of Charles I. Ere this Sir William Dick's second son, Andrew, had been appointed Sheriff of Orkney and Zetland in his brother John's place; and, upon the event of his second marriage, he obtained a charter from Charles I., in conjunct fee with his spouse, Jean Leslie, of the lands of Holland, with the manor-place, the 'towmailles, quoyes, quoylands, outbreckes, nesis,' fishings, tenants, etc., in the Isle of Stronsay, parish of St. Nicholas, sheriffdom of Orkney, which were resigned by William Henrysoun of Holland, with consent of Margaret Grahame, his spouse, and which the king incorporated into the free barony of Holland, with manor-place of Holland as principal messuage, the feu-duty to the King being 'thric calders of barley and four barrels of buller, with suits and presences at the head courts of the said sheriffdom, with the customary services.' Failure for three years running in payment of the duties involving loss of the charter, which dated from Linlithgow, 6th March 1646.[1]

This was a very critical period in the history of Scotland, owing to the enormous loans granted to the state by the nobles, who sacrificed houses, lands, and money most freely for their country's service. Most of the landed estates in the kingdom then became so heavily mortgaged that in some cases they never reverted to the original owners. Among the staunch loyalists who made considerable sacrifices for Charles I. was William, seventh Earl of Morton, in return for which he obtained, in 1643, a grant in the form of a wadset of the Earldom of Orkney and Zetland, which had reverted to the Crown on the execution of Earl Patrick, redeemable on payment of the sum advanced to the king, viz., £100,000 Scots.

Weary and worn with the warfare between the Church and the State, the Earl of Morton retired to his newly acquired territory in the northern isles, and there he died on 7th August 1648, succeeded by his eldest son, Robert, whose honours were but short-lived, for he also died in Orkney on the 12th November of the following year, having survived the beheading of his royal master, King Charles, barely ten months. His young son, William, inherited the

[1] *Register of the Great Seal*, 1634-1651, No. 1622.

Earldom of Morton only, for his grandfather, Earl William, having found himself unable to sustain the duties and burdens of the Earldom of Orkney, had resigned it into the hands of the King in July 1647. It is strange that both the Dick and the Lauder families should at this time, quite independently of each other, have become financially complicated with the Earl of Morton's affairs, though these families were not united by marriage until the next century. Among the first charters of Charles II. we find him granting 'to Mr. Andrew Dick, lawful son of Sir William Dick of Braid, knight, and his heir or heirs of the first or second marriage, and their heirs and successors equally, the lands and Earldom of Orkney, south and north isles thereof, with superiorities, tenants, palaces, towers, and mills; offices of justiciary, sheriffdom, foudrie, and admiralty therein by sea and land (the Lordship of Zetland being excepted), which the late William, Earl of Morton, resigned on the 16th July 1647, redeemable by the heirs, successors, and assignees of the said earl for 100,274 merks, 10s., paying the proportion of the duties contained in the charter of the said earldom.' Signed at Edinburgh, 15th August 1649.[1]

On the previous day the king had also granted another portion of the Earl of Morton's estate in payment of a bond to Bailie Lauder (Sir John Lauder of Fountainhall), merchant-burgess of Edinburgh. The lands mentioned in the charter are so extensive and so varied in their character that it must have been a terrible downfall to the Morton family to have been under the necessity of contracting such a sweeping mortgage; and as it happened only a few months after the death of Earl William, we can well understand that such a crushing blow must have hastened that of Earl Robert also. The Morton estate, granted under legal reversion to Bailie Lauder, consisted of the lands and barony of Aberdour, with the burgh harbour and castle, etc. (*and a number of other lands in Fife*); also the barony of Kinross, including the loch and castle of Loch Leven (*and a number of other lands in Kinross-shire*); also some islands in the Orkney group, viz., Wallas and Hoy—the latter unequalled for picturesqueness in the whole of Great Britain or Ireland—with its mighty precipices of stupendous perpendicular rock; also South Ronaldshay, and the lands of Birsay, with its old castle built by Lord Robert Stewart, and the pertinents of these islands, in so far as they belonged to the king, or to William, Earl of Morton (deceased), or to the late Patrick, Earl of Orkney. This charter also included the right to a sum of £30,000 sterling, for which the Earldom of Orkney had been mortgaged to the Earl of Morton. All these lands were apprised from Robert, Earl of Morton, for £8910, 16s. 6d.[2]

[1] *Register of the Great Seal*, 1634-1651, No. 2135.   [2] *Ibid.* 1634-1651, No. 2134.

THE DICKS OF ORKNEY

One really wonders, after reading this long charter and the innumerable names (with which we have not tried our readers' patience), what could have been left as a patrimony for young William Douglas, ninth Earl of Morton, from whom Cromwell, as Protector of the Commonwealth, wrested even the semblance of an estate by annexing also the wadset of the Lordship of Zetland in 1657.

Mr. Andrew Dick appears, however, to have retained his connection with Orkney for more than twenty years: for when he was knighted by Charles II. in 1663 he is called 'Sir Andrew Dick of Craighouse and Northfield in Orkney.' This estate of the lands and island of Northfield he had acquired by a letter of alienation and disposition from his father, Sir William Dick of Braid, in 1651,[1] his father having acquired it from William Henrisoun of Holland, under reversion for payment of £5557, 11s. 3d. Scots, on the 19th November 1641. It was very comprehensive, including the lands of Towmailles, with rents, etc., of Sailnes and Sand, Nosse and Bousta, also Nouster and Holland, Udiesland, Skorrie, and others, all in the Sheriffdom of Orkney, which Charles II. confirmed to him in 1663, the year of his knighthood. After his death his nephew, Captain Andrew Dick, was appointed, on the 30th July 1669, Steward Principal and Chamberlain of Orkney and Zetland; and in 1678 he was elected to represent these islands in Parliament. In the list of members he is mentioned as 'Captain Andrew Dick, Steward-Convener for Orkney and Zetland Stewartry, third son of Mr. John Dick, fiar of Braid,'[2] thus putting his identity beyond all question. Captain Andrew married the daughter of an old Perthshire family, Francisca Nairne, by whom he had one son, William, and a daughter called Jean, who afterwards became the wife of Adam Sinclair, seventh Laird of Brew.[3] Before his death Captain Andrew Dick acquired a considerable amount of property in the old town of Lerwick, and extensive lands in the Shetland Isles, which, in 1701, descended to his only son, William Dick, called of Fracafield, from the village near Lerwick which gave the designation to the family until 1774. But the office of steward did not pertain to any of the Dicks after the death of Captain Andrew.

James, eleventh Earl of Morton, having been a zealous partisan for the union of the kingdoms of Scotland and England, he was requited for his services in 1707 by a renewal of the grant of the Earldom of Orkney and Zetland, and his nephew James, fourteenth Earl of Morton, also obtained an irredeemable right to the Earldom and Lordship of the Isles in 1742. 'On the abolition of heritable

---

[1] *Registrum Magni Sigilli*, Lib. lx., No. 388.   [2] Johnson's *Members of Parliament*.
[3] *Zetland Families*, by Francis J. Grant, W.S., Carrick Pursuivant of Arms, p. 15.

jurisdictions in 1748 he was awarded £7147 as compensation for the loss of his office as Steward and Justiciar of Orkney and Zetland. In 1766 he disponed his whole rights in these islands to Sir Laurence Dundas, Bart., of Kerse, in the county of Stirling, for £63,000.'[1] But long ere all this had taken place, the intercourse between landlord and tenant in the isles was on a much more genial footing, noblemen, even of the highest rank, taking a pride in visiting the crofts from time to time, no matter how small the holding of the tenant, and they would condescendingly partake of such refreshments as were offered them, however simple—'sweet milk, curds and cream, or even *churn milk*.'[2] Such was the reigning hospitality of these northern regions. One of the most interesting of the ancient customs that have now become obsolete was the '*directing of the cross*,' as it was then termed, which is analogous to the old Scottish 'Fiery Cross' of the Highlands, but in those far-away, primitive lands it was more frequently enforced for religious purposes than for warlike gatherings.

When, at the command of the minister, the sheriff, the justice, or the bailie, the Fiery Cross had been ignited, it could neither be extinguished nor laid down until every parish had been convened or admonished as to its intent and purpose. From hand to hand it passed, and with all sacred diligence from village to village, each messenger simply repeating to the next relay the words of the proclamation it symbolised. The penalty in default of the same was £16.[3]

Another of these 'Acts maid be the Sheriffs for the weill of the country,' commencing, '*Court holdin be me, Robert Sinclair of Saba, bailzie of St. Androis, at the Cheppell of Tolhope, upon the tenth day of March* 1666,' ordained the furnishing of a certain amount of heather by every householder in each parish, that it might be placed on the hill 'called Hamnihill, above the house of Horrie,' to be set on fire as a safety 'beacon,' or for giving the alarm at the appearance of strange ships, 'under the paine of fourtie schilling Scots,' and also that a constant watch of four men should be maintained on the hill, each household in the parish relieving their neighbours in turn, 'ilk four-and-twentie hours,' 'under paine of ten punds Scots.'[4]

The carrying out of these regulations and several other acts as quaintly minute, anent the weighing of goods, the selling of fish, the keeping of dogs, the riding of other men's horses, and cutting and stealing their tails, the harbouring of idlers and beggars, the punishing of vagabonds, and the hiring

---

[1] *Zetland Families*, by Francis J. Grant, W.S., Carrick Pursuivant of Arms, p. 15.
[2] Gunson's *Ancient and Present State of Orkney*.
[3] *Orkney Papers*. [4] *Antiquarian Magazine*.

THE DICKS OF ORKNEY

of Shetlanders to strangers, all came within the duties of the sheriff-depute and his bailies, who administered justice in all cases, both civil and criminal.

But, as far as we know, after the death of Captain Andrew Dick, none of the Fracafield family were ever appointed sheriff or bailie. This, however, did not expatriate the Dicks from Shetland or Orkney. They remained as residents there for more than seventy years, being landowners and landlords in the burgh of Lerwick and the surrounding parishes; and as at that time their estates were pretty equally divided between the mainland of Orkney and the mainland of Zetland, a by no means insignificant point of interest to them must have

OLD WINDMILL, NORTH RONALDSHAY.

been the rock-bound islet, miscalled 'Fair Isle.' Standing in mid-sea, half-way between Kirkwall and Lerwick, it is easily seen from afar in *fair* weather by its conical height; but for months it is enshrouded in mist, becoming a source of endless danger to the hapless mariners, lured to their fate by the strong gales, with neither warning-bell nor beacon-light to intimate their doom. In olden times, upon its summit, called 'Ward Hill,' the heather fire was kept ablaze; and 'the ruins of the guard-house can still be seen, where centuries ago the lonely watchman spent many a weary night, ready to kindle his signal-fire at the approach of a hostile sail.'[1]

> 'Upon each mountain s rugged height
> Gleamed luridly the watch-fire's light,
> Isle signalled unto isle.'

To this day the islanders point out the spot where, in 1588, *El Gran Grifon*,

[1] *Art Rambles in Shetland.* By J. T. Reid.

THE DICKS OF ORKNEY

one of the mighty ships of the great Spanish Armada, became a total wreck, with the loss of nearly a hundred lives. If those among the Spaniards who were rescued with the Duke de Medina found but meagre fare upon this almost barren island, they would also find still more meagre welcome when they began to devour not only the scanty supply of sheep and fowls, but also the very ponies of the poor islanders, some of whom, we are told, under cover of night hid their beasts in the rocky caves known only to themselves.

SCALLOWAY CASTLE.

SIR WILLIAM DICK OF BRAID, PROVOST.

TO WILLIAM DICK BAILLIE

ANAG. I WILL MACK EID

'*I will make aid*, since I by grace have strength
And hopes (by Christ) to conquis Heaven at length.'

An Acrostick Sonnet

'W Vpon those tops wher Vertue lives with Fame,
I would as worthy, there ingrave thy name,
L est that thy knowledge, which deserves renoun
L y unadmired into oblivioun.
I n full desire the contrae thou inherit ;
M ount therefore Fame into the highest spheare,
D eclare his doings daily maire and maire.
I s it not hee who by his Actions all
C an serve the King still, readie at a call?
K now also that the compass of his care
   By all men is accounted wondrous rare,
   Since for his wisdome and his vertues sake,
   This Kingdom scarcely can afford his make.
   Wherefor it must bee, and I may vow
   That God his actions alwayes doth allow.'

AD EUNDEM

'I askt the Eccho if it would
Thy gifts descrive to me,
Thou had no match it plainly told;
And it can no wayes lie.'

W. M.
(Col. William Mercer)
1637.

CHAPTER V

SIR WILLIAM DICK OF BRAID, KNIGHT

'With mortal crisis doth portend
His life to appropinque an end.'
SCOTT.

N order to resume the thread of Sir William Dick's remarkable career, we must go back to the time when he settled his eldest son John in the Sheriffdom of Orkney, which was in 1628. But it was not until March 1631 that Sir William commenced his extensive acquisition of landed property, his first purchase being Sanct-Geiliegrange;[1] the whole transaction having been arranged during a game of golf on the Braid Hills, and his son John came down from Orkney to be present at the ceremony of infeftment, which took place in the garden of the manor-place.

By this time the five sons had all grown to manhood, and it was natural that Sir William should suppose they would soon be desirous of settling themselves in life. Consequently, with his ever-increasing wealth, he determined to secure a comfortable home for each of them: but before doing so, he resolved to extend the domain of the patrimonial estate by purchasing a barony for his eldest son, and relegating the Grange to a younger one. It was in the month of August of the same year, therefore, that he fixed upon the estate of Braid, which lay

DICK COAT OF ARMS.

upon the east side of the Penicuik road. Situated in the picturesque valley of a woodland glen, a site of unsurpassed natural beauty, this estate com-

[1] See chapter iii.

SIR WILLIAM DICK OF BRAID, KNIGHT 47

prised both rocks and hills and upland meadows, farms and fishings, mills and mill-lands, all and sundry as resigned by Sir Robert Fairlie and his spouse, Lady Margaret Dalmahoy, with the consent of Alexander Fairlie, their eldest son and heir-apparent—the same Fairlie family who, in 1603, had purchased Bruntsfield Manor from Sir Alexander Lauder of Hatton.

Judging from the description given of its boundaries, the Braid estate must have been very comprehensive. It was divided into Aver and Nether Braid (now called Upper and Lower), and it included the Mains of Braid, with the manor-place; also Briggs of Braid and Braid Craig, Blackford, Greenbank, Plewlands, Smiddigrein, Egypt, etc., with all the cottages and crofts, tenants and vassals, arable lands and pasture lands—many broad acres most beautifully blended with upland and lowland scenery.

These lands were erected by the King into a free barony, and from this estate Sir William took his title, Braid House becoming henceforth the principal family residence, with this proviso, that Dame Elizabeth Moresoun, his wife, should renounce her conjunct fee in the manor-place and lands of Sanctgelegrange, accepting in lieu thereof an annual rent of 2000 merks from the Grange lands during her life.[1] The reason for this proviso became apparent within the next twelve years, during which Sir William obtained no less than eight charters under the great seal, not for self-aggrandisement, but for the future apportioning of his seven children. With his barony he also obtained the honour of knighthood from King Charles, for the many faithful services he had rendered to the Crown. But of a baronetcy there is not the slightest mention made in any of the documents; in proof of which not one of his sons took the title of *Sir* after his death, unless especially knighted by the King, as in the case of Sir Andrew, his second son. This is a very important fact, which seems to have been overlooked by the Dicks of Fracafield.

When Sir William purchased the beautiful estate of Braid, the heir-presumptive, his eldest son John, was alive, but he died thirteen years before his father. It may have been at the family home that he passed away, for he was buried at Greyfriars—not at Kirkwall in Orkney. He died, also, at the time of the family's greatest prosperity. One by one his younger brothers all married, and were settled by Sir William in fine estates of their own. But the patrimonial barony of Braid was the most beautiful of all. Situated in a lovely den between the Blackford and the Braid Hills, the manor-house was even then a veritable hermitage in its seclusion.

The present building is not the actual homestead purchased by Sir William

[1] *Register of the Great Seal*, 1620-1633, No. 1843; also Appendix, Note III.

Dick, for it was almost entirely rebuilt in 1780 after the Gordons of Cluny got possession of it. The chief attraction, however, was not the mansion but the estate. The rocky crags and pastoral hills, the wooded dells and wimpling burns, all beauties of nature's own forming, and therefore the historical associations connected with its name still cling to its surroundings. The far-famed 'furzy hills of Braid,' well known in Scottish lore as the halting-place of Edward I. and the hunting-ground of King James and 'his barons braw.'

The records of the property go pretty far back, showing that the manor was possessed by Henry of Brade, a family of note in the early annals of Midlothian. After the Henries the Fairleys became Lairds of Braid, and continued to hold it for many generations. In 1528 they sold part of their lands to Robert Bruce of Bynnings, and the rest of the estate Sir William Dick purchased in 1631 from Sir Robert Fairley, whose son Alexander had married Martha, daughter of John Knox and Margaret Stewart, who was the youngest daughter of the ' good Laird of Ochiltree.'

As John Knox was fifty-seven, and Margaret Stewart only a girl of sixteen when he took her unto himself as his second wife, she was still in the prime of her young womanhood when he died in 1572, ten years later; consequently we find her shortly after as the wife of Sir Andrew Kerr of Faudonside, with whom Alexander Fairley made the contract for his marriage with Martha Knox, her daughter.

We mention this because upon their marriage Martha Knox and Alexander Fairley had been infefted, in conjunct fee, in the lands of Over-Braid,[1] and consequently she had a voice in consenting to the sale of the property to Sir William Dick.

After Sir William became settled in his Barony of Braid, he installed his two merchant sons, William and Alexander, who were co-partners with him in business, as *fiars* of their future patrimony—the former of Sanctgelegrange, the latter of Plewlands. In 1637 his son William married Janet M'Math, the daughter of a wealthy merchant in Edinburgh, descended from the ancient family of M'Math of that Ilk in Dumfriesshire. At the time of her marriage with William Dick she was the childless widow of Thomas Bannatine, merchant-burgess, from whom she had inherited a goodly fortune.[2]

---

[1] Contract, dated at Lintoun, 7th April 1584, between Alexander Fairlie, son and apparent heir to Robert Fairlie of Braid, on the one part, and Andrew Ker of Fawdounsyde and Martha Knox, his gudedaughter, on the other part, as follows :—' Alexander is to marry the said Martha before 31st May next, and to infeft her in conjunct fee in Over-Braid, and Andrew Ker is to pay 1000 merkes with Martha as tocher.' Registered on the 25th June 1584 (*Register of Deeds*, vol. xxii., fol. 224).

[2] Appendix, Note IV.

SIR WILLIAM DICK OF BRAID, KNIGHT 49

As 'Lady Grayng,' wife of the first Baron of Grange, Janet M'Math eventually became 'the guardian angel' of the old manor-place. But during the past year stirring events had been taking place in the city, and though peace reigned in Sanct-Gillie-Grange, there was tumult in Sanct Gillie's Kirk. A royal mandate had been issued by Charles I., and intimations thereof were given from every pulpit in the town, announcing that the *liturgy* would be read on the following Sunday in all the churches. A large concourse of people consequently gathered in St. Giles' '*Cathedral*' to hear the Dean of Edinburgh officiate, in presence of the Lord Chancellor, the Lord Treasurer, the Privy Council, the Judges, and the Magistrates. No sooner was the Prayer-Book opened and the service commenced, than the first clash of opposition was raised by an old 'kail wife' called Jenny Geddes hurling her cutty-stool at the Dean's head. This was the signal for a general uproar, and a regular pitched battle ensued with sticks and stones; heads were broken and windows smashed, the bishops themselves barely escaping with their lives. This happened in 1637, the same year in which Janet M'Math and William Dick were married, and that memorable 23rd of July was ever after called 'Stoney Sunday.' Little did Jenny Geddes, the heroine of the 'cutty stool,' dream of the turmoil her onslaught of the Dean of St. Giles had raised in the city. The very atmosphere became ablaze with fiery zeal—not for righteousness, but for *creed*, that cold and cruel substitute for religion. Yet there were men on either side ready to lay down their lives for it, and Scotland's sons awoke like giants to show the world their powers of endurance. Father against son, and brother against brother, they meted out the bitterness of religious animosity : for the old persecuting spirit, which had been lulled for a space, now revived with fourfold rancour—not nation against nation, but man to man, they fought the same fight all over again beneath another banner. The cry was no longer, 'Down with the Papists !' but 'Down with the Prelates !' ' For God and the Kirk !' ' Join the Solemn League and Covenant !' and, lest any should escape confiscation or fire, men gripped each other by the throat as it were, demanding, ' King or Commonwealth ?'

Stormy political scenes, therefore, must the ancient walls of the Manor-House of Grange have often witnessed at this period, it being not only a central *rendezvous* for the Royalists, but also for those zealous Covenanters who had joined Sir William Dick of Braid's party, he being one of the most active leaders, on account of his substantial wealth and influence ; for it was universally acknowledged that Sir William was a man of great integrity and prudence, combined with an indomitable spirit. Every enterprise which he undertook had repaid him a hundredfold.

All this wealth was centred in a small warehouse in the Luckenbooths, under the shadow of St. Giles. So rapidly did he coin money, that he was supposed to have discovered the alchymist's secret of the philosopher's stone. Writing upon this point, Sir Thomas Dick Lauder says, ' He had the power of coining money, we mean not only metaphorically but in reality, for we are possessed of a very pretty copper coin of his, with the insignia of Commerce on one side, surrounded by the motto, "FORTUNA COMES VIRTUTI," and on the obverse a house, with his name, in the legend surrounding it, "WILLIAME DICK OF BRAID." So wealthy was he that his effects in money and landed estates amounted to no less a gross sum than £226,000 sterling—being nearly equal to two millions of money at the present day—which his descendants have documents to prove.' We can well understand, therefore, why this opulent merchant should have been chosen Provost of Edinburgh at this critical period— the same year in which the 'Solemn League and Covenant' was so enthusiastically signed by thousands of people in the Greyfriars' Churchyard, Sir William Dick being among the foremost, having already joined with the Earl of Montrose and other loyalists in defence of the religious liberties of their country. Four of Sir William Dick's sons—John, Andrew, William, and Alexander—signed the Covenant and joined the League with their father, the youngest son, Lewis, being at sea. It was at the close of his provostship that Sir William made ' a settlement of his affairs, and a disposition of part of his effects to be divided among his children amounting to about 600,000 merks.' A statement of his whole heritable and moveable estate was also drawn up about this time by his fourth son, Alexander,[1] showing the sources from whence he drew his large income. So extensive were his possessions, that it is said he could ride on his own land from Linlithgow to North Berwick.

His town residence was the splendid edifice in the High Street, then known as ' the mansion of Adam Bothwell, Bishop of Orkney,' who once possessed the ancient Barony of Broughton, and whose name has been handed down to posterity as the man who performed the ominous marriage ceremony between the infamous Earl of Bothwell and the unfortunate Mary Queen of Scots on the 15th of May 1567. There is very little of the former splendour left, but the building itself is still standing occupied as business premises. It was here Sir William Dick resided during his term of office as Provost of the city in

[1] Appendix, Note V.

SIR WILLIAM DICK OF BRAID, KNIGHT 51

1638-1639, but that the mansion was his own is proved by the disposition of sale after his death, and its title in the City Records as 'Sir William Dick's Land.' This period stands recorded in the annals of Sir William's life as the acme of his career. In the prime of life, the prime of wealth, and on the pinnacle of fame; honoured and honourable, sought of peers, and blessed by the people; his badge, '*Pro Rege, Lege, et Grege*,' upon his knightly banner, and his Motto, '*Publica salus nunc mea merces*,' the standard of his deeds.

Yet so zealous had Sir William now become for the Covenant, that he was ready to sacrifice everything for the national welfare 'and the purity of true religion freed from the vain inventions of man'—but when Cromwell appeared on the scene, as the avowed foe to monarchy, 'worthy, faithfu' Provost Dick' (as douce Davie Deans calls him) being loyal to the backbone, and hating the usurper and his ironsides even more than he hated Episcopacy, he was induced to advance for the preservation of his Prince and State the sum of £20,000 for the service of King Charles. By this ill-advised transaction Sir William Dick fixed his own doom, for the royal cause was already on the wane, and he was thereby classed among the malignants, gaining the ill-will of the triumphant usurper, who in retaliation ordered a bill of payment to be drawn upon him, cruelly fleecing him of £65,000 sterling. 'No less than £180,000 sterling in hard cash was taken from him in this way.' Truly Davie Deans was right when he said, 'In those days folk did see men deliver up their siller to the State's use as if it had been as muckle sclate stanes,' his own father having seen them 'toom the sacks o' dollars out o' Provost Dick's window intill the carts that carried them to the army at Dunse Law; and if ye winna believe his testimony, there is the window itsel' still standing in the Luckenbooths, at the airn stanchells, five doors abune Advocate's Close.'[1]

Thus it came to pass that Sir William Dick, the merchant prince of Edinburgh, suddenly became a penniless debtor. Very like a stroke of the magician's wand does the sequel to all his brilliant successes appear, strikingly portraying the freaks of Dame Fortune's fickle favours. So sweeping was the downfall that every one connected with him took part in his misfortune. The Barony of Braid and his other estates were swallowed up in heavy mortgages, some of them being sold at a five years' purchase, and his whole family rendered destitute.

It was at this crisis that Dame Janet M'Math, his excellent daughter-in-law, stepped into the breach, and, with her own inherited wealth, paid off the bond on

---

[1] *The Heart of Midlothian.* By Sir Walter Scott.

SIR WILLIAM DICK OF BRAID, KNIGHT

'Sanct Geilie-Grange,'[1] 'and saved one roof-tree to cover the defenceless heads of the stricken family. No wonder Sir Thomas Dick Lauder calls her 'the guardian angel, for whose memory we have an especial and grateful respect.'

At the redeemed homestead of the Manor-Place of Grange, therefore, Sir William Dick, his wife, and his son's children at length found shelter and hospitality; for his eldest son John having died in 1642, and his youngest son Lewis in 1646, their widows and children were bereft of their portion also, and of all means of support. But not even here in the seclusion of the old manor could the ill-fated Knight of Braid find rest—so unceasingly was he tormented by his creditors—his very life in danger from day to day. With bowed head, therefore, he left his native city and his wife and suffering family, and travelled to London to try to recover from the Parliament some of the large sums of money lent to the Government on their own security, hoping personally to accomplish the redress which even the most influential friends had failed to obtain. For Lord Loudon, the High Chancellor, who devoted his talents to the Covenanters, had already sent a l ter[2] to the House of Commons, complaining of the non-payment of the promised reimbursement of £40,000 due to Sir William Dick of Braid in 1644. But it had had no effect, though followed by the most pathetic petitions sent on his behalf. After ten years of this weary waiting and sore disappointment, personally attending upon the ' *Three Parliaments*,' he at length recovered the small sum of £1000 out of the £80,000 due to him by England and Scotland.

[1] '1654, March 27.—At Edinburgh, the Commissioners for Administration of Justice to the People of Scotland, ordains infeftment to be given under the Great Seal to Janet M'Math and her heirs and assignees heritably of the lands of Overgrange—with the pertinents and the 18 acres of arable land of the Sheines, called of old, Sanct Gillie-Grange, with the yeard, orchard, and place of the Scheynes, houses and biggings now waste, and pertinents thereof, lying between the rest of the lands of Sanct Gillie-Grang on the West and South, and the Common Muir of Edinburgh on the North and East, acquired by William Dick from Archibald, Lord Napier of Merchiestoun, and all pertaining heritably to the deceased William Dick, and wherein William Dick, his son, is lawfully charged to enter heir in special. If these lands or any of them are held in chief of Sir William Dick of Braid, these letters are to be directed to him to infeft Janet M'Math therein. Similar letters are to be directed to the Provost, Bailies, Council, and Community of Edinburgh as superiors of the lands of Nether Grange, with the parts and portions of the Burgh Muir acquired by the said Sir William Dick from the deceased Mr. John Cant, sometime of St. Gilliegrange, and Mr. Andrew Stevinsone, present minister at Dunbar, with the Manor-Place of Grange, and also in certain properties in Edinburgh, all which have been apprised at the instance of the said Janet M'Math, for a debt of 35,000 merks of principal, and 1750 merks of sheriff fee.'— *General Register of Decreets of Apprisings*, vol. viii.

It is stated that summons was served upon the said William Dick in the house of the said Janet M'Math, his mother, on the 7th March 1654. The lad could only have been sixteen years of age, and the debt, as we have already seen, was that incurred by his grandfather for the State. This purchase of the Grange Manor by Janet M'Math saved her son the imprisonment endured by his cousin, William Dick, heir of Braid.

[2] Manuscript Letter, signed, 'Loudon Cancellaruis, J.P.D., 1st May 1644,' in the Signet Library.—Appendix, Note VI.

This sum was instantly swallowed up by the creditors, still leaving him absolutely penniless '*in his great old age of seventy and five years*,' So destitute was his condition in November 1655 that a small sum weekly was allotted to him by the Government '*for the supply of his present necessities*;' but even then the debtor's law stepped in, and by the malice of some petty creditor, this *very small sum* was seized, and he himself cast into prison. The State, for which he had sacrificed his all, meanwhile finding it convenient to forget him. And the Commonwealth allowed him absolutely to die 'for want of the common necessaries of life.' During all those anxious years, his children and grand-children, numbering in all fifty persons, were bereft of everything—many of them reduced to a state of complete destitution, had it not been for the kind-ness of Janet M'Math, his daughter-in-law, whose generosity again shone forth most conspicuously. Never in its most palmy days had Sanct-Geilie-Grange been a more saintly haven of rest; for with unstinted hospitality this motherly woman opened her purse, her heart, and her home to the little ones crying for bread. Most truly of her might it have been written :—

'Through suffering and sorrow thou hast passed
To show us what a woman true may be.'

Amidst all this affliction there is some feeling of relief in knowing that the aged sufferer, Sir William Dick, had at least the comfort of a visit from his affectionate wife, Dame Elizabeth Morrison, and some of his children, in his miserable prison—though they were unable, in their own penury and distress, to supply his need or heal his broken heart.

He died in the debtors' prison at Westminster on the 19th December 1655, and his poor dead body would have been refused a decent burial had it not been for the timely intervention of the 'guardian angel' of the family, who undertook the whole expense of the funeral,[1] bringing the remains of the ex-Provost of Edinburgh back to his native city. The spot to which Janet M'Math, in the 'goodness of her heart,' transported the body of Sir William Dick from his prison at Westminster was close to the north wall in the Greyfriars' Churchyard, in the ground he himself had purchased for his family tomb fifteen years before, and where his first-born had been laid to rest.

[1] 'We are in possession of a very curious document,' writes Sir Thomas Dick Lauder, in his *Scottish Rivers*, 'the bill for Sir William Dick of Braid's funeral, paid by his daughter-in-law, Janet M'Math, of the family of M'Math in Dumfriesshire, who was wife of William of Grange, his third son. Not only do we owe to this lady's wealthy private exchequer and excellent heart the possession of this very curious discharged account, but many others of a similar description, and this piece of land on the Jordan also' (meaning the redeemed estate of the Grange of St. Giles'. Among the family papers we saw a letter from Sir William Dick in London to Janet M'Math, his daughter-in-law, at the Grange, and another from Sir Andrew Dick, his son, after the death of his father; but as Sir Thomas Dick Lauder, the present baronet, was on the Continent at the time, we could not procure a copy of them.

Of his burial on that spot the Council Records[1] give unquestionable proof, but, unfortunately, at present there is not the slightest sign of any tombstone marking the place, all trace of it having disappeared in the excavations which were made on that side of the churchyard when the new entrance from the north was formed with the steps leading down to it. Among the number of historically interesting burial-places, therefore, which have been thus completely lost sight of, we must also reckon that of Sir William Dick of Braid, the merchant prince who was Provost of Edinburgh in the eventful years of 1638-1639. Still, we cannot but regret that the devoted patriotism of such a man should find no record even among the nation's memorable tombs, though all true patriots feel

'The glory of one fair and virtuous action
Is above all the scutcheons on their tomb.'

There is ample corroboration of all these sad facts in the rare old pamphlet printed soon after the death of the unfortunate knight, Sir William Dick, which, with several other documents anent the same subject, forms a unique folio volume in the Signet Library. Pathetic indeed are the appeals it contains, as set forth in the petitions sent to headquarters[2] concerning payment of the large sums due by the State to Sir William Dick and his family. This pamphlet is entitled,

THE
Lamentable ESTATE and diftreffed CASE
Of the Deceafed
Sr William Dick
IN
SCOTLAND,
And his Numerous
FAMILY and CREDITORS
FOR THE
COMMONWEALTH

[1] *Council Records of Edinburgh*, 1606-1726, vol. xv. fol. 163. See also Appendix, Note VII.
[2] Appendix, Note VI.

PUBLICA FIDES, NUNC MEA SERVITUS.

He whom you see thus by vile Sergeants torn,
Was once his Countries pattern, now their scorn;
Whilst into Prison dragg'd, he there complains;
Who least deserves, doth soonest suffer Chains.

And who for Publick doth his Faith engage,
Changes his Pallace for an Iron Cage.
Then adde: To shew his undecoming Fate
He had been free, had he not serv'd the State.

B Wil. Dick.

SIR WILLIAM DICK OF BRAID, KNIGHT 55

and the 'Preface to the Reader' commences thus: '*Honorable and Courteous Reader, That your eyes may affect your heart, you have here presented to your view (the Mirror of his Age among men of his Quality) the deceased Sir William Dick, Mayor of Edinborough in Scotland—Renowned both at home and abroad as a Famous Merchant.*' The writer then enlarges upon Sir William's public virtues, his munificence, and his self-denial for the common weal, also his creditable standing among men while holding a clear conscience towards God, with more '*Ellogies and Declarations*' than some readers may care to peruse; but for those who should desire to do so we give a copy of the tract in the Appendix. The most interesting feature of this old pamphlet lies in the typical representations of the prosperity and adversity of the ill-fated knight, as portrayed in the three copper-plate engravings, which have now become very scarce[1] (here reproduced by kind permission).

Plate I. represents Sir William Dick, richly attired, on a prancing steed, close to the shore at Leith, evidently superintending the unlading of one of his rich argosies, which has five decks, with port-holes all puffing out smoke. Sir William is surrounded by his followers, and below his horse's feet lie several bags with a clasped hand on each, all lying wide open and the gold coins pouring out. In the upper part of the picture there is a fort and the old city of Leith, with a band of soldiers, a crowd of people, and flags flying. There is also a small engraving at the left-hand corner representing Sir William Dick as Lord Provost, attended by his guard of twenty-four mounted soldiers. At the top of the plate are the Latin legends, 'PUBLICA · SALUS · NUNC · MEA · MERCES,' 'PRO · FOEDERE · REGE · ET · GREGE,' 1640—Sir William being at that time in the height of his prosperity. The plate is signed at the right-hand corner, 'Rob. Vaughan, Sculp.,' and at the foot of the print are some curious verses.

Plate II. shows Sir William Dick in prison, with his hands and feet chained, and his wife and children weeping round him. Three of Cromwell's soldiers are standing on guard. There are chains and handcuffs, a birch rod, and a whip with several leather thongs, having a little spur attached to each, besides other instruments of torture lying on the floor—painfully reminding us of what the poor imprisoned Covenanters had often to endure. The signature

---

[1] Sir Walter Scott mentions this pamphlet in Note R. to the *Heart of Midlothian* as being very rare at that time, the only copy he had seen costing thirty pounds; but even that is far below the large price given by the Writers to the Signet for their unique folio volume. Sir Thomas Dick Lauder, seventh baronet, found this old pamphlet so valuable and interesting as a relic of his ancestor, Sir William Dick, that he most patiently and artistically made a perfect pen-and-ink facsimile of it—copying every line of the three engravings and every word of the letterpress, forming a neat folio volume, which is still highly prized by his descendants.

56   SIR WILLIAM DICK OF BRAID, KNIGHT

of the engraver is 'Guli. Vaughan,' and the motto is 'PUBLICA · FEDES · NUNC · MEA · SERVITAS.' There are two descriptive verses below the print, signed 'Will. D.'

Plate III. shows Sir William dead and lying in his coffin, with his wife and children weeping over him. Knowing his age to have been seventy-five, we may naturally conclude that the younger children, a boy and a girl, are his grandchildren. The background consists of pillars and arches. The legend below is, 'ET · SINE · BUSTO · IACO · SEPULTUS.' The verses are signed in full— 'Will. Devaux.'

In looking carefully over this plate, it is not difficult for us to determine who the various personages were intended to represent. The elder lady is said to be dame Elizabeth, Sir William's spouse, and the younger one standing beside her is undoubtedly meant for Janet M'Math, with her only son, William Dick of Grange, and two of the grandchildren. The young man at the head of the coffin is most likely intended for Sir William's second son, Sir Andrew Dick, who was in London at the time, with his only daughter, Elizabeth ; the young lad at the foot probably being the eldest grandson, William, heir to the Braid estate, whose father, Mr. John Dick of Orkney, died in 1642.[1]

[1] The eminent antiquary, David Laing, LL.D., writing to Sir James Gibson Craig, to whom this folio volume belonged, in 1854, says, 'I return you Sir William Dick's volume, with many thanks. *The Lamentable Estate* is the finest copy I have seen.' Bryan, in his *Dictionary of Painters*, in giving the lives of Robert and William Vaughan, the engravers, also mentions that he had in his possession the three plates engraved by them for the small folio pamphlet describing the sufferings of Sir William Dick of Braid, and that it was even then very scarce.

SIR WILLIAM DICK'S COIN.

ET SINE BUSTO IACEO SEPULTUS.

See him expos'd to th' curtesie of the Skie,
Who for his Countrey durst do more then die.
His helpless Issue now survive to tell,
Their Father di'd without a parallel.
Since Miserable, Naked, and Forlorn,
Went to the Grave as he was born.

Of this brave man, it onely may be said,
Not here he buried lies, but here he's laid:
Such strange il-boding Epitaphs to scan,
Will wound a State more, then an Army can;
For who'll trust private men, if States endure,
To see him wretched, who made them secure.
       Wil. Devaux.

CHAPTER VI

THE HEIRS OF BRAID AND DICKS OF FRACAFIELD

'Love can hope when reason would despair.'

N the death of Sir William Dick in 1655, his grandson William, eldest son of Mr. John Dick of Orkney, fiar of Braid, became heir to the barony of Braid, but the inheritance was merely nominal, for he never possessed one fraction of his patrimony. Instead of 'lands and gear,' the poor young man simply inherited his grandfather's debts and liabilities, with a legacy of poverty and imprisonment, which he endured for many years before the injustice of his case gained any sympathy from the creditors, or his petition[1] for protection made any impression on the Parliament. In fact, his whole life seems to have been spent in seeking redress from the State with no ultimate success whatever. His brother, Mr. John Dick, about two years younger than himself, appears to have gone to London and entered some mercantile firm, from whence he endeavoured to assist his unfortunate elder brother, whose case it is sad to find was rendered more pitiful by the unnatural conduct of his uncle, Sir Andrew Dick of Craig House, who, in consequence of the imprisonment of the heir, took upon himself the representation of the family.

In the Signet volume already mentioned, among the petitions relating to Sir William Dick, there is a later tract entitled, 'The Suffering Case of William Dick, Esq., grandson and heir of Sir William Dick of Braid, with others of his Family, by the intolerable oppression of Sir Andrew Dick—an unnatural brand thereof—Humbly tendred (for redresse) to the Honourable Members of the Parliament of England.' From this tract, which is too long to transcribe in full, it is evident that after the death of Sir William the small sum which had been allotted for a short time to supply the old man's '*present necessities*' was withdrawn; and his second son Andrew had again petitioned in the name of the family that some support might be continued to them, '*until further satisfaction*

[1] Appendix, Note VIII.

THE HEIRS OF BRAID AND

was made.' Orders were accordingly issued by Charles II. for the payment of £5 per week to the family of Sir William Dick, to be charged on the Treasury of England, and paid to Sir Andrew Dick *for their use*, as he was living in London at the time.

This sum Sir Andrew punctually received, but most unjustly retained for his own use, utterly ignoring the right of his elder brother's heir and other members of the family to any portion of it, though many of them were in a sadly distressed condition; especially the young heir of Braid, who was at that time still incarcerated in the Tolbooth for the debts due in reality by the State. Sir Andrew, tacitly denying his nephew's existence, got possession of the papers relating to the public debt, and claimed the same as due to himself as ' *Sole Son, Executor, and Representative of the deceased Sir William.*'

This statement being in a measure false, was most misleading; for though in 1669 Sir Andrew was sole *surviving* son of Sir William Dick, he was not *sole* representative while the three sons of his elder brother were living. The petition, therefore, goes on to beg 'protection for the person of William Dick, heir,' in the first place, from his uncle Sir Andrew, and secondly, from his grandfather's creditors, seeing he can offer them no security whatever, they being already in possession of all he should possess, and everything whereby any satisfaction could be procured, '*except flesh and bones.*' And it winds up with an earnest appeal to the honourable members of the House that the petition may be read before the Parliament dissolve, '*the desperate disease calling for a present remedy.*'

The petition was lodged by his brother John with the clerks in the full hope of obtaining a favourable response, '*as an Act of great Justice in a Supream Power, Debitor for sums of money contracted for the good of the whole Nation.*'

No pecuniary alleviation appears to have followed this petition for Mr. William Dick, but he was evidently granted release from confinement; and it is also evident that Sir William Dick's two sons, Andrew and Alexander, had both been in a measure bound towards the creditors of their father in being cautioners upon some of the earlier mortgages, and consequently it became doubly hard upon the young heir that he, who had had no part in the contracting of the liabilities, should be the one to bear the brunt of the penalty in default of the same.

But we do find a disposition granted by Sir William Dick himself on the 13th December 1651, whereby 'for the better payment of his creditors,' and for the relief of his sons' cautioners, he disposes to Sir Andrew and Mr. Alexander Dick, 'for their respective interests in the lands and barony of Braid and not

DICKS OF FRACAFIELD

otherwise,' also, 'in so far as they were bound for the said father,' not only the lands of North Berwick and Heugh, but also the lands of Braid, Blackford, Greenbank, etc., and in general 'all the lands belonging to the said Sir William Dick within the kingdom,' wholly and solely for the creditors. This disposition [1] was ratified by Charles II. on the 14th June 1672, fifteen years after the death of Mr. Alexander Dick, which left Sir Andrew sole executor upon this particular bond, and places his subsequent behaviour in a somewhat better light, though it is still clearly evident, however small a redress was gained from the Crown, he invariably got the lion's share. Whatever may have been the immediate result of the petition with regard to Sir Andrew's injustice towards his nephew, we cannot say ; but we do know that had it not been for his aunt, Janet M'Math, Dame Dick of Grange, this penniless, nominal laird would have undoubtedly died in the debtors' prison, like the old knight of Braid, his grandfather. It is gratifying, however, to be able to add that, after the death of his aunt, he gained the affection and sympathy of Elizabeth Duncan, a lady who linked her fate with his in 1678, and cheered the few remaining years he had to live ; but his constitution was so completely broken down that he soon passed on to a much 'better inheritance,' leaving her with one young son, William, born in 1679, also called the 'heir of Braid.' But the lands of Braid never returned to the Dick family ; they were too heavily mortgaged, and consequently they remained in the family of the Brouns of Gorgie.

As to the young heir of the third generation, the early part of his life was passed, like his father's, in poverty, his mother petitioning first King James and then King William for the righting of their wrongs ; and as Mrs. Elizabeth Duncan was too poor to educate her son, he eventually entered the 3rd regiment of the foot-guards, and became captain under the Duke of Argyle, fighting so bravely at the battle of Almanza, in Spain, in 1707, that he was afterwards promoted to be fort-major and deputy-governor of New York. It was there he *assumed* the title of baronet, as heir-male to his great-grandfather,[2] Sir William Dick of Braid, who, however, was invariably styled *Knight* and *never Baronet*. In course of time, by his tact and energy, Major Dick acquired both lands and money in the States ; then settling down on his own plantation, he shortly after married the widow of Captain Foulis, but at his death in 1733 he left no son to heir the assumed title, and his whole estate passed to his only daughter,

---

[1] *Registrum Magni Sigilli*, Lib. lxiv. No. 274.
[2] *The Baronage of Scotland*, by Douglas, who utterly ignores the second and third sons of John Dick, eldest son of Sir William Dick of Braid, the existence of whom, however, is fully evidenced by public documents, and also by the public positions accorded them.

THE HEIRS OF BRAID AND

Agnes, and the representation of the family to his cousin, William Dick of Fracafield, only son of Captain Andrew Dick, third son of John Dick, fiar of Braid, advocate, who was the eldest son of Sir William Dick of Braid, knight.

We learn from the testament-dative of Mr. John Dick of London, the second son of Mr. John Dick of Orkney, that the money which supported him and his brother, the unfortunate heir, came from Janet M'Math, 'Lady Grayng,' and their uncle William, first Baron of Grange, for in this will Mr. John acknowledges his indebtedness to them for £2000, and also 1200 merks to his own wife Agnes Dick, according to their marriage-contract. John Dick died childless in 1681, his wife surviving him; and the will was given up by Captain Andrew Dick, brother-german to the deceased and his executor-dative, being confirmed on the 13th January 1682.[1]

Mr. William Dick, who became the representative of that branch of the family in 1733, was then in his fifty-fourth year, having been 'born at Kirkwall, where he was baptized on the 5th November 1679.' He married Barbara Sinclair, and had two sons, Robert and William, and two daughters, Barbara and Ursilla. The former married 'Gilbert Neven of Sconsburgh in 1728,' and had two children, Helen, and James, who was born several years after, and died in infancy, having been 'baptized at Sound, in Yell, 1st January 1742.' 'Helen was served heir to her father on the 1st December 1746. She married Robert Mitchell, shipmaster, Zetland, in 1752, and died in 1808.' Mr. William's daughter Ursilla 'married Laurence Sinclair of Goat,'[2] and had two daughters, Margaret and Elizabeth.

Of the other branch of the Fracafield family, the Dicks of Wormadale, we hear little except that William Dick, eldest son of Walter Dick of Wormadale, was a notary public, and Commissary Clerk of Zetland in 1676. He was twice married, each time to the daughter of a Zetland laird—first, to Janet, daughter of John Mitchell of Westshore, and secondly, to Grizel, daughter of Robert Robertson of Gossaburgh. His only son, Andrew, died before him, and his daughter Janet married Arthur Nicolson of Lochend, a family connection. The property of Wormadale was inherited by Andrew Dick, who was served heir to his grandfather William in 1728. In the Lerwick Kirk-Session Record we find this William Dick was made a member of the Session in January 1724; and on the 2nd of May of the same year another entry says, 'The moderator reported that Wormoodale Desired to Borrow £200 Scots, viz., in Danes species out of the Poor's Box, for which sum he Obliges himself to give his Personal

[1] Commissariat of Edinburgh, *Register of Testaments*.
[2] *Zetland County Families*. By Francis J. Grant, W.S., Carrick Pursuivant of Arms.

DICKS OF FRACAFIELD

Bond. xxx *Granted.*' Mr. William Dick's district for visitation as an elder was allotted to him, on the 10th August 1724, being ' fixed from the manse to the end of the town.' At his death in 1728 the loan does not appear to have been repaid, judging from the entry of 1731, November 10, 'The Session obtained security for the existing loan to Andrew Dick in the shape of bills from Mr. Sinclair, merchant at Whiteness, and James Mitchell of Gerlesta.' This was William Dick's grandson, who on more than one occasion stood godfather to the Rev. John Hunter's children. Wormadale seems to have been a small house of about six rooms, quite of the ordinary type—unhewn stone and *harled*—about five and a half miles from Lerwick, near Wormadale Hill. Mr. William Dick of Fracafield had also evidently settled in Lerwick, as he is mentioned in the Kirk Session Records on the 4th January 1725 as desiring ' further accommodation in the Kirk of Lerwick for erecting a loft above his own seat upon the east side of the Pulpit.' We are surprised to find that his younger son William was not baptized there until 28th March 1737—the same year that Robert, the elder son, had his fifth child baptized—which would naturally lead us to suppose the two sons were not by the same mother, there being nearly thirty years difference in their ages.

The eldest son, Robert Dick of Fracafield, on succeeding his father, recommenced the sending of petitions to the King, praying for payment of the old debts due by the State to his ancestor, Sir William Dick of Braid, but with no better success than his predecessors. He married Janet Dickson, and had no less than nine children,[1] each of whom was duly baptized at Lerwick by the Episcopal clergyman, Rev. John Hunter. His eldest son Charles was only eight years old when his father died, and an action of sale for debt was brought against him ' as heir of his father, at the instance of Andrew Ross, Steward Depute and Chamberlain of the Earldom of Orkney. This action dragged through a weary course of thirty years, during which time most of the parties and council, and several of the judges, before whom the process came, died. At length, on the 24th December 1774, decree was obtained, and the estate of Fracafield brought to the hammer. From the decreet of sale something is learnt of the extent of the family possessions, and they are said to include

---

[1] Their names as entered in the Register being :

1. ' Barbara, baptized September 1731.
2. Douglas, baptized 8th August 1732.
3. Frances, baptized December 1735.
4. Charles, baptized 13th October 1736.
5. James, baptized 27th January 1737.
6. Andrew, baptized 24th December 1738.
7. Christina, baptized 21st July 1739.
8. and 9. Twins, Thomas and Elizabeth, both baptized 8th July 1740.'

For these Kirk-Session extracts I am indebted to the courtesy of James Shand, Esq., of Trinity.

lands in no less than thirteen parishes, viz., Tingwall, Quarff, Burra-Lunnasting, Delting, Northmaven, Gulberwick, Whiteness, Weisdale, Whalsay, Dunrossness, Lerwick, and Bressay. The rental of the whole lands is stated to be £509, 19s. 4d. Scots; and the price realised being £12,098, 8s. 6d. Scots, the creditors, whose debts amounted in all to £48,565, 15s. 9d. Scots, must only have received a dividend of about five shillings in the pound.'[1]

After this painful winding up of his father's estate, Charles Dick left Shetland as a complete bankrupt, taking with him his wife, Martha Montgomery, and his two sons, William and Page-Keble. Finding some employment in London, he finally settled down in the Southern Metropolis, and in 1805 had so far recovered himself that 'he took opinion of counsel on the question of serving himself heir-male of the family.'

This must have been in consequence of the death of Sir John Dick (great grandson of Captain Lewis Dick, fifth son of Sir William Dick of Braid) to whom the presentation of the family had been assigned in 1768, when it was supposed that no male-heir of the elder branch was living.

But the question does not appear to have been settled in Mr. Charles Dick's lifetime; for we find his eldest son William, when he had reached his fifty-sixth year, having risen to be Major in the East India Company, was served heir to his ancestor, Sir William Dick of Braid, in 1821, and thereupon assumed the title of *baronet* which Sir William never possessed, being at all times, and in all public records simply styled *knight*, after the year 1641,[2] but never baronet. The well-known genealogist, Mr. Francis Grant, Carrick Pursuivant of Arms, a very good authority upon all such matters, in alluding to this title of baronet, says, 'This was quite a delusion, for it has been amply proved that no such baronetcy was ever granted to the family.'

Whether the assuming of the title had anything to do with his marriage would be difficult now to decide, but it is strange that the major should have remained a bachelor until his fifty-seventh year, and then entered the connubial state just three months after having established himself as Sir William Dick, Bart. He was married on the 27th April 1821, and his bride was Caroline, daughter of John Kingston of Rickmansworth, Herts, widow of

---

[1] *Zetland County Families.* By Francis J. Grant, W.S., Carrick Pursuivant of Arms, who also informs us that the estate of Fracafield was purchased by Peter Innes, merchant in Lerwick, for £1900.

[2] The two deeds which mark the change are (1) No. 989 *Reg. Mag. Sig.*, dated 15th September 1641, in which he is designated simply 'Merchant-burgess of Edinburgh,' and an Act of Parliament, vol. v. p. 424, dated 17th November 1641, in which he is styled 'Sir William Dick of Braid, *Knight.*' From the circumstances recounted therein it appears as though King Charles I. had conferred the dignity upon him that very day.

DICKS OF FRACAFIELD 63

Lieut.-Colonel Alexander Fraser. But there was no son to heir the title—only one little daughter. Major Dick died at the age of 85, and was succeeded by his brother, Sir Page-Keble Dick, in 1840, as eighth Baronet, according to Debrett, but Burke does not recognise the title at all. Sir Page-Keble Dick also lived to a good old age; having married an English lady called Nancy, daughter of Richard Partridge of Birmingham, by whom he had an only son. He died in 1851, aged eighty-two, at Port Hall, near Brighton, the family residence, and was succeeded by his son, 'Sir Charles William Hookaday Dick, ninth Baronet, who was born in 1802, and married in 1835 to Elizabeth, daughter of George Chassereau, Esq., of Brighton.'[1] They had four daughters—Louisa-Sebastianna, Fanny-Matilda, Phœbe-Maria, and Amelia-Nancy, and one son, Henry Page, born 1853. From all accounts fortune does not seem to have favoured the descendants of John Dick, fiar of Braid, after they lost all their Orkney and Shetland lands in 1774; not having taken to commerce like their burgess ancestor, Sir William Dick of Braid, they do not seem to have been able to retrieve their losses from an accumulation of debt, inherited with the additional burden of delicate constitutions.

The following notice in the *Pall Mall* on Tuesday, 5th December 1876, of the death of the ninth Baronet of Port Hall, revived in the public mind the old story of the financial reverse in the fate and fortune of the worthy old Provost of Edinburgh and Knight of Braid. 'Sir Charles William Hockaday Dick, Baronet, died on Sunday at Brighton, at the age of seventy-four years. Sir Charles was for some years Custodian of the Brighton Museum, and on losing that post when changes were made in the Institution, he sank into poverty, which was aggravated by the long-continued illness of members of his family. One of the late baronet's ancestors, Sir William Dick, warmly espoused the cause of the Royalists in the time of Charles I., and besides indirectly losing thereby a fortune of about £200,000 actually advanced for the service of the king a sum of over £50,000. An act was subsequently passed making this a debt due from the public, but the amount was never repaid. After considerable delay and much exertion a pension of £132 per annum was granted to the family in the reign of Charles II., 'until such time as his Majesty should take course with the principal.' His Majesty never did 'take course with the principal,' and in 1845 the pension itself was struck off the list. Frequent efforts were made to induce Parliament to restore the annuity, but without results. Sir Charles leaves a widow, two daughters, and a son, Henry Page Dick, who is a clerk in one of the local banks, and who succeeds to the title 'as

[1] Debrett's *Baronetage*.

THE HEIRS OF BRAID AND

Sir Henry Page Dick, tenth Baronet of Port Hall, Brighton. He was married in 1880 to Eliza, third daughter of J. Hylden, Esq., of Tufnell Park, London. They bear the Arms of the Dick family, and their motto, 'Publica salus nunc mea merces' (The public safety is my reward), is still the same as in the old engraving of Sir William Dick of Braid, printed in 1640.

As there is no fine old Scottish manor-house to describe in connection with Capt. Lewis Dick, fifth and youngest son of the old Knight of Braid, we will conclude this chapter on the descendants of his eldest brother John, by narrating a few of the facts recorded of him, thus uniting the first and the last links in that family chain. Having taken to a seafaring life in his youth, Lewis Dick received no lands of his father in patrimonial fee; but in lieu thereof he obtained, on his coming of age, 40,600 merks, and he must have distinguished himself very early in his naval profession, as he soon rose to be commander of a frigate of war.

Like his four elder brothers, Captain Lewis Dick widely extended the family circle by his matrimonial alliance, whereby he connected himself with several of the Scottish nobility; viz., the Earls of Hopetoun, Bothwell, and Haddington, and also the Marquess of Bute; his wife being Margaret, daughter of Sir James Foulis of Colinton, Bart., whose grandmother was Mary, daughter of Sir John Lauder of Hatton. Some few years later his father-in-law, Sir James Foulis, being among those actively engaged in the civil war subsequent to the death of Charles I., he was one of the band of nobles betrayed into the hands of the English, and taken prisoner to London. His companions were 'the Earls of Leven, Crawford, Marischall, and Lord Ogilvy, besides several other gentlemen of rank.' After the restoration of Charles II. Sir James Foulis was appointed Lord Justice-Clerk, under the title of Lord Colinton.

Captain Lewis Dick made a home for his bride at West Newton, Northumberland, where their only child, Andrew, was born, and where the Captain himself died in 1642, six years before the sad death of his father, Sir William Dick of Braid, at Westminster. This child Andrew lived to become squire of West Newton, and he in turn married an heiress, Mary Scot, in 1672, and left an only son, Andrew, to inherit his estate. Andrew Dick, Esq. of West Newton, married Janet Durham in 1715, and continued the male line of Captain Lewis Dick, though of his three sons only the second son, John, survived him. He had been brought up as a merchant, and went abroad in 1739, residing for some time in Holland, the old headquarters of the foreign traffic of the Dicks. He married Anne, daughter of Joseph Bragg, Esq., of Somersetshire. Many years after he had been appointed British Consul in

DICKS OF FRACAFIELD

Tuscany by King George II., when he was about fifty years of age, the following interesting notice appeared in the *Scots Magazine* for 1768 :—

'*Edinburgh, March 14th.*—John Dick, Esq., His Britannic Majesty's Consul at Leghorn, was served heir to Sir William Dick of Braid, Baronet. It appeared that all the male descendants of Sir William Dick had failed except his youngest son, Captain Lewis, who settled in Northumberland, and who was the grandfather of John Dick, Esq., his only male descendant now in life. Upon which a respectable jury unanimously found his propinquity proved, and declared him now to be Sir John Dick, Baronet. It is remarkable that Sir William Dick of Braid lost his great and opulent estates in the service of the public cause and the liberties of his country, in consideration of which, when it was supposed there was no heir-male of the family, a new patent was granted to the second son of the heir-male, which is now in the person of Sir Alexander Dick of Prestonfield, Baronet. The Lord Provost and Magistrates of this city, in consideration of Sir John Dick's services to his King and country, and that he is the representative of that illustrious citizen, who was himself Lord Provost in 1638 and 1639, did Sir John the honour of presenting him with the freedom of the City of Edinburgh. After the service an elegant dinner was given at Fortune's to a numerous company, consisting of gentlemen of the jury, and many persons of distinction, who all testified their sincere joy at the revival of an ancient and respectable family in the person of Sir John Dick, Baronet.'

There must have been no family intercourse for many years between the Dicks of Northumberland and the Dicks of Orkney and Zetland, otherwise it could hardly have been possible for Sir John Dick, great-grandson of Captain Lewis Dick, *fifth* son of Sir William Dick of Braid, to have been served heir to his ancestor, when Charles Dick of Fracafield in Zetland was living, he being great-grandson of Captain Andrew Dick, *third* son of Mr. John Dick, fiar of Braid, who was the *eldest* son of Sir William Dick, Knight of Braid.

Mr. Charles Dick eventually protested against this assignation, but being bankrupt, as we have seen, he had very little influence at Court; however, upon the death of Sir John Dick without male heirs, being a widower, the matter remained undisputed, and Major Dick, eldest son of Mr. Charles Dick, obtained the position of representative of the ancient family of the de Dykes.

DICK COAT-OF-ARMS.

CHAPTER VII

THE BARONS OF GRANGE AND THE SETONS OF PITMEDDEN

'The grassy court, the mossy wall,
Vault, bartizan, and turret tall,
With weeds that have o'ergrown them ;
Though silent as the desert air,
Yet have their eloquence, and bear
Mortality upon them.'

SETON BOOK-PLATE.

N coming back to the old manor-house, we find that, notwithstanding the sorrows and hardships which the unfortunate family of Sir William Dick had been called upon to endure in their youth, causing many of them to find an early grave, yet the records show that the old walls of Sanct Geilie-Grange rang from time to time with the joy-bells of mirth and marriage, followed by births and baptisms.

The twice widowed Janet M'Math had lived to see her only son, William Dick, second Baron of Grange, also twice married. His first wife was the daughter of Sir John Leslie of Newton, one of the senators of the College of Justice, a younger son of Andrew, fourth Earl of Rothes (whose portrait is still at the Grange House), but this lady died within a few years, leaving him with two daughters only : Anne and Janet, each of whom were eventually sought in marriage, the elder by Peter Leith, Esq., of Craighall, and the younger by Mr. Munro Carnegy, advocate.

The second wife of the Laird of Grange was *Charles*, daughter of Robert Leslie of Kinclaven, third son of Patrick, Lord Lindores, whom he married in 1674. She was cousin to his first wife, and bore him another daughter, and one little son and heir.

But the aged grandmother never saw the boy, for at the close of the year 1678 that large-hearted woman, the heroine of the Grange, who had survived Sir William Dick and her second husband twenty-three years, entered her haven of rest, passing away most peacefully at a good old age, having won

THE BARONS OF GRANGE AND SETONS OF PITMEDDEN 67

for herself the best of all *in memoriams*: 'Many shall rise up and call her blessed.'

The double monogram, I.M.T.B., on the apex of the magnificent tomb she had erected in the Greyfriars' Churchyard to the memory of her first husband,

JANET M'MATH'S TOMB, GREYFRIARS' CHURCHYARD.

Thomas Bannatine, puts it beyond all doubt that she was buried beside him, whose virtues she had recorded in the following quaintly-worded epitaph :—

HODI·MIHI ; CRAS·TIBI

'Vita quid hominus? Flos, umbra et fumus arista ;
Illa malis longa est, illa bonis brevis est.'

'To-day is mine, to-morrow yours may be ;
Each mortal man should mind that he must die.'

'What is man's life? A shade, a smoak, a flower.
Short to the good, to the bad doth long endure.'

'If thou list that passeth by,
Know that in this tomb doth ly
Thomas Bannatine ; abroad
And at home who served God.

> Though no children he possest,
> Yet the Lord with means him blest.
> He on them did well dispose,
> Long ere death his eyes did close.
> For the poor his helping hand,
> And his friends his kindness fand ;
> And on his dear bedfellow,
> Janet M'Math, he did bestow,
> Out of his lovely affection,
> A fit and goodly portion.
> Thankful she herself to prove,
> For a sign of mutual love,
> Did no pains, no charges spare,
> To set up this fabrick rare—
> As Artimise, that noble Dame,
> To her dear Mausolus' name.'

'He died 16th July 1635. Of his age 65.'

Here, therefore, below this monument, we feel assured, rest the mortal remains of Janet M'Math, who in her youth was the loving spouse of Thomas Bannatine. The initials were no doubt added as the crowning point after her death, for there was no room on the face of that elaborate tomb to carve her name in full. Most truly 'her record was on high.'

A few months after her death, on the 9th of April 1679, her son, William Dick, inherited her estate, being, as the record puts it, 'served heir of Janet M'Math, his mother, widow of William Dick of Grange, in the lands of Over-Sanct-Gelie-Grange, with the Manor-Place of Grange, etc., and eighteen acres of arable land of Sheines, of old termed Sanct-Geile-Grange, with the garden of Sheines.'[1]

His term of holding was not very long, however, for in sixteen years his own boy became the baron. On the 6th May 1695 he was served heir to his father in the same lands, with the 'orchard garden.' This orchard came close up to the walls which formerly surrounded the Convent of St. Katherine of Siena, which had been built on part of the Grange lands, and the same spring had supplied the manor-house and the Sisters of St. Katherine with pure drinking-water. From them it was called the 'Ladies Well,' but it never possessed the miraculous qualities attributed to the healing oil of the 'Balm Well' of St. Katherine at Liberton, to which the Sisters had made a yearly pilgrimage. These ancient wells and aged thorn-trees, which are invariably to be found on old estates, always carry with them a large amount of popular interest, serving, as they do, from generation to genera-

[1] Maidment, from the *Retours*.

tion, as indisputable landmarks when the whole surrounding district has been built upon.

William Dick, third Baron of Grange, being only a youth when his father died, he fortunately escaped entanglement in the politics of the period, just when the nation's indignation was at its height owing to the infamous massacre of Glencoe, an act of savage vengeance as cruel as it was perfidious. This calamity being followed immediately by the widespread disaster of the Darien scheme, combined with the continued injustice shown by the State to the lawful appeals of the young heir of Braid, his cousin, undoubtedly helped to form the political bias of the lad, who in after life proved his Jacobite sympathies so openly. These sympathies were greatly augmented by his alliance with Dame Anne Seton, third daughter of Sir Alexander Seton of Pitmedden, and Margaret, daughter and heiress of William Lauder, Esq., brother of Sir John Lauder, Lord Fountainhall, thus forming the first link in the matrimonial chain between the Dicks and the Lauders. Sir Alexander Seton had five sons and five daughters, each of whom inherited the staunch loyalty of their ancestors to the Stuart family. Of the five sons, three were physicians ; and William, the eldest, being M.P. for Aberdeen, he was one of the commissioners appointed to treat about the union between England and Scotland in 1706. Of the five daughters, four became intimately associated with the Grange of St. Giles, while the eldest, Lady Elizabeth Seton, married Sir Alexander Wedderburne, second Baronet of Blackness, Forfarshire, whose nephew was governor of Broughty Castle for the Chevalier de St. George in 1715. It is only natural to suppose that the five little maidens, born and brought up in such a Jacobite home as Pitmedden, would form their matrimonial alliances with devoted royalists. Their grandfather, Sir John Seton of Pitmedden, had been shot through the heart by a cannon-ball while carrying the standard of King Charles against the Covenanters at the battle of the 'Brig o' Dee' in 1639. Of this they were constantly reminded by the addition to their coat-of-arms of a heart with drops of blood issuing from it. The family crest being: a demi-man in military habit, holding the banner of Scotland, with the motto on an escrol above, '*Sustento sanguine signa.*'

This was carved over the original doorway of the old mansion-house of Pitmedden, which is still standing in its fine old policy, about a mile and a half from the picturesque village of Pitmedden, near Udny. But the old halls are uninhabited, bare and silent now, and the antique sun-dial looks very solitary on the lawn in front of the house, the greater part of which has been modernised of late years, and consequently, partly bereft of its clinging ivy, so characteristic of these old baronial residences. Pitmedden had been acquired by the Setons of Meldrum and Mounie in 1598, and has remained in the family close on three hundred years.[1]

Two magnificent cedars of Lebanon at the back of the house bespeak its age; but the chief beauty of the place is its old garden and its unique gateway, with its ornamental pillars and double steps, approached by a covered way of overarching boxwood, the growth of many generations, to form which they must have been trees of a goodly size even in the days of the five little ladies whose after-lives became so intimately linked with the ancient Grange of St. Giles.

SUN-DIAL, PITMEDDEN.

At that time Scotland was in a strangely unsettled state owing to the union of the two kingdoms in 1707, which had caused much ill-feeling and discontent in the north, especially among the Jacobites, who regarded the treaty as an effectual barrier to the restoration of the Stuarts, and consequently were determined to oppose it by inviting the Chevalier de St. George, son of the exiled monarch, James II., over to Scotland, in order to frustrate the settlement of the succession to the throne on the Elector of Hanover. Their hopes on this point were strengthened by the fact that, since the death of the young Duke of Gloucester, the only surviving son of Queen Anne, she had manifested a decided leaning towards the claims of her brother, the Chevalier, to the throne of his father. The sudden death of the Queen, however, in 1714, and the immediate proclamation of George I., put an end to all their plans for the time being. But we must pass on to 1745, when Prince Charles Edward, the grandson of James II., came to Scotland to test the strength of the Jacobites, still hoping to secure the crown for his father, the Chevalier de St. George. We all know how fortune seemed to smile upon the young prince at first, and how gallantly he held his Court in the palace of his forefathers at Holyrood after the battle of Prestonpans; how he encamped on the banks of Duddingston Loch, and slept at an inn in the village. Every event of that eventful year has been indelibly engraven upon the history of the nation, and to many it entailed the loss of both life and lands.

[1] It has lately been sold to Alexander Keith, Esq., of Chopelton, Ellon, Aberdeenshire, by Sir William Samuel Seton, ninth Baronet of Pitmedden and Cushnie. The sale was effected in 1893.

GARDEN GATEWAY, PITMEDDEN.

Three of the Seton family, and their cousin, Sir John Wedderburn, joined the prince's Life-Guards under Lochiel. But Dame Anne Seton and William Dick of Grange had then no son to enlist in the Stuart cause, the only surviving child of their marriage being their daughter Isobel, who, upon the death of her brother, was styled 'Dame Isobel Dick, heiress of Grange.'

In 1725, when their only son James was alive, a new grant of the estate had been obtained, settling the succession upon him as heir-apparent, and also arranging the portion of his sister Isobel. This charter is of peculiar interest, and very clear in its application; it reads thus:—

'King George grants to William Dick of Grange in liferent, and Dame Anna Seton, his spouse, in security and payment to her of the free annual rent of 2000 merks, payable to her after the death of the said William Dick, and to James Dick, their eldest lawful son, in fee, and his heirs-male; whom failing, any other sons to be born between the said William Dick and Anna Seton, and their heirs-male. Whom failing, the heirs-*female* of the foresaid James Dick, and of any other heirs-male above mentioned. Whom failing, to Isabella Dick, the only lawful daughter of the said William Dick and Anna Seton, and her heirs-male, whom failing, the heirs-*female* of the said William Dick and Anna Seton, and their heirs-male: Whom failing, the heirs-*female* to be born of the daughters of the said William Dick, according to the order above written; the eldest heir-female always succeeding without division, under the conditions at length after specified—the 18 acres of the arable lands of "Sheynes," formerly called St. Geillie Grange: with the garden, orchard, place of Sheynes, and buildings now ruinous and pertinents, lying between the other lands of St. Geillie Grange on the west and south, and the common muir of Edinburgh on the east and north, and in the parish of St. Cuthbert's and shire of Edinburgh. Which lands formerly belonged to the said William Dick, and were resigned by him for this regrant, reserving his liferent and power to install vassals and feuars; and also reserving the interests of his spouse as above.'

This charter, however, is specially burdened with provisions to the younger children of William Dick and Anna Seton, viz.: To the said Isabella Dick, their daughter, 15,000 merks, if there be no other younger children surviving at the time of their death; but if there are, it is reduced to 10,000 merks, and each other child receives 8000 merks, these being payable by the said James Dick. If Anna Seton predecease her husband, the 2000 merks payable to her in the case of her survival is to be released to James by his father, and James is not to burden the lands without his parent's consent. To be held of the Crown for payment to the chaplain of St. Stephen's Altar in the metropolitan church of Glasgow, 10 merks.

There is also a general confirmation of all contracts and dispositions and charters, etc., in favour of the said William Dick and his authors and predecessors, which is also valid to his son James—dated at Edinburgh, 12th February 1725.[1]

As no other children were born to William Dick and Dame Anna Seton, their only daughter, Dame Isobel Dick, as heiress of Grange, inherited the whole estate upon the death of her father, third Baron of Grange, in 1755. At that time she had been married over twenty-four years to her cousin-german, Sir Andrew Lauder of Fountainhall; who does not appear to have espoused the cause of Prince Charlie; and consequently, as we shall see, his horses and pistols were requisitioned, which seems strange enough, when we consider that both his own mother and his wife's mother were of the Seton family.

Of the numerous family of Sir Andrew Lauder and the heiress of Grange, the two elder sons, William and John, died young. Dame Isobel Dick, therefore, with the consent of her husband, disponed her estate of Grange to her third son, Andrew, according to the Register of Entails for 1757—a precautionary measure taken to prevent the recurrence of the sad experience of Sir William Dick of Braid; as, in the old form of entail, 'an estate so protected could not be attached by creditors.' It might be burdened by bonds and debts, but it could not be alienated from the heirs of entail. Dame Isobel's death occurred most unexpectedly the following year (1758). Lady Lauder of Fountainhall, as she was then called, appears to have died at the Grange House, which was still occupied by her mother, Mistress Anne Dick (Dame Anna Seton), to whose care she confided her younger children. Her third and eldest surviving son, Andrew, being of age, he accordingly inherited his mother's estate, and taking his place as head of her family, he became Andrew Dick, Esq., fourth Baron of Grange—residing there during his father's lifetime. Dame Isobel was buried in the family tomb at Old Greyfriars.

Ere the close of another six years, sorrow again entered the old home of Sanct Geilie-Grange, and Mistress Anne Dick passed away, in 1764, on the 2nd day of April, at one o'clock in the morning, surrounded by a number of her grandchildren. Mistress Dick was in her eighty-eighth year, and deeply regretted. She was buried in her own family vault at Seton Chapel. The administration of domestic affairs at the Grange then fell into the hands of her youngest sister, Dame Jean Seton, who in her youth had presented a white rose to Prince Charlie. She, like her elder sister, Dame Isobel, had remained unmarried, but was by courtesy now called 'Mistress Jean Seton' by her nephews and nieces, with whom she lived until her death, which occurred early in 1768.

[1] *Registrum Magni Sigilli*, Lib. xcvi. No. 143.

On the 29th January Mr. Andrew Dick of Grange had written to his sister, Miss Jean Lauder, at Fountainhall, to tell of the distress they were in on account of the continued indisposition of Mistress Jean Seton. After mentioning her want of appetite, he startled them by saying, 'She was suddenly taken very ill yesterday afternoon, and alarmed the whole family. She dropt down on the floor in a fit, and was immediately carried to bed, when after recovering a little she vomited excessively a great mixture of corrupted blood and bile— a very dangerous symptom. Mr. Ingles was sent for immediately, and stayed here all night. She is this day a little easier, and I hope will continue so, for if she should have more returns of the last fit, her life will be in imminent danger.'

The writer then goes on to speak of his father's health, having heard that he also had been indisposed; but he hoped it would not prevent his brother Archy being sent to Haddington School at Candlemas. The next tidings from the Grange conveyed to the family at Fountainhall the sad news of Mistress Seton's death, and the vault at Seton Chapel was again opened to lay her outward form beside that of her elder sister. She was sadly missed at Sanct Geilie-Grange, but Mr. Andrew Dick's cup of sorrow was not yet full, for in the following year his father's illness became so serious his life was despaired of, and notwithstanding the best medical attendance and the most dutiful nursing from Miss Jean, he succumbed to his complaint, and Sir Andrew Lauder was buried beside his spouse, Dame Isobel Dick, whom he had survived eleven years.

Mr. Dick of Grange, being the eldest surviving son, came into the estate and title as Sir Andrew *Lauder-Dick*, sixth baronet, and from henceforth the Lairds of Grange were entirely merged in the Baronets of Fountainhall, and the arms of Dick quartered with the rampant griffin of the Lauders.

CHAPTER VIII

PRINCE CHARLES EDWARD AT THE GRANGE

'A wee bird cam' to oor ha' door,
He warbled sweet and clearly,
And aye the o'ercome o' his sang
Was " Wae 's me for Prince Charlie ! "
Oh ! when I heard the bonnie, bonnie bird,
The tears cam' drappin rarely ;
I took my bannet aff my head,
For weel I lo'ed Prince Charlie.

Quo' I, " My bird, my bonnie, bonnie bird,
Is that a tale ye borrow ;
Or is 't some words ye 've learnt by rote,
Or a lilt o' dool and sorrow ? "
"Oh ! no, no, no ! " the wee bird sang,
" I ve flown sin' mornin' early,
But sic' a day o' wind and rain !—
Oh ! wae 's me for Prince Charlie ! "'
WILLIAM GLEN.

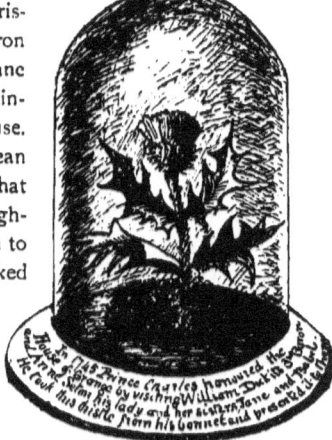

PRINCE CHARLES' THISTLE.[1]

CONSIDERING the devotion of the 'gallant Setons' to the house of Stuart, and the confiscations endured by the Dick family as Royalists during the Commonwealth, it is not surprising that William Dick, Baron of Grange, and his lady, Anne Seton, should have had the honour of entertaining Prince Charles Stuart at the Grange House. The younger sisters, Miss Isabel, and Miss Jean Seton of Pitmedden, were also present on that festive occasion, and danced with his Royal Highness. The youngest of these ladies was chosen to present the Prince with a pure white rose, plucked from a bonnie bush in the garden ; the roots of which are still flourishing and casting up new shoots from year to year, bearing royal roses to this day.

On accepting the rose, the Prince is said to have gallantly taken the thistle from his bonnet and presented it to the young lady.

This thistle is still preserved with the greatest care—being hermetically sealed under a small glass shade, with the following inscription engraved on a goldplate, on the margin of the stand :—

[1] The little sketch of this heirloom was taken with the kind permission of Lady Anne Dick Lauder.

PRINCE CHARLES EDWARD AT THE GRANGE

'In 1745 Prince Charles honoured the House of Grange by visiting William Dick, its third Baron, and Anne Seton, his lady, and her sisters, Jane and Isabel. To mark the regard of his family from Queen Mary downwards for that of Seton, he took this thistle from his bonnet and presented it to the ladies.

'He afterwards received them at breakfast at Holyrood, and distinguished them at the Court.'

The Grange Loan, along which Prince Charles Edward rode on that time-honoured visit to the old manor-house, was at that period, and especially at that season of the year, one of the most charming roads within the suburbs of Edinburgh, passing as it did thro' green fields with running brooks and hedgerows all aglow with autumn tints—while the hills beyond were a glory of gorse and heather. At present it is shorn of many of its rural charms; still the fine old trees that overarch it make it a delightful walk on a summer afternoon, when the chequered shadows fall softly on the grass-grown footpath. Until recently its rustic beauty was enhanced by the picturesque cottages in connection with the old lodge at the Grange House. They were a never-ending source of delight to the eye—with their outside stairs, white-washed walls, and crow-stepped gables. The wee windows were almost hidden under the luxuriant masses of dark green

PRINCE CHARLIE ROSEBUSH.

ivy, contrasting so splendidly with the fine broken reds and russets of the quaint old roofs—partly tiled and partly thatched, with an incomparable background of trees of every hue, colour, and form, so artistically combined that they were a constant theme for landscape painters—Sir George Harvey himself, when President of the Royal Scottish Academy, immortalised them in the background of his '*Bowlers*.' But all are not gifted with the artist's unbounded love of tumble-down picturesqueness, and therefore we can quite believe the gatekeeper may after all prefer the trim new lodge to live in. There is no accounting for taste. However, these thatched cottages stood there at the time of our story, in the days when royalty graced the halls of old 'Sanct Geilie-Grange,' a hundred and fifty years ago. But 'Bonnie Prince Charlie's' festivities in 'Auld Reekie' were not of long duration, neither were his royal manifestoes and proclamations, which appeared from time to time in the *Caledonian Mercury* for the months of September and October of the year 1745. The authoritative tone in which some of these were worded would sound strange enough to many ears in 1746, but the description therein given of the Prince himself exactly suited the temperament of his Highland followers, though we of the nineteenth century might think it more heroic than royal for a Prince to be able 'to eat a dry crust, sleep on pease straw, take his dinner in four minutes, and win a battle in five.' Still there is no denying that Prince Charles Edward was just the kind of hero that the Scottish populace could adore, and enthusiastic Jacobite ladies become passionately proud of—which accounted for the marvellous way in which, without bloodshed, he entered the Capital of Scotland and quietly took possession of the royal palace of his ancestors at Holyrood. It is interesting to note that his route on that memorable occasion lay almost within the radius of the estates of the Dicks and the Lauders. From Corstorphine to Greig's Mill, on to Braid-burn, from thence to the Burghmuir, resting at the Bore stone (the old Banner Stone of Flodden), then turning eastward and riding along the old Grange Loan, he passed the Grange House, with its Ivy Lodge and overarching trees, then skirting by St. Roque's through fields to Priestfield, he entered the King's Park by a breach in the wall, and crossed the Hunter's Bog. 'On reaching the eminence below St. Anthony's Chapel and Well, when for the first time he came in sight of the old palace, he alighted from his horse, and paused to survey the beautiful scene. Then descending to the Duke's Walk (the favourite resort of his grandfather) he halted for a few minutes to show himself to the people, who now flocked around him in great numbers, with mingled feelings of curiosity and admiration. Loud huzzas came from the

Old Cottages, Grange Loan. 1865.

crowd, and many of the enthusiastic Jacobites knelt down and kissed his hand. He then remounted his horse—a fine bay gelding presented to him by the Duke of Perth—and rode slowly towards the Palace. On arriving in front of Holyrood he alighted, and was about to enter the royal dwelling when a cannonball fired from the Castle struck the front of James V.'s tower, and brought down a quantity of rubbish into the courtyard. No injury was done, however, by this gratuitous act of annoyance, and the Prince, passing in at the outer gate, and procceeding along the piazza and the quadrangle, was about to enter the porch of what are called the Duke of Hamilton's apartments, when James Hepburn of Keith, who had taken part in the rising of 1715, "a model of ancient simplicity, manliness, and honour," stepped from the crowd, bent his knee in token of homage, and then drawing his sword, raised it aloft, and marshalled the way for Prince Charles up the broad flight of stairs.' Tall, handsome, fair, and noble in aspect, the Prince excited the admiration of all those fearless Jacobites, who were ready to lay down their lives for him as the heir of the Stuart race. The ladies compared him to Robert Bruce, and used all their arts and industry to favour his cause, which suddenly rose like a star, but ere long was 'quenched in blood on the Muir of Drummossie.'

KING'S STABLES, CULLODEN MOOR.

From some curious papers in the Dick Lauder charter-chest, we gain some idea of the manner in which Prince Charles obtained arms and ammunition for his followers. 'The papers are contained in an old pocket-book, which was found on the road near Tranent in the year 1745. It seems to have dropped from the pocket of Mr. George Gordon of Beldorney, who appears to have been an officer in the Prince's army, in command of a party sent to search the gentlemen's houses of East Lothian for arms and horses.'[1] As several of the

---

[1] This information is on the outside of the packet, in Sir Thomas Dick Lauder's handwriting.

persons and places mentioned therein were closely connected with the Lauder family by marriage, we will transcribe the documents in full.

The first document is 'the *Warrant* for his proceeding on the expedition on which he was now sent, which has the Prince's seal attached to it.'

'CHARLES, Prince of Wales, etc., Regent of Scotland, England, France, and Ireland, and the dominions thereto belonging, to GEORGE GORDON, Gentleman.'

'These are empowering you to search for all horses, arms and ammunition that you can find in the custody of, or belonging to, any person or persons disaffected to our interest, and seize the same for our use—for the doing of which this shall be your Warrant.—Given at Holyrood House, the eighteenth day of October 1745, by his Highness' command, MURRAY.'

After this follows the instructions given to George Gordon of Beldorny.

'You are to take the Musselburgh Road through Inveresk by Carberry, Cousland, Wind-Miln, Ormiston Park and House of Muir, where old Mr. Wight lives. You turn to the east from this place to Fountainhall, Sir Andrew Lauder's house. The stables are above the house—these secure in the first place, and if you please, Mr. Currie's house, who lives hard by them and has arms. Don't forget Sir Andrew's horse furniture and pistols, which will be in his house. You may likewise ask for arms. His horse is a bay gelding, I believe.

'From this place you march south, through Templehall and Preston, to Nether Keith. Leave your Horses at ye Change House which is upon the road, and without delay go up to the house; but before you enquire for Mr. Ker of Keith, detach two men to secure the granary, where the horse stands. This granary is a little to the westward of the house in the garden. Send one man to the west end of it, which is without the garden. Show him your warrant, and order him to open the garden door, and give you the key of the granary: take no saddle from him, but tell him if you please who you are, and you will be made very welcome.

'From this you go through Upper Keith to Johnston Burn, belonging to Bailie Crokat. If you find no horse here worth while, take a saddle.

'You must return from this place to Upper Keith again, cross the water at Humby Miln, pass Humby, because his horses are taken already, and go to Leaston, the stables are just before the gate. Secure them. Here you may expect something, but deal gently with him, and take only the best.

'When you go east by Kilda and Newtoun to Newton Hall: if Mr. Newton has not sent his horses away with his friend the Marquis of Tweeddale, he will have something worth your acceptance. His wife is a very fine woman, and a Stewart, a ffriend of John Roy Stewart. Judge for yourself whether you go there or not. From this place you return again, and come to Newhall, Lord George Hay's house. You may call here, but I'm afraid everything will be put out of the way.

'From thence you go to Eaglescairney. Enquire for a cropt-eared bay gelding, hollow-backed—here you may get a good fowling-piece or two. Then you go to Clerk-

PRINCE CHARLES EDWARD AT THE GRANGE

ington, take a guide along with you, and go first to Blackhouse, which is the Mains; leave a guard here, and go down to the house. Mr. Cockburn has a good gelding and a gray Galloway, with good furniture—and if he has any good work horses, take them, as he is a declared enemy. The stables are betwixt Blackhouse and ye House of Clerkington, opposite the pigeon house, upon your right hand as you go down to the house.

'Mr. Watkins of Kidsbuts—two brown mares and a gray: his stables just at ye back of ye house.

'Mr. —— at Rachael —— in Giffordhall.

Sir Francis Kinlock at Gilmerton, his son Sheriff of East Lothian. Some good horses, a fowling-piece or two.

'The Laird of Congleton some good horses—as likewise his good brother Mr Hepburn at Beanston.'

The next paper consists of 'Memoranda, which seem to have been made by Mr. George Gordon during his expedition.' There are twenty-six entries in

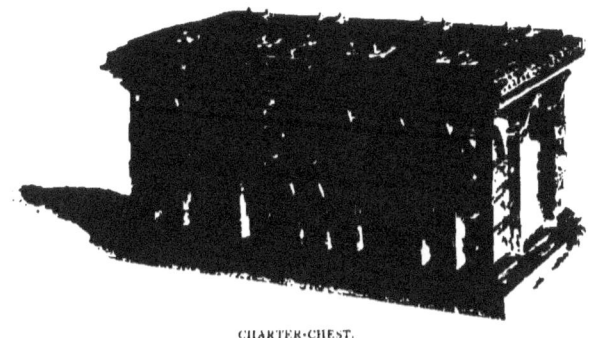

CHARTER-CHEST.

all, none referring to the above names, and in almost every instance the record is, Mr. or Mrs. —— depones he or she '*neither has nor knows of any arms*,' or else, as in No. 18, 'Mr. Geds nor his lady at home.'

No. 21 is one of the few exceptions:—'Mr. Andrew Thomson depones he has no arms, but has a saddle with his brother'—and the last paper in the pocket-book is a letter referring to the above:—

'EDINR., 31 *Oct.* 1745.

DR BROTHER,—Give the bearer my seddel, and oblige your servant,

ANDREW THOMSON.

To James Thomson,
Brewr. in Edinr.'

even descended to the article of dress. From a perusal of this act one would be led to conclude that the Government trembled at the figure of tartan or shape of a philibeg. The garb which the Caledonians had worn from the earliest ages of their nation—the garb to which they were attached by the affection which is natural towards the peculiarities of one's native country, and for the objects to which one has been habituated from his earliest years—was prohibited, both as to stuff and shape; and, of course, a stop put to almost the only species of manufacture in the country.'

'To wear a philibeg of any sort, or a coat or greatcoat made of tartan, subjected the wearer, whether *man or boy, upon being convicted by the oath of one witness, before any justice of peace, to imprisonment without bail for six months. But for the second offence to banishment for seven years to any of the foreign plantations.*'

The religious restrictions were even more stringent, and caused the deepest animosity.

'When princes meet, astrologers may mark it an ominous conjunction, full of boding, like that of Mars with Saturn.'

CULLODEN HOUSE.

CHAPTER IX

SCOTTISH CELEBRITIES AT THE GRANGE

'Entering his closet, and among his books,
Among the great of every age and clime—
A numerous court—turning to whom he pleased,
Questioning each, why he did this or that,
And learning how to overcome the fear
Of poverty and death.'

FTER the death of Mrs. Jean Seton, and the subsequent removal of Mr. Andrew Dick to Fountainhall upon the demise of his father, Sir Andrew Lauder, fifth Baronet, in 1769, the Manor-House of Grange was shut up for a while. The sweet, old-fashioned flowers drooped, but the ivy grew apace, deftly clothing the ancient walls with a beauty all its own, and the faithful rooks still nestled in the fine old trees. Then came a period when strangers leased the house and grounds, some of the fields being let to Lord Cockburn's father, who lived at Hope Park. The manor-house was leased by John Forrest, merchant-burgess of Edinburgh, who had married Jane, third daughter of Sir Walter Riddell, Bart., of Riddell in Roxburghshire. Their third son, James, became a Writer to the Signet, and in 1779 he married his cousin Catherine, only daughter and heiress of James Forrest, Esq., of Comiston, in the village of Colinton, Midlothian, who was descended from Mr. Alexander Forrest, 'Provost of the Collegiate Church of St. Mary-in-the-Fields, near Edinburgh,' in 1613. According to Peter Williamson's first Directory published for this city, Mr. James Forrest, the writer, must have gone to live in Milne's Court in 1773, which was at that period the fashionable quarter for lawyers and judges; and from the same authority we find he removed from thence to Lauriston Lane, where he was residing in 1805, with an only daughter and a son, also called James, who was elected Lord Provost of Edinburgh in 1838, and created a baronet in honour of the Queen's coronation that year.[1] Mr. James Forrest, the writer, died in 1820, but we do

[1] We shall have occasion to mention Sir James Forrest, Bart., in connection with the Queen's visit to Scotland in 1842.

not know if his father, John Forrest, died at the Grange House, or when the family vacated it. It could not have been later than 1790, for it is a well-authenticated fact that the Manor-House of Grange was tenanted at that period by the celebrated Dr. Robertson, the historian—a man of whom Lockhart says, 'His genius would have made him an object of reverence in any age and country.' His father, the Rev. William Robertson, was minister of Old Grey-friars, to which church Dr. Robertson was also nominated in 1761—shortly before he was appointed Principal of the University of Edinburgh. The thirty years during which he held this office appears to have been the most brilliant period of its history—for the city of Edinburgh had never before boasted of such a constellation of literary stars—not only among doctors and divines, but it was an age also of able judges and clear-headed lawyers, celebrated historians and deep-thinking philosophers. Names of world-wide celebrity filled every post of honour. In this brotherhood of talent we find Fergusson and Hume, Cuming and Blair, Cullen and Hunter, Gregory and Munro, Henry Mackenzie (the 'Man of Feeling') and James Macpherson of 'Ossian' notoriety; whilst those noted on the bench were Lord Kames and Lord Hailes, with the eccentric Lord Monboddo and Fraser Tytler, known as Lord Woodhouselee. But the central figure at all their social and intellectual gatherings was ever the genial doctor, Principal Robertson, leader of the Church Assembly and foremost among ecclesiastical politicians. Born with the gift of eloquence, he was one of the most popular preachers of the day, and also the most noted historian in Britain. He published his celebrated *History of Scotland* in 1759, for which he received the sum of six hundred pounds for the two quarto volumes; but before he had completed his *History of America* the value of literary work had risen so rapidly that in 1777 he received £4500 for it. Yet by some his earlier work on the Reign of the Emperor Charles V. is considered a much more valuable tribute to the historical literature of the period. In his younger days the doctor had been a most zealous volunteer, notwithstanding his ordination to preach the gospel of peace and his actual nomination to a church. But the Jacobites, against whom he would fain have fought had his services been accepted in 1745, were much better pleased to receive his volleys from the pulpit in 1755, with a friendly shake of the hand in all good fellowship afterwards—for his moderation as a church leader in after-life became one of the chief causes of his great popularity.

The high intellectual standing of the University of Edinburgh owed much to the indefatigable labours of Principal Robertson, and by no means the least important of his services was his long struggle to obtain larger and more suitable buildings for the college over which he presided, though he did not live to see much more than the new foundation-stone laid.

At the time that he fraternised so warmly with Dr. Johnson, he was living in the picturesque quadrangle of the old University, entered by College Wynd, where he remained located until 1788. Brilliant indeed was the circle of talent to which James Boswell of Auchinleck introduced his bosom friend in that scrambling old college square, the entertainment offered by their genial host, Dr. Robertson, being truly an intellectual feast, given with proverbial Scottish hospitality; and so masterly was the conversational power of each of these learned doctors, that the elegant dinner parties and social suppers became a veritable tournament of words—cultured English *versus* 'good, honest, natural Scotch.' Dr. Robertson had been the first to drink wine with the 'Old Dominie' on his arrival in 1773, and the first to greet the renowned traveller on his return from the Hebrides.

Shortly after Dr. Johnson's visit, the old, rickety college quarters occupied by the professors being pronounced unsafe, Dr. Robertson removed with his family to Whitehouse Loan, and from thence to the Grange. But it was some years previous to this that his niece, Miss Eleanor Syme, had married Mr. Henry Brougham of Brougham Castle. The young couple resided for a time in a flat at the corner of the Cowgate, overlooking the Greyfriars, where the celebrated statesman, Lord Brougham, was born. To him the old Manor-House of Grange was a favourite resort during his uncle's life, when, in company with Henry Cockburn and other lads of his own age, he rambled through its fields and orchards; for, with all his erudition, Dr. Robertson had a most kindly way with young people.

Very pleasing are the reminiscences of the last few years of the Doctor's life at the Grange, as given by Lord Cockburn in his *Memorials*, he having been very intimate there as a boy. 'Many a happy summer day,' writes he, 'had his grandson, John Russell, and I in that house. The Doctor used to assist us in devising schemes to prevent the escape of our rabbits, and *sometimes* (but this was *rarely*, and with strict injunctions to us to observe that moderation which Mrs. Robertson could never make himself practise) he permitted us to have a pull at his *favourite* cherry-tree.' Strange little figures they would appear to us now, these youngsters, climbing fruit-trees, feeding rabbits, and chasing each other through this old-fashioned garden, in their antiquated 'High School apparel,' consisting of 'a round black hat, a shirt fastened at the neck by a black ribbon, a cloth waistcoat, rather large, with two rows of buttons and buttonholes, so that it could be buttoned on either side, which, when one side got dirty, was convenient; a single-breasted jacket, which in due time got a tail and became a coat; brown corduroy breeches, tied at the knees by a showy knot of brown cotton tape; worsted stockings in winter, blue cotton stockings in summer, and white cotton for dress; clumsy shoes, made to be used on alternate feet daily, with brass or copper buckles.'

SIXTEENTH CENTURY GARDEN AT THE GRANGE.

The coat and waistcoat were always of glaring colours, such as 'bright blue and scarlet,' or 'grass-green and scarlet.' 'No such machinery as what are now termed braces or suspenders had then been imagined.'

Lord Cockburn also gives us a very graphic description of the old Doctor himself from a boy's point of view. He says:—

'The Doctor was a pleasant-looking old man, with an eye of great vivacity and intelligence, and a large projecting chin. A small trumpet was fastened by a black

SCOTTISH CELEBRITIES AT THE GRANGE

ribbon to a buttonhole of his coat, and he wore a rather large wig, powdered and curled. He struck us boys even from the side-table as being evidently fond of a good dinner, at which he sat with his chin near his plate, intent upon the real business of the occasion. This appearance, however, must have been produced partly by his deafness, because when his eye told him that there was something interesting, it was delightful to observe the animation with which he instantly applied his trumpet, when having caught the scent, he followed it up, and was the leader of the pack.'

It was within the walls of this quiet retreat at the Grange that the worthy Doctor laid down his pen, and gently passed on to the higher life, on the 11th June 1793, in his seventy-first year. He was buried at Greyfriars, where thousands had heard him lift up his voice for God's truth and his country's weal. His tomb is one of the most imposing monuments in this ancient churchyard; it stands at the north-east corner, very near to Jane M'Math's, with the Castle of Edinburgh in the distance.

Among other Scottish celebrities associated with the Grange of St. Giles we also find the name of Sir Walter Scott, but not as a dweller therein. His first appearance within its precincts must have been while he was attending the Old High School, where he shone most conspicuously in the playground as an inexhaustible story-teller, his young memory overflowing with the Scottish legends and Border tales he had heard from his grandfather at Sandy Knowe, which he delighted to relate to his admiring school-fellows. He says of himself, 'On the whole I made a brighter figure in the *yards* than in the *class*.' It was, no doubt, this love of adventure which made him on one of his boyhood's visits to the Grange House secretly determine to climb the stone pillars at the north entrance, and triumphantly face those rampant griffins, to discover for himself whether their outstretched tongues were '*veritable paint or veritable flame*.'

It is very questionable if at present one visitor in a hundred knows anything about the griffins, so luxuriantly have the trees and evergreens enshrouded them; but Master Walter Scott certainly satisfied himself that the fiery dragons were harmless before his minister, Dr. Robertson, went to live at the Grange. Scott's parents had been regular attendants at Old Greyfriars for many years, and the two families were on closely intimate terms. Still, often as Sir Walter must have visited the old manor between his youth and manhood, never did his footsteps wander thither in his declining age, after his princely dream of Abbotsford had been shattered, and the antiquated Sanct Geilie-Grange of Dr. Robertson's day had been converted into the baronial residence of his much esteemed friend, Sir Thomas Dick Lauder. The traditional story which has been for some time afloat, that Sir Walter frequently sat at the drawing-room window overlooking the bowling-green, with a little child, the youngest pet of the household, upon his knee, is purely apocryphal; for the mighty 'Wizard of the North' had been struck down with paralysis in 1830, and Sir Thomas did not come to live at the Grange House until 1831, though we were shown the exact spot, and the very chair Sir Walter was supposed to have sat upon, which resolved itself at once into a pictorial representation of the scene. But upon inquiry at headquarters we soon discovered that historical traditions require a much better foundation for their authenticity than mere fictitious hearsay, dates being stubborn facts to deal with. Still, there really is some truth in that portion of the story which associates the honoured name of Scott with little Miss Beatrice Dick Lauder, the youngest daughter of Sir Thomas; but the incident itself took place at Abbotsford, and not at the Grange.

The intimacy between the two families was such that visits were frequent between Relugas and Abbotsford. Shortly before Sir Walter's last illness, three of the daughters of Sir Thomas Dick Lauder were staying at Abbotsford; the youngest being a very tiny, sensi-

THE GRIFFIN GATEWAY AND OLD NORTH ENTRANCE AT THE GRANGE.

tive little lady, towards whom Sir Walter in his large-hearted, grandfatherly way was most tenderly chivalrous, taking the child on his knee every evening at bedtime and saluting her affectionately with a 'good-night' kiss. Little Miss Beatrice, who considered this her father's privilege alone, was quite indignant that she should be treated as a baby. In after-years, however, she learned to prize as a tender memory the endearing caresses of the renowned Sir Walter Scott of Abbotsford.

This great name had become as a household word in the Lauder family, not only on account of the warm friendship between Sir Walter and Sir Thomas, but also on account of the similarity in their choice of literary subjects.

It had been said 'that the freedom and felicity of Sir Thomas's style approached nearer to that of Sir Walter Scott than any contemporary instance that can be adduced'; but that was not the only point they had in common, for with all his love of chivalry, Sir Walter's own words about the 'cultured rich' might have been written by Sir Thomas himself, whose creed in life and literature had also 'the democratic touch of a big heart, with the pride of the Scottish laird and gentleman.' 'Let me tell you,' said Sir Walter one day, in writing to Miss Edgeworth, 'that I have had the privilege of knowing some of the most celebrated men and women of my time, and that I have derived more satisfaction and comfort from the conversation and example of the poor, unlettered, hard-working people, than from all the wisdom of the learned folks. I have heard finer sentiments and seen finer lives among the poor people than I have ever seen or heard of anywhere outside the pages of the Bible. Believe me, my dear, all human learning is mere moonshine compared with the culture of the heart.'

'Dear Scott!'—we repeat it reverently, as it came from the sorrowing soul of his mutual friends, whose reminiscences of this, the closing period of his life, are full of the most tender sympathies. Sir Thomas Dick Lauder had barely been one short year at the Grange ere the funeral knell of Sir Walter sounded throughout the length and breadth of Scotland. 'Scott is dead!' they cried, and every voice repeated it; for truly, as Lord Cockburn had said, 'Scotland never owed so much to one man.'

As it fell to the lot of Sir Thomas to witness and describe the funeral procession as it passed from Abbotsford to Dryburgh, we cannot do better than close this chapter on Scottish celebrities with a few passages from his own account of it.

'Alas!' he writes, 'with what sadness do we recall that day when his funeral obsequies took place, when we followed his remains in humble sorrow from

Abbotsford, while the towers and gables and pinnacles of the mansion were smiling beneath the mellowing rays of the September sun, as if unconscious that the master spirit which called them into being had for ever fled from them.'

During the ceremony, performed by Principal Baird, Sir Thomas, being overcome with grief and the heat of the crowded room, stepped out into the porch to seek the air, and here, while holding sacred communion with past memories, 'footsteps came slowly and heavily treading through the small armoury. They were those of the servants of the deceased, who with full eyes and yet fuller hearts came reverently bearing the body of him whose courteous welcome had made that very porch so cheerful to all.'

Sir Thomas was the only eye-witness of this pathetic part of the funeral duties, accident giving him the privilege which was lost to the crowd within. Uncovering his head he stood subdued by an indescribable feeling of awe as the corpse was carried out so tenderly and silently by those who had loved and honoured the master, not another hand being allowed to touch the coffin, which was plain and covered with a black cloth. It had an ordinary plate upon it with this inscription, 'Sir Walter Scott of Abbotsford, Bart., aged 62.' Grateful for having been allowed to witness this scene, Sir Thomas again took his place among the mourners, and followed the mortal remains of Sir Walter from the house of Abbotsford, where all his earthly affections had been centred. The procession of carriages, as it wound its way eastward towards Melrose, extended over a mile.

In his published account,[1] Sir Thomas Dick Lauder gives a beautiful and graphic description of the silent sorrow and tokens of national sympathy so universally manifested as the cortège passed solemnly along the route to Dryburgh.

Six years later Lord Cockburn pens another testimony to the eternal abiding of true friendship—his heart still wailing for his friend. 'Dear Scott! when he was among us we thought we worshipped him, at least as much as his modesty would permit. And now that he is gone, we feel as if we had not enjoyed or cherished him half enough. How we would cling to him if he were to reappear! It is a pleasure which the next generation may envy that I still hear his voice and see his form. I see him in the Court, and on the street, in

---

[1] *Tait's Magazine* for November 1832.

company, and by the Tweed. The plain dress, the guttural burred voice, the lame walk, the thoughtful, heavy face with its mantling smile; the honest, hearty manner, the joyous laugh, the sing-song-feeling recitation, the graphic story—they are all before me a hundred times a day.' And we can only add, Adieu! Sir Walter, Scotland loves thee still!

THE SCOTT MONUMENT.

CHAPTER X

SIR ANDREW DICK OF CRAIGHOUSE

> Up ! lady fair, and braid thy hair,
> And rouse thee in the breezy air.
> Up ! quit thy bower, late wears the hour,
> Long have the rooks caw'd round the tower.'
>
> JOANNA BAILLIE.

AS we have now seen the ending of the direct male line of John Dick of Braid and William Dick of Grange, the eldest and third sons of Sir William Dick, Knight, of Braid, it will be necessary, in order to complete the family circle, to add a few facts about the other three sons—Andrew, Alexander, and Lewis—the two elder of whom obtained lands in fee from their father prior to his reverse of fortune. Being so closely connected with Sanct-Geilie-Grange, the thread of their lives has in a great measure been interwoven with the events already recorded; for they, with the other members of the family, assuredly shared its hospitality in the days of Janet M'Math.

We have already had occasion to mention the second son, Andrew Dick, with regard to the petition sent to Parliament on behalf of his nephew, the young heir, William of Braid, and also in connection with the burial-ground in Greyfriars' Church-

ANCIENT PILLAR FROM ENTRANCE-GATE, CR

SIR ANDREW DICK OF CRAIGHOUSE 93

yard;[1] but from what we have thus gathered, he does not appear to have been at all like his father, the worthy Provost. On the contrary, there is a metallic ring in his grasping, money-loving nature, which is completely at variance with the large-heartedness of the Dicks. Still he seems to have been a man of note in his day, reaping honours and position, more perhaps on account of his father's virtues than his own. He was bred to the law, and became an advocate in the Court of Session; and having married his cousin Christina, only daughter and heiress of Henry Morrison, a wealthy merchant-burgess of Edinburgh, with her he received a large accession to his estate, '4000 merks of yearly rent in houses in Edinburgh, and 59,000 merks in money.' But their married life was of short duration, and their only son William died very young. Upon the death of his wife Christina, Mr. Andrew Dick was left with one little daughter, called Elizabeth.

In 1642 his elder brother, John Dick, also died, leaving his appointment in Orkney vacant, and the following year Mr. Andrew was elected to the Sheriffdom. In 1646 he extended the family circle by taking unto himself as his second bride, Jean Leslie, whose sister afterwards became his nephew's wife. They were both daughters of Sir John Leslie of Newton, younger son of Andrew, fifth Earl of Rothes.

In the same year King Charles I. granted a charter to Mr. Andrew Dick, Sheriff of Orkney and Zetland, and to Jean Leslie, his spouse, in conjunct fee, of the lands of Holland, with the manor-place, and the 'towmailles, quoyes, quoy landis, outbreckes, nesis,' fishings, tenants, etc., in the Isle of Stronsay, parish of St. Nicholas, and Sheriffdom of Orkney, resigned by William Henrysoun of Holland and his wife Margaret Grahame. This estate the King incorporated into the free barony of Holland, with its manor-place as the principal messuage. For which the yearly payment to the King as superior was 'three chalders of barley and four barrels of butter, with suits and presences at the head courts of the said Sheriffdom, with the customary service.' Failure for three years running in payment of the duties involved loss of the charter, which was signed at Linlithgow, 6th March 1646.[2]

Knowing as we do the large sums lent by Sir William Dick of Braid to the State, it is not surprising to find that Mr. Andrew Dick was also induced in the days of his financial prosperity to lend 100,000 merks to the Earl of Morton (he being at that time Earl of Orkney) upon what he considered good Government security. But there was nothing financially secure in those days, though the great family disaster did not occur until after the death of Charles I., which took place in January 1649.

[1] Appendix, Note VII. [2] *Register of the Great Seal*, 1634-1651, No. 1622.

94 SIR ANDREW DICK OF CRAIGHOUSE

On the 22nd of May of the same year Charles II. also granted to Mr. Andrew Dick of Holland, Sheriff of Orkney, and Jean Leslie, his second spouse, in conjunct fee, the lands and 'Manor-Place of Craighous,' in the shire of Edinburgh, '*anciently by union in the barony of Newbotle.*'[1]

This seems to be the first acquisition of Craighouse by Andrew Dick, who is generally supposed to have received it in patrimony from his father, Sir William, but this charter does not in any way lead to such a conclusion. It is distinctly stated that it 'belonged to Mr. Alexander Dick, son of Sir William Dick of Braid, Knight,' who had received it by charter from 'John Rutherford and Janet Nasmythe, his spouse,' 1642;[2] and that he had resigned it into their hands, they having reserved the power and right to dispone it, showing that Mr. Alexander's possession could only have been on leasehold, though the price thereof was to be paid to him by his brother Andrew. The feu-duty remained the same, 'payment to the King of 6 merks, and duplication on entry of heirs, with a prohibition of alienating or mortgaging the lands without the King's licence.' This was a very important clause, and accounts for the estate being still in the possession of Mr. Andrew Dick in 1663, long after the wholesale bankruptcy of the family. Mr. Andrew seems to have been the only one of the five sons of Sir William who could hold the purse-strings tight and make events subservient to his own profit.

The confiscation of the Earl of Morton's property resulting in the mortgage of the whole lands, and the Earldom of Orkney, held by that nobleman, being wadset to him, is mentioned in the Orkney chapter; for, in consequence of the heavy loans granted to the King by the Earl, he appears like many others to have got beyond his depth in the national sea of debt. After the Restoration, the Earldom of Orkney, as feu-farm, Charles II. also granted to Mr. Andrew Dick, then Sheriff of the islands, for 100,274 merks, 10s., being redeemable by the heirs of the Earl for the same sum. This charter[3] was granted to Mr. Andrew on the 15th of August, the same year in the spring of which he had bought Craighouse, 1649. But the quaint old House of Craig had a history long before it was purchased by Mr. Andrew Dick.

There appears to have been a charter anent the lands of *Craiglokart* as far back as the reign of David II. It was in favour of James Sandilands, and most likely it included the ancient square tower of Craiglockhart, still standing as a picturesque ruin upon the roadside, the history of which is completely buried in oblivion.

---

[1] *Register of the Great Seal*, 1634-1651, No. 2057.
[2] *Ibid.* No. 1252.   [3] *Ibid.* No. 2135.

SIR ANDREW DICK OF CRAIGHOUSE

Its massive walls, six feet thick, with a narrow doorway and a very narrow stair leading up from the vaulted room below to the storey above, all mark it as a place of defence in early Scottish history.

Perhaps that narrow subterranean passage at Craighouse, which is said to be of such considerable length, so well built, and so strongly arched, that Dr. Hill Burton 'believed it to be as old as the Romans,' may have originally been connected with this old keep in those dark and troublous times when dirks were rife and shelter scarce.[1] In its earliest days Craighouse evidently belonged to the Abbey of Newbattle, for in 1528 a charter is granted by 'Edward, Abbot of Newbotle, with consent of the chapter,' for good service, to Hugh Douglas, burgess of Edinburgh, and Mariota Broun, his spouse, 'of their lands commonly called Craghouss, with the pertinents, lying near Edinburgh, and within the Sheriffdom thereof, between the lands of the Laird of Braid, called the Plewlands, on the east, the lands of Craiglokhart on the west and south, and the lands of Merchanstoun on the north parts.' They are also bound not to alienate nor mortgage the lands without the liberty of the superiors; and also to attend their courts when summoned by their officers.[2]

By this document it is very clear that though the lands of Plewlands belonged to the Barony of Braid, Craighouse did not, and the frequency with which it changed hands during the next hundred and twenty years proves it to have been at this period more of a burgher's feu-farm than a baronial residence.

The first attempt at any external decoration of the building was in 1565, when it came into the hands of the Symson family. As was usual at that period, upon the marriage of the owner of an ancient keep or manor-house, it underwent a complete restoration; and then the initials and date, with the coat-of-arms, were superadded. In this instance we find over the original entrance doorway, in the old tower of Craighouse, the initials L.S.C.P., 1565, ascertained to represent the names of Laurentius Symsone and his wife, Catherine Pringle of Craiglatch. Whether this be the same person who is

---

[1] But of its existence there is positive proof as late as 1878, for while the builders employed by the managers of the Edinburgh Asylum were examining the walls and foundations in the back or stable court of Craighouse, 'they came upon a secret subterranean passage, very strongly built, with stone-arched roof and sides, about three feet wide, and from four to five feet high. This passage or tunnel skirts the west or outer wall of the new wing of the house, it then turns round the north front to the north-east, towards Edinburgh, and finds its exit in the adjoining field, under an old tree, some distance from the house,' not far from the old dove-cot.*

[2] *Registrum de Newbotle*, pp. 282-284.

* From a local magazine called the *Morningside Mirror*, 1878.

mentioned in the *Retours* in 1603 as 'Laurentius Symsone, hæres *Alexandri Symsone de Craighous, patris in terris de Craighous*,' we cannot say; or this may be the grandson of the former Laurentius, whose title seems indisputably carved on the stone.

It is difficult to reconcile this date of possession on the part of Laurentius Symson with the following story from Pitcairn's *Ancient Criminal Trials*, which seems also to be very precise as to date and locality. It affirms that on the 17th December 1600, John Kincaid of the Craighouse, a turbulent sort of a youth, went with a party of friends, and several followers, all clad in armour, and armed to the teeth with swords, pistols, and daggers, to the house of Bailie John Johnston, in the village of the Water of Leith, and bursting open the doors, they forcibly abducted Isobel Hutcheon, a quiet, peaceable widow, and carried her off to Craighouse. Fortunately for the poor woman, King James VI. was riding at the time in the fields close by, with the Earl of Mar, Sir John Ramsay, and others. Seeing the commotion, the King sent Mar to inquire the cause, and hearing the truth, he despatched Ramsay also, and some of his attendants, to Craighouse to secure and rescue the widow. They, meeting with resistance, threatened to set fire to the building if the woman was not instantly released. For this outrage John Kincaid was tried on the 13th January 1601, and fined 2500 marks, payable to the treasurer; and it is also stated that he forfeited to the King 'his brown horse.'

Five years later this same turbulent youth is entered as successor to his father, Sir James Kincaid of that Ilk, Knight, in the lands of Craiglockhart; but it does not say, *and Craighouse*, therefore it must only have been held on lease. This seems the more likely, as in 1636 it is still in the possession of the Symsone family; for Charles I. then grants it in feu-farm to James Nasmyth, merchant-burgess of Edinburgh, and Christian Boyd, his spouse, upon the resignation of John Symsoun of Craighous, with consent of Janet Johnstoun, his wife. The deed is dated at Edinburgh, 14th November 1636.[1]

There is another story of Craighouse which is also difficult to allocate, the events transpiring in 1569, only four years after the name of Laurentius Symson had been placed over the entrance-door. But since Mr. Robert Chambers has given it a place in his *Traditionary Scottish Stories* as belonging to this old mansion, we can only conclude that the Symsons may have owned Craighouse as mid-superiors, but did not live in it during those tragical years of civil warfare. One thing, however, is certain, the name of Stephen Brunt-

[1] *Register of the Great Seal*, 1634-1651, No. 608.

SIR ANDREW DICK OF CRAIGHOUSE

field[1] is on record as an adherent of Queen Mary, and consequently strongly opposed to the Regent Moray. The main points of the story are as follows:—

It would appear that the old House of Craig was besieged for two months, in 1569, by Sir Robert Mowbray of Barnbougle, who had attached himself to the cause of Moray against the Queen, then a prisoner at Lochleven. In the month of December Craighouse was taken, and the captain, Stephen Bruntfield, was captured. Under promise of protection, he was being conducted as a prisoner to Edinburgh Castle, when Mowbray, breaking his word, barbarously slew him on the links, called in consequence Bruntfield Links.

It is stated that the widowed lady of Craighouse had been a Maid of Honour to the Queen 'from her early years, that she was educated in France, and had left the Court to become the wife of Bruntfield'; and also that her name was *Marie Carmichael*. This is decidedly *traditional*. The Queen may have had an attendant of that name, but it certainly was not one of her childhood's Maries, whose names, Mary Livingstone, Mary Fleming, Mary Seaton, and Mary Beaton, are too well certified historically for any lover of romance to change any of them into Hamilton or Carmichael, notwithstanding the old ballad, which says—

> 'Yestreen the Queen had four Maries,
> The night she'll hae but three :
> There was Marie Seaton, and Marie Beaton,
> And Marie Carmichael, and me.'

It is well known that the sad story of this ballad had reference to a young French maid and the French physician at the Court of Holyrood, after the Queen's marriage with Darnley; and it is quite possible that the post of Maid of Honour may have been given to a 'Marie Carmichael,'[2] after the marriages of Mary Livingstone and Mary Fleming. But though tradition affirms it, history is silent upon the matter.

However, the story says that the lady of Craighouse had been attached to the Court of Queen Mary, and the loyalty of her husband warrants the belief. We can only give an epitomised version of the sad sequel to the barbarous murder of Stephen Bruntfield, but even that will suffice to show the dark side of society in that age of bitter feuds, and the mortal strife in which

---

[1] According to Sir David Lindsay, the Burnfields or Bruntfields were vassals of the Bishop of Glasgow during the fifteenth century; and in the sixteenth century they were a numerous clan in the Merse.

[2] Most probably the daughter of 'John Carmichael of Meadowflat, who sat in Parliament in 1560.'—*Workman's MS.*

most of our old mansions have played a part. The young widow, it seems, remained at Craighouse, with her three infant sons, unmolested, but the whole tenor of her life was changed. She shut herself up in a special apartment, hung round with black cloth, illuminated solely by the light of a lamp. Here, with no other society than that of her little children, and the periodic visits of her priestly confessor, she passed her days.

In such gloomy surroundings, brooding over her husband's cruel death, and the wrongs of her imprisoned Queen, no wonder that the mind of the poor lady became unhinged ; and in the blankness of despair, there rose an all-engrossing passion, the desire for *revenge*. For this she lived, and for this she reared and trained her three beautiful boys, sending them each in turn over to France, the school of chivalry, that they might be perfect in the use of arms.

Every feeling being thus warped, even maternal love and hope were crushed beneath that deadly hydra-headed monster, *hate*. To this hatred for the murderous Mowbray the solitary widow sacrificed each gallant youth on his return from France.

Stephen, her first-born, challenged and fought the laird of Barnbougle in single combat, in the King's Park, where he fell beneath the sword of his adversary. Roger, the second son, also fought and died, leaving the murderer still victor.

When Henry Bruntfield, the third and last surviving son, returned to his native land, his widowed mother, so far from endeavouring to hinder his burning desire to avenge the death of his father and his brothers, she is said to have urged him to the combat in the following words :—' Only yesternight I dreamed that your father appeared before me. In his hand he held a bow and three goodly shafts—at a distance appeared the fierce and sanguinary Mowbray. He desired me to shoot the arrows at that arch-traitor, and I gladly obeyed. A first and a second he caught in his hand, broke, and trampled on with contempt. But the third shaft, which was the fairest and goodliest of all, pierced his guilty bosom, and he immediately expired. The revered shade at this gave me an encouraging smile and withdrew. My Henry, thou art that *third arrow* which is at length to avail against the shedder of our blood.'

It was with difficulty young Bruntfield obtained permission from the King to enlist against Mowbray for the third time in mortal combat ; but at length he prevailed, and the duel was appointed to take place on Cramond Island, opposite Barnbougle Castle, in the presence of the Duke of Lennox and several other courtiers.

SIR ANDREW DICK OF CRAIGHOUSE

'At a little distance upon the sea lay a small decked vessel with a single female figure on board.'

Fierce and desperate was the fight between the gallant youth and the ferocious, unwieldy laird; but at length the deadly struggle came to a close, for Mowbray fell heavily to the ground, and Bruntfield, although exhausted with the loss of blood, had just sufficient strength to thrust his dagger beneath the breastplate of his fallen foe. A loud shout immediately proclaimed him victor; and instantly there arose an unearthly scream from the anchored vessel, and in a few minutes the remorseless widow of Stephen Bruntfield fell upon the neck of her victorious son. But the culmination of the revenge she had yearned twenty long years to accomplish was more than she could bear. She expired in the arms of the avenger of his race.[1]

Such is the story traditionally attached to Craighouse of the Plewlands, which is said to have been haunted ever since by the 'Phantom Lady,' who walks there nightly, wringing her hands in an agony of remorse, but who is only seen by moonlight. If all this did really take place in connection with Craighouse, it must have been under the superiority of the Symsons, who, according to the Records, only resigned their right over it in 1636 to James Nasmyth, who within six years had again to sell part of the lands[2] to Mr. Alexander Lowis in liferent, and Mr. Ninian Lowis, his son, in fee, and afterwards to surrender his whole claim to Robert Inglis, a merchant in London for a debt of £10,495, 19s. 8d.[3] Charles I. on the same day, 29th Sept. 1642, regranting the lands to Elizabeth Spence, daughter of the late John Spence, merchant burgess, under legal reversion, for 6240½ merks.[4] Then follows, on the 2nd Nov. of the same year, the charter already mentioned to Mr. Alexander Dick, from John Rutherford and Janet Nasmyth, his wife; Alexander Dick, Laird of Heugh, resigning his right seven years later in favour of his elder brother, Mr. Andrew, the second son of Sir William Dick of Braid. Craighouse then

---

[1] This story is very differently told in Anderson's *MS. History of Scotland*, in the Advocates' Library. It is there stated that the murder of Stephen Bruntfield did certainly take place on the 22nd December 1596, not on the burgh links, however, but near the crags at St. Leonard's—and the murderer's name is given as James Carmichael, the Laird of Carmichael's son—and Stephen Bruntfield is styled Captain of Tantallon Castle—instead of Master of Craighouse. It would almost appear as though the names had been reversed in the tradition, making it seem probable that Carmichael's father had lived at Craighouse, and that Stephen Bruntfield had married his sister, Mary Carmichael, who, after the murder of her husband, returned to her former home, and shut herself up in the gloomy manner described in the story. The *MS. History* also records the combat, but states that it was Adam Bruntfield, a younger brother of the murdered man, and not his son, who slew Carmichael on Barnbougle Links before 5000 spectators—the judges being the Duke of Lennox, Sir James Sandilands, the Laird of Buccleuch, and Lord St. Clair.

[2] *Register of the Great Seal*, 1634-1651, No. 1281.
[3] *Ibid.* No. 1239.   [4] *Ibid.* No. 1241.

became known as the manor-place of Sir Andrew Dick of Craighill, and truly a more beautifully situated home he could not have chosen for his bonnie young bride, Jean Leslie of Newton. The view from the avenue gate is still enchanting, but in those days there was nought to intercept or mar the lovely prospect of undulating slopes, rich meadow lands, and golden fields of grain; with a stretch of distant scenery which could not be surpassed by any homestead in the whole of Midlothian. And what a wealth of beauty, never old and ever new, in the glorious sunsets, flooding the hills with crimson and amethyst across the shores of Fife.

At the time of Mr. Andrew Dick's purchase of Craighouse, Sir William, his father, was still living as Knight of Braid, and his other two surviving sons were Lairds of Grange and Heugh. But within the next five years the financial crash came, and the humiliating experiences which almost wiped them all from off the face of the earth.

It was at that crucial period, when, after the death of his grandfather, the young heir of Braid was at starvation point, languishing in prison, held there by Sir William's creditors, that his uncle Sir Andrew, who practised more of law than equity, seems to have kept his own head above water, by not only pocketing the very pittance the Crown grudgingly repaid for the maintenance of the whole family, but also his pride in accepting the honour of Knighthood from Charles II. '*in consideration of the loyal services of his late father,*' Sir William. In this charter he is called 'Sir Andrew Dick of Craighouse and Northfield in Orkney.'

The two sons, Lewis and George, born of Sir Andrew's second marriage, both eventually entered the army—and Sir Andrew himself lived to see his only daughter Elizabeth, by his first wife, twice married. Her first husband was Thomas Boyd, Esq. of Penkill, and the second was Mr. James Dunbar; but she had no children by either.

When the eldest surviving son Lewis inherited his father Sir Andrew's estate, he was a captain in the British Army, married to an English lady, Jane Sangster, by whom he had an only son called Alexander, and a daughter named Jane. George Dick, who was born in 1654, was also a British officer, but he died young, leaving an only daughter called Nicolas.

Captain Lewis Dick appears to have lived very little in this country, owing to his military profession, and the active service required in those days, on account of the Monmouth Rebellion, and the Duke of Marlborough's illustrious campaign with the confederates abroad. But after his death his son Alexander

SIR ANDREW DICK OF CRAIGHOUSE

Dick became connected with the ancient families of the Scotts of Rossie, and the Hopes of Craighall, Ceres, by his marriage in 1710 with Margaret, daughter of Patrick Scott of Rossie, and his wife, Margaret Hope, daughter of Sir Archibald Hope of Rankeillor (grandson of the famous Sir Thomas Hope, King's Advocate for Scotland in the reign of Charles II.).

There is every reason to believe that Craighouse passed out of the hands of the Dick family at this time, as it became the property in 1711 of one George Porteous, a herald painter, who made considerable alterations upon it, adding a new wing, and then letting it for £100 Scots yearly.

Alexander Dick, Esq., of Clermiston, near Corstorphine, died in 1729, leaving one son, Patrick, a lad about eighteen years of age, and two younger daughters, Janet and Anne, but Mr. Patrick did not live long after he came of age: he died in the flower of his youth, unmarried, and in him ended the whole male line of Sir Andrew Dick of Craighouse, second son of Sir William Dick, Knight of Braid. Janet Dick, the elder sister, heired her brother, and shortly afterwards romantically married her cousin, Doctor Alexander Cunyngham, fourth son of Sir William Cunyngham of Caprington, whom we shall have occasion to mention in another chapter in connection with the Prestonfield branch of the family.

Before doing so, however, it will be interesting to note a few of the worthies who inhabited old Craighouse after it had passed entirely from the possession of the Dicks.

On looking over the records we find it changed hands very frequently towards the end of the last century. In 1726 it belonged to Sir James Elphinstone, who made further additions to it, and embellished the east doorway with his coat-of-arms impaled with those of his wife, Dame Cecil Denholm of Westshields.

It is very likely the date 1746, which is carved over the lintel of one of the west windows, marks another transition period, when Craighouse passed into the Lockhart family—in the person of Alexander Lockhart, Dean of the Faculty of Advocates (afterwards Lord Covington)—for three years later we find it was the scene of a brilliant marriage in high life. His eldest daughter, Rebecca, being married at Craighouse on the 13th Sept. 1749 to James Hay, Lord Boyd, thirteenth Earl of Errol, one of the most popular noblemen of his period. 'His stature was six feet four inches, and his proportions most exact.' Dr. Johnson always declared that 'he resembled Homer's character of Sarpedon —he looked so like an antient hero.' Sir William Forbes, when speaking of him, said: 'Were I desired to specify the man of the most graceful form, the most elegant, polished, and popular manners whom I have ever known in my long intercourse with society, I should not hesitate to name James, Earl of Errol.' 'He was adored by his servants, a blessing to his tenants, and the darling of the whole country.'

Five years after the marriage, their only child, Lady Mary, was born; but, before she was seven years old, her mother, Lady Rebecca died, and her father marrying again the following year, the child came to live with her grandparents, passing most of her young days at Craighouse. Here, when she was scarcely sixteen, Lady Mary Hay was married to General John Scott of Balcomie, Member of Parliament for Fife.[1] Her father, the Earl of Errol, died at Calendar House on the 3rd of July 1778, in his 53rd year—'beloved, honoured, and regretted — leaving not one enemy behind him.' His brother, Charles Boyd, had been involved in the 'Prince Charlie' Rebellion in 1745; but having made his escape to France, he remained there for twenty years. He returned, however, in 1766 and resided at the patrimonial residence, Slains Castle, Aberdeen, escaping the fate of his father, the Earl of Kilmarnock, who was beheaded in 1746 on Tower Hill for the same offence of high treason. Strange to say, James, Earl of Errol, his son, being of the Stuart blood-royal, 'officiated as Constable of Scotland at the coronation of George III. in 1761.' It is said 'that he neglected by accident to pull off his cap when the King entered, and apologised for his negligence in the most respectful manner; but his Majesty entreated him to be covered, for he looked on his presence at the solemnity as a very particular honour.'

OLD STONE OVER DOORWAY, CRAIGHOUSE.

A few more years saw the Lockharts pass from Craighouse, and then it became the property of the Gordons of Cluny, who had already ac-

[1] Douglas's *Peerage*.

quired and rebuilt the Braid Hermitage, the first estate of the worthy Knight of Braid.

But it is doubtful if any of the titled owners of this rambling old mansion were ever as widely known as the celebrated John Hill Burton, LL.D., the Scottish historian, who resided here for many years in the latter half of this century, this distinguished author being equally famed in the literary world of law, history, and politics. The intellectual gatherings that were held beneath his hospitable roof were most *recherchés*, and he gave to the venerable place a peculiar charm all his own which never failed to delight his guests. Judging him by the depth of his scientific and political works, and his celebrated History of Scotland, few could imagine the wealth of anecdote, and the large-hearted, sympathetic kindliness that graced his conversation as host and entertainer, which is not always the case with very intellectual men; and in private Mr. Burton literally lived among his books. At Craighouse every room was lined with the innumerable volumes of his extensive library, which had taken him his whole life to collect, and which it almost broke his heart to part with. Many a midnight lamp had he burned in their all-engrossing company; but we cannot say if ever, during the small hours of the morning, he troubled himself about the nocturnal wanderings of the 'Phantom Lady.' It is not likely, for the ghosts of the past that would visit him would be sure to be historical characters of some note, crowding round his fertile brain in order to get themselves immortalised by his illustrious pen. That pen is silent now, and the masterly hand that guided it is at rest. Craighouse, like 'Sanct Geilie-Grange' of old, has undergone many changes of late, but it is still a quaint, 'auldfarrant' kind of mansion, approached, as of yore, by its beautiful avenue of venerable trees.

For some years before Dr. Hill Burton took it, it stood tenantless, and in a very dilapidated condition, bidding fair to become a perfect ruin—gaunt and silent, but for the cawing of the rooks and the nightly hooting of the owls. The garden became a wilderness, and the wooded slopes the frequent resort of wandering waifs and gipsies. The fine old corbie-stepped roof was the only part of the building that gave any outward sign of life; and here the yearly tenants were the starlings and the swallows, who built their nests in unmolested peacefulness and security. But a change at length came over the scene, and with repairs and alterations came also human voices ringing through the deserted halls, and human forms were soon seen flitting within its chambers. Then it was known to the wayfarers and holiday pedestrians who loved its seclusion that Craighouse of Plewlands was *let*.

Loving hearts brought back the feeling of home, and tender hands stayed the ravages of Time within the quaintly-beautiful garden—almost solemn in the depth of its shadows and the stateliness of its hedges and magnificent trees. The dear, old-fashioned flowers lifted their drooping heads again, and the grassy banks around them soon regained their softness and their verdure. But a weird and eerie influence had crept about the place, which it never wholly lost especially about the lower apartments, the whole under-flat being vaulted, and at that time very dark and gloomy—fearfully suggestive of rats.

CRAIGHOUSE.

Such was the old Manor-House of Craig when the managers of the Edinburgh Asylum bought the property in 1878. And great, indeed, have been the changes that have passed over it since then. The ancient walls of solid masonry are still intact, and the interior of the old mansion has been restored, beautified, and rendered habitable, with the most praiseworthy discrimination and regard to its former characteristics. Every sixteenth and seventeenth century feature has been retained, and many of its former beauties brought to light in the course of the restoration. For instance, when the workmen stripped off the modern wallpaper, canvas, and plaster, they discovered eleven curious old paintings on the original oak-panelled walls, all in the decorative style of a

SIR ANDREW DICK OF CRAIGHOUSE 105

former period, with 'temples, columns, trees, fountains, waterfalls, caves,' etc., which had been hidden from view for many long years. It is difficult at present to tell whether they were painted by George Porteous, the herald painter who had made considerable additions and alterations to the old manor-house in 1711, or whether they were executed in honour of the brilliant marriage of Lord Covington's daughter, Rebecca Lockhart, to the Earl of Errol in 1749. If the latter, they were most probably the work of James Norrie, the celebrated panel-painter, who, during the early part of the last century, had artistically decorated the walls, ceilings, doors, and shutters of most of the fine old mansions in and around Edinburgh with landscapes, fruit and flowers; some of which were executed with great spirit and artistic skill. The latter supposition appears the more probable, as the paintings seem to have been surrounded with a framework of rich carving in wood, the usual method in which James Norrie finished his panels. Unfortunately their genuine antique appearance attracted the covetous attention of some dishonest fellows among the workmen, for, out of the eleven panels discovered, eight were stolen, leaving only three to grace the walls of that most charming room in Old Craighouse within which the original old-fashioned fireplace has also been brought to light from beneath the modern partitions which concealed it, thus giving an air of quaintness to the whole apartment.

At present there is a feeling of sombre unity and appropriateness in the entire scheme of colour and decoration throughout the whole of the old building; and its baronial character is preserved by the circular stone stair to the ancient keep, with its carved lintel, already mentioned, and the date 1565. The original doors of solid oak, all studded with big iron nails, are still doing duty at the entrance, showing also the iron bolts and huge locks which remind us of the days when it took its part in the city's civil wars.

But of the new buildings erected upon a magnificent scale, at an enormous expense, on the surrounding land acquired by the managers of the Edinburgh Asylum, we can say little in such a short historical sketch as this. It would take an entire chapter to describe the palatial magnificence of the central mansion alone, with its princely Tudor hall and chapel, its splendid ballroom and unique music gallery; also its extensive and highly decorated corridors, drawing-rooms, and dining-rooms, with endless wards all furnished and complete with every modern luxury and comfort. While for outdoor recreation and exercise there are hundreds of acres of hill and moorland; orchards and gardens all enclosed and laid out in walks; with bowling-green and pleasure-

106   SIR ANDREW DICK OF CRAIGHOUSE

grounds, and seats at every point from which the distant view is most exceptionally fine.

Such are the mighty changes that have taken place in the surroundings of Craighouse since the days in which it belonged to the family of Sir William Dick, Knight of Braid. The old familiar gateway has lately been removed, but the ornamental pillars are standing erect as sentinels within the grounds. While the lordly trees still nightly whisper the same old story; and cooing doves still wing their flight around the ancient dove-cot which has for centuries past marked Craighouse of the Plewlands as a baronial property.

OLD LINTEL STONE, CRAIGHOUSE.

CHAPTER XI

ALEXANDER DICK, LAIRD OF HEUGH, AND THE BARONY OF PRIESTFIELD

> 'Early they took Dun Edin's road,
> And I could trace each step they trode ;
> Hill, brook, nor dell, nor rock, nor stone
> Lies on the path to me unknown.
> Much might it boast of storied lore.'
>
> SCOTT.

MR. ALEXANDER DICK, the fourth son of Sir William Dick of Braid, like his older brother William, Baron of Grange, was a merchant-burgess of Edinburgh. The patrimony which his father had designed for him, and which he only received in fee, consisted of the lands of Heugh near North Berwick. This estate Sir William acquired in March 1634, ratified by Charles I. in 1641, but the charter confirming it to his son, commencing '*Alexandro Dick, filio, Dom. Wilhelmo Dick de Braid*, etc., is dated 21st Nov. 1642.'

These lands had been under the superiority of the family of Sir John Home for some generations past, but they appear to have been resigned into the King's hands about this time, and new grants issued under reversion. It is not necessary to enter into the special tenure of the leaseholds, which are sometimes rather complicated ; but in order to understand the extent of the lands and the rights belonging to Sir William and his son at North Berwick, we will transcribe certain portions of the charter to 'His Maj[ties] Lovit Sir William Dicke of Braid,' whereby he grants to him

DOVE-COT HEUGH, NORTH BERWICK.

ALEXANDER DICK, LAIRD OF HEUGH

the Mains of North Berwick, with the manor-places and houses, yards and orchards, dove-cots and fishings, with all the pertinences. The farm-lands, or farm-acres, with the links, extending in all to fifteen husband-lands (390 acres), with the teinds of the fishes of the harbour of North Berwick. The west part of the town of North Berwick, called the Nungaitt (west of the stream called Clertie Burn), with tofts and crofts and the grain mill of Linton, on the water of Tyne, in the constabulary of Haddington. Also the Grange of Breiche in the parish of Calder; the aisle of Langbeland,

RUINS OF THE PRIORY, NORTH BERWICK.

with the rights of patronage of the chaplainries and altarages, called Lady altar, Rood altar, and St. Sebastian's altar, founded of old within the parish kirk of North Berwick, together with the teinds of the lands mentioned, and also of the Law-meadow, North Berwick Law, and the mill-crofts of Kinteith. The lands called Horsecruik, Puntoun, Muirefauld, Slingabak, Puntounrig, Punton-myre; the North Meadow of *Heuche*, near North Berwick, and the lands of Bonytoun and Greensyde, *being parts of the said William's lands of Heuche*, in the parish of North Berwick. All which were formerly incorporated in one barony of North Berwick, and were resigned by Mr. James Durhame of Kynnell, and Sir John Home of North Berwick, with consent of Sir George and Mr. Patrick Home, his sons, and of Alexander Home of Rowanstoun. The above lands were incorporated anew by the King into the free barony of North Berwick, to be held in feu-farm for the payment of £68, 6s. 8d. for the lands, and £20 for the advocation and teinds.[1] Many of the names mentioned here have now completely disappeared, but they serve to give evidence of the extent of the leasehold acquired by Sir William, to which were added in June 1642 the parsonage and vicarage teinds of the lands of Crag, Balgonie, and Gleghorn,[2] also in the parish of North Berwick. The whole of these lands had been disponed by Sir John, Sir George, and Mr. Patrick Home to Sir William Dick, besides some acres belonging to Anna and Helen Home.

There is no doubt whatever but that this extensive East Lothian property was included in the lands given up to Sir William's creditors at the time of the family's misfortune, for, as before stated, the Manor-Place of Grange was the only rooftree that was not sold or mortgaged.

The sole remaining trace of the original homestead of Mr. Alexander Dick is a gable-end built into the wall of the large farmhouse still bearing the name of 'The Heugh.' Upon this gable there is the complete outline of a good Gothic arch, of sufficient size to warrant the supposition that it once formed part of a chapel window. We could, however, learn nothing with regard to its history; but the old dove-cot is still standing in a field close by, beneath the shadow of North Berwick Law. There is no doubt about its originality, for the country-folk would as soon think of '*dinging doun the kirk*' as of demolishing one of these ancient landmarks, attached to every baron's castle-keep or tower in the land. It was a well-known prediction among them that if the dove-cot fell, the lady of the manor would die within the year. Moreover, in the sixteenth century its possession and its position marked the status of the family, for no man was allowed to build or hold a dove-cot, 'unless he had lands to the value of ten chalders of victual yearly, within two miles of it.' Frequently the '*doo-cot*' stands erect, sheltering whole colonies of white-winged inhabitants long after the manor-house has disappeared.

There is not much that is special to relate about the doings of Alexander Dick, the Laird of Heugh, beyond his signing the Covenant with his father, Sir William Dick, and assisting him in all his mercantile enterprises; for, though a merchant-burgess of Edinburgh, he does not appear to have figured in any great public capacity either in that city or in North Berwick.

From the public records we know that he possessed Craighouse on lease-hold for the first seven years of his married life, and that his wife was Helen, daughter of Sir James Rocheid of Innerleith, Bart., after whom he named his only son, James, who could only have been a youth at the time of his father's death in 1657. Mr. Alexander Dick also left his widow with two little

[1] *Register of the Great Seal*, 1634-1651, No. 103. [2] *Ibid.* No. 1151.

ALEXANDER DICK, LAIRD OF HEUGH

daughters. Janet, the eldest, was born in 1653, as entered in the Edinburgh Register of Births; and among the witnesses of her baptism we find Sir Andrew Dick, her uncle, and her Orkney cousin, Mr. John Dick. She eventually married George Gordon of Woodhall, Esq., and her younger sister, Ann, married into the Sydserfe family of Collegehead. Young James Dick, like his predecessors, betook himself to commerce, and entered the business firm established by Sir William Dick and his merchant sons, occupying the same business premises in the Lawnmarket at the sign of 'The Anchor,' which in course of time became known as the firm of Dick and Cuningham,[1] his partner being Sir Hugh Cuningham of Crosshill, Bart. But, if we would learn somewhat of the baronial home of the fourth link in the family chain of the good old Knight of Braid, we must traverse the city of Edinburgh from the extreme west to the extreme east, and pause within the precincts of the fine old Manor of Prestonfield (or Priestfield as it was then called), this being the first property acquired by Mr. James Dick, his grandson.

The barony of Priestfield, with its tall mansion, is of very ancient date, its written records reaching far back into the Wardlaw family, who continued their superiority over the lands of Priestfield until 1509.

In 1485 sasine in terms of a charter had been granted by James Wardlaw of Riccartoune, as mid-superior, to Adam Cant, eldest son and heir-apparent of Henry Cant of Brownisfield, and to Agnes Tod, spouse of Adam, in conjunct fee, of the lands of 'Preistisfeild,'[2] but in 1509 James Wardlaw acknowledges by a letter of obligation[3] that he had sold his superiority of these lands to 'ane

[1] This firm eventually became that of 'Craig Brothers,' of which Mr. John Heiton of Darnick Tower, in his *Castes of Edinburgh*, writes as follows:—'We find that the business of the firm of *Craig Brothers* (with change of names) dates back to before 1638, at which time it was in the hands of the celebrated and wealthy William Dick—better known as Sir William Dick of Braid—the forebear of the Dicks of Prestonfield—then denominated "a foreign merchant," who was Provost of Edinburgh in 1638.'

It appears again in his grandson, Sir James Dick of Prestonfield, 'city merchant,' and Provost of Edinburgh in 1681. About this time Sir Hugh Cuningham of an Ayrshire family was taken in, and the firm was Dick & Cuningham, at the sign of the Anchor in the Lawnmarket. Intermarriages joined the partners in family relations, hence the present name of Dick-Cuningham of Prestonfield. The business thence descended till we find it in the hands of one of the Cuninghams in 1790, who reversed the firm into Cuningham & Dick, by taking in William Dick, a cadet of the family of the Dicks, described as residing at 'the Brigs of Braid.' On the death of Cuningham, Dick carried on the business himself, and on his death in 1798, it was purchased by John Turnbull, the late City Chamberlain, who ultimately assumed John Craig (one of the brothers Craig) as a partner, the firm being now Turnbull & Craig. On the retirement of Mr. Turnbull, Archibald Craig joined his brother, and since that period two other brothers, William and Robert, have been assumed, constituting the present firm of 'Craig Brothers.'

On further inquiry we find this building was occupied in 1859 by Messrs. Clapperton & Co., and since their removal to the new town it has been designated 'Stewart's Arcade'; the firm of Messrs. Craig Brothers & Co. being transferred to Chambers Street.

[2] *Memorials of the Earls of Haddington*, by Sir William Fraser, 'Abridgment of Charters,' 316, vol. ii. p. 239. [3] *Ibid.* p. 243.

wourschipfull man, Walter Chepman, burgess of Edinburgh,' and on resigning them into the hands of James IV., 'he obliges himself to warrant Chepman in the superiority, and to deliver to him within eight days his "ald charter" granted to the late Gilbert Wardlaw, his predecessor, or a copy narrating that the lands are held directly of the King, *blench* for a pair of gloves, to be presented at the feast of St. Giles in St. Giles' Kirk. A penalty of a hundred pounds Scots is imposed for failure of warrandice.' Walter Chepman was a man of wealth and influence, holding a high position in the State, his house being in the ecclesiastical quarter, which was then the aristocratic part of the Cowgate, between Blackfriars' Wynd and Strichen Close. In a charter under the Great Seal,[1] granted to him three months previous to this transaction, he is styled by the King, 'Our well beloved and familiar Walter Chepman, burgess of Edinburgh,' to whom and to his spouse, Agnes Cokburne, he grants the lands of 'Ewirland' in *Cramond Regis* (at that time the King's hunting-seat, now called Barnton), the service to be rendered for these lands being that of presenting water from a silver ewer (*seruicium laracri*) should his Majesty desire it.

Adam Cant, to whom the lands of Priestfield were feued by James Wardlaw of Riccarton, was descended from a very ancient family, the Cants of Cant's Close, which belonged to them for many generations, with various other landed properties in the vicinity of Edinburgh and county of Midlothian, but they did not retain their feu-charter of Priestfield for more than thirty-seven years.

Adam Cant had been Dean of Guild in 1450, but, dying childless, his nephew, Henry Cant of Over-Liberton, grandson of Henry Cant of Brounisfield, became his heir, and as such he signed an obligation in favour of his 'traist freynd,' Maister Thomas Hamilton, who had married his father's sister, Margaret Cant. This grant was to the effect that whenever the granter shall in any way obtain sasine of the lands of Priestfield, lying in the sheriffdom of Edinburgh, and of the land and tenement lying in the wynd called Cant's Close, within the burgh of Edinburgh, on the north side of the High Street, 'fornent the entre of Sanct Gelis Kirk, callit "the stynkand stile,"' which lands and tenement belonged to the late Adam Cant, brother of the granter's father, and now belong to his widow, Agnes Tod, in conjunct fee, or his heirs and successors, he will give infeftment to Mr. Thomas Hamilton and his heirs of the lands of Priestfield, to be held of the granter in free blench, only doubling the blench specified in the charters of the lands; also of the burgh land and

[1] This charter is dated at Edinburgh, 5th January 1509-1510. See also *Memorials of the Earls of Haddington*, by Sir William Fraser, vol. ii. p. 243.

tenement, reserving to Henry Cant the frank-tenement for life. This obligation is granted for a sum of money (not stated) of which Cant discharges Hamilton. It is dated at Edinburgh, 28th May 1519, and signed, 'Henry Cant, w^t my hand at the pen.'

Seal attached contains a shield bearing a bend (apparently engrailed) between a mullet in the sinister chief, and a crescent in the dexter base, and the legend, ' S. Hendrici Cant.'

This grant was not carried into effect for three years, when, for a certain sum of money paid down, Agnes Tod, the widow, having then become the wife of John Prestoun, signed a contract with his consent on the 2nd September 1522, renouncing her conjunct fee in Priestfield and Cant's Close in order that they might be disponed by Henry Cant to 'Maister Thomas Hammylton,' reserving to herself the frank-tenement only. Henry Cant of Over-Liberton then resigned these lands of Priestfield into the hands of Walter Chepman as superior in favour of Mr. Thomas Hamilton of Orchardfield. The document was signed and sealed on the 5th February 1522-23.[1]

These may appear somewhat dry facts, but they are nevertheless of interest to our subject, seeing it was from this same family of Cants that Sir William Dick purchased the Grange Manor in 1631.

In that year also an aisle was added to the church at Duddingston for the use of the 'Laird of Prestonfield,' his tenants, and his servants, the whole estate of Priestfield having been disjoined from the kirk and parish of St. Cuthbert in the previous year, and annexed to those of Duddingston. A more picturesque village kirk could not be desired, being one of the very few Norman churches of the twelfth century now left. Its position is unique, standing on an eminence overlooking the placid lake, where the stately swans sail majestically among the water-reeds, the whole scene being one of sweet sylvan beauty, the peacefulness of which is seldom equalled.

In 1597 Priestfield was occupied by Sir Thomas Hamilton and his eldest son, Thomas, who afterwards became first Earl of Haddington, but he still continued to reside at the Manor-House of Priestfield, where he died in 1637, leaving it to his brother, Sir Alexander Hamilton, a soldier of rare distinction, who also died there in 1649, bequeathing it to his daughter, from whom Sir Robert Murray purchased it in 1670. Such is the pedigree of the tall, antiquated mansion which Sir James Dick purchased in 1677. On the 2nd of March of the same year Sir James was created a baronet of Nova Scotia, by royal patent. This honour was conferred on him for two reasons: first, because

[1] *Memorials of the Earls of Haddington*, by Sir William Fraser, vol. ii. pp. 247-248.

of his acknowledged merit as a good citizen; and, secondly, in appreciation of the loyalty and sufferings of his grandfather—a sort of tardy reparation by the State, for which Sir James Dick of Prestonfield paid pretty heavily in cash, as also did his cousins who were similarly honoured. In 1679, two years later, Sir James was elected Provost of the city of Edinburgh. A new act had just been passed, declaring the period of election to be for *two* years only, owing to

DUDDINGSTON LOCH AND CHURCH.

the tyrannical use which had been made of the office by his predecessor, Sir Andrew Ramsay of Abbotshall, who had been Provost for fifteen years in succession.

A few years before he purchased Priestfield, Sir James Dick had married Dame Anne Paterson, daughter of Andrew Paterson of Dunmore, county Fife, and their eldest child, Janet, was born in 1672, at whose baptism we find two of his mother's brothers, the Rocheids of Craigleith. The birth of the son and heir, who came two years later, was a matter of great rejoicing. He was called James, after his father and his grandfather, and among those present at his baptism was his cousin, William Dick, second Baron of Grange, the only son of Janet M'Math. In due course several other children followed in rapid succession ; but in slow procession, one by one, they departed, even the son and heir, leaving only the eldest girl, Janet, to inherit her father's estate, as Baroness Dick Cunynghame, after she became the wife of Sir William Cunynghame of Caprington. But many stirring events transpired in her father's life ere that time came, which we shall relegate to another chapter.

OLD PILLAR OF ORIGINAL ENTRANCE TO PRESTONFIELD.

CHAPTER XII

SIR JAMES DICK OF PRESTONFIELD, THE WISE PROVOST

'The steir, strabach, and strife,
Whan bickerin' frae the brochs o' Fife,
Great bangs o' bodies, thick and rife,
    Gaed to Saint Andros toune.
And wi' John Calvin in their heids,
And hammers in their hands, and spades,
Enraged at idols, mass and beads,
    Dang the Cathedral doon!'
                                    WILLIAM TENNANT.

SHORTLY after he had obtained the Provostship, political circumstances brought Sir James Dick into royal notice. The Duke of Albany and York, on account of his openly expressed Roman Catholicism, had been advised to retire into Scotland as King's Commissioner, there to await the result of the Bill of Exclusion.

Sir James Dick being Provost as well as one of the most influential citizens of Edinburgh, he naturally took an active part in the Duke's reception in the Scottish metropolis. Having sailed from Woolwich on the 20th October 1680, his Royal Highness, after weathering a 'mighty storm,' reached Kirkcaldy on the 26th. He crossed from Burntisland to Leith on the 29th, from whence, 'in much solemnitie, he was conveyed to the Palace of Halirudhous.' 'Great preparations had been made for his entrance into the Scottish capital: he was conducted in regal pomp through the Watergate, then the royal entrance; sixteen companies of trained bands, in full uniform, were called out upon the occasion, and sixty men selected from them, accoutred and apparelled in their best manner, were appointed his bodyguard. An entertainment was given him by the magistrates, which cost nearly thirteen hundred pounds sterling, an enormous sum in those days, and in the then depressed state of Scotland.'[1] Lord Fountainhall tells us that it was upon the Duke's first visit to the castle that 'Mons Meg was riven in the shooting.' This was naturally deemed a very bad omen, and the fact of its having been fired off

[1] Maitland's *History of Edinburgh*, p. 101.

by an English gunner, the Scots resented it extremely. The chronicler quaintly adding, ' *We thinking he might of malice have done it purposely, they having no canon in all England so big as shee.*'

But a few months later the remembrance of this evil omen was cast into oblivion by another fortuitous event, also considered prognostic of the Duke's future, which Lord Fountainhall, whose observation nothing seemed to escape, sums up very briefly thus :—' In the end of Februar 1681 we heard that of 4 Lyons in the Tower, 3 of them dyed, and the Lyon remaining was that which was designed " the Duke of York's Lyon," *whereon every one made ther observe.*'

The same chronicler's own 'observe' on the 14th of October of the same year is equally concise. 'The Duke of York's birthday was keeped at Edinburgh with more solemnities and more bonfires than the King's used to be. *So prone are flatterers to adore the rising sun.*' The Scottish nobles had, indeed, from the first landing of the royal Commissioner, shown themselves most assiduous in their loyal attentions to him ; his grave and lofty bearing, combined with the most courteous dignity of manners, accorded well with their ideas of royalty, and raised the standard of their own punctiliousness. James, Duke of York, was in every respect a more noble Prince than his unstable brother, King Charles. His very sincerity in upholding his religious convictions gained for him the staunch adherence of the Highland chiefs, who tendered their allegiance to the grandson of their own King James VI. most willingly.

But the Duke was also anxious to win the favour of the populace, in order to secure his title as a Stuart to the kingdom of Scotland, in case his adherence to the Catholic faith excluded him from reigning in England upon the death of his brother, Charles II. Consequently many of the atrocities enacted against the Covenanters during the administration of the odious Duke of Lauderdale were considerably ameliorated, though we know that, as ' King's Commissioner,' the Duke was forced to preside at the trials by torture that went on in those dread, dark halls below the Parliament House when *Bluidy Mackenzie* was King's Advocate. The horrors of those days we need not repeat. They are burnt into the history of the human race, for such things ever have been since men first began to differ about the dogmas of religious creed. Fiendish cruelty on the side in power, with heroic endurance and stoic martyrdom on the other. To counterbalance the unpopularity of these severities, a splendid Court was held at Holyrood, where the royal Duke and his proud Duchess, Mary d'Este de Modena, presided with all the luxury and display of continental courts, which, in the eyes 'of gay cavaliers and high-born maidens,' contrasted most agreeably with the hitherto straitlaced decorum,

SIR JAMES DICK OF PRESTONFIELD 117

stately manners, and rigid reserve of fashionable society in the Northern capital. We are told that tea was introduced for the first time into Scotland on these occasions, being offered by the Duchess, as something unique, to the Edinburgh ladies. It had been imported into England some few years previous to this as a foreign luxury; but its fabulous price made it a *liqueur* rather than a beverage, even at royal levees. We can hardly imagine it possible that the refreshing plant so indispensable to our *afternoon-tea* could have been sold in London in 1657 at £10 and £5 per pound, with a duty of 5s. on each pound. No wonder they boiled it to extract the costly juice from each individual leaf. Some even ate the concocted leaves, taking it to be some rare Chinese vegetable.

The Duke of York's daughter, the Princess Anne (afterwards Queen of England), assisted at these royal entertainments at Holyrood, and thus acquired a liking for this costly ' *Tcha*,' as it was called ; for Pope tells us the '*great Anna sometimes counsel took and sometimes tea.*'

Returning to the politics of the period, it is worthy of note that though the Duke of York in his staunch Roman Catholicism was most severely disposed against Presbyterianism of every shade and degree, yet we find, for his brother's sake, the Episcopalians met with more than tolerable toleration. This naturally fostered a spirit of animosity and retaliation in all classes, manifesting itself in unruly outbursts among the students of the University, the schoolboys, and the apprentices, who in all ages proverbially fan into flame the smouldering ashes of any party spirit. They commenced by wearing 'a badge of *blew ribbans* in their hats, with these words embroidered on them, "*No Pope*," "*No Priest*," "*No Bishop*," "*No Atheist*," while some of the Episcopalians wore "*red ribbans*" with the words, "*I am no Phanatick.*"' 'As if,' writes Lord Fountainhall indignantly, 'all who declare against popery were *Phanaticks !*'

The College of those days was a very different institution, both externally and internally, from the Edinburgh University of the nineteenth century. It was the only '*perfectly Protestant*' College in Scotland, consequently upon a different basis from those of St. Andrews, Aberdeen, and Glasgow. It was called the 'Royal College of King James,' he having granted the foundation charter and elected himself its godfather, with the promise of an endowment to his '*god-bairne.*' There is a good anecdote told of the Scottish Solomon in connection with the meeting in Stirling Castle in 1617 for the grand '*Disputation*' of learned men from this University in presence of the King. At the close of the discussions 'one who stood by told his Majesty that there was one of the company of whom he had taken no notice, *Mr. Henry Charteris*, Principal of the Colledge (who sate upon the President's right hand), a man of exquisite and universal learning, although not so forward to speak in publick in so august an assembly.' 'Well,' answered the King, 'his name applieth very well to his nature, for *Charters* contain much matter *yet say nothing*, but put *great purposes in men's mouths.*'[1] It appears his own chartered promise of a '*god-bairne gift*' belonged to one of those '*great purposes*,' for it never travelled any further than the King's own mouth—the '*god-bairne*' never saw it.

In order to establish King James's College many old and very interesting buildings were demolished, while others, belonging to the Ancient Kirk, 'originally called *St. Mary's-in-the-Fields*,' were retained and made use of for the University, 'the gateway of which was at the head of the College Wynd, with a lofty bell-tower, and the first five words of the AVE MARIA in Gothic characters cut upon its lintel, as it was the original portal of the Kirk of Field.'[2] It was in this old University, with its irregular courts and straggling buildings of various dates, that most of the learned men of Scotland for three centuries obtained their education and passed their degrees, while the younger and more boisterous students carried on their fanatical pastimes and riotous pranks. As a striking instance of this we may mention the serious riot that took place on Christmas day 1680, two months after the Duke of York's arrival, Sir James Dick of Priestfield, grandson of Sir William Dick of Braid, still being at that time Provost of Edinburgh. It appears that the most fanatical among the young men at the College, imbued with the persecuting spirit of the age, determined to show their anti-popish zeal by burning an effigy of the Pope at Yuletide. Accordingly, with unexampled effrontery, they placarded through the town a most seditious advertisement, which could not fail to cause a serious disturbance in the city if it were seen by any of the Duke of York's household. But what did these thoughtless young rascals care about broken heads so long as they got their Yuletide frolic carried out? This is their wild advertisement, recorded by Hugo Arnot:—

'These are to give notice to all Noblemen, Gentlemen, Citizens, and others, that We, the Students of the Royal College of Edinburgh (to show our detestation and abhorrence of the Romish religion, and our zeal and fervency for the Protestant), do resolve to burn the effegies of Anti-Christ, the Pope of Rome at the Mercat Cross of Edinburgh, the 25th of December instant, at Twelve in the forenoon (being the festival of Our Saviour's nativity). And as we hate tumults as we do superstition, we do hereby (under pain of death) discharge all robbers, thieves, and bawds to come within 40 paces of our company, and such as shall be found disobedient to these our commands, *Sibi Caveant*. By our special command, Robert Brown, Secretary to all our Theatricals and Extra Literal Divertisements.'

---

[1] Sir Alexander Grant, *Story of the University*. [2] James Grant, *Old and New Edinburgh*.

SIR JAMES DICK OF PRESTONFIELD

Sir James Dick immediately set about trying to prevent the whole affair: he had the ringleaders seized by the Town Guard while in their beds, and forthwith imprisoned in the Tolbooth; and the rest of the students were made to promise to the Regents of the College that they would give up their foolish intention. So little reliance, however, could be placed on their promises, that the city on Christmas eve had quite the appearance of a beleaguered town, being patrolled all night by the foot-guards and the city militia, while at the College and the Palace the guards were doubled. Notwithstanding all this, with boldness worthy of a better cause, the young rebels mustered on Christmas morning in the High School Yard, and in spite of Provost, Principal, Regents, and guards, they carried their effigy of '*his Holiness, with triple Crown and Keys,*' in triumph down the High School Wynd; then, hearing the tramp of the Grey Dragoons under command of the fierce old General Dalzell, they hastily set fire to it, at the corner of Blackfriars' Wynd, in front of Cardinal Beaton's house, and fled for their very lives. The soldiers were ordered to beat out the flames, and rescue the 'Pope,' but this they knew would be no very agreeable undertaking, guessing the combustible nature of his composition; and so, not being over desirous of such an inglorious martyrdom, they contented themselves with battering the image at a safe distance, when lo, its head rolled off amidst the shouts of the street boys and the jeers of the rebel students, seven of whom were apprehended and brought to justice by Sir James Dick. In consequence of which we find the following quaint entry in Lord Fountainhall's Diary:—

'11*th January* 1680-1.—The mansion house of Priestfield besyde Edinburgh, belonging to Sir James Dick, provost of Edinburgh, was in this evening about 7 or 8 o cloak, brunt: whither by casuall accident and negligence, or designedly by præcogitat malice, could not weill be determined. Some jaloused the scooll boyes at the Colledge, because he had imprisoned some of them for their frolique of burning the Pope.'[1]

As threats against the magistrates had been previously uttered aloud in the streets by the students, Sir James Dick very naturally took it for granted it was the '*scooll boyes,*' especially as some of them had been seen near Priestfield House that evening, 'with unlighted links in their hands, and one with a lantern.' The gates of the College were therefore ordered to be shut, and the students were all banished to a distance of fifteen miles beyond the city. In ten days, however, they were permitted to return, on condition that their parents became liable for their better behaviour in future. Sir James Dick

[1] Fountainhall's *Historical Observes.*

120   SIR JAMES DICK OF PRESTONFIELD

having a friend at Court in the Duke himself, his house at Priestfield was rebuilt within six years from the public treasury, and the date of its completion, 1687, placed upon the pediment of the centre dormer window, and the

HIGH SCHOOL WYND AND CARDINAL BEATON'S HOUSE.

initials of Sir James Dick, and his spouse, Dame Anne Paterson of Dunmore, on either side.

Burnt out one year, we are told that the worthy Provost barely escaped drowning the next, on his return from London with the royal Duke in 1682.

SIR JAMES DICK OF PRESTONFIELD

'Of this disaster the following extract of a letter, dated 9th May 1682, from Sir James himself to his correspondent in London, gives some interesting particulars ':—

'At seven o'clock in the morning of Sunday last, the man-of-war called the *Gloucester*, Sir John Berry captain, where his Highness was, and a great retinue of noblemen and gentlemen, whereof I was one; the said ship did strike in pieces, and did wholly sink upon the bank of sand called the Lemon and Oar, about some twelve leagues from Yarmouth. This was occasioned by the wrong calculation and ignorance of a pilot, which put us all in such consternation that we knew not what to do; the Duke, and the whole that were with him, being all in bed when she struck; the helm of the said ship having broke, and the man being killed by the force thereof at the first stroke. When the Duke had got his clothes on, he inquired how things stood, she being sunk nine feet of water in the hold, and the sea coming in at the gun-ports: and all the seamen and passengers were not at command, every man studying his own safety, forced the Duke to go out at the large window of the cabin, where his little boat was ordered quietly to attend him, lest the passengers and seamen should have thronged so in upon him as to drown the boat; which was accordingly so conveyed, as that none but Earl Winton, and the President of the Session (Sir George Gordon of Haddo, afterwards Earl of Aberdeen), with two of his bed-chamber men (one of these was John Churchill) went with him, but were forced to draw their swords to hold people off. We seeing his Highness gone, did cause tackle out, with great difficulty, the ship's boat, whereon the Earl of Perth got in, and then I went by jumping off the shrouds, into the boat: the Earl of Midleton, immediately after me, did jump into the same, upon my shoulders: withal there came the laird of Touch, with several others, besides the seamen that were to row. . . . Among them that were left were my Lord Roxburgh, and Laird Hopetoun and Mr. Littledale, Roxburgh's servant, and Dr. Levingston, the President of the Session's man; all being at the place where I jumped, but could not follow, since it seems they concluded more safety to stay in the vessel, than to expose themselves to any other hazard; all which persons in an instant were washed off and all drowned. There perished in this disaster above two hundred persons.'[1]

After this miraculous escape Sir James Dick was again elected Provost of Edinburgh for 1683, in which capacity he appears to have given universal satisfaction. This fact alone bespeaks no little tact and ability in those days, so full of bitter animosities, wherein the ever recurring religious feuds fostered the growth of cringing hypocrites and secret spies—every man holding his hand in readiness to grasp his sword, none knowing whom to trust, nearest neighbours often the deadliest foes. Looking back historically from our present standpoint, we cannot help wondering how much rancour, ill-feeling, and bloodshed might have been spared both countries had that royal Duke quietly slept beneath the waves at Yarmouth.

[1] Burke.

But what would Scottish bards have done without their 'bonnie Prince Charlie'? Ah! well, there are wheels within wheels which few mortals can understand, and every human life fits in as an indispensable spoke somewhere.

When next we hear of Sir James Dick, wise Provost though he be, we find him in the Law Court; the case in point being one concerning the swans on Duddingston Loch. Some time before Sir James purchased Prestonfield, John, Duke of Lauderdale, had put some swans upon the lake. These swans, after the death of the Duke, his widow, Elizabeth Murray, daughter of the Earl of Dysart, and the Duke's second wife, claimed as hers by right of inheritance; which being disputed, she caused some of them to be carried off and put in a secure place under lock and key. Sir James, considering that he had acquired the swans with the loch, proceeded forthwith to their retreat, and, breaking open the door, took back the birds to Duddingston and set them afloat again. This so enraged the Duchess that she raised an action of damages against him, and gained her case. Sir James, in retaliation, had the whole flock of poor innocent swans chased entirely off the loch; but it is pleasant to be able to add that they were speedily befriended by the interference of the Duke of Hamilton, as Heritable Keeper of the Palace of Holyrood, who protested that all wildfowl or animals upon the boundary of the royal park belonged to the King; whereupon they were quietly restored to their watery home, their fledglings, and their nests; and perhaps, for all we know, they are the veritable ancestors of those which delight our eyes to-day and test the powers and the patience of our artists. This case must have caused considerable interest among the citizens of Edinburgh, if in their day the picturesque loch were as freely resorted to by pedestrian pleasure-seekers as it is with us at present—we might almost say, in all seasons and in all weathers, for in summer we see groups of children scattered upon its banks feeding the beautiful swans, while lovers saunter along the shore basking in Love's sunlight; anglers, meanwhile, wandering to and fro fishing for perch and pike. Mischievous boys, too, *cela va sans dire*, who, with the aid of their canine companions, delight in chasing the pretty black coots from among the water-reeds, or in flinging some unwilling puppy, for the good of its health, among the stately lords of the loch, sailing forth majestically in full plume. But when King Frost appears, the scene is changed, and the sparkling ice is covered with enthusiastic skaters, morning, noon, and night; for, should the Queen of Heaven withhold her pale and silvery lamp, we behold a transformation scene by torchlight.

Such was the outcome of the lawsuit of Sir James Dick of Prestonfield, who was called the wise Provost of Edinburgh, though it is very doubtful if the

SIR JAMES DICK OF PRESTONFIELD

students of 1681 would have indorsed the title—at least not until they had reached the years of discretion. There is one wise thing, however, which Sir James certainly did, and that was the carting away of heaps upon heaps of decayed rubbish from the filthy streets and thoroughfares of the city. What he

CHILD FEEDING SWANS.

thus philanthropically commenced for the good of the public became eventually an incalculable boon to himself and his posterity ; for the spreading of all this refuse upon the marshy banks of Duddingston Loch so enriched his lands, that their fertility increased in a marvellous degree ; and this superiority of soil has been sustained down to our own day.

SIR JAMES DICK OF PRESTONFIELD

It appears, however, that the loch has greatly diminished in extent, for in those days it was twice its present size, owing no doubt, as Lord Cockburn tells us, to the regular cutting down of the reeds close to the ground, 'by means of short scythes with long handles.'

The healthfulness of the marsh may be dubious, but of its picturesqueness there can be no doubt, nor yet of its forming a most attractive feature in the Prestonfield estate.

This estate lost its chief charm to Sir James Dick when his last surviving son and heir-apparent passed away; for, with all his worldly prosperity, the Baronet of Priestfield could not keep sorrow from his hearth, nor death from entering his door. His only remaining child was his eldest daughter, Lady Janet, wife of Sir William Cunyngham of Caprington.

In 1699, therefore, Sir James Dick 'made an entail of his estates of Prestonfield and Corstorphine to the second and younger sons successively of his daughter, Lady Janet,' and on the 22nd March 1707 he resigned his baronetcy, obtaining a new patent from Queen Anne, the title and dignity of which was to descend according to the entail of his estate,[1] they so succeeding being obliged to bear the name and arms of Dick.

Some men might have been apt to think that, having thus satisfactorily settled their worldly affairs, they would be expected to slip quietly away to their forefathers; but Sir James lived twenty-one years after making this settlement, and only when he had reached the good old age of eighty-five did he pass peacefully onward, leaving his title and estates to William, third son of his daughter Janet and Sir William Cunyngham. Sir James Dick was the last of the male line of Alexander, fourth son of Sir William Dick of Braid.

In the picturesque little church of Corstorphine, founded in 1427, there still exists a memento of Sir James Dick as laird of the barony. This consists of one of the silver cups used at the Communion, which was gifted by him six years before his death. It has the following inscription engraved upon it:—
'23 May 1722. This Silver Cup is given as ane free gift by Sir James Dick, Baronet, and Heritor and Patron of the Church of Corstorphine, and that for the use and service of the said Church: the weight thereof being 30 unces, 7 drop and ane half.'[2] The height of the cup is a little over seven inches, the same as

---

[1] Charter of Baronetcy patent. 'Queen Anna grants to Sir James Dick of Prestonfield and his heirs-male, whom failing, to the heirs-male of Lady Janet Dick, his daughter, spouse of Sir William Cuningham of Caprington, in terms of the entail of Sir James Dick's lands and estate of Prestonfield, the title, honour, and dignity of Knight-baronet, with all privileges pertaining thereto.' Patent dated at Kensington, 22nd March 1707.

[2] Corstorphine Kirk-Session Records. See Appendix, Note IX.

SIR JAMES DICK OF PRESTONFIELD

the companion cup, which was provided by the other heritors. They are valued as being the last of the mazer shape, with the Edinburgh hall-mark. The maker's name was John Seatoune, the date of whose 'freedom' or full admission to the Corporation of the Goldsmiths' Craft was 1688. These cups were made by him in 1717, and nominally presented by the heritors to the church in 1719, though they did not come into use until 1722.[1]

[1] This information has been kindly given by Mr. Alexander Brook, F.S.A. Scot.

COMMUNION CUP

CHAPTER XIII

PRESTONFIELD MANOR

'It was a shady and sequestered scene,
Like those famed gardens of Boccaccio,
Planted with his own laurels, evergreen,
And roses that for endless summer blow ;
And there were fountain springs to overflow
Their marble basins, and cool, green arcades
Of tall o'erarching sycamores, to throw
Athwart the dappled path their dancing shade.
                                                    HOOD.

HE family into which the old manor of Prestonfield was entailed consisted of six sons and four daughters.

The eldest son, Sir John Cunyngham, one of the most learned and most polished gentlemen of the period, did not succeed his father in the estate of Caprington until 1740. (This estate had at one time been the seat of the great warrior and Scottish hero, Sir William Wallace, and it was even then considered ancient.[1])

The second son, James, died young, leaving William his grandfather's heir. He became second Baronet of Prestonfield, as Sir William Dick, in 1728.[2] His father's family belonged to the Conynghames of Kilmaurs, whose fourteenth century ancestor, Sir William de Conynghame, had married Eleanor Bruce, and was styled Earl of Carrick during her life. From him also sprang the Earls of Glencairn.

The young baronet, Sir William Dick, being thus of noble descent, and coming from a home of much refinement and learning, he had been fully prepared, and was ably fitted to undertake the duties and offices which his inheritance of the title entailed upon him. But the most remarkable event in his after-career, certainly, was the fearlessness with which he wooed and wed the fair and eccentric Miss Anne Mackenzie, whose wild pranks had so often astonished and scandalised the prim aristocratic inhabitants of St. James's Court in the Lawnmarket, where she was born. She seems to have inherited the daring and assurance of her grandfather, Sir George Mackenzie of Rose-

---

[1] Burke's *Peerage*. [2] The new charter of entail was granted in 1735. Appendix, Note X.

PRESTONFIELD MANOR

haugh (the fierce, red-handed foe of the Covenanters), mingled with a large share of the talented wit of her father, Sir James Mackenzie of Royston. Very little, however, of either maiden coyness or common propriety appears to have been combined with it. Not content, as ladies in the present day, with masquerades and fancy balls, within the limits and usages of society, this fair girl donned the attire of a cavalier in the open streets, and 'went about the town at night in search of adventures,' taking her maid with her, dressed as her squire. Sometimes these frolicsome follies ended most unpleasantly, and the *would-be gallant* found herself incarcerated in the city guard-house, locked up like any common brawler or disturber of the peace. Instead of this taming her wild spirits, she exulted in her folly, and only wrote witty verses at the expense of her enemies. How Sir William had the courage to take unto himself this accomplished madcap as a bride is difficult to conceive; for even as Lady Anne Dick her name was a byword for egregious eccentricities. Though born in the family town-house in St. James's Court, the greater part of her youthful days were spent at the manor-house of Royston, built beside the ruins of the old castle at Granton. This estate having been entailed upon her father by George, Viscount Tarbat, first Earl of Cromarty. Could it have been the proximity of her home to the restless, ever-changing sea that had inspired Lady Anne with such witching love of freedom from all the trammels and conventionalities of society? May be, for in her wildest moods it would have been hard to tell which struggled most to overstep the bounds—Lady Anne or the surging waves that lashed the rocky barrier below the castle walls. A sturdy old castle it must have been many centuries before Miss Anne Mackenzie was born to climb its turret stairs; and a fine old ruin it still is, with a most delightful old-fashioned garden, wherein strangers have received the kindliest welcome. But the unique sea-gate, with its magnificent iron-wrought filagree, which was one of its chief attractions, is no longer there. In Lord Cockburn's day it was 'the grandest gate in Scotland.' Its noble pillars, capped with a ducal coronet, still remain to tell the story of their former grandeur. When the Duke of Argyll acquired Granton Castle from the Hopes of Craighall, and Royston from Sir James Mackenzie, Lady Anne's father, he made it one of the finest estates near Edinburgh, and named it after his eldest daughter, 'Caroline Park'—not in honour of Queen Caroline, as is generally stated, for Queen Caroline died in 1737, three years before the Duke of Argyll and Greenwich purchased this estate. But he had christened his eldest child Caroline after the Queen, he being at that time Field-Marshal of all the forces of King George II. This daughter married the Earl of

PRESTONFIELD MANOR

Dalkeith, and with her the property went into the Buccleuch family. The Duke of Argyll dying without male issue, his English title descended to his eldest daughter Caroline, she being 'created Baroness Greenwich on the 28th August 1767.'[1]

The fine old manor-house of Royston, with its broad staircase and magnificent filagree work, passed out of the Mackenzie family just one year before the death of Lady Anne Dick, to whom it had been as a paradise of perpetual delight in her youth.

Sir William Dick only survived his eccentric wife, Lady Anne, five years and a half, dying in 1746 childless; and in consequence he was succeeded in the Barony of Prestonfield by his brother Alexander.

Being fourth son of Lady Janet Dick, heiress of Prestonfield, there did not appear much likelihood in his youth of Sir Alexander inheriting his grandfather's estate, but the proverbially 'unexpected' always does happen in the matter of inheritance. This estate comprised not only Prestonfield and Cameron, but a considerable amount of land at Cramond, and also in Corstorphine, where the magnificent sycamore tree of Sir William Dick, the worthy Knight of Braid, still stands in the centre of the village. At one time it was reckoned the largest in Scotland.

In autumn, with its golden foliage, it forms a living monument to the

ROYSTON CASTLE.

[1] Burke's *Peerage*.

PRESTONFIELD MANOR   129

memory of Scotland's beautiful Queen, Mary Stuart; it being an oft-repeated tradition that she brought over from fair Touraine, her dowry lands in France, the first little sycamore tree seen in Scotland. This she planted in the garden at Holyrood, and from it have sprung all the beautiful groves of sycamores in the land—veritably a numerous progeny, and right royal trees they have become, as those at Prestonfield can testify.

Sir James Dick's grandson, Dr. Alexander Cunyngham, who succeeded his

GRANTON FROM SILVERKNOWES.

brother, Sir William Dick of Prestonfield, was a well-known physician in the county of Pembroke, where he had been successfully practising medicine for many years. He had taken his degree at Leyden in 1725, having studied under Dr. Boerhaave,[1] and had also travelled over a great part of the Continent to complete his education; passing especially through Italy, remaining some time in Rome storing his mind with the beauties of foreign art and literature, which gave him the culture and refinement for which he was so justly distinguished. Dr. Alexander Cunyngham did not continue his professional duties after he was called back to his native country to become Sir Alexander Dick, yet in 1756, ten years after inheriting the title of Baronet of Prestonfield, he was unanimously elected President of the Royal College of Physicians of Edinburgh, which honour was conferred upon him for seven

[1] Douglas, *Baronage of Scotland*.

R

years consecutively; 'and upon his retirement the Fellows, as a testimony of the sense which they had entertained of his eminent services, hung up a portrait of the ex-President in the hall—a mark of distinction never previously bestowed upon any member whatsoever.'[1] Of this College Sir Alexander had been a member for thirty years, having been made a Fellow in 1727, after his return from Holland as Dr. Alexander Cunyngham.

He married his cousin, Dame Janet Dick, granddaughter of Sir Andrew Dick of Craighouse, in 1736. Her brother Patrick, as we have already stated, was the last of the male line of Sir Andrew, the second son of Sir William Dick of Braid, so that, as in the case of the fourth son, Alexander, the estate and name again descended to a daughter 'Janet.'

It is not stated how many children filled the nest of the young doctor and his lady, Miss Dick of Clermiston; but, judging from the date of her marriage and the time of her death in 1760, it is evident that some must have predeceased her, for she left only two daughters to her sorrowing husband, the elder of whom, also named Janet, was born in 1749, and the other, an infant called Anne, was born in 1759. The fact of having no son to heir his title and estate must have induced Sir Alexander to give a stepmother to his little ones, by forming another matrimonial alliance in 1762, though he had by that time attained his fifty-eighth anniversary. Subsequent events, however, proved the wisdom of his choice, for he enjoyed twenty-five years of uninterrupted companionship and wedded felicity with Dame Mary Bulter, eldest daughter of David Bulter, Esq., of Pembroke, by whom he had three sons, William, John, and Robert, and also three more daughters. This merry band of children filled the glad sphere of Prestonfield with new ties and new relationships, intensifying the enthusiastic interest with which Sir Alexander embellished and improved his estate.

Duddingston Loch came in for a considerable share of his attention. To his boys it was a never-failing source of recreation, between fishing, shooting, boating, and skating; but to the baronet himself it offered a wider field of pastime and antiquarian research, one discovery after another turning up as he dredged the loch for marl. At length, finding he had made a goodly collection of ancient fragments of bronze swords, spear-heads, and other stone implements, besides a quantity of human skulls and bones of all sorts, he presented the whole of these antique specimens to the newly formed Antiquarian Museum, where they are still to be seen among its curiosities under the heading of 'Bronze Leaf-shaped Swords.'

[1] Burke's *Baronage*.

This was in 1780; but the planting and enclosing of parks had been going on for many years; indeed, Sir Alexander himself tells us that many of these trees he and his brother William planted in 1727, which was the year before his grandfather, Sir James Dick, died. Plantations being very rare in Scotland at that time, this was, doubtless, one of the chief points on which the baronet and Dr. Samuel Johnson agreed so well; for among the illustrious visitors entertained at Prestonfield by Sir Alexander Dick was the learned Doctor, when he came north at the pressing invitation of their mutual friend, Mr. James Boswell of Auchinleck. But as Dr. Johnson's visit to Scotland was one of the *great events* in the annals of 'Auld Reekie' in 1773, we cannot do justice to it at the tail-end of a chapter, and shall therefore reserve it for our next.

Before proceeding with it, however, we will take note of some of the leading landmarks on the Prestonfield estate, among the most beautiful of which we would unquestionably class its magnificent yew-trees, planted a few hundred years, most likely, before Sir Alexander's day—the living product of centuries of sunlight and rain.

There is as much truth as imagination in the thought that Scotland's beautiful Queen, Mary Stuart, must have often sat beneath their kindly shade with her four maiden Maries, in the days when Priestfield belonged to the loyal house of the Hamiltons, seeing they were then, as they still are, the hereditary keepers of the Palace and Park of Holyrood.

It seems much more probable, therefore, that Queen Mary visited Priestfield Manor and the gardens adjoining her own park than that she slept three nights at Sanct Geilie-Grange, then the home of John Cant, the wealthy merchant-burgess.

But, even so, it is not possible to say that Mary Stuart *occupied* any portion of the present *house* of Prestonfield, seeing it was almost entirely rebuilt after the fire of 1680. There is no doubt, however, about its connection with Prince Charles Stuart, during his stay at Holyrood and his encampment at the village of Duddingston. The loyalty of the Dicks to the House of Stuart was as unimpeachable as that of the Setons, with whom Sir Alexander's cousin, the Baron of Grange, was at that time allied by marriage. The Prince's reception and entertainment at the Grange House we have already narrated; but Sir Alexander Dick was not Baronet of Prestonfield until the year following the memorable 1745; therefore it must have been Sir William, his brother, who received Prince Charles at Priestfield Manor, where the royal guest-chamber is still called 'Prince Charlie's room.'

The Prestonfield estate owes to Sir Alexander Dick's love of horticulture the fact that Priestfield was the first 'improved property' in Midlothian; and very proud the aged baronet was to show his beautiful gardens and grounds to the great lexicographer, who was equally fond of horticulture, and an ardent lover of trees. His admiration for Sir Alexander's garden was unbounded—with its long, smooth lanes of turf, called bowling alleys; the high clipt hedges, with parterres of flowers—ending in the most charming landscape views of Duddingston Loch and Craigmillar Castle,—acres of lawn, soft as a Persian carpet, an avenue of stately trees, and plantations all enclosed. Orchards in full bearing, fruit and vegetables in abundance, with flowers of every hue; and, to crown all, a luxuriant crop of Chinese rhubarb of the true species, a perfect rarity, the first that had been successfully grown in Britain, and which the London Society for Promoting Arts and Commerce gratefully acknowledged in 1774 by sending Sir Alexander Dick a gold medal, as it was at that time most highly prized for its medicinal virtues.

The mansion in which Sir Alexander received Dr. Johnson prior to his famous 'Tour to the Hebrides,' and also on his return, was the same four-storeyed house which had been rebuilt by the Government for Sir James Dick, his grandfather. The date of its completion, 1687, was carved on the centre window of each gable, and on the dormer windows on either side the initials S·I·D and D·A·P (Sir James Dick and Dame Anne Paterson), the pediments being surmounted with the Scotch thistle and the family crescent. Instead of the usual crow-stepped gables so universal at that period, we find the coping and terminals much more ornamental. The original doorway before the present handsome porch was built was at the south side of the house; at present it is converted into a window with the old moulding still reaching to the ground, and the antique sun-dial which then stood beside it is now in the garden. Not in Sir Alexander Dick's garden; that has vanished—not, however, before it was immortalised by Lord Cockburn; for this fine old garden at Prestonfield, which Sir Alexander Dick bequeathed in all its beauty to his son Sir William, was one of the happy hunting-grounds of Lord Cockburn when a boy. His graphic description of it is even now more interesting since the scene has changed. He says, 'All between the loch and the house was a sort of Dutch garden, admirably

SUN-DIAL, PRESTONFIELD.

kept. Besides the invariable bowling-green, which formed the open-air drawing-room of all our old houses, it had several long, smooth lanes of turf, anciently called *bowling-alleys;* parterres and lawns interspersed; fountains, carved stone seats, dials, statues, and trimmed evergreen hedges. How we used to make the water spout! There was a leaden Bacchus in particular, of whose various ejections it was impossible to tire.'

As Lord Cockburn was born in 1779, it is not likely he ever saw the aged baronet, Sir Alexander Dick, himself; it is of his son that he writes when he says, ' My father was a friend of Sir William Dick of Prestonfield, who flourished when I was a boy. A great sportsman, handsome, good-natured, and (which goes a great way with me) a first-rate skater. We were the only boys (*and how we were envied from the hillside!*) who were always at liberty to play in his grounds and to use his nice boat.'

What sunny memories these old-fashioned gardens conjure up years after the merry voices that echoed within them are silently hushed! But we look in vain for this identical garden in which these last-century boys ran riot among the bees, the birds, and the flowers, wandering down to the edge of the loch where the boat was moored.

These landmarks have long since been removed, for the old garden, as such, virtually disappeared when upon its site the present circular stables were built by Sir Robert Keith Dick-Cunyngham, seventh Baronet. These stables, beautifully covered with masses of ivy, are decidedly unique as seen from the Queen's Drive round Arthur's Seat, giving quite the appearance of an enclosed village —with their numerous stalls, where in days of yore fifty high-bred horses were housed and fed, for other members of the Prestonfield family have been great sportsmen as well as Sir William Dick, Henry Cockburn's hero. The entrance to the stable buildings is quite a feature on the Prestonfield estate; picturesquely placed below the south brow of Arthur's Seat, the arched gateway is substantially built, like one of the old city ports, and opposite to it there is a drinking fountain, the frequent resort of a whole colony of white-winged doves and pretty silver-hued pigeons. Some of the original massive holly hedges intercept the view of the stables from the tennis-court and the mansion; and in this direction there are also some very fine unclipt evergreens. Truly Sir Alexander Dick would have been justly proud of his beautiful trees could he have seen them in their present magnificence.

Though we have no intention of narrating the history of the Dick-Cunyngham family, yet, as Prestonfield Manor, their baronial residence, has been so closely allied with Sanct Geilie-Grange in the past, we cannot close this slight historical record of it without mentioning the uninterrupted succession of the noble family to whom it still belongs.

Sir Alexander Dick died in November 1785, aged 83. His eldest son, Captain William Dick, who succeeded him, was born in 1763. He had joined the Grenadier Guards at the age of sixteen; and shortly after coming into his estate, he married Miss Johannah Douglas, heiress of Garvaldfoot, in the county of Peebles; but dying suddenly on the 19th November 1796, he left her a young widow with four children under age—one son and three daughters. He was succeeded by his son, Sir Alexander Dick, fifth Baronet, then a boy

PRESTONFIELD HOUSE

of nine, who only bore the title eleven years and a half, dying unmarried in 1808. His initials, 'S · A · D 1805,' are carved upon one of the stones taken from Clearburn House when it was demolished some few years ago. It stood within the Prestonfield estate, upon the lower boundary of the grounds, past which the Clearburn rivulet used to flow. It had been occupied by various members of the Dick family from time to time. Upon the death of Sir Alexander the title reverted to his uncle John, second son of Sir Alexander (Cunyngham) Dick and Lady Janet Dick of Clermiston. Sir John Dick (Cunyngham), sixth Baronet, also died unmarried, four years after he succeeded to the estate, which passed to his brother, Robert Keith, third son of Sir Alexander Dick.

PRESTONFIELD MANOR 135

Sir Robert Keith Dick-Cunyngham, seventh Baronet, who succeeded in 1812, appears to have taken the same deep interest in the old Barony of Priestfield as his father, Sir Alexander Dick. He not only transferred the gardens and built the circular stables, but also improved the property at Cameron, the jointure appendage of the Prestonfield estate, where Dame Janet Dick, Dowager Lady Cunyngham, had resided. Sir Robert also changed the boundary wall of Prestonfield on account of the public road passing too near the house. For this purpose he obtained a special grant, on condition that a new public road was formed, and a substantial wall built along the enclosure.

In January 1829 Sir Robert succeeded to the Baronetcy of Caprington, in Ayrshire, upon the death of his cousin, Sir William Cunyngham, and was in consequence thereafter styled Dick-Cunyngham. His lady was Harriet, daughter of Thomas Hanmer, Esq., of Stapleton, in Gloucestershire; and of their five sons the eldest, William Hanmer, joined the King's Dragoon Guards, and the next two entered the Honourable East India Company's civil service at Bengal.

In one of the grass parks beside the garden there is a mound with a group of trees upon it, beneath the shelter of which stands a monumental obelisk, erected to the memory of a son and a daughter of Sir Robert Keith Dick-Cunyngham and his spouse. The inscription tells us they both died abroad—the daughter at Baden-Baden in 1834, and the son in India in 1847.

Sir Robert died two years later, and was succeeded in 1849 by his eldest son, Sir William Hanmer, who had married Miss Susan Steuart, daughter of J. A. Steuart, Esq., of Urrard, Perthshire, fourteen years before coming to the estate. Their eldest son, Robert Keith Alexander, became ninth Baronet in 1871. In 1864 he married Sarah Mary, only daughter of William Hetherington, Esq., of Birkenhead, Cheshire. Sir Robert Keith Alexander Cunyngham, seventh Baronet of Lambrughton and Caprington and ninth of Prestonfield, died at Polefield, his Cheltenham residence, on Sunday night, 2nd May 1897. The deceased baronet was born on the 21st December 1836, and was educated at Edinburgh Academy and at Bonn. He was a lieutenant in the 93rd Highlanders, and went through the Indian Mutiny, where he was severely wounded, receiving the medal and clasp for his services in the campaign. Sir Robert left three sons and three daughters, the eldest son, William Henry, succeeding to the title.

Sir William Dick-Cunyngham, tenth Baronet, was appointed to the command of the 2nd Gordon Highlanders in February 1897. The translation of

Major Dick-Cunyngham, V.C., 1st Argyll and Sutherland Highlanders, to this command was most unexpected, 'he having only a few days before parted company with the battalion to which he has now returned, and under whose colours he received his baptism of fire and Victoria Cross—on his promotion to field rank.'

OLD STONE AT PRESTONFIELD, WITH THE DATE OF RECONSTRUCTION (SAME AS OVER THE DORMER WINDOWS OF THE OLD MANSION).

CHAPTER XIV

DR. JOHNSON'S VISIT TO EDINBURGH

'For modes of faith let senseless bigots fight;
He can't be wrong whose life is in the right.
In faith and hope mankind may disagree,
But be our one concern broad Charity.'

ANON.

F all men intellectually and morally great, there is not one upon whose social character there has been a greater diversity of opinion than upon that of Dr. Samuel Johnson, whom James Boswell calls 'the Great Lexicographer,' 'the Mighty Moralist,' but whom his father, the Laird of Auchinleck, designates 'the Auld Dominie,' 'that Jacobite fellow.'

With all his pedantry, ostentatious dogmatism, and uncultivated manners, Dr. Johnson was unquestionably a most popular man among the *literati* of both kingdoms,—the mainspring of his popularity being his sharp, clear, terse, robust, and graphic power of treating every imaginable or unimaginable subject with the most convincing result, in the ordinary course of conversation. Of this, Boswell at all times took the greatest advantage during the Doctor's visit to Scotland; and, by dint of storing his notebooks and his diary with the polished and unpolished gems of thought which fell continually from this ever-flowing fountain, literally made Johnson himself the expounder and recorder of his own Memoirs.

EDINBURGH CASTLE.

Sir Alexander Dick, the distinguished Baronet of Priestfield, was one of those who so thoroughly appreciated Dr. Samuel Johnson's brilliant conversational powers and extensive learning that he not only invited him to dinner several times, but also to become his guest for a few days, notwithstanding his ungainly appearance and decidedly overbearing manners.

History doth not affirm that Lady Mary Dick reciprocated her lord's admiration of the worthy Doctor. We rather doubt it; but, whatever may have been her outspoken or private opinion, there can be no doubt, if all the strange stories related of him by Mrs. Thrale, or even Boswell himself, are true, her sense of propriety must have been considerably shocked at times with his bluntness and ill-breeding. Mrs. Boswell had already braved her husband's displeasure, and eased the vexation of her mind by calling the uncouth friend whom Boswell idolised, '*a great brute!*' adding, with extreme warmth, 'I have seen many a bear led by a man, but I never before saw a man led by a bear.'

Not very flattering, certainly, to either party; but there is no accounting for taste—the ladies would have preferred a little less learning and a little more courtesy—less of the 'dominie' and more of the gentleman. And who can blame them when we read the graphic description of him given by Macaulay, or the faithful Dutch-like transcripts of his modes and manners stereotyped by Boswell himself? Dr. Samuel Johnson was then in his sixty-fourth year, a perfect encyclopedia of knowledge, a sort of walking dictionary in a very rough binding. Most uncouth in appearance, slovenly in dress, irascible in temper, easily provoked, and blessed with an appetite that would have astonished a ploughboy. His voracious attachment to legs of mutton and broiled chickens, and his capacity for stowing away enormous quantities of everything he took a fancy to, such as hotch-potch, honey, clotted cream, tea, etc., was simply alarming. It appears, however, that this capacious eater, who never did anything by halves, could also fast when he chose. 'But when he did not fast,' as Macaulay says, 'he tore his dinner like a famished wolf, with the veins swelling in his forehead, and the perspiration running down his cheeks; he scarcely ever took wine, but when he drank it, he drank it greedily and in large tumblers. Everything about him—his coat, his wig, his figure, his face, his scrofula, his St. Vitus' dance, his rolling walk, his blinking eyes, his insatiable appetite for fish sauce and veal pie with plums, his mysterious practice of treasuring up scraps of orange-peel, his morning slumbers, his midnight disputations, his contortions, his mutterings, his gruntings, his puffings, his vigorous, acute, and ready eloquence, his sarcastic wit, his vehemence, his insolence, and his fits of tempestuous rage,' all make it a marvel that this 'Ursa Major,' with a voice that out-roared all disputants, should have been so fêted and warmly received by many of the highest in the land. There never was a more palpable instance of the superiority of mind over matter. Much of the homage thus paid to his

DR. JOHNSON'S VISIT TO EDINBURGH

erudition was no doubt due to the enthusiastic praise of his friend Boswell ; but much more to the true ring of the metal itself. For with all his eccentricities and profound learning, Dr. Johnson was benevolence personified, and as true as steel. Very likely he had profited by the hard beatings he himself tells us he got at his dame school at Lichfield, and the still harder blows of misfortune in the school of adversity in his youth.

It must have been a rare sight to have seen the aristocratic Boswell and the 'Auld Dominie' walking up the High Street arm in arm. Johnson's gigantic frame, corpulent and unwieldy, clad in his 'full suit of plain brown clothes, with twisted-hair buttons of the same colour, a large, bushy, greyish wig, a plain shirt, heavy top-boots, and a very wide brown cloth greatcoat,' with pockets which, Boswell says, 'might have almost held the two volumes of his *folio* dictionary.' At the same time he always carried a huge English oak stick, calling forth the simile of 'Hercules and his club.'[1] All the while his fashionable young friend was 'eternally blustering about the dignity of a born gentleman,' he, James Boswell, Esq., of Auchinleck, never forgot he had a pedigree which dated back to King David I. It would be much easier to imagine than to describe the astonishment depicted on Mrs. Boswell's face when these two bosom friends arrived at the spacious and elegant apartments at St. James's Court, in the Lawnmarket, on that 'dusky night' in the month of August. Contrary to their ordinary habits at such a late hour, Mrs. Boswell had prepared tea for their southern guest, knowing his peculiar love for this beverage—morning, noon, or night. This attention rendered him so affable and engaging, that her husband says 'his conversation soon charmed her into a forgetfulness of his external appearance.'

Judging from its after-effects, and the subsequent correspondence, we rather fancy the charm eventually became more effective when the charmer was absent. Very likely when Boswell made that eulogistic remark, he was thinking of his own first interview with the great lexicographer in Temple Lane, as he had recorded it in his journal ten years before.

Tuesday, 24th May 1763, he writes :—' I boldly repaired to Johnson. His chambers were on the first floor of No. 1 Inner Temple Lane. . . . He received me very courteously, but it must be confessed that his apartment and furniture and morning dress were sufficiently uncouth. His brown suit of clothes looked very rusty; he had on a little old shrivelled, unpowdered wig, which was too small for his head ; his shirt neck, and the knees of his breeches, were loose ; his black worsted stockings ill-drawn-up, and he had a pair of unbuckled shoes by

---
[1] This simile is most strikingly apparent in his monumental statue in St. Paul's Cathedral.

way of slippers. But all these slovenly particularities were forgotten the moment he began to talk.' Tea and talk! What would Dr. Johnson's life have been without his tea and his table-talk? How exultingly he calls himself 'a hardened and shameless tea-drinker, who has for twenty years diluted his meals with only the infusion of this fascinating plant, whose *kettle* has scarcely time to cool, who with tea amuses the evening, with tea solaces the midnight, and with tea welcomes the morning.'

Mrs. Boswell truly did her share in promoting his happiness in this respect while he was her guest. His breakfast, which lasted from ten in the morning till one or two o'clock, was a constant levee; and though Boswell himself could not be present all the time, on account of his duties in the Court of Session, he says, ' My wife was so good as to devote the greater part of the morning to the endless task of pouring out tea for my friend and his visitors.' Endless indeed! when we remember that Johnson himself took *thirteen* cups at a sitting—and tea was tea in those days—though not quite 60s. a pound, as it was in 1707. Johnson might well say *tea-kettle*, since the tea was always *boiled*, though by this time even the populace had learned to use the liquid only, and not eat the leaves, as many of the nobility had done in 1680, believing it to be some rare garden vegetable.

It is very evident that notwithstanding Mrs. Boswell's dislike to Johnson's personality, she was most attentive to his comfort, even vacating their own large airy bedroom for his accommodation, that he might enjoy the magnificent view across the Nor' Loch.

It had taken the Doctor some months to make up his mind to start on this northward journey—but who can wonder at it, considering that in 1763 there was only one stage-coach running between London and Edinburgh, leaving each city but once a month, and taking from twelve to sixteen days to perform the journey? This state of matters may have been slightly improved by the year 1773, so as to reduce the weary days from sixteen to ten, but it was not until 1783, ten years after the Doctor's visit, that the journey was accomplished in five days. Competition having then started fifteen coaches weekly. What would the worthy 'auld dominie' have thought, had any one told him that in 1883, a person who supped in Edinburgh could breakfast in London the next morning—and the horses being made of iron feel no fatigue?

One of the most interesting places connected with Dr. Johnson's Edinburgh visit is the White Horse Close, where Boswell met him on his arrival. This was the terminus for the London stage-coaches, and at that time the best inn and hostelry in the city.

DR. JOHNSON'S VISIT TO EDINBURGH

It is amusing to think how soon the tempestuous temper of the burly Englishman was roused on Scottish soil, for Boswell found him in a violent passion because the waiter had taken the liberty of sweetening his lemonade without the use of sugar-tongs. 'The Doctor in his indignation threw the lemonade out of the window, and seemed inclined to send the waiter after it.' Yet this irate philosopher thought nothing of helping himself with his fingers out of the sugar-bowl in the most aristocratic society. Upon one occasion of his doing so, the lady quietly ordered the sugar-bowl to be removed from the table. When the Doctor had finished his tea, he angrily dashed his cup into the fireplace, the astonished lady exclaiming, 'My set of best china ruined!' 'Madam,' coolly replied Johnson, 'I never supposed you would use anything after me.'

Another unpardonable practice of this extraordinary man was lifting the candles out of the candlesticks if they did not burn brightly, then turning them upside down, allowing all the sputtering grease to drop on his hosts' good carpets, much to the disgust of the ladies who so graciously entertained him for their husbands' sake. Can we wonder that after nine days' stay this unattractive visitor had occasion to write, 'I know Mrs. Boswell wished me well to go.' Strange to say, Boswell, in his unbounded admiration for the great scholar, seems to have been blind to these annoyances, for he ingenuously says, 'In this he showed a very acute penetration. My wife paid him the most assiduous and respectful attentions while he was our guest; so that I wonder how he discovered her wishing for his departure. The truth is,' he adds apologetically, 'his irregular hours and uncouth habits could not but be disagreeable to a lady,'—a verdict which a few others besides Mrs. Boswell no doubt freely indorsed. Unfortunately mind and manners do not always agree.

One day when the Earl of Eglinton, a relation of Mrs. Boswell's, was regretting to Dr. Robertson that Johnson had not been educated with more refinement, and lived more in polished society, 'No, no, my Lord,' said Signor Baretti, 'do with him what you would, he would always have been a bear!' 'True,' answered the Earl with a smile, 'but he would have been a *dancing bear*.' It is pleasant to add that Goldsmith, who knew him better than any of them, maintained that with all his roughness of manner, no man alive had a more tender heart. 'He has nothing of the bear but his skin,' said he; and in this Boswell heartily acquiesced. Nothing, however, could exceed the kindness and hospitality with which Dr. Johnson was received and entertained by the brilliant literary circle of the University and the landed gentry of Auld

Reekie—notably among whom were Sir William Forbes, Lord Hailes, Lord Elibank, Lord Cullen, the Earl of Eglinton, Sir Alexander Dick, Dr. Blair, Dr. Gregory, David Hume, Principal Robertson, and many others, not forgetting Lord Monboddo, a man as learned, as upright, and as eccentric as Johnson himself.

The old Doctor was immensely proud, on his return to London, to enumerate to his friends, with a certain consequential air, the number of titled people at whose houses he had been dining. But the story *par excellence* which he never failed to repeat was what 'the lady of quality' had said to him one day at dinner. This lady was Susanna, the lovely Countess of Eglinton, then in her eighty-fifth year; who told him she was married before he was born, and consequently might have been his mother; thereupon playfully adopting him as her son, and embracing him affectionately when they parted. To a man like Johnson in his sixty-fourth year, this was an indelible honour. Very likely the Countess of Eglinton, who was a staunch Jacobite, felt a sense of kinship to the man who had been chivalrous enough to espouse the cause of a Stuart in such an assemblage of Lords of the Session as were gathered around the festive board, when Johnson exclaimed with warmth and indignation, in reply to Boswell's lament over Scottish independence, 'Sir, never talk of your independency, who could let your Queen remain twenty years in captivity, and then be put to death without even a pretence of justice or your ever attempting to rescue her; and *such a Queen*, too, as every man of any gallantry of spirit would have sacrificed his life for.'

Dr. Robertson, Principal of the Edinburgh University, was perhaps the friend next to Boswell himself who most warmly welcomed Dr. Johnson to the Scottish capital. 'I long to take him by the hand,' he writes, which he certainly did most cordially, showing him over the old historic buildings and through the library of the ancient College, trudging up and down creaking stairs, in and out of the closes at the back of the tall lands in the High Street. At that time Principal Robertson lived in the old College buildings, in one of its irregular quadrangles, to which there were two entrances—one at Potterrow Port, and the other at the head of College Wynd, which was the main road to this queer, scrambling old University. The gateway was unique, being surmounted by a quaint square tower, upon the front of which had been sculptured the Burgh Arms, wanting the supporters. Upon the lintel below there was a beautiful inscription in Gothic characters, AVE MARIA, GRATIA PLENA, DOMINUS TECUM, a relic of more ancient times; this having been the original entrance to the old Kirk-of-Field, on the site of which the first College

DR. JOHNSON'S VISIT TO EDINBURGH 143

had been built in 1581. This queer old gate with its bell-tower stood exactly opposite the house in which Sir Walter Scott was born.

LAWNMARKET AND WEST BOW.

'A scene of grave yet busy life,
Within the ancient city's very heart,
Teeming with historic memories, rife
With a departed glory stood apart.
High o'er it rose St. Giles's ancient tower,
Of curious fretwork when the shadow falls,
As the pale moonbeams through its arches pour,
Tracing a shadowy crown upon the walls.'

Little did Dr. Johnson think, as he and Boswell passed up and down the wynd, in and out of those rickety buildings, talking of all the mighty deeds of the past, that the future Wizard of the North was peeping down upon him with two-year-old curiosity, from a lop-sided dormer-window in the antiquated house opposite. Of these historic buildings every vestige has been swept away; reminiscences of their picturesqueness alone remaining with those who were fortunate enough to sketch them before they were demolished. Infinitely more classic in character was the city of Edinburgh that Johnson traversed in his day, for every land of the High Street was a story in stone, and every footprint from the Lawnmarket to the Nether-Bow was planted on historic ground. The widespread demolition of these antique landmarks had not then commenced, and to Dr. Samuel Johnson 'Edina' was truly the 'Queen of Cities,' even though at that time its romantic beauties had not been immortalised by the facile pen of Sir Walter. The Luckenbooths were still there, a huge pile of buildings, jammed into the middle of the High Street, at the end of which there stood the old Tolbooth, very ancient and very grim; but the deep emotion which the thrilling story of *The Heart of Midlothian* called forth was unknown to the 'auld dominie,' for Effie Deans had not seen the light and Scott was still an infant.

Strange to say, notwithstanding its quaintness and authenticity, John Knox's House had little charm in the Doctor's eyes, judging from his remark to Boswell about his burial-place. They had been to St. Andrews to see the ruins of the magnificent Cathedral of St. Regulas, when Boswell, inadvertently showing his ignorance, asked the verger where John Knox was buried. 'In the highway, I hope,' retorted Johnson; 'I have been looking at his *Reformations.*' Little did he or Boswell think that such a sacrilegious supposition had become a stern reality, and that they themselves had daily walked unheedingly over the grave of this 'Apostle of the Scots'; for the Parliament House had been built in 1632 upon the old churchyard of St. Giles, where John Knox had been buried nearly a hundred years before, amidst the tears and lamentations of a large concourse of citizens and nobles. Not one of the young advocates passing in and out of the Parliament House in 1773 ever guessed that a few feet in front of the statue of Charles II., and many feet below the pavement of Parliament Square, lay the mortal remains of 'the man who never feared the face of man.' No tomb or memorial then marked the grave, which was absolutely 'in the highway.' The initials [1] I · K · 1572, have since the re-erection of the statue of Charles II., been cut on the pavement; but how few passengers even now think of the stern reformer as they tread above his desecrated resting-place.

[1] See tailpiece-vignette.

BIRTHPLACE OF SIR WALTER SCOTT, COLLEGE WYND.

DR. JOHNSON'S VISIT TO EDINBURGH

' Knox slumbers there,
Mingling with border chiefs that stilly sleep,
And churl and burgher bold, and haughty peer,
And those a people wept for, sharing now
The common lot, unhonoured and unknown.
. . . Thrice desecrated burial-place !'

Far otherwise was it with the ancient tomb of the Boswells of Auchinleck, upon which was signed that memorable document, 'the Solemn League and Covenant.' It had become one of the lions of the city, visited by hundreds of good Presbyterians frequenting the kirkyard between sermons, and it was pointed out to the worthy Doctor, with no small pride, by James Boswell, as the resting-place of his ancestors—but the 'auld dominie' took far more interest in the eloquent and polished address of his friend Dr. Robertson, from the pulpit of Old Greyfriars, than in any tomb save that of the martyrs.

The bond of friendship between Samuel Johnson and Dr. Robertson never wavered from that first Sabbath they clasped hands and drank wine together. Many a brilliant conversation they had in the old college library, all subjects being alike to them—ecclesiastical, political, or philosophical, it mattered little. But Dr. Robertson was invariably the more genial, and Johnson the more dogmatic of the two.

Much as the 'auld dominie' loved talking, he was almost as nimble with his feet, when his unbounded curiosity prompted him to action or his interest was keenly awakened. No place of note in Edinburgh remained unvisited and no relic unseen. But of the mysterious Scottish regalia he only heard in whispers. In his day that room in the castle was more closely barred than any haunted chamber.

Dr. Webster of the Old Tolbooth Kirk volunteered to be his guide through the steep closes of the Canongate, where many of the oldest and most historical houses were to be found, but sometimes the ascent or descent was more than the unwieldy frame of the Doctor had bargained for; but then many of his titled lady friends lived up in these high lands, issuing forth from time to time to take an airing in their sedan chairs, or to make a call in some neighbouring close. All this was delightfully new to the Londoner—such many-storeyed, heavenward-built houses he had never seen before. And the Doctor did like seeing things with his own eyes: it never satisfied him to look through other people's spectacles, no, not even at his ghosts.

It is a strange psychological fact that this man who was morally brave enough at all times to speak the truth even in the most minute particular, and

T

had no fear of the supernatural, yet was in bondage throughout his whole life to the fear of death.

In these two points lay the greatest strength and the greatest weakness of his character. Nothing made him more irascible than to be thought old or infirm, consequently he would climb steep ascents unassisted, and mount difficult stairs with alacrity. On one occasion, when two of his companions only half his age submitted to be carried on men's shoulders from the boat to the landing-place at Icolmkill, he sprang into the sea and waded vigorously out.

The three things which appear to have fixed themselves in Dr. Johnson's mind as supremely peculiar to Scotland, were, oats being used as food for men, the absence of tree plantations and hedges, and the mysterious gift of second sight, for which he had always had a 'dim veneration.' He returned from the Hebrides with his faith in it considerably increased; and when attacked for his so-called credulity by the more rigid Presbyterians, Boswell ever stood on the defensive side of his friend. Indeed, his own words were almost prophetic when he said that 'second sight was no more connected with superstition than *magnetism* or *electricity*,' seeing that hardly one in ten thousand had then heard of either the one or the other,—words which are now, after the lapse of a century, in every one's mouth, and part of every one's scientific creed.

Dr. Johnson would willingly have travelled many hundred miles to find himself in a *bona fide* haunted house. One day Boswell in a merry mood asked him if he would not start if he saw a ghost. 'I hope not,' replied the Doctor; 'if I did, I should frighten the ghost.'

On his return from the Hebrides Dr. Johnson again visited his friend, Sir Alexander Dick of Prestonfield; and when four years later he published his *Journey to the Western Islands of Scotland*, he sent a copy to his kind host, receiving a most eulogistic critique from the baronet, with a warm invitation to return. But the Doctor's health was beginning to fail, and all thoughts of leaving home again in search of perilous adventures had vanished.

The following letter from Sir Alexander Dick to Dr. Samuel Johnson was written from Prestonfield, February 17th, 1777 :—

'SIR,—I had yesterday the honour of receiving your book of your *Journey to the Western Islands of Scotland*, which you were so good as to send me, by the hands of our mutual friend, Mr. Boswell of Auchinleck, for which I return you my most hearty thanks; and after carefully reading it over again, shall deposit it in my little collection of choice books, next our worthy friend's *Journey to Corsica*. As there are many things to admire in both performances, I have often wished that no travels or journey should be published but those undertaken by persons of integrity and capacity to judge well, and describe faithfully, and in good language, the situation, condition, and manners of the countries passed through. Indeed, our country of Scotland, in spite of the Union of the Crowns, is still in most places so devoid of clothing, or cover from hedges and plantations, that it was well you gave your readers a sound *monitoire* with respect to that circumstance. The truths you have told, and the purity of the language in which they are expressed, as your *Journey* is universally read, may, and already appear to have a very good effect. A man of my acquaintance, who has the largest nursery for trees and hedges in the country, tells me that of late the demand upon him for these articles is doubled, and sometimes tripled. I have, therefore, listed Dr. Samuel Johnson in some of my memorandums of the principal planters and favourers of the enclosures, under a name which I took the liberty to invent from the Greek, "*Papadendrion*"—Lord Auchinleck and some few more are of the list. I am told that one gentleman in the shire of Aberdeen, viz., Sir Archibald Grant, has planted above fifty millions of trees on a piece of very wild ground at Monimusk. I must inquire if he has fenced them well before he enters my list, for that is the soul of enclosing. I began myself to plant a little, our ground being too valuable for much, and that is now fifty years ago; and the trees, now in my seventy-fourth year, I look up to with reverence, and show them to my eldest son, now in his fifteenth year, and they are full the height of my country-house here, where I had the pleasure of receiving you, and hope again to have that satisfaction with our mutual friend Mr. Boswell.

'I shall always continue, with the truest esteem, dear Doctor, your most obliged and obedient humble servant, ALEXANDER DICK.'

In 1784 when poor Dr. Johnson was in a very reduced condition of body from long-continued asthma and dropsy, he says in one of his letters to his ever faithful friend Boswell, 'Ask your physicians about my case, and desire Sir Alexander Dick to write me his opinion.' Which Sir Alexander evidently did, though the letter itself is not given us; but Boswell says, 'I transmitted him a letter from that very amiable baronet, then in his eighty-fourth year with his faculties as entire as ever, and mentioned his expressions to me in the note accompanying it. "With my most affectionate wishes for Dr. Johnson's recovery, in which his friends, his country, and all mankind have so deep a stake."'

The direct medical advice given by this eminent physician seems to have comforted the suffering invalid, who writes from London, March 2nd, 1784, 'Return Sir Alexander Dick my sincere thanks for his kind letter, and bring with you the *rhubarb* which he so tenderly offers me.' This plant, now so common in our kitchen gardens, was at that time quite a rarity, and highly prized by the medical faculty for its medicinal virtues. But the Doctor was too far spent for any healing, save the transition of spirit. With his affectionate yearning towards his old Edinburgh friends there came a power of endurance

and a degree of patience as remarkable as 'the continuance of those wondrous powers of mind which had raised him so high in the intellectual world.'
His sufferings ended on the 13th December 1784.

> '... From his cradle
> He was a scholar, and a ripe and good one,
> And to add greater honours to his age
> Than man could give him, he died fearing Heaven.'

STONE OVER BURIAL-PLACE OF JOHN KNOX.

PART II

CHAPTER XV

THE LAUDERS OF LAUDER AND BASS: AS WARRIORS

'Scotland, involved in factious broils,
Groan'd deep beneath her woes and toils.'

'Years dark have followed darker years,
And treason's clouds and faction's fears,
And Scotland's blood and Scotland's tears,
And sordid rivalry.'
The Harper's Song.

E shall not attempt to lay before our readers the widespreading branches of a genealogical tree—for, naturally enough, the longer the pedigree, the more intricate the branches thereof; but it is well that we should at least glance over the earliest records of the Lauder family, for by so doing we come upon those valuable old charters upon the rights and privileges of which so much stress was laid from the thirteenth to the sixteenth centuries—though to the generality of non-participators, they simply mean long scrolls of parchment in black-lettered Latin, almost indecipherable; and it is fortunate for some of us when we come across any of these ancient family jewels in a modern setting. Such is the old charter telling us how one portion of the Bass Rock came into the family of the Lauders, the other half having already belonged to those feudal barons as far back as the eleventh century—held direct from the Crown, whereas this charter is purely ecclesiastical in its granting and in its holding. It was granted by William Lamberton, Bishop of St. Andrews, to Robert Lauder, one of the brave companions of Sir William Wallace.

COAT-OF-ARMS.

'To all men by whom this charter shall be seen and heard, William, by the grace of God Bishop of St. Andrews, wishing salvation in the Lord:

'Know ye that we, valuing highly our Church's advantage, have granted, and by this our present charter have confirmed to Robert de Lawedre, for his homage and service, the whole of *our part* of the island in the sea which is called the Bass, near to *Aldham*, in Lothian: to HOLD and TO BE HOLDEN by the said Robert and his heirs, from us and our successors for ever, with all liberties, commodities, and easements, and with the pertinents, freely and quietly, in all and by all, without any reservation; paying therefore, the said Robert and his heirs, to us and our successors at Tynnyngham (Monastery) at the term of Whitsunday yearly, one pound of white wax in name of feu-farm, for all lands, services, and demands which can be exacted or demanded by us and our successors for the said island with the pertinents.

'Therefore we, William, and our successors, do hereby warrant, maintain, quiet, and defend to the aforesaid Robert and his heirs, *our aforesaid part* of the island of the Bass, with the pertinents of the same for ever—and that against all men and women. In testimony whereof, we have made and appointed our seal to be fixed to this present charter.

'Given at Wedale,[1] the fourth day of June, in the year of our Lord 1316, before these witnesses—Lords William and William, by the grace of God of Melrose and of Dryburgh, with the Lords Abbots, James of Douglas, Alexander Stuart, Henry Sinclair, Robert Keith, Esquires, and others.'

This ancient charter was written in Latin in ten and a half lines in the beautiful and distinct character of the period on a small piece of parchment 10¾ inches by 4½ inches. The seal had at some time been torn off, but vestiges of its having been there still remained. Its companion, the charter of confirmation by Johannes de Forfar, the Prior of the Convent of St. Andrews, was also beautifully written in fifteen lines, in the same character, in the same year, the parchment being 11½ inches by 5½ inches. The seal of the monastery appended to it remained in good preservation for five hundred and twenty years, during the whole of which time these charters were in the possession of the family.[2] Of their beauty and their antiquity Sir Thomas Dick Lauder, seventh Baronet, was justly proud, but in his remarks upon this seal, he says that in the impression as given by Anderson,[3] 'a smaller cross, under the cross on the right hand, is awanting,' which is to be found on the seal itself.

These documents prove that the father of this Sir Robert de Lawdre already

---

[1] The present village of Stow is situated in the centre of the district formerly called Wedale, or '*the Vale of Wo*,' which anciently belonged to the Bishops of St. Andrews.

[2] We regret to say the original deeds were stolen in 1836 and never recovered; but Sir Thomas Dick Lauder, seventh Baronet, had fortunately taken copies of them himself for his *Genealogical Roll of the Lauder Family*, from which we obtained these dimensions.

[3] J. Anderson's *Diplomata et Numismata Scotiæ*, Plate C, right-hand figure at the bottom.

possessed the most important part of the island of Bass, which was in itself too small a territory to be divided or to be held by two masters.

The ancestors of Sir Robert de Lawedre, the assignee of the Lamberton charter, had been established in Scotland from the time of Malcolm Canmore, who, after his coronation in 1056, granted lands to all those barons who had assisted him to recover the throne. One of these Anglo-Norman barons who signally distinguished himself by his prowess in the field against Macbeth at Birnam Wood, was Robertus de Lavedre. For these services he was rewarded with large grants of land in Berwickshire and the Lothians, and also a portion of Macbeth's lands in Morayshire. He fixed his chief seat in the beautiful dale of the Leader, naming the district, by royal command, after his own surname— Lauder-dale; and henceforth he became known as Lawedre of that ilk. Of these lands he and his heirs were appointed hereditary bailies by the King at the Parliament of Forfar; at which time also the newly crowned Sovereign changed the Scottish thanes into earls, granting them extensive lands and royal privileges with their titles.[1] To the barons also he gave the right of '*pit and gallows*,' by which they had the power to erect gibbets for the men and draw-wells wherein to drown the women whom they adjudged worthy of death upon their own lands. Many of the oldest charters contain the words, '*cum fossa et furca*'—under which pretext, in lawless times, unwarrantable cruelties were perpetrated with impunity.

From this period there is no special record of the family for some years, but in 1188 we again come upon a Robertus de Lavedre among the Scottish nobles who accompanied the Earl of Huntingdon, brother to William the Lion,[2] to the East, to fight beneath the banner of the cross, under the standard of Richard Cœur-de-Lion. They called it the '*Holy War*,' to rescue the sacred sepulchre at Jerusalem from the hands of Saladin, Sultan of Egypt. It was the third crusade, and all Europe was in arms against the Saracens, kings and emperors fighting side by side—Frederick the First of Germany, Richard of England, and Philip Augustus of France; while Pope and prelates preached remission of every crime to those who won an unmolested passage for the pilgrims to the East. Fired with enthusiasm, thousands braved death and danger most triumphantly for the glory of the Church and the honour of knighthood. Millions, it is said, flocked to this crusade, leaving all to win their spurs, or to work out the salvation of their souls, but thousands of every nationality only found a grave beneath the burning sun of Palestine. A few hundreds did return to their families and their homes, and among that few was our brave

[1] Holinshed, pp. 277, 278. [2] Nisbet's *Heraldry*, folio, p. 351.

crusader, Robert de Lavedre, who is styled fifth Baron. Beyond this we know nothing of his after-life; nor can we tell whether Johannes de Lavedre of Popil was his brother or his son, but the existence of such a person seems to be proved at any rate by a long charter granted by his son, Alexander de Lavedre of Popil, to Gilbert Cockburn for sixteen years' possession of certain lands, in consideration of a certain loan of money in his extreme necessity. The document itself, having been returned to the Lauder family, shows the debt was liquidated. In it the father and son are styled, 'Alexandro de Popil filius et hæres Johannis de Popil,' and it is dated, 'anni gratiæ MCCLXX.'[1]

The lands of Popil were situated in the parish of Whittinghame, in East Lothian, and belonged to the Lauder family for many generations. It seems to have been given off at an early date to a second son of Bass, for we find all through this century and the next, Lauders, Lairds of Popil, co-existing with the Barons of Lauder and Bass, the chief of the family.

The Alexander de Lavedre above mentioned appears to have had a son John, whose existence is also proved from the same document in the following words: 'Per modum dicta terra ut supra scriptum est remaneat ad Johannem filium meum et heredem—sicut in ejus hereditate in tota vita sua,'[2] which, freely translated, tells us that '*In this way the said land above described shall remain to John, my son and heir, to be his inheritance during the whole of his life.*' He must have lived between the years 1250 and 1290, succeeded by several generations of Lauders of Popill, whose names are much more varied than those of the Lairds of Bass.

For instance, in 1359, 'William Landels, the Bishop of St. Andrews, confirmed to the nuns of Haddington a toft and a garden, with eleven acres of land, in Popil, which had been granted them by Patrick, the son of Roger de Lawdre of Popil.'[3] Again, in 1450, we find James II. granting to David de Lawdre, uncle of Robert de Lawdre of Edringtoun, the lands of Popill in Haddingtonshire, which the said Robert resigned in the hands of the King as Earl of March, to be held by David and Mariota, his wife, and survivor of them, and their heirs-male, for payment to the King, as Earl of March, of two pairs of gilt spurs at Popill at the feast of St. Michael the Archangel. This is dated at Edinburgh, 25th April 1450.[4] Then again, in 1493, a suit was moved in Parliament by David Lawder of Popill against several persons for casting down the mill-dam of Popill nine years before. The Lords found that those persons

---

[1] The writ in the charter-chest of Sir Thomas Dick Lauder is written in a clear Saxon character on a piece of parchment eleven inches wide and six inches deep. The seal has evidently been roughly torn off.
[2] Lauder Roll.   [3] Chalmers's *Caledonia*, vol. ii. p. 488.
[4] *Register of the Great Seal of Scotland*, 1424-1503, No. 343.

had done wrong, and ordered them to rebuild the mill-dam and to pay the complainant three pounds yearly for nine years past, in lieu of the profits of the mill of Popill.[1] These records show the decided connection between the Lauders of Popill and the Lauders of Edringtoun and Bass—the eldest son of Lauder and Bass taking Edringtoun during his father's lifetime.

Returning to the chief of the family, we find Sir Robert de Lavedre, probably the son of the crusader, witnessing a charter of John de Mautelant to the Abbey of Dryburgh, and William de Lawedre of Lowther witnessing a grant by Alexander III. This William was sheriff of Perth in 1251,[2] but what relation he bore to the Laird of Bass, whether eldest or second son, is not stated, but we know that the heads of the Lauder family of that period were as often called of that ilk as of the Bass.

But of the next chief, Sir Robert de Lawedre, Laird of Congalton and Bass, we have much more detail, as he was the inseparable associate of Sir William Wallace, the grand champion of Scotland, his faithful companion in arms, and his trusty friend from the beginning of his career to the sad ending of his heroic life. Sir Robert defended his fortress of Bass with great determination against Edward I., and in his staunch loyalty to his country none could seduce him from his allegiance.

> 'Nayne couth him trete, knycht, squier nor lord,
> With King Eduward to be at ane accord.'[3]

Such was his eagerness to march with Wallace against Cospatrick, Earl of Dunbar, who had espoused the English cause, that he would rather have lost his beloved Bass than have been denied this gratification.

We find him again present with his hero at the famous battle of Stirling Bridge in 1297, wherein Wallace gained a most complete victory over John de Warenne, Earl of Surrey, and in which the ill-fated and much detested Sir Hugh Cressingham was slain at the very outset as he led the van of the doomed Englishmen who attempted to cross the bridge. Better had they listened to the advice of the Scottish traitor, Sir Richard Lundie, and never set foot upon that long, narrow wooden way, which led them like sheep to slaughter and a watery grave.

> 'A hidwyus cry amang the peple raiss,
> Baithe horss and men in to the wattir fell.
> The hardy Scottis that wad na langer duell
> Set on the laiff with strakiss sad and sare.'

---

[1] *Parliamentary Records*, 376. [2] Burke's *Baronage*.
[3] Blind Harry's *Wallace*, Book viii. line 65. In this poem, by 'Henry the Minstrel,' Lauder's exploits with Wallace are frequently mentioned.

Wallace, on foot, with the '*grate scharp spere he bare*,'[1] was in the thickest of the fight, and with his own hand slew Cressingham, the King's treasurer. Ten thousand slain and seven thousand drowned without mercy, left but a poor straggling remnant to that invading army, who set fire to the bridge in order to prevent the Scots from pursuing them. This old wooden bridge stood about a mile above the spot where the present stone one was shortly after erected— for Stirling being at that time the key to the Highlands, the bridge necessarily formed an indispensable highway.

Daring exploits and marvellous successes followed this unexpected victory; and we find Robert de Lawedre is often mentioned as being among those Scottish knights who, in the hour of their country's need, rose grandly to the occasion.[2]

'Like master, like servant,' was never more apparent than in those feudal days when, according to the allegiance of the greater barons to their sovereign, so in exact ratio was the fealty of the lesser, who were their vassals and dependants. One influential baron meant a few hundred stalwart men-at-arms to do his bidding, thus making every knight and baron his own protector and avenger.

But no band of trusty knights or squires could avail against treachery. A traitor in the person of a supposed friend betrayed Scotland's magnanimous champion to King Edward, his bitterest foe. It is said when Wallace found himself overpowered and betrayed by Sir John Menteith, before his hands were bound, he threw his mighty sword into Robroystone Loch, and forthwith he was exultantly taken to England, there 'to thole his martyry,' as Wyntoun, the chronicler, calls it. Thus died on the 23rd August 1305 Scotland's grandest warrior, who to his last hour as boldly defended his country's rights as when he nobly fought for her freedom from oppression.

Not many years later, in 1311, his faithful companion Lawedre, Laird of Bass, died, and was buried within the ancient church on the shore at North Berwick. According to Nisbet, his tomb was still to be seen in the aisle of the ruined kirk[3] as late as the year 1722: the inscription, which at that time was quite legible, is rendered as follows :—

'*Heir · lyes · ye · good · Robert · Lauedre · Ye · greate · Laird · of · Congaltoun and · ye · Bas.*' MCCCXI.
'HIC · JACET · B^{us} · ROBERTUS · LAVEDRE · M^{ns} · D^{vs} · DE · CONGLETON · ET · LE BASS · QUI · OBIIT · MENSE · MAII.' MCCCXI.

---
[1] Blind Harry's poem, Book vii., lines 1170 to 1214.
[2] Abercromby's *Martial Atchievements of the Scottish Nation*, Edin. 1711, vol. i. p. 529, folio.
[3] Nisbet's *Heraldry*, p. 443, folio 1722.

This old church stood close to the harbour, and was of a very early date. At present the site is used as the coastguard station, and is simply a sea-girt grassy mound with a stone wall or rampart built below it to check the inroads and havoc of the sea, which had for many years been making most unseemly ravages into the very graves of former generations. The church itself had been built upon a sort of islet, or peninsula, connected with the mainland by a span of arches. In 1656 the church and bridge had become so ruinous that the kirk-

RUINS OF THE AULD KIRK ON THE SHORE AT NORTH BERWICK.
(*Drawn by Gros. in 1722.*)

session 'resolved rather to change the site of the parish church than to rebuild the arches or bridges connecting it with the shore.' After the erection of the new parish church in the seventeenth century, the auld kirk was abandoned and fell into ruins; the only portion of it now remaining is the strongly built vaulted porch which served as a mortuary chapel as long as the burial-ground was permitted to be used. Here in the centre of this grassy mound is a flat stone marking the entrance to the old family vault of the Lauders of the Bass which was then within the aisle of the church, beside that of the Douglases of

Tantallon. There is no sign, however, of the antique tombstone of 'the great and good Sir Robert de Lauedre' who died in 1311, having fought at the battle of Stirling Bridge in 1297. But as many of the ancient families had removed the tombstones of their forefathers over to the new kirkyard after the violent storm of 1774, this stone would probably be among them. At present it is quite lost sight of, unless it be among those very ancient-looking, ponderous

OLD PARISH CHURCH, NORTH BERWICK.

slabs which were cleared out of the roofless aisle of this second parish church some few years ago, and are now leaning face-in against the tower wall.

From this brave old knight and his crusading ancestor have sprung the long line of the Lauders of the Bass,—thirty-three of whom are said by Sir Andrew Lauder to have been called Sir Robert, making it very difficult for us to distinguish one from the other, were it not for some special appellation given to them from time to time to denote some special service, or from the respective dates of their writs and charters.

But charters alone are dry reading compared with the stirring events of this warlike period in Scottish history, wherein the Lairds of Bass by loyalty obtained their prominent position—sharing as they did the dangers and the honours of

AS WARRIORS

the Border wars, and the exploits of William Wallace, Robert Bruce, the Black Douglas, and his brave companion-in-arms, Randolph, Earl of Moray, in the liberating of Scotland from the English yoke.

Ever and anon in the romantic adventures and hairbreadth escapes of Robert Bruce we find a Lauder comes to the fore, and is rewarded by lands for 'good service' done to the King; which in those non-recording days would have been swept into oblivion had it not been for these old family writs. It was thus Sir Robert de Lawedre acquired Pencaitland,[1] Colden, and the mill of Lethberd, on three separate occasions shortly after 1306, that memorable year in which Robert Bruce was crowned. The lands thus granted were invariably those forfeited by the previous owners for want of allegiance in time of war.

This is the same Sir Robert de Lawedre whom we mentioned at the beginning of this chapter in connection with the Lamberton charter. He was the eldest son of the 'great Laird of Congalton,' who had inherited one-half of the Bass—the other half being granted to his son by the Abbey of St. Andrews in 1316, five years after the 'good laird's death.'

Sir Robert, the recipient of this grant, appears to have also inherited the valour and prowess of his progenitors. He had been the follower of Sir William Wallace as squire in his father's lifetime, and fought bravely in the repulsion of Edward II. from Scotland; also in the subsequent reprisals made by Robert Bruce in the north of England. He had been appointed Justiciary of the Lothians and the south of Scotland by King Robert; and as such he was one of the plenipotentiaries who signed the truce between those two monarchs in 1323.[2] Negotiations for this peace had been going on for three years—the first embassy of knights having received a safe-conduct in 1320. Among these we find two of the witnesses of the Lamberton charter, and also the name of the eldest son of Sir Robert de Lawedre, who was attached to the train as a page[3] —preparing him for the duties he was soon after called upon to fulfil according to the oath administered to those who had by chivalry won their knighthood.

The oath of a knight was very binding, and ran as follows:—

'I shall fortify and defend the true, Holy, Catholick and Christian Religion presently professed, at all my Power.

'I shall be loyal and true to my Sovereign Lord the King his Majesty, and do Honour and Reverence to all Orders of Chevalry, and to the noble Office of Arms.

---

[1] Charters, *Register of the Great Seal*, No. 55, p. 11, No. 62, p. 12, No. 89, p. 17, 1206-1424. See Appendix, Lauder Charters.
[2] Rymer's *Fœdera*, vol. iii. p. 1022.   [3] *Ibid.* p. 809.

'I shall fortify and defend Justice to the uttermost of my Power, bat[1] Fewd or Favour.

'I shall never fly from the King's Majesty my Lord and Master, or his Lieutenant in Time of Battel, or Medly with Dishonour.

'I shall defend my native Country from all Aliens and Strangers at all my Power.

'I shall maintain and defend the honest Adoes and Quarrels of all Ladies of Honour, Widows, Orphans, and Maids of good Fame.

'I shall do Diligence wherever I hear tell there are any Traitors, Murtherers, Rovers, and Masterful Thieves and Outlaws, that suppress the Poor, to bring them to the Law at all my Power.

'I shall maintain and defend the Noble and gallant State of Chevalry with Horses, Harnesses, and other Knightly Apparel to my Power.

'I shall be diligent to enquire and seek to have the knowledge of all Articles and Points touching or concerning my Duty, in the Book of Chevalry.

'All and sundry the Premisses I oblige me to keep and fulfil. So help me God ; by my one Hand, and by God himself.'[2]

The truce of 1323 was brought about by the intervention of Sire de Sully, the French envoy, who had been captured with the English prisoners in Yorkshire, and who offered to mediate a peace between the two nations, providing King Robert granted him liberty to go back to England. In the national document, drawn up in old French and dated at Newcastle-on-Tyne, 3rd May, anno 1323, the names of the nobles and churchmen witnessing it are all set forth ; and among those on the part of the Scottish King are William Lamberton, Bishop of St. Andrews (the same who granted the charter of the Bass) and Thomas Randolph, Earl of Moray. The two attesting knights are Sir John Menteith and Sir Robert de Lawedre, senior.

But the cessation of hostilities between the southerners and the Scots was not of long duration, for in the Border lands fierce encounters were constantly taking place, cattle being lifted, towns pillaged, and whole villages burned to ashes. A sudden check, however, was given to the almost incredible exploits and feats of valour performed by Lord James Douglas and Thomas Randolph, Earl of Moray, by the news of the cruel murder of Edward II. by his own nobles.

The shock seems to have affected the aged frame of King Robert, now worn out by disease. Satiated with war, and ill at ease in his body, he assembled his lords and barons, and proposed a final treaty of peace with the young King Edward III.

Again we find Sir Robert de Lawedre the chosen ambassador for the ratification of the treaty concluded at Edinburgh on the 17th March 1327.[3] One of

---

[1] Without. [2] Works of William Drummond of Hawthornden.
[3] Robertson's *Index*, folio, p. 101.

its conditional clauses was that a marriage should take place as soon as possible between David, eldest son and heir of the King of Scots, and Johanna, sister of the King of England, both being under age. Hugh, Earl of Ross, and Robert de Lawedre, Justiciary of Lothian, by special command were present at Northampton in 1328, and took the oath of peace as proxies for King Robert. They swore 'on the soul of the Bruce' that the Scottish King would sacredly maintain the peace and hold to all the stipulated articles of the treaty with regard to the marriage and the dowry.

Upon the return of Sir Robert Lawedre to Edinburgh, his son Robert was appointed Justiciary of 'that part of Scotland on the North side of the Water of Forth,' his estate being in Morayshire. With this office he also received an additional pension of £20 per annum—evidently for good service rendered to the State. We might almost be tempted to think this was intended for Robert Lawedre, senior, were it not for the confirmation charter granted by King David II. thirty-five years later.[1]

King Robert Bruce died on the 7th June, the year following the treaty of peace, and was succeeded by his son David, a child of three years of age, during whose minority, which commenced in 1329, Sir Robert Lawedre elder of Bass and his son showed themselves to be men of sterling merit, with considerable authority in the lands over which they held almost unlimited jurisdiction in virtue of their baronial rights and their high office in the State.

In a charter granted by Randolph, Earl of Moray, to John, Earl of Angus, of Morthyntoun[2] in 1331, to which Sir Robert is witness, he is simply called *Roberto de Lawedre, Militibus, Justiciario Lowdonie*'; but at an inquest held by him at Aberdeen on the 10th September 1333 he is styled Sir Robert Lawedre, '*Chamberlain of Scotland.*' The inquest was 'in reference to the second teinds of the bishopric in the Sheriffdom of Banff, and that of the Lordship of Conveth (in Inverkeithing parish); one part was in the hands of the Earl of Moray, another belonged to Sir Archibald Douglas, and a third to Sir Walter Ogilvie.'[3] Most likely this meeting of adjustment took place in consequence of the death of Sir Archibald Douglas two months before at the battle of Halidon Hill, at which both Sir Robert Lawedre of the Bass and his eldest son were present, though the former was too far advanced in age to be able to dismount with his armour on, and therefore he took no active part in the fight.

[1] Confirmation by King David II. of the gift by his father Robert I. to Sir Robert de Lawedre of an annual pension of £20 from the proceeds of the Justice Courts north of the Forth. Dated at Dunfermline, 1st October, thirty-fourth year of reign (1363). *Register of the Great Seal*, 1306-1424, No. 67, p. 31.
[2] *The Douglas Book*, by Sir William Fraser, K.C.B., LL.D. Charters, No. 16, p. 14.
[3] *Ibid.*, vol. ii. The Douglas Correspondence, p. 587.

Upon this occasion the Scots had, unfortunately, with national predilection, chosen the sloping hillside as their vantage-ground, thus exposing themselves as defenceless targets to the irresistible volleys of the famous English archers stationed in the marshy valley below.

An ancient MS. tells us 'the arrows flew thick as motes in a sunbeam,' and the Scots fell by thousands beneath that fatal shower, 'which no mail-coat could brook.'

Sir Robert the younger (styled of Quarrelwood, and also Captain of Urquhart) fought most bravely at this disastrous battle on the hill. He was in the third division of the army, under Sir Archibald Douglas,[1] then Regent of Scotland in place of Sir Andrew Murray, who was a prisoner; but Sir Archibald himself was among the slain at Halidon. He was a younger brother of Sir James Douglas, called the 'Good Lord James,' who had gone in 1330, with a band of Scotland's noblest warriors, to carry the heart of Bruce to the Holy Land. A sacred mission, no doubt, in that crusading age of chivalry; but Scotland's need of all her bravest sons at that period was very great, the young King David being a mere child, and his southern foe waxing stronger day by day. Immediately after this defeat near Berwick, Sir Robert de Lawedre, Laird of Quarrelwood, hastened to the north to occupy and garrison the Castle of Urquhart, on Loch Ness, which, by his brave defence, completely defied the power of Edward III., and stands recorded in our annals, associated with the name of Lauder, as one of the five strongholds of Scotland which the English could not take.

These fortresses were:—1st, The Castle of Dumbarton, held by Malcolm Fleming of Cumbernauld; 2nd, the Castle of Loch Leven, by Alan Vipont; 3rd, the Castle of Kildrumy, defended by Christian Bruce, 'a venerable matron, sister of Robert I.; 4th, the Castle of Urquhart, by Robert Lauder: and 5th, the Peel or Tower of Loudoun, on the borders of Carrick, kept by John Thomson, a man of lowly birth, but of approved valour.[2]

Urquhart has long been a complete ruin, but the strong square tower is still in excellent condition, bidding defiance to wind and weather as it rises picturesquely over the deep waters of Loch Ness, standing on the western shore, midway between Fort Augustus and Inverness. The ruins of the castle are most extensive, occupying a considerable portion of the sloping peninsula in the bay of Urquhart. The situation is beautified by the woods of Glen Urquhart on the west, and Ruiskie woods to the south.

[1] This Sir Archibald Douglas had married Donnagilla, the daughter of Marjory Cuming, sister of John Baliol.—*Douglas Peerage.*
[2] Boethius, Book xv. chap. 5; and also Hailes' *Annals*, vol. ii. p. 168.

AS WARRIORS 163

We are not told how long the aged knight, Sir Robert de Lawedre, who had been Governor of Berwick Castle, lived after the battle of Halidon Hill. We know that he received his Berwick fees, from the entries in the accounts of Sir Alexander de Seton, collector of the burgh of Berwick at that period, for in them we find: Item, 1329, 'Paid to Robert de Lawdre balance of his fee of fifty marks, £6, 13s. 4d.'; and also the next year: 'Paid to Robert de Lawdre for his fee due at Martinmas, £33, 6s. 8d.' But the next entry evidently refers to his son: Item, 'Allowed to accountants for the fishery of Eidermouth, now in possession of Sir Robert de Lawdre by right of inheritance, £40, 0s. 0d.'[1]

URQUHART CASTLE, LOCH NESS.

However, there is every reason to believe that the Baron of Bass named among the Scottish Commissioners appointed in 1335 to treat of peace between King Edward and young David Bruce was the aged Justiciary of the Lothians, though, in consideration of his extreme age, his brave son, the Captain of Urquhart Castle, would be sent as his proxy. These Scottish Commissioners were 'Andrew Moray, William de Keith, Robert Lawder, and William Douglas.'[2]

There is strong evidence of its having been the elder Sir Robert Lawedre of Bass that was appointed Commissioner, as he had been confirmed in his office of Justiciary only the previous year (1334) by Edward III. himself, in his regulating of the Government after his victory over the Scottish nation. Not

[1] *History of Berwick.* By John Scott, Esq.   [2] *Fœdera*, t. iv. p. 677.

that Sir Robert had accepted the post as an honour bestowed by the enemy of his country and his King—his patriotic soul would have spurned such a deed; but having been established in the office by King Robert Bruce, the duties pertaining to which Lawder had faithfully performed for so many years that the English monarch deemed him the fittest person to continue to hold it; these duties not being military, but for the judicial administration of the established laws of the country. No Englishman, therefore, could have filled the post of Justiciary of the Lothians; but all the strongholds and castles which had surrendered to Edward were garrisoned and commanded by English soldiers.

Robert Lawedre junior had also shown himself a man of good capacity for law and order, as well as a good soldier in arms, or he would not have been appointed by King Robert as Justiciary of the North of Scotland in 1328, which post he held for more than fifty years. Therefore we see that Sir Robert Lawder (who was styled of Quarrelwood[1] during his father's lifetime to distinguish him, both being called Sir Robert) had already become a person of note before he inherited the Bass.

He it was who had been taken prisoner at Jedburgh in 1332, the winter before the battle of Halidon Hill, when 'Baliol's party was waylaid and attacked by an ambush under the command of Archibald Douglas, which, however, was discovered and routed, while Baliol reached Kelso in safety. In this skirmish it is said Robert of Lawder the younger was taken with others. There must have been an exchange of prisoners shortly after, for we soon hear of him again fighting under the Douglas banner, after John Baliol's undignified ride to Carlisle. The Scottish leaders having heard from their spies of Baliol's imprudent march from the fortress of Roxburgh to the comparatively defenceless town of Annan, they resolved on a surprise, which was boldly conceived and promptly executed. Marching over-night, the Scots arrived at Annan in the early morning, and finding the hapless Baliol and his followers in their beds, slew about a hundred of them. Baliol himself escaped again, but in such haste that with one limb clothed and the other naked he threw himself on a bare-backed steed, and thus fled to Carlisle. His brother, Sir Henry Baliol, who slew many of the attacking party with a stout staff, was at last, with several other knights, overpowered and slain.'[2]

Were it not for their judicial position, and their close connection with the

[1] Its first designation was 'Quarry-wood in Moravia,' so called from a rich quarry of freestone in the adjacent hill, which was once covered with a large oak wood.
[2] *The Douglas Book*, by Sir William Fraser, vol. i. p. 205.

Church, we might well be surprised at the frequency with which the chiefs of the Lauder family appear as witnesses to many of the important royal charters granted under the Great Seal at this period, especially such as had reference to the Abbeys of Dryburgh and Melrose, and those granted by the Earls of Douglas and Angus, those powerful houses so nearly allied to the throne. Between the years 1333 and 1381 several of these documents have not only the name of Sir Robert de Lawedre of Bass appended, but also that of his son, Sir Alan. When, in 1370, the brave defender of Urquhart Castle appears to have had occasion to sell part of his land 'in and near his burgh of Lauder,'—the purchaser being Thomas de Borthwicke, a near relative of the family,—among the witnesses are John Mautelant (Maitland) of the Lauderdale family of Thirlestane Castle, and his brother William. This charter is also attested by Sir Robert's son Alan, and his grandson, '*Roberto filio Alani tunc Ballio de Lawedre.*'[1] This Alan de Lawedre was one of the bravest knights that ever drew sword; famous in all martial exercises, renowned in feats of chivalry, and foremost in his country's service. He was known as the Constable and Keeper of Tantallon Castle, one of the Douglas strongholds. Trained under the banner of the good Lord James, he won his spurs most nobly. Few leaders could boast, as Douglas did, that he had fought seventy battles, out of which fifty-seven were victorious, and not a scar had marked his face.

Sir Alan is reputed to have set out for the Holy Land with Lord James Douglas and the heart of Bruce, and also to have died fighting with him in Spain[2] in 1330. Family records, however, prove that to have been impossible. He may have gone forth with that chivalrous band in the flower of his youth to win his spurs; but he must undoubtedly have returned again with those who brought back the body of Lord James, for not only does he witness several of the Douglas charters after that event, but still further, he himself obtains no fewer than eight charters under the Great Seal between the years 1370 and 1381.

The first of these had been granted to him by the High Steward of Scotland, grandson of Robert Bruce, as Baron of Renfrew, before he became King, and therefore before the year 1370. In it he is styled Alan de Lawedre, tenant of Whytslaid, and the confirmation charter, granted by Robert II., is dated at St. Andrews 13th June 1371.[3] In it, 'for his good and faithful services rendered, and to be rendered, to the King,' the lordship and lands of Whytslaid

[1] Lauder Family Roll in Charter-Chest. [2] Burke's *Baronage*.
[3] *Register of the Great Seal*, 1306-1424, p. 81, No. 277.

166   THE LAUDERS OF LAUDER AND BASS

are bestowed upon him and his heirs, with all the profits of the courts, and their issues, the annual rents, farms, and duplicands, and for the yearly payment to the Barons of Renfrew, if required, 'one penny silver' at the feast of the Nativity of St. John the Baptist.

On the same day King Robert also confirmed the charter by Malcolm, son of John, son of Nigel of Carrick, to Alan de Lawedre of his whole lands of Mertoun, which formerly belonged to the late Alan le Zouch, with half of the Mains of Lawedre, and half of the fulling mill, which had belonged to the late Sir John de Baliol; also the whole land of Newhyggyng, in the Constabulary of Lawedre, shire of Berwick-on-Tweed.[1]

The next charter is a grant by Sir Hugh of Eglynton to Alan de Lawedre for homage and service of the lands of Norton, in the barony of Ratho.[2]

From the next two charters we find that Sir Alan must have taken unto himself a wife before the year 1366. The chosen lady was Alicia Campbell, daughter of Sir Colin Campbell of Loch Awe, of the Argyll family, who had also obtained large grants of land for military services rendered to the family of Bruce both in Ireland and the north of Scotland.

The charter by William, Earl of Douglas,[3] to Alan de Lawedre contains a Precept of Sasine for the lands of Wormotstoun to him and his wife, Alicia Campbell, conjointly; and they are both mentioned also in the grant given by the King himself, while Steward of Scotland, of the two carucates (200 acres) of land in the town of Norton, in the Barony of Ratho, which had belonged to Ibbok and Minote of Norton, the ancient tenants.[4]

Shortly after this, in 1374, the King, Robert II., gives an annual pension of £10 sterling to Sir Alan de Lawedre, from the proceeds of the justice courts south of the Forth, in consideration of the labour of his office of clerk of the Justiciary Rolls.[5] This post appears to have been in the family of the Lauders of Bass for at least three generations already. By purchase Sir Alan appears also to have acquired the lands of Westhall and Northlaw of Ratho, besides

[1] *Register of the Great Seal*, 1306-1424, p. 82, No. 278.   [2] *Ibid.*, p. 82, No. 279.
[3] *Ibid.*, No. 280. See also MSS. of the Duke of Hamilton—Historical Manuscripts Commission, p. 208, No. 126. 'William, Earl of Douglas, Lord Wallace of Lauderdale, and of the regality of Lauder, to our beloved cousin William de Lyndsay, greeting:—We command and authorise you to cause to be publicly given to Alan de Lawedre and Alice his wife conjunctly, and the longer liver of them, by their Bailie, heritable sasine of the whole lands of Wormotston, with the pertinents, within our Regality of Lauder, which lands Fergus of Airth, our true tenant thereof, resigned and returned by staff and baton duly and lawfully in our hands; saving the right of third parties following the tenor of our charter completed in his favour: Which to do we commit to you our full power and special mandate for the office of a good Bailie by these presents: In testimony whereof we have caused our seal to be affixed to these presents, dated at Edinburgh 28th July 1366.
[4] *Register of the Great Seal*, p. 82, No. 281, 1306-1424.   [5] *Ibid.*, No. 29, p. 101.

those of Plats from Thomas Cripney and William Elphinstone,[1] but the two most important of all his charters were that of the whole town of Haltoun from John de Halton, on the 26th July 1377, confirmed by Robert II. to Sir Alan and Alicia his spouse, in fee and heritage for the customary service,[2] and that of Brownisfelde acquired in 1381, which we mention in another chapter.

Of Sir Alan's five sons, three were soldiers and two were bishops, of whom we shall subsequently speak.

At this early date we do not find many domestic incidents recorded— beyond the mere facts of deaths, births, and marriages—and yet now and again among these old manuscripts we come upon an episode which reads like a whole family history, condensed into two small parchment scrolls, such as the 'Instrument of Sasine,'[3] anent the lands of Auldcathie, a village near Winchburgh, in the Sheriffdom of Linlithgow, and the 'Retour of Inquest' after the death of Katrina Lauder. From these papers we gather that Katrina, heiress of the Barony of Howman and Swynset, near Jedburgh, and of Crailing, near Kelso, both in the county of Roxburgh, married John Lauder, son of Sir Robert Lauder of the Bass, eldest son of Sir Alan; but in a few years she died (1424), leaving four little daughters—Mariota, Beatrice, Christian, and Elizabeth. The *eldest* and the *youngest* were nominated heirs of their mother, Katrina Lauder, in all her lands, but the reason for this distinction is not given. We only know that on the death of their father, John Lauder, a few years later, the lands were held by the King (James I. of Scotland) for the children, who became wards of Chancery. On the death of Sir Robert Lauder of the Bass, their grandfather (1436), the three elder daughters were left joint heiresses in the lands of Auldcathie. The Sheriff of Linlithgow being commanded to 'infeft' them, they were, according to the old Scotch legal custom, presented with *earth* and *stone*, as symbols of legal delivery and possession.

As they came of age, they each received their portion of the estates. Mariota (by some called 'Marion Lauder') inherited the 'Chemys' or Manor-House of Howman, and a quarter of the whole barony, also half of Swynset, the other half belonging to her youngest sister, Elizabeth, with a quarter of the lands of Howman—but by the time she was old enough to take possession of her inheritance, the three elder sisters had divided the lands of Auldcathie, and married into the ancient families of Home, Rutherford, and Wardlaw.

[1] *Halton House.* By J. R. Findlay, Esq. [2] *Register of the Great Seal*, 1306-1424, p. 48, No. 104.
[3] Historical MSS., Athole and Home, p. 109.

CHAPTER XVI

THE LAUDERS OF BASS AS CHURCHMEN AND AMBASSADORS

'My spreit hartlie I recommende
In Manus tuas Domine;
My hope to thee is to ascende
Rex quia redemisti me.'
                              SIR DAVID LINDSAY.

UDGING from some of their earliest records, it is evident the Lauders were as well known in the church as in the Camp. It is no matter of surprise, therefore, for us to find that Sir Alan de Lawdre, one of Scotland's bravest warriors, should have been the father of two bishops (William, Bishop of Glasgow, and Alexander Lauder, Bishop of Dunkeld), for in those days the most renowned statesmen were the churchmen, on account of their scholarship.

But it is not often we find three brothers holding such high positions of responsibility in the State at the same time— for out of the five sons of Sir Alan, the eldest, Sir Robert de Lawedre of Lauder and Bass, was Lord Justice of Scotland ; William, Bishop of Glasgow, was Lord Chancellor ; and Alexander, before he was Bishop of Dunkeld, was an ambassador. There is

ARMS OF BISHOP LAUDER ON GLASGOW CATHEDRAL.

not much recorded of the latter, who was promoted from the rectorship of Ratho to the Bishopric of Dunkeld, in May 1440,[1] and who died in Edinburgh in October of the same year. He was buried in the old kirk of Lauder, near Lauder Fort. It is far otherwise with William Lauder, his elder brother, of whom the ecclesiastical records take considerable note. He was Archdeacon

[1] Milne's *Vitæ Dunkeldensis, Ecclesiæ Episcoporum*, p. 19.

THE LAUDERS OF BASS 169

of the Lothians, when on the death of Bishop Matthew he was promoted to the Bishopric of Glasgow, by Pope Benedict XIII., without the election of the Chapter, who, however, did not dispute his appointment.'[1] Upon four different occasions he received a safe-conduct for travelling through England, on the King's commission : twice while Archdeacon (in 1405 and 1406), and once as Lord Chancellor in 1423 ; and also as Bishop of Glasgow in 1424, the year before he died.[2] From family records there seems to be no doubt of his being the third son of Sir Alan de Lawedre and Alicia Campbell ; but Mr. Cosmo Innes speaks of his parents as 'Robert and Annabella de Lawedre.' This may have arisen from his State relationship to King Robert III. and Annabella Drummond his Queen.[3]

Bishop Lauder lived in the old Episcopal palace, which stood near the cathedral, a famous old building even then, for in 1300 it had witnessed much of the strife and bloodshed of the usurping days of Edward I., who had installed Anthony Beik, the warrior bishop of Durham, in the Bishopric of Glasgow, and Earl Percy had at the same time taken possession of the Bishop's Palace. Sir William Wallace, Scotland's champion, indignant at such flagrant usurpation, soon came to the rescue of St. Mungo's city, and with a band of his brave followers, gave battle to the English invaders in the High Street, at which their leader, Lord Percy, was slain and the southerners completely routed. Some years after this, in 1345, Bishop Rae built the first stone bridge across the Clyde, in Glasgow, at which time also the cathedral was undergoing considerable repairs and enlargements. When Bishop Lauder was nominated to the see, the foundation of the chapter-house had been commenced, but the old wooden spire, which had been struck by lightning and destroyed in 1400, was still untouched. Upon these portions Bishop Lauder left his mark so unquestionably, that his work has never been disputed, though the full extent of it is undefined ; for when he died Bishop Cameron took up the work, and carried it to fuller completion. It is therefore clearly evident that those portions bearing the Lauder Arms are justly attributed to him, and these arms are seen in two places on the same level, on the exterior of the western wall of the chapter-house ; within which the Lauder griffin is again very prominent upon the dean's seat.

In the semi-darkness of this vaulted chapel it is not easy to study the beautiful carving on this ancient relic of bygone times, which is well worthy of close scrutiny, for the chisel has been used upon it with great effect and

[1] Innes's *Sketches of Early Scotch History*.   [2] Rymer, vols. viii. p. 445, and x. p. 298.
[3] We do not find the name Annabella occurring in the Lauder family, until about 1598, when Sir Alexander Lauder of Halton married Annabella Bellenden of Auchnoule.

Y

artistic skill. The old griffin of the Bass stands out boldly on the shield. His twofold character—half lion and half eagle—is most skilfully pourtrayed. Above the Lauder Arms and the Gothic ornament, there is a fine old inscription in abbreviated ecclesiastical Latin, which has puzzled even well-read antiquarians, from time to time. It stands thus:—

> Wilms · fuda^t · istut · capilm · dei
> GULIELMUS · FUNDAVIT · ISTUT · CAPITULUM · DEI
> *William founded this Chapter of God.*[1]

At the intersection of the ground arches of the vaulted roof of this chapter house, there are two fine bosses carved with the arms of James II. and his Queen, Margaret of England.

INSCRIPTION OVER DEAN'S SEAT CHAPTER HOUSE, GLASGOW CATHEDRAL.

Bishop Lauder also built the stone tower of the cathedral, up to the main parapet, upon the battlement of which his arms are again seen—with the pastoral staff above the shield, and a mullet at each corner as a mark of cadency, showing him to be the third son of the House of Bass. The Glasgow Cathedral, and that of St. Magnus in Kirkwall, are the only two in Scotland which entirely escaped the frenzied destruction of ecclesiastical buildings at the

[1] We are indebted to the kindness of Mr. P. M'Gregor Chalmers, author of *A Scots Mediæval Architect*, for the translation of this old inscription from our own sketch—and also for a most interesting visit to the cathedral, Mr. Chalmers being thoroughly conversant on all points historically and architecturally connected with the 'Laigh Church' in the Crypts. He also kindly pointed out the various places where the arms of Bishop Cameron appear, on the ceiling and pillar completed by him after the lapse of two hundred years, when he roofed over the chapter-house built by Bishop Lauder.

AS CHURCHMEN AND AMBASSADORS

time of the Reformation. This was owing to the wisdom of the civic authorities in taking down every semblance of a cross, a virgin, or a saint. Among the ecclesiastics of the Lauder family (and they were a goodly number) we find much more variety in the Christian names than among the Lairds of Bass. For instance, in the charter by James, Earl of Douglas and Marr, to the Monks of Melrose, dated 27th July 1388, mention is made of three churchmen— Thomas Lawder, Master of the Hospital of Soltra, Robert de Lawdre, Canon of Glasgow, and another Thomas Lawdre, a priest; and we frequently find the names of Hector, Gilbert, and Maurice Lauder as witnesses. There were no less than five bishops in this family within eighty years. William, Bishop of Glasgow, who died in 1425; Alexander his brother, Bishop of Dunkeld, who died in 1440; Robert, Bishop of Dunblane in 1447; George, Bishop of Argyll in 1462; and Thomas Lauder, another Bishop of Dunkeld, who died in 1481.[1]

The latter was preceptor to King James II., and founded an altarage in St. Giles' Church to St. Martin in 1449; he also endowed a chaplaincy of the 'Holy Cross Isle' in Sanct Geilis Kirk in 1480. Among his munificent acts it is further recorded that he purchased a mansion in Edinburgh, to be used as the Palace of the Bishops of Dunkeld—by himself and his successors. This mansion stood in the Cowgate, almost opposite the Archiepiscopal Palace of the See of St. Andrews, at Blackfriars' Wynd, more generally known as 'Cardinal Beaton's House.' From all accounts, Bishop Lauder's palace was truly a most extensive mansion, with large gardens attached to it, running back nearly to the old town wall.

A very different kind of dwelling was the Hospital of Soltra, of which Thomas Lauder was 'Master' in 1388. It is one of those historical relics of the past which have earned a sacred place in the heart of all lovers of human brotherhood. It stood on the top of a steep hill in the Lammermoor range; and what is now a mere fragment in the private burying-ground of the Maitlands of Pogbie was once a church, an hospital, and a village. As far back as 1164 this silent, desolate ruin upon a heather-clad hill was the traveller's St. Bernard of Scotland, and many were the weary feet, and the hungry, soul-sick bodies that found rest and food and shelter with the solitary monks of the Lammermoors at Soltra. The hospital, which with pious zeal King Malcolm reared, was doomed to destruction in 1561, and given over to the 'Reformers.' As the shattered walls fell in, the monks fled, but the inhabitants of the few lowly huts, called the village of Soutra, clung with Scottish pertinacity to their thatch and their heather, until not one man remained to tell its ancient story.

[1] *Workman's Manuscript.*

It was from this mountain monastery at Soutra that Thomas Lauder, Bishop of Dunkeld, emerged to take his place at Court as the preceptor of the young King. He was also succeeded by another, Thomas Lauder, as Master of the Hospital of Soltra, for we find in a charter of 1459 that should the lawful male heirs of John Lauder of Burngrange fail, a certain portion of land in the Cowgate was to pass to the Master of Soltra and his successors in fee. Dempster, who wrote in 1600, gives us a very lucid account of this ideal bishop. He says : [1]—

'Thomas Lauder, Bishop of Dunkeld, was the most eminent, the most pious, and the most learned prelate of his age, not only of that see, but of anywhere else in that kingdom. It was during his time that Alexander Mill the Canon lived, who wrote the Acts of that Church in the must lucid and erudite manner. He it was who instructed James II. in the arts of goodness. He received the episcopate against his will in the sixtieth year of his age, but he did not on that account flee youthful labours, for besides preaching every week in the most learned manner, he restored the ecclesiastical discipline and the manners of his clergy, by example, precept, fear, and punishment. He distributed the territory of his Church on both sides of the Tay, and ruled the district so diplomatically, that neither the negligence or rapacity of his predecessors, nor the carelessness of his successors, could harm the see. He restored, increased, and erected anew the sacred buildings with incredible zeal and magnificence. He provided a sacristy with gold and silver vessels, and furnished it with precious vestments ; he increased the number of the canons, founded chapels, established and endowed musicians from his own resources ; spanned the Tay with a notable bridge, and built a bell-tower from the foundation ; and with no less ability than was visible in his other acts he wrote *The Life of John the Bishop*, who is treated of in Book ix. of this present work, and who, after having been appointed to St. Andrews after seven years' delay of the Roman Curia, died Bishop of Dunkeld, irradiated with the glory of miracles. He also wrote one volume of sacred lectures, a work on the Gospels, and the Canons of his Church. He died on the 4th November 1481, aged eighty-six, having ruled his see for twenty-six years.'

From the earliest date of their history and in each successive generation one or other of the younger sons of Lauder Tower, Bass, or Halton entered the Church ; and we find ecclesiastical patronage, a parsonage, or a manse attached to each of their estates for the benefit of these younger sons, who often ranked with their elder brothers in Parliament as lords in the Church, through all the changes and vicissitudes of Scottish ecclesiastical affairs. Nor could they pass through these vicissitudes without taking part in some measure with the frequent embroilments of Church and State ; for it is remarkable how invariably we find at this period a marked man of the Lauder family fulfilling some high office of trust in the various capacities of soldier, bishop, or ambassador.

[1] Translated from *Hist. Eccles. Gentis Scotorum*, Book XI. vol. ii. p. 441. See also Frontispiece.

AS CHURCHMEN AND AMBASSADORS

There are several instances on record in which they acted also as ambassadors-extraordinary—a title by which the highest diplomatic ministers were distinguished—being sent on very special occasions by one Sovereign to the Court of another.

Of the sons of Sir Alan de Lawedre, who died in 1401, Sir Robert Lawdre, his eldest son, Laird of Lauder and the Bass, and Sir Robert's younger brother, William, Bishop of Glasgow, who was also Lord Chancellor, were both sent to the Court of Henry V. of England to treat concerning the liberation of the Scottish King, James I., who ever after called this sturdy knight 'our Loveit of the Bass.' Lauder's seal, a '*Griffin segreant*,' is still extant, appended to an instrument dated 16th July 1425.[1] As a mark of distinction he is also called '*Robert with the Boreit Whynger*,' evidently implying that he was a fearless knight as well as a faithful ambassador. There is no want of proof, however, of the trust and confidence reposed by crowned heads upon the most momentous occasions in several of the members of this ancient family. In a safe-conduct granted for diplomatic purposes in 1423 by King Henry VI., the above 'Robertus de Lawdre de Basse, chivaler,' and his brother James, are both mentioned; and from an old manuscript of Sir Andrew Lauder's we find that 'in the late collection of the French King's treaties of peace and alliances for 300 years back, the contract of marriage betwixt Louis XI. of France, then Dauphin, and Margaret, daughter to James I., King of Scotland, in 1436, is there recorded from the original; and one of King James's ambassadors for the treaty of marriage at Paris, insert in that contract, is Edwardus de Lavedre; *for so it was then syllabieate and spelled*.' This important official document was therefore undoubtedly signed by Sir Edward de Lawdre, Sir Robert's eldest son, whose brother Alan was, according to Holinshed, also sent as an ambassador to France, not by the King, however, but by William, the young Earl of Douglas, who had just succeeded his father, Archibald Douglas of Drumlanrig, in 1439. His first public act, we are told by Godscroft, was to despatch Sir Malcolm Fleming of Cumbernauld and Sir John Lauder (all the early writers call him Alane de Lawedre) to the French Court to do homage for the Duchy of Touraine. The messengers are said to have been well received, and to have given their oath of fidelity on behalf of the earl, who thus obtained the confirmation of his right to the dukedom. Shortly after their return to Scotland, the Earl of Douglas, who was not eighteen years of age, and his brother David, a lad of twelve, were inveigled to Edinburgh Castle by Chancellor Crichton,

[1] *Descriptive Catalogue of Impressions from Ancient Scottish Seals* (Maitland Club), by Henry Laing. 4to. Edinburgh, 1850.

under pretence of being made companions to their youthful Sovereign, King James, then only eight years old ; and there they were treacherously put to death without trial or warning, beyond the ominous placing of the black bull's head upon the table at the feast to which they had been so perfidiously invited. Speechless with astonishment, the brothers were bound, led out to the courtyard of the castle, and beheaded, in spite of the imploring tears of the young King, to whose retributive account, however, in after years, this crime was laid. Four days later Sir Malcolm Fleming, the faithful friend of the murdered earl, shared the same fate,[1] but Alane de Lawedre escaped, very likely through the intervention of Bishop Lauder, the King's preceptor. It is not surprising that we find Alan's name coupled with that of Sir William Lawder of Haltoun among the knights in the retinue of another Earl of Douglas a few years later, when he had succeeded his brother Edward as Laird of Bass. Later on, when the town of Berwick was surrendered by Henry VI. of England to James II. of Scotland,[2] the Castle of Berwick was at once put into the charge of Robert Lawder of Edrington, an important official and soldier, son and heir of Bass. For this charge Lawder received 200 marks per annum, and he kept his position uninterruptedly for thirteen years at least, from 1460 to 1474, when he was succeeded by 'David, Earl of Crawford, one of the most influential servants of the Scottish King.' But within two years we find James III. granting letters to Robert Lauder of Edrington, again appointing him 'Keeper of the Castle of Berwic-on-Tweed' for the next five years and further, during the King's pleasure, with the same annual pension of 200 marks, dated 20th January 1476-1477.'[3] The office of Chief Customer was also given him, which posts he retained until the last year of the Scottish occupation, when Patrick Hepburn of Hailes had possession of the fortress, which he was forced to surrender to the English on the 25th August 1482.

This was the last of Scottish rule in Berwick. Five years previous to this event Sir Robert Lawder, younger, whom King James III. calls 'son of our Loveit of the Bass,' had been appointed, with Sir Alexander, Lord Hume, Sir Adam Blackadder of that ilk, and the Lyon King, to conduct to Edinburgh, from the English Court, the persons who were conveying from Edward IV. 2000 marks as an instalment of his daughter Cicely's portion. This Princess had been affianced to the young Prince James, Duke of Rothesay, in 1474, both being children under age ; but according to the articles of the treaty, a certain

---

[1] *The Douglas Book.* By Sir William Fraser, K.C.B., LL.D.
[2] *History of Berwick.* By John Scott, Esq., Rector of the Grammar School.
[3] *Register of the Great Seal of Scotland,* 1424-1503, No. 1276.

AS CHURCHMEN AND AMBASSADORS 175

sum of money was to be paid in Edinburgh yearly by King Edward as her future dowry, until the fulfilment of the marriage. This money was delivered to the English messengers intrusted with the conveyance of it in presence of the Scottish commissioners, who were then also responsible for its safety and the lives of the messengers, for which purpose they carried a safe-conduct from their King.

This curious document we find worded as follows, commencing, 'Anno Domini 1477, Edward IV. an. 16—Pro dote pretacta et salvo conductu':—

RUINS OF THE CASTLE OF BERWICK-ON-TWEED.
(*From a Drawing by Grose in 1722.*)

'James be the Grace of God King of Scottis til the serviteurs of our derrast Bruther, the King of Ingland, Bringers of the money aught to us be our said derrast Bruther of this terme of the Purification of our Lady callit Candilmas, after the forme, tenoure and effect of the Indentures maid betwixt him and us, Greting—Wit ye us to have sende for the traist sicklier and souner convoying and keping of yhon in the Bringage of the said money to us, our traist and wele belovite cousin, Alexander Lord Hume, Robert of Lawder of Edrington, sonne and apperande are til oure Loveit Robert Lawder of the Bass, and Adam

Blackachetir of that Ilk, quhilks persons, or any two or one of them togither,'[1] were to form the safeguard of their passage to and from Scotland.

Such a commission at that period was no sinecure. Two thousand marks did not mean a Bank Order safely deposited in a secret pocket. It did not even mean gold and silver coins, if we may judge from a letter written by the Duke of Norfolk to Lord Cecil seventy years later upon the same subject of money transference.

'For God's sake,' writes Norfolk, 'when you send us more money, let it be sent in gold, or new silver. This last you sent was in *pence*, two pences, and old testoons!'

Well might he complain. Only imagine £22,000 being sent from London to Stirling in copper coins!

It took eighteen days, with three carts, twenty-two post-horses, twelve men, and two guides, besides the constables to watch it at night. 'Altogether this transference of £22,000 cost £112, 11s. 8d.'[2] And though this special instance took place in 1547, we may safely conclude that the roads were as bad, and robbers as plentiful in 1477, making it no holiday matter for the responsible persons intrusted with a royal transference. The state of the country can be easily imagined when we remember that in the reigns of the early Stuart Kings the borderland was such a hornet's nest of thieves, 'that watchers were kept along the whole border; and at every ford by day and by night, settlers, watchers, searchers of watchers, and overseers of the watchers were appointed. Besides these cautions, the inhabitants of the marches were obliged to keep a certain number of *Slough Dogs*,' or what we call Bloodhounds. 'The Chief officers, bailiffs, and constables throughout the district being directed to see that the people kept their quota of dogs and paid their contributions for their maintenance.'

Persons who were aggrieved, or who had lost anything, were allowed to pursue the '*Hot-trode*' with horn and hound, with hue-and-cry, and 'all other accustomed manner of hot pursuit.'[3] Yet one of these old border barons, we are told, lost 5000 sheep in one night, showing very forcibly the necessity for all this precaution, the mosstroopers being the terror of the limits of both kingdoms.

The confidence, therefore, which the King at this time so decidedly manifested towards the Lauders of the Bass, speaks volumes for their downright

---

[1] Chalmers's *Caledonia*, vol. ii. p. 283, and Rymer's *Fœdera Anglicæ*, vol. xiii. p. 41.
[2] *History of Berwick*. By John Scott, Esq., Rector of the Grammar School.
[3] Pennant's *Tour*, p. 68.

AS CHURCHMEN AND AMBASSADORS 177

trusty troth and leal-heartedness, which was as firm in its integrity as their own sea-girt rock. Young Robert Lauder of Edrington, who was thus intrusted with his sovereign's financial affairs, could only have been King's Squire in 1477. His father, Sir Robert Lawder, 'our Loveit of the Bass,' had just been reappointed Governor of Berwick Castle, which King Edward was eagerly waiting an opportunity to recover. This opportunity James III. soon gave him by breaking the treaty of marriage between his son and Lady Cicely in 1479, which led to a renewal of the war, and the gathering of 50,000 men at the King's command at Lauder Burgh, where the meeting of the nobles in Lauder Kirk, headed by Archibald, Earl of Angus, culminated in the ignominious death of Cochrane and the other royal favourites on Lauder Bridge. But the crowning point of the national disaster was the complete loss of that bulwark of the eastern marches—the town of Berwick—in 1482.

We are not told in what manner the Lauders acted upon the special occasion of these stormy doings in and around their bailieship of Lauderdale: but their position must have been somewhat difficult at times, considering the judicial office they held in the Burgh, and the military service their land charters called forth.

There must have been many clashings of duty, and also many qualms of conscience during the struggles so frequently occurring between the powerful house of Douglas and the King, for it is very evident from charters[1] extant that at this period the Earls of Douglas both owned and forfeited in rapid succession the Lordship of Lauderdale. But of the loyalty of the Lauders there was never any doubt, nor do we find them at any time losing lands by forfeiture on that account.

Shortly after the sad death of James III. in the miller's house at Sauchie, after the battle of Sauchie Burn, we find the young commissioner, Sir Robert Lauder of Edrington, acquiring the lands and tower of Beil,[2] very probably in anticipation of his marriage; for had the charter been granted after that auspicious event, his wife's name would in all probability have been conjoined with his and that of his heirs, whereas it simply says:—' James IV. grants to his squire, Robert Lauder of Edrington and his heirs, the lands of Bele, Johnscleuch and le Clyntis, with the tower, fortalice and mill of Bele, in the Barony of Dunbar, and constabulary of Haddington; also the lands and mill of Mersintoun, with the over and nether tofts thereof in Berwickshire, resigned by

[1] *Historical Manuscripts Commission*, Charters 15 and 16, p. 17.
[2] Which the family retained until 1768.

Z

Hugh de Dunbar of Bele: paying yearly one penny silver in name of blench. Dated at Linlithgow, 12th September 1489.[1]

When next we hear of the Laird of Edrington and Beil, he has taken for his bride Isobel Hay, second daughter of John Hay, twelfth Baron of Yester, by his wife Elizabeth, sole heiress of George Cunninghame of Belton. And it is very evident that the bridegroom's aged father and mother, Sir Robert Lawder of Bass, and Agnes Faulaw of Fallow Hall in Cheshire, were both alive at the time, and indeed for some few years after, for in 1491 James IV. confirms a mortification by Agnes Faulaw, spouse of Robert Lauder of Bass, of fifteen merks from tenements in Edinburgh and Leith for masses at the altar of the Virgin Mary in the parish church of St. Andrew the Apostle, in North Berwick, for the soul of King James III., and her late husband William Carreboris. It is made with her present husband's consent, and sealed with his seal, at Le Craig on the 20th October 1491.[2]

The children of Robert Lauder of Edrington and Beil by Isobel Hay were, as far as we can ascertain, two sons and a daughter—Robert, Henry, and Margaret Lauder. Robert succeeded to the Bass after his father, and is specially known by his indenture from the preaching friars of Dundee, which we shall mention shortly. Mr. Henry Lauder is usually styled of St. Germains. He was advocate to King James V., and also to his daughter Queen Mary. He is often mentioned in the Sederunt Books, and in *Liber Decretorius*, being one of the seven lawyers authorised by Parliament in the first erection and institution of the College of Justice, by Act 64, Parliament 1537. On the 13th January 1538, King James wrote the following letter to the Court:—

'Rex—Chancellor, President, and remanent Lords of Session, it is our will, and we charge you, that ye, incontinent, after the sight hereof, admit our Lovit familiar Clerk, Mr. Henry Lauder, our Advocate, to sit and remain in our Council House, to hear and see delivering of Bills, giving of Interlocutors, Decisions, and Determinations of all Causes, and Actions, swa that he may hear and know such things as shall happen to occur that concerns us, exceptand always the Actions and Causes for the whilks he beis Advocate, and speaks for at the Bar allenarly.'[3]

In consequence of this letter, 'the Lords took his oath to be secreit, and received him into the Inner House.' He is mentioned as brother of Robert Lauder of Lauder and Bass, in the indenture of the monks of Dundee. Henry Lauder, known as Lord St. Germains, died in 1560 according to his testamentdative. His death is also noticed in the following entry in Lord Hailes

[1] *Register of the Great Seal of Scotland*, 1424-1503, No. 1045.
[2] *Ibid.* No. 2068.   [3] *Register of Testaments.*—Edinburgh.

catalogue:—'1561, November 12. Mr. John Spence appointed—title Condie: predecessor St. Germains deceased.' His sister Margaret Lauder was the second wife of Alexander Hume of Polwarth, fourth Baron; and their three daughters were—Margaret, married to Patrick Hepburn of Craig; Catherine, married to Robert Pringle of Pringle; and Isobel, Abbess of North Berwick. Lord St. Germains' eldest son was served heir to his father on the 30th May 1562. In the deed he is styled 'Gilbert Lauder, son and heir to the late Mr. Henry Lauder of Sanct Germains—Advocat quhile he levit to our Soverane Ladie.'[1] With reference to the peculiar indenture of Sir Robert Lauder of Bass, his descendant Sir Thomas Dick-Lauder writes as follows:—'The curious indenture in my possession, handed down to me among the ancient parchments of my family, not only establishes the existence of this Robert Lauder but also proves that the family of Lauder of Lauder, and Lauder of Bass continued to be one and the same, at least until after his time. The indenture is dated in the year 1531. It is written in twenty lines, in the more modern German hand, on a piece of parchment about 11½ inches wide by 9 inches high. It has those indentations at its upper part which marks it as cut from the other part of the indenture, viz. that which remained with the parties with whom it was entered into, which would at any time have proved the identity of that corresponding part, which indentations give the name of indenture to this species of written contract.

'At the bottom of the writing are the signatures of nine friars of the convent of Dundee.

'The following is an accurate copy of this curious document, as far as I can depend on the accuracy of my own deciphering':—

'We frier John Gregory Provincial of ye friers Predicators within ye Realme of Scotland, Prior and Observant of ye place of ye said ordo of ye Burgh of Dundee, to all & sundry quhais knowledge in Christs salvation. Greeting in God everlasting. Amen. Forasmeikle as ane nobill man, Robert Lauder of Bass, with nowrit money in gold deliverit be his Bruther to our said place of Dundee, ten pounds annualrent zeirlie to be lifted and resavit be us ye saidis Prior and Convent of Dundee, and our Friers Predicators. That is to say ellevin merks to be lyfted and resavit zeirlie at twa times in ye zeir be us of ye landis of Kilduntane lyand within ye sherifdome of Fyfe, and foure merks siclyke zeirlie to be lyftit and resavit at ye said twa usual times in ye zeir be us of ye landis of Cyr, lyand within ye Barony of Segyden and Sherifdome of Perth, as is at more length exprest in the Charters maid to us heretofore.

'Wherefore freelie we bind us ye said Prior and Convent, and our successors to say daily ane mess, be ane of ye brether of our said place of Dundee, for ye said Robert

[1] *Index of Deeds,* vol. v. No. 233.

Lauder of Bass and his progenitors, and successors, & to say oulkly and ilk fest day in ye honor of ye glorious Virgin Moder of Christ, ye devote pros, ane gloriosa, & sing ever ilk zeir after the deths of ye said Robert Lauder of Bass, ane amberfare, yt is to say placebo, and dirige, with ane mess of ye requiem after. Afterwards zeirlie ye day of ye said Robert's deth, ye whilk day mess to be said, ane gloriosa, oulkly to be sung ane amberfare, with mess of ye requiem, as said is to be sung zeirlie for ye said Robert Lauder of Bass.

'Anext is ane sequele binding to ye foresaid ten pounds annual rent given to our foresaid place in perpetual almens, as said is, requiring us to resave ye foresaid almens with ye said bynding, ye whilk we have resavit, & be thir presents resavis, byndand us and our successors Prior and Observant of our said place of Dundee to do ye said suffrage, as is alswa exprest.

'In witness hereof we have houng our Priory sele, togidder with our subscriptions manual to ye Predicators Indentures, and it to remain with ye said Robert Lauder and his airse, and that by part to remain with us and our successors for them & their's information of this our present bond & obligation.

'At our said place of Dundee ye twenty aught day of November ye zeir of God Ane thousand fyve hundred & thretty ane zeirs.

'Frater JOHANNES GREGORY, Prior, manu. p.p.a.
'Frater ALEXANDER BARCULAY, Prior, manu. p.p.a.
'Frater JOS. CRECHTON SUPPER, manu. p.p.a.
'Frater WALTER GREY, manu. p.p.a.
'Frater ALEXANDER DOUGALL, manu. p.p.a.
'Frater DAVID LYNDSAY, manu. p.p.a.
'Frater PETER FORFAR, manu. p.p.a.
'Frater WILLIELMUS LORIMER, manu. p.p.a.
'Frater LAURENTIUS CHRISTIE, manu. p.p.a.'[1]

Robert Lauder, the granter and holder of this curious old document, was a great supporter of the Queen-Regent, Mary of Guise, doing good service for her in East Lothian against the English, and also in upholding her authority in opposition to the Lords of the Congregation. He married Alison Cranstoun of Cranstoun, and from deeds extant he must have had four sons—William, John, Robert and Alexander; but it is also very clear from the same source that John the second son was illegitimate, and not the son of Alison Cranstoun; for, on the 15th February 1531, James V. granted 'letters of legitimation to John Lauder, natural son of Robert Lauder of the Bass,'[2] in order that he might eventually inherit a portion of his father's estate, which as a bastard he could not do. Sir Robert had evidently made provision for the separating of the Lauder lands from the Bass estate long before his death, desiring to apportion each of his sons therein, leaving Lauder Tower and the Forest to his eldest son William as chief, and the Bass estate with the East Lothian lands to his second

---
[1] Family Roll, Charter-Chest of Sir Thomas Dick Lauder.
[2] *Register of the Great Seal*, 1513-1546, No. 1136.

son. That this son was called John, and not Robert, is clearly evidenced by the charter itself, which Sir George Mackenzie distinctly affirms bore, '*Joanni Lauder, filio secundo genito de Lauder Tower*'; and in after years, when a dispute arose as to which should take precedence, Lauder Tower or Bass, this charter was brought forward to prove that, of the two branches after the division which took place in 1561 upon the death of Sir Robert Lauder, the last Baron of Lauder and Bass combined under one representative, Lauder Tower was chief and Bass younger, which fact was also manifested by the junior branch changing the supporters of the arms, taking angels in lieu of the two white lions of the chief, and the new motto: '*Sub umbra alarum tuarum.*' But the reason of this son John not appearing in the succession as Laird of Bass became apparent in his father's lifetime, for he entered the Church, became Archdean of Tweeddale, notary-public, and secretary to Cardinal Beaton. He

ARMS, LAUDER (BASS).

officiated at the consecration, by the Cardinal, of the little chapel on the Bass rebuilt upon the site of the original one which supplanted the cell of St. Baldred. John Lauder, 'secretarius,' was well known in his day as the bitter accuser and opponent of George Wishart the martyr, who was burnt in front of the castle of St. Andrews, the Cardinal himself pompously conspicuous among the onlookers.

Robert, the younger son of Sir Robert Lauder, was therefore made Laird of Bass, and inherited the East Lothian lands; and with his patrimony he also inherited the Lauders' loyalty to the house of Stuart, for his name appears among those who gathered in defence of Scotland's hapless Queen on Carberry Hill in 1567. Holinshed's *Chronicle* tells us: 'There were with the Queene and Bothwell, the Lords Seiton, Yester, and Borthwike, also the lairds of Wauchton, Bas, Ormiston, Weaderburne, Blackater and Langton. They had with them also two hundred harquebusiers waged, and of great artillerie some field peeces. Their whole number was esteemed to be about 2000.'[1]

[1] Holinshed, vol. v. p. 624.

This Laird of Bass was twice married, and had a large family, eight sons and three daughters, from whom a numerous progeny descended. As far as we can judge from the various records, it would appear as though the eight sons and two of the daughters belonged to the first wife Mariota, after whom the eldest daughter was named. In 1569 she became the wife of Thomas Otterburn of Reidhall,[1] and her sister Margaret married Mr. Edward Aitkyn in March 1573.[2] Her tocher was 3000 merks, half to be paid by Sir Robert before the marriage, and the other half on the 1st of May 1575. Of the sons the eldest was Sir Robert Lauder, Knight of Popill; the second, John, of Beil; third, James, Dean of Restalrig; the fourth, George, an advocate, afterwards Laird of Bass; then came Alexander and William, Arthur of Scuney, and Patrick of Gervat. Besides these we read of two illegitimate sons, William and Henry; to the latter his father left £200 in his will, to the former he gave a land of houses in North Berwick.

On the 12th September 1556 a strange document was registered about 4 P.M., 'whereby Robert Lauder of the Bass, younger' (whose wife Mariota could only have been dead a year or two) 'discharges Mr. George Strang, Mr. Michael Robesone, Mr. Henry Kinross, Mr. John Robertson, and all others, from registering a contract and obligation made by him to Patrick, Earl Bothwell, and Jane Hepburn, his daughter, "anent the Contract of Marriage with the said Jane"; and he appoints Mr. Robert Heriot to pass and discharge the persons aforesaid from acting as his procurators in this matter; and to do such other things as are necessary therein. This was done in the garden of Thomas Lauder, in the burgh of North Berwick, who is a witness thereof.'[3] From this deed we are led to suppose that a betrothal or promise of marriage had taken place between Sir Robert Lauder and Jane Hepburn, which for some reason Sir Robert declined to fulfil; and the authoritative way in which the breach of promise was carried out in the presence of the notary-public of the burgh, makes it appear as though he had both right and reason on his side. However that may be, two years later we find the gallant knight choosing another lady for his second wife, and this time most effectually, for the marriage-contract was registered on the 22nd August 1558, the bride being Elizabeth Hay, half-sister to the late John, Lord Hay of Yeister,[4] to whom the usual dowry lands were assigned. Some years later, when Sir Robert had settled his worldly belongings and apportioned his first wife's children, he increased the liferented portion of his second spouse by giving her a charter of

[1] *Index of Deeds*, vol. xxiii. No. 408.
[2] *Ibid.* vol. xlii. No. 92B.
[3] *Register of Deeds*, vol. i. f. 440.
[4] *Ibid.* vol. iii. p. 144.

AS CHURCHMEN AND AMBASSADORS 183

the lands of Clintis in Haddington.[1] Their only daughter, Elizabeth Lauder, was married 'in face of holy Kirk' to David Prestoun, eleventh Baron of Craigmillar,[2] at Yuletide 1575, her tocher being 5150 merks, the disposal of which was particularly provided for; and the bridegroom's uncle, George Prestoun, who had been living at Craigmillar Castle, had to vacate it and the lands and mains of Craigmillar, for the entering of the young couple. The dowry portion of Elizabeth Lauder from her husband was the liferent of the 'lands of Prestoun, with the pertinents thereof, lying on the Water of Esk,'[3] near Edinburgh. This marriage of his favourite daughter only took place six months before the death of her father, Sir Robert Lauder of Bass.

Ten years previous to this the eldest son and heir-apparent of Bass, the Laird of Popill, had been married to his stepmother's niece, Margaret Hay, daughter of William, Lord Hay of Yester, she being the young widow of James, seventh Lord Borthwick. Upon which occasion the bridegroom, Sir Robert, according to the custom of the times, resigned his lands, manor-house, and mills of Popill into Queen Mary's hands, to be regranted in their united names. These lands the Knight of Popill held of the Queen for payment of two pairs of gilt spurs. The charter and contract of marriage was dated February 1566—signed at Beill, one of the old family towers belonging to the Laird of Bass. Among the witnesses we find another churchman of the Lauder family, Mr. George Lauder, rector of Auldcathy.

A few years later, the young Laird of Popill made a further settlement in favour of his wife, in case he should predecease her, some of his lands being already mortgaged. This was in 1574; and the next year, to the great grief of his family, he was dead. As his little son Robert had already predeceased him, and also his brother John, who was next in succession, his death opened up quite a chapter of domestic events, about which a considerable amount of mystery still hangs; and as it is entirely from the Council Records we gather our information of the circumstances, it is natural to suppose there was much behind the scenes which never would be made known. One thing, however, appears very certain—which is, that James, the third son of Sir Robert Lauder of Bass, had in some way angered his father to such an extent that he actually imprisoned him in his tower at Beill, which seems all the more extraordinary in that he was a dignitary in the Church, being Dean of Restalrig. This Deanery was not dissolved by Act of Parliament until 1592, though by order of the General Assembly of 1560 the church itself had been ordered to be

[1] *Register of the Great Seal*, 1546-1580, No. 2334. [2] *Index of Deeds*, vol. xiv. No. 410.
[3] *Register of the Great Seal*, 1546-1580, No. 2540 (MS. Lib. xxxiv. No. 403).

'raysit and utterly casten doon,' as a 'monument of idolatry,' on account of its numerous statues and saintly images. We may conclude, therefore, that as James Lauder was still styled Dean of Restalrig in 1575, he must have been the last of that order. Whether it was a religious offence, a political offence, or a domestic offence which had roused his father's ire we are not told, but we may safely conclude from the sequence that it was not an unpardonable offence. From the Register of Council we extract the following :—' Apud Edinburgh, 12th March 1572.—Anent oure Soverane Lordis letters rasit at the instance of Maister James Lauder, Dene of Restalrig, makand mentioun that quhair Robert Lawder of Bass his fader in the moneth of December last bipast, tuke and apprehendit him, and as yet haldis and detanis him in strict firmance and prisoun—within his place of Beill—the said Maister James being oure Soverane Lordis fre liege man, and will not suffer him to pas at his fredome and libertie at his pleasour, without he be compellit.' The said Robert Lawder is therefore charged 'to put the said Maister James to fredome and libertie furth of the said ward, on paine of rebellioun and putting of him to the horn.' From the tenor of this complaint and its issue, we can plainly see that the cause of the incarceration was both political and religious. Sir Robert Lauder, Laird of Bass, was a staunch Queen Mary man. He had already been put to the horn as a rebel for defending her on Carberry Hill, and he unquestionably adhered to the old form of faith; whereas his son, the ex-Dean, on losing his living and position in the Church, had evidently embraced the reformed doctrines and joined the Lords of the Congregation, or he could never have appealed to them as their 'free liege man.'

The very fact of Sir Robert having lent the sum of £2000 to Queen Mary and her husband, Lord Darnley, in 1566, to assist them in raising funds to resist the rebellious Lords, and also his sturdy refusal in 1569 to sell his rocky nest on the Bass to Regent Moray, in order that this isolated stronghold might become the future prison of his dethroned sovereign, made the Lords of the Congregation place his conduct to his son in the very worst light. Not that we would by any means defend it, knowing so little of the circumstances, but subsequent events tend greatly to unfold the fact that James Lauder, the Dean, had been, and still was, a tool and a spy in the service of the Regent.

The death of Sir Robert Lauder, Knight of Popill, without an heir-male, brought this Mr. James into a different relationship towards his father—that of eldest surviving son and heir-apparent—in consequence of which Sir Robert immediately entered into a legal contract with him. This contract is so important in its bearings, and so very explicit to those who can read between the lines, that we feel we must transcribe it in full :—

AS CHURCHMEN AND AMBASSADORS 185

'Registration on 24th October 1575 of a contract dated at Edinburgh and Beill 20th October 1575, between Robert Lauder of Bass, Mr. James Lauder, his son and apparent heir (and brother and heir to the deceased Sir Robert Lauder of Pople, Knight), and Mr. George Lauder, his brother-germain, with the advice and counsel of James, Earl of Morton, Regent, Archibald, Earl of Angus, Sir John Bellenden of Auchnoull, Justice-Clerk, Mr. James MacGill of Rankeillor-Nether, Clerk Register, and Mr. David Borthwick of Lochill, His Majesty's Advocate, and others, loving friends and favourers of the said Robert's auld house of Bass, procuring the weill, preservation and continuance thereof, with his bairns and posterity, that is to say, The said Mr. James undertakes as speedily as possible, on his father's expenses, to enter heir to the said Sir Robert, his brother; and the father undertakes by resignation to denude himself of all lands and others possessed by him in which his said deceased eldest son was not put in fee, whereupon the said Mr. James shall immediately take possession thereof; and if his father die before the resignation is made, Mr. James is, after his death, to serve himself heir and take infeftment thereof. Further, Mr. James undertakes by advice of his father, my Lord Regent, my Lord Angus, Mr. George Lauder, Moreis Lauder, burgess of Dunbar, Sir James Forrester of Corstorphine, Knight, John Swyntoun of that Ilk, Thomas Otterburne of Reidhall, Mr. James Makgill of Rankeillor-Nether, Sir John Bellenden of Auchnoull, Knight, and Mr. David Borthwick of Lochill, or most part of them, to join himself in marriage with an honest and agreeable party, as shall be thought convenient by them, and provide her with a competent provision, to which the said Mr. George binds himself to consent. Then whatever tocher shall be received with her shall be used for the redemption of such lands of the house as are mortgaged, and the overplus is to be delivered to his father to be used at his pleasure. The father obliges himself not to sell any of his lands or reversions to any person whatsoever, so that they may in time be redeemed. After the said Mr. James and his spouse have been provided in a conjunct fee, he is forthwith to make resignation of all in his superior's hands for a regrant thereof to the said Mr. George and his heirs-male, reserving the liferent and a reasonable terce to his spouse should he predecease her; and providing that if Mr. James has heirs-male of his own body, it shall be lawful to such heirs to redeem the lands from the said Mr. George and his heirs by payment of a rose-noble, and Mr. George binds himself on getting his charter to grant a reversion to this effect and for this payment, but always without prejudice to his liferent of the lands of Little Spotte, Priestlaw, and also of the teinds of Little Spott, to be enjoyed by him after his father's death. Should Mr. James have no sons, but daughters, Mr. George binds himself to pay to them, if one, 5000 merks, if two, 4000 merks each, if more, 10,000 equally among them at their marriage. Mr. James on his father's death promises to renounce in favour of Mr. George his interest in the lands of Little Spott and Priestlaw. He also obliges himself *not to put any keeper in the house and Isle of Bass other than a sure and tender friend of the family*, and that by advice of the said friends.

'As Mr. James has no means, his father agrees to pay the expenses of his entering to the lands, also to give him a pension of 500 merks yearly till he is married, paying the same quarterly in Edinburgh, to begin at Martinmas next; and after he is married to give him and his spouse a competent maintenance. *If Mr. James sell his pension the deed shall be null.* But Mr. James voluntarily obliges himself to refrain from all alienations of the lands and other property or pension, or injuring the patrimony and estate in any way, except only the lawful use thereof, and Mr. George comes under a similar obligation.'[1]

That such a contract should have been deemed necessary between father and son plainly indicates that there had been something radically wrong and unnatural in the son's previous conduct towards his father.

That he should be so completely penniless is also strange, even making allowance for the loss of his Church living by Reformation reversal, for he had been in possession for many years of the large house, gardens, and orchards of Restalrig, independent of the college prebendaries, whose houses and gardens lay nearer to the church. His own house and grounds he had let on lease to his brother William in 1570.[2] Such was the state of matters when Sir Robert himself died in June 1576. He had lived to see all his daughters well married; of his sons three had predeceased him, and the only one who seems to have been a thorn to his peace of mind was Mr. James, the dean.

According to his last will and testament Sir Robert Lauder's goods and gear amounted to £8240, 6s., and the debts due to him brought it up to £10,663, 12s. 8d. His own debts amounted to £3648, 1s., among which was £33 to Mr. George Lauder, his son, for a year's teind of Petcokis, and also £80 to Dame Margaret Hay, Lady Bass, younger, the widow of Sir Robert of Popill for a year's rent of Panshiellis, £80. His will was drawn up and dated at Beill on the 9th November 1575, within three weeks after the contract he had made with his son James. In his will Sir Robert Lauder appoints Elizabeth Hay, his spouse, James Forrester of Corstorphine, Knight, and Mr. James M'Gee, Clerk of Register, his executors. He had already infeft his son Arthur after his mother's death in an annuity of 100 merks of the lands of Scuney; but he bequeaths him 1000 merks in a very indefinite way, ordaining it to be paid out of the tocher of the bride of Mr. James, but unfortunately for Arthur, the lady was never chosen. The other 500 merks left him were more sure, seeing they were

[1] *Register of Deeds*, vol. xiv. fol. 322.
[2] At Edinburgh, 19th October 1570, King James the Sixth confirms a charter made by Mr. James Lauder, Dean of Restalrig, and the prebendaries of the College thereof, by which, for certain sums of money and other gratitudes, they set in feu-farm to his brother, William Lauder, elder, and his heirs and assignees, the large mansion and house occupied by the said James and Adam Logan, with lands, houses, buildings, enclosures, gardens, and orchards adjacent thereto, belonging to the said dean, and with the houses, buildings, gardens, orchards, lands, meadows, and enclosures belonging to the said prebendaries, and each of them in the territory of Restalrig, near the church thereof, and shire of Edinburgh. Paying annually to the said dean and prebendaries £8, and also to the Baron of Restalrig certain annual rents or feu-duties due to him therefrom, also with duplication of the feu-duty on the entry of heirs. The charter contains Precept of Sasine and is dated at Restalrig, 12th October 1570. Witnesses, Christopher Knowis of that ilk, George Mak, and John Levinax.—*Register of the Great Seal*, 1546-1580, No. 1934.

to be paid by his executors, 'in full satisfaction of his bairns' part of goods both of his late mother and himself.' Sir Robert also ordains '500 merks to be paid to his son, Patrick Lauder, together with the 1000 merks for which he has sasine of the lands of Garvet.'

Further, he leaves to Margaret Lauder, daughter to the late Alexander Lauder, his brother, 300 merks, and to Walter Lauder, her brother (Notary Public), £100, and 'to each of the five bairns of John Lauder, his late son, £40.' To his natural son, Henry Lauder, £200.

'He further desires that, seeing his children are now provided for, his free gear be divided into three, one part to belong to himself, the second to his wife,

THE BASS.
'Dread rock, thy life is two eternities,
The last in air, the former in the deep.'

Elizabeth Hay, and the third to his daughter Elizabeth, to whom he also leaves and dispones his part, being the rest of his whole goods and gear.' Which testament was confirmed and registered on the 19th April 1577, the year after his death.[1]

According to the terms of the contract of 1575, in which both James Lauder and his brother George were parties, Mr. James had resigned the whole of the lands to which his father had entered him as heir, in favour of Mr. George, for the payment of certain annuities, in consequence of which they had been regranted to Mr. George by the King, and he was now served heir to his father as Laird of Bass; but of Mr. James Lauder's marriage we find no mention. He appears to have died in August 1682 at Utterstoun, and his will was given up by his brother, William Lauder, for registration on the 27th July 1683.

[1] Commissariat of Edinburgh. *Register of Testaments*, vol. lix.

THE LAUDERS OF BASS

Sir Robert Lauder, who died in 1576, was the last Laird of Bass who bore the baron's title by feudal tenure. His two successors were Mr. George Lauder, his fourth son, and his grandson (also Mr. George Lauder), the last of the long line of the ancient Lauders of Bass, to whom from 1056 to 1649

> 'The royal grant through sire to son
> Devolved direct *in capite*.'

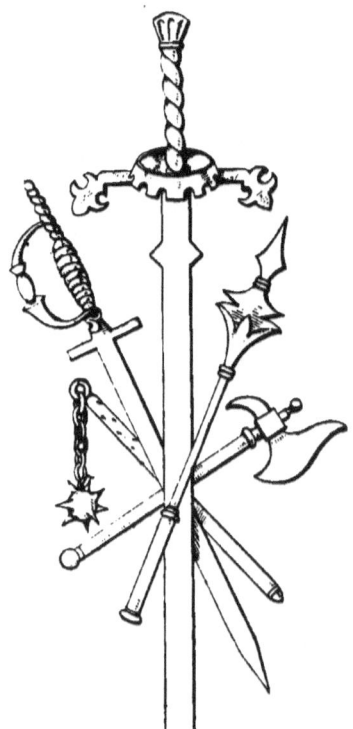

OLD WEAPONS—LAUDERS OF BASS.

CHAPTER XVII

THE CASTLE OF BASS

'The Solan's home—
Stupendous Bass!'   DELTA.

ESIDES exciting the cupidity of kings, the mighty Bass appears to have called forth the admiration of all the earliest travellers in Scotland. Hector Boethius calls it 'Ane wonderful craig, risand within the sea, with so narrow and strait hals that no schip nor boit may arrive bot allanerlie at ane part of it. This crag is called the Bas; unwinnable by ingine of man.' Even as far back as 1405 its strong fortress was used as a temporary place of safety for the young Prince James when fleeing from his unprincipled uncle the Duke of Albany. King Robert III., thus relying on the staunch loyalty of Sir Robert Lauder, whom the Prince ever called his 'loveit of the Bass.' From this 'grim throne of Solitude,' he set sail for France, under the care of Walter Wardlaw, Bishop of St. Andrews, and Henry St. Clair, second Earl of Orkney; but as we know the ship was intercepted at sea, and the Prince was carried captive to England in the ninth year of his age, where he remained for nineteen years, and it was his '*loveit of the Bas*' who obtained his release.

The remains of this fortress or castle still form an interesting feature of the Bass, but the oldest building on the island is the little chapel dedicated to St. Baldred, who is said to have made his abode in a cell on that spot as early as 606. These hermits were wonderful men for finding out the strangest and most inaccessible places to live in, as though lured by nature's deepest solitude, or lulled by her wildest storms.

Those were the days of primitive *Christianity*, not civilisation's intellectual *Christianism*. The first hermits were zealous men, who wrought for the pure love of God; saints truly, but not by canonisation. That kind of human homage had no existence in the early Church; it sprang up mushroom-like, as pride and spiritual ambition grew apace. There was no *Saint* Baldred then, he was simply 'the Hermit of the Bass,' praying and fasting there in solitude from time to time ; and when teaching and preaching along the coast he was called 'the Apostle of the Lothians.' 'Following the example of John the Divine, he resided in solitary places, and betook himself to the islands of the sea.'

Boece says St. Baldred died on the Bass Rock; but from all accounts he was buried at Auldhame, a fact of which the common people seem very proud even to this day, although, according to the old chronicler, they had to share the honour with Tyninghame and Prestonkirk. The legend is best given in his own quaint fashion :—

'There lived in these daies [606] that holie man Valdred a Scotish man borne, but dwelling amongest the Picts, whome he instructed in the right faith, and therefore was named the Doctor of the Picts. He departed out of this life within the Iland called the Basse, lieng about two miles off from the maine land within the sea, where the Forth hath entrie betwixt the same Ile, and an other called the Maie. There were three parishes fell at contention for his bodie, as Aldham, Tininghame and Preston—so far foorth, that they were at point to haue fought about it ; but that by counsell of some discreet persons amongst them, it was ordeined that they should continue in prair for that night, and in the next morning stand to th' order of the Bishop of the Dioces, who was come thither the same time to be present at the buriall. The next day in the morning there was formed *three heires with three bodies* decentlie covered with clothes, so like in all resemblance, that no man might perceive anie difference. Then by commandment of the Bishop, and with great joy of all the people, the said severall bodies were carried severallie unto the said three severall churches, and in the same buried in most solemne wise, where they remaine unto this day in much honor with the common people of the countries neere adjoining.'

Holinshed adds as a marginal note, ' A miracle if it be true.'

Rev. Dr. Thomas M'Crie, junior, in his *History of the Bass*, states that the ' Parish Kirk in the Craig of the Bass ' was consecrated in honour of St. Baldred so late as 1542, when it is more than probable the present structure was first erected under the patronage of that notorious enemy of the Reformation, Cardinal Beaton. The following is our authority :—

'1542. The v day of January, M. Vilhelm Gybsone, Byschop of Libariensis and Suffraganeus to David Beton, Cardynall and Archbysschop of Sant Andros, consecrat and dedicat the paris kirk in the craig of the Bass, in honor of Sant Baldred, bysschop and confessor, in presence of Maister Jhon Lauder,[1] Arsdene in Teuisdaill, noter publict.'[2]

---

[1] This Mr. John Lauder was secretary to Cardinal Beaton, and the bitter accuser of George Wishart the martyr in 1545.
[2] *Extracta e variis Cronicis Scocie*, p. 255. Printed for the Abbotsford Club, 1842.

THE CASTLE OF BASS

This chapel was unquestionably built upon the site of the original cell of St. Baldred, already marked by the walls of the pre-Reformation chapel, which was incorporated into this 'parish kirk' consecrated in 1542; for Hugh Miller,[1] after his visit to the Bass, points out the difference in the various ages of the masonry, showing the great antiquity of the older part. Jean de Beaugné, the personal friend of Sieur d'Esse, who was sent by Henri II. of France to help Mary of Guise to expel the English after the battle of Pinkie, gives us a very full and interesting account of this wonderful deep sea crag in 1547. He calls it '*L'Isle des Magots*' on account of the large white birds, like swans, that make their nests there. The Scots, according to Beaugné, 'received it as a fact that the hundred, or hundred and twenty soldiers who formed the ordinary garrison of the Castle of Bass, which is built on the island, lived for the most part on nothing else than the fish daily carried thither by these birds; and burned no other wood than what these wild geese brought in spring to build their nests with, this being sufficient to last them for a whole year.'

If such was a fact in the sixteenth century the solan geese have become more economical in their habits with the march of civilisation, for they are now said to dispense with nests altogether, for the most part laying their eggs on the bare rock, and firmly agglutinating them to this hard bed by what might be called *eggshell solder*. Any old nests that are found appear to consist entirely of moss and dried grass.

Beaugné's account of the position of the castle is very lucid. 'The island,' he says, 'on which the castle is situated, is an impregnable rock, of small extent, fashioned by nature of an oval shape, with but one approach, and that on the side of the castle, so very difficult that it can only be gained by very little boats each following the other, the island being surrounded by rocks covered by the sea, which none except those acquainted with the place can avoid. The island is so little inviting and so uneven that till you come to the castle wall itself, you cannot plant the foot on level ground; and this is so much the case that (as I have often myself seen) when the captain's servants wished to enter, it was necessary to throw down a thick rope to help them in the ascent; and when they have reached the foot of the wall with the utmost difficulty, a basket is let down in which they are drawn up, and this is the only means of entering that castle. There used to be a postern, but it is now banked up and built in, in an incredible manner, and the rest of the castle is so constructed that it seems to rise sheer from the sea.'

From all these early accounts it must indeed have been a most uncomfort-

[1] *Geology of the Bass.*

able, unenviable dwelling. Taylor, the water-poet, also mentions it in 1618, but more from a culinary and profitable point of view, having been well entertained at the Castle of Auldhame, in a little village upon the coast. He writes: 'Among our viands that we had there, I must not forget the *Soleand goose*, a most delicate fowle, which breeds in great abundance in a little Rocke called the Basse, which stands two miles into the sea. It is very good flesh, but it is eaten in the form as wee eate oysters, standing at a side-boord, a little before dinner, unsanctified without grace; and after it is eaten it must be well liquored with two or three rowses of sherrie or Canarie sacke. The lord or owner of the Bass doth profit at least two hundred pound yeercly by those geese—the Basse it selfe being of a great height, and near three quarters of a mile in compasse, all fully replenished with wilde-fowle, having but one small entrance into it, with a house, a garden, and a chappell in it, and *on the toppe of it a well of pure fresh water.*'[1] This remarkable well being one of the wonders of the sea-girt rock, it is frequently mentioned. Sir Thomas Brereton, who visited it in 1636, says: 'Here is excellent fresh water in this isle, a dainty, pure spring, which is to be the more admired.' Another English traveller (John Ray) writes: 'They make strangers who come to visit it *Burgesses of the Basse*, by giving them to drink of the water of the well, which springs near the top of the rock, and a flower out of the garden thereby.' Many people of our own day, judging from present appearances, doubt the existence of this '*pure spring*' entirely; but it is not the only instance of the complete disappearance of what was once an apparently inexhaustible supply of pure water, nor yet the only instance of a *fresh spring* on a rocky, sea-girt island—witness Inchcolm and Cramond Islands. However, there is no doubt of the excavated *well* itself being there, which visitors to the Bass can see for themselves, but as for the *delicious, sparkling water*, it is, alas, too truly a matter of faith. Water there certainly is, but we doubt if any one would care to be made a 'burgess of the Bass' by venturing to taste it. Hugh Miller says he found the old well 'to be full to overflowing with a brown, turbid fluid,' which he calls '*dilute tincture of guano*,' and such it is still, judging from the odoriferousness of it. It has also been called 'cold infusion of undressed mutton,' a sheep having fallen into it and been left to decay. No wonder it smells! and we cannot be surprised that people say there is no *pure spring* on this 'mighty high rock placed in the sea,' though there are still 'some sheep, some kine, and some coneys; and as to the '*Solene Geese*' and other wild-fowl, it is quite true that at certain times they '*do*

[1] I am indebted for these extracts from the early travellers to the valuable and comprehensive collection of *Early Travels in Scotland* contributed to Scottish history by P. Hume Brown, LL.D.

THE CASTLE OF BASS

make such a noise as that you may hear them and nothing else a mile before you come to them.' Every one who has sailed round the Bass can testify to that.

Such was the inaccessible, impregnable nest of the Lauders, when the family was divided into two branches at the death of Sir Robert de Lawder of Bass in 1561, who, having only two surviving sons, left the title and estates of Lauder to William,[1] the elder son (who eventually rose to the Bench as Lord Lauder), giving the Bass and the lands of East Lothian to his namesake, Robert, the younger son, who thereupon added another to the long list of the Lairds of Bass called *Robert Lauder*; and he is distinguished as having been with Queen Mary on Carberry Hill when she was taken prisoner by the rebel lords, in June 1567, in consequence of which we find in the Register of Council for 1st September 1567: 'Robert Lauder of the Bass is cited to deliver the hous, fortalice, and Isle of Bas to the officiaris, executouris hereof, within xlviii houris next efter the charge.' Which request he certainly did not comply with, knowing it was by no means an easy task for them to dislodge him from his sea-girt rocky fort. After his death we find Lady Bass, his widow (who was Elizabeth Hay of Yester), suing Sir John Stewart of Traquhair for the sum of £2000, lent by Robert Lauder of the Bass in 1566 to Queen Mary and the King (Lord Darnley), to which transaction he, with three other nobles, had become cautioner. The rest having died in the meantime, the whole burden fell upon the Laird of Traquhair, who declined to pay, and was accordingly summoned by Lady Bass, and the decision was given against him at Stirling Castle, March 21st, 1578-9,[2] by the Lords of Council and Session.

In 1569 the Earl of Morton and his confederate, James Stuart (the Regent Moray), had each endeavoured *privately* to obtain the isolated stronghold of the Bass, both being dead set on finding safe quarters for the future incarceration of their dethroned Queen, who had already eluded their vigilance by

---

[1] In Burke's *Baronage* he is by some mistake called Richard, but Lord Fountainhall calls him William.

[2] 'Stirling Castle, 1578-9, March 21st.—Complaint by Sir John Stewart of Troquhar, Knight, as follows : He is sued before the Lords of Council and Session by David Preston of Craigmillar and his curators in the matter of an " obligation " upon the payment of twa thousand pundis, money of this realm, borrowit be the King and Quene (Mary and Lord Darnley), his Hieness darrest fader and moder, fra umquhile Robert Lawder of Bass. At the time of the loan they deliverit their obligatioun in the word of Princes, and for thame, thair aires and successouris, and fand umquhile Sir Symon Preston, of that ilk, fader to the present Lord of Craigmillar, and umquhile Alexander Hamilton of Innerwick, cautioneris, as alsua umquhile George, Erle of Huntlie, and the Lord of Troquhair to relief thame.

'Subscrivit with thair handis and under thair signet, MARIE R., HENRY R., etc., at Dunbar, 16 March 1565.'

The 'complaint' is taken from the Register of Council ; and the deed of obligation to Robert Lauder of Bass, from the King and Queen of Scotland, is in the *Register of Deeds*, vol. viii. No. 279.

2 B

THE CASTLE OF BASS

making her escape from Lochleven Castle. But though outwardly to all appearance they seemed 'hand and glove' in any transaction against their sovereign, privately each had his own ambitious projects to serve in the matter, as will be seen by Wishart of Pitarrow's speech to Regent Moray about this same grim, '*solitary Bass*':—'I hear say my Lord of Morton is

CASTLE OF BASS.

> 'Mark the lone rock that grandly studs
> The melancholy main—
> The raving winds, the foaming floods
> Burst over it in vain.
> In age majestic as in youth
> It stands unchanged—secure
> Symbol immortal of the truth,
> They conquer who endure.'
>
> G. J. DUNPHIE.

trafficking to get the house of the Bass, which if he does, he will stop some devices your Grace knows; and therefore were I in your Grace's stead, I would go between the *cow* and the *corn*. I tell you the Auld Crag is a good starting-hole; at least it will serve to *keep them that you would be sure of*.'[1]

[1] Richard Bannatyne's *Memorials of Transactions in Scotland*, 1569-1573.

THE CASTLE OF BASS 195

In 1581, while Queen Mary was still a captive in England, her son James VI. visited the Bass, of which he appears to have been granted temporary possession, with his suite. On expressing his earnest desire to secure it entirely for the Crown, the royal offer of purchase was as stoutly refused by George Lauder as it had been on a former occasion by his ancestor, Robert Lauder of Bass, whose outspoken reply to the King's great-grandsire was very characteristic both of the period and also of the sturdy independence of the Scotch barons. But his Majesty retiring with a good grace, George Lauder got the 'Auld Crag' back again. And this was evidently accomplished without offence, for we find King James, two years later, ratifying a most lengthy document in favour of Mr. George Lauder of Bass anent the 'Solangoosifera Bassa of the Forth,' in which we see that even at that time (1583) this rocky fortress was used as a baronial place of imprisonment, and also that the solan geese and other wild-fowl frequenting the island formerly were, as they still continue to be, the private property of the owner of the Bass. This 'Ratificatioun of ane Act of Secreit Counsaill in favouris of the Laird of Bass, maid upon the xxj day of Januar, the zeir of God J^m V^c fourscoir thre zeiris, to Maister George Lauder of Bass,' was to forbid the slaying, destroying, or snaring of '*Solane Geiss*' by strangers upon pain of a fine of £20—half of which was to belong to his Majesty, and the other half to Mr. George Lauder, or his heirs. If the delinquent were unable to pay the fine, he was to be imprisoned on the Bass for the space of one year at his own expense, his goods being sold for that purpose. Seeing that the King was to share in the mulct of the plunderer, proclamation thereof was ordered to be made at the Market Crosses of the following towns: 'Dundie, Abirbrothok, Montrose, Santandrois, Craill, Anstruther, Pittenveme, Sant Monanis, Weymis, Dysart, Kircaldie, Kingorne, Brunt-Iland, Aberdor, Inverkething, and utheris sey townis on the north side of Forth'; also at the towns and havens of 'South-ferie, Cramond, Leith, Fischerraw, Saltpains of Prestoun, North-beruik, Dunbar, Skaitraw, and Aymouth.' In this year (1583) Mr. George Lauder of Bass had some matter of dispute with Mr. Alexander Home of North Berwick Mains about the possession of the lands called Farm Acres of North Berwick, in which Home had raised an action against Lauder in the Court of Session, and also before the Commissaries of Edinburgh, for spoliation of the teinds of the lands of Balgone and Craig. The matter being appointed to arbitration, the judges' arbiter acquitted Mr. George Lauder and Thomas Otterburne of Reidhall, his brother-in-law, who was his cautioner. In another case also, which was brought up against Mr. George, in which his cousin, Maurice Lauder, was his cautioner, the judges also gave it in his favour, finding that Mr. George Lauder and his predecessors were in their right in the matters disputed.[1] These land disputes were of frequent occurrence, and almost unavoidable where the lands were so scattered and open, and the owners very often politically at feud with one another, as the Homes and Lauders repeatedly were.

In February of the year 1588-9 Mr. George Lauder of Bass, upon his marriage with Isobel Hepburn, eldest daughter of Sir Patrick Hepburn of Wauchton, resigned his lands of Popill and Wester Spot into the King's hands as superior, for a regrant in conjunct fee with his spouse, heritably to descend to the heirs-male, whom failing, to the next-of-kin bearing the name and arms of Lauder.[2]

There is scarcely a year from his marriage to his death but what Mr. George Lauder's name appears in the public registers in one way or another. Lands regranted, lands forfeited for non-entry, lands mortgaged, and lands sold or apprised. The charters are too numerous and too tedious to be transcribed; we can only give the sum-total of the main facts, relegating any special charter to the Appendix among the family documents.

In 1591 the Tynynghame lands were confirmed to Mr. George Lauder of Bass, who is called the King's Councillor; and in a very long charter[3] anent all his lands, the Barony of Beill, with fortalice, manor-place and mills; the lands of Popill, and the mill of Mersingtoun; lands of Crag and wardlands of Tynynghame, with the principal mansion, fortalice, dovecot, etc. etc., and the lands of Lochhouses, besides many others, are all regranted and confirmed to him in 1597-8, by King James the Sixth, for himself and as administrator and tutor of his son, Henry, Prince and Steward of Scotland, Duke of Rothesay, Earl of Carrick, Lord of the Isles and of the Barony of Renfrew. In this elaborate document Mr. George is styled the King's '*familiar councillor,*' showing the Laird of Bass still retained the royal favour, adhering faithfully to the Crown. Five years before this, on the 1st of May 1593, he had been at a convention of the nobles and barons at Holyrood, and there signed a resolution for the more rigorous prosecution of Earl Bothwell and his adherents.

As this conclusive charter of 1597 is the first in which the name of George Lauder, son and heir-apparent of Mr. George Lauder, appears as heritor of his parents, we conclude the confirmation of these enumerated lands was given on his behalf, the year of his birth affirming his heirship; which charter was also ratified with others by the Archbishop of St. Andrews, with consent of his chapter, in 1609. Mr. George Lauder died in 1617, leaving his wife, Isobel

[1] *Register of Deeds,* vol. xxii. f. 37.
[2] *Register of the Great Seal,* 1546-1580, No. 1628.   [3] *Ibid.* 1593-1608, No. 688.

THE CASTLE OF BASS

Hepburn, as his executrix and administrator for their son—appointing her with others to act for him while under age. Their names are often coupled together in the Tyninghame Church Records as 'George Lauder of Bass, and Dame Isobel Hepburn his mother.'

Money seems to have been much more scarce than land with this branch of the family, especially at this period, judging from their constant difficulties anent the payment of teinds and taxes. 1626 still finds the young laird contending with his inherited creditors; and, as Charles I., like his father King James, was very anxious to possess 'the Auld Crag,' he took the first opportunity to enforce the law against the family who held on so firmly to their rocky nest. But unfortunately for them, their revenues had decreased and their taxes increased in inverse ratio, leaving them virtually upon the rocks, not only domiciled but also financially.

Considering the instructions given by Charles I. to the President of the Session, 10th November 1626—'that you cause prosecute our right concerning the Bass with all expedition for effectuating of that end you have from us '—it is not surprising to find, two years later, a warrant sent out against them, on behalf of their creditors. This document, which is characteristic of the period, we shall transcribe, or at least a portion of it :—

'Apud Halyrudhous, secundo Decembris 1628.—*Inter alia*, "Forsameckill as the King's Majestie being informed that George Lauder of Bass, and Dame Issobell Hepburne, Ladie Bas, his mother, doe stand rebellis and at the horne, at the instance of diverse thair creditors, and that notwithstanding thairof they peaceablie bruke and injoy some of thair rentes, and remain within the Crag of the Bass, presooming to keepe and mainteane thame selffis, so to elude justice and executioun of the Law : his Majestie wes thairupon moved by his letter direct to the Lords of his Privie Counsell to give strait ordour and command that charges sould be direct for delyuerie of the Bas, apprehending of the rebellis and committing thame to waird within the Tolbuith of Edinburgh thairin to remane, ay and untill they sould give full satisfactioun to thair creditors, and procure thame selffis relaxt from the processe of horne—ffor obedience whairof the said Lords have caused charge the said Laird and Ladie Bas to compeir before thame to answere upoun their rebellioun, with certificatioun if they failyed, the said Lords would proceed against thame with the most rigorous executioun, and under the greatest panes that the lawes of the kingdom in such a caise would allow.—And the saids Laird and Ladie Bas compeirand be Mr. Alexander Hepburne, indweller in Edinburgh ; he produced a petitioun subscryved with their hand, purporting thair hard and desolate estait, and testifieing thair reddie willingnesse to give unto thair creditours ententment, if the said Lords would be please to graunt a warrant unto thame for thair saulf repaire to the burgh of Edinburgh to deale with thair creditours without danger of the law."'

This warrant appears to have been granted '*betuixt the twentie day of December instant, and the twentie day of Februar nixtocum*,' providing that within that time the said Laird and Ladie Bas gave satisfaction to their creditors, 'otherwise this warrand to be void, of no strength, force, nor effect, from thenceforth and for ever.' Sufficient satisfaction of some kind must therefore have been given, as they appear to have secured their safe holding of the 'Auld Crag' for another twenty years, which was probably due to their having preferred to sell their estate of Tyninghame to meet the demands of their numerous mortgages. It is painfully evident that George Lauder, the last Laird of Bass, simply inherited the debts of his forefathers. The lands were all too heavily bonded for any chance of redemption. And it is sad to see how rapidly those bonds were called up, and land after land belonging to this fine estate put to the hammer. In 1618 Beill had been mortgaged to Sir Ludovick Craig of Riccarton, Knight, and another bond was taken up by Mr. John Paip in 1623 for 5400 merks; but the very next year, Thomas Hamilton, Earl of Melrose, obtained a charter of the same lands of Beill and Popill, which were apprised from George Lauder of Bass. This charter the earl must have resigned in favour of Sir James Hamilton of Priestfield, Knight, his son; for on the 29th June 1625, 'Charles I. for himself, and as Prince and Steward of Scotland,' granted to Sir James and his heirs and assignees, the north side of the Bass, the lands of Beill and Popill and others, redeemable within seven years, which were apprised for £5000 by Mr. Nicholson, younger, advocate. There is also a charter of these lands, dated 27th September 1625, to Thomas Lord Binning,[1] which is only another title of Sir Thomas Hamilton's, who with the approbation of the Crown, afterwards changed his title of Earl of Melrose to that of Earl of Haddington. The Tyninghame estate was sold in June 1621 to John, Lord Murray of Lochmaben, who afterwards became Earl of Annandale, and he eventually resold it to the first Earl of Haddington, as we shall see in the next chapter. But these sales only postponed the fatal day when the Lauders were reluctantly obliged from sheer force of circumstances to part with their impregnable nest, 'the mighty Bass,' the ancestral home of so many generations. In 1649 it became the property of the Earl of Haddington and Hepburn of Waughton conjointly. All the poetry and fascination that had so long encircled the 'Auld Crag' from its early days of chivalry, now vanished with the Lauders. The ancient castle was no longer the home of the Barons of Bass and their 'bairns,' but just a strong fortress on an inaccessible rock, with every discomfort and privation imaginable. It soon changed hands again, being purchased by Sir Andrew Ramsay of Abbotshall in Fife, who was at that time Provost of Edinburgh. Sir Andrew knew well what he was about when

[1] *Register of the Great Seal*, 1620-1633, No. 879.

THE CASTLE OF BASS

he bought the island for £400 from the Laird of Wauchton, and sold it to the Government for £4000 in 1671. Thus the 'Auld Crag' became at last a State prison, under the administration of the odious Earl of Lauderdale, in the reign of Charles II.; and the ancient Chapel of St. Baldred, its patron saint, served the garrison as a magazine. At present an arched staircase leads down underground from the nether end of the Castle, to what was formerly the bastion, at the foot of which is the entrance to an awful cavern, dark, damp, and dismal, the rugged sides and roof of which are cut in the bare rock itself. In this

PRISONS OF THE BASS.

horrible pit and other hideous dungeons, the champions for religious freedom in Scotland groaned and died, leaving their faith as a legacy to the nation. Of their endurance and their sufferings we need not speak here, for who has not heard of '*the prisons of the Bass*'?

> 'And from that rugged, lonely spot, ascended rich and rare,
> The incense of the contrite heart, the sacrifice of prayer;
> And angels from the heights of Heaven did look complacent down
> On honoured heads that soon should wear the martyr's glorious crown.'

Later on, the impregnability of the Bass Rock was well tested: it being the last place in Scotland that surrendered to King William III.

The captain, a zealous Jacobite, held out against the Government for a considerable time, and only capitulated when sheer starvation stared in the face of the few remaining of his brave men. Even at the last, by a clever stratagem he was able to make his own terms. He had still in reserve a few bottles of the best French wine, a little brandy, and some very fine biscuits. These he placed, in an off-hand way, before the Commissioners sent by the Government to treat with him, begging them just to help themselves freely, as there was no scarcity of provisions on the island, and he was quite determined not to surrender unless he had his own terms. Of course the Commissioners on their return gave an account of their liberal entertainment, and also that the place still appeared to be well manned; for part of the Governor's stratagem had been to hoist upon muskets and spears, all the old hats and coats they could find in the garrison, and place them along the walls, so that the men in the receding boats should see them and report accordingly; which they did, and the most honourable terms were thus obtained for the staunch defenders of the Bass, 'with the testimony of having done their duty like brave men.'

This grim, sequestered rock had been but a short time in the possession of King William before some Jacobite officers were confined in the State prison upon it. By some means they contrived to surprise and overpower the garrison, and, establishing themselves forthwith as its defenders for King James, they again bade defiance to the English Government. They managed for some time to escape detection, and received supplies of food and ammunition from their Jacobite friends on shore; and, making use of the boats that belonged to the island, they even had the audacity to blackmail merchant ships entering the Firth. At last 'a squadron of English ships of war' was actually sent to reduce the place, but their guns did so little damage to this precipitous crag, they were obliged to retire to a safer distance from its more successful missiles, and convert the siege into a strict blockade. All food-supplies now ceased, for it was death to any man supplying provisions to the rebels. This did not prevent a Jacobite gentleman named Trotter (a relative of John Trotter of Mortonhall) from making the attempt, for which he was seized and condemned to death; 'the gallows being erected opposite the Bass, that the garrison might witness his fate.' But the garrison had no intention of witnessing anything of the kind; so they fired a cannon from the island, just at the time of the execution, scaring the executioners from their post. This did not save their poor friend's life; it only delayed his death, for he was hanged elsewhere, and a stricter watch set over the Bass, in consequence of which the garrison were finally obliged to surrender, having retained it from June 1691 till April 1694. Their bravery was so far acknowledged that their lives were spared, and they were admitted to honourable terms. From this time forth, the fortress was dismantled, and the guns and ammunition all cleared away, leaving the island to the undisputed possession of the solan geese—its first and rightful owners—who still remain unevicted. But even they, geese though they be, find the 'Auld Crag' very undesirable winter quarters, and migrate to southern latitudes in the autumn, departing as soon as their young broods are strong enough on the wing to undertake such a long journey. They return to their island home early in

TENANTS OF THE BASS.
'The air was dirkit with the fowlis
That cam with yammeris and with yowlis,
With shrykking, screeking, skrymming scowlis,
And meikle noyis and showtes.'   DUNBAR.

May, weather permitting, and commence to build their nests in every crag, crevice, and corner. They arrive like a mighty swarm of bees—
'Thousands upon thousands, an innumerous throng,
Darkening the noontide with their winnowing plumes';
the deafening sound of their unmusical whirring and screaming being such, that once heard, few ever desire to have it *encored*.

THE CASTLE OF BASS

The solan geese live principally on herring, which accounts for their fishy taste; and it is said that the male can carry home five or six herrings at a time for its mate and her young ones, having a dilatable pouch something like the pelican. In this they differ from the sea-gulls, and also in their manner of mounting into the air. Notwithstanding the thousands there are of them, the female lays only one egg once a year. It is of an elongated form, and bluish-white in colour. These facts, though somewhat digressive, are not irrelevant to our subject, seeing that for five centuries these 'tenants of the Bass' were unquestionably the most profitable vassals of the old feudal Chiefs of Bass, requiring neither food nor clothing from their lordly masters, yet never failing to bring in a goodly revenue year by year,

'Amid the bleak and barren solitude
Of that precipitous and sea-girt isle.'

CHAPTER XVIII

LADY BASS AND THE LAUDERS OF TYNINGHAME

'Lo! on that mound, in days of feudal pride,
Thy towering castle frown'd above the tide.'

N the days of their prosperity the Lairds of Bass only occupied their island fortress in the summer months, retiring to a family residence on the mainland during the winter. That this was not the house in the High Street of North Berwick which they also possessed, we have full proof, but the manor-house at Tyninghame, which, according to the following documents, they leased for more than fifty years, and afterwards purchased. The first statement we find is the 'Lease by Andrew Forman, Archbishop of St. Andrews, Primate of Scotland, granting to Robert Lauder of Bass, Knight; Robert Lauder, his son and heir-apparent; Robert Lauder, son of the said younger Robert; and Adrien Lauder, son and heir-apparent of Walter Lauder, to the longer liver of them and their heirs and assignees, all and sundry the barony and lands of Tyninghame, with the mains, town, husbandlands belonging to said town, cotlands, brewlands, mill-lands, Giles-croft, Staneflat, loch, rabbit-warren, etc., for the term of nineteen years from the date of the lease, to be held of the Archbishop of St. Andrews and his successors *freely*, for the following payment yearly:— For the mains, £20 Scots; for the loch and rabbit-warrens, 40s.; for the husbandlands, £10; for the cotlands, brewlands, mill-lands, Giles-croft and lands of Staneflat, £10, 6s. 8d. Scots, and other dues according to the rental, dated 28th July 1517. St. Andrews, Metropolitan Church.'

This and two other similar documents are in the Haddington charter-chest.[1]

'The feudal title of Sir Robert Lauder, Knight, to Tyninghame was completed by charters from John Maitland, Archbishop of St. Andrews, in the years 1569-1570,' as specified in the old inventory of Tyninghame writs.

Thirty-six years later another charter was granted, through Sir Patrick

[1] Sir William Fraser's *Memorials of the Earls of Haddington*, vol. ii.

Hepburn, to Sir Robert Lauder's son by 'Andrew Melville, Provost, Principal of the College of St. Mary, or the New College of the University of St. Andrews, therein granting to *Mr. George Lauder of Bass* the Kirklands of Tyninghame, with mansion, houses, etc., in the lordship of Tyninghame, regality of St. Andrews, constabulary of Haddington, and sheriffdom of Edinburgh, to be held to the said George and his heirs-male and assignees whomsoever, heritably and irredeemably of the said Patrick Hepburn's superiors in the same, and the successors in feu-farm and heritage for ever, for payment of £10, 11s. 6d. Scots in name of feu-farm, with duplicand at the entry of each heir.' The contract is dated at Edinburgh, 28th June 1606, and attested by Sir Patrick Hepburn of Wauchton, Knight; Mr. John Hepburn, his brother; John Lauder in Tyninghame; with Robert Lyntain, Advocate; David Anderson, Writer, and others. Written in the office of David Anderson, Writer, Edinburgh, dated at St. Andrews 2nd July 1606.

This is the same Mr. George Lauder of the 'Solangoosifera' document, who, notwithstanding the lands he and his wife, Isobel Hepburn, Lady Bass, possessed at Beill and Tyninghame, 'Knowis, Kirkhill, Tusche, Wester Lochous, and Wester Spot,' was constantly increasing the number of his creditors. A great part of these lands having been mortgaged to the different persons who had at various times lent the family large sums of money under reversion, which debts Mr. George Lauder, junior, and his mother afterwards inherited, as also their proportionate share of the taxes on these lands for all church and parish expenses. In June 1617 their share alone of the subscriptions raised for the providing of sacramental vessels for the communion and baptism in the kirk at Tyninghame amounted to £121, 5s.; or, as it is quaintly stated in the Record: 'Suma of money to be payit be the Ladie Bass, six scor pundis, ane pund, five s.' This was by no means a voluntary contribution, and following immediately upon the death of her husband, the Laird of Bass, it came as a heavy tax upon the widow.

But kirks were paramount in those days. Daily services commenced at eight o'clock in the morning, and on Communion Sabbaths at six A.M. Fines were frequent, and penance for even small offences very heavy. Congregations were held together by strong discipline, with very little voice in church matters. Session rules were very stringent and oppressive in the Covenanting days of yore. Christ's yoke was not made easy, nor was the burden of His beautiful commandment, 'Love one another,' made light; and we look in vain for the 'Charity which covereth a multitude of sins,' when, 'in face of holy kirk,' poor shrinking women were made 'to stand besyde the place of repentance the

THE LAUDERS OF TYNINGHAME 205

whole tyme of Divine service; and after singing of the second Psalme, to confess publicklie upon their knees' the failings of their tongues. Ministerial duties savoured more of the police-court than of the fold of the Gentle Shepherd; their pastoral tasks were onerous, and the surveillance of soul and body unceasing; for however edifying to the inner man the length and weight of the Sabbath services appointed by the Assembly, they certainly were a weariness to the flesh. Whatever would these holy Covenanters have said had they seen the real Jesus of Nazareth walking in their cornfields upon the Sabbath day?—'To the jougs, away with Him!' and yet these very men were ready to lay down their lives for the *Christ* of their *Covenant*; and none more zealous, more earnest, and more patriarchal than Mr. John Lauder, who laboured and loved, lived and died in the rustic village of Tyninghame, ministering faithfully in the ancient Church of St. Baldred for fifty-two eventful years, during which time he made himself felt as a power in the pulpit, a sympathiser in every home, and a terror to the boys and the fishers on the Sabbath-day. No boy dare look at 'a bool' within miles of his district, and no fisher dare place a lobster-pot on a Sunday, though he might set his nets for herring with impunity. Why this distinction we know not, but of this we may feel assured, that the whole of the lower creation were truly grateful for the twenty-four hours of absolute rest if the men were not; especially the poor horses, for none at Tyninghame dare yoke a horse within those twenty-four 'Sabbathe houres' under very heavy penalties; but, strange to say, *abstaining* from work on 'Yoole-day' was reckoned as great a sin as working on the Lord's day.

Still, for all this strict surveillance of ministers, elders, and schoolmasters, we cannot help noticing that the people in general were not any better behaved then than they are at present in some of the very wildest parts of Ireland. Fighting at a marriage was no uncommon practice, and fighting in the kirk itself was almost as frequent. On one of these uproarious occasions a man deliberately threw his neighbour over the gallery. No wonder they required to have two pairs of '*jougs*' at Tyninghame—one at the Church and another at the Market Cross. With what satisfaction the patriarchal minister must have entered his minute in the Record a few Sabbaths after that scrimmage: '*Order weel keipit—God be praise!*' A true father of his flock was this zealous minister of the beautiful little Church of St. Baldred at Tyninghame.

Of the old village we have no knowledge beyond what we gather from the past records; for all the places mentioned by the kirk-session have vanished like a dream in the night, leaving but a faint memory of what was then so real.

And very real it does become to us again in the pages of *An Old Kirk Chronicle*, in which Mr. Hately Waddell brings before us the kirk chronicler himself as a living, breathing spirit, and yet a man withal who identifies himself in every minute particular with the social doings of his people. His record opens in 1615 and closes in 1650. Mr. John was a Lauder, and his brother, 'Maister Robert Lauder,' was minister of the adjoining parish of

WHITEKIRK.

Whitekirk. St. Baldred's at Tyninghame, Prestonkirk, and Whitekirk were the three most ancient churches in that part of the country. There was also an old chapel and churchyard at Auldhame which formed part of the estate of the Lauders of the Bass for many years.

These brother ministers were the sons of the Bailie of Tyninghame, Mr. John Lauder, of the elder branch of the family, who died in 1621, about six years after his son John was nominated to the church at Tyninghame. Their widowed mother lived at Haddington, and Mistress Jean Lauder, one of the sisters of this large and united family, kept her brother's house at Tyninghame Manse until she was married, on the 19th February 1629, to Mr. George

THE LAUDERS OF TYNINGHAME 207

Forrest, in consequence of which, the following year, Mr. John, the minister, took unto himself a wife. On Sunday, 7th February 1630, he was married to Elizabeth Haitlie at Whittinghame, the bride taking possession of her new home on the Friday after. Mr. John's brother, Alexander Lauder, was chaplain and tutor at Whittinghame. He appears to have died young, deeply regretted. His death is recorded with quaint simplicity by his elder brother, the chronicler:—

'December 21, 1628.—Alexander Lauder, my brother, depairtit this lyff, and sleepit maist sweetlie in the Lord, betwixt sevin and aucht houris at nicht, at Whittinghame, in my lord of Whittinghame his hous: and was brocht doune in ane hors litter to Tyninghame upon Tysday, the twentie-third of December, to his buryall besyd his father and brother, many accompanying him, bothe gentlemen and utheris.'

Not only the births, deaths, and marriages of the village were faithfully entered into the minute-book, but all village delinquencies, village quarrels, and village disasters—good crops and bad crops, floods and storms. There is a refreshing touch of nature in the simple routine of the life of this village pastor from the time of his marriage to the death of his wife. Her people lived in the beautiful valley of the Merse, and sometimes we find this affectionate couple riding pillion together on the old manse-horse, going to visit Elizabeth Haitlie's mother and friends. It does not say whether the two bairnies, John and Alexander, went with them.

One of the saddest and most pathetic entries in that thirty years' record is that which tells of a death and baptism on the same day at the manse: 'Upon the 5th day of November, being Tysday, 1639 yeirs, about 7 hours in the morning, Elizabeth Haitlie, spouse to Maister John Lauder, minister at Tyninghame, departit this lyfe. The said day ane sonne bapteisit to Maister John Lauder, minister, lawfullie named James. Bapteisit be Maister Robert Lauder, minister at Whitekirk.' Mr. Alexander Lauder and Robert Lauder, portionar of Tyninghame, witnessing.

At the fall of the next year Mr. John Lauder lost his mother, Alison Caldclaithe; but we hear no word of a second marriage.

Warriors were more in quest than wives at that time—soldiers and preaching being paramount. Even the Church records bare their weekly testimony to the warlike state of the country; and the beautiful little village Church of St. Baldred was filled from time to time with the regiments passing to and fro.

May 26th, 1639, we are told: 'This day Mr. James Rowe, minister to Montrose his regiment, prieched heir befor noon, and Mr. John Lauder efter noon, many soldiers being present, both Montrose his regiment, and many westland soldiers, who heard the Word attentively and reverentlie. They removit this toune on Wednesday nicht. . . . 20th June—The Scottishe camp removit from Dunse Law and came to Dunglas. Ane peace was concludit on the Tysday. Praised be God!'

But alas! it was not of long duration, for in September 1642 Mr John Lauder again writes: 'The sword raging throughout all Christendome; but more barbarouslie in Ireland, and daily more threatened in England, through the lamentable division between the King and his Parliament, tending to the subversion of religion and peace in all the three kingdoms.'

Shortly before Mr. John Lauder was appointed one of the chaplains to the army, he mentions that the Earl of Argyll worshipped in his little church on his way to hold a court in that district.

The whole of Bailie Lauder's God-fearing family were staunch Covenanters, having 'subscrybit the Covenant at Edinburgh'; and during the Parliamentary wars both the ministers, Mr. John and Mr. Robert Lauder, were separately ordered to join the Scottish army, then encamped at Durham. The elder brother, minister of Tyninghame, was appointed chaplain to the East Lothian Regiment, commanded by the Laird of Wauchton, a Hepburn, whose son was lieutenant-colonel. One of the Parliamentary statutes[1] ordained 'that preachers be chosen, the fittest in the presbyteries, for the army; not too learned, but men who have greater fancy than judgment; vehement and zealous in their utterance, and who dare sometimes play the souldiers, to keep the army in the fear of God and exhort them to service, comforting them in extremities'; and 'that all swearing and blasphemies be discharged under grievous punishment, through the whole camp.' Mr. John Lauder marched with the soldiers from place to place, camping out with them, sleeping and preaching in the fields, from the 5th July to the 27th August 1641, on which day he writes his first entry again in the Record Book:—'Friday, 27th August. I cam to Dunbar; and about eleven hours in the forenoon I maid ane exhortation to Wauchton's regiment in the kirkyard of Dunbar; and so the regiment was disbandit, and I cam to Tyninghame saiflie that nicht, at seven hours at evening; and preached on Sunday.'

This seems a simple statement, very simply told, but in reality it must have been quite a jubilee in the parish, seeing they had had no '*preiching*,' only '*reiding*' from the schoolmaster, since the minister went to the camp. He does not tell us his text, but we may be sure it was thoroughly to the point, for

[1] Appendix, Note XII.

'Maister Johne Lauder' of Tyninghame had always been famed for the aptness and appropriateness of what he called his '*pertinent texts*' for remarkable occasions ; such as, ' Disastrous floods from storms and ocean-tide,' ' The trumpet-blasts of war,' ' The burning of warlocks and witches,' and the ever fruitful theme of the Covenant, besides the numerous ' Solemne Fasts to be keepit ' throughout the land, for the sins and the follies of the nation.

Between the Lady and the Laird of Bass, the bailie, the public notary, and the two ministerial brethren, the Lauders had it all pretty much their own way in this district; but in matters of Church discipline there was a constant warfare going on between the manor and the manse. Lady Bass appears to have been very often in arrear with her tithes, and as often in a state of bristling resentment from the strict oversight and interference of the elders with regard to her servants, she differing considerably from them in her judgment as to what was, and what was not, *lawful* to be done on the ' *Sabbathe Day*.' She was fined on several occasions for these overt acts of her domestics. At one time they had baked some bread for her on a Sunday, she being in Edinburgh, expecting it to arrive on the Monday ; at another time her grieve answered one of her letters on Sunday, as it was important she should get it as soon as possible. For these and other such like offences the fines were pretty heavy, but they were always forthcoming, though the tithes were not, which the Record very clearly states: ' Given be the Ladie Bass for penaltie of her servand quha brak ye Sabbothe, 18s.' (February 4th, 1621). In fact, Lady Bass considered the family very much aggrieved by the Archbishop of St. Andrews, and also by the Presbytery of Dunbar, in their apportioning part of their lands to the minister of Tyninghame for a manse and a glebe. The matter had eventually to be brought into court to be settled ; which it was, in favour of Mr. John Lauder, the minister, by Act of Parliament.

Robert Lauder of Gunsgreene was Bailie of Tyninghame in 1641, and Mr. Robert Lauder, who was notary public, was always styled 'portionar of Tyninghame,' from his charter of certain acres in the Lordship of Tyninghame received from Mr. George Lauder of Bass. He was uncle to Mr. John Lauder the minister, and his brothers, Robert, George, and Alexander, so frequently mentioned in the records. From the names of Patrick Hepburn of Smeaton, George Hepburn, son of Sir Robert Hepburn of Aderstone, Alexander Lauder and William Lauder, in Dunbar, who were witnesses at the baptism of this Mr. Robert Lauder's son George, it is evident that he was on friendly terms with his relatives in the district. We find him also appearing at all public meetings and Church convenings on behalf of Lady Bass and her son, Mr. George Lauder ;

especially about this particular period, when the pecuniary troubles of the Laird and Lady Bass came to a climax. Being utterly unable to meet the demands of their mortgagees, they were compelled most reluctantly to yield to a sale of their beautiful estate of Tyninghame, which passed out of their hands on the 2nd June 1621, being purchased by John, Lord Murray of Lochmaben (afterwards Earl of Annandale) 'for 200,000 merkes.' Seven years later Lord Murray resold it to the first Earl of Haddington for the same sum he had paid to the Lauders. Sir William Fraser says there are still several old folio volumes bearing the name of Lauder of the Bass in the library of Tyninghame, which were no doubt acquired at the last purchase of the estate in 1628.

The national chronicles of this period were anything but cheering—1621 was memorable as a year of drought and consequent famine; 1637 was a year of much sickness; and 1639 a year of war and bloodshed, with universal mourning and sore privation. But the sorrows of Lady Bass were drawing to a close. The sale of the Manor of Tyninghame, and the constant worry of the creditors, evidently hastened her death, for she was at that time a woman over seventy years of age, though of an indomitable, unyielding spirit. It was well for her that the mortal span of life did not permit of her seeing the fatal year 1649, when the ancestral nest on the auld crag passed into the hands of the Earl of Haddington, who had already purchased their old home at Tyninghame.

The next record of any great interest concerning the Bass is dated April 1651, when a requisition was sent to the keeper, 'that the Bass might be made secure for the registers, as it had been in a former day of calamity'; and it is added, 'The Laird of Wauchton, to whom that strength belonged, being personallie present, most gladly offered to receive them, promising utmost care to secure and preserve them from all danger.' In 1652 these records were ordered by Cromwell's Parliament 'to be packed in a cask and sent to the Tower of London, there to remain in the same custody that the other records that came out of Scotland are.' Consequently many of our Scotch records were burnt in the House of Commons in the conflagration of 1834.

'The former day of calamity' mentioned above was the battle of Dunbar, 3rd September 1650, after which the highly prized ancient Bible, which had been presented to the church at Tyninghame by John, Lord Murray, and the bell and public records had all been deposited on the Bass for safety. The Record[1] for November 2nd, 1651, tells us that 'Twa pounds, eight shillings were given to Johne Nisbett, debursed by him for bringing out the *mort-cloth* and Church Bible out of Tantallon, and carrying them from thence in and out of the

[1] *Churches of St. Baldred.* By A. J. Ritchie.

Bass.' This seems to be the last of Mr. John Lauder's interesting records, comprising the most minute events in the parish for the space of thirty years; giving us a wonderfully concise picture of Scottish life in a rural district in the seventeenth century. The births, deaths, and marriages in his immediate family and that of his three brothers, his two sisters, Jean and Isobell, and their respective cousins, are all duly recorded. Mr. John Lauder the minister's brother George died in 1644, and his brother Robert was evicted, with his schoolmaster, under the new liturgy; but was eventually restored to his benefice, in conjunction with his son George, in 1674. Mr. John Lauder lived to see the restoration of monarchy, and the introduction of Episcopacy, in the reign of Charles II. How he managed to keep his charge and escape the fate of his ministerial brethren who were confined in the stronghold of the Bass, is not recorded. He died at Tyninghame in 1662. In 1676 we find Mr. George Lauder, formerly of Bass, appealing to the brethren 'on behalf of the old bridge of Whitekirk,' which was in a most ruinous condition; and as it was evidently one of the legal uses of money left for 'pious purposes' to build bridges with it, his request was granted, especially as the church at Tyninghame had always maintained a supervision of its own old wooden bridge over the Tyne, which had at an early date replaced the primitive stepping-stones and the ferry-boat. There is a very rustic flavour about the annual church entries '*for cartloads of whins from the Law*,' to lay upon the bridge at Tyninghame; but naturally enough parish ministers with their glebe acres were as much interested in such matters as the farmers.

There is no mention made of Mr. George Lauder ever having been married, so that with him the younger branch of the Lauder family seems to have died out, all the land having melted away bit by bit, 'till it ended in a quantity only sufficient to furnish a resting-place for the bones of its proprietor.'[1]

There is a manuscript volume in the Advocates' Library, in which the famous Maggie Lauder figures as a woman of masculine capacity and a heroine of no small degree. The anecdote is as follows:—

'There hath been a tradition in the burgh of North Berwick and county about, handed down from father to son, that when Oliver Cromwell, that grand usurper, hypocrite, and great wicked man, lay with his army encamped about Dunbar, before the battle of Doonhill, that he sent a party to North Berwick, where Sir Robert Lauder, then of the Bass, had his house, with barnyard and other office houses. The party entered the barn, where the corn was sacked up ready to be carried out to be sown. The party having offered to carry off the corn for the use of their master, the Lord Protector (as they called

[1] Sir Thomas Dick Lauder, *Scottish Rivers*.

him) and his army, Sir Robert's servant went into the house and acquainted Mistress Margaret—*alias* Maggie Lauder—Sir Robert's sister, who had the management of his family affairs. She immediately ordered the sharpest knife and a flail to be brought to her, and went into the barn, where, after upbraiding the men, she ripped up the sacks, and managed the flail with such dexterity that she beat off the party; for which she most deservedly may be accounted amongst the greatest and most glorious heroines of that age. Sir Robert was obliged to abscond because he was a Royalist.'

The recorder of this tradition could hardly have been aware that the last Sir Robert Lauder of Bass died in 1597, and consequently never did, and never could have either seen or heard of such a being as the 'grand usurper' and 'wicked hypocrite' Oliver Cromwell. Had he written 'George Lauder, late of the Bass,' the story might have gained full credence, for he was an old bachelor and needed some such kindly dame as 'Mistress Margaret' to look after his household affairs. As for Sir Robert, truly enough he was denounced as a Royalist, but unfortunately it was for his loyalty to Queen Mary, not Charles II. It is also traditionally stated that the 'bonnie Maggie Lauder' of Anster Fair, who danced to the pipes of Rob the Ranter was none other than the *sonsy* daughter of this same Sir Robert Lauder, Laird of Bass. If this old ballad was written, as it is said, by Francis Semple of Beltrees in 1642, then may it not also refer to this doughty heroine of the flail?

A very different heroine is the 'bonnie Maggie Lauder' of William Tennant's exquisitely humorous poem, also called 'Anster Fair,' in the time of King James V., wherein he relates how 'Fair Maggie's hand was won by mighty Rob the Ranter.'

To enable us to understand how much the present princely mansion, gardens, and policies at Tyninghame differ from the very moderate dimensions of the old manor-house in the days of Lady Bass, we must not forget that the original village of Tyninghame, and the church in which the recorder, Mr. John Lauder, preached, now lie buried beneath the green sward and the magnificent trees within the enclosed policy immediately surrounding the house; not a vestige of the old village remaining to tell us the site of the market cross or the village manse; the only fragment of stonework left being two beautiful Norman arches of the ancient church of St. Baldred, erected long prior to the Reformation, and which for many generations stood in the centre of the parish kirkyard. This relic of the past is so carefully enclosed by trees and evergreen shrubs as to be at certain seasons of the year perfectly hidden from view, and being scrupulously guarded from visitors to the grounds very few even know of its existence. The reason for this great seclusion is its sacred-

THE LAUDERS OF TYNINGHAME 213

ness in the eyes of the noble proprietors, who have for three centuries made it their family burying-ground, and a more secluded and restful 'God's-acre' could not be found ; the very soil is sacred, and the elements palpitating with memories of the past, with nought but the morning hymns of the feathered tribes to break the stillness of the air. Within this sequestered spot there is an ancient tomb, with a recumbent form, weather-beaten and defaced. The

ANCIENT TOMB IN THE RUINS OF ST. BALDRED'S CHURCH AT TYNINGHAME.

universally accepted tradition is that the effigy represents an abbess—name unknown. History in this instance is more silent than the grave, for here the very stones speak for themselves.

In the first place it is difficult to conjecture why the lady has been called an abbess, seeing that the whole style of dress is undoubtedly that of a lady of rank about the period of James II. or James III. Had the lady been an abbess, whatever may have been the degree of her former position in society, she would unquestionably have been portrayed in the habit of her religious order. The heraldic bearings also refute the supposition, and disclose more than a mere name could have done; for history is sometimes written in stone, which if men forget the stones do not. To begin with, the lady's dress is decidedly that of a person of position and importance, and the head-dress, such as was worn by the nobility in the fifteenth century; at which time the caul was usually made of some quilted material, such as satin or cloth of gold, richly embroidered, and set with precious stones, the whole being covered with a veil, supported on wires bent in front to the shape of a heart, with double lappets behind the head.

Notwithstanding the dilapidations of this sculptured figure, these characteristics are most clearly discernible, with careful scrutiny. The dress with its ample folds has been beautifully decorated, having also a girdle of that period set with jewels, passing round the waist, and then falling almost to the feet. The necklace is also a marked feature, from which is suspended a large lozenge-shaped locket or brooch—decidedly not a cross, as it unquestionably would have been had the lady been an abbess.

Lying at her feet, as was most customary on the tombs of the nobility at that time, are the sculptured remains of two of her favourite dogs—one apparently a greyhound, and the other a small poodle or lap-dog. With careful examination, the limbs and position of each are quite discernible to those versed in monumental effigies.

In front of the tombstone, below the slab on which the figure reclines, are several shields, which it is impossible to decipher with any degree of accuracy, seeing they are at present sunk half-way below the surface of the earth, which has been increasing about them from generation to generation, even to the extent of entirely covering the base of the beautiful pillars of the Norman arches. But there is not the slightest doubt about the four centre shields being bordered with cinquefoils, and the first shield on the right being charged with a fer-de-moline.

Had the lady been attired as an abbess, it would not have been difficult to conjecture her personality, for there had been several prioresses in succession, both from the Lauder family and that of Home, in the convent at North Berwick, but the heraldic bearings on the upper part of the tomb put identity past all conjecture. Startling as the assertion may appear, we feel these coats-of-arms warrant our assuming that so far from being an abbess, this silent, mysterious lady was the wife and widow of two husbands. If our rendering is at all correct, we would still further say that we believe the lady was none other than Mary Douglas, Dowager Countess of Angus, who afterwards became the wife of Sir John Carmichael, who died in 1436. Such a bold assertion no doubt demands proof—historically and heraldically. We can only give the links as we have searched them out, knowing full well that nothing short of a marriage certificate can be deemed *infallible* in proving the identity of wives and widows.

We will commence, however, with the heraldic shields, and then follow up the historical links; because, armed with these, it will be much easier to make the stones speak for themselves. As seen in our illustration,[1] this ancient monument bears three shields, the uppermost being charged with the old Douglas arms, the three stars wonderfully distinct, but the heart somewhat defaced. The shield to the right is blank, which also has its own significance. The shield to the left bears the arms of Carmichael of that ilk, which as given by Sir David Lindsay is 'Argent, a fess wreathed, azure and gules.' In this instance the shield is placed on a banneret, with a star decoration. This also marks the personality of the bearer, and renders the second shield necessary, because no husband could impale his wife's arms with his own on an ensign or banner, it being used exclusively for combatants in battle or tournament; and according to Sandford, 'No husband impaling his wife's arms with his own can surround the shield with the Order of the Garter or any other order.' The fact of this decorated banner-shield being upon the lady's tomb, proves her to be the widow of the bearer of it, and at her death her own family coat-of-arms would undoubtedly be placed upon her tomb, in conjunction with it, if she were titled in her own right. The escutcheon, therefore, reveals the family, while history unfolds the name.

In order to unravel this silent mystery, we must take a glance at some of the chivalrous events transpiring at that particular period; and fortunately we need not search in vain, for it is an historical fact that Sir John Carmichael of that ilk joined the band of Scottish warriors who were sent to the assistance of Charles VI. of France against the English. Setting forth, therefore, under the banner of Archibald, Earl of Douglas, in whose lordship his lands of Kirkmychel lay, Sir John was present at the battle of Beaugé in Anjou, in April 1422, where he signalised his valour by unhorsing the Duke of Clarence, the English general, who was immediately slain by the Earl of Buchan and others, thus deciding the fate of the day in favour of the united French and Scottish armies. By this achievement Sir John Carmichael attained the highest martial honour, being made a knight-banneret on the field of battle, and having

[1] Taken with the kind permission of the Earl of Haddington.

broken his spear in the encounter with the Duke, he obtained also the addition to his family arms of a hand holding a broken spear, which is still the crest of his descendants. These honours he received from Archibald Douglas, as Commander-in-Chief of the Scottish army ; but King Charles of France also bestowed upon him the Order of the Star, the highest dignity in the rank of chivalry which France could bestow, the King himself being one of the thirty knights of the order.

The Carmichael arms, the banneret and the star of France, are all clearly visible on the old tomb at the ruin of St. Baldred's church at Tyninghame. But what about the lady? Simply this, that all heralds appear to agree in stating that Sir John Carmichael married the Countess Dowager of Angus, and Burke calls her ' Mary Douglas of the Angus family,'[1] showing the paternal line from whence she came. The chief difficulty now lies in the identification of the special Mary Douglas—and to find which of the innumerable branches of the Douglas family she belonged to. There are several Maries among them ; but seeing we have no register of births and baptisms about that date (1400), and heralds make a point of ignoring the daughters of ancient families, unless they were heiresses, we shall only venture to suggest that she might probably be the youngest daughter of James, Earl of Abercorn, seventh Earl of Douglas—whose eldest son William was stabbed by King James II. at Stirling Castle. Her tomb, however, being at Tyninghame would lead us to suppose that as a Douglas her maiden home would be Tantallon Castle ; and we have no hesitation in saying that we believe the effigy to represent the said Mary Douglas, Countess Dowager of Angus, and also that she outlived her second husband, Sir John Carmichael. This the heralds have registered, by the position of the upper shield, and the blankness of that on the right-hand side.

The story they tell us in the language of heraldry seems to be, that when at his death this shield of Sir John Carmichael was placed on the tomb to the left, not being able to impale the paternal arms of his wife, they were naturally placed opposite, on a separate shield—which could only bear the simple Douglas coat, as widows who married a second time could not continue to quarter the first husband's arms with their own. Which fact seems also to help in confirming our supposition as to the identity of the lady—for the Fer-de-Moline, or cross-crosslet on the first shield on the base, represents an Umfraville —whose interesting family history we have not space to enter into here, but who were undoubtedly summoned to Parliament as Earls of Angus at that period ; and Godfrey, the last of that race bearing the title, was slain at Beaugé

---

[1] Burke's *Extinct Peerage*, p. 105 ; also, *The Scots Compendium of the Peerage*, vol. ii. p. 108.

CHANCEL ARCH OF ST. BALDRED'S CHURCH, TYNINGHAME.

THE LAUDERS OF TYNINGHAME

in 1422, the title lapsing until it was bestowed by the King on the Stewarts eventually passing into the Douglas family through Margaret, daughter and heiress of Thomas Stewart, Earl of Angus, marrying William, Earl of Douglas. The blank shield still further elucidates our theory of Lady Mary Douglas. If, as we suppose, the Douglas arms were sculptured on the corresponding shield to Sir John Carmichael's at his death in 1436, they would unquestionably have been *erased* in 1455, at the time of the rebellion of the Douglases, after the assassination of their chief by the King, when the whole family rose in arms, and were denounced as rebels, attainted and banished the kingdom, their arms being publicly torn and reversed. The complete smoothness of this blank shield points to its having been deliberately erased, and the arms obliterated by a mason under command. This fact alone is sufficient to warrant our assumption that the lady was a daughter of the house of Douglas, and that the upper shield bearing her own arms was placed on the tomb with her effigy, after her death, when the Angus branch of the Douglas family had been pardoned and restored to their honours and kingly favour.

This fine old tomb must have formed a most interesting feature in the interior of the beautiful little Norman church in the days of the warrior knights and barons of Bass. But the Church of St. Baldred was standing long before the Lauders came to the Bass in the twelfth century, and the Monastery of Tyninghame also, from whence they received their charter, and at which they yearly delivered their 'pound of white wax.' It was considered ancient even then, having been founded by 'Saint Balthere the anchorite,' popularly known as St. Baldred of the Bass, who died in 756. We are told by Simeon of Durham that the Lindisfarne diocese, in which this monastery was situated, extended 'from the Tyne to the Tweed, including the district of Teviotdale.... Its possessions beyond the Tweed consisted of the districts on the north bank from the sea to the river Leader, and the whole land which belonged to the Monastery of St. Balthere, which is called Tyninghame, from the Lammermuirs to the mouth of the river Esk.' The chronicle of Melrose informs us that 'immediately after he had burned and plundered the Church of Saint Baldred in Tyninghame, King Anlaf died.'[1]

The present ruined arches, therefore, evidently belong to a church which must have been re-erected or restored before the eleventh century, for the privilege of sanctuary was granted to Tyninghame by pious King David, making it quite a little city of refuge with its monastery and its 'protection stone' at the church altar. Being on the highway between Edinburgh, Dunbar,

[1] *An Old Kirk Chronicle.* By Rev. Hately Waddell.

and Berwick, St. Baldred's shrine was frequented by ambassadors and bishops, pilgrims and crusaders, whose arms and banners were blessed at the altar. In those days, at the first sound of the reading of the 'Gospel of Peace,' each crusader rose and pointed his sword towards 'the Book' in token of his oath to defend it by force of arms. The pillars of the beautiful Normanesque arch of the chancel still bear the marks of the consecration of Scottish dirks and daggers, which, to ensure victorious use upon their southern foes, were sharpened

RUINS OF ST. BALDRED'S CHURCH, TYNINGHAME.

on the pillars nearest the altar. These arches are all that is now left of this mediæval church, which appears to have been about eighty-five feet long, divided into four spaces which Mr. John Lauder in his records designates 'roumes.' These rooms had seats on each side, and the one in the chancel had two lofts or galleries, one for the Earl of Haddington and the other for the Laird of Scougal. The Lauder seats were exactly opposite the tomb of Lady Mary Douglas, on the north side of the church, not far from the pulpit, which was placed almost under the eastmost arch; and the door for the minister to enter by is supposed to have opened out of the apse to the south. The church

THE LAUDERS OF TYNINGHAME

was not fully seated, the whole centre being left for the women, who brought their own 'stoules' or 'creepies.' The portion between the west arch and the entrance door, which extended out from it, was used as a school on week-days, the schoolmaster living in the steeple or bell-tower, where stray wanderers and waifs were also lodged. Higher up the 'dowes' found shelter, and sometimes lower down, for Mr. John Lauder tells us 'the beadle' got an allowance 'for pouther tae shoot the doos because they filet the seats.' In the early days this steeple had no 'big bell.' There was the usual handbell, which was rung four times every Sunday through the village to summon the flock to the various services, and also on funeral occasions, when the beadle walked in front of the cortége with ominous din. The jougs for delinquents were placed at the kirk door, that all entering might take warning; and the indispensable 'stool of repentance' stood inside the church, a 'wooden erection raised on turf and stone,' close to the pulpit, from whence the culprit was most solemnly exhorted and admonished, condemned and absolved, 'in presence of the pepill publicklie.'

It was through the instrumentality of Maister John Lauder that the 'great bell' was procured for the steeple, though it was presented by the 'Richt Honourable Johne Murray in 1625; after which any one desiring the 'big bell' to be rung for a burial had to pay 'ten shillings Scots, the one half thereof to belong to the beadle for the ringing the said bell, and the other half to the poor.' Mr. John never forgot the poor, and when the church funds were low, he helped them most willingly out of his 'ain purse.' The 'hinging of the bell' cost £159, 8s. 6d. Scots. The church tower is supposed to have been about seventy feet high; and the bell was rung from the outside, with a strong rope, which Mr. Waddell tells us was 'turned every six months and changed every year.' When the church was cleaned and 'decorit,' Mr. John Lauder added a new pulpit, also out of his 'ain purse'; but the communion cups and baptismal basins were got by subscription, or what was then called 'stent.' The new tokens were not struck until three years after the death of Maister John.

The church stood in the churchyard, and the village stood close to the church and the river, east and west, the manse being at the west end, in the main street of the village. There were small hamlets here and there of a few houses each, the inhabitants mostly depending on fishing; and for their accommodation, and that of the children going to and from school, a ferry-boat was instituted and kept up by the kirk-session, the old stepping-stones in times of flood being both dangerous and impassable, which Æneas Sylvius, the Pope's nuncio, found in 1435. When going on pilgrimage to the holy well at Whitekirk, he had to walk barefooted for ten miles over frozen, rocky ground, going round from the Monastery of Tyninghame by Prestonkirk, and over the old bridge, which was repaired two hundred and thirty years after by Mr. George Lauder. This holy well of Black Agnes, the founder of Whitekirk, has been entirely lost both for church and people for many a long day—

> 'A little lowly hermitage it was,
> Down in a dale, hard by a forest's side,
> Far from resort of people that did pass
> In travel to and fro—a little wide
> There was an holy chapel edified,
> Wherein the hermit duly wont to say
> His holy things each morn and eventide.
> Thereby a crystal stream did gently play,
> Which from a sacred fountain welled forth alway.'
> SPENSER.

Very little of the present princely mansion at Tyninghame can be said to have belonged to the Lauders of the Bass. Some portions of the outer walls, when it was enlarged by Lady Bass in 1617, have been incorporated with the new building, which was completed about 1830; but the whole policy has been remodelled upon the site of the ancient village. Of the monastery, church, and farm not a vestige is left as a landmark but those two exquisite Norman arches in the sacred mausoleum of the noble house of Haddington.

TEMPLAR'S TOMBSTONE, TYNINGHAME.

The well-known magnificent gardens at Tyninghame extend over seventeen acres of ground: a perfect marvel of colour arrangement in each successive season.

To those who revel in landscape beauty, nothing could be more delightful than a drive through the lovely Binning woods, which stretch along the coast for more than two miles and a half,—the sylvan enterprise of Thomas, sixth Earl of Haddington, resulting in the present magnificent scenery, so picturesquely interspersed with woodland, river, rock, and sea.

The pretty little village of Tyninghame has all the rural charms of cottages overgrown with roses and honeysuckle, whose 'gardens shine with apple-bending boughs; where the white lilies mingle with the rose.' It was in this

THE LAUDERS OF TYNINGHAME

village that the present Earl of Haddington discovered an ancient Templar tombstone serving as a doorstep to one of the cottages. His lordship had it removed from its desecrated position to the burial-place within the ruin of St. Baldred's Church. It appears as though the two ends of the stone had been shortened in order to make it fit the cottar's humble threshold. The following measurements of its present dimensions were taken by Mr. Brotherston, head gardener on the estate, whose genuine antiquarian taste and genial kindliness greatly enhanced the pleasure we experienced in examining these bygone relics of generations long since buried beneath the ancestral trees of Tyninghame. The length of the Templar stone is 2 feet 11¾ inches, the width being 1 foot 9¾ inches. The stem of the cross is from 2 to 3 inches wide, and the length from tip to tip 5¼ inches.

WHITEKIRK TOKEN, AND BOSS
FROM THE PORCH.

CHAPTER XIX

THE LAUDERS OF HALTOUN AND BRUNTISFIELD

'One age is now: another that succeeds
Extirping all things which the former breeds;
Another follows that, doth new times raise,
New years, new months, new weeks, new hours, new days:
Mankind thus goes like rivers to the spring,
And in the earth all have their burying.'
                                WILLIAM BROWNE.

HE Halton branch of the Lauders descended from Sir Alan de Lawedre and Alicia Campbell his spouse, daughter of Sir Colin Campbell of Loch Awe, ninth of the Argyll family. Sir Alan had purchased this extensive estate, which is designated as '*the whole town of Haltoun with the pertinents*,' from John de Haltoun, the King's true tenant, in consequence of the said proprietor having fallen into very distressed circumstances. The charter was granted by King Robert II. as 'Baron Ratho, and superior thereof,' signed at Kyndrocht on the 26th July 1377,[1] just three years after the same lands had been leased by the King to John de Haltoun, whose deed was signed and sealed at 'Skoone.'

Sir Alan, whose acts we have already recorded, evidently lived until 1401, as in that year William de Naper, fourth Baron of Merchiston, Constable of Edinburgh Castle, witnessed a charter to Alan de Lawedre, who must have been fully ninety years of age at the time. Of his five sons, the eldest, Sir Robert, inherited Lauder Tower

COAT-OF-ARMS—LAUDER OF HALTOUN.

[1] *Registrum Magni Sigilli*, 1306-1424, p. 148, No. 104.

THE LAUDERS OF HALTOUN AND BRUNTISFIELD 223

and the Bass; and George, the second son, became first Baron Lauder of Haltoun. He had already obtained 'the lands of Sornefawlache, at Greinhill, in the Barony of Wistoun,' from Sir James Sandilands of Calder by the resignation of Marion Pittendreich.[1] Sir George de Lawedre married Lord Douglas's sister,[2] and had one son, Alexander, who succeeded him In 1408 Sir Alexander, second Laird of Halton, married Elizabeth Forster, daughter of Sir John Forster of Corstorfyne, and according to custom he resigned his lands at Ratho into the hands of his superior, to obtain a regrant in the conjunct names of himself and his spouse. The deed is granted by Robert, Duke of Albany, the governor, on the 17th December in the parish church of Dundee, and Sir Alexander's uncle, William, who had that year been nominated Bishop of Glasgow, witnessed the charter.[3] Both nephew and uncle went to England together in 1423 on the same embassy, William Lawdre being then also Chancellor of Scotland.

Sir Alexander Lawdre of Haltoun is mentioned again as obtaining a safeconduct from Henry VI. on the 30th November 1433;[4] but he must have died the following year, judging from an entry in the Chamberlain Rolls, at the date 5th June 1434, on which day a sum of money (£13, 6s. 8d.) is entered as 'received from Thomas Cranstoun from the lands of Haltoun and Norton belonging to the heir of the late Sir Alexander de Lawdre, Knight, within the shire of Linlithgow, for the term of Pentecost only, in the year 1433, and he debits himself with nothing for the term of Martinmas following, because the said heir entered and took possession of the lands.' This was Sir William Lauder, third Laird of Haltoun, whose name is mentioned in the passport for the safe-conduct granted by Henry VI. in 1450 to the Earl of Douglas and his retinue, on their way to and from Rome, the earl having resolved to travel and also to remain some time in England, being out of favour in Scotland owing to his having on various occasions openly manifested his contempt for the young King's authority. 'In personal wealth and power, the Earl of Douglas not only approached to, but greatly exceeded the King himself,' who had mortally offended him by taking from him the important post of Lieutenant-General of Scotland, because it had afforded him such unlimited power that he had become too ambitious and very dangerous to the State.

As the Lauders of Haltoun were connected by marriage with the Douglas family, they appear upon several occasions to have sided with the earls in their rebellion; but the Lauders of the Bass were invariably staunch in their loyalty

[1] Robertson's *Index*, p. 144.
[2] *Peerage*, Crawfurd, p. 91.
[3] *Registrum Magni Sigilli*, 1306-1424, p. 239, No. 42.
[4] Rymer, vol. x. p. 537.

to the Crown. Upon this occasion, however, there seems to have been a Lauder from both branches in the earl's retinue—Sir William Lauder of Haltoun, and Sir Alan de Lawedre of Bass. The latter we have already mentioned in connection with the Douglas embassy to the court of Charles VII., King of France, as having been sent with Sir Malcolm Fleming to do homage for the Duchy of Touraine. Buchanan and Godscroft call him John; but Holinshed and all the early Scottish historians call him 'Alane of Lawder.'[1] Another reason for the malcontentment of the Earl of Douglas at that time was the favour shown at court to Lord Crichton, who had brought home the young Princess Mary of Guelder as Queen. Now Crichton was the avowed foe of the Douglases, as shown in the treacherous murder of the young Earl William and his brother David in Edinburgh Castle, cousins to this William, who was eighth Earl of Douglas, and fifth Duke of Touraine. Retiring to his own castle therefore in disgust, the earl determined to go to Rome, it being the year of the Pope's jubilee.

'Thither the Earl of Douglas went,' writes Abercromby, 'and with him his second brother, Sir James (who, being bred a scholar, was, though not in orders, expectant of the Bishopric of Dunkeld), as also the Lords Hamilton, Gray, Seton, Salton, Oliphant, Forbes, Urquhart of Cromarty, Fraser of Philorth, *Lawder of Bass* (previously called Alan Lawder[2]), Campbel, Calder, etc. These noblemen and gentlemen were so very numerous and so well equipped, that as they made a very noble figure in their passage through Flanders and France, so they filled even Rome itself with the expectation of their arrival. The Earl of Douglas was more particularly honoured and caressed wherever he came, the fame of his ancestors being yet fresh in those countries, and their services at Beaugé, Verneuil, etc., in the highest esteem with the French King Charles, who still lived and gratefully remembered them.'[3] In the meantime Douglas's enemies at home availed themselves of his absence to injure his reputation with the King by accusing him of flagrant acts of misused power while in office as Lord-Lieutenant. He was consequently summoned to appear in judgment, at which his brother and his vassals rebelled; but they were won back to their allegiance by the King's clemency. Not so the earl, whose anger was roused by the ill reports set afloat, which even 'reached the ears of the Scots pilgrims at Rome,' so that many of his followers deserted his standard, for which reason he desired the passport from King Henry VI. on his return to England, for a safe-conduct for himself and his still numerous retinue, which

[1] Holinshed, vol. v. p. 429.
[2] Abercromby's *Martial Atchievements*, vol. ii. p. 328. [3] *Ibid.* pp. 349, 350.

passport 'promised them protection and safety within King Henry's territories during the space of three years.' Besides his own name, and that of his brother Sir James, we find 'Sir James Hamilton, Sir Alexander Home, Sir William Cranstoun, Sir Nicholas Campbel, John Clark, Andrew Gray, *William Lawder* (of Haltoun), Thomas Cranstoun, Andrew Kerr, Charles Murray, George Haliburton, John Doddes, John Greenlaw, George Finlaw, *Alan Lawder*, and James Bishop'; who with eighty more in their company, 'whether noble or ignoble,' as the record has it, are promised protection. The Earl of Douglas had far too much ambition to remain voluntarily at the English court for three years; therefore, within less than one year we find him in Scotland again, and reinstated in the King's council and favour. In April of the following year, 1451, his love of travel, pomp, and show is again in request, and he is sent by King James to Newcastle to confer with the English monarch about the breaches of the late truce. This time the train consisted not of his own retinue merely, but those also who were joined with him by the Sovereign in his commission—a goodly company of the highest nobles in the land, among whom were the Bishops of Dunkeld and Brechin, the Earls of Angus and Crawford, the Lords Sommerville, Montgomery, Glammis, and Gray, Sir John David of Murray, and Alexander Nairn of Sandford. But very little real business appears to have been done, Douglas having an eye to his own personal desire to retain the good-will of the English King in his already meditated revolt against James II., in case he or his followers might require it; consequently, the next month after his King's commission, he obtained another safe-conduct for himself and his own retinue, and one year's protection from Henry. Besides the earl's three brothers—Sir James Douglas, Archibald Douglas Earl of Moray, and Hugh Douglas, Earl of Ormond—there are several knights and gentlemen, and among them still the same two members of the Lauder family —Sir William Lawder of Haltoun, and Alan Lawder of Bass. We mention this because of the after-result. This protection included also sixty-seven retainers, 'armed or unarmed, on horse or on foot,' and most of the names enumerated in the document were afterwards engaged on the side of Douglas in his rebellion. But it is of Sir William Lauder of Haltoun that we would speak; and it is somewhat difficult to say what his real position was with regard to the King and Douglas, but an old chronicle distinctly tells us that he was the messenger chosen the following year by the King to request the presence of the Earl of Douglas at the court held at the Castle of Stirling. We are not told whether Sir William Lauder knew that this invitation was of no good import to the earl, or whether being a friend he was simply chosen to throw Douglas off his guard, for the earl had indeed good reason to fear the King's resentment, having made himself most obnoxious by his late cruelty in putting to death Lord Colville, Sir John Herries, Sir John Sandilands of Calder, and particularly Maclellan, called the 'Tutor of Bomby.' According to the baronial rights of pit and gallows these death-warrants passed muster as *executions*, but in reality they were revengeful, cold-blooded murders, and as such the King regarded them; but according to the feudal law, there was no redress but reprisal. There is no reason to believe, however, that King James had any other premeditated intention in his request than the immediate curbing of the earl's power by making him break his iniquitous bond with the Earl of Crawford called 'Beardie,' or the 'Tiger-Earl,' from his ferocity, and the Earl of Ross, whose extensive domains in the north of Scotland gave him almost royal authority. These three earls combined possessed by far the larger share of the King's dominions, and had made an alliance to show their contempt of the King's authority, 'that they would take part in each other's quarrels against every man, *the King himself not excepted.*'

Douglas knew full well that his daring breach of all the laws of equity had made him many enemies among the nobility, especially in his last dastardly murder of Maclellan, the guardian of the young Lord of Bomby (ancestor of the Earls of Kirkcudbright). Maclellan was one of those who, in his true loyalty to his Sovereign, refused to join the earl's league, defying his threats, which so enraged Douglas that he assaulted his castle, took him prisoner, and carried him off to his stronghold at Thrieve, situated on an island in the river Dee in Galloway—a castle with as bad a reputation as that of Earl Patrick Stewart at Scalloway. The King was greatly concerned when he heard what Douglas had done; and, in order to prevent Maclellan from sharing the fate of Colville and Herries, he wrote a letter himself to the Earl of Douglas, 'entreating him as a favour, rather than urging as a command,' that he would deliver Maclellan into the hands of his uncle, Sir Patrick Gray. Sir Patrick went in person with the letter to Thrieve Castle. 'Douglas received him just as he had arisen from dinner, and with much apparent civility, declined to speak with Gray on the occasion of his coming until Sir Patrick also had dined, saying, "It is ill talking between a full man and a fasting."' But this courtesy was only a pretence to gain time to do a very cruel and lawless action. Guessing that Sir Patrick Gray's visit respected the life of Maclellan, he resolved to hasten his execution before opening the King's letter.

Thus, while he was feasting Sir Patrick with every appearance of hospitality, he caused his unhappy kinsman to be led out and beheaded in the courtyard of the castle. When dinner was over, Gray presented the King's letter, which Douglas received and read over with every testimony of profound respect. He then thanked Sir Patrick for the trouble he had taken in bringing him so gracious a letter from his Sovereign, especially considering he was not at present on good terms with his Majesty. 'And,' he added, 'the King's demand shall instantly be granted, the rather for your sake.' The Earl then took Sir Patrick by the hand, and led him to the castle-yard, where the body of Maclellan was still lying.

'Sir Patrick,' said he, as his servants removed the blood-stained cloth which covered the body, 'you have come a little too late. There lies your sister's son, but he wants the head. The body is, however, at your service.'

'My lord,' said Gray, suppressing his indignation, 'if you have taken his head, you may dispose of the body as you will.'

But when he had mounted his horse, which he instantly called for, his resentment broke out, in spite of the dangerous situation in which he was placed. 'My lord,' said he, 'if I live, you shall bitterly pay for this day's work.' So saying, he turned his horse and galloped off.

'To horse and chase him!' cried Douglas; and if Gray had not been well mounted, he would in all probability have shared the fate of his nephew. He was closely pursued till near Edinburgh, a space of fifty or sixty miles.'[1]

Such being the man, it is easy to understand why King James chose Sir William Lauder of Halton, a friend of Douglas, to carry his invitation to the earl, which invitation the earl boldly accepted, on condition that he received a safe-conduct under the Great Seal, signed by the King, pledging his promise that he should be permitted to go to the Court at Stirling Castle and return in safety. Thus protected against personal danger he forthwith set out with Sir William Lauder, and was received graciously by the King, with whom he dined on the following day, the King's real desire being to bring back this powerful noble to his allegiance.

At seven o'clock in the evening supper was served, after which the King led Douglas to his private room, that he might amicably expostulate with him in regard to the treasonable bond he had formed with Crawford and Ross, begging him to relinquish the treaty and return to his former loyalty to the Crown. Douglas absolutely refused to give up the bond, and when the King rose to his dignity and commanded him, the earl only became the more stubborn and haughty in his refusal, which so exasperated the King that, in a fit of passion, he exclaimed, 'By heaven, my lord, if *you* will not break the league *this* shall';

[1] Sir Walter Scott's *Tales of a Grandfather*.

lifting his dagger and plunging it in the earl's throat. Among the few nobles who were present was Sir Patrick Gray, who had sworn vengeance for the death of his nephew: he immediately struck the earl upon the head with his battle-axe, and then several others of the King's bodyguard also stabbed him until the corpse was covered with twenty-six wounds. The unfortunate earl, thus taken unawares, expired without uttering a single word, and another black deed was recorded against the House of Stuart for their retributive harvest in the future.

Whether Sir William Lauder had wittingly or unwittingly participated in the assassination of Douglas we cannot say, but having been made the decoy duck, he was treated by the Douglases as the accomplice of the King, against whose perjured name and broken passport they vented the first outburst of their rage, 'with the sound of five hundred horns and trumpets' paraded through the town. Then James, the eldest brother of the murdered earl, succeeded to the title; and, 'burning for revenge, he took up the quarrel of his house with the King; and Scotland was plunged afresh into a civil war from the Border to the Moray Firth.'[1]

Halton House, which was then a fortified tower, was immediately besieged by the Douglases and taken; but it was eventually recaptured by the Lauders with the King's aid, who sent a large supply of ammunition and men to their assistance. It is even stated that the great *bombard* which was placed on four carts and drawn by a large number of horses, sent by the King, was none other than the famous 'Mons Meg,' which had been forged by the Galloway blacksmith for the siege of Thrieve Castle. There is no doubt whatever about the expense of this coming to the rescue of Halton being paid by the State, for we read in the Chamberlain Rolls[2] of an account being rendered in 1453 at the Exchequer, 'for the hire as well of men as of horses at Haltoun in the time of the siege of the same: and for iron caps, called salattis, given to the servants and archers of the King, and for pitch, bitumen, and carts for the carriage of divers beams, and for the wages and expenses of masons and carpenters present at the Tower of Haltoun.' Considerable damage at the hands of both besiegers and besieged was done to the tower, for which the presence of Mons Meg may in part be answerable; for truly Meg was 'muckle-mouthed,' having an opening two feet three inches and a half wide, from which proceeded a roar more terrible than that of Thisbe's lion, and what was much more effectual, huge bullets made of Galloway granite, which in time drove the Douglases from Halton and also from that dread Castle of Thrieve.

[1] Hill Burton.   [2] Vol. iii. pp. 574, 576; also vol. v. p. 606.

Halton Tower in those days was very like the old Keep of Niddry Castle, built in the same style, at the same period, 'consisting of three storeys with very thick walls, a number of closets and recesses, and a spiral staircase lighted by narrow arrow-holes, winding up sixty feet.' The lower part was merely a large dark chamber massively vaulted in stone, and evidently strongly stanchioned at the window—probably the guardroom of the original fortalice, where the prisoners awaited their summons to 'pit or gallows.'

The year 1454 was one of unparalleled calamity for Scotland. The Douglas war-cry resounded throughout the length and breadth of the land, carrying fire and sword and all the miseries of a civil war in its wake, aggravated by an equally dreaded visitation of pestilence and famine. It was as though the bitter cup of desolation could not be reckoned full unless it were overflowing. Silent hearths, burning crops, and wasted fields, instead of the songs of the reapers and garners filled with golden grain. Truly it was no petty quarrel between the Douglases and the King. Still, rivers of Scottish blood could not wipe out that murderous stain of treachery from the royal shield, and only when two of the brothers—Archibald, Earl of Moray, and Hugh, Earl of Ormond— were slain, and James, Earl of Douglas, with his third brother, John, Lord Balveny, had sought refuge and protection in England, did the banished dove of peace return, and not even then with folded wings. Shortly after this (1460) King James himself was killed by the bursting of a cannon at the siege of Roxburgh Castle; but James Douglas remained an outlawed exile for nearly twenty years.

Sir William Lauder of Haltoun died in 1452, the same year that the Earl of Douglas was assassinated, most likely while defending his tower at Haltoun, and he was succeeded by his son, Sir John Lauder, Knight, fourth Laird, who appears to have passed a considerable portion of his time in France. In 1464 he and his kinsman, Alexander Forster, with three other barons and thirty attendants, received a safe-conduct from King Edward IV. for the purpose of visiting the shrines of Picardy. His wife's name is not mentioned in either Peerage or Baronage; but his daughter Mary married Sir James Foulis of Colinton, whose only son left a daughter, Margaret, who married Captain Lewis Dick, R.N., fifth son of Sir William Dick of Braid, Knight. Sir John Lauder's eldest son, Sir Alexander, also obtained a protection from Edward IV., and joined his father's party on their return journey after visiting these shrines, whether for healing, or for the performing of sacred vows and donations after the past tragical events is not stated, but Haltoun Tower and all the adjacent lands belonging to the Lauders of Halton must have been in a forfeited condition for a while, as we learn from James II.'s charter to his Queen, Marie of Guelderland, in 1452,[1] that it was in consequence of the forfeiture of the deceased William de Laudre of Haltoune that the King granted to his consort, 'for the dear love he bear her,' the free barony or special regality of all the lands of Haltoune, with the manor-place, also the temple lands of Newtoun, the Plat, Weschal, Nortoun, and the North Raw of Rathou, with the mill thereof, and the annual rents of the town of Gogar, in the sheriffdoms of Edinburgh and Renfrew,' besides the lands of *Brounysfelde*, which had also belonged to the Lauders of Haltoun from 1381.[2]

We cannot wonder that the sons retired to France under these conditions. However, after the death of James II., we find them returning, and obtaining a regrant of their lands in Peebles from James III. in 1472, upon the occasion of the marriage of William Lauder, son and heir-apparent of Sir Alexander Lauder of Haltoun, Knight. These lands comprised Easter and Wester Wormotstoune, and Over and Nether Kedstoune, which Sir Alexander resigned in favour of his son William and his wife Mariota.[3] This was in the month of August, and exactly ten years later, William having died before his father, the King grants to the second son, George, now heir-apparent, and to his wife Katherine, conjointly, some of the lands of Halton, and part of Norton in the Barony of Ratho, which Sir Alexander Lauder, his father, had resigned. This deed is dated 25th August 1482,[4] and in 1490 the King restored the lands of Bruntsfield to Sir Alexander; Henry Cant, to whom they had been leased, personally resigning them.[5] Sir George Lauder had evidently already won his spurs, as he is called the Knight of Quhitslaid (Whitslaid), which property belonged heritably to the second son of the Halton family.

Alexander, the third son, who was a burgess of Edinburgh, upon his

[1] *Register of the Great Seal*, 1424-1503, No. 544.
[2] Brounsfield Charter by King Robert II. to Alan de Lawedre of the lands of Boroumore, with the pertinents, which belonged to the deceased Richard Broun of Boroumore, within the shire of Edinburgh, and which he resigned in the granter's hands, who had thereupon by charter infeft the deceased William de Lawedre, brother of the said Alan, therein by charter. To be held of the granter in fee and heritage for payment of one silver penny at the Boroumore at the feast of St. John the Baptist yearly, if asked, in name of blench. Dated at Edinburgh, 4th June 1381.—*Register of the Great Seal*, 1306-1424, p. 162, No. 8.
[3] *Register of the Great Seal*, 1424-1503, No. 1069. [4] *Ibid.* No. 1517.
[5] *Ibid.* No. 1988; also *Acta Dominorum Concilii*, 1478-1495, p. 146.

Acta, *11th October* 1490.—'In the action and cause pursued by Alexander, Laird of Hawtoun, Knight, against Henry Cant, burgess of Edinburgh, son and heir of the deceased Adam Cant, for the wrongous deferring to resign and upgive the lands of Brownisfield, with their pertinents, contrary to the form of the said deceased Adam's reversion made thereupon, and for the costs and skaith sustained by the said Henry therethrough ; both the said parties being personally present, the letter of reversion made by the said deceased Adam, together with the letter of tack under the seal of the said Alexander made to the said Henry Cant for the term of five years of the same lands, at length seen, heard, and understood, the Lords of

OF HALTOUN AND BRUNTISFIELD 231

marriage with Janet Paterson, in June 1497, obtained a grant from his father, Sir Alexander Lauder, of the lands called 'East Ploughlands of Nortoun, in the town and territory of Nortoun, in the Barony of Ratho'—to be held by them conjointly, from the granter, for two pennies in name of blench. These lands had previously been a portion of the patrimony of George, the second son, who, upon entering into his inheritance as heir-apparent of Halton, in place of his elder brother William deceased, consented to the disposing of them to his younger brother Alexander—who on the 14th August of the same year acquired from his father by purchase, for himself and his wife, Janet Paterson, 'the lands of *Brounisfield*,' with the manor-house and gardens, park, herbarium (or kitchen garden), with the houses, etc., 'except one perticate of land at the east end, adjoining the ditch thereof, in the common muir of Edinburgh.' The purchase-money is not mentioned, but the feu was simply 'a red rose in name of blench,' to be given annually. Among the witnesses to the deed are 'Sir George Lawder (Knight), son and heir-apparent of the granter; Alexander Lawder of Burngrange; Sir Gilbert Lawder, Vicar of Twyname;[1] Robert Lawder, William Lawder, and Thomas Lawder; also John Forestare of Nudri, and Archibald Forestare, his brother.'[2]

The deed is dated and signed at 'Haltoun' (14th August 1497), proving that whatever damage the tower had sustained in the siege, it was sufficiently habitable to be the residence of Sir Alexander and his family. These charters were not confirmed by the King, James IV., until 1516, and during the interim, Sir Alexander Lauder of Haltoun had been Provost of Edinburgh for the years 1501, 1502, and 1503.

After his death in 1505, Sir George Lauder of Whitslaid, his son, became Sir George Lauder, sixth Laird of Haltoun, but the knight does not appear to have been as wealthy as the burgess, for while his brother Alexander was buying estates and serving the King, Sir George was getting terribly in arrear with his rents and feus; and thus we find letters directed, on the 12th May 1508, for distraining him for payment of £20 annually, for nine years preceding 1505, for the rents, etc., of the lands called Bissats, Bells, and Aytoun lands.[3]

This was the year in which Mr. Alexander Lauder was chosen provost of

Council decreets and delivers that the said Henry Cant shall freely resign and upgive in our Sovereign Lord's hands all and sundry the said lands of Brownisfield, with their pertinents, in the most secure wise that can be devised by the said Alexander; like as at more length is contained in the said reversion. They also ordain that the said Henry Cant shall enjoy the tack of the said lands of Brownisfield for the next five years, commencing from Whitsunday last past, when payment of the sum contained in the reversion was made.'

[1] Twyname in Kirkcudbright, formerly called Campstoun. It has an old castle beside the mains.
[2] *Register of the Great Seal*, 1424-1503, No. 3019.   [3] *Ibid*. No. 3224.

the burgh (1508), and for good service rendered to the King, James IV. grants him an extensive addition to his lands—incorporating them into a free barony, whereby he became Sir Alexander Lauder of Blythe, the lands being those of Thirlstane and Tullosfew, with their dependencies as follows:—'Thirlstane Maynes, Ernisheuch, Egrop, Windeparke, le Heuch, Blythe, Hatherwik, Garmuir, Over Tullos, Nether Tullos, Dodhous, and Simpryn in Berwickshire, which had belonged to William Maitland of Lethingtoun (grandfather of the then existing Sir William Maitland of Lethington), but which had fallen into the King's hands by reason of non-entry of the heir for over twenty-five years, the default amounting to £2861, 15s. This Barony of Blyth was to be held by Alexander Lauder and his wife Janet and their heirs, for service at the head court of the shire of Berwick, within the bailiary of Lauderdale, after the feast of St. Michael, and it was also stipulated that redemption of the lands was reserved to Sir William Maitland of Lethington, within seven years [1]—the bypast rents to be paid to Sir Alexander Lauder or his heirs.

According to the custom of the age, Sir Alexander consecrated a portion of his wealth by dedicating it to the honour of God, founding an altar in the church of St. Giles, on the 30th April 1509,[2] subsequently endowing a chaplainry in this new chapel, which was near the south-western corner of the church, and dedicated to Gabriel the archangel.

This mortification, which is confirmed by the King on the 17th August 1513, consisted of 'an annuity of 15 merks out of the annual rent of 24 merks, derived from that tenement of land of the late Robert Laudere, in the High Street of Edinburgh,[3] with another annuity of 5 merks, and 9 merks in addition to the former sum—also 32s. and 2 merks from other lands for masses, candles, etc.' This deed is witnessed by Mr. James Lawder, and Gilbert Lawder—most probably the same Vicar of Twyname already mentioned, both of whom were sons of Lauder of Haltoun. It is distinctly stated that this donation was granted by Sir Alexander, 'with consent of his wife, Janet Patersoun'—who voluntarily increased it by four merks in her widowhood. The symbolical carvings and ornate pillars supporting the beautifully groined roof of this chapel, made it one of the finest features of the old cathedral of St. Giles, before it 'fell a prey to the Reforming zeal of 1559.' It is still called Lauder's Aisle. Sir Daniel Wilson says, 'It consisted of two arches extending between the porch and the south transept; and in the south wall, between the two windows, a beautiful altar tomb was constructed under a

[1] *Register of the Great Seal of Scotland*, 1424-1503, No. 3348.
[2] *Ibid.* No. 3455.
[3] *Ibid.* No. 3878.'

deep recess, on which a recumbent figure had, no doubt, been originally placed, although it probably disappeared along with the statues and other ancient decorations,'[1] when 'the images and altaris of Sanctgeilis Kirk were distroyit and brint.' Sir Daniel Wilson, among other writers, mentions that Alexander Lauder of Blyth 'filled the office of Provost in the years 1501-1503 ; and again in 1508-1510,' which statement at first sight seems quite feasible, and arises from the frequent occurrence of the name Alexander, in the Halton family, without any other distinctive appellation. The fact of their names being thus entered on the old manuscript 'List of Aldermen and Provosts of the city of Edinburgh, whose names are on record from the year 1296 to the Union of Scotland and England in 1707,'[2] makes it appear even more probable. Had the proper designation of Haltoun or Blyth been appended to the name of 'Alexander Lauder,' this error would never have arisen, for in the public records it is clearly stated that Sir Alexander Lauder of Haltoun, who granted a charter to William Ker of Yare, on the 16th April 1504, was Provost of Edinburgh, one of the witnesses being 'Alexander Lawder, son of the said Alexander, Provost of Edinburgh.'[3]

Sir Alexander Lauder of Haltoun died in 1505, being succeeded by his son Sir George ; the Alexander here mentioned as witness was the third son of Haltoun, and he did not obtain his Barony of Blyth until 1509, in the charter of which it is narrated that it was granted by James IV. for 'the good services of his servitor, Alexander Lauder, Provost of Edinburgh.'

He had been elected the year before for three years, and was again re-elected in 1511-1513, when he was succeeded by Archibald Douglas, the aged Earl of Angus (renowned at Lauder Bridge as 'Bell-the-Cat') under whose banner he marched at the head of the burghers to the fatal field of Flodden, where Sir Archibald lost his two sons and two hundred followers of the name of Douglas. In the long list of noblemen who died with King James 'in that infortunate battell,' we find 'Sir Sander Lowder, and Sir George Lowder'[4]— their younger brother James being also killed.

Thus both the houses of Halton and Blyth, which had given provosts to the chief burgh of Scotland for nine years, lost the heads of their respective families in one day. Sir George Lauder of Haltoun was succeeded by his

---

[1] *Memorials of Edinburgh*, by Sir Daniel Wilson, p. 386.   [2] See Appendix, Note I.

[3] James IV. grants confirmation, on the 2nd May 1504, of a charter by Sir Alexander Lawder of Halton, selling to William Ker of Yare the lands of Mertoun with its fishings in the water of Tweed, and in 'le lowis' of Mertoun, in the bailiary of Lauderdale and shire of Berwick ; to be held of the said Alexander under the King. Dated at Edinburgh, 16th April 1504; and among the witnesses is Alexander Lauder, son of the said Alexander, Provost of Edinburgh.—*Register of the Great Seal*, 1424-1503, No. 2787.   [4] Holinshed's *Chronicles*, p. 482.

son Sir William, as seventh Laird. He had been married the previous year to Agnes Henderson, having received at the time of his marriage a grant of land from his father, viz., the property of Over and Nether Kidstoun, and Easter and Wester Wormestoun, with the mills thereof, and also the hill called 'the Grene Meldoun,' in the shire of Peebles—Sir George retaining 'his own liferent and a reasonable terce to his wife, with the exception of forty merks' worth of the said lands, which the said William and Agnes were to hold as in fee. Sir George had also reserved the right to pasture his cattle on the hill. This contract was dated at Edinburgh, 29th January 1512-13.

But the astounding national calamity which took place at Flodden the following year carried sorrow and dole to every mansion, tower, and cot in the land—peer and peasant, baron and burgher, all suffered alike in this formidable crisis. Scotland's crown again descended to an infant, and John, Duke of Albany, his father's cousin, was made Regent of the realm. Born and brought up in France, he naturally drew to those of the Scottish nobles who could speak his language and carry themselves with the polished bearing of the French court. Consequently we read of Sir William Lauder of Haltoun finding favour with the Duke, and in consideration of his father's, his grandfather's, and his uncle's services, he obtained the relief of all his lands lying in the shires of Edinburgh, Berwick, and Peebles, in 1515, and also licence 'to fortify and re-edify his house at Haltoun, and appoint porters and other officers thereat.' This deed was dated and signed at Stirling, 'sealed with the unicorn' in absence of the King's seal. The restoration and rebuilding accordingly commenced at once, and, as Mr. Findlay says, 'To this period does the great central tower belong, which, in spite of alterations and encrustments, is a fine example of the peel-tower or keep, showing on a ground-plan something like a cube with a smaller one set alongside of it. There is no date affixed to any part of it, to show if it is five centuries, or only three and a half centuries old—the difference between 1515 rebuilt, or 1377 when John de Halton sold the estate to the Lauders.'[1]

The Earls of Bothwell had evidently from time to time had several transactions, both friendly and unfriendly in their tenor, towards the Lauders of Halton ; and at this period some of Sir William's lands were leased from the earl, the 'tack' having been granted to Sir George Lauder in 1512 for sixteen years after date.

Sir Alexander Lauder of Blyth, who died at Flodden, does not appear to have left any sons to inherit all his wealth and property ; or, if so, they must

[1] *Halton House.* By J. R. Findlay, Esq.

have died before the year 1528, at which date his nephew, Sir William Lauder of Haltoun, is mentioned in a charter as his acknowledged heir.[1]

In 1531 we find Sir William both buying and selling land. On the 22nd June he sold the Mains of Over Gogar to the King's servitor, James Aitkinhead;[2] and on the 24th November he purchased the lands of Stewartoun in Peeblesshire, from William Stewartoun of that ilk, and among the witnesses are Gilbert Lauder of Bawbardy, and Robert Lauder of Burngrains.[3]

Two years later Sir William's son and heir, another Alexander Lauder, took unto himself a wife, with the consent and approbation of his father, who settled upon the young couple a goodly portion of landed estate, to be held of the King, which estate comprised all the lands of the Mains of Over Gogar, and the lands of Newbigging in Lauderdale, with the lands of Nether Kydstoun in Peeblesshire.[4] The contract was signed on the 24th February, and confirmed by the King, James V., on the 28th February 1533-4. The bride was Janet Borthwick, daughter of Lord Borthwick of Borthwick Castle, who had been one of the guardians of the King in his infancy. In three years Halton House was again the scene of another wedding, and Helene Lauder, Sir William's daughter, was married to Michael Scott, son and heir-apparent of Sir William Scott of Balwery,[5] an ancient family of great power and ability, one of whom, in 1280, was the famous Wizard, Michael Scott, Baron of Balweary, whose extraordinary discoveries in science and chemistry gained for him the notoriety and reputation of a magician. The gross ignorance of the period in which he lived, fostered among the people that love of the marvellous which not only made them believe the stories they invented, but also to invent stories past all belief. Even the devil himself became most philanthropic in those days, aiding 'Auld Michael of Balwearie' to form a substantial road through Locher-Moss in the short space of one night. The magical powers of Sir Michael have clung to his name for centuries, when all he did as a benefactor to his race has been buried in oblivion. This may account for tradition assigning him two tombs—one for his deeds, no doubt, and the other for his bones. The first is said to be in King David's Abbey at Holme-Cultrane, but the second, which is in Melrose Abbey, is of world-wide fame, for who has not heard that

'Within it burns a wondrous light
To chase the spirits that love the night'?

---

[1] *Register of the Great Seal*, 1513-1546, No. 572.
[2] *Ibid.* No. 1037.
[3] *Ibid.* No. 1097.
[4] *Ibid.* No. 1367.
[5] *Ibid.* No. 872.

During the whole minority of James V. Scotland was in a continuous state of internal dissension and party strife: the very streets of Edinburgh were filled with the brawlings and mortal combats between the powerful houses of Angus and Arran, or the Earls of Huntly, Moray, and Home. The Lauders of Lauder and Halton were frequently mixed up in these quarrels; and, as each sided with their own party, it often caused dissensions among themselves. But nothing of any great moment occurred in the family until after the death of King James, when the English wooed the infant Queen with fire and sword, and Edinburgh, under the Earl of Hertford's guns, became 'a mass of blackened ruins.'

During that stormy period Sir William Lauder, who had 're-edified his fortalice of Haltoun,' died, and was succeeded by his eldest son, Sir Alexander Lauder, Knight, who had married Janet Borthwick. Sir Alexander was one of those who, fighting bravely to repel the English, 'was felled at Pinkie in September 1547,' as we are told in an old manuscript,[1] and his son William came into the estate. Sir William was a young man at the time, without much stability of character, and, judging from his after-career, easily influenced by those about him. His first desire was to strengthen the fortifications of Haltoun, and in order to accomplish this he placed himself under an obligation to William Sinclair of Roslin, and John, Lord Borthwick, and Agnes, Countess of Borthwick. He obtained the Writ for Fortification on the 26th April 1557,[2] and on the 28th he registered a Bond of Obligation, acknowledging that he had received from John, Lord Borthwick, 200 merks, which he promises to repay at Martinmas next. This was dated at Haltoun, and witnessed by Robert Lauder and Stephane Lauder.

In March 1562 Sir William was suspected of siding with the conspirators under Darnley, Ruthven, and Douglas, and we find his name appearing on that tremendously long list of 'personis delaitit of the slaughter of David Riccio.' There does not appear to have been any forfeiture, however, as, in the month of June of the same year, Queen Mary granted a charter to Alexander Lauder, son and heir-apparent of Sir William Lauder of Haltoun, of 'the lands of Quhytlawis and Burngrains, with mills, multures, woods, fishings, and tenants, etc., in Berwickshire, which Robert Lauder of Burngrains resigned'; it also included 'all action of non-entry and recognition which the Queen might have anent these lands.'[3]

A few months previous to the murder of Riccio, when every truly loyal

[1] Family Roll, by Sir Thomas Dick Lauder. [2] *Register of Deeds*, vol. ii. 77, 1554-1581, No. 120*b*.
[3] *Register of the Great Seal*, 1546-1580, No. 1418.

OF HALTOUN AND BRUNTISFIELD 237

heart was attuned towards Scotland's beauteous Sovereign, on the first yuletide spent in her own kingdom since her childhood, Alexander Scott, a connection of the Lauders of Halton by marriage, wrote an elegant little poem of twenty-eight stanzas, inscribed—

A NEW YEAR GIFT TO QUEEN MARY WHEN SHE
CAME FIRST HOME, 1562

I

'Welcome, illustrate Ladye, and our Queen;
Welcome our Lion with the Fleur-de-Lis;
Welcome our Thistle with the Lorraine-green;
Welcome our rubent Rose upon the rise;
Welcome our Gem and joyful Genetrice;
Welcome our belle of Albion to bear;
Welcome our pleasant Princess maist of price!
God give you grace against this good New Year.

. . . . . .

XXVIII

Fresh, fulgent, flurist, fragrant, flower formose,
Lantern to love, of ladies lamp and lot;
Cherry, maist chaste, chief carbuncle and choice,
Sweet smiling Sovereign shining bot[1] a spot.
Blest, beautiful, benign, and best begot,
To this indite please to incline thine ear:
Sent by thy simple servant, Sanders Scot,
Greiting great God to grant thy Grace good Year.'

As an instance of the petty feuds that sometimes took place between the Lauders of Halton and their cousins the Lauders of Lauderdale, we need only mention that of June 1565, when Sir William Lauder of Haltoun sued William Lauder, son and heir-apparent of Gilbert Lauder of Bawbardeis, for 'violent occupation of his lands and cattle.' This seems strange enough when we are reminded sixteen years later that Sir William of Haltoun endeavoured to defraud his own son and heir of his patrimonial estate by selling it to this same William, son of his brother Gilbert. The charter[2] was absolutely confirmed by James VI. at Dalkeith on the 28th June 1581, by which Sir William Lauder of Haltoun sold to William Lauder, son and heir-apparent of Gilbert Lauder of Balbardeis and his heirs, 'the lands of Haltoun, with the castle and manor, the lands of Plat, Westhall, and Northraw, with the mill at Kirkmylne, and multures and sequels thereof; three-quarters of the lands of Norton; the town and mains of Over Gogar, with mill, tenants, etc.; the lands

---

[1] Without.   [2] *Register of the Great Seal*, 1546-1580, No. 226.

of Brounisfield, in the shire of Edinburgh; Over and Nether Kidstones, with their mill; Easter and Wester Wormeston, half of Stewartoun, Brunelaw, and Brigend, in Peebles; lands of Newbigging, Rogerislaw, Blaksaidis, half the mill of Lauder, lands of Quhitlaw and Burngrange, in the bailiary of Lauderdale, Berwickshire; and the rest by annexation, in the barony of Renfrew.' The reddendo to the King as Prince and Steward of Scotland for one-quarter Norton and for Quhitslaid was one penny in name of blench; and for the rest, *ward-holding* with the customary services. Among the witnesses were Thomas Lauder, another son of the said Gilbert, and William Lauder, a merchant in Kelso, whose wife was Janet Bell. Whatever may have been Sir William's reason for thus disinheriting his eldest son, it is not here mentioned; but an Act of Parliament was obtained in 1585 'for annulland the infeftment maid to Gilbert Lauder of Balbardeis and his sone of the landis and leving of Haltoun.' In this Act the complaints of Alexander Lauder, son and heir of Sir William of Halton, are set forth, showing that the said Gilbert had, by imposing on the simplicity of his father, fraudulently induced him to consent to a pretended sale, whereby the lands and baronies of Haltoun were conveyed to him or his son William, to the utter exclusion of his own son Alexander, the complainer, and fiar thereof. The complaint goes on to state that the 'said William, father of said Alexander, has renuncit his lyferent to the said William Lauder; whereupon he has set purpose to sitt down upon the haill landis, mains, and heretaiges, and to exclude the said Alexander and his posteritie perpetually thirfrom, the lyke quhairof has nocht ben sene within this Realme in na aige past.' Parliament took the same view as Mr. Alexander, and declared the infeftments thus complained of null and void. The interdict was registered on the 2nd August 1586.

One would be inclined to think this was quite sufficient to prevent all further intercourse between the families, instead of which, having once established his right to the inheritance of the Halton estate, Mr. Alexander voluntarily becomes a party with his father in a contract between Sir John Maitland of Thirlestane, the King's secretary, and his uncle, Gilbert Lauder of Balbardeis, his wife, Elizabeth Lauder, and their son William, for the sale of the lands of Quhitslaid and Brighauch, with the grain and fulling mills, woods and fishings within the bounds of Lauderdale, to the said Gilbert for the sum of 5500 merks, and two pennies silver yearly in name of blench to Sir John Maitland. This deed [1] was confirmed by the King on the 30th July 1586, and ratified on the 2nd August, the same day as the interdict for the sale of Halton.[2]

[1] *Register of the Great Seal*, 1546-1580, No. 1016.   [2] *Register of Deeds*, vol. xxiv., 406.

OF HALTOUN AND BRUNTISFIELD   239

In the following month a matrimonial contract was entered into between Mr. Alexander Lauder and Marie Maitland, sister of Sir John Maitland of Thirlestane, and third daughter of the deceased Sir Richard Maitland of Lethington. Upon their marriage they were installed in the lands acquired from Sir William Lauder of Halton, which were to be held by them, and the survivor, and their children, whom failing, by James Lauder (of Muircleuch), brother of Alexander, and his heirs, whom failing, by the same William Lauder, son of Gilbert of Balbardies.[1] It is not necessary to enumerate all these Ratho lands again, suffice it that Halton Castle and Bruntisfield Manor in Edinburgh were both included, Sir William reserving his liferent.

It is interesting to note that Marie Maitland's father, Sir Richard, who died the year before her marriage, was one of the most noted men of that period. After having been for many years employed in the State by James V., Regent Arran, and also by Mary of Lorraine, he lost his eyesight, and ended his days as the 'Blind Baron.' Sir Richard, who had been a poet of no mean degree in his day, also 'tuned his ancient lyre to give his fair liege lady a quaint poetic welcome and sage counsel on her return to her Scottish Realm'; but we can only give the closing stanza—

> 'And though that 1 to serve be not so able
> As I was wont, *because I may not see*,
> Yet in my heart I sall be firm and stable
> To thy Highness, with all fidelitie—
> Aye praying God for thy prosperitie.
> And that I hear thy people, with high voice
> And joyful hearts, crying continually :
> *Viva Marie ! très nobil Royne d'Ecosse !*'

This Sir Richard Maitland was the aged baron who, in his seventy-fourth year, had his Barony of Blythe harried of 5000 sheep and cattle in one night by an English captain and his marauding band. This was in 1570, and the 'Blind Baron' lived to be ninety.

But we must now return to Halton ; and in the registration of a contract which is in the form of a 'Decreet Arbitral,'[2] we shall find a somewhat feasible solution to the mystery concerning the unnatural sale of Mr. Alexander Lauder's inheritance by his father. This deed of arbitration between Sir William Lauder and his son Alexander is dated 25th January 1587-8, following on a submission, dated 8th August 1587, which shows that there had been an action of divorce raised before the Commissaries of Edinburgh between

[1] *Register of the Great Seal*, 1546-1580, No. 1031.   [2] *Register of Deeds*, vol. xxii. fol. 193.

Sir William and his wife, Dame Jean Cockburn; and for removing 'sclander' arising thereby, and providing Dame Jean in the meanwhile with a competent maintenance, this reference to arbitration had been made. The judges, arbiters chosen by Sir William Lauder of Haltoun on the one part, and Alexander Lauder, his son and apparent heir, taking upon him the burden for his mother, Jean Cockburn, spouse of said Sir William, on the other part, were Mr. John Lindsay, parson of Menmure, Mr. John Graham, parson of Killearn, Mr. John Cockburn of Ormiston, and John Cuningham of Cuninghamhead, who had married Barbara, daughter of Sir William Lauder and Lady Jean Cockburn, on the 25th November 1577.[1] The judges ordained Sir William to lease to his son Alexander the lands of Bruntisfield and Gogar Mains for the lifetime of Sir William, for payment of 10 merks yearly, which Sir William forthwith did. Mr. Alexander undertaking to observe the leases and tenants already set by his father; but exception was made of an annual rent of £35 secured over Bruntisfield to the late Gilbert Dik, burgess of Edinburgh, and another of £50, with one of 48 merks secured over Gogar Mains, which Sir William was to relieve his son of. It was agreed that if the said Dame Jean predeceased Sir William, this contract should *ipso facto* expire. In return for this, Lady Jean was to abandon the process of divorce, and Sir William also was to stop all legal proceedings against his wife.

This was a very sad domestic episode—the only one of the kind we find recorded in all the preceding generations of the Lauders; and it must have sorely embittered the family intercourse, as Lady Jean Cockburn lived for some years with her eldest son Alexander at Bruntisfield, whereas his father Sir William resided with their second son James and their unmarried daughter Susanna at Halton. From an old manuscript [2] of Lord Fountainhall's we find that 'Sir William Lauder of Halton was on an assize in 1589'—seven years before his death, which took place in November 1596, according to the date of his last will and testament,[3] which was given up by 'the said James and Susanna, his lawful son and daughter, and executors to him.'

Sir Alexander Lauder, Knight, succeeded as tenth Laird of Halton; but his young wife, Marie Maitland, had died just six months before his father, leaving him 'administrator to Richard, Jane, and Helen Lauder, their children,' as executor to their late mother. No mention is made in the will of the eldest

[1] *Record of Deeds*, vol. xxi., 245*b*.
[2] A curious manuscript of excerpts of criminal cases by Sir John Lauder of Fountainhall, described as 'being in folio, closly wrot with his own hand, and consisting of 427 pages.'—Family Roll, by Sir Thomas Dick-Lauder.
[3] Commissariat of Edinburgh. *Register of Testaments*, vol. lix.

son Alexander, he being heir-apparent of his father. The '*free gear*' left to be divided among the three younger children was £1041, 13s. 4d.[1] Sir Alexander Lauder was not long in providing a stepmother for his young family, and the lady who became his new partner in life was Annabella Bellenden, sister of Sir Ludovick Bellenden of Auchnoule and Broughton, after whom they named their first-born son Ludovick.

The time had now arrived in which the mansion-house and lands of Bruntisfield were separated from the Halton estate, passing completely away from the Lauders. It had been the jointure-house of the Haltoun family for many generations; but in 1603, most probably on the death of his mother, Lady Jean Cockburn, Sir Alexander sold it to John Fairlie, of the family of Braid,[2] with the consent of his second wife; and in consequence of her having been liferented in Bruntisfield Manor, Sir Alexander 'granted to his spouse, Annabella Bellenden, the lands of Westhall and Ratho in contentation thereof,' the deed being witnessed by Sir Ludovick Bellenden and his brother Walter.[3] Several charters then followed in rapid succession, whereby many of the Halton lands changed hands at this epoch, and others were purchased for the younger sons. The mains of Over Gogar were sold to Mr. Patrick Bannatyne, W.S., Mr. Alexander Lauder, younger of Halton, Lady Marie Maitland's eldest son, witnessing the transaction, on the 29th June; and on the 9th July of the same year, 1610, these lands of Over Gogar, etc., were resold by Mr. Patrick to Ludovick Lauder, the eldest son of Sir Alexander by Lady Annabella Bellenden. This could not have been in anticipation of his future marriage, as the lad was only twelve years old; most likely it was for his patrimonial inheritance on his coming of age, as on the same day his parents also made him fiar of their lands of Lekbernard or Halhouse, with the manor, mills, mill lands, etc., as resigned by Sir James Foulis of Colingtoun,[4] whereas at the same time they settled the manor of Halton and lands of Norton upon his half-brother Alexander, the heir-apparent, in conjunction with his future wife, Lady Susanna Cuninghame, daughter of James, Earl of Glencairn, the Laird of Halton simply reserving his liferent.[5] Some of the lands were held of Prince Henry as superior, and some of the King, James VI., who confirmed the charters.

---

[1] Commissariat of Edinburgh. *Register of Testaments*, vol. lix.
[2] *Register of the Great Seal*, 1593-1608, No. 944.
[3] *Ibid*. No. 137.   [4] *Ibid*. Nos. 326 and 327.
[5] These lands still included Westhall and Northraw of Ratho, also Kirkmylne, Priestslands and Plat, in the Barony of Ratho; Newbigging, Rogerlaw, Blaksydes, half the mill of Lauder, Burngragne, and Quhitlaw, in Lauderdale; Wester Wormestoun or Cringiltie, Easter Wormestoun, Over and Nether Kidstone, Stewartoun, and Brumelaw and Brigend, in Peeblesshire.—*Ibid*. No. 345.

Four years later, 1614, that portion of these lands which lay in Lauderdale was sold to John, Lord Thirlestane, and Lady Isabella Seytoun, his spouse, with the mutual consent of Sir Alexander Lauder, senior, and his son Alexander, the fiar of Haltoun, to be held of the said Alexander Lauder, junior, for payment yearly of £33, 6s. 8d.[1] feu-duty. This was Mr. Alexander's last charter, as he died shortly after, leaving a young widow and no son to take possession of the title and property. In 1621 we hear of the aged Sir Alexander Lauder of Halton, his father, as being one of the commissioners appointed by James VI. '*for the planting of kirks where kirks is yet unplanted.*'

The next intimation we find is in an old manuscript of Retours,[2] under the Letter L.: 'Lawder, Mr. Richard, served aire to Alexander Lawder, fiar of Haltoun, 18 May 1625. Alexander Lawder, elder of Haltoun, was their father.' This is the son Richard mentioned in Lady Marie Maitland's will, who must have been about thirty-five years of age when he came into his elder brother's inheritance. Judging from a grant by King Charles I., on the 9th April 1633, of some lands in Peeblesshire[3] which Mr. Robert Burnet acquired and Mr. Richard Lauder resigned, there had been some transactions about them between Richard Lauder and Brice Semple of Cathcart and Jean Lauder, his spouse, which Jean is evidently Mr. Richard's sister, who is also mentioned in their mother's testament-dative.

The next charter in point of date is a very interesting one, as it brings us again in contact with the other branch of the Lauder family, viz., the Lauders of Bass, who were at this period in the midst of their financial difficulties, their lands dwindling away bit by bit. The simple facts it gives us are as follows:—Charles I., for himself and as administrator to his son Charles, Prince and Steward of Scotland, etc., grants to Mr. Richard Lauder of Haltoun and his heirs and assignees whomsoever, under legal reversion, the north half of the isle and hill of the Bass, the lands of Elboth, Auldcastell, and Blakdykes, and others, including Easter Pencaitland in the constabulary of Haddington, which belonged to George Lauder of Bass and Isabella Hepburn, Lady of Bass, his mother, and were apprised by John Park, merchant-burgess of Edinburgh, for £2283 odds, who assigned the process to the said Richard. Dated at Edinburgh, 18th January 1634.

Three years after this Mr. Richard Lauder also bought up the lands of Over Newtoun from his half-brother, John Lauder, described as 'lawful son of

[1] *Register of the Great Seal*, 1593-1608, No. 1208.
[2] A curious old manuscript, entitled, 'A account of the haill Nobilitie and several of the Gentrie that have been served aires to ther predicessors from 1550 to 1708.'—Family Roll, by Sir Thomas Dick-Lauder.
[3] *Reg. Mag. Sig.*, 1620-1633, No. 2160.

OF HALTOUN AND BRUNTISFIELD 243

the late Alexander Lauder of Haltoun.'[1] He was full brother to Sir Ludovick Lauder, and Colonel George Lauder, the soldier-poet, of whom Dr. Laing says in a note on *Caledonia's Covenant*, written by Colonel Lauder in 1641, 'This is another poem by George Lauder. He was younger son of Lauder of Halton, in Midlothian, by Mary, daughter of the venerable Sir Richard Maitland of Lethington. After finishing his studies at the University of Edinburgh, where he was 'laureated' in the year 1620, our author embraced a military life, and appears to have accompanied the ill-fated expedition to the island of Rhé in France, under the Duke of Buckingham, in 1627.'[2] Dr. David Laing has evidently been under some mistake with regard to the parentage of Colonel George Lauder. He was undoubtedly the son of Sir Alexander Lauder of Halton, but not by his wife Marie Maitland, as she died in 1596, and his name is not mentioned in her will; besides, Colonel George is said to have been born in 1600. He was the second son of Sir Alexander by Annabella Bellenden, his second wife, who was still living when the young soldier left his home in 1622 —verified by his own words in his *Valedictory Address on leaving Scotland*, commencing—

    'Launcht from my native shore, forth in the world's great maine,
    No stormy blast of Fortune's frownes shall drive me home again.'

    'Thus fraughted with desire farre distant shores to see,
    Scotland farewell! I goe to seeke what is ordained for me.'

    'The World my country is through which I 'le wand'ring goe,
    And think my Home where ere I come, the Heavens command me so.'

    'I scorn the Idol wealth, which all the world adores—
    To worship Earth's unworthy drosse, a worthy mind abhorres.'

    'Let Fortune's minions laugh, who have no God but gold,
    And let the world say what it will, thus Lauder is resolv'd.'

    'Farewell, then, famous shire! where first I saw the light;
    Great Britain's garden, Louthiane, I must forgoe thy sight.'

    'Farewell, my worthy sire! the honor of thy race,
    Whose shining glory doth eclipse thy grandsires with disgrace.
    Heavens make thee happy here, and grant thee Nestor's yeares,
    Then give thee Life's eternal joys above the rolling spheares.'

    'Farewell, my loving Dame! from out whose fertill wombe
    This body free from all the markes of Nature's scorn did come.
    Long may thou live in joy, and long enjoy thy mate,
    To sympathise with him in all—health, honors, happy fate!'

---

[1] *Register of the Great Seal*, 1634-1651, No. 686.
[2] *Fugitive Pieces of Scottish Poetry, Seventeenth Century*. Edited by David Laing.

'Farewell, fraternall twigs, that from one stocke do spring,
All happiness befall you here, that earthly bliss can bring.'

. . . .

'Farewell, deare Virgin Dove! whom as my life I love,
Sweet Sister, whom I wish both faire and fortunate to prove.'

. . . .

Then to 'Arete,' his 'soul's sweet mistress,' he adds—

'And thou, O Faire, Farewell! well may thou, faire, farewell—
It's only thee I grieve to leave, whose want I 'le ever feel.
The Heavens upon thy head powre out their joyes and blisses,
And grant thee glad accomplishment of all thy choycest wishes.
Let Fortune do her best to please thee evermore,
And wondering Earth admire thy worth, whose like was ne'er before.
Though I Earth's wand'ring guest a vagabond do stray,
And must, alas, forgoe thy face—fates call me so away—
Yet time shall trie the truth of my (deare love) to thee;
And in my Song I 'le praise thee so, that all the world shall woo thee.
Againe, faire Faire, farewell! though last on thee I call,
Yet thou art first into my thought, both first and last of all;
And if I ever chance those northern coasts to see,
And find thee, as I never doubt, of this same mind to be,
With thee I 'le anchor then, and leave the stormy maine,
And for thy sake henceforth I vow ne'er to launch forth again.
                                                    LAUDERO.[1]

'EDENBOROUGH, 1622.'

During his military career George Lauder wrote a goodly number of spirited poems and several epitaphs in verse, but he remained away abroad many years, chiefly residing in Dutch Brabant at Breda, where a number of his poems were printed. Being a born soldier, he rose to be colonel of his regiment, and took every opportunity of extolling the hardy life of a military man over the fashionable foibles and follies of the votaries of society. In his *Scottish Soldier* he says—

'Let painted puppies, womanish conceates,
Court monkies, which on favour's smile awaits,
Fard, frize and painte; for me I never seeke
To have a better collour on my cheeke
Than when the dust and sweate doe hide my face—
Methinks such grimness is a souldier's grace.'

Colonel Lauder became the intimate friend and companion of William Drummond of Hawthornden, upon whose death in 1649 from heart-break at the beheading of his beloved Sovereign, Charles I., Lauder wrote a most lengthy

[1] 'Georgius Lauderus, ex antiquissima Lavderorum. Familia de Halton, oriundus, Scotia descedens. Kalend. August. Patriæ, Parentibus, & Amicus vale dicit.'—From a manuscript volume in the Library at New Hailes, ed. Dr. David Laing.

OF HALTOUN AND BRUNTISFIELD 245

and elaborate elegy or classic pastoral, eulogising his friend 'Damon,' whose departure he most deeply deplored. George Lauder had evidently been engaged for twenty years in foreign service, 'worn with weary toil of wandering,' as he himself puts it, when his own son crossed 'the maine' to tell him of Drummond's death.

'Tears drown'd his eyes, his hoary head he hung ;
And at the name of Damon fainted—so he loved his Fame.'

Colonel Lauder's own epitaph was written in 1670 by Sir Alexander Wedderburn, who was grandfather of Sir Alexander Wedderburn who married Elizabeth Seton, eldest daughter of Sir Alexander Seton of Pitmedden, twice linked to the Fountainhall branch of the Lauder family.

Colonel George Lauder's half-brother, Mr. Richard Lauder of Halton, had no son to inherit his large estate, and of his two daughters, Jean and Elizabeth, the younger one became mistress of Halton. The elder sister married Sir Thomas Elphinstone of Calderhall in 1650, and received her dowry and patrimonial portion in money. As we do not purpose following that collateral branch of the Halton family, we shall only mention that upon the splendid tomb of the Elphinstones on the west side of the Greyfriars' churchyard, there is a tablet with the following inscription:—

'HEIR · IS · BURIED · JEAN · LAUDER · ELDEST · DAUGHTER · TO · THE
LAIRD · OF · HALTOUN · LADY · CALDERHALL · WHO · DYED
ON · THE · 2 · DAY · OF · JUILLY · 1672.'

Elizabeth, the younger sister, married Charles Maitland, younger brother of the Duke of Lauderdale, after whose death Mr. Maitland succeeded him as third Earl of Lauderdale, and his countess, Elizabeth Lauder, became lady of Thirlestane Castle. But this was not for many years after their marriage in 1652, in the contract of which Mr. Richard Lauder settled the whole of his landed estate upon them and their lawful heirs ; and as he died very shortly after their union, they took immediate possession of Halton, which was thus incorporated into the Lauderdale possessions. Ere long the old fortalice changed its venerable appearance, and with the addition of expansive wings, ornamental turrets, balconies, and balustrades, it grew from a fortified tower into a magnificent mansion. Sir Charles Maitland, as Lord Halton, did much for the beautifying of the estate by the laying out of the grounds and the decoration of the interior and exterior of the building, which, judging from the dates upon those portions built by him, would be completed between 1664 and 1675. His brother the Duke of Lauderdale's taste in such matters, as displayed in the princely magnificence of Thirlestane Castle and his classic residence at Ham, had a marked influence upon him—not that they were upon the most amiable terms with each other by any means. Bishop Burnet, who knew them personally, when writing of them in 1671, says, 'The Earl of Lauderdale had for many years treated his brother, the Lord Halton, with as much contempt as he deserved, for he was both weak and violent, insolent and corrupt.'

The Duke himself had not much to boast of in sweetness of disposition, moderation in speech, elegance of manner, or knightly bearing. The same bishop tells us 'he was very big, his hair red, hanging oddly about him. His tongue was too big for his mouth, which made him bedew all that he talked to, and his whole manner was very unfit for a court.' And yet this rude, blustering, red-hot persecutor had wooed and won two wives—the last Duchess being equal to three. Scotland is not likely soon to forget the doings of the Duke of Lauderdale, whose name is so opprobriously coupled with that of Sir George Mackenzie—it being difficult to say which of the two used the most blasphemous language in sending multitudes of staunch Covenanters '*to glorify God at the Grassmarket.*'

This is the man whom Lord Fountainhall quaintly describes as 'the learnedest and powerfullest Minister of State in his age'; and truly his magnificence was princely, but his princely extravagances not only involved his own estate in Lauderdale, but caused his brother, Lord Halton, to sell off a great part of his newly acquired lands in and around Ratho to help him out of his financial difficulties; but Halton remained intact, and to this day the initials of Charles Maitland and Elizabeth Lauder are conspicuously prominent, for, as Mr. Findlay points out, they are to be seen in at least four places. 'On the pillars of a side gateway they stand out in bold relief, sharply chiselled as of yesterday. The two dial-plates bear their monograms, and also the iron flag of the vane which surmounts the tower, veering about in the wind for over two hundred years.' On the southern front of Halton House the fourteenth century arms of Sir Alan de Lawedre are still to be seen. In all the seventeenth century descriptions of Haltoun the gardens are specially noted. Sir Robert Sibbald in 1683 calls it 'the noble dwelling of Haltoun, the residence of the Earle of Lauderdale, where are fine gardens and a large park, with a high wall about it'; and in another account [1] it is spoken of as the principal seat in the parish of Ratho: 'a venerable old house, with extensive gardens, and surrounded with large plantations of at least 800 acres of ground.' This was

[1] *Statistical Account of Scotland.* By Rev. James Robertson.

OF HALTOUN AND BRUNTISFIELD 247

in 1793, and Mr. Findlay says, 'In the title-deeds the pleasure-grounds were described as embracing 240 acres, and the gardens fully six acres.' These gardens, after being for one hundred and twenty years the pride of the Maitland family under six Earls of Lauderdale, were for many years let to a market-gardener. This is the usual fate of these fine old baronial gardens when the expense of keeping them up becomes too great. At one time

HALTON HOUSE.

Halton could also boast of several ponds, the resort of herons and all sorts of wild-fowl and the beautiful kingfisher, in the days when hawking was in its prime; indeed, the same writer tells us that 'Halton was the last of the regular old hawking establishments that existed in Scotland.' In the days when, in its splendid hospitalities it vied with the Earls of Hopetoun in providing 'upwards of fifty bedrooms and stabling for seventy horses,' no residence in the Lothians, west of Edinburgh, except Hopetoun House, could compare with Halton, famed for its beautiful pargeted ceilings, its evergreens, and its fountains. It was one of the old-fashioned gardens in which Lord Cockburn revelled when his friend, Lord Jeffrey, was tenant of Halton—writing 'his reviews in a little gilded closet'; for of all the large number of *large* rooms in this great rambling house at his command, Lord Jeffrey chose the little 'gilded closet' as his study.

But as it is simply with regard to its immediate and collateral connection with the Lauder family that we have narrated the history of Halton House, we shall not enter into any of the more modern details, interesting though they undoubtedly might be to all lovers of Midlothian lore. For a full description and statistical account of this venerable mansion, with its nineteenth century owners and tenants, from its sale by James, eighth Earl of Lauderdale, in 1792, to Miss Scott of Scotstarvet for £84,000, to its purchase by the Earl of Morton, with its 500 imperial acres, in 1870, for £42,000, for his son, Lord Aberdour, we would refer our readers to the charming work [1] on the subject published by J. Findlay, Esq., who was for some years himself a tenant of Halton House, and made the history of it a special study. We must not omit to mention, however, that the intermediate purchaser was the Rev. Thomas Randall, D.D., who, on the death of his maternal uncle, Mr. Davidson of Muirhouse, to whom he was served heir, became Dr. Davidson, whose son, Captain Davidson, lived for some time at Halton, and endeavoured to restore it to its pristine magnificence. This was in 1820, after Lord Jeffrey had left it and gone to his 'beloved Craigcrook.'

Among the illustrious tenants of Halton House, besides Jeffrey and Captain Davidson, we find it was occupied for a short time by Mr. Archibald Constable, the celebrated publisher; also by Sir David Wedderburn, Bart., Postmaster-General for Scotland, and Mrs. Grant of Congalton, all familiar names in the Lauder family. For many years, however, it remained tenantless and neglected, owing to the great expense of keeping up such a large establishment and such extensive garden grounds, in which everything grew in such rank profusion that not only walls but balustrades and vases were all overrun in the most artistic fashion. It is even said that the house was offered rent free to Mr. James Leslie, C.E., if he would undertake the payment of the window-tax alone. Bereft of its former grandeur and shorn of its magnificence, Halton is still a charming place, with its historical landmarks and its old-world associations.

Before closing this chapter we cannot refrain from adding a few facts about the old Manor-House of Bruntisfield after the Lauders parted with it in 1603, long linked as it had been with Haltoun; for 'Brounisfelde' (so it was anciently called when Richard Brown, its first recorded owner, sold it to Sir Alan de Lawedre in 1381) had been the *dower-nest* of each successive bride of the

[1] *Halton House*. By J. R. Findlay, Esq. Published in 1875.

OF HALTOUN AND BRUNTISFIELD

Lauders of Haltoun for two hundred and twenty-six years; and the thickness of the original walls still tell their own antique story. The date 1605, carved with the initials I · F—E · W over several of the windows also commemorates the fact of its passing into the hands of John Fairlie and his spouse, who considerably enlarged the original building, which is still incorporated with the present mansion. Many years after his death, a charter was granted in 1696, by King 'William and Queen Mary, to John Fairlie's great-grandson, William Fairlie, now of Brounsfield, and his lawful heirs, of the lands of Brounsfield with manor-place, etc., which formerly belonged to the deceased Alexander Lauder of Haltoun, and were by him with consent of Annabella Ballandene, his spouse, in terms of a Contract of Alienation made by them with the deceased John Fairlie, burgess of Edinburgh, and William Fairlie, afterwards Sir William Fairlie, his son and apparent heir; dated 1st and 20th July 1603—registered in the Books of Council and Session, 26th August of that year—resigned at Edinburgh in favor of the aforesaid William Fairlie, now of Brounsfield as heir served and retoured to the said William Fairlie of Brounsfield his grandfather—which service was before the bailies of Canongate on the 1st April 1679.' The charter is dated at Kensington, 29th April 1695.[1] On the 26th July 1695 there is another charter whereby this William Fairlie sold Brounisfield to George Warrender of Lochend, who was at that time bailie and afterwards Provost of Edinburgh, under three sovereigns: King William, Queen Anne, and George I., who created him a baronet in 1715.

For the following interesting facts in the subsequent history of Bruntisfield, after it was purchased by George Warrender of Lochend, we are indebted to the courtesy of Miss Warrender, daughter of Sir George Warrender, sixth Baronet of Bruntisfield and Warrender Park, who has kindly permitted a few extracts to be taken from her charming little book, *Walks near Edinburgh*, in which she tells us that the Warrender family is of French extraction, descended from a 'De Warrender who came from Picardy in the train of Mary of Guise,' and also that Sir George Warrender, Provost of Edinburgh, who purchased the estate of Bruntisfield, 'by degrees also acquired other lands lying contiguous to Bruntisfield, by purchase from Rigg of Riggsland, Biggar of Whitehouse, and Dick of Grange; and these form the property of Bruntisfield as it now stands. Miss Warrender then adds:—

'The Lauders of Haltoun became extinct in the seventeenth century, and their representation devolved on the Maitland family by the marriage of Elizabeth Lauder, the

---

[1] *Registrum Magni Sigilli*, vol. lxxiii. fol. 166, No. 195.

heiress of Haltoun with Charles, third Earl of Lauderdale. That descent we have inherited through my father's mother, Lady Julian Maitland;[1] so that after a lapse of nearly three hundred years, the descendants of the original possessors inhabit the old house again.

'After the purchase of Bruntisfield by George Warrender, it remained for nearly a hundred years in possession of the younger branch of the family, which came to an end in 1820, by the death of Hugh Warrender, an old bachelor, who was Crown Agent for Scotland. He was succeeded by his cousin, my grand-uncle, the Right Hon. Sir George Warrender, M.P., who, on taking possession, discovered the existence of a secret room. The house was then thickly covered with ivy. Lee, the Royal Academician and

BRUNTISFIELD HOUSE.

Architect that Sir George had brought down from London with him, was the first to suspect its existence, from finding more windows outside than they could account for. An old woman who had charge of the house denied for a long time any knowledge of such a room, but, frightened by Sir George's threats, she at length showed them the narrow entrance that was concealed behind a piece of tapestry. This was torn down and the door forced open, and a room was found just as it had been left by some former occupant; the ashes still in the grate. Whether, as one story said, it had been used as a hiding-place in troubled times, or whether, according to another legend, it had been the room of a dearly loved child of the house, after whose death it had been hurriedly shut

[1] Lady Julian-Jane Maitland, fourth daughter of James, eighth Earl of Lauderdale; married in 1823 to John Warrender, Esq.—Burke's *Baronage*.

OF HALTOUN AND BRUNTISFIELD

up never to be entered again by the broken-hearted parents, there are now no means of knowing; but the blood-stains on the floor point to some darker tragedy, and a tradition still lingers, that, not long after the discovery of the room, a skeleton was found buried below the windows. It is still known as the ghost room, though nothing has been seen at any rate for many years. . . . Bruntisfield is the last of the old houses in the immediate vicinity of Edinburgh which is still inhabited by its owners.'

The present baronet is Sir George Warrender, sixth of the line, married in 1854 to Helen, daughter of Sir Hugh Hume Campbell, seventh Baronet of Lauderdale.

SUCCESSION OF THE LAUDERS OF HALTOUN OR HALTON, TAKEN FROM AUTHENTIC PUBLIC RECORDS AND FAMILY WRITS.

Progenitor, Sir Alan de Lawedre, who married Alicia Campbell, daughter of Sir Colin Campbell of Lochaw.

1377. Haltoun acquired; inherited by second son.

1400. First Laird of Haltoun, Sir George de Lawedre—married sister of Lord Douglas; succeeded by eldest son.

1408. Second Laird, Sir Alexander—married Elizabeth Forster, daughter of Sir John Forster of Corstorfyne; sent on embassy to England, 1423, and again in 1433; succeeded by eldest son.

1434. Third Laird, Sir William—married . . . ; obtained safe-conduct from Henry VI. in 1450; King's Messenger in 1452; succeeded by eldest son.

1452. Fourth Laird, Sir John—married . . . ; obtained safe-conduct, 1464; daughter Mary married Sir James Foulis of Colinton; succeeded by eldest son.

1465. Fifth Laird, Sir Alexander—married . . . ; regrant of lands in Peebles, 1472; Bruntsfield restored, 1490; eldest son William died before 1488; succeeded by second son.

1505. Sixth Laird, Sir George of Whitslaid—married Katherine; was killed with his brother, Sir Alexander Lauder of Blythe, at the battle of Flodden, 1513; succeeded by eldest son.

1513. Seventh Laird, Sir William—married Agnes Henderson; rebuilt and fortified Halton, 1515; daughter Helene married to Michael Scott in 1536; succeeded by eldest son.

1537. Eighth Laird, Sir Alexander—married Janet Borthwick; died at the battle of Pinkie, 1547; succeeded by eldest son.

THE LAUDERS OF HALTOUN AND BRUNTISFIELD

1547. Ninth Laird, Sir William—married Jean Cockburne; accused of being among the conspirators concerned in the murder of David Riccio, 1562; divorced 1587; succeeded by eldest son.

1596. Tenth Laird, Sir Alexander—married, 1st, Mary Maitland, third daughter of Sir Richard Maitland of Lethington, and 2nd, Annabella Bellenden, sister of Sir Ludovic Bellenden of Auchnoule and Broughton; sold Bruntsfield Manor, 1603; eldest son, Alexander, fiar of Haltoun, married Lady Susanna Cuninghame, daughter of James, Earl of Glencairn, in 1610, and died before his father, who was succeeded by his second son.

1625. Eleventh Laird, Richard Lauder, Esq., served heir to his brother. He had two daughters, Jean and Elizabeth: Jean married Sir Thomas Elphinstone of Calderhall in 1650, and Elizabeth married Charles Maitland in 1652. He was afterwards third Earl of Lauderdale. Upon them and their heirs Mr. Richard Lauder settled his estate of Halton in 1652.

SITE OF LAUDER TOWER.

CHAPTER XX

THE ANCIENT BURGH OF LAUDER

'A blending of all beauties; streams and dells,
Fruit, foliage, crag, wood, cornfield, mountain, vine,
And chiefless castles breathing stern farewells
From grey but leafy walls where Ruin greenly dwells.'

BYRON.

HIS truly ancient and oft-renowned royal burgh of Berwickshire is pleasantly situated on the river Leader, in a hollow at the foot of the heath-clad Lammermoors.

The natural scenery of the surrounding district is twofold in its character, consisting of the upland ridge of unfertile moorland, where nought but the purple heather blooms, and the low-lying valley of the richly cultivated Merse, watered by the Leader, which rises in the hills about four miles above Lauder, and flows through Lauderdale for nine miles and then falls into the Tweed below Drygrange—commemorated in the old Scottish song of 'Leader Haughs and Yarrow':

'Sing Erslington and Cowdenknows,
Where Humes had ance commanding,
And Drygrange, with the milk-white yowes,
'Twixt Tweed and Leader standing.
The bird that flees through Redpath trees,
And Gladswood banks ilk morrow,
May chant and sing sweet Leader Haughs
And bonnie Howms of Yarrow.'

The 'Leader Haughs' or meadows were famed in feudal times for breeding the stateliest Scottish steeds, and early in the thirteenth century Cowden-Knowes was the Parnassus of Scotland.

Here Thomas 'the Rhymer' met the Fairy Queen. Ercildoune, which stood on the banks of the Leader, about two miles above its junction with the Tweed, was the home of Scotland's earliest poet, famous for his prophecies and his poems as far back as 1283. But it is the home of a still older feudal baron, Robertus de Lawedre, that we are in search of at '*Leader Burgh*,' 'the Lauder Tower family being the chief stem springing directly from and representing the first Lauder, who came into Scotland with Malcolm Canmore.'[1] Halton and Bass were only branches springing severally from the same root. The principal headquarters of the family, therefore, in the days of its feudal power, was Lauder Tower, and then the Castle of the Bass. Of the former not a vestige now remains, the site itself having long been used as a market garden.

This ancient stronghold stood in the main thoroughfare of the burgh of Lauder, within sight of the old Tolbooth, where for generations these hereditary bailies of Lauderdale held their court. The spot is still known as the 'Tower Gardens.'

The early records are not very decisive as to the exact extent of the lands granted to Robertus de Lavedre in the vale of the Leader, but it is self-evident they could not have been anything like so extensive as they subsequently became in the fourteenth and fifteenth centuries, during which period, by grants and by purchase, the numerous branches of the Lauders of Lauder, including the Lauders of Halton and Bass, added considerably to their possessions. That they had from the very first powerful neighbours in the district around them is also evident, for we find the De Morvilles, the Maitlands, the Dunbars, and Sir James Douglas eventually obtaining rights and privileges within the regality of Lauderdale. With the De Morvilles, Maitlands, and Dunbars we sometimes find the Lauders at dagger's point; but with Sir James Douglas and his successors they were ever on the most friendly terms, the basis of their friendship being loyalty to their King and country.

It is surprising that the learned author of *Caledonia* gives us so little information about the first settling of the Lauders in the Lauder valley. Were it not for Rymer's *Fœdera*, Boethius, and Holinshed, we might almost suppose the Malcolm Canmore grant of land to be a legendary story, though it is as well attested as the first earldoms in Scotland.[2]

The paucity of records in the eleventh century no doubt accounts for this. What Mr. George Chalmers tells us about Lauder is a whole century later. He says, 'Lauder as a kirk town is as ancient as the reign of King David, if not older'; but if it really was a *kirk town* in 1152, some one must have built the kirk. Now we know the Lauders built Lauder Tower, but we find no direct mention of a chapel, though the next paragraph would lead us to suppose that it was the usual custom to build one on the territory granted by the King. '*Like the other great settlers*,' says Mr. Chalmers, 'Hugh Morville having obtained a district, built a castle, a church, a mill, and a brewhouse for the con-

Genealogical Roll of the Family of Lauder of Lauder Tower, by Sir Thomas Dick-Lauder, seventh Baronet. [2] Holinshed's *Chronicles*, p. 277.

THE ANCIENT BURGH OF LAUDER 255

venience of his followers' in the 'territory of Lauder, on the Leader water'—a very wide designation. It is very evident, however, that the ancient family of De Morville did settle in some part of Lauderdale, and that they held large possessions there for many years.

In the reign of Malcolm IV., before the death of Earl Henry in 1152, we find the King confirming a grant of the tithes of the mill of Lauder to the canons of Dryburgh, which they had derived from Hugh de Morville. Now this Hugh de Morville died in 1162, having been the first Lord High Constable of Scotland, under King David; and his territorial right in Lauderdale descended successively to two male heirs, and to a long succession of female heirs, who introduced the Lords of Galloway, the De Quincys, and the Baliols.'[1]

Holinshed tells us that 'Rowland, Lord of Galloway, married the sister of William Moorvill, Constable of Scotland, who dying without issue, Rowland obtained the same office by inheritance in right of his wife, from whom did issue Alane, Lord of Galloway, and Constable of Scotland by inheritance from his mother'[2] (1183); and we know that Devorgilla, eldest daughter of Alan, Lord of Galloway, married Sir John Baliol, grandfather to the King, who was crowned at Scone. This explains how the right of patronage of the church of Lauder was resigned by 'John Baliol and Devorgilla, his spouse, in 1268, for the benefit of the canons of Dryburgh, with *the site of the chapel to the same church of Lauder belonging*'[3]—the Baliols evidently representing the De Morvilles at that period.

We can find no mention of any other church within the burgh of Lauder than the old kirk which formerly stood near the castle, then called 'Lauder Fort,' but now Thirlestane Castle, the seat of the Earls of Lauderdale. May it not have been, therefore, that the lands granted to Hugh de Morville lay in that direction, and that the castle built by him would be this old historic fort, destroyed during the English invasion, and rebuilt and fortified by Edward II. in 1324?

We know that Baliol forfeited his vast estates eventually, and that the greater part of them were bestowed by King Robert Bruce upon James, Lord Douglas, who had so ably supported him; and also that King Robert, in 1371, granted to Alan de Lawedre half of the mains of Lauder, with half of the fulling mill which had belonged to the late Sir John de Baliol, in the constabulary of Lauder.[4] This locating of the lands proves that they had at some time

---

[1] Chalmers's *Caledonia*, vol. ii. p. 221.   [2] Holinshed's *Chronicles*, p. 325.
[3] Chart, Dryburgh. Lauder as a mother-church had formerly two chapels of its own: one at Kedslie and another at St. Leonard's.   [4] *Register of the Great Seal*, 1306-1424, p. 82, No. 278.

belonged to the De Morvilles, for the office of Constable was hereditary in that family, as the bailieship of Lauderdale was in that of the Lauders. The Constable of Scotland was an officer of high dignity. 'He had two great prerogatives: first, the keeping of the King's sword, which the King when he swore fealty delivered to him naked, and thence the badge of the Constable is a naked sword; secondly, the absolute and unlimited command of the King's armies while in the field, in the absence of the King—a command, however, which did not extend to castles and garrisons. He was likewise judge of all the crimes committed within two leagues of the King's house, which precinct was called 'the *Chalmer of Peace*.'[1]

These historical facts make it more than probable that the original Castle of Hugh de Morville, as Lord Constable of Scotland, would be the same Lauder Fort which was so often besieged by the English and retaken by the Scots, the whole county of Berwickshire being one continuous scene of stramash and strife throughout the Border wars.

After the battle of Bannockburn King Robert Bruce, in consideration of the great loyalty and faithful services of Gilbert de Haye, Lord of Errol, granted him a large portion of the lands which fell to the Crown; and also in consequence of the forfeiture of John de Baliol and the De Quincys, the high office of Chief Constable of Scotland becoming vacant, the King, by royal charter, dated 12th November 1315, granted the same to Gilbert de Haye and his heirs for ever; but as there is no mention of the Castle of Lauder, it is not likely that it was included with the office, especially as we find Lord Gilbert and several of his successors were buried in the Abbey Church of Cupar.[2] It is very evident, however, that during this stormy and unsettled period the lands of Berwickshire and the jurisdiction thereof changed hands frequently, both by forfeiture and by donation. Some of these changes are so intricate in their tenure, and the discrepancies of the narrators so confusing, that we shall not attempt to enter into them minutely; suffice it for our purpose to mention the

[1] *Encyclopædia Britannica*.
[2] The noble Earls of Errol have retained the office of Lord High Constable of Scotland up to the present day, it having been expressly reserved to them by the Treaty of Union, as the following protestation on the 7th January 1707 affirms:—'I, Charles, Earl of Errol, Lord High Constable of Scotland, do hereby protest, That the office of High Constable, with all the rights and privileges of the same, belonging to me heritably, and depending upon the monarchy, sovereignty, and ancient constitutions of this kingdom, may not be prejudiced by the Treaty of Union between Scotland and England, nor any article, clause, or condition thereof; but that the said heritable office, with all the rights and privileges thereof, may remain to me and my successors entire and unhurt by any votes or Acts of Parliament whatever relating to the said Union: And I crave that this my protestation may be recorded in the Register and Rolls of Parliament.'—*Scots Compendium of the Peerage of Scotland*, vol. i. pp. 184-188.

domains and holdings of the Lauders themselves as we find them recorded in and around the ancient burgh of Lauder.

Of one thing we may be very certain : they never possessed the old Castle of Thirlestane on the Leader, nor did Lauder Fort ever belong to the Lauders. Of the very earliest history of Thirlestane we know nothing, therefore it could not possibly have been built by the Lauders, or it would have been mentioned among the family writs. The records of the Maitland family, however, go far to substantiate the belief that it belonged to them from its foundation. History and Scottish ballad both prove its antiquity, and that as far back as 1250 it belonged to Sir Richard Maitland, who so bravely defended it in his old age against the English. Like most of these old thirteenth century warriors, we find him granting land and pasturage at Thirlestane to the Abbey of Dryburgh in 1249; and in one of the most authentic ballads given by Sir Walter Scott in his *Border Minstrelsy*, we read of 'auld Maitland' and his brave doings. The poem seems to have delighted Sir Walter by its concise accuracy; and as it brings before us a wonderful picture of the times in which those feudal barons, who were next-land neighbours to the Lauders of the Tower, lived and fought, we cannot refrain from subjoining a few of the verses :—

'King Edward rade, King Edward ran—
I wish him dool and pyne !—
Till he had fifteen hundred men
Assembled on the Tyne.

'And thrice as many at Berwicke
Were all for battle bound,
Who, marching forth with false Dunbar,
A ready welcome found.

'They lighted on the banks of Tweed,
And blew their coals sae het,
And fired the Merse and Teviotdale
All in an evening late.

'As they fared up o'er Lammermore,
They burned baith up and down,
Until they came to a darksome house !
Some call it Leader-Town.

'"Wha hauds this house?" young Edward cry'd,
"Or wha gi'es 't ower to me?"
A gray-hair'd knight set up his head,
And crackit right crouselie.

> '"Of Scotland's King I haud my house :
> He pays me meat and fee ;
> And I will keep my good auld house
> While my house will keep me."
>
> 'They laid their sowies to the wall,
> Wi' mony a heavy peal ;
> But he threw ower to them agen
> Baith pitch and tar barreil.
>
> ' With springalds, stanes, and gads of airn
> Amang them fast he threw,
> Till mony of the Englishmen
> About the wall he slew.
>
> ' Full fifteen days that braid host lay,
> Sieging Auld Maitland keen,
> Syne they ha'e left him hail and fair,
> Within his strength of stane.'

And the ruins of this 'auld strength of stane' are still standing upon the hill about two miles and a half from the burgh of Lauder, the river Leader meandering lazily through the march below, passing also in its course King Edward's Fort at Lauder-town, to which the Maitlands removed somewhere about 1585, in Chancellor Maitland's day. He was younger brother to Sir William Maitland of Lethington, Queen Mary's Secretary. Their ancestral home at Thirlestane having become too antiquated, darksome, and ruinous, the family vacated it, after beautifying and considerably enlarging Lauder Fort, which King James V. had used as a hunting seat, and to which the Chancellor eventually gave the patrimonial name of Thirlestane Castle.

As such it remains to this day; and the ancient fortress has now become one of the most princely palaces in Scotland, noted for its massive towers and imposing grandeur, which is due to the taste and wealth of the notorious Duke of Lauderdale. These facts become interesting as connected with the history of the Lauders, even though Lauder Fort never belonged to the Tower family ; because we know that Charles Maitland, third Earl of Lauderdale, brother and successor to the Duke, married Elizabeth Lauder, his second cousin, the only daughter and heiress of Richard Lauder, Esq. of Halton, in 1652, thus uniting the estate of Halton with the earldom of Lauderdale. This was the second marriage between the Halton family and the Maitlands—Alexander Lauder having married the Chancellor's sister.

But there never seems to have been much cordiality between the Lauders of the chief line and the Maitlands of Thirlestane. Petty feuds and petty

THE ANCIENT BURGH OF LAUDER

strifes were constantly recurring, causing jealousies in judicial matters as long as the bailieship of Lauderdale remained with the family at the Tower. It is commonly believed that the original town of Lauder stood at one time on the common moor, on the east side of the road leading from Lauder to Stow. If so, it is probable that the first lands of the Lauders lay more in that direction, as in their earliest charters they designate the burgh of Lauder as theirs, being their baronial territory, whereas the lands of the Maitlands of Thirlestane and

MUIRCLEUCH RUINS.

the de Morvilles each lay in an opposite district. The extensive ruins of an old castle which belonged to the Lauders of Muircleuch, down in the glen at the march between Muircleuch and Newhouses, and the ancient tower at Whytslaid, which descended for generations in the family of Sir Alan de Lawedre, prove that their lands stretched far beyond the precincts of the present burgh of Lauder.

The exact date when this ancient town was built is not known, but that it must have been at an early period is evidenced by the wall of defence with which it was enclosed. A small portion of this wall is still standing; and the four entrances to the burgh were called 'ports.' In the olden time the Lauders of the Tower would probably have the defence of that on the western side, as William Lauder, one of the bailies, whom we shall have occasion to mention, was styled 'Will of the West Port.'

There is one point, however, of which there can be no doubt, viz., that in whatever situation the lands granted to the Anglo-Norman settlers may have been, they were invariably held of the King for homage and service, which feudal tenure continued in vogue in Scotland up to the sixteenth century, if not later. In the history of property and of persons there are two periods of great importance in the Scottish annals: the first is from the reign of Malcolm Canmore to that of David I., when so many strangers settled in North Britain; and the second is the reign of Robert Bruce, when the contest for the Crown produced so many forfeitures, which were granted to the spirited supporters of the successful King.[1] There were also two elements in the mediæval ages which counteracted the abuses of the growing power of the feudal barons over their vassals and dependants—these were the Crown and the Church; for which reason we find the King courting the alliance of all the principal town communities by erecting them into royal burghs, with certain privileges for military service.

The town lands of Lauder were therefore thus erected into a royal burgh by William the Lion between 1165 and 1214. The laws and customs in the early days of the burgh were primitive in the extreme, and many quaint charters were granted by the King to the burgesses.

One of the privileges of the 'Acre System' adopted by the burgh, and made binding upon each burgess, consisted in his being entitled to put out one cow, one horse, and eight sheep on the burgh common. One cowherd, it seems, was sufficient for the whole township. About sunrise he went through the village blowing a horn, and the owners turned out their cattle, which were driven by the lad on to the common, at some little distance from the burgh, and left there to graze until sunset, when they were again collected by the herd, who brought them back to the main street. Sounding his horn vociferously, he there left them, each cow finding its own way to its own berth.

The horn has been handed down from generation to generation, and the practice continued for centuries.

It is easy to see how in turbulent times whole herds of the burghers' cattle could be driven off by the moss-troopers, or the foraging scouts of an invading army, without the possibility of redress.

[1] Chalmers's *Caledonia*, p. 223.

NOTE.—*The circular abutment beside the Cottages is the only remains of the old Town Wall.*

THE ANCIENT BURGH OF LAUDER

It is not necessary for us to enter into the peculiar tenure of the land ; suffice it to mention that as 'the early charters were lost in the anarchy of the Border wars, a charter of *Novodamus* was given by King James IV. in 1502, confirming the rights and privileges which the burgesses had enjoyed for more than three hundred years.'

The land which belongs to the burgesses extends to seventeen hundred acres. But only one privilege or burgess right goes to each holder, however many 'acres' he may have. A 'burgess acre' does not mean merely one acre in extent—it means one 'holding.' For instance, the seventeen hundred acres of burgh land is divided into a hundred and five burgess acres, for which there are only fifty burgesses. Of these holdings or 'acres,' the Earl of Lauderdale has thirty out of the hundred and five, but 'each burgess must at least have one *acre* which he may cultivate as he pleases ; but the part of the common effciring to it must be cultivated, so far as rotation is concerned, as the magistrates and council direct, so that the whole land may terminate in pasture at the same time.' This is applicable to the 'in-field land,' that is, land which has been broken up, and been in cultivation. The 'common,' or what is called 'out-field land,' is pastured in common, and the stock upon it is managed by a committee of burgesses, and the proceeds divided. The number of 'acres' cannot be increased, and a new burgess can only be admitted when an old one is retiring, or disposed to sell his 'acre.' The price of an 'acre' ranges from £150 to £350 or so, according to the size, situation, and quality. It may measure from one and a half to three and a half imperial acres. The money does not go to the burgh, but to the burgess selling it, as he paid for it on entry.

To this day in Lauder burgh, the 'acre' mode of tenure is the same ; managed partly by the individual, and partly by the magistrates and council. Sir Henry Maine considers the burgh of Lauder as the best and most complete example of the 'community system' extant in Scotland.

Of course many of the primitive customs are at present obsolete. For instance, what community in our day would tolerate the following curious monopoly ?—' No one shall bake or brew in the burgh, except John Lauder, the bailie thereof.'

The ancient custom of 'Riding the Marches' has also been abolished in Lauder, though still continued in some Scottish towns. It was formerly considered a very necessary precaution, when the burghs were not enclosed. We are told that—' Once a year, on the King's Birthday, the bailies, council and burgesses mounted on horseback in front of the Tolbooth, and drank his

Majesty's health, and then set off to ride round their ground.' 'At various points the burgess-roll was called, and witnesses were present who could thus give evidence where the burgesses rode, the law presuming they were within their own property.' One of these roll-call places is on the west side of the Stow road, and is marked by a high cairn.

LAUDER PARISH CHURCH, AND SITE OF MARKET CROSS.

The riders 'went past the school to Woodheads march; passed westward, returning along Whitlaw and Trabrown march, and home by the west. Within three quarters of a mile from home, they halted for a race. Those who could not hold on, got some one who could to ride his horse, and the whole came down at a furious pace to the Town Hall.' Dangerous frolic to the public and to themselves—and serious accidents occasionally happened.

This boisterous ceremony was usually allowed to be a season of excessive feasting and drinking; 'the bailies, council and burgesses, all dining together in the evening.'[1] The town of Lauder was at one time a place of considerable importance politically; and the Scotch Parliament occasionally met there in the 'old kirk at the castle.' There was also a market cross at which public proclamations were made in the olden times; it stood in the main street, or market-place, a few yards west from the Tolbooth stairs, nearly opposite the present parish church. One of the peculiarities of Lauder burgh is a backway for carts, running the whole length of the town. It is said by some that the gates were locked at an early hour nightly, after which all the traffic was required to enter by one gate only, and the backway afforded access to it. Here they also had that primitive kind of curfew, called the 'town drummer,'

[1] For the foregoing remarks on the tenure of the burgh land, and also much of the local information anent the customs of the burgh, we are indebted to the courtesy of Mr. Broomfield, the well-known solicitor there, who has kindly permitted us to make use of the MS. notes which his father, the late Mr. Thomas Broomfield, had prepared for the *Berwickshire News*, 1892.

who went through the streets every night at eight o'clock, beating his drum most vigorously—repeating the performance again in the morning between five and six o'clock, to waken the inhabitants. As clocks and watches were not in vogue in the days of the curfew bell, this rude reveille was pardonable enough then ; but one can hardly believe that such a barbarous practice was only voted a nuisance, and stopped, about forty or fifty years ago : such however is a verified fact.

Before proceeding to mention a few of the historic events which have kept the name of Lauder burgh so fresh in the memory of all lovers of old chronicles, it may be well, perhaps, for us to learn somewhat of the rights and privileges which constituted a thirteenth century royal burgh. A very brief study of the pages of the various writers on this subject will soon bring before us the most interesting and prominent points in these ancient laws and customs ; without which it is not easy for us to understand the life and freedom of a burgher in the Middle Ages, compared with the servile bondage of the non-freed agricultural labourers and tenantry.

Royal burghs were undoubtedly the only centres of freedom in Scotland in the twelfth, thirteenth, and fourteenth centuries—'*as freedom was then understood.*'

They constituted the freedom of the Crown from the evil consequences of the non-allegiance of rebellious nobles, on the one hand ; and the freedom of the burghers from the oppression and tyranny of the great barons, on the other. For which reason the site of a royal burgh was always chosen with due regard to its proximity to a royal castle, or a cathedral with a monastery, and if possible with the advantage of a harbour, for trade by sea or river. When the town was established on the royal demesne, the houses, grounds and privileges were held directly from the Crown—it was then called 'the King's burgh.'

'No man could be a King's burgess, according to the burgh laws, unless he did service to the King for at least one rood of land—known as his *burrowage.* He was bound to defend it, and to pay to the King five pence a year for every rood so held.'

'On admission, every burgess had to swear fealty to the King, and to the bailies, and to the community of the burgh.'

The 'burgess-roll had to be produced at the court or *eyre* of the great chamberlain, who, as representing the sovereign, periodically visited the royal burghs—supervised their conduct, and disposed of appeals from the decisions of the burgh magistrates.'[1] In the early days of burghal development, the

[1] Early Scottish Burghs. *Scottish Review,* vol. ii. 1883.

annual payments by the burgesses to the Crown, and all fines and issues of the burgh court were collected and paid over to the Exchequer by a Crown officer, known as the bailie, who seems moreover to have exercised a certain civil and criminal jurisdiction within the burgh.

After a time the Crown, in order to raise money, adopted the practice of *farming* the rights of levying rents and customs to certain individuals for a fixed sum, which was no doubt one of the reasons of the deadly feuds between the bailies by fee, and the hereditary baronial bailies of Lauderdale; for all burghs were not royal burghs—there were also burghs of regality, burghs of barony, and bishops' burghs. The King granted all charters in his own burgh, but he only *confirmed* those that were granted by a lord, whether lay or ecclesiastic. 'A grant of regality was the highest that could be given to a subject. It took as much out of the Crown as the sovereign could give: in fact, it invested the person who received it in the sovereignty of that territory.' Such were the early grants given to the noble houses of Douglas and Angus, enabling them to bid defiance to the throne, which necessitated the increase of royal burghs to counteract their influence and power. For 'every burgess was required to provide himself with military weapons, and to take part in the periodical musterings and weapon-shawings which were proclaimed and supervised by the magistrates of the burgh.' He was bound also to defend his own burrowage and to take his share of watch and ward, not only in defence of the town, but of the kingdom. Strangers therefore of any nationality could settle down as Scottish burgesses in a 'King's burgh,' providing they became amenable to all the laws and regulations, paying the customary fees, and doing the required service. Even bondmen could enter under certain conditions, for 'the burgh laws proclaimed that if any man's *thrall*, baron's or knight's, came to a King's burgh, and bought a burrowage and dwelt in it for twelve months and a day without challenge of the lord or of his bailie, he should be evermore free as a burgess within that burgh, and enjoy its freedom.' But this was not an easy matter, even though burgess-ship could be bought—the buying was often the most difficult part of the accomplishment. A bondman might escape into a town and elude observation for a time, but unless he brought with him the means of purchasing a tenement, and actually acquired it, his residence was ineffectual.'[1] Then again, property in those days could not be sold 'except in the presence of witnesses, encumbered with all the formalities prescribed by the law'; so that it is 'almost inconceivable that any bondman, or person attached to the soil of an estate, could realise the means wherewith to purchase a

[1] *Scotland under her Early Kings*, by E. W. Robertson.

burrowage, without the knowledge and challenge of his lord.' But through the good-fellowship and assistance of the other burgesses it did sometimes happen; and after a bondman had remained his full time and acquired his freedom, constant residence in the burgh was not required as an indispensable condition of his burgess-ship, only non-residents did not enjoy the full amount of the rights and privileges. Every burgess, however, was bound to attend the three head courts of the burgh, held after the Feast of St. Michael, Yule, and Easter, and another imperative duty was that of '*Watching the Burgh*.' The arrangement for this was as primitive as the 'Curfew Drum.' An officer appointed by the burgh went his nightly round, and with a stout staff struck the door of each house which was bound to provide a watchman for that night, who was expected to step forth, fully equipped with two weapons, ready to watch the burgh, 'wisely and busily, from curfew to sunrise.'

In turbulent times this post was no sinecure, even though the curfew forbade all men but those in authority from leaving their homes after nightfall, 'except to fetch a priest to a sick man, to go to the mill, or to do the bidding of their lord';[1] and even under these circumstances, he who was abroad after dark, when called to halt, was bound to declare openly the reason of his absence from home. In King David's reign robberies were so frequent, and cattle-lifting so general, that he considered the watch-dog of such paramount importance that he enacted a special law with regard to it. Whoever killed a watch-dog was bound to watch its master's house for a year and a day, and become answerable during that period for any losses that might be incurred.

One of the burghal regulations in order to keep up the dignity of the magistrates was the prohibiting of 'any Provost, Bailie, or Bedell, from making bread, or brewing ale for sale'; and with regard to the burgherhood, the same law 'excluded from its privileges every dyer, butcher, or tanner, who worked at his calling with his own hands.' He could only superintend as 'a Master.'

As no royal burgh was complete without a castle, neither was any burgh complete without its hospital, especially in the days when leprosy was so prevalent in Scotland—said to have been brought over by the crusaders from the East. The rules with reference to lepers were very stringent, and Lauder burgh was no exception. Any person struck with leprosy had to be removed immediately without the walls of the town, to the 'leper-spittal' on the moor; and if it were discovered that any one had sheltered a leper within the burgh, he was fined the full forfeiture of his whole burrowage. And yet, strange to

[1] *Scotland under her Early Kings*, vol. i. p. 260.

say, though a leper dared not upon pain of death be seen to enter any town, he was not forbidden '*to sit at the gate and beg*.'

The rights of the burgh consisted chiefly in matters of jurisdiction, and the privileges in mercantile and personal affairs. Every burgess had a right to be tried by his peers. He might decline the jurisdiction of any court outside the burgh, even the King's court, and demand, when challenged in any suit, to be tried in the court of his own burgh, before his alderman or bailie. At the same time it was necessary that he should *appear* when cited before a King's court, out of due respect to the King's authority, otherwise he could not claim his privilege. But 'no burgess could be summoned by a King's officer unless accompanied by an officer of the burgh.' Neither could any person if arrested by a King's bailie 'be removed beyond the liberty of the burgh, either to the castle, or any other prison, unless he failed to find surety.' And in the matter of levying food and funds for the garrison of the castle at any time, the castellan could not require a burgess to lend him goods of greater value than forty pence, or for a longer period than forty days.[1] It was also the right of every burgess, when he went on pilgrimage with the sanction of the Church, whether to the Holy Land or a distant shrine of any sacred place, that 'his house and means were declared to be in the *King's peace*, and in the *Bailie's peace*, until his return.'

Every offence committed by a burgess had to be settled in the court-house of his own burgh, whether that offence related to the King, the constable of the castle, or any noble of whatever degree or locality, and the jury must consist of men of his own community. This constituted his right of freedom from all thraldom but the laws of the royal burgh he belonged to. By no means an insignificant right in the feudal days of baronial 'pit and gallows.'

The castellan also held a court at the castle gate, at which all within and without the burgh who had any grievance against the castellan himself, or any of his retainers, had to appear and make their complaint, and to abide by the decision of that court.

As all lands in a royal burgh were held of the Crown, each holder of a certain tenure or amount of land had to render forty days' service on castle guard, but no constable could summon a knight to perform castle guard whilst he was serving in the King's army, either at home or abroad ; nor could he exact a fine at any time, if a proper substitute, a liege man, was forthcoming who would voluntarily perform the service. It is easy to see, under these conditions, how galling the service could be made at times, and what scope it

[1] 'Early Scottish Burghs.'—*Scottish Review.*

afforded for adding fuel to the smouldering ashes of the constant feuds between the knights of Lauder Tower and the constable of the castle at Lauder Fort. It was a continual warfare between burgh rights and the supreme power of an unscrupulous regality. The two mills also—the grain mill and the fulling mill, of which, in the earliest days of the burgh, the castle had the one half, and the tower the other—were a prolific source of altercations and reprisals. Being situated, the one below the fort, and the other beyond the old castle of Thirlestane, and both upon the banks of the Leader, the fishings of which stream sometimes belonged to the one family and sometimes to another, according to their grants and forfeitures, it became an easy matter for the vassals on the one side or the other to cause annoyance and injury by diminishing or increasing the volume of the water by blocking up the mill-dam; for which reason in troublous times burgh mills and baronial mills were usually watched by night and by day. Besides these mills driven by water, there were also in suitable situations windmills for grinding the corn, though in many districts the rude hand-mill was all they had for many centuries, laboriously worked by the upland bondmen.

As royal burghs were expressly designed to foster the spirit of peace, commercial enterprise, and good brotherly fellowship, one of the duties imposed upon each member of the community was that of helping his neighbour when in trouble. For instance, if a burgess had been misbehaving and was arrested at any place beyond the burgh, either for debt or misdeed, his brother-burgesses were bound to go and bail him out. If the prison were within the sheriffdom, they had to do it at their own cost, if beyond the shire, at the cost of the accused. If, after being kept 'in fastening in his own house for fifteen days,' he could find no surety for his good behaviour, he was committed to the prison of the burgh tolbooth. Trading in merchandise of every description was exclusively confined to the burgh, and commerce was rigidly forbidden to every class except burgesses and 'sons of burgesses, so long as they remained in family with their fathers.' No churchman, noble, baron, or secular person whatever outside of the burgh community could trade. None but burgesses could buy wool, or dye it, or make it into cloth, or even cut up the cloth. And, strange to say, no one but a burgess could have an oven on his land, or keep a hand-mill, or make any article whatever for sale ; and all wholesale merchandise had to be presented in good faith 'to the burgh merchants at the market cross.'

One of the greatest privileges granted by William the Lion was 'freedom from toll and lastage, and from pontage and passage to all royal burgesses and their heirs, within and without all the havens in the kingdom on both sides of the *Scots Sea*,[1] as the Firth of Forth was then called. This was an immense boon to traders. From the very earliest charters the burgesses were vested in the absolute property of their holdings, and the succession of their heirs fully secured on the principle of primogeniture. Bastardy alone precluded inheritance. To burgesses of energy and talent, therefore, the way was open to wealth and influence, and many of them acquired high positions among the landed class ; some eventually becoming provosts of the various royal burghs, marching at the head of the burghers to battle, and being honoured with knighthood for good service rendered to the King. In the burgh records we find this to have been the case both in the Dick and Lauder families, even before their intermarriage. The stirring reminiscences of the old Border warfare in Lauderdale alone would fill not one but many volumes, its every hill and valley teeming with memories of marching armies, with warlike barons, knights, and squires performing prodigies of valour ; whilst on the other hand, the poets sing of the beauties of its hills and dales, the whimpling streams, the moorland and the heather, and antiquarians love to wander among its ancient keeps and towers, their every footprint burning with historic lore. It is a great pity there is so much uncertainty about the exact site of the old Lauder Bridge of historic fame, over which Cochrane and his companions, the King's unworthy favourites, were so ignominiously hanged by the nobles assembled with the army of King James on the banks of the Leader in 1482. It is one of the episodes in the history of the burgh which can never fall into oblivion. 'The shallow waters of the Leader winding in devious folds' must have presented anything but a sleepy condition with 50,000 men encamped around the royal tent. It is very evident this spot under these peculiar circumstances was chosen for various reasons as most suitable for the carrying out of the lynch law against the six ill-fated favourites, whose national crimes were decidedly augmented in the eyes of the great nobles of that chivalrous age by the fact that not one of them was really a '*gentleman*' in name, mind, or manners. The only one among them whose father had been knighted was young Ramsay of Balmain ; this, and his extreme youth, weighed considerably in his favour as he clung to the King, who put his arm round him, and begged his life from the stern Sir Archibald Douglas, whose feudal superiority in the surrounding neighbourhood gave a specious appearance of justice to the red-handed punishment of the King's minions.

> 'I mean that Douglas, fifth of yore,
> Who coronet of Angus bore,

[1] 'Early Scottish Burghs.'

' And when his blood and heart were high,
Did the third James in Court defy,
And all his minions led to die
On Lauder's dreary flat.'

So utterly detested had they been by the commoners that the very soldiers exultingly offered the ropes of their tents and the bridles of their horses to assist in the execution of their hanging. This black deed accomplished, the nobles proceeded to secure the King's own person; and the house in which he was captured was still standing in the main street a few years ago. Instead of marching against their ancient foe the southern King, the assembled army returned with the lords to Edinburgh, carrying their own King back as a prisoner; young Ramsay of Balmain being permitted to accompany him and to remain in the castle, where the King was placed under '*a gentle and respectful degree of restraint*,' so potent were these feudal lords in feudal times. But the affection of King James for his rescued favourite appears to have been more permanent than was usual with so weak and fickle a monarch, dating as it did from his schooldays. In a letter[1] from Lord Fountainhall to his son, Sir John Lauder, we find him mentioned as follows :—

'John Ramsay, son to the Laird of Corstoun, in Fife, and of Janet Napier, his wife, being ane handsome young boy, was made choice of to attend King James III. at the Grammar-School. There was pains taken for another gentleman's son who was bred in the High School of Edinburgh, and both read and wrote better; yet the young King thinking John had more the mien of ane gentleman, preferred him—the choises of such princes being like Rehoboam's, not so much founded on merit as fancy, and ane similitude of humours; and I have observed friendship and acquaintance contracted betwixt boys at school to be very durable, and so it proved here. For King James III. made him one of his cubiculars, and then Captain of his Guards; with this extravagant privilege that none should wear a sword within two miles of the King's Palace, without his special warrant and licence, which caused him much envy and hatred. But for supporting him against the same, he first knighted him, and then gave him the lands of Kirkanders in Galloway, Terrinean in Carrick, Gorgie in Lothian, and Balmain in the Mearns. All which lands his posterity hath sold, or been evicted from by recognitions except Balmain.'

When the King was his own master again, after the insurrection of Lauder Bridge, he created his young favourite, Sir John Ramsay, Lord Bothwell—that most fatal title to all who ever held it, be it Hepburn or Stewart. But after the

[1] Dick-Lauder Charter-Chest, Letter, dated 3rd April 1691.

King's tragic death the Parliament annulled that title, and Ramsay was simply called 'the Laird of Balmain' to the end of his days.[1]

What part the Lauders took in this lawless administration of capital punishment we are not told; upon this point the family records are silent. But it does seem a little incongruous that all the secret meetings of the disaffected nobles should take place in the auld kirk at the fort when the burgh could boast of a tolbooth or council house: it almost leads us to suppose that the Lauders of the Tower were on the King's side of the quarrel. This auld kirk, which is now completely demolished, stood about sixty yards from Lauder Fort. There is a very old sycamore tree still standing which marks the approximate site. In this ancient chapel the Bailies of the Tower worshipped for more than five centuries, and here they buried their dead for many generations.

[1] These facts are in a measure interwoven in the past history of the Lauder connections, seeing that this same John Ramsay was ancestor to Lord Fountainhall's father-in-law, Sir Andrew Ramsay of Abbotshall.

CHAPTER XXI

THE LAUDERS OF LAUDERDALE

'A house there stands on Leader side
Surmounting my descriving,
With rooms sae rare, and windows fair,
Like Daedalus' contriving.
Men passing by do aften cry,
In sooth it hath no marrow:
It stands as fair on Leader side,
As Newark does on Yarrow.'

NICOL BURNE.

O discuss the ancient burgh of Lauder without recalling the history of these old bailies would be like acting *Hamlet* and leaving out the ghost; for in all royal burghs the office of baronial bailie was analogous to that of chief alderman in England. In the earlier ages the position was hereditary, and the title one of honour and distinction, the duties being those of chief civil magistrate in the King's burgh, with judicial and legislative authority, held of the Crown direct. At the same time it appears evident that in higher criminal cases the bailies of the burgh were subject to the unlimited jurisdiction of the sheriff, who was chief man of the shire. The office of Sheriff-depute of Berwickshire was vested for life in the powerful family of the Homes from 1447, which was the occasion of the bitterest animosity at times, notwithstanding the frequent intermarriages between the contending families of Lauder and Home. A simple case in point occurring as early as 1476 when a cause was moved in Parliament at the King's instance, against two bailies of Berwick Tower, for taking out of the King's irons two persons who had been put in by the sheriff.[1] It is also stated that Patrick, Lord Hailes, was then Sheriff of Berwickshire, and Oliver Lauder of Lauder his deputy. If so, he must have been acting in his capacity of hereditary bailie of Lauderdale, in concert with Sir Alexander Home, tenth Baron of Home, his own son-in-law, for Mariota, daughter of Sir Robert Lauder of Lauder and Bass, had married Sir Alexander Home, ninth Baron,

[1] *Parliamentary Records*, 208.

and their eldest son Alexander had married his cousin, Oliver Lauder's daughter, also called Mariota.

All that we know of this Oliver Lauder of Lauder Tower seems to be from the *Parliamentary Records*, for we find him in 1473 raising an action against David Pringle, 'touching the thirling of the lands of Pilmuir to the milne of Lauder.' The half of this mill, which had originally belonged to the De Morvilles, had been granted to Sir Alan de Lawdre by King Robert in 1371. The case in question was referred by the lords' auditors to an inquest, but the proceedings were stopped in consequence of the letters of King James III. How the matter was eventually settled is not stated, but it would appear as though it must have been in favour of Oliver Lauder, as after his death in 1489 we find the Pringles, or Hoppringles, again molesting the heirs of the deceased in the 'Wardlands pertaining to the King by the death of Oliver Lauder of that ilk,' which his son and nephew laid claim to as belonging to them in virtue of a composition thereof made to them by the Lord Treasurer and componitors, whereas James Hoppringle claimed them as now belonging to him by a gift from the King. A most unlikely gift from such an avaricious monarch as James III., and for which they could produce no charter, proof, or letter, so that the lords decided again in favour of the Lauders—Robert Lauder of Bass and Robert Lauder of Muircleuch—who had paid the customary entry fees as heirs of Oliver Lauder, James Hoppringle being forbidden to molest them in the labouring of the lands otherwise than by process of law if he had any just claim.[1] As to the fulling mill, records prove that it remained in the family up to 1633. This mill was one of the most important of the 'pertinents' attached to a barony, in some sense almost as essential as the grain mill itself, for if the men of the community had to be fed, so also had they to be clothed. Not that Lauder is ever mentioned as a manufacturing town; but the people themselves had learned the art of spinning and weaving from the first settlers, making use of their home-grown wool from the sheep which roamed the surrounding hills and pasture-lands. It was not long ere Scotland became famous for its woollen cloth, trading with the Flemish weavers who came over in the twelfth century; and then every barony had its kirk and its mills, the flour mill for the grain and the fulling mill for the wool—so called from the fuller's earth used in the cleansing of the oil out of the cloth, which was then beaten with heavy wooden mallets turned by a wheel until it was well purified and sufficiently shrunk for use.

Mill-lands, brewlands, and fishings were also very important items in the

[1] *Acta Dominorum Concilii*, 1478-1495, 9th April 1489, p. 120.

THE LAUDERS OF LAUDERDALE 273

home industry and home produce of a baron's revenue, with a band of retainers to feed and money invariably at a low ebb.

We can well understand, therefore, how petty encroachments from unscrupulous neighbours would cause strife and brawling among the dependants on either side, when the barons themselves were ever ready to defend their legal rights, or their supposed rights, by the sword. It needed a stout heart and a strong hand to hold one's own in those days when right and might were so sorely at variance, for family feuds were often as deadly as those of the veriest outside foe. With regard to the lands of the Lauders of that ilk, we must not forget to mention the Forest of Lauder, concerning which the family possessed so many charters, and which was quite distinct from the Ettrick Forest, the regality of which belonged to the House of Douglas. The Forest of Lauder appears to have been the original grant to Robertus de Lavedre, being included in the bailiary of Lauderdale, within which the burgh of Lauder was erected, with its tower, kirk, mills, and council-hall. Whatever lands the younger sons inherited, the Forest seems always to have descended with the Tower to the eldest son for more than five centuries.

In 1525-6 we find the succession is still the same : 'Robert Lauder of that ilk grants to his eldest son, Robert Lauder, and his heirs, his lands of the Forest of Lauder, with half of the mill of Lauder, also his lands of Dalcoif, with tenants, etc.,' all which lands, in the bailiary of Lauder, are confirmed to him by a charter of James V. on the 11th January 1525, the deed being witnessed by Andrew Lauder, brother-german of the granter, and Richard Maitland of Lethington.[1]

Sir Robert Lauder, younger of that ilk, upon his marriage with Alison Cranston, resigned his lands, as was usual, into the King's hands, who thereupon quitclaims them, and re-confirmed them to Lauder and his spouse conjointly on the 29th July 1538. This is the same Sir Robert Lauder of Lauder and Bass, whom we have already mentioned in a former chapter as having obtained that curious indenture from the Preaching Friars of Dundee. Bass and Lauder Tower, up to his death in 1561, had always been represented by the same chief, but he in his will having left the Tower and Lauder lands to his eldest son William, and the Bass and East Lothian lands to his younger son Robert, the succession was henceforth carried on by two distinct branches ; and whereas the arms of Lauder Tower had been previously borne with the name of Bass equally, whilst the two estates were vested in the same representative, so now were they retained by the elder branch only, with the

[1] *Register of the Great Seal*, 1513-1546, No. 344.

original supporters, two white lions—and for heraldic difference the junior branch of Bass took angels as supporters and a gannet for crest, with the motto, SUB UMBRA · ALARUM · TUARUM ·[1] ('under the shadow of thy wings').

This Sir Robert Lauder, the last Baron of Lauder and Bass combined, had ever been the faithful adherent and supporter of Mary of Guise in her warfare and contentions with the Lords of the Congregation; therefore it seems more than probable that the William Lauder who 'maid a litill farsche and play,' to be acted before the Queen-Regent, Mary of Guise, in 1554, was his eldest son, William Lauder, called the Laird of Lauder, to distinguish him from his brother, the Laird of Bass, which William, a few years after the division of the lands, became one of the Lords of Session, as Lord Lauder.[2] Though there is very little information given with regard to him, yet there is quite sufficient to prove his identity. He is mentioned by Lord Fountainhall, his great-grandson, as the 'Laird of Lauder,' and also by Sir Andrew Lauder in one of his private MSS. thus: 'In 1570 and afterwards, I find William Lauder of that ilk, one of the Lords of Session,' and the date of Lord Lauder's resignation is given by Lord Hailes as the 9th July 1575, when Mr. James Meldrum was appointed in his place. Another important fact, also given in Lord Fountainhall's MS., is the marriage of William, Lord Lauder, to 'Mary MacDougall, daughter to the Laird of Mackerston,' whose coat of arms is enrolled [3] as 'a Lyon collared with a broken crown about his neck, in memory of killing the tyrant Nothatus by Dovalus,' governor of Brigantia.[4]

If such is an heraldic fact, it must certainly be one of the oldest coats extant in Scotland, seeing that Nothatus was the ninth governor of Scotia, reckoning from Cecrops, king of Attica, reaching so far back into the dark ages that it requires a very powerful search-light to find his name. As we find heralds differ as well as historians on the subject of genealogy, we shall, as far as possible, follow the succession of the Lauders of that ilk at this period from the holograph notes of Lord Fountainhall, who was himself the representative of the family to whom and of whom he wrote, and consequently admitted by all to be the best authority. From him, however, we only learn the names of his own particular branch, and their relationship to each other, with the coats of arms of the various families with whom they intermarried. The quaint manner, also, in which these relationships are set forth often cause a considerable amount of ambiguity. For their absolute identity, therefore, from their land charters, we have to search the public records.

[1] See illustration, chap. xvi. p. 181.
 In Burke's *Baronage*, erroneously called 'Richard.'
[3] Sir George Mackenzie's *Heraldry*, p. 3.
[4] Holinshed's *Boethius*, p. 46.

THE LAUDERS OF LAUDERDALE

It appears that Lord Lauder and Mary M'Dougall had two sons—Robert, who succeeded him, and William. Robert married Magdalen Home, and William married Elizabeth or Jean Ballenden of Lasswade.

Of these two sons we find little recorded; but their marriages were of great import in the future transactions of their respective sons. Robert's eldest son became Laird of Lauder, as Robert Lauder of that ilk. He was an advocate, and in 1589 he married Margaret Borthwick, resigning his lands, with the Forest of Lauder, half the grain-mill, and the whole of the fulling-mill in the lordship of Lauderdale, to obtain a regrant of them in conjunct fee with his spouse and their future children in heritage. William, his brother, had three sons, William, James, and Andrew. William, the eldest, who had in his youth been nicknamed 'Will o' the West Port,' performed the duties of the hereditary bailieship of Lauderdale, whereby he was often brought into very unenviable connection with the lawless doings of the landowners, both great and small, and incurred much ill-will through the adjudication of the fines and penalties consequent on his office of bailie. Feuds and disagreements were of constant occurrence between the Lauders and the Maitlands, the Homes, the Cranstouns, and the Hoppringles, with each of whom they were closely related by marriage.

These feuds came at length to a terrible climax in the month of March of 1598. There had been fierce animosities going on for some time between them, both in political and social matters. Unfortunately, the Laird of Lauder and his cousin the bailie were both young men, headstrong and firmly rooted in their sturdy independence, which could ill brook the taunts and arrogance of Alexander, Earl of Home, in his capacity of Sheriff of Berwickshire, or the pride of the Maitlands of Thirlestane, to whom the Lauders of Halton, now in the ascendant, were allied. Whether there was at that special time a prisoner of either of these families being tried in the burgh court-house, we know not, for the cause of the catastrophe seems to have been lost sight of in the startling event itself.

It is a well-authenticated historical fact that in the year 1598 the Earl of Home and his armed followers came to the town of Lauder seeking Bailie William Lauder, commonly called 'Will of the West Port,' who no doubt had good reason, from past experience, to suppose their desire to find him was of no friendly import. We are distinctly told he was administering justice in the Tolbooth at the time; whereupon the Earl's party attempted to burst open the door, and upon their refusal to desist, Lauder fired a pistol from a small window, killing John Cranstoun, one of the men. The rest of the party then set fire to the main entrance, thinking thus to prevent his escape; but the bailie, in attempting to rush out through the side door which led to the vaulted prison below the hall, was hacked to pieces, though some say he was 'dirked while on the bench.' James, one of his brothers, besides several of those with him, were also slain, among whom was Robert Lauder of that ilk, his cousin the laird. The combined clans of Home and Cranstoun then fired the Tolbooth, but the thickness of the walls prevented much damage being done

OLD TOLBOOTH, LAUDER.

to the building itself—only the upper floorings and part of the roof being destroyed.

Mr. Broomfield, a very good authority, says: 'The burgh records in the clerk's office go back about three hundred years, and no mention is made of the Hall and Tolbooth till 1770, when the roof was slated in place of thatched, as it had been before that time. If a new Tolbooth had been built within three hundred years, mention was sure to have been made there; and the present Hall is believed to be the veritable Tolbooth where "Will of the

West Port" was murdered.' The walls are very thick, and the vaulted under-story is still arched of stone. There is nothing picturesque about the old building whatever, but it is interesting to us as being the only building at present standing within the ancient burgh which is unquestionably connected with the Lauders of Lauder Tower—for in this ancient court-house each Bailie Lauder in succession for many generations transacted his official duties.

The fact of the perpetration of this barbarous murder was evidenced in court thirteen years later, which Lord Fountainhall mentions in his *MS. Excerpts from the Criminal Registers*: 'Anno 1611—Lindsay, *contra* Carruthers, sometyme servand to my Lord of Sanquhar. He takes him to a remission, granted in November 1606 to Alexander, Earl of Home, Lord Jedburgh and Dunglas, Sir John Hume of Hutton Hall, knight, Mr. Samuel Hume, his brother, Thomas Tyrie, tutor of Drumkelso, etc. etc., wherein the King pardons them all for the treasonable burning of the Tolbuith of Lauder, and killing William Lauder, in Anno 1598, called William at the West Port. (This was my good-sire's eldest brother; he was bailzie at the time, doing justice at the time in the Tolbuith.) The King pardoned them because the said Earl had satisfied the said burgh of Lauder for the said slaughter and burning.'

Lord Fountainhall then adds—'My good-sire [*i.e.* grandfather] was immediately made bailzie upon his brother's slaughter. William left a daughter behind him, that was married to Thomas Calderwood's father; a daughter of hers again is married to William Scott in Dalkeith.'[1]

The satisfaction given was the payment of so many merks into the burgh treasury, the sum varying according to the status of the murdered man. In this instance, William Lauder was hereditary bailie of a royal burgh, and therefore in the King's service, for which, and for the burning of the King's council-house, there would also be indemnification required.

The fact of Andrew Lauder, the youngest and only surviving brother of the deceased bailie, taking his place immediately, proves that the bailieship of Lauderdale was still hereditary in the family; but, from all accounts, the place had been made so hot for him with rancour and ill-feeling that, 'in order to shun any further blood,' he had to take flight for his life to his mother's people at 'Leswaid.' There, we are told, he married 'Polton's daughter as his first wife.' The lady was Janet Ramsay, daughter to David Ramsay of

[1] This extract from Lord Fountainhall's MS. was sent to Sir Walter Scott in a letter, by Charles Kirkpatrick Sharpe, Esq., of Hoddam, in 1824.

Hillhead, son of Ramsay of Polton, a cadet of the Dalhousie family. This Andrew Lauder is styled of Melvin Mill, and he afterwards became a merchant in Edinburgh.

The direct cause of the tragic raid on the Lauders is not stated, but there is full evidence of its having been a matter of family jealousy, which had caused an unrelenting feud of many years' standing, notwithstanding that the two powerful clans of Home and Cranstoun were both related to the Lauders, and the intermarriage of the cousins very frequent. The commencement of the feud appears to date as far back as October 1488, the first year of the minority of James IV. The conspirators, whose rebellion had caused the death of James III. at Beaton's Mill, seizing the opportunity of the non-age of his son, determined to hold the reins of government, and enrich themselves by the impoverishing of those who had become their enemies by appearing in arms in defence of the late King. This they accomplished by fines and forfeitures, after which supreme rule of special districts was distributed among themselves. 'To Lord Hailes and Alexander Home, the heir of Lord Home, were assigned the Merse, Lothian, the wards of Haddington, Linlithgow, and *Lauderdale.*'[1] *Supreme rule* gave power of life and death, which allowed full scope for the elastic conscience of men who could imbrue their hands in the blood of their King, soon finding a pretext for clearing up old family feuds in the same way when fertile lands were coveted ; for, though Lauder burgh was unquestionably the headquarters of the Lauders of that ilk, a glance at an old map of Berwickshire soon discloses the extent of the lands possessed by them in the surrounding neighbourhood, and so firmly were they rooted to the soil, and so loyal were they in their fealty to the Crown, that it was no easy matter even for the combined forces of those in power to wrest their lands from them legally. Hence the high-handed onset of the armed followers and the treacherous use of the dirk, which only increased the feud, and was eventually the means of fugitating the last of the ancient line of the Lauders of Lauder Tower in 1643, as we shall see further on. Lord Home, the father of Sir Alexander Home, who perpetrated the murder of William Lauder in the Tolbooth, had been appointed Lord-Chamberlain before the year 1513, and was one of the few who returned alive after the battle of Flodden Field, but, as Holinshed tells us, he received no sympathy, being severely reproved as the cause of all the mischief at Flodden, having behaved himself, not as a captain, but as a traitor and enemy to his country.[2] Upon that fatal day three of the Lauders were killed—Sir Alexander Lauder of Blythe, Sir George

[1] *Caledonia*, vol. i. p. 282.   [2] Holinshed, p. 482.

Lauder of Halton, his brother, and also James. Lauder of Burngrains, their younger brother.

The Lauders of Halton and the Lauders of Lauderdale were very closely allied in those days, the younger sons of Halton having lands at Whitslaid and Burngrains, contiguous to the lands of Lauder Tower, sharing by contract the grain-mill and the fulling-mill on the Leader.

Robert Lauder of that ilk, who was killed, with his brother William, in the Tolbooth Raid on the 5th March 1598, had only been married nine years, and he left a widow with seven children, the youngest an infant, and the rest all under age, their mother, Margaret Borthwick, being appointed tutrix. The children are all named in the laird's last will and testament, which he had made on the 5th March 1595, and by it it seems evident that the three daughters, Elizabeth, Jane, and Barbara, were older than the four sons, William, Robert, Richard (and John, who was born after 1595). Whatever the extent of Robert Lauder's lands may have been at the time of his death, the money left to the children was simply £867, 13s. 4d.; but, unlike many of the Lairds of Bass, his debts only amounted to £5. He was buried in the 'Auld Kirkyard' near Lauder Fort; and his youngest and only surviving brother, Andrew, was appointed bailie. Mr. Andrew, as before stated, did not remain long in Lauder after the murder of his brother William and the death of Robert, the Laird, whose children all being young, the whole family left the burgh for a time, leaving the old Tower silent and deserted. A strange fate seemed to hang over it from that time forth, for it never regained its prestige, and the family also dwindled as though a sudden blight had come over them. There was no head to take the lead; the chief was a boy, and the widow bowed down with grief.

Mr. Andrew settled with his mother's relatives in Lasswade, and took a wife, as we have seen, from the house of Polton. By Janet Ramsay of Hillhead he had only one son, John, afterwards Bailie Lauder, the first baronet of Fountainhall; but he was married a second time to Isobel Borthwick, by whom he had several children.

Young Robert Lauder, the heir to the Tower, was entered in the estate in due course; and having passed through his studies as a lawyer, he obtained his degree and became an advocate. He afterwards married Ann MacDougall of the Mackerstoun family, into which his grandfather William had married. In 1614 we find him taking his place as chief of the family at the marriage of his eldest sister Elizabeth, who married Thomas Redpath, heir-apparent of Thomas Redpath of that ilk. Their marriage portion consisted of the lands of Wronklie, the charter of which was witnessed by the bride's two brothers,

Robert Lauder of that ilk, and the youngest, called John. Three years later, and the estate of Wronklie passed by purchase into the hands of Ralph Ker, who also obtained the office of bailie of Lauder.

In 1624 we find Robert Lauder of Lauder mentioned as being on an assize in the case of a man called Adie Usher, who was hanged for theft; and again in 1627, when a man Purves was sentenced to transportation for stealing a horse. It is further stated that 'Robert Lauder of that ilk is cautioned that he should attend the Goodman of Johnstonburn till they were all in readiness to goe off the country to serve in the wars; and the Justice ordains the said Goodman to pay to Andrew White, jailor in Edinburgh, his fees.'[1] From a charter anent the forest lands of Lauder, it is evident that Robert Lauder of that ilk had a son and heir born in 1627, and that he resigned his lands in the lordship of Lauderdale in his favour, to be held of the King, with the provision that 'whenever Robert Lauder, senior, on forty days' warning, paid of Rose-noble[2] of gold in the parish kirk of Lauder, or consigned the same in the hands of a responsible man in the parish of Lauder, he should have regress to the said lands.'[3]

It does not appear as though this redemption-money was ever paid, for in a very few years we find the whole of these lands are chartered to Mr. Peter Arbuthnett, servitor of John Maitland, Earl of Lauderdale, with the consent of Sir William MacDougall of Mackerstoun, curator and uncle of Robert Lauder, jun.

Whether this had anything to do with the final quarrel between the Lauders and the Maitlands, we cannot say. Lauder Fort had all been remodelled and renovated by Chancellor Maitland before 1595, and when John, second baron, was raised to the Bench as Lord Thirlestane, the Fort changed its name to Thirlestane Castle—its lord soon after becoming first Earl of Lauderdale. This was in 1624; and it is not difficult to foresee that all lands surrounding the Castle would henceforth be coveted, and every opportunity seized for evicting previous owners by not granting the renewal of the charters in the lordship and regality of Lauderdale. Bit by bit the lands were drawn into the one large estate, which from a barony became a dukedom, and the princely mansion of the notorious Duke of Lauderdale rose like a palace of the *Arabian Nights* in all the magnificence of its gorgeous display in art and classic adornment, encircled by all the natural beauties of a unique situation. What occasioned the serious quarrel between Mr. James Maitland of Auchinchamper

---

[1] Lord Fountainhall's *MS. Excerpts from the Criminal Registers*, pp. 110 and 121.
[2] Rose-noble, a gold coin worth 6s. 8d., stamped on one side with a rose.
[3] *Register of the Great Seal*, 1620-1633, No. 1833.

and the Laird of Lauder Tower we cannot now discover, but fierce words must have passed before it came to fiercer blows with keen-edged weapons; and Mr. James was so worsted in the battle that he was mutilated for life. If this fray took place in Lauder, Mr. Robert does not seem to have sought the protective rights of a burgher in his native place. Nor can we wonder under the circumstances, with a Hume for sheriff and a Maitland for judge, that he should have preferred fugitation with his whole family rather than seeking mercy from the foe of his house. Again Lord Fountainhall takes note of him: 'Anno 1643. Robert Lauder of that Ilk, Anne MacDougall his spouse, and Robert Lauder their son, for mutilation of Mr. James Maitland of Auchinchamper are denounced fugitives for not finding caution.'

The mystery which enshrouds this sad affair Heaven's High Tribunal alone can unveil. We leave it deeply regretful that it should be a death-knell which closes the door of the first of the ancient homes of the long line of Lauders, since the days they fought so bravely for Malcolm Canmore against the usurper Macbeth. That Robert Lauder revisited the home of his forefathers is monumentally evident, for he came to lay the silent form of his only son in the auld kirkyard, close beside Thirlestane Castle. The stone he raised to the memory of the last Lauder of Lauder Tower stands as a witness to the extinction of the oldest branch of the elder line of the Lauders of Lauder and Bass :—

HIC·JACET[1]
ROBERTUS·LAUDERIUS·FILIUS·
UNICUS·ROBERTI·LAUDERII·
ANTIQUÆ·DOMUS·DOMINI
BENŒ·SPEI·ADOLESCENS·
OBIIT·ANNO·DOMINI·1649·
R [shield] L

'Lonely mansion of the dead !
Who can tell thy varied story?
All thine ancient line have fled,
Leaving thee in ruin hoary.

'Thou hast had thy day of pride ;
Martial squadrons rank'd before thee ;
Towering high and flaunting wide,
Gilded banners beaming o'er thee.

---

[1] 'Copied from a gravestone in Lauder Churchyard on the 13th September 1792 by Sir Andrew Lauder-Dick, Bart., of Fountainhall, in presence of his son, Thomas Lauder-Dick.'

'Heroes came and tilted near;
  Beauty claim'd thee for her dwelling;
  Evening pilgrims paused to hear
  Tones of mirth and music swelling.

'Thou hast had thy day of strength,
  Braved the tempest in its thunder,
  Scorned invasion, but—at length
  Time hath rent thy walls asunder!'
                                        DELTA.

In reference to this monumental stone and epitaph, Sir Thomas Dick-Lauder gives a most interesting account in the Family Roll. He says:—

'On the 12th September 1792 my father, Sir Andrew Lauder-Dick, and I went to Lauder together for the purpose of making a search for some of the relics of the Lauders. I was then a boy of eight years old, but the work my father was engaged on filled my young mind with the deepest interest. We sought eagerly for some remains of the ancient family fortalice of Lauder Tower, and were directed to the site where it had stood, in a garden still known by the name of Tower Garden, close by the east side of the present church of Lauder. But, alas! we found not a remnant of the hearths of our ancestors, and the only fragment which now remains of it is a single freestone about two feet square, having the family arms and supporters on it, which seems to have occupied a position over some gateway. This was brought from Lauder to Fountain-hall soon after the purchase of the latter estate by Sir John Lauder, which, for the sake of preservation, was built by my father into the inside wall of the garret at Fountainhall, where it still remains. We looked in vain even for foundations—not a trace was left! The massive walls and towering buttresses, which had so long kept out the furious flood of many a border foray, had given place to the more humble sub-divisions of the kitchen garden. Whilst ruminating on the metamorphosis, my father was addressed by a man of the name of Lauder—who was at that time about eighty years of age—who told him that he well remembered a large portion of the old tower or keep of the building remaining for many years, until the old walls were pulled down to clear the ground.

'In the adjoining churchyard the old man showed us an ancient gravestone, which, though so much injured by time as to occasion some little difficulty in deciphering, was clearly and satisfactorily made out at last. It was the monumental stone of the Robert Lauder who was the last of this chief line of the Lauders of Lauder. My father carefully transcribed it. There was a much defaced coat-of-arms between the last two capital letters R. L. The head of the griffin was visible, but a Latin inscription which followed bade defiance to my father and to the parish schoolmaster whom he called to assist him. It was on the death of this Robert Lauder that the first Sir John Lauder of Newington, Edrington, and Fountainhall, Baronet, succeeded to the chieftainship of the family, and it was then that the Lord Lyon King-at-arms gave him the supporters of the family.

'The old man whom I have mentioned as our willing cicerone at Lauder, and who

THE LAUDERS OF LAUDERDALE 283

seemed to be delighted to get any one to listen to what apparently so much interested himself, told us that this monumental stone had been brought from the old churchyard, near Lauder Fort, in the year 1673 to that in which the present church now stands. He said he remembered to have seen more stones with Latin inscriptions upon them and the name of Lauder, but so old and defaced that he could not make them out.'[1]

The present parish church was erected in 1673 by order of Parliament in the reign of Charles II. It has no pretensions whatever to ecclesiastical grandeur, or even architectural beauty—not even quaintness: it is one of those plain, substantial, homely buildings which mark the severely rigid Covenanting period. We found the old tomb of the last heir to Lauder Tower still erect, but even

TOMB OF THE LAST LAIRD OF LAUDER TOWER, LAUDER CHURCHYARD.

more weather-worn and illegible; and on close examination we came to the conclusion that the letters R. L., with the shield and griffin between and the almost obliterated Latin inscription below, must have been added after the death and burial of the last laird himself, Robert Lauder of that Ilk.

There was also another tomb near it, the front of which had some emblematical carving upon it which looked centuries old; but on the other side of the stone there is an inscription firmly cut. It ran as follows :—' Elizabeth Young, spouse to Andrew Lauder, who died 21 of Nov. 1754, aged 72 years. Also their children, one son and one daughter, who died young.'

[1] Sir Thomas Dick-Lauder's Manuscrip'.

Had this Elizabeth Young been the wife of the old man called Lauder who was himself eighty years of age in 1792, he would have mentioned it to Sir Andrew Lauder at the time of their search; but it is not improbable that he was ere long laid beside her, as the last of that generation of the Lauders of Lauderdale, whose branches from the old root were many and wide-spreading. We cannot undertake to formulate their genealogical tree; but the following list of names, verified from authentic records, will demonstrate the truth of the remark 'wide-spreading':—

LAUDER BRANCHES

The Lauders of Lauder and Bass (re-presented by the same chiefs from 1056 to 1561).
Lauders of Haltoun.
Lauders of Popill.
Lauders of Beil.
Lauders of Quarrelwood, Morayshire.
Lauders of Edringtoun, Berwick.
Lauders of Dunbar.
Lauders of Gunsgreen.
Lauders of that Ilk (after separation, 1561 to 1649).
Lauders of Bass (after division).
Lauders of St. Germains.
Lauders of Muircleuch.
Lauders of Whitslaid.
Lauders of Park.

Lauders of Carolside.
Lauders of St. Leonards.
Lauders of Bounoche.
Lauders of Wormestoun.
Lauders of Burngrains.
Lauders of Over Gogar.
Lauders of Halhouse or Lekbernard.
Lauders of Peebles, Over Kidstone.
Lauders of Tyninghame.
Lauders of Scuny.
Lauders of Blyth.
Lauders of Bruntisfield.
Lauders of Ratho, Norton.
Lauders of Haddington, Le Crag.
Lauders of Easter Pencaitland.
Lauders of Fountainhall.
Lauders of Grange.

Well may we ask of these ancient homes, 'Whence hath fled thine ancient glory?'

The Lauders of Beilmouth, an offspring of the Bass, retained possession of their estate until 1768, and the Lauders of Carolside up till about 1795. The laird of Carolside was the last of the name of Lauder who owned lands on the Leader. Of him Sir Thomas Dick-Lauder writes:—

'This gentleman was so remarkable for his style of dressing that he went in Edinburgh by the name of "*Beau Lauder*," a title which rather flattered than annoyed him. We can just recollect him as being followed by the boys whilst walking the streets as a very old man, with a cocked hat, gold-headed cane, scarlet coat, lace ruffles, embroidered waistcoat, satin shorts, white silk stockings, and gold buckles on his shoes richly set with stones. Poor man! his fate ultimately was a very sad one; for, if our recollection serves us right, he was accidentally burned to death sitting in his chair, as he then was in a helpless state.'

The Lauders of St. Leonards were burghers and agriculturists. It was one of the oldest of the family settlements, having an old tower or keep like

BURN GRANGE.

Whitslaid, but not nearly so extensive as Muircleuch. It had, however, at one time a chapel and a burying-ground. There is still an old inscription built into the farmhouse wall over one of the windows:—

DEUS · EST · FONS · VITÆ ·

the testimony of those who in ages past worshipped here 'in spirit and in truth.' More than five centuries have elapsed since first the walls of this chapel of St. Leonards echoed to the requiem chant for the dead, or the soul-stirring

Te Deum for victory over southern foes, when Leader-town was a place of note, a very battlefield of kingdoms. Now it might well be called 'Sleepy Hollow,' so primitive is the imprint of a past century. So easy-going and quiet, one might almost fancy every day was Sunday, and the inhabitants of the two-storeyed houses and the simple little thatched cottages were taking their indoor Sabbath rest.

OLD STONE FROM LAUDER TOWER.

PART III

CHAPTER XXII

SIR JOHN LAUDER, FIRST BARONET OF FOUNTAINHALL

'Blest too is he who can divine
Where the real right doth lie,
And dares to take the side that seems
Wrong to man's blindfold eye.
. . . . . .
'For Right is right, since God is God,
And Right the day must win;
To doubt would be disloyalty,
To falter would be sin.'
FABER.

THE younger branch of the ancient family of the Lauders of Congalton and the Bass having declined in the seventeenth century, they gradually died out, as we have seen.

But it is with the elder, and at present only remaining branch, that the story of 'Sanct Geilies' Grange' is concerned; and we find the connecting-link in the person of Andrew Lauder, who settled at Lasswade in 1595. He was the third son of 'Robert Lauder of that ilk, and his lady, Elizabeth (Jean) Ballenden, daughter of Ballenden, Laird of Leswaid.' It was his elder brother, William, called 'Will of the West Port,' who was killed by the Homes and the Cranstons, with several others of his kindred, 'when they brant the Tour of Lauder in 1598.'[1]

LORD FOUNTAINHALL'S BOOK-PLATE.

Mr. John Lauder, the eldest son of Andrew Lauder of Lasswade and Janet Ramsay of Polton, became the wealthy merchant-burgess of Newington, who acquired all the lands of Fountainhall, Temple Hall, Mutton Hole, and Peaston Burn, in the county of Edinburgh, eventually erecting them into a barony. He is usually styled Bailie Lauder, to distinguish him from his son, Sir John Lauder, who was knighted in

[1] Maidment's *Analecta Scotica*.

1681, six years before his father obtained the honour and title of Baronet. The Bailie was a prudent, purpose-like man of business, and endowed with great tact, which enabled him to steer clear of the political controversies so prevalent in his day. He amassed a large fortune, and made many influential friends. The circle of his family connections was very extensive, as one can easily imagine, seeing he was three times married, and became the father of twenty-three children. His first wife was Margaret

FOUNTAINHALL.

Speirs, by whom he had two sons, Andrew and James, and one daughter. She died after the birth of her second son, James, in 1643. His second wife, whom he married in 1645, was Isobel Ellis, daughter of Alexander Ellis of Mortonhall and Margaret Uthward (commonly called Edward), whose father, Nicol Uthward, was Dean of Guild in Edinburgh, and her grandfather was Provost in 1592. The family of Eleis or Ellis dated back for several generations prior to the reign of James IV., and were notably connected with the Setons of Parbroath and the Nisbets of Dirleton.[1] Isobel Ellis bore her husband, Bailie Lauder, fourteen sons within twenty-two years, and after her death he married again in 1670. His third wife was Margaret Ramsay, daughter of George Ramsay of Iddington, in the county of Berwick. Young and beautiful she may

[1] See Appendix, Note X. Holograph notes of Sir John Lauder, Lord Fountainhall, in the Dick-Lauder charter-chest.

FIRST BARONET OF FOUNTAINHALL 291

have been, as old men's brides so often are, but she soon proved herself to be the proverbially unjust stepmother towards the children of the former marriage, seeking eventually to obtain everything for her own son George, to the detriment of the lawful heir and his younger brothers, William, Andrew, and Colin. These alone, it would appear, lived to reach man's estate out of the fourteen sons of Isobel Ellis. William became a physician, and Colin[1] a merchant. Sir John Lauder, the eldest, had already married his cousin, Janet Ramsay, and left the paternal home the year before his father's third marriage; and as both of the sons of Bailie Lauder's first wife had also died young, and the only daughter, Catherine, had married into the Blythswood family long before that unfortunate event, no mention is ever made of them in any of the subsequent family papers.

Margaret Ramsay appears to have been a heartless, worldly woman—one who, having first insinuated herself into the affections of the old Bailie, led him captive at her will, holding full sway at Fountainhall. Judging from the letters written about her, and the far from complimentary terms in which she is described by her stepsons, she must have made the patrimonial home anything but a paradise. From the very first she began to sow discord between the children of the former marriage and their father, and eventually endeavoured to rob them of their birthright. For many years she incessantly wearied her husband by her inordinate ambition, constantly urging him to procure a knight-baronet's patent; and when at length the old man complied with her importunate request, she, with the assistance of her father, George Ramsay of Iddington, and her brother-in-law, Doctor Trotter, had the deed made out so that it should descend to her eldest son George, then a child. As soon as the Bailie became aware of what she had so fraudulently done, he openly declared his dissent to the transaction, and appointed another patent to be obtained running in the natural channel of his lawful heirs. This so enraged the ambitious woman that she became almost mad with jealousy, and resolved at all hazards to get possession of that new patent, which had been left in the hands of Mr. Robert Lauder to be testified. Setting off, therefore, post-haste to Edinburgh, she reached Mr. Lauder's house at eleven o'clock at night, and forcing herself and her accomplices into his presence, she declared 'she would have his heart's blood' if he did not deliver up the patent at once. Such violent effrontery met with its own reward, and the patent was placed in safer legal quarters, until the matter was decided by the court. This was in the month of May 1688. Still unabashed, Margaret Ramsay allowed her malice to carry her so far as to

[1] From whom Dr. William Preston Lauder is descended.

denounce Sir John Lauder in open court as an enemy to the late King James, and disaffected to the present Government, hoping thereby to see him relegated to the prisons of the Bass. In consequence of this defamation, she actually, with the assistance of her brother-in-law, procured another patent, with the title descending to her four sons, George and his three little brothers, successively, and at their death to become extinct, declaring that she hoped to live to see her stepsons all rooted out, 'they and their posterity, from off the face of the earth.' By threats she expected to overpower the decision of her aged husband in favour of his elder sons; terrifying him by attempting to stab herself in his presence if he would not comply with her unreasonable requests, and threatening to drown herself and her children if any of the other sons came near the house.

No wonder the poor, tender-hearted old man was often heard to declare with much sorrow, 'that her marriage had made him wearie of his life.' Could any thorn in the flesh have been greater than this uncongenial spouse, whose fraudulent ways and evil doings are all set forth in the quaint phraseology of the period by Sir John Lauder in the memorial sent to Parliament in 1689-90.[1] The details narrated in the memorandum for this document would furnish data sufficient for a three-volume novel, so thoroughly did Margaret Ramsay bear out the character of the worst type of stepmother.

They seemed to need pretty strong language in those days, for Lord Fountainhall says, ' She studied by all the diabolical acts that feminine malice could inspire to alienate the said John Lauder's affection from his children.' She certainly showed a most pitiful want of courtesy to her indulgent husband, never allowing him to be alone one minute with his elder sons, by intruding herself and her relations most insolently at all times and seasons, following him like a spy from room to room, lest he should put his hand to paper to sign any document in their favour. But what kind of daughter could one expect from such a father as George Ramsay of Iddington—a man who could lend himself to the embezzlement of the money intrusted to him, then lay the blame upon another, and who could break open the Bailie's cabinets to search for papers, and force the old man, by threats, to alter his will, demeaning himself to fraud and forgery of dispositions, with a man upon his deathbed!

Of what avail was all this unjust scheming? Retributive justice swiftly overtook them all. Right at length became might, and pride was humbled in the dust.

[1] See Appendix, Note XIII. Holograph notes by Sir John Lauder; Memorandum anent the patent and libel case, in the Dick-Lauder charter-chest.

FIRST BARONET OF FOUNTAINHALL

A charter was granted by Parliament on the 25th of January 1690, testifying that Sir John Lauder, knight, eldest surviving son of Sir John Lauder of Fountainhall, first baronet, was heir to the title and dignity of a knight-baronet, to which he accordingly succeeded at the death of his father—on the 2nd April 1692, in his ninety-sixth year, his youngest son David being born when he was eighty-three years of age. The family mansion-house of Fountainhall was then quitted for ever by Margaret Ramsay. Of the three sons, George, Archibald, and David—for whom she had acted in such a disgraceful manner—only one lived to inherit the estate of Iddington, and his death is registered in 1704, 'on the 4th February, Archibald Lauder, Lord of Idington.' He was born in 1679, and consequently was only twenty-five. Of the two daughters, Margaret, the eldest, died, and the younger one, Elizabeth, married John Cuninghame of Woodhall.

Sir John Lauder now became chief of the family, having obtained a decreet annulling the first patent—a most lengthy but valuable document, which is preserved in the charter-chest with both the baronetcy patents, one sealed and the other showing the marks where the seal had been torn off and cancelled. The parchment also is much damaged, apparently by 'having been thrown into the fire to destroy it, but suddenly snatched out again.' Both of them have the red and white ribbons, the tinctures of the family coat, attached to them, but only the true one bears the imposing 'Great Seale.'

After assisting the heralds to prepare an escutcheon for the burial of his father, the first baronet of Fountainhall, Sir John Lauder, wrote the following epitaph for his tomb :—

> 'Honorabilissimi Domini D. JOANNIS LAUDER Senioris a Fountainhall.
> Equitis Baronteti. Epitaphium.
>
> 'Lauderum laudes moruit qui mille recondit
> Hic Tumulus ; lachrymas fundere jure derit.
> Cana fides, stabilis pietas, prudentia solers,
> Forma venusta sonis, consociata jacent.
> Heu Virtutis honos, cunctarium et copia rerum,
> Tristia non fati pallere jura queunt !'
>
> 'G. SKENE, *Rector*.
> 'J. DUFTRIS, *Scholos*.
> 'Edinburgenæ.'

Sir John Lauder, second baronet of Fountainhall, who thus took possession of his patrimonial home, was the eldest son of Isobel Ellis and Bailie Lauder. He was born in Edinburgh in 1646, and was consequently forty-six years of age at his father's death. He was brought up to the law, and after finishing

294 SIR JOHN LAUDER

his studies at the University of Edinburgh, he was sent to complete his education abroad. From his own manuscript journal, written during his residence in France, it appears 'that he set out on horseback from Edinburgh on the 26th March 1665, and reached London on the 1st of April.' There he spent six days in visiting the most remarkable objects in the metropolis; after which he, along with some companions, 'sailed down the river to Gravesend, proceeded by post to Dover, crossed to Calais, and from thence hastened to Paris.' His expenses between Edinburgh and Paris he reckoned as having come to £9 sterling. He remained at Poictiers from 28th July to the 14th April of the following year studying the French law, afterwards returning to

BARONETCY PATENT—LAUDER, 1688.

Paris *via* Cambray and Valenciennes. Shortly after, taking a 'voyage through Holland and Flanders,' he visited Brussels and Antwerp, then settled down for some time in Leyden to complete his studies. Finally, he took boat at Mardyke and sailed for Rotterdam, returning to Scotland on the 9th November 1667.[1]

The diary which Mr. John Lauder began on leaving home at the age of twenty, he continued uninterruptedly to the end of a long life, forming those voluminous manuscripts of which we shall speak presently. His marriage took place two years after his return from Leyden, having first taken his position as a member of the Faculty of Advocates. His wife, as before stated, was his first cousin, Janet, daughter of Sir Andrew Ramsay of Abbotshall,[2] at that time proprietor of the Bass and Provost of Edinburgh. The marriage seems to have been a

---

[1] Preface by Dr. David Laing in *Historical Notices of Scottish Affairs; Selected from the Manuscripts of Sir John Lauder of Fountainhall, Bart.*

[2] The portrait of Sir Andrew Ramsay, Bart., of Abbotshall, who died in 1688, and that of his daughter Janet, the wife of Lord Fountainhall, are both at the Grange House.

very happy one, and most auspicious in every way for the youthful bridegroom, then in his twenty-fourth year, his father-in-law being a man of influence and wealth. Besides being Provost of the city and a Lord of Session, he filled the office of 'Rector and Governor' of the University. This office had been combined with his provostship in 1665, owing to the high-handed disturbance he had caused in consequence of a son of his having been chastised severely with the birch-rod by one of the Regents of the College. From that day corporal punishment was abolished in the University—to the corporeal delight of the students, no doubt, but to the utter dismay of such godly parents as practically believed in the wisdom of Solomon about sparing the rod and spoiling the child. It is more than likely the Provost's son was spoiled already, though Sir Andrew was not always so considerate of the feelings of other people's sons when called upon to exercise his civic authority. On the contrary, he was deemed a very violent-tempered man. It was in the month of May of that same year, 1665, that the anniversary of the birth and restoration of Charles II. was celebrated with national rejoicings, in which Sir Andrew took a prominent part as Provost.

It is amusing to note with what suavity they combined preaching, praying and feasting upon such royal occasions, and how much loyalty was stimulated by the royal wine which flowed liberally 'for divers hours at eight conduits, to the great solace of the indigent commons,' around the Mercat Cross. Here they also erected a green arbour, loaded with oranges and lemons, for the Provost and members of the Council, among whom was Bailie Lauder, at that time an influential, active man.

One of the most memorable sights of that gala-day of universal hilarity, amidst the firing of guns, the blowing of trumpets, and the drinking of royal healths, was the strange procession of the old *Blew Gownis*.

These 'Bedesmen,' as they were at first called, originated in the fifteenth century, and consisted entirely of such aged paupers as had a claim on the royal bounty on account of their military service. During the Commonwealth they had shared in the universal wreck of all things pertaining to royalty, but at the Restoration the 'Blew Gownis' were by no means forgotten; and in this royal birthday pageant they formed a picturesque and foremost group. Thirty-five in number, they corresponded to the age of the reigning monarch, their number increasing yearly until his death, each man receiving a corresponding number of shillings in his new leather purse, made by the King's glover. When they had all marched in procession up the Canongate, 'telling their beads' for the good of the King's soul, and praying for long life to him (disinterestedly, of course), they assembled in the parish church of St. Giles, heard the sermon, and then received their usual allowance of bread and beer, and also their new gowns. The loyal feelings of the people being especially intense upon this the first anniversary after the Restoration, the 'Blew Gownis' had an 'unco guid' time of it.

Two years later, Sir Andrew Ramsay received a letter from Charles II., stating that in future the chief magistrate of Edinburgh should be permanently styled 'Lord Provost,' with the same rank and precedence as the Lord Mayor of London and Dublin. This and other honours he doubtless obtained through having 'recommended himself to the good graces of the Duke of Lauderdale,' who had so much interest at Court. Some time after, Sir Andrew was also created a Lord of Session, in return, it is said, for £17,000 extorted as gifts from the town of Edinburgh.[1] In reference to some of his civic acts, Alexander Grant says, 'he must have been a very potent Lord Provost, who probably had things all his own way, for he appears to have held office no less than fifteen years; but,' he adds, 'it is a pity that with so much influence he had not greater wisdom.'[2]

The country was in a most oppressed and distressed state at that time, owing to the perilous position people of all ranks were placed in with regard to the enforced abjuration of the Covenant, and the obnoxious Test Oath, which no thinking person could conscientiously sign, owing to its inconsistency with itself, the second clause completely contradicting the first. This oath was tendered to the Earl of Argyle, as a Privy Councillor, in 1681, he declaring that he took it *'so far as it was consistent with the Protestant faith.'* This explanation or qualification was considered tantamount to high treason, and the Earl was consequently thrown into prison, tried, found guilty, and most unjustly condemned to death. Sir John Lauder, being a zealous Whig, was chosen counsel for the Earl, with six others, and barely escaped imprisonment himself for his boldness in defending him. Argyle's sentence, however, was deferred for a time, he having escaped out of prison, in the dusk of a drizzling, foggy December evening, disguised as a page, holding up the train of his daughter-in-law, Lady Sophia Lindsay. How keenly one can sympathise with the noble fugitive's trembling dismay when the scrutinising sentinel at the castle gate seized him roughly by the arm as they were passing from under the archway. In his agitation the Earl dropped the lady's gown in the dirt, but she, with admirable presence of mind, snatched up her train from the slosh and mud, and in a pretended rage, threw it in Argyle's face, calling him

[1] *History of the University.* By Alexander Bower.   [2] Grant's *Story of the University.*

reproachfully a 'careless loun,' so besmearing him that his features were not recognised.[1]

Notwithstanding that the earl's honours were withdrawn, his life and estates forfeited, his arms reversed, and a price put upon his head, Sir John Lauder remained his firm friend and defender still. Upon his recapture, he was one of those who sorrowfully beheld his execution at the Mercat Cross, on the 30th June 1685. In recording his daily *Observes*, he writes :—

'After this many things were done in mockerie of the Test. Even the "*Scoollboyes*" held this iniquitous trial up to ridicule, in illustration of which the children of Heriot's Hospitall, finding that the dog which keeped the yairds of that Hospitall had a publick charge and office, they ordained him to take the Test, and offered him the paper; but he, loving a bone rather than it, absolutely refused it : then they rubbed it over with butter (which they called ane explination of the Test, in imitation of Argile) and he licked off the butter, but did spit out the paper; for which they held a jurie on him, and, in derision of the sentence against Argile, they found the dog guilty of treason and actually hanged him.'[2]

So much for the tender mercies of the rising generation as statesmen.

Sir John Lauder was returned to the Scottish Parliament, in 1685, for the county of Haddington, and for twenty-two years he continued to represent it. It was about five years after Sir John had been honoured with knighthood that his lady, Janet Ramsay, died—27th February 1686. Her death touched him very deeply, and for some months he nursed his grief most assiduously. Still, notwithstanding the undoubted affection he bore her throughout the seventeen years of their wedded life (to say nothing of his bitter experience of the malevolence of his own step-mother), yet, the following year, he wooed and married again, his second wife being 'Marion Anderson,[3] daughter of Anderson of Balram, in the parish of Aberdour.'

As a senator of the College of Justice, Sir John Lauder took the title of Lord Fountainhall from his patrimonial residence, and by this title he is most widely known, especially in connection with his folio volumes of law 'Decisions.' Altogether he was a very remarkable man, both in appearance and mental calibre : keen-witted and shrewd, full of logic and learning, unquestionably the most distinguished lawyer of his day. As Lord Fountainhall, he had been made a Lord of Session in 1689, and one of the Lords of Justiciary in 1690. A seat on the bench was also offered to him in 1692, but he bluntly refused it, because he was denied permission to prosecute the inhuman perpetrators of the

---

[1] Law's *Memorials*.   [2] Fountainhall's *Historical Observes*.
[3] 'March 26th. Sir John Lauder of Fountainhall, Advocate, and Dame Marion Anderson, by warrant of my Lord Bishop, to Mr. Alexander Ramsay.'—Family Roll and Register of Marriages.

diabolical massacre of Glencoe, which had been most perfidiously carried out on the 13th of February of that year. For forty-four years Sir John Lauder was indefatigable in recording every interesting law case or historical event that came under his observation, so that his manuscripts were most voluminous, and a perfect encyclopædia in themselves of events transpiring between 1660 and 1701. These valuable manuscripts appear to have been strangely scattered after his death, when his splendid library was sold by public auction [1]—some of his writings having been actually rescued from being used as waste paper in a tobacconist's shop. The serious loss this would have been to the literary members of the nation can well be imagined by those who have dipped into the stream of knowledge, so quaintly poured forth in the quarto volumes published at various times by the Bannatyne Club. That several of the manuscripts have been irrecoverably lost is very evident from Lord Fountainhall's own record of a volume called *Miscellanie Historicall Collections, digested into Annals (in imitation of Tacitus) by order of tyme, as they occurred from the year* 1660 to 1680,' and which Dr. Laing says 'has hitherto remained undiscovered.' The second volume, or continuation, ranging from 1680 to 1685, proves how interesting the first must have been. Imbued with the religious feeling of the age, the motto 'JEHOVAH PORTIO MEA' is inscribed on the title-page. On looking over these 'Historical Observes,' one cannot help feeling astonished sometimes at the offhand way in which Lord Fountainhall sums up in a few quaint words some of the most terrible events passing immediately before him, as though the very sight of that hideous '*Maiden*' had rendered death too familiar to affright. With the same concise deliberation he relates a ghost story, a law case, or the execution of a covenanter—all in one breath as it were. He certainly gives us to understand that he lived in an age of merciless persecution, gross injustice, and inordinate extortion, to say nothing of its superstition, fanaticism, and bribery. His remarks upon people and ordinary occurrences are so shrewd and so pithy, that it is difficult to resist the temptation of quoting a few of them. Who, for instance, would imagine that the following obituary related to the man whose administration had made all Scotland tremble for so many years?
'24 of August, 1682, dyed John Maitland, Duke of Lauderdale, the learnedest

---

[1] In volume ii. Maidment's *Analecta Scotica*, p. 72, there is a notice of the sale of Lord Fountainhall's books, among which are mentioned 'a very clean and full copy of the Acts of the Parliaments of Scotland, called the *Black Acts.*' A 'copie of Tindal's Bible complete in 1551.' *Martyre de la Reyne descosse*, by Blackwood in 8vo, printed 1558. *The History of King Robert Bruce*, printed at Edinburgh, 1670, 8vo. 'This edition of Bruce is even become rare, but the best, which is the first, and very rare, is that of Edinburgh by the famous printer, Andro Hart, in 1620 (first 1616, second 1620), who at the same time printed the *History of Wallace.*'

FIRST BARONET OF FOUNTAINHALL

and powerfullest minister of state in his age. Discontent and age were the ingredients in his death, if his Duchesse and Physitians be freed of it; for shee had abused him most grossly, and got all from him shee could expect.' And again, who would take this entry, dated December 1684, to have been written by a long-headed, cool, matter-of-fact lawyer?—'We ware troubled with the rumours of visions and apparitions, viz.: a shower of blew bonnets seen in the air at Glasgow and evanished when they came neir the ground'—after which he adds, 'a little ghost and spectre appears at Rosneth (one of my lord Argile's houses, where Athole has got his locality, and placed a garrison of fifty men); it beats the sojers sometimes, and bids them make good use of their tyme, for it shall not be long'; and then, as though conning it over, the wise judge writes: ' *But many of thir things are forged.*'

Lord Fountainhall must have had a good deal of *hearsay* experience in '*thir things*,' seeing he was at the bar when his father-in-law, Sir Andrew Ramsay, had the notorious wizard, Major Weir, and his unfortunate sister, Grizel, brought to trial for witchcraft, 'Maister John Sinclare, minister of Ormestoun' (a village a few miles from Fountainhall), being one of the witnesses against them. These poor, wretched maniacs were strangled and burned in the month of April, 1670, their very names remaining a terror in the neighbourhood of their dwelling, in the West Bow, for more than a century afterwards. Could it be otherwise when ten of these so-called witches, as aged and as crazy as poor Grizel Weir, were burnt at the stake in Edinburgh that same year? No wonder that John Lauder, the leading advocate, should have been '*troubled about thir things*,' since these trials for witchcraft continued to the very end of his long life, the last burning of a witch in Scotland taking place in Dornoch in 1722. Nor was Lord Fountainhall the only one among the Lords of Session who dipped into the subject of ghosts and second-sight:[1] even the notorious Duke of Lauderdale himself was interested in the subject; and, had it not been thought too closely allied to witchcraft, many in Scotland would have openly owned their belief in it. But the iniquitous laws against witchcraft were not repealed until 1736, and, alas for humanity! even then the Associated Presbytery of the Seceding Ministers actually appealed against this tardy act of justice in 1743, making it a matter of public prayer, counting it as a national sin, ' contrary to the express word of God.'

It is remarkable how invariably, in all transition periods wherein men waver on the borderland between fanaticism, superstition, and agnosticism, in all ages

---

[1] There are several interesting letters on second-sight in the correspondence of Samuel Pepys, 1699, and also in the *Life of Dr. Samuel Johnson.*

300   SIR JOHN LAUDER

and in all countries these so-called magical waves inundate society. Call it witchcraft, necromancy, sorcery, fetichism, or any other *ism* we please, it is all one with the popular revivalisms which periodically sway the masses like a mighty rushing torrent. It is just as though all the mental foulness of so many generations had to be stirred up and spiritually evaporated before the clear, transparent waters of a new life dispensation could flow into the thirsty souls of the children of progressive humanity.

It is very evident no nation has ever yet stamped out the belief in witchcraft by hempen cord or burning fagot, and they never will. Old Father Time, the greatest wizard of them all, will teach the people by and by how to transform witchcraft into wisdom.

But we must crave our readers' pardon for this digression, and return to our record of Sir John Lauder, whose quaint diary sent us off on the witches' track. We now come to a period in his life when it did seem as though Sir John's posterity was going to be 'swept off the face of the earth,' as Margaret Ramsay had desired, so many of his children one after another having died young; nevertheless, like his father the Bailie, he lived to see his children's children growing up around him.

Four years after the family returned to Fountainhall, his eldest son, John Lauder, married his cousin, Margaret Seton, third daughter of Sir Alexander Seton of Pitmedden, he being then in the twenty-sixth year of his age; but the wedding bells did not ring again until 1710, when the next surviving son, David, also a young advocate, married Margaret Maxwell, daughter of Sir John Maxwell of Pollok. Two years later their sister, Helen Lauder, also married her cousin, George Ogilvy, fourth Lord Banff, whose aunt, Helen Ogilvy, had been married to Sir Robert Lauder of Bielmouth in 1694. Sir Robert was the last landed proprietor of that branch of the family, the estate passing from them in 1768. It had been purchased in 1489 by Sir Robert Lauder of Edrington and the Bass, so that we can well understand why the old painting of Biel House should present such a different style of architecture from the present elegant mansion, with its chapel, and its lovely terraces, overlooking the Papana river, as now possessed and occupied by Lady Mary Hamilton Ogilvy.

Knowing Lord Fountainhall to have been a man of most precise habits and such a voluminous propensity for pedigrees and diary writing, it is rather surprising that there should not be among the family manuscripts a greater number of his holograph records upon the family history prior to his own day. There are, it is true, some interesting letters to his eldest son narrating certain events as transpiring among his ancestors, but most of the minutely written pages are devoted to paternal advice, and setting forth the genealogies of his own father and mother, with an elaborate account of the coats-of-arms belonging to each branch.[1] There is another subject in which he also took a particular interest, and that is, the tombs of his ancestors and progenitors, which in his day were to be found at Lauder, North Berwick, Pencaitland, and Greyfriars. Sometimes we find him readjusting his burial rights with the Kirk Session, such as at Pencaitland, in 1707, and Old Greyfriars. But the petition anent the Greyfriars was not presented until the 18th of June 1719, and not being a matter for the Kirk Session, it was sent 'Unto the Right Honourable the Lord Provost, Bailies, and remanant Magistrates and Council of the good Town of Edinburgh.'

It was a piece of ground lying on the north-west corner of the Greyfriars' Church, which had been allotted in 1669 to his father, Sir John Lauder, 'to be a burial-place to him and his family and descendants in all time coming,' which burial-place had become buried in ashes when the church steeple was blown up by an explosion of gunpowder on the 7th May 1718, the town having used the steeple as a powder-magazine with the most disastrous consequences. In repairing the damages and rebuilding the church, the town agreed to enlarge it by taking in so many feet westward, which distance would completely cover Sir John Lauder's burial-place, making what was formerly *without* the church to come *within* it. This he begs they will take notice of, and allot him the same proportionate piece of ground *within* the church, on the spot *where the ashes of his family lay*, adding appealingly, 'I must declare to your Honours, I am much more concerned in that piece of ground where my dear Parents and nearest Relations ly, than in all the Dust in the World'... 'therefore 'tis humbly craved that your Lordship and Honours will ratify and confirm my Right to these my Ashes ... and your Petitioner shall ever pray,' etc. Which petition was speedily granted, this having been the burial-place of the Lauders of Lauder from the period of its removal from Lauder Tower in 1598, and consequently contained the remains of William Lauder and his wife, Elizabeth Ballenden of Broughton: of their son, Andrew Lauder of Lasswade, and his wife, Janet Ramsay of Polton: of their son, Sir John Lauder of Newington and Edrington, first Baronet of Fountainhall, who died in 1692, and his spouse, Dame Isobel Ellis of Morton Hall: Lord Fountainhall's own mother, and also a goodly number of their young children. In less than three years Lord Fountainhall's own body was laid beside them, this remarkable man having died at his town residence in one of the ancient closes in the Lawnmarket in 1722, at the age of

[1] See Appendix, Note XIV.

seventy-six. His eldest son, Sir John Lauder, succeeded him as third Baronet of Fountainhall.

The family town residence 'stood where Mylne's Court now stands, and its gardens went quite down the steep bank at present covered by the Mound, to the southern margin of the North Loch of Edinburgh, the ground being laid out in terraces one below another.'[1] Sir Thomas Dick Lauder gives us a very graphic picture of the aged judge living there in his latter days, from an account which he received from Miss Innes of Stow, whose mother was one of the daughters of David Lauder, Esq., of Huntly Wood, Lord Fountainhall's younger son, who had married Margaret Maxwell of Pollok. David Lauder and his wife both died early, leaving two infant daughters, co-heiresses, who were brought up by their grandmother, Lady Maxwell. These two little orphans used to go regularly every Saturday to visit the old Lord, their paternal grandfather, who 'sat in an antique chair in an apartment hung with gilded leather, the furniture being of the old-fashioned, richly carved description, especially a cabinet on the top of which grinned a real human skull, that failed not to make a strong impression upon the minds of his grandchildren. Before dismissing them he invariably made them kneel before him, and putting their heads between his knees, he gave them his blessing in the most solemn and patriarchal manner. He then bestowed a shilling upon each of them; but no sooner had they reached the ante-room, where their Abigail was waiting for them, than she pounced upon them like a hawk and rifled them of the money.'[2]

[1] *Scottish Rivers*, by Sir Thomas Dick Lauder.
[2] One of these little girls married Mr. Innes of Stow, and the other, Miss Jean Lauder, married Dr. Patrick Cumin of Relugas, whose granddaughter became the wife of Sir Thomas Dick Lauder, seventh Baronet of Fountainhall.

CHAPTER XXIII

THE BARONETS OF FOUNTAINHALL

'The mosses of thy fountains still are sprinkled
With thine Elysian water-drops.'

SIR JOHN LAUDER, third Baronet, succeeded his father, Lord Fountainhall, in the estates and title in 1722. He was already a man of mature age, and had celebrated his silver wedding, the previous year, with Margaret Seton, the daughter of Sir Alexander Seton of Pitmedden, Bart., one of the Senators of the College of Justice, as already mentioned; but Sir John Lauder does not appear to have attained to any special dignity in the Court of Session, nor yet to have made himself in any way conspicuous in public events. He was strictly orthodox in his principles, though most of the members of his wife's family were staunch Jacobites. He only enjoyed the old home and his titled inheritance about six years. He died in 1728, and his place as head of the Lauder family was taken by his eldest son, Sir Alexander, who had always remained under the paternal roof, being unmarried, and of a delicate constitution. He died two years after his father, leaving the estates to his younger brother, Sir Andrew Lauder, fifth Baronet, whose life was more historically eventful. This was in 1730, when the greater part of Scotland was in a state of ferment on account of the number of men of rank and influence who were attainted or in exile in consequence of the Jacobite rising; but Sir Andrew Lauder held firmly to the Government, thus escaping the fines and forfeitures of his Highland friends. In September 1736 a fresh disturbance of another type took place in Edinburgh, startling all classes of society—when the mob, taking the law into their own hands, set fire to the Tolbooth, the historic 'Heart of Midlothian,' and, bursting open the

THE HEART OF MIDLOTHIAN.

doors, dragged forth Captain Porteous from his place of concealment up the chimney of his prison cell, and hanged him forthwith to a pole from a window at the corner of the Grassmarket. The charge against him was having fired on the people at the execution of Wilson the smuggler, whom they had tried to rescue. Captain Porteous had been reprieved by Queen Caroline, hence the conspiracy, called by the lynchers 'an act of justice.' As soon as their victim was dead the mob dispersed, throwing down their arms in the streets, and leaving the town as silent and peaceful as though no riotous doings had taken place. All this was done without the slightest opposition, in the clear autumnal twilight; and though the Government offered a reward of two hundred pounds for the discovery of any person concerned in the riot, not a ringleader was taken.

It was generally suspected that many of the actors on this occasion were men of rank and social position, judging from the audacity of the scheme, and the prudence and secrecy with which the whole plan was carried out. Arnot says: 'The clothes which appeared under their different disguises, as well as the conduct and deliberation with which their plan was executed, bespoke many among them to be superior to the vulgar, and that the violence they committed proceeded not from the rash and unpremeditated concert of a rabble'—rash enough, at any rate, to terrify the whole of the peaceful inhabitants of the city. There is a fine representation of the death-scene, called 'the Porteous Mob,' in the National Gallery of Scotland, painted by the late Mr. James Drummond, R.S.A., which is very characteristic of the period.

The next great political event was the Jacobite Rebellion of 1745, and the landing of Prince Charles, his stay at Duddingston, and his residence at Holyrood Palace. This we have mentioned in a former chapter, in reference to Sanct Geilies' Grange; and also that this same Sir Andrew Lauder of Fountainhall was the first to have his horses and pistols requisitioned, notwithstanding his connection with the 'noble house of Seton' through his mother, Lady Margaret Seton, and his wife's mother, Mistress Anne Seton, her sister—Mrs. Dick of Grange—whose only daughter he had married, making the third generation of cousins intermarrying in the Lauder family within sixty years. It is not often that father, son, and grandson each marry their cousins, but at this period it so happened; for Lord Fountainhall had married his cousin, Janet Ramsay of Polton, in 1669; Sir John Lauder, his eldest son, married his cousin, Margaret Seton of Pitmedden, in 1696; and Sir Andrew Lauder, their third son, also married his cousin, Dame Isabel Dick, heiress of Grange, in 1731, a year after he had succeeded to the baronetcy. Lord

THE BARONETS OF FOUNTAINHALL 305

Fountainhall's daughter, Helen Lauder, had already followed her father's example and married her cousin, George Ogilvy, fourth Lord Banff, in 1712. These closely interwoven conditions no doubt accounted physiologically for the greater number of their children being so delicate in constitution and dying in their infancy ; but it is not easy to comprehend how their families should have differed so much in politics, some being such staunch Jacobites and others not.

Sir Andrew Lauder's wife died in 1758 ; but shortly before her death, as already mentioned in chapter vii., she disponed her property and estate to her third son Andrew, her two elder sons having predeceased her.

Mr. Andrew Lauder, upon being served heir to his mother, took the name of *Dick*, as head of Sanct Geilies' Grange, living there with his mother-in-law and his aunts of the Seton family until the death of his father, Sir Andrew Lauder, at Fountainhall in 1769, when he inherited the title and both estates, being henceforth Sir Andrew Lauder-Dick, sixth Baronet of Fountainhall and fourth Baron of Grange.

His position as chief over his younger brothers and sisters required him to leave the Grange House and return to the patrimonial home. Young, wealthy, and good-looking, he appears to have been a universal favourite among the neighbouring gentry, but at that time there was not even a rumour of his marriage. In the month of May 1771 Sir Andrew paid a visit to London, going from thence with his cousin, Mr. Cumin, to Paris for two months. Many interesting traits in his character are to be gleaned from his long letters to his sister, Miss Jean, during his absence, he never failing to exhort her to be particularly attentive to her young sisters and brothers—for Dame Isobel Dick, Lady Lauder, had left a numerous family at Fountainhall. Notwithstanding his affection for the old home, Sir Andrew was absent that year the whole of the lovely summer months, when the gardens and the woods were most attractive ; but he was never oblivious of Miss Jean's comfort, nor his own desire that his household should be ordered aright. Many and sundry are the directions and messages sent to Mrs. Johnstone the housekeeper, and to the butler about the wine cellar, and the bottling of the malt liquor, besides other domestic manufactures. In those days every gentleman's family had set times and seasons for the wine-making, the brewing, and herb-drying, the fruit gathering and fruit preserving, all on a large scale, entailing a considerable amount of time, care, and attention, the responsibility always falling in some measure upon the lady of the house, no matter how large the retinue of servants might be.

Among Miss Jean Lauder's numerous correspondents, her cousin, Miss Jane

Innes, appears to have been the most frequent and most prolific. Her racy letters are full of pithy remarks upon men and manners in general, and the dispositions of certain persons in particular. She christened the manor-house of Fountainhall '*the Monasterie*,' always designating the family as the 'brothers and sisters,' Miss Jean being lady abbess, evidently in playful reference to the bachelorhood of the lord and master of the establishment. In one of her letters, dated 5th August 1769, she gives a graphic account of the fall of the North Bridge while in course of erection, owing to the heavy rains, which had loosened the earth about the abutments to such an extent that the whole of one end collapsed on the third day of that month. 'Is not this fall of our bridge a most dismal catastrophe?' she writes. 'It is the only subject of conversation here, and nothing can be more melancholy. They talk of a child having been dug from the ruins yester night, and that it was then alive; but this is incredible. There is no depending on any account. Each new-comer brings a new story, and contradicts what was told you before; but I would fain hope that none have actually lost their lives but Miss Dundas, Mr. Fergus, and that child. Their relations certainly deserve our sympathy; but let us be thankful that of the many who were entombed in the ruins so small a number have perished, and that we ourselves have escaped. The bridge used to be a general rendezvous about that time of night, and thus every one was miserable until they heard that their friends were safe. The whole night there was a confused noise in the streets, some running from curiosity, and others with distraction, to inquire after their vagrant children; in short, you can paint nothing to yourself more dismal or shocking.'

As far as could be ascertained, there really were only five deaths out of the large number of persons who were literally dug out of the ruins. This sad event was a sore trial to Mr. Mylne, the architect. The bridge was commenced in August 1765, and was to have been completed by midsummer 1769; but, in consequence of the loss of time and increased expenses, it was not opened for passengers until 1772. The sum contracted for the building of the bridge was £10,140, and Mr. Mylne undertook to uphold it for ten years, but when finished it was found to have cost £17,354. These facts are interesting at this special time, when the same bridge is being reconstructed on a wider scale. It is also worthy of note that, besides being used for traffic, the old bridge formerly served the purpose of a place of confinement, for in 1774 we read that the magistrates issued a proclamation to the effect that all beggars found in the streets 'would be imprisoned in the dark vaults beneath the North Bridge, and there fed on bread and water.'

In another letter from Miss Jane Innes to her cousin, Miss Jean Lauder, she tells us that Sir Andrew returned from Paris in the month of August (1771), 'not only much improved in his looks,' but, as she puts it, after describing his visit to her mother, 'he has not in other respects travelled in vain.' His letters and journals recounting his foreign adventures were evidently so entertaining that his sister, Miss Jean, was quite envied by her companions upon the receipt of them; but Sir Andrew revelled in the freedom of his bachelorhood for another ten years at least, for it was not until 1782 that he married Dame Elizabeth Broun, daughter of Thomas Broun, Esq., of Johnstonburn, lineally descended from the family of Hartrie, or Hertrie, of Peebles and Lanark, a very old family, which had been twice royally connected by marriage. It was John Broun, Laird of Gorgiemylne, who acquired by royal charter the lands and barony of Braid after the decease of Sir William Dick, which charter was again confirmed to him and his heirs by another royal charter of Charles II. in 1681.

The year following the marriage of Sir Andrew Lauder-Dick and his lady, Elizabeth Broun, a little daughter was born, whom they named Agnes, but she died as an infant, and in 1784 Sir Andrew's desire for a son and heir was fulfilled, and they called him Thomas, after his maternal grandfather. The juvenile days of this young representative of a noble race were passed at Fountainhall, whose brooks and burns and woodland glens were a never-ending source of delightful recreation from the time he could mount a fence, or climb a tree, fish for trout, or ride that wonderful Highland pony called Jenny, 'which for symmetry of action, and speed and endurance,' according to his own testimony, 'was not to be matched in the three Lothians by any quadruped of her inches.' Sir Andrew proved himself to be a most indulgent, and at the same time a most exemplary father to his motherless boy—for Lady Elizabeth died three years after his birth. All Sir Andrew's strong affections were consequently centred in his little son. He shared his childish amusements, making him also his daily companion in his walks, thereby encouraging him in all natural manly sports, and winning his boyish confidence, while allowing him sufficient freedom of action to develop his own individuality and independence of spirit. He had no desire, however, to make him a fox-hunting laird, though 'Jenny' was allowed at times to do her best at following the hounds in those very juvenile days, and many a good scamper over hill and dale she gave him; but as the years increased such sport was discouraged for the milder ploy of angling. Then came the college days, and the keen love of art, the awakening to literary endowment, and the choice of a profession. To such a student of nature the law had no attraction ; to travel and gain knowledge seemed to the future baronet the acme of bliss, but that meant an independent fortune, which he knew at that time he did not possess, so, like the most of the young nobility of his age, Mr.

THE PATH THROUGH THE WOODS.

Thomas Lauder-Dick entered the army, joining the 26th Cameronians, 'a marching regiment' as he calls it, making him a pedestrian by profession when he felt himself to be a born rider. But few in his regiment were better fitted for the martial exercise, owing to the long walks over moss and moor he had been accustomed to take with his father, rising with the dawn and tramping mile after mile to reach some favourite stream, then angling from pool to pool until the day was far spent, making their homeward retour in the cool of the evening with baskets heavily laden.

While on the march with his regiment, Mr. Thomas Lauder wrote home regularly to Sir Andrew, his father, very long and interesting letters with the most minute accounts of his travels, his doings, and his entertainments at the various military stations. Some of these letters are well worthy of transcript, did space permit, showing that in all his wanderings and manifold experiences his affections remained firm to his native land and his home circle. He also kept up a constant correspondence with Miss Charlotte Cumin, his cousin, at Relugas, who eventually became his bride after he had quitted the army at his father's request, and settled down to a literary career. Dame Charles Anne Cumin, as the lady was then called, was the only daughter and heiress of George Cumin, Esq., of Relugas, great-grandson of Lord Fountainhall. To

THE BARONETS OF FOUNTAINHALL 309

her father she had ever been as the 'apple of his eye,' his one great aim in life being her tender upbringing and careful education; but he did not live to share in the joy of her happy union, for he died in 1804.

The marriage took place in 1808, amid great rejoicings, in the lovely home of Relugas, in Morayshire, which had just been enlarged and beautified. Here, in this garden of Eden, the young couple continued to reside with the bride's mother, Mrs. Cumin, whose maiden name was Susanna Judith Craigie Halkett,

WAITING FOR THE YOUNG LAIRD.

being the eldest daughter of Colonel Craigie Halkett of Hall Hill, Fife. Though Sir Andrew Lauder sorely missed the companionship of his only son, who had just entered his twenty-fourth year at the time of his marriage, still the intercourse between the families was so constant and so friendly that he soon found new life and new interests springing up within the circle of Relugas. He lived to see three infant daughters come like sunbeams to gladden his son's home, and each of them return to the angel-land ere a son was born to inherit the name of

Lauder. Then came three more little daughters and another son before Sir Andrew Lauder-Dick, in his eighty-fifth year, resigned his lands and his title to Sir Thomas. He died at Fountainhall on the 16th November 1820, and was buried in the family tomb at Greyfriars.

From the succession of Sir Thomas we notice the change in the name from Lauder-Dick to Dick-Lauder. The reason for this is thus explained. Andrew Lauder, son of Dame Isobel Dick, inherited the Grange at his mother's death during his father's lifetime, and he was in consequence called Mr. Dick, his father being Sir Andrew Lauder of Fountainhall. When he died, Mr. Dick of Grange, *alias* Lauder, became Sir Andrew Lauder-Dick, but his son, Mr. Thomas Lauder, at his death inheriting both estates, took his title as Sir Thomas Dick-Lauder, seventh Baronet of Fountainhall and fifth Baron of Grange, the Baronet taking precedence.

The baronial manor of Fountainhall, which Sir Thomas Dick Lauder inherited from his father, Sir Andrew, lies in the parish of Pencaitland, thirteen miles from Edinburgh, and about two miles south from Ormiston station. It is in no way connected with the village of Fountainhall, near Stow, as one might naturally suppose.

After passing through the picturesque village of Ormiston, with its red-tiled

OLD CROSS AT ORMISTON VILLAGE.

roofs, its French-looking boulevards, and its quaint stone cross, the road leads directly through the woodlands to the old mansion-house, which stands upon the rising ground above the woods of Ormiston and Woodhall, forming as it

THE BARONETS OF FOUNTAINHALL

were one extensive policy. Seen above the trees, this antiquated, sixteenth century residence has a much more imposing appearance, but from an artistic point of view it gains in picturesqueness when approached from the south-east. It stands within gardens and shrubberies, the oldest portion of the building being clothed with ivy, rich purple clematis, and a wealth of climbing roses.

Like most of these Scottish family residences which have been added to from time to time, Fountainhall is very irregular in its structure—a curious compound of old and new, which gives it that quaint, old-fashioned look, the original stone walls being still kept up with plastering and harling without the least pretension to architectural adornment of any kind. It never was a place of defence, and consequently there is no strong tower nor castellated exterior, as in many of the Scotch baronial mansions.

The entrance door, which is fully arrayed with genuine knobs and nails, is comparatively small, and placed below an overhanging turret with a circular stone stair which leads

OLD HALL AND ENTRANCE TOWER.

to the roof, from whence a magnificent panorama of the surrounding country is obtained. The oldest portion of the building dates back to the fifteenth century, and consists of four storeys, while some of the later additions have only two or three. There are a few old carved stones, but the most interesting is one which belonged to the Lauders of the Bass. It has evidently had an ancient shield bearing their heraldic griffin upon it, though at present it is so much defaced by age as to be almost undecipherable. The latest addition to the building is only two storeys high, and it must have been built before Fountainhall was acquired by Bailie Lauder, as the date of its erection, 1638, is upon one of the windows with the monogram M.D.P., being the initials of some member of the Pringle family from whom Sir John Lauder purchased it. This portion, with its outside stair, is both picturesque and of historical interest, being the entrance to a large apartment or hall known as Lord Fountainhall's reception-room. This hall is pretty much in the same condition now as it was when his descendant, Sir Thomas Dick Lauder, described it fifty years ago in his *Scottish Rivers*.

Writing of his great-great-grandfather he says :—' To illustrate the manners of his times, we may mention that the room in which he sat at Fountainhall is above forty feet long ; the walls, now consisting of bare masonry alone, were probably then covered with tapestry, but it has never had any ceiling, the eye having been permitted to wander upwards amongst the bare rafters through the void overhead till it rested on the wood under the slates.' And such it still is, only in Lord Fountainhall's time it had also an inside stair communicating with the rest of the house, which it has not at present. The name of Fountainhall was taken from the number of beautiful springs to be found in the neighbouring woods. Some of them are fine mineral springs, strong and pure, their medicinal qualities being fully attested. There is a story told in the family which proves the strong impregnation of iron in the waters of one at least of these famous wells. It happened in the college days of Sir Thomas, who always spent his holidays at Fountainhall with his father, Sir Andrew. One evening as he was passing through the glen on his way to visit a neighbouring friend, he was tempted by the cool, refreshing stream of pure translucent water to take a copious draught. On arriving at his destination his friends looked at him in amazement. They had heard that he had not been very well lately, but they were shocked at his appearance, wondering what manner of complaint could have so metamorphosed his handsome features in so short a time. In blissful ignorance as to the cause of their surprise, Sir Thomas himself was perfectly unconcerned, until he beheld himself in a mirror, when lo! his lips were as black as ink! He had taken a strong cup of tea before starting, and a still stronger dose of sulphate of iron on the way. This accident led to his eventually making a chemical analysis of the waters, which he afterwards

THE BARONETS OF FOUNTAINHALL 313

published.[1] Besides this special mineral well there are many others; and also the 'Butter Well,' so called because, on account of its delicious coolness, the butter was placed in it during the summer months as a refrigerator.

The 'Ladies' Well' also is another of these sparkling gems nestling in the ferny glade, and giving forth an inexhaustible supply of the purest water for the use of the manor and the manse.
A sweeter 'Wishing Well' for lovers' tryst could not be desired in the lovely month of 'leafy June.' But what of winter's lengthy calendar, when old King Frost holds sway and every sparkling drop is an icicle?

WISHING WELL IN THE GLEN.

The usual appendage which marks a baronial dwelling of the sixteenth century is not amissing at Fountainhall, for the old dovecot stands beneath the stately trees as of yore. But what is most unusual, it has a fine specimen of the 'Jougs' fixed into the wall. This ancient instrument of ecclesiastical and baronial discipline was more generally affixed to the parish church or the nearest tolbooth. In 1592 it had been enacted that 'irons and stocks were to be provided in every parish for the punishment of idle beggars and vagabonds,' and we know the kirk at Pencaitland certainly adhered to the law in this respect, as the jougs are also to be seen there yet. But as Lord Fountainhall was a Judge in the Court of Session as well as an elder in his parish church, it is hard to say whether this 'ancient terror of evil-doers' was most frequently used upon Church or State

[1] 'Account of the Aluminous Chalybeate Spring at Fountainhall,' Thomson's *Annals of Philosophy*, vol. viii. 1816, No. 43, p. 3. These waters contained from 60 to 80 parts of sulphate of iron in the 100.

2 R

delinquents. But it is very evident, as Miss Dunlop once tritely remarked, 'there was a disposition in the country in those earlier times to punish sin on the person of the sinner, rather than make them a burden on the tax-paying public.' Certainly they had a fearsome array of personal punishments, and it would be a difficult question to decide which of them—the Branks, the Jougs, the Stocks, the Ducking-Stool, or the Whipping-Post—was most dreaded by those sixteenth-century miserable sinners.

THE JOUGS AT THE KIRK.

This ancient parish church at Pencaitland, so intimately connected with Fountainhall, dates back to 1213, and undoubtedly the oldest part of it bears the moss-grown appearance of its remote age, so does the peculiarly *earthy* odour of the interior. For artistic tomb-seekers and antiquarians there is not a more picturesque old kirkyard in the kingdom. It is a perfect treasure-house of mossy stone relics with the quaintest carvings and epitaphs, of every form and dimension, legible and illegible.

The church itself stands upon rising ground, embosomed in a grove of tall trees, with a high wall enclosing it from the road which leads down to the manse, situated on the sunny slope of the brae, completely nestled amid shrubs and flowers, with the river Tyne flowing at the foot of the garden. The river also divides the parish into Easter and Wester Pencaitland. The former is by far the more picturesque end of the village, with its old church and pretty cottages clothed with ivy and creeping plants, its ornamental, though modern, schoolhouse, and its quaint rural post-office. But Wester Pencaitland boasts of its ancient Market Cross, and the old-fashioned, weather-beaten sun-dial surmounting it, similar in form to that upon the oldest portion of the parish church, wherein the beautiful memorial window of stained glass has been placed to the memory of the late Lady Ruthven of Winton House. Within this parish church, below the steeple-loft, was the ancient burial-place of the Fountainhall family when Sir John Lauder became the possessor of the estate but not having had occasion for its use, no claim had been made for its appropriation until 1707, when Lord Fountainhall sent in a petition to the kirk-session, which was entered in the session record as follows—

'26th May 1707.—This day it was represented by my Lord Fountainhall that the burying-place belonging to his predecessors and authors, heritors of the lands within this parish of Pencaitland, now possessed by the said Lord Fountainhall, was in the west end of this church of Pencaitland, below the loft and before the bell-steeple; and therefore craved this Session to give their concurrence to his having possession of the said burying-place.'

None, however, of the Lauder family rest there, with the exception of very young children, the usual place of entombment being their own vault at Greyfriars; but here lie the mortal remains of many of the ancient family of George, Lord Seton, who owned the first baronial castle of Winton, and was connected by marriage with the Lauders.

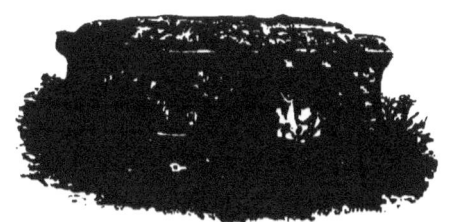

OLD TOMB, PENCAITLAND.

CHAPTER XXIV

RELUGAS

'There is a spot of earth supremely blest,
A dearer, sweeter spot than all the rest.
Where shall that land, that spot of earth be found?
Art thou a man? a patriot? Look around,
And thou shalt find, howe'er thy footsteps roam,
That land's thy country, and that spot thy Home!'
J. MONTGOMERY.

LET us now return to Relugas, that lovely spot on the Findhorn near Forres, where Sir Thomas Dick Lauder and his lady lived for twenty-three years in a perfect garden of Eden.

Few appreciated its peacefulness and its beauties more than his intimate friend Lord Cockburn. 'Could I recall past days,' he writes, 'I would not leave *one* unrecalled that ever I spent with Sir Thomas, especially at his former paradise of Relugas, at the junction of the Divie and the Findhorn. . . . I used to visit him almost yearly at Relugas, one of the most beautiful spots in Scotland; and what a combination of pleasures was there in the kindness and hilarity of that family and in the scenery of that Eden!—the long river-walks of the forenoon, amidst the glories of the woods of Darnaway and Altyre, and the long evenings of domestic mirth by which each happy day was at last brought to a close.'

Some faint idea of the beauty of those river-walks can be gleaned from the description Sir Thomas Dick Lauder himself gives of them in all their glory before the fearful destruction caused by the Morayshire floods in 1829:—

'Entering the Relugas property from the Dunphail march, a branch of the pleasure-walks led down the left bank of the Divie for about two miles, quite to the point of its junction with the Findhorn. Having had some severe lessons from former floods, especial care had been taken to conduct the line at an elevation considered by every one to be quite beyond all risk of injury. The rocks and recesses of the wooded banks, and the little grassy slopes, were covered in a wild way with many thousand shrubs of all kinds, especially with laurels, rhododendrons, azaleas, lilacs, and a profusion of roses, which were thriving vigorously and beginning to bear blossoms, whilst the rocks were covered with the different saxifrages, hung with all sorts of creepers, and enamelled with a variety of garden flowers, all growing artlessly as if sown by the hand of nature. The path was therefore considered to be not unworthy of the exquisite scenery through which it led. But the flood of the 3rd and 4th of August left not one fragment of it remaining from one end to the other. Not a tree, or shrub, or flower, or piece of soil, nay, or of moss or lichen, is to be seen beneath that boldly and sublimely sketched line of flood that appears on either side, and from end to end of these rocks, like the awful handwriting of God on the Wall.'

Notwithstanding the damage done to Relugas by this awful flood, the beauties of Nature still left are sufficient 'to captivate strangers, and to make them wonder how there could have been anything to regret; yet ten thousand points of locality are now lost on which hung many long-cherished associations with the memory of those who can never return to sanctify the new scenes resulting from the late catastrophe.'

OLD GARDENER, DUNPHAIL.[1]

The character of the scenery around Relugas is wild and grandly picturesque, owing to the boldness of the lofty rocks below and the luxuriant woods above. The lovely banks of the Divie and the Findhorn are a life-long school of landscape-painting to all lovers of the majestic in Nature.

The romantic walks in this beautiful neighbourhood are most minutely described by Sir Thomas in his *Scottish Pictures*,[2] where he also gives a quaint portrait of the old gardener at Dunphail, Simon Roy, 'the political as well as natural historian of the district,' who appears to have been a personage

[1] From a pencil sketch by Sir Thomas Dick Lauder, lent by his daughter, Miss Cornelia Dick Lauder.
[2] Published in Constable's *Edinburgh Magazine* for February 1822, page 210.

of no mean size and importance, especially in his Sunday garb. 'Clad in his light grey coat, of ample fold, decorated with velvet collar that once was black, and large saucer-shaped buttons that once shone with all the glitter of carved steel; his long peeled staff in his right hand, and his left reposing in his bosom; his thin figure bent forward, and the high features of his pale spare countenance shaded by his flat bonnet, and wearing a holy air of resignation and piety,' as he frequently walked side by side with Sir Thomas on a Sabbath morning through the winding paths of the glen on their way to the little village church—old Simon holding forth with all the garrulity and freedom of age, telling 'long stories of the last lairds of the castle, intermixed with endless harangues on rural economy, bees, blossoms, gooseberries, and caterpillars.'

The principal points of interest in the immediate vicinity of Relugas, which stands, as it were, on a peninsula between the two rivers, were at that time the Divie Falls, Macrae's Loup, and the beautiful 'Mill Island,' with its Doric temple, its rustic bridges, its lofty ornamental trees, its grassy glades and winding walks, with a cascade at one end, and the castellated Otter's Rock at the other, all formed to please the eye and delight the senses—a most sequestered spot, a very hermitage of peace and beauty. But the flood came, and finding it a garden of Eden, it left it a desolate waste of waters. In one night it 'vanished, like the scenery, in a dream.' Near to this, at the back of the house, rises the conical hill of Doune, beautifully wooded, and laved at its rocky base by the Divie, which can be seen from the windows on the north side of the house as it pursues its course along the soft green lawns and garden banks which slope towards it, ere it passes under the Divie Bridge on its way to join the Findhorn.

The only ancient relic on the Relugas grounds is one of those vitrified forts of early times which have caused so much discussion since 1777 in Scottish Antiquarian Societies.

Many were the choice subjects depicted in this lovely neighbourhood of hill and valley by the Rev. John Thomson of Duddingston, as he wandered through glade and glen with Sir Thomas Dick Lauder, who was himself an indefatigable draughtsman both with pen and pencil, recording scenes and places sought for in vain after that terrible flood. Money could never estimate the loss sustained by Sir Thomas and his family in this unparalleled calamity, for no sum could compensate for the total destruction of the living beauties of Nature which had been planted, fostered, and cherished with such tender care for so many long years.

It was not, however, the devastations within the domain and pleasure-grounds of Relugas which first induced the transplanting of the Dick Lauder family to Edinburgh ; it was the ever increasing requirement of College educational advantages for the sons, who were growing up, and superior accomplishments for the daughters also ; for which reason Sir Thomas, in making choice between his two Midlothian family mansions of Fountainhall and the Grange, fixed on the latter.

But at that period the Grange House was by no means in a condition befitting a baronet's residence, being cramped in dimension and antiquated in appearance ; but the necessary work of reconstruction had already begun on a grand scale, and in the interim Sir Thomas wrote one of his most popular works, a detailed account of 'the Morayshire Floods,' which was published in 1830, and dedicated in the following manner to his friend Lord Cockburn, who was at that time one of the leading Advocates at the Bar :—

'To Henry Cockburn, Esq. of Bonally.

'MY DEAR COCKBURN,—As you are answerable for the infliction of this volume on the public, you must not be surprised that I now claim for it the protection of your name, so universally known and respected ; and, at the same time, afford myself an opportunity of acknowledging the many obligations I owe to your long and steady friendship, and of manifesting my admiration of your private virtues, and the pleasure and pride with which I subscribe myself, my dear Cockburn, your warmly and sincerely attached, THOS. DICK LAUDER.

'RELUGAS, 17th June 1830.'

That it was no easy matter to have undertaken such a work we can gather from the information given by Sir Thomas's second daughter, Miss Cornelia Dick Lauder, who, as a young girl, had been an eye-witness of the great disaster.

Many are the interesting stories she has related to us of this event ; but it will be much more delightful to our readers that we should quote some of her own words, penned at the request of the publisher of the new edition of her father's work. 'Well do I recollect,' she writes, '"the Flood" of Monday, 3rd August 1829. We, the school-room children of the family, after lessons were over, sat at the window looking out upon the trees bowed by the wind, the gloomy sky, and pelting rain, wondering if we should ever get out again. I remember also the excitement caused by the message that the rivers were up "beyond the memory of man." It was not at first intended that we should go out at all ; but our pleading looks touched my father, who could never bear to see us disappointed, and we were accordingly sent to equip ourselves in our old pelisses of the winter before, covering our heads with boy's caps, for umbrellas were impossible in the wind.

'I think we must have looked very like a troop of ragged Highland terriers as we joyfully followed my father down the garden. And very full of glee we were, until we stood with wonder and awe beside the raging Divie. Then, indeed, our joyous tones were hushed ; no sound could be heard but the mighty voice of the waters. One after another, the large trees bent over like willow wands, and on the surface of the flood were for " a moment seen, then gone for ever."

'We followed my father up the river, to a place above the Divie Fall, where an incident occurred which has not been recorded in *The Moray Floods*. The river-walk at this point was at a great height above the ordinary course of the stream, but in its flooded condition the river was raging along quite close to it. My two sisters, ignorant, as we all were, that the walk was undermined, were standing on it, gazing with wonder at the river. An English gentleman, one of our visitors, who was out with us, possessed by what seemed to us all a vain fear, called to them and entreated them to return to where the rest were standing. They did not hear him, and remained gazing on the flood. My father, who had himself no doubts as to the safety of their position, could not, however, bear to see the anxiety of his friend, and shouted to his daughters to come back. They immediately obeyed, and the whole party turned up the bank. Happening just then to look round, I saw the portion of the walk on which my sisters had been standing break away and fall into the raging torrent. My father's kindness of heart had thus mercifully saved himself a great sorrow.'

After beautifully describing the junction of the rivers before and during the flood, Miss Dick Lauder goes on to say : 'Darkness alone drove us home that night. Next morning we wandered forth again, retracing our steps of the evening before. Reports of the devastation at Dunphail, and anxiety about its inhabitants, made my father continue his walk up the Divie, and with sorrow we gazed on the destruction there. I remember that whilst so engaged, the sun, which had been struggling through the clouds, suddenly burst out upon the scene. It seemed, like Noah's bow in the heavens, to say, " Comfort yourselves ; all is over ; it shall not be so again."'

A much needed gleam of hope after three nights and two days of unintermitted rain—descending, not in drops, but in sheets of water.

The sights and the sounds which met them on all sides were grandly appalling, and so deeply impressive as never to have been forgotten ; fraught also with more danger to Relugas than seemed possible at first from their apparently safe vantage-ground, for the bridge, the offices, and stables narrowly escaped being carried away. In dread of this, Sir Thomas himself, the coachman, the gardener and his men, sat up the whole night. After the devastating flood had entirely ceased, Sir Thomas, urged by the entreaties of his friends (in particular by those of Lord Cockburn), undertook to write an account of it.

Miss Dick Lauder says : ' The task soon became a labour of love. Information poured in from all sides ; but my father himself visited all the scenes of devastation reported to him, making frequent expeditions on horseback for days at a time to places he could not otherwise have reached, for rivers had to be forded where bridges had been carried away.

'At last the book was finished, but was considered by the publishers too voluminous for publication on a subject supposed to be only of local interest. It was a hard task for my father, but after demurring for a while he patiently set himself to the work of rewriting and condensing a book which has proved one of his most estimated works.'

It is still, notwithstanding its curtailment, a book of 230 closely printed pages, with sixty-four illustrations, reproduced from Sir Thomas's inexhaustible sketch-books, and several maps.[1]

One of the most painful incidents of 'the Moray Floods,' so graphically therein described by Sir Thomas, is that of the sad fate of Charles Cruikshanks, an innkeeper of Aberlour, whose death seems to have enlisted the sympathies of the whole neighbourhood, from the peculiarly trying circumstances and prolonged suspense attending it. At the first rising of the flood he had gone out on a float to try and save his own and his neighbour's hay ; but the waters rose so rapidly at the meeting of the currents that he lost all control of his raft, which was being hurried into the whirlpool, when with swift dexterity Cruikshanks caught hold of the topmost branches of a tree and clung there for his very life, calling aloud for help. Boat after boat approached the spot where the poor man was suspended aloft between the raging waters and the stormy sky ; but every effort to reach him was unavailing ; no boat could live in such a whirlpool, and as darkness fell upon the scene, his brave companions reluctantly gave in, ominously whispering among themselves, ' His hour has come.'

Throughout the whole of that fearful night the cries of the wretched man were heard by his frantic wife and her friends upon the shore, growing fainter and fainter, sometimes entirely lost in the booming sound of the wind and the waves. But at dawn there came a long shrill whistle across the watery waste, to tell them he was still in life ; but the voice was gone, and ere the sun rose

---

[1] The original publishers in 1830 were Messrs. A. and C. Black, Edinburgh ; but the new edition brought out in 1873, with the Introductory Note by Miss C. Dick Lauder, is published by Mr. R. Stewart, High Street, Elgin.

the flood had covered the very tree-top and the man; not a landmark was to be seen.[1]

Fortunately the sweeping destruction which took place all along the rocky banks of the Divie and the Findhorn did not extend to the lovely flower-gardens and wooded walks immediately surrounding the mansion-house of Relugas. Visitors came and went as usual, friendly courtesies were exchanged, and the same open-hearted hospitality was dispensed. Authors, poets, painters, judges, all found Relugas a perfect paradise.

On the 27th of that memorable month of August, Principal Baird came from Forres to visit his friend Sir Thomas Dick Lauder. When he reached the Divie Bridge, just as they were crossing it, he called out to the post-boy to stop, that he might enjoy the beautiful scenery. 'Na, na, sir!' roared out the lad, smacking his whip, 'these are owre kittle times to be stopping on brigs.'

Dunphail, the beautiful property of Mr. Cumming Bruce, adjoining Relugas on the Divie side, suffered fearfully from the floods, owing to its position in the valley, though the house itself stood six hundred feet from the ordinary course of the river.

About six o'clock on the evening of that terrible Monday, 3rd of August, the river had risen so much as to carry away two handsome wooden bridges, one for carriages and the other for foot-passengers; and when an embankment at the upper end of a large island in front of the lawn gave way, it allowed a mighty torrent to pour down towards the elegant mansion, which had only just been completed at a great cost, and which, Sir Thomas says, was 'one of the happiest efforts of Mr. Playfair's classical taste.' The rapid increase of the flood so alarmed the family that the carriage was ordered, and Mrs. Cumming Bruce and her daughter induced to seek safer quarters. Gradually tree after tree and mass after mass fell with thundering booms into the seething torrent, which by eleven o'clock had risen within *nine feet* of the front foundation, and within *four paces* of the foundation of the kitchen tower.

The furniture was then hastily removed in carts, piled up promptly, with most astonishing dexterity; and although this was accomplished on a dark night, amidst the roar of waters and ceaseless rain, by the aid of lanterns alone, not one article was lost, and not even the most delicate drawing-room ornament broken.

The last bank fell in within one yard of the whole structure, and then every living soul quitted the building—Mr. Cumming Bruce and his people

[1] Miss Dick Lauder has a picture representing this incident, painted by the Rev. John Thomson of Duddingston, with the figure of Cruikshanks put in by Sir James Grant.

retiring to a safe distance to watch with anxious hearts the fall of the beautiful mansion. But the word had gone forth, 'So far shalt thou come, and no farther,' for *there* the flood ceased, and the home was saved.

There is a pretty little story related of Dobbin, the Dunphail pony. Being old, and a great favourite with the family, he was pastured on the green sward of the beautiful island in the river. This island had never been known by the oldest man in the place to have been flooded; but when the crash of the embankment was heard, and patch after patch of green pasture disappeared, a great excitement arose as to poor Dobbin's safety.

Sir Thomas, who tells the story, says : 'Dobbin, now in this twenty-seventh year, and in shape something like a 74-gun ship cut down to a frigate, was seen galloping about in great alarm as the wreck of roots and trees floated past him; and as the last spot of grass disappeared he was given up for lost. At this moment he made a desperate effort to cross the stream under the house— was turned head over heels by its force—rose again with his head up the river, made boldly up against it, but was again borne down and turned over. Every one now believed him gone, when, rising once more, and setting *down* the waste of water, he crossed both torrents, and landed safely on the opposite bank.'

Bravo, Dobbin of Dunphail! a water-kelpie could not have done it better. Near to this spot, just below where the Dorback falls into the Divie, there is a huge block of stone, weighing about a hundred tons, which never moved one hair's-breadth during the whole of the raging flood, which swept everything else before it. It now stands as a landmark in the river whence islands have ceased to exist.

One universal cause of thankfulness throughout this unparalleled calamity caused by the extensive flooding of so many rivers, was that out of the hundreds of human lives snatched from the watery waste, only eight persons fell a sacrifice to the raging torrent. This seems almost incredible when we read how the deluge 'poured down the furrowed sides of the mountains in a thousand cataracts, like the mighty hosts of God's destroying angels,' sweeping the accumulated riches of the numerous valleys off to the ocean in different directions at the same moment, and how, 'throughout the whole windings of each respective strath all was sudden dismay, clamour, and dread, —some struggling to escape with life from the devouring waves; some pent up in their tottering dwellings with the shadow of death around them ; others hanging to their crazy and toppling roofs, suspended over the depths of eternity, while bold hearts were stirred up to do daring deeds, and all the finer feelings and magnanimous virtues of humanity were excited and called into activity.'

Only a few short hours before, and all was peaceful abundance and smiling prosperity where now 'gaunt Famine sits brooding over the new-born wastes'; and yet Sir Thomas tells us that, 'heavily as the dispensation descended on people of all ranks, neither complaints nor murmurs were heard to arise.'

Hundreds of people flocked north to view the scene of desolation, and many were entertained at Relugas. Among these visitors in the spring after the floods was Mr. John Browning, an English poet of some note, whose name bespeaks his fraternal relationship to Robert Browning, the most truly original but least understood poet of this century. Mr. Browning had come to Morayshire with a very high-sounding, eulogistic introduction to Sir Thomas. Miss Dick Lauder remembers him well, and tells an amusing incident of his wild enthusiasm over the beauties of the place. Very early the morning after his arrival, she happened to be looking out of the window, and saw the figure of a man running at full speed along the garden-walk towards the water, with the tails of a long flowing dressing-gown flying in the wind. Just in time for breakfast, the same gentleman returned, quite breathless, presenting Sir Thomas with an original poem, 'To the Waters of Relugas,' in admiration of which he had spent the last hour, without even knowing the name of the river. Before leaving, however, he re-wrote the poem, with a new title, as follows:—

'FAREWELL TO DIVIE.

Divie! ceaseless is thy singing,
Thy topazian waters bringing
Pearls which, o'er the rude rocks flinging,
In the sun's eye thou dost hang.
Sweet it is to sit and view thee,
Sweet to watch the pebbles thro' thee,
Sweet it is to sing unto thee
Songs, where minstrel never sang.

I would bear thee my devotion,
Bless thee, hurrying to the ocean,
And, with not serene emotion,
Tune for thee a parting lay.
Brighter days shall glide before thee,
Silence muse no longer o'er thee,
Thou shalt find a minstrel worthy
When I wander far away.

'J. BROWNING.

'To SIR T. D. LAUDER, BART.,
May 1st, 1830.'

Upon his return to London the poet sent the following little note, with two books, to his kind host at Relugas :—

'MY DEAR SIR THOMAS,—I herewith send you two little volumes of mine, which, if you will place on the shelves of your library, may serve to hang a slight memory upon of those, to me, most interesting days I spent at Relugas.—With kindest compliments to Lady Lauder, believe me, my dear Sir Thomas, yours ever truly,

'JOHN BROWNING.

'LONDON, 14th May 1830.'

It was at Relugas, the same year as the great flood, 1829, that Sir Thomas Dick Lauder first became personally acquainted with Hugh Miller, 'the journey-

OLD ROCK IN THE FLOOD.

man mason of Cromarty,' whose literary genius had been discovered by Miss Dunbar of Boath, Forres, an old lady who had been of great service to him in lending him books and poems. She eventually introduced him to Sir Thomas in reference to a book of poems she had induced him to publish ; but as the interesting correspondence between Sir Thomas and Hugh Miller himself did not take place until the Baronet had removed to the Grange House, we will reserve it for another chapter.

With what fond regret the family departed from Relugas, with its woods and vales, its winding rivers and lonely glens, it is easy to imagine, for had it not been the bridal home of Lady Lauder and the birthplace of her numerous olive-branches? To sell it seemed impossible, so the beautiful Eden was let to Mr. Fitzpatrick and his young bride.

Not many years passed, however, ere it was besought by Mr. William Mackelligan, who had been born and brought up in a cottage on the estate. As a young man he went off to China, and being successful in business, he returned with a fortune, determined, if possible, to fulfil the dream of his life, which was to become lord and master of Relugas. Accordingly, he made overtures for the purchase, which being accepted, he was duly installed; but his aged parents still continued to live in their simple home in the valley. Mr. Mackelligan soon found, however, that it took somewhat more than he had at all anticipated to keep up an estate like Relugas; consequently he was obliged ere long to part with it, and it was eventually bought by Mr. George Smith, of the Carrington family, in whose possession it still remains.

THE GRANGE HOUSE FROM THE BOWLING-GREEN.

CHAPTER XXV

THE GRANGE HOUSE AS A BARONIAL RESIDENCE

'A palace is measured from east to west, or from north to south, but a book is measured from earth to heaven.'—JOUBERT.

WITH the aid of builders, masons, carpenters, plumbers, painters, and gardeners, under the transforming influence of that eminent architect, Mr. W. H. Playfair, in less than five years the external form of 'Sanct Geilie Grange,' *as such*, became a memory of the past. With consummate skill this antiquated twelfth-century Grange of St. Giles was completely hidden within the elegant seventeenth-century mansion designed by Sir Thomas Dick Lauder, with his cultured taste and architectural knowledge. The whole of the original building is still there, but added to in such a way as to make it the *central* portion of the present structure; consequently some of the inside walls are more than six feet thick, having been the outside walls in former days; and, notwithstanding its modern interior elegance, it still retains many of its ancient characteristics. Seen from the garden terrace or the bowling-green, it now presents a most picturesque appearance, with its broken sky-line of turrets and crow-stepped gables. The high chimneys and battlemented keep, with the pedimented dormer windows, also combine to enhance the artistic effect; and the architectural beauty of the whole structure is considerably increased by the projecting balconies and substantial stone steps leading into the garden. Formerly the house consisted of three storeys, except the very oldest portion, and that was four storeys in height, to which altitude the whole building has now been raised by Sir Thomas, and the two western turrets were erected to give uniformity to the outline, and weight to its baronial character, besides adding to the strength of the ancient gable.

But to give a proper idea of the extensive improvements in the exterior and interior arrangements, it will be better to commence, as the builders themselves would do, at the basement, for the present vestibule, the inner entrance-hall, the wide staircase, with its massive balustrade and lofty window, all form part of the later additions, besides two ranges of apartments, and an inner stair to the upper storeys. The outer offices and servants' accommodation on the ground floor were also considerably extended.

Above the front portal are the sculptured arms of the Dick-Lauder and Cumin families, supported by the white lions, with the date of the reconstruction, 1827. The door is of massive oak, studded in the antique fashion, and just behind it there formerly stood a very remarkable-looking seat, called in bygone Scottish homes 'the lang settle.' This we shall mention among the relics. Several old carvings from Elgin Cathedral, and some of a still more ancient date, are hung upon the walls of the vestibule and inner lobby; they are chiefly connected with the abbots and bishops of the Lauder family. There is also a well-executed medallion bust representing Bishop Lauder, who was preceptor to James II. of Scotland, and promoted to the See of Dunkeld in 1452.[1] Immediately below this carved head stand two shield-shaped hall chairs, with emblazoned backs, each having two long spears, one on either side, firmly supported to the back by iron rings, a fashion prevailing in the 'rough and ready' period called the 'good old fighting days.' There are two chairs precisely similar in the lobby at Lauder House. Some well-arranged groups of battle-axes, shields, and spears are to be seen in every available space, besides a facsimile of Wallace's two-handed sword, a mighty weapon, but for whom it was made we cannot tell. There it stands, however, a most creditable-looking *in memoriam* of Sir Robert de Lawdre of the Lamberton charter, whom history affirms was the associate of Sir William Wallace. Above the first landing hangs a large picture, eight feet by five, entitled 'Le Roi boit,' painted by Jordaens, the subject being taken from one of the ceremonies of Old Twelfth Day as it was celebrated in France, no one at the feast being allowed to drink until the chosen 'King of the Bean' had first set the example, but the moment his glass had touched his lips a unanimous shout arose, 'Le Roi boit!'—this signal of '*The King drinks*' being followed in most cases by universal riot and uproar, which is vigorously portrayed in the painting.

As we mount the ample staircase several of the old 'Barons of Grange' and their stately Dames look down upon us from their respective frames on the wall, among which we find the portraits of the five daughters of the Seton family who entertained Prince Charles Stuart at the Grange House. That of Dame Isabel Seton is particularly interesting. She is painted in a blue silk dress embroidered with silver,[2] the silk of which it is spun having been wound off the cocoons by her own hands from the silkworms she had reared and fed

[1] Frontispiece.   [2] This dress, which we have seen, is still carefully preserved in the family.

SIR THOMAS DICK LAUDER, SEVENTH BARONET OF FOUNTAINHALL, AND HIS LADY.
From a painting by W. Nicholson, R.S.A.

in a little house in the garden, now called the apple-house. The hall where these pictures hang is lighted from the east by a lofty double window, through which the early morning sun streams with rosy-coloured rays, ofttimes tinting their bygone faces anew with the glowing look of youth and beauty.

Among the family portraits at the Grange there are many historically interesting, representing persons of note and dignity, men who held high public offices in their day,—such names as Sir William Dick of Braid, Sir John Leslie of Newton, and General Leslie, Lord Newark, Sir Andrew Ramsay of Abbotshall, Sir John Lauder, Lord Fountainhall, Sir Alexander Seton of Pitmedden, and Sir John Cockburn of Ormiston, besides many others which we shall enumerate in the Appendix.[1]

The present dining-hall was originally two rooms, the drawing-room and dining-room of the old manor-house. Having retained more of its antique character, it is not so lofty as the modern drawing-room. The walls are panelled in oak, and the ceiling is ornamented with transverse mouldings, with a bold cornice, also of oak, corbelled, with some quaintly carved heads of monks and abbots. This substantially-furnished and comfortable-looking room is forty-five feet long by eighteen broad, and well lighted on the south and west by three large windows, with stone balconies, and one smaller one to the north. The walls are also hung with a number of interesting old family portraits, and some valuable bevelled mirrors in antique frames, besides several sculptured shields and emblematical devices. Over the mantelpiece there is an exquisite picture of Sir Thomas Dick Lauder, seventh Baronet of Fountainhall, and his Lady, painted by W. Nicholson, R.S.A. Some of the old-fashioned Scotch arm-chairs are superb; one in particular, which, from its height, size, colour, weight, and importance, looks as if it must have played its part as a dais-throne in Prince Charlie's time; but most of the finely carved black oak cabinets and furniture at present in the Dick-Lauder family are similar in design to that of Randolph, Earl of Murray.

We now come to the principal feature of the nineteenth-century portion of the building—the spacious drawing-room, which is entirely new, and decidedly modern in its elegant and tasteful adornment, but which bears withal an air of charming adaptation to its mediæval surroundings. The walls and ceiling are of *oak*—strangely at variance, one would be apt to suppose, with all our modern ideas of a drawing-room,—but its character is admirably sustained; weight and sombreness are completely transposed into subdued richness and harmony by its space, the loftiness of the moulded ceiling, and the immense

[1] Appendix, Note XV.

flood of light which permeates every portion of this delightful room from two lofty windows, the southern one being a magnificent oriel reaching from the floor to the ceiling, and extending almost the whole breadth of one side of the room, giving an airiness and grace which is most effective. From the balcony of the western window there is a flight of steps leading from a turret into the garden, a very romantic spot, the stone seats being surrounded with ivy, and overarched by one of the most graceful laburnum trees imaginable, a perfect blaze of golden tassels in the spring. Among the many pleasing reminiscences of the drawing-room at the Grange we must not omit to mention the dramatic and musical entertainments given by the young members of the family to their numerous friends. The western oriel with its large recess was most admirably adapted for the erection of the stage, with drop-curtain and footlights complete, and nothing could be more convenient for the performers than the position of the Library, both with regard to stage exit and dressing-room. The performers were always strictly confined to the family circle, assisted by the French governess, and it was usual to represent two short plays, one in English and the other in French, at each entertainment, — all the necessary stage duties of manager, costumier, scene-painter, prompter, etc., being willingly undertaken by the young ladies themselves, even to the composition of the play sometimes. 'The Daisy Bridge,' for instance, a play in two acts, was written expressly for the 'Grange Salon Theatre' by Miss C. Dick Lauder.

OLD FAMILY CHAIR.

At Relugas, the children being all very young, the comedies had been simple in character, such as 'L'Enfant Gaté,' par Madame la Comtesse de Genlis, 'Vanity Punished,' 'The Sword,' 'L'Aveugle de Spa,' 'King Alfred,' 'L'Isle

Heureuse,' ' La petite Glaneuse,' etc.; but at the Grange House the *répertoire* increased in elaboration, and upon one occasion 'The Beacon,' by Joanna Baillie, was so admirably represented that the aged authoress wrote a beautiful letter to Miss Dick Lauder, thanking her for the artistic interpretation of her idea, as rendered by herself and her sisters with the aid of their brother, Mr. George Dick Lauder.

The Library, which is so conveniently situated between the drawing-room and the dining-room, was formerly the external limit of the building on the southern side, and it still retains its original six-feet-thick walls, as seen by the depth of the recessed doors, on either side, opening into each of the apartments. In this secluded room centres all the literary interest of the Grange House, and in it Sir Thomas Dick Lauder himself wrote several of his later works, especially *The Queen's Progress* in 1842, and those interesting articles for *Tait's Magazine*, called 'Scottish Rivers,'[1] which end so pathetically.

Passing out through the dining-room on to the landing, by means of an inner stair built over the entrance porch, we ascend to the older portion of the Grange. This stair also communicates with all the apartments on the second, third, and fourth storeys. The room immediately above the drawing-room was Sir Thomas Dick Lauder's own bedroom. It is a charming room, with an air of quaintness about it, and a most delightful view of wood and vale to be seen from the broad substantial balcony at the double window. Adjoining this apartment was Lady Dick Lauder's boudoir, with the most unique recess imaginable, formed by the round turret, which looks very like the *bowers* we read of in mediæval romances, from which plighted maidens waved a last adieu to their departing knights, or wedded dames watched anxiously in times of war for the return of their absent lords. Then there is the White Room, which has the date 1727 on the pediment of the dormer window, the Pink Room, the Green Room, the Daisy Room, the Lilac Room, and the long upper Day Nursery, which had been dedicated to the memory of Janet MacMath and her husband, William Dick, first Baron of Grange, by placing their united monograms W. D., I. M., and the date of their marriage, 1637, over each of the dormer windows.

The *small* apartment called 'Queen Mary's Room' is in the third storey of the square tower, and is only reached through another room by descending a few steps.

Of the four turrets which now flank the southern and western gables only two originally belonged to 'Sanct-Geilie-Grange,' as shown in the view of it

[1] These articles were collected into a small volume, and republished by his second daughter, Miss Cornelia Dick Lauder, in 1879.

given by Sir Thomas Dick Lauder himself in a sketch [1] which he took in 1825 before commencing the extensive alterations he had planned. The chief interest, however, which is still centred in one of these older towers, lies in the oft-repeated assertion that it is haunted. Of this we shall speak in another chapter on Traditional Stories.

BELFRY TOWER, GRANGE HOUSE.

At present the entire pleasure-grounds and gardens are included within five or six acres; but they have been laid out with much artistic taste; and are thoroughly in keeping with the character of the place. The luxuriance of the ivy bespeaks generations of growth and culture—indeed, we could quite well believe that the stately arch at the bend of the avenue, so densely clothed with it, might have originally formed part of the prior entrance to the inner precincts of St. Geilic-Grange, therefore we consider the stone with the ancient Burgh Arms upon it (already mentioned in connection with Dr. Robertson and the Old College) has been most appropriately given such a conspicuous place thereon. The parterre and grounds immediately within view of the principal windows are laid out in terraces and flower-borders, with tazzas and smaller vases picturesquely placed, while the steps in every direction add greatly to the effect, conveniently leading from the higher to the lower walks, and also down to the beautiful bowling-green, with its sheltering evergreens and ornamental statues, where in the days of the Reform Bill politics and pleasure were so enthusiastically combined. The four graceful statues which stand facing north, south, east, and west, upon the bowling-green, were presented by Alexander Mitchell Innes, Esq. of Ayton Castle, as a marriage gift to the family from whence he took his beautiful bride, Miss Charlotte, the third surviving daughter of Sir Thomas Dick Lauder. 'I have taken one maiden,' he quietly remarked, 'and left you four!'

[1] See p. 357.

AS A BARONIAL RESIDENCE

Some of the happiest summer days of the young people at the Grange House were spent upon the bowling-green; one might almost say, and summer nights too—for it was frequently converted into an *impromptu* ball-room, and many a merry dance was tripped by moonlight upon its soft green velvety carpet. The school-room piano was carried out by the young gentlemen on their shoulders, garden chairs were placed round the circle, and the candles set for the pianist. Then no sooner were the first notes of some fascinating waltz or Highland Schottische struck than the merry young couples floated away in the mazy dance, like fairies on the green, quite beyond the sound of the music, keeping tune with their voices, and returning to the starting-point in high glee, to find they had kept in perfect time with the piano.

Upon a higher level than the bowling-green is the old southern approach to the House, in the centre of which stands the Warrick Vase.

THE WARRICK VASE AVENUE.

The archway of this original entrance can still be traced in the outside wall, though the aperture is built up.

There is another feature of interest connected with the Grange Manor which we cannot pass by unheeded. Beyond the bowling-green, in the shady nook where 'the Monk's Seat' is embowered, we find what is called 'the Dogs' Cemetery,' where lie in undisturbed repose the household pets of the Dick-Lauder family, each with a history of its own, and some of them with special virtues most pithily recorded in verse. The most interesting of the epitaphs is that of the noble ' Bronte,' who well deserves the foremost place :—

> From Newfoundland his high-bred fathers came,
> Lords of the sea—BRONTE his gallant name
> To reasoning man ensample he mot be,
> For who so free from vice and sin as he?

> Urged by his generous heart, a youth to save
> He dived—and dragged him from the whelming wave—
> But all, alas ! too late—No life remained ;—
> The weeping mother to her bosom strained
> The noble dog : then be not too severe
> If o'er this turf where Bronte lies we drop a tear.
>
> Vth Julii MDCCCXXXVIII.

The prose version of this pathetic story, as related to us by Miss Dick Lauder, is quite worthy of repetition, for Bronte was truly a hero as gallant as his name. One evening the butler had taken the dog as usual for a stroll in the surrounding fields, near by which lay a disused quarry half filled with water, such as in former days they ducked the poor old witches in. At this point Bronte became violently excited, running round the banks, barking furiously. No amount of whistling or calling could induce him to leave the spot ; and when the servant went back for him he perceived something struggling in the water. On his throwing a stone into the dark stagnant-looking pool the noble animal made one bound forward, leaping from the heights into the water below. Unerringly he swam towards the form, and seizing it by the clothes, commenced with great effort to return to the bank ; but from the evident weight of the lad the clothing gave way and he lost his grip, so the boy sank below the surface. Still undaunted, the brave dog dived a second time, and brought the youth up with a firmer grasp, boldly swimming towards the shore, nor relaxed his hold until he had laid the unconscious boy upon the rocky bank. By this time a crowd had collected, and some medical students who were playing cricket in the adjoining field came to the rescue ; but all their efforts to resuscitate the form were unavailing, life was extinct : and the sad burden was borne to his mother's house, she being a widow. The next day the poor woman called at the Grange and asked if she might see the dog that had so nobly tried to save her boy, and when Bronte appeared, all unconscious of his heroic deed, the sobbing mother just put her arms round his neck and hugged him.

Knowing this to be only one instance of the noble deeds of the gallant Bronte, can we wonder that such a tender-hearted philanthropist as the late Sir Thomas Dick Lauder should have deemed the faithful animal worthy of a monumental record after death ? The epitaph itself is more truthful than half the fulsome panegyric stones erected in the adjacent cemetery to hundreds of misused human lives.

The next stone in point of date is that of 'Rattle,' a well-trained setter with a pedigree. Many a fine day's chase he had enjoyed with his enthusiastic master, and more than likely he assisted at that memorable fox-hunt at Crichton Castle, where the hounds poured out of a narrow window one by one like a falling cataract, and Reynard escaped to cover. Rattle's tomb is even more imposing in appearance than Bronte's, having his effigy carved upon the

DOGS' CEMETERY.

top from a drawing of him taken by Sir Thomas, who also wrote his quaint epitaph :—

    Of Nero's blood,
    A Cocker good,
  Old Rattle dashed thro' brake and cover ;
  Nor feared mishaps
  Though caught in traps.
  His legs were broken five times over.
    But Death's fell snare,
    Ne'er known to spare,
  He slowly wound around his wizzen.
    So Hare and Roe
    May fearless go
  Since Rattle lies in Death's cold prison.
    6th September 1840.

Judging from the record on the next tombstone, 'Raith' appears to have been distinguished simply by loving and being loved, for it says :—

'Here lies the King Charles Spaniel
RAITH,
For twelve years the pet of the Grange House.
9th August 1847.

Passing from this shaded spot through a postern in the dividing wall, we emerge into the avenue close beside the present gateway to the Grange House, with its circular arch and crested turrets, which was also built in 1827 by Sir Thomas Dick Lauder, who changed the position of the original avenue, making it to sweep with a graceful curve beneath the ancestral trees, which stand like protecting sentinels guarding the old homestead of so many generations.

SUN-DIAL, GRANGE HOUSE.

THE AVENUE, GRANGE HOUSE.

SIR THOMAS DICK LAUDER, BART.

From a painting by Robert Scott Lauder, R.S.A. Photographed by Mr. Marshall Wane.

CHAPTER XXVI

SIR THOMAS DICK LAUDER, BART.

'Scorner of wrong, and lover of the right,
Compounded all of nobleness he seemed,
And was indeed the perfect, gentle knight
The poet dreamed.'
ALFRED AUSTIN.

IR THOMAS DICK LAUDER, seventh Baronet of Fountainhall, for whom and by whom the Grange Manor had been thus metamorphosed, was the honoured and chivalrous representative of a long race of Scottish noblemen, his whole appearance, bearing, and mien tallying with his pedigree—his handsome features, expressively lighted up by a pair of 'honest, fearless, happy blue eyes,' and his nobly-formed head, surmounted with a wealth of long fair hair, carelessly thrown back in picturesque masses. No truer man ever trod on Scottish soil—equally true with peer or people, and a staunch supporter of all Liberal reforms. Among his most intimate friends we find such well-known names as Lord Jeffrey of Craigcrook and his inseparable companion, Lord Cockburn of Bonally, Lord Rutherfurd of Lauriston Castle, Sir James Gibson-Craig of Riccarton, Sir John Dalrymple, Professor Wilson, and Dr. John Brown —most of whom, following the fashion so prevalent in the earlier part of this century, had converted some fifteenth-century castle, or old square tower, into a picturesque baronial residence. At each of these charming abodes they

DICK LAUDER COAT-OF-ARMS.

visited in turn, revelling in the sculptured relics of the past, so delightfully commingled with the natural beauties of the present.

With what relish Lord Cockburn speaks of them all, especially his much-loved Bonally! His description of the renovation of the Grange House is short, but pithy; and his having known it so well in its primitive condition in Principal Robertson's time makes it all the more interesting.

'Fifteen years ago,' he writes this in 1845, 'the Grange House was a tall grey keep, with an old garden, on different levels, joined by balustraded stairs, all in bad order. It is now an excellent house, with the garden preserved, but greatly improved. The old approach, which was from the north, and nearly inaccessible, has been given up for the more striking one from the west, and the place is rich (perhaps too rich) in evergreens, statues, vases, stairs, balustrades, terraces, and a delightful bowling-green. No time-honoured mansion was ever touched by a more truly antique hand.'

It would indeed have been strange if the home Sir Thomas Dick Lauder had specially designed had not been intrinsically picturesque and artistic. From his youth up he had always been a most prolific draughtsman. Most of his earlier works are illustrated with his own hand, and many are the graphic sketches from his pencil scattered among his friends. His frequent companion in art was the Rev. John Thomson of Duddingston, at whose pretty manse, overlooking the loch, Sir Thomas was a constant visitor.

On one occasion, while Thomson was busy at work on a picture, seated on a camp-stool under the shadow of a rock, Sir Thomas with characteristic dexterity sketched his friend's portrait,[1] in an off-hand, easy way, which is highly valued for its truthfulness by the admirers of the pastor-painter, lying at whose feet, not sleeping, but keenly alive to his responsible position of *coat-and-colour-box guardian*, is our canine hero Bronte. As an artist Sir Thomas was a keen observer of Nature, every phase of which touched him, from the sky overhead to the flowers at his feet; but human hearts never failed to touch him most.

Among his reminiscences of those matchless scenes he gazed upon with an artistic eye during his mountain rambles with his friend Henry Cockburn, none seems to have moved him more than the sight they came upon one bright September Sabbath, towards sunset, as the last rays of the setting orb fell upon the rustic groups of the people of Menstrie, picturesquely clustered upon a grassy knoll to the east of their sweet village, all intent upon 'Divine Service.'

[1] This sketch is at present in the possession of Miss Dick Lauder.

SIR THOMAS DICK LAUDER, BART.

Lord Cockburn, noticing this in his Diary, says : 'Sir Thomas and I waited at a little distance and heard four verses of a psalm sung. The mingling of the voices at such an hour, in such a scene, combined with the recollections of the hill-folk, was most solemn and delightful.'

As a politician, undoubtedly the principal event with which Sir Thomas Dick Lauder's name is associated is that of the Reform Bill, and many were the memorable political gatherings which again took place beneath the roof-tree of the Grange of St. Giles.

It might have turned out a very serious affair to many had this Bill not passed ; for Sir Thomas himself, Henry Cockburn, Lord Jeffrey, and Sir James Gibson-Craig would all have been impeached. We are told the warrant had already been made out against them. The monster meeting in favour of the Bill took place in St. Ann's Yards, the field immediately to the east of Holyrood House—Sir Thomas Dick Lauder presiding. An eye-witness says : ' There were probably 30,000 present. Yet the people behaved with perfect obedience to the laws—no rioting, no indecorous language ; the grave and silent masses felt they were on the eve of a popular crisis.' None more painfully interesting had occurred in Britain since 1688. On the 6th August 1832 Lord Cockburn writes enthusiastically : ' The regeneration of Scotland is now secured ! Our Reform Bill has become law !' The ceremony called the Reform Jubilee took place at Edinburgh on the 11th August on Bruntsfield Links. About forty thousand were present, besides the fifteen thousand in procession. It was a glorious sight, improved by a splendid day. The people sang ' God save the King,' ' Rule Britannia,' and ' Scots wha hae wi' Wallace bled.' This part of the ceremony appears to have been sublime and effective, the last song particularly, which was sung as Scotsmen alone can sing it, with the earnestness and devotion of a sacrament.

On the 15th September 1834 the Whigs testified their gratitude to Earl Grey by a public dinner, at which both he and Lord Brougham were present. The Earl's arrival in Edinburgh was literally a national triumph, almost equal to a Royal progress. The magistrates and trades all turned out in procession, with bands and banners, conducting him in state through a moving mass of human beings, while every ridge, pinnacle, and window was teeming with heads and waving with handkerchiefs. As a popular demonstration of popular joy this spectacle was considered by many to have been a finer sight than even the arrival of George IV. It was a national tribute to moral dignity, truth, and honour. No man ever more justly earned the esteem of the whole nation than Earl Grey. His political opponents even could not but admire his honourable and consistent career. At the time of this public reception he was the guest of the Earl of Stair at Oxenfoord Castle.

As there was no hall in the city large enough to hold the company at dinner, Lord Cockburn says, 'we gallantly resolved to make one, and I doubt if such a structure was ever reared before in so short a period, for in twelve days (three of them one ceaseless torrent) a wooden edifice above 100 feet square, perfectly comfortable and handsomely decorated, was produced; the floor was matted, the side walls and roof lined with canvas, painted and adorned by no less an artist than Roberts; the raw beams which supported the roof made, by coloured cloth, into beautiful columns; and, in short, the whole interior was as elegant as if there had been no hurry about it. It was like one of the creations of the *Arabian Nights*. The whole was lighted by gas, chiefly from a splendid lustre taken from the Theatre. Including about 240 ladies, there were nearly 2800 persons in the "Pavilion," as it was called. All got in by sections of thirty ranged in the area, and moving off by ballot without any tumult, and all were well accommodated. There could not have been a more inspiring spectacle. It was the homage of Scotland to its greatest public friend.'

This Pavilion was erected in the eastern compartment of the High School, just below the Calton Hill, on the south side, and the chair was occupied by Archibald, Earl of Rosebery, K.T., in the absence of the Duke of Hamilton.

In 1835 Earl Grey visited Sir Thomas Dick Lauder at the Grange House, and in right royal style he commemorated his visit by planting an oak-tree in a conspicuous spot in the avenue, upon the bank on the north side, not very far from the grand ivy-clad arch. It is still called 'Earl Grey's Oak,' and a fine healthy tree it is, although only a baby-tree as yet, in its sixty-second year, compared with the venerable giants that surround it.

The most prominent names among the first leaders of the Whig party in Scotland were Henry Erskine, the Right Hon. William Adam, Lord Gillies, John Clerk, and David Cathcart, each of whom became Judges; Archibald Fletcher, Malcolm Laing, and John M'Farlane, Advocates; but Sir James Gibson-Craig, Lord Jeffrey, Lord Cockburn, and Sir Thomas Dick Lauder had entered the lists later on.

The favourite resort of all these literary men was the Meadows, along the avenues of which they met daily to talk of politics and religion; for political opinion was strong in those days, and manifested itself even in dress—'shorts, silks, and buckles,' with powdered wigs, *versus* the 'gaiters and natural locks of Jacobinism.'

SIR THOMAS DICK LAUDER, BART.

The most conspicuous figure among the latter was Sir Thomas Dick Lauder, with his fair flowing locks and his formidable-looking 'agrarian club,' who, according to universal testimony, was one of the most chivalrous and at the same time most gentle of political warriors.

His versatility seems to have been as great as his popularity. His friends sometimes regretted that he had not been born poor, for then his talents would have had full scope, making him all the more famous, either as a musician, an artist, a geologist, or a first-rate land-surveyor.

Of all the Whig leaders he was the greatest favourite with the mob, and so liberal in his 'Whiggism' that he could keep the very Radicals in order. His picturesque appearance alone was sufficient to captivate the populace. His untiring energy and large-hearted philanthropy made him first and foremost in all public proceedings, 'insomuch that strangers judging from newspapers might suppose that he ruled everything in Edinburgh.' As a landowner he was ever honourable, not in title only, but in deed and in spirit, his acts at all times overflowing with equity and kindness, and his conversation brimming over with mirthfulness and genuine Scottish humour.

A striking instance of his popularity with the students took place immediately after that memorable 'monster meeting' in St. Ann's Yards. The blue carriage containing Lady Lauder and several of the children was standing at a short distance from the crowd, awaiting Sir Thomas, but as soon as the people began to cheer the last speaker a band of the students rushed forward, took out the horses, and drew the carriage in triumph the whole length of the Canongate, right up into Charlotte Square, Lady Lauder being the whole time in fear and trembling lest some accident should happen to mar the day's brilliant success, but the young gentlemen kept on assuring her there was no danger. 'Trust us, Lady Lauder,' they repeated again and again. 'Trust us, no harm shall befall you.' True enough they landed in perfect safety, and from that day forward the very sight of the blue carriage made 'their soles itch to become the horses.' 'Well do I remember the light-blue coach with the white liveries,' writes Dr. John Brown in one of his charming letters to Miss Dick Lauder, 'and the young daughters, so like a posie of flowers beside the beautiful mother.'

Another interesting incident, which happened a few years after Sir Thomas and his Lady came to the Grange, is mentioned in Lord Cockburn's Diary, but it must be given in his own words, or the charming breadth and simplicity would be lost:—

'*16th May* 1836.—There was an annular eclipse of the sun yesterday afternoon.

'The public attention had been long called to it, and Dr. Chalmers had had the goodness to propose that as the phenomenon would happen on a Sunday between two and three in the afternoon, service should be put off to a later hour than usual. This advice was generally followed, and the eclipse owed no small part of its fame to the novelty of the kirks not meeting at the ordinary time. It was a beautiful spectacle. The day was warm and cloudless; the people all out, principally on the hills and fields— almost every one with a bit of darkened glass. . . . I was on the top of the tower at the Grange House, with Sir Thomas Dick Lauder and his family. There was something very impressive in the obscuration. The blaze of the brightest day became like the cold thoughtful dawn of a summer morning a little before sunrise. . . . There were no stars visible (which was said there would be) with the naked eye, nor were animals (as was also predicted) amazed; at least the cows, horses, and sheep on the Grange fields never abated a single munch of their young juicy grass. A bantam cock on the tower crowed frequently, which was held at the time to prove that he thought it the twilight of the morning. But he crowed as vigorously when he walked into the dining-room some hours afterwards in the glare of the western sun. He was tame, and seemed to crow whenever he was entertained.'

The next day Lord Cockburn conscientiously adds to his entry: 'I find that I'm wrong about the stars. We saw none, but other people did.'

At a large public dinner given on the 19th March 1838 to Sir William Allan, the Scottish historical painter, upon the occasion of his election as President of the Royal Scottish Academy, Sir Thomas Dick Lauder was in the chair as usual. It is interesting to note how very frequently he fulfilled the office of chairman during the last fifteen years of his life. There was hardly a public meeting of any importance in Edinburgh at which he was not asked to preside. His natural flow of language, and the goodly store of wit and anecdote at his command, made his presence always delightful.

The intercourse between Sir Thomas and his friends was at all times harmonious and sympathetic. Among those on intimate terms with him were Professor Wilson (known as Christopher North) and his brother, Mr. James Wilson, 'one of the most genial of men,' in whose company he sailed round the North of Scotland in 1842. Sir Thomas's interesting Diary, in which he describes each place of note as they journeyed, was afterwards published in two volumes, entitled *A Voyage round the Coasts of Scotland and the Isles.*

In the same year he also wrote an account of the Queen's first visit to Scotland with Prince Albert, a 'Royal Progress' famed for its banquets by day and its bonfires by night, a national rejoicing equal to a second Coronation, which lasted from the 1st until the 15th September. The magnificent spectacle of the blazing heights as the Royal Squadron sailed up the Forth has never been surpassed. Sir James Forrest of Comiston, who was created a Baronet at the Queen's Coronation in 1838, was still in office as Lord Provost in 1842. The two most prominent events in which his name appears in an official capacity as connected with the Royal visit are so opposite in character that we might almost call the one sublimely ridiculous and the other sublimely grand. In the first Sir James became most conspicuous by his absence, for though we can hardly credit it possible that Her Majesty, after so much national preparation, should land at Granton Pier, and there be no Provost, no Bailies, and no Councillors to receive her, yet such was the fact; nor were any of these worthy civic dignitaries to be seen at the newly-erected barrier through which the Queen was to enter her northern capital after receiving the silver keys of the city. How this happened none could tell, for there was certainly no lack of loyalty. But the Queen rose early that morning and the Provost did not. Her Majesty left the royal yacht with the Prince Consort at five minutes to nine, instead of between ten and eleven o'clock, which Sir James had been told the evening before would be the most probable hour. But though the Provost was not there His Grace the Duke of Buccleuch was, and so were the people, thousands upon thousands of them, loyally cheering to welcome our Sovereign Lady as her carriage passed through the crowd.

The enthusiastic zeal with which the Chief Magistrate and Councillors tried to overtake their morning tardiness caused no little merriment throughout the day, and ere night fell the whole city rang with a parody on the old Jacobite song 'Hey, Johnny Cope,' the new version being:—

> 'Hey, Jamie Forrest, are ye waukin' yet?
> Or are your Bailies snorin' yet?
> If ye are waukin' I would wit
> Ye'd hae a merry, merry mornin'!
> . . . . . .
> The Queen she's come to Granton Pier,
> Nae Provost and nae Bailie here,
> They're in their beds I muckle fear,
> Sae early in the mornin!
> Hey, Jamie,' etc.

This song with its many verses flew like wildfire from street to street, the refrain being kept up unremittingly for a whole fortnight. Even Royalty smiled at the parody, though the young Queen graciously took upon herself all the blame of the misadventure by saying they had been pleased to change their arrangements in order to make a formal visit into the city from Dalkeith Palace on the following day—which they did, and Sir James then had the honour of making his eloquent speech while presenting the silver keys to Her Majesty; to which the Queen replied with her usual grace and sweetness, 'I return the keys of the city with perfect confidence into the safe keeping of the Lord Provost, Magistrates, and Council.'

The following day Sir James Forrest's name was again immortalised at the magnificent ceremony of the laying of the foundation stone of the Assembly Hall by the Grand Master and the Grand Chaplain of the Grand Masonic Lodge while Her Majesty and suite were at the Castle.

The inscription on the plate which was deposited in the stone was as follows :—

'To the glory of GOD, in honour of the
QUEEN.
On the 3rd day of September in the year of our Lord
MDCCCXLII.,
The day of our most gracious Majesty
QUEEN VICTORIA
Visiting the City of Edinburgh,
The Right Hon. Sir James Forrest of Comiston, Bart.,
LORD PROVOST,
The Rev. David Welsh, D.D., Moderator of the Assembly,
The Foundation Stone of this superb structure, to be called
VICTORIA HALL,
For the use of the
GENERAL ASSEMBLY OF THE CHURCH OF SCOTLAND
Was laid by
The Right Hon. Lord Frederick Fitzclarence, G.C.H., etc.,
Grand Master Mason of Scotland,
In presence of the Grand Lodge and other Masonic Lodges.
JAMES GILLESPIE GRAHAM, Esq. of Orchill, Architect.
JOHN LIND, Master Builder of the Hall.
The length of Building from East to West, 141 feet.
Height of Spire over the Entrance, 241 feet.'

Her Majesty held her Royal Levee on Monday the 5th September at Dalkeith Palace, the residence of His Grace the Duke of Buccleuch, instead of within the ancient halls of Holyrood, as was at first arranged, owing to an unfortunate alarm of fever in that district. This was the source of much chagrin and disappointment to many, as all the arrangements had been completed on the grandest scale, and the Royal apartments had been gorgeously refurnished.

On the day of the Queen's arrival four thousand persons, irrespective of rank or class, were admitted to the Duke's grounds, that a most loyal shout of welcome should greet the Royal visitor as she drove up to the Palace.

The number of carriages which arrived at Dalkeith Palace on the day of Her Majesty's reception of the Scottish nobility and gentry amounted to four

SIR THOMAS DICK LAUDER, BART.

hundred, forming a cortège more than three miles in length. By this we can understand how numerous were the presentations.

Lady Lauder and her four daughters, the Misses Susan, Cornelia, Isabella, and Maddalena Dick Lauder, were each presented by the Countess of Rosebery, whereas their sister Charlotte, who had been married shortly before to Alexander Mitchell Innes, Esq. of Ayton Castle, was presented by the Duchess of Roxburghe. We are also told that among the ladies who distinguished themselves at this memorable levee by the grace and dignity of their comportment was Lady Lauder, who had already won the reputation of being the most elegant minuet dancer of that period. But an amusing scene took place with one of the young ladies, who evidently could not emulate her mother's calm and measured demeanour. After making her obeisance in due form, and gracefully kissing Her Majesty's hand, she stepped back with well-trained skill until she had reached the prescribed distance, then, with an intense feeling of relief, she turned and absolutely ran, in her nervous haste ignoring the Prince altogether. Becoming suddenly ashamed of her precipitous retreat, she looked back apologetically, just in time to see Prince Albert smiling at her trepidation, which smile, gracious as it was, did not tend to lessen her confusion.

We have no intention of following our then youthful Sovereign Lady Queen Victoria throughout her enthusiastic progress among her loyal Scottish subjects, for the whole routine of the Royal journeyings, the princely entertainment at Taymouth Castle given by the noble Marquis of Breadalbane, and the Royal visit to Drummond Castle, have each been most delightfully recorded by Sir Thomas Dick Lauder in his interesting and elaborate volume on the subject; but there are one or two little incidents we should like to mention in connection with the book itself which we know have not been published before, seeing they are taken from the private letters of Sir Thomas to Lady Lauder, who had gone to Harrogate with her daughters for change of air in the summer of 1843, while Sir Thomas was busily occupied at the Grange House revising and sending off the proof-sheets of the *Royal Progress* for Her Majesty's perusal.

In a letter dated 6th July he writes: 'I am now done with the *Queen's Progress*, so far as my labours are concerned. The corrections in the last slips sent to Her Majesty had reference to the effects of the sea on herself and the Prince. But although she must necessarily have had every desire that they should be carried into effect, Anson[1] says that he is authorised to

---

[1] Honourable G. E. Anson, Treasurer of the Household to His Royal Highness Prince Albert.

say that if the alterations will increase either trouble or expense the narrative may be left entirely as it is. Is not this a most amiable trait? Of course I altered the passages, and I hope made them better than they were before.'

Sir Thomas had evidently in his first copy given Prince Albert the credit of being a good sailor, which, from his own confession, it appears he was not, so the corrected passage now reads as follows:—

'The Prince suffered a good deal from the sea; indeed, he was seldom, if ever, altogether free from nausea; but Her Majesty, who has been more used to the element, and from her earliest years attached to the amusement of sailing, stood the voyage extremely well, and was rarely, if at all, in any degree seriously affected by it. The Queen may indeed be called an excellent sailor in all respects, for the directions which she gave to the Commander-in-Chief as the several vessels approached the steamer at the Nore were as distinct and professional as if she had been many years in naval command.'[1]

In another letter to Lady Lauder, dated 17th July, Sir Thomas writes: 'Constable[2] this morning tells me that the Queen never receives persons to present books, nor Prince Albert either, but George Anson thinks that in this instance the Prince will break through this rule'—which he evidently most graciously did, as the following extract from a letter dated a week later clearly testifies: 'Constable had a long interview on the 20th with Prince Albert, when he presented the royal copies of the *Royal Progress*. The Prince expressed himself delighted with the book, examined the original sketches very carefully, making appropriate remarks upon each. He said he should like to show the sketches to Her Majesty, and that Constable should hear from him next day. Constable then goes on to say: "His Royal Highness's manner is so perfectly unaffected that he put me at once at my ease, which was very fortunate, as it enabled me to answer all his questions distinctly, which I am sure modesty (*mauvaise honte*) would not otherwise have permitted."'

These presentation copies to Her Majesty must have been most gorgeously bound—in Royal tartan and gold—judging from the splendid quarto volume which Lady Lauder found awaiting her on her return to the Grange House in September, sent at the dying request of George, Lord Abercromby, second Baron of Aboukir.

Two years later a most imposing sight was witnessed by Sir Thomas Dick

---

[1] The Queen's voyage to and from Scotland, between Woolwich and Granton, had been made in the *Trident* steam-vessel, preceded by the *Black Eagle* and *Rhadamanthus* war-steamers, Sir Edward Bruce being Admiral of the Squadron.

[2] This was Thomas Constable, printer of the *Royal Progress*. He was a son of Archibald, the well-known publisher, occasionally referred to in this work.

Lauder and his family from the top of the tower of the Grange House. This was the complete destruction of Old Greyfriars Church by fire in the month of January 1845. It took place on a Sunday morning, and Hugh Miller appears to have been the first to notice the smoke issuing from it as he was passing Heriot's Hospital towards the church a little before ten o'clock. In an incredibly short space of time the blaze of light cast over the city was magnificently grand. The roaring of the flames, the crashing of the beams, and the heavy thud of the falling slates as shower after shower descended, soon attracted a vast concourse of people, startled by such unusual sounds in the calm silence of a Sabbath morning. As they approached the fearful conflagration, the low murmurs of the awe-stricken crowd mingled with the shouts of the firemen. 'A sea of fire continued to rage within the area of the building; such, however, was the intensity of the heat that not a fragment of the charcoal remained.' Ere long the space occupied by the Old Greyfriars was left as bare as the floor of a quarry, and the adjoining church of the New Greyfriars soon presented even a more melancholy appearance. 'From every window issued a tongue of fire that rose fierce and high, making a grandly lurid spectacle of flame and smoke, leaving in its track a desolate ruin, all charred and chipped. The huge gaping window of the eastern gable looked as if Knox's rascal multitude had been hammering upon it for a week.'

Two sculpturesque forms appear to have struck the poetic imagination of Hugh Miller during the conflagration. One might almost call them Life and Death. The first he describes thus: 'The pinnacle on the eastern gable—a pyramidal mass of stones, whitened and cracked amid the flames, and throwing off splinter after splinter into the fiery area below, assumed a striking resemblance to a human figure, that, standing unmoved where the conflagration raged most fiercely, seemed the very genius of the scene.' The second picture he gives us is by no means so pleasant: 'On an ancient and very fantastic monument beside the window there stands in prominent relief a tall figure of Death, in the common skeleton form, and armed with the all-destroying scythe. The grim sentinel kept his place bravely. He has borrowed from the conflagration a darker grin, and the smoke seems to have coiled thickly in the hollow of his open ribs, but he has caught no scathe from the fire; and when the vast bolt of flame roared from the opening beside him, and the graves were blazing at his feet, he must have furnished no inadequate resemblance to his prototype, the "goblin full of wrath" described by Milton.'[1]

Sir Thomas Dick Lauder, from his higher vantage-ground, saw with sorrow

[1] *A Voice from the Greyfriars.* By Hugh Miller.

and dismay the fiery destruction of the Old Greyfriars, where he and his family had so often worshipped, and where the ashes of his immediate forefathers lay. The building itself, 'like an old martyr, had closed its history in smoke and fire,' after having witnessed some of the grandest and most striking scenes recorded in Scottish ecclesiastical annals.

THE OLD TOLL AT THE CAUSEWAYSIDE.

CHAPTER XXVII

LITERARY WORK OF SIR THOMAS DICK LAUDER AND HUGH MILLER'S CORRESPONDENCE

'Whate'er he did was done with so much ease,
In him alone 'twas natural to please ;
His motions all accompanied with grace,
And Paradise was opened in his face.'
DRYDEN.

HE agitation and excitement consequent on the passing of the Reform Bill had barely subsided ere the interesting correspondence commenced between Sir Thomas Dick Lauder and Hugh Miller about books, and the publication of his first work, *The Traditional History of Cromarty*. As these letters have never been published before, some of my readers may be glad to see the unfolding of another phase of the mind of this truly great man, and hear his own criticisms upon himself and his work. Naturally enough the keynote of almost every letter is gratitude to Sir Thomas for the efforts he had been making to bring the MS. under influential notice. On the 12th April 1833 he writes from Cromarty :—

'HONOURED SIR,—I want words to say how deeply I am impressed with your kindness and condescension, and how much I feel honoured by the manner in which you have been pleased to express yourself regarding my humble labours.

'The long-continued easterly winds have so shut up the bay of Cromarty that none of the traders that frequent it have sailed from it for the last three weeks. The trading smack *Ness*, however, is now preparing to quit it on her voyage to Leith, and I have given my manuscript to David M'Kenzie, one of the sailors, who is to get it conveyed to the Grange House. Would it were more worthy of your perusal !'

This packet duly arrived at its destination, and after perusal the MS. was submitted by Sir Thomas to other competent judges also ; but it was the month of October before the criticisms reached Cromarty, and relieved the author's anxious mind. In the beginning of the following June, 1834, Hugh Miller again writes :—

'If ever my Traditions get abroad, I find they will be all the better for having stayed so long at home. Since sending you my manuscript I have thought of alterations which will materially improve some of the chapters, and as these chapters occur so early in the work that the reader would probably derive from them his first impressions of the whole, the emendations may be of some importance. That I may avail myself of them it is necessary that my manuscript be sent me by some one or other of the Leith traders. . . . I blush to think of the world of trouble to which, through your own goodness, I have subjected you,' etc.

The next letter is written a few weeks after, and is dated

'CROMARTY, 25*th June* 1834.

'HONOURED SIR,—Your goodness overpowers me; I have skill enough partly to express what I think, and language enough partially to commemorate what I imagine, but my *feelings* have no vocabulary, and I can only reiterate that I am neither insensible of your kindness nor ungrateful for it. Enclosed in your letter of October last you transmitted to me Mr. Thomson's truly flattering opinion of my manuscript in his own hand, and I need not say how much gratified I was by praise of so high an order, from one whom the gentleman I have the honour of addressing regards as one of the first literary judges of the day. He is less known, however, in this part of the country than either you, sir, or Professor Wilson, and his opinion consequently cannot be deemed of such weight. The Professor's decision on my History, if at all favourable, would be of incalculable value to me; a statement of your own, however brief, of perhaps more value still.

'I have had to-day a highly gratifying and truly kind letter from Mr. Forsyth of Elgin. He enters warmly into my scheme, and is sanguine that I shall succeed. He has secured for my Prospectus (which I think I shall send to press in about a fortnight hence) the names of London, Glasgow, Aberdeen, and Banff booksellers. I myself am acquainted with those of Inverness and Tain, and I trust I may calculate, through you, on Mr. Black for Edinburgh.

'I am very slightly acquainted with Allan Cunningham, and shall, I think, write to him. No one better knows the hopes and fears of the literary aspirant, or has felt more exquisitely what it is to be encouraged in the contest by the notice of those whom the world conspires to celebrate. We are both pilgrims passing along the path which leads right through the wicket, only he has reached the garden of Beulah, whereas I am still struggling in the mud of the slough, and have giants and wild beasts, and perhaps even Apollyon himself, to contend with. I trust it will not fare with me as with the poor fellow who, instead of entering by the wicket, climbed over the wall; and also that at the gate of the glorious city my roll (though the signature does look a little doubtful) will not be pronounced a forgery. Again I blush to think how much I have cost you in postages,[1] but in Cromarty there are no franks, and opportunities by travellers going south do not occur once in a twelvemonth. I little dreamed when I first wrote you, rather more than a twelvemonth ago, of the immense amount of trouble to which I was subjecting you.—I am, honoured Sir, with sincere and grateful respect, your obedient humble servant, HUGH MILLER.

'To SIR THOMAS DICK LAUDER, Bart., Edinburgh.'

---

[1] Each letter of this correspondence is marked 1s. 0½d.

The next extract is from a letter dated 3rd September 1834, in which Hugh Miller says :—

'There is a philosophy of tradition and a poetry of common life which do not lie quite at the surface, and in writing some of my earlier chapters I had too little of the miner in me to penetrate to where they lay.'

Then, speaking of his prospects, he goes on to say :—

'I have been a good deal in luck ever since I resolved on giving my History to the public. The Messrs. Anderson of Inverness have just brought out their *Guide to the Highlands*, a work which cost Murray a hundred pounds in advertisements alone. In the article "Cromarty and Wick" there are long extracts from my letters on the Herring Fishery, and very flattering notices of the writer, with an allusion to my intended volume, which, from the interest attached to the *Guide* in this part of the country, both from its intrinsic merits and the character of its authors, will, I am certain, be worth fifty pounds to me expended in advertisements. Is it not a lucky circumstance that this work and my Prospectus should have appeared in Inverness in the same week?'

From this Prospectus it appears that Hugh Miller was anxious to bring out his book by subscription, three hundred subscribers at seven shillings and sixpence each being the number he hoped to obtain. Writing about the opinions of the press, he says :—

'Provincial criticism is so timid a thing that I don't at all like it. It would even say of the *Iliad* that it was a very passable sort of poem, considered as the production of a poor old man who was blind and a beggar, and of *Tam o' Shanter* that as the composition of a ploughman it was really *pretty well*.'

There is a break in the correspondence with Sir Thomas after this letter, in consequence of Hugh Miller's visit to Edinburgh, and his personal interview with the Baronet. This important event is best told in his own words, as related by himself in *My Schools and Schoolmasters*, where, after describing his journey from Cromarty, he says :—

'I had transmitted the manuscript of my legendary work several months before to Sir Thomas Dick Lauder, and as he was now on terms in its behalf with Mr. Adam Black, the well-known publisher, I took the liberty of waiting on him to see how the negotiation was speeding. He received me with great kindness, hospitably urged that I should live with him so long as I resided in Edinburgh, in his noble mansion, the Grange House, and as an inducement introduced me to his library, full charged with the best editions of the best authors, and enriched with many a rare volume and curious manuscripts. "Here," he said, "Robertson the historian penned his last work, *The Disquisition*, and here," opening the door of an adjoining room, "he died." I of course declined the invitation. The Grange House, with its books, and its pictures, and its hospitable master, so rich in anecdote, and so full of literary sympathies, would have been no place for the poor pupil-accountant.[1] Sir Thomas, however, kindly got Mr. Black to meet me at dinner, and in the course of the evening that enterprising bookseller agreed to undertake the publication of my work on terms which the nameless author of a volume somewhat local in its character, and very local in its name, might well regard as liberal.'

From the dining-room of the Grange House, therefore, Hugh Miller stepped over the Rubicon, and entering the literary world, he became a member of the society known as 'men of letters.' After his return to Cromarty the correspondence recommenced, and the letters became more frequent and still more interesting; but the first epistle conveyed the sad news of the death of his old friend and benefactress, Miss Dunbar of Boath, of whom he says, in writing to Sir Thomas :—

'Her heart was one of the warmest and least selfish I ever knew. I was employed in writing to her, with all the freedom which her goodness permitted to me, when the letter reached me which intimated her death. My thoughts were so cast into the conversational mould that I could almost realise her presence, and had she suddenly expired before me I could not have been more affected.'

The next experience Hugh Miller relates in his letter dated 6th July 1835 is even more startling, for, as he says, 'it is very rarely that one has to tell the *living* how much they have regretted them as dead.' This circumstance he explains as follows :—

'The bank here has occasionally to remit large sums of money to a neighbouring town, and as the road is lonely, and runs at one place for several miles through a deep wood, I have had to provide myself with arms, and to act as messenger. I had half completed one of these journeys when the fearfully circumstantial account of your sudden death first reached me. A thunderbolt could not have appalled me more. During the whole of my walk homewards I was like a man haunted by a spectre. There is no time when the force of contrast is more strongly felt than when we have to regret a deceased friend or benefactor. An apparition of the scene at the Grange House on the evening I had the happiness of spending there was continually rising before me. I saw the kind and hospitable landlord, and the attached and amiable family, and every time the darker scene rushed into my mind—a scene of grief and bereavement—there was the infliction of a pang. On my arrival in Cromarty, however, I attained to a happier mood. I had just stepped out of the ferry-boat when a little old man, the most Whiggish of all my acquaintances here, after perusing my face for half a minute, and then seizing hold of my hand, addressed me with a "Take heart, boy! it's all a trick of the rascally Tories. Sir Thomas is as much alive and as well as I am."

---

[1] From the age of sixteen to thirty-two Hugh Miller worked as a journeyman mason, but from thirty-two to thrity-eight he was a pupil-accountant.

'I could fain see the fellow horsewhipped who gave birth to that report.
'Accept my warmest thanks for your exertions on my behalf; it will be ill with me when I cease to remember them. May I request you to tender my respects to Lady Lauder. Whig as I am in my principles, I find I am a true Tory in my feelings, and never was I more conscious of this than when at the Grange House. It will be long ere I forget that the lady who then showed me so many kind attentions is a descendant of one of the most ancient and celebrated of all our Scottish families.'[1]

As we can only transcribe one more of these interesting letters, we shall choose that of the 12th September 1837 as being more directly in touch with the literary work of Sir Thomas, to whom he writes in reference to some books the Baronet had lent him :—

'Need I say that I have been delighted with your legendary volumes—that I have read them with an avidity only equalled by that with which I used to devour for the first time the fictions of Scott. By the way, this intense feeling of interest, now that the mighty Minstrel breathes no longer, is becoming of comparatively rare experience, and one therefore luxuriates the more in it when it occurs. You have infused a new spirit into the dry bones of tradition. They lay in heaps, choking up the vista of the past, a true valley of visions to you ; but now that the breath of genius has passed over them, they stand up, an exceeding great army. I am delighted with the breadth and boldness of your pencil. There is exceeding power, too, in the concluding pages of "Christy Ross" —so much, indeed, that I am mistaken if it does not stand alone in our literature. Dr. Drake's well-known fragment, written with the acknowledged purpose of exciting terror by what he terms the "interference of simple and natural causation," is tame and commonplace in comparison. I find frequent traces of poor Christy in this part of the country, where her wayward and eccentric habits and manners seem to have left a deep impression. I have often heard how she lived solitary in the old Castle of Cambscurrie on the edge of the Dornoch Forest, sewing for herself a mantle of mice-skins, and how very frightful a thing her readily exercised hospitality used sometimes to prove. I am informed that the woman who tended her in her last illness and laid out her corpse for the grave is still alive.

'In the legend of "Allan with the Red Jacket," as in the story of "Christy Ross," I recognise an old acquaintance. But the Allan of your legend is a much better fellow than the Captain M'Donald of the tradition, though I daresay I should make some allowance for the hereditary prejudices of the person from whom I received the latter. She was a M'Kenzie, some of whose ancestors, as they had resided for centuries within less than a mile of the Chapel Kelliechrist, might probably have fallen victims to the fiery revenge of the M'Donald. I wish you could have heard some of her stories. She was like Christy Ross, a wild maniac, and used to spend whole nights among the ruins of the chapel, conversing, as she used to say, with her father's spirit ; but her madness was of the kind which, instead of obscuring, seems rather to strengthen the purely intellectual powers. Her malady seemed but a milder kind of genius, and so, mad as she was, I used to deem her conversation equal to that of most women in their senses. I scraped an acquaintance with her when working as a mason prentice about sixteen years ago, in

[1] The Comyns of the days o. Bruce.

the neighbourhood of Kelliechrist. She had taken it into her head that I was some great person in disguise, and used to come to me every evening after work was over to consult me on such questions as the Origin of Evil and the Eternal Decrees, and others of equal *simplicity* and *clearness*. I gave her, of course, the benefit of all my metaphysics, whether doubtfully bad or bad beyond doubt, and got in return sets of the finest old stories I have met with anywhere. How her eyes used to brighten when she spoke of the "bloody and barbarous M'Donalds" and the fearful raid of Kelliechrist! She was sister to that Mr. Lochlow of Lochcarron, the modern prophet of the Highlands, of whom you cannot fail to have heard, and in some respects she must have closely resembled him. But she is gone, and many a fine old story has died with her. Her fate was exactly that of Christy Ross as described in your legend. When fording the river Conan in one of her wildest moods she was swept away by the stream and drowned, and her body cast upon the bank a day or two after. The Christy Ross of authentic story died, I believe, in her bed.

'I had the pleasure last winter, when on a two days' visit to Elgin, of seeing the Priory of Pluscarden, which you have so beautifully described in your tale of "The Rival Lairds," and a painting could not have recalled it more vividly to my recollection. I saw much that pleased me during my brief visit, and I also enjoyed much, for the occasion was a joyous one—my marriage. I had Mr. Isaac Forsyth of Elgin for my guide. I saw the Lady Hill, with its rock-like ruin and its extensive view; the Museum, with its spars and its birds; the splendid Institution so redolent of the showy benevolence of the present age, and the still more splendid Cathedral, so redolent of the showy piety of former times; but, above all, it was the hermit-like Priory in its sweet half-Highland, half-Lowland glen, with its trees and its ivy, and all the exquisite innumerable combinations of the simple and the elegant, that impressed me most strongly. I found, too, that my companion, whose taste has been much more highly cultivated than mine, was quite as much delighted with it. You, who are yourself so happy in your domestic relations, will not be displeased to hear that, after having enjoyed for full five years all that a lover enjoys in courtship, I now possess all that renders a husband happy in a wife. I have now been rather more than eight months married, and am as much in love as ever.

'But I wander sadly. I sat down to say how much I was delighted with your fascinating volumes, and lo ! here I am descanting on courtship and marriage. On the first perusal of your work I was particularly struck by two circumstances—your amazing breadth of pencil, if I may so express myself, and the peculiarly Celtic character of your work. I see nought of the Saxon in it ; all is wild, irregular,—gigantic achievement, chivalrous to the extreme ; human daring in "love strong as death, hatred as cruel as the grave"; and your broad, bold style of narrative and description seems the best possible to consort with this character.

'Accept evermore my warmest thanks for the entertainment it has given me, and believe that I am, honoured Sir, with sincere gratitude and respect, your humble friend and obedient servant, HUGH MILLER.

'TO SIR THOMAS DICK LAUDER,
    Of Grange and Fountainhall, Baronet.'

In 1840 Hugh Miller came to Edinburgh as editor of the *Witness* newspaper, and the literary friendship thus commenced continued up to the death of Sir Thomas, whose interest in the peculiar genius of Mr. Miller increased with each new publication of his scientific and geological works. But much as he admired him as an earnest student and indefatigable writer, he esteemed him even more highly as a man, for his high-minded honesty, broad liberality, and sincere reverence for truth.

It was not solely upon the legendary portion of Sir Thomas Dick Lauder's work, however, that the Baronet and Hugh Miller had so much in common. The basis of their lifelong sympathy was their mutual love for geology. Hugh Miller was only a lad of sixteen, working as a journeyman mason, when Thomas Lauder, Esq. of Relugas, read his paper on the 'Parallel Roads of Glen Roy' before the Royal Society on 2nd March 1818[1]—two years before he succeeded to the baronetcy of Fountainhall. The valuable information in this paper was suggested to him by an accidental ramble through that valley in the course of a pedestrian tour in the West Highlands during the previous August.

To show how much this scientific work was appreciated by a scientist nearly sixty years later, we will transcribe a passage from the *Times* newspaper of Saturday, June 10th, 1876:—

'ROYAL INSTITUTION.—Last evening Professor Tyndall closed the season of the Friday evening discourses by a lecture on the "Parallel Roads of Glen Roy." The chair was taken by the King of Hanover, and the lecture theatre was crowded. Among the audience were the Spanish Ambassador and Lord A. Russell, Lord and Lady Claude Hamilton, the Baron von Wrangeil, Lord Stanley of Alderley, Lady M. Egerton, the Marchioness of Anglesea, the Countess of Rosse, Mr. and Mrs. Spottiswood, and a large number of distinguished scientific men. In the course of the lecture, Professor Tyndall, in making reference to Sir Thomas Dick Lauder's paper, read before the Royal Society in Edinburgh, says, "There is no man, in my opinion, connected with the history of the subject who has shown in relation to it this spirit of penetration, this force of scientific insight, more conspicuously than Sir Thomas Lauder Dick. Two distinct mental processes are involved in its treatment: firstly, the faithful and sufficient observation of the data, and, secondly, that higher mental process in which the constructive imagination comes into play, connecting the separate facts of observation with their common cause, and weaving them into an organic whole. In neither of these requirements did Sir Thomas Lauder Dick fail."'

The Professor then proceeded to point out the relative position of Glen Guoy, Glen Roy, and Glen Spean from a diagram made by Sir T. Lauder Dick, and to describe the way in which he had examined the district and arrived at his conclusions, which is all given at length in the *Times* newspaper. When

[1] Article on the 'Parallel Roads of Lochaber,' in the *Transactions of the Royal Society*, vol. ix. Part I.

Miss Dick Lauder noticed the account of this lecture she wrote to Professor Tyndall expressing the pleasure it had given to herself and her sisters to find how thoroughly their father's scientific work was estimated by him; to which letter she received the following reply:—

'18th June 1876,
'HEATHFIELD PARK, HAWKHURST.

'DEAR MADAM,—It will give me great pleasure to send you a copy of my brief essay as soon as it is in print.

'Your father's insight as regards the Parallel Roads of Glen Roy won my respect and admiration long ago. It gratified me much to have an opportunity of saying this in public. That gratification is now enhanced by the knowledge that what I have said regarding their father has given satisfaction to the daughters of Sir Thomas Dick Lauder. —Faithfully yours, JOHN TYNDALL.'

The untechnical summary of this very interesting scientific paper consists in the discovery of three natural parallel roads which extend for several miles through the three glens above mentioned in the wilds of Lochaber. These three paths are upon different levels, the lowest being the least distinct, but throughout their whole length they are perfectly parallel to each other, running horizontally along each little nook and cleft of the hills. Sometimes these roads are narrow, and sometimes from sixty to seventy feet in breadth. The precision of their parallelism first led Sir Thomas to study the geological formation of their surroundings, which suggested the conclusion that the valley below them was the bed of a lake in past ages, the waters of which had gradually subsided at three distinct intervals, leaving these parallel roads as rock testimonies to future generations.

Sir Thomas also wrote an interesting account of the district round Portree, giving an accurate description of the wonderful mountain of Quiraing. Messrs. Black, the publishers of *The Picturesque Tourist of Scotland*, acknowledge their indebtedness to him for the perusal of this MS. journal, and also for the use of a pen-and-ink drawing of that unique mountain, from which they have produced a most beautiful engraving. The literary correspondence between Sir Thomas and Mr. Archibald Constable also commenced in 1822, concerning a second publication of Lord Fountainhall's manuscripts, a volume of which had already appeared under the title of *Chronological Notes of Scottish Affairs*, chiefly from Lord Fountainhall's Diary, with a preface and explanatory notes by Sir Walter Scott. This compilation not having given universal satisfaction, it was proposed that 'a more copious selection of the miscellaneous MSS.' should be undertaken by his lineal descendant, Sir Thomas Dick Lauder, in which work Sir Walter Scott again offered his willing services, and the agreement was finally settled, Sir Thomas promising to put together such incidents and materials as he possessed into the form of a biographical sketch—the two volumes to be called *Historical Notices of Scottish Affairs*. It appears from the preface that 'this work had actually proceeded at press to page 304 in 1825, when the misfortune of the publisher put a stop to the enterprise.' Several years later Sir Thomas's transcripts were placed at the disposal of the Bannatyne Club, who took up the subject, and in 1848 carried the work to

OUTLINE SKETCH OF GRANGE HOUSE BY SIR THOMAS.

completion; but the new volume was prefaced and edited by Dr. Laing, the eminent antiquarian, Sir Thomas having laid down his pen, and gone to his long rest ere it was finished.

It is not possible for us to enumerate the various literary works of Sir Thomas in this chapter, but we hope to append a catalogue of them further on.[1]

During the last eight years of his life Sir Thomas Dick Lauder had full scope for the use of his artistic taste and scientific knowledge in his appointment as Secretary of the Board of Manufactures and Fisheries in Scotland, being at all times an active promoter of public improvements. Among his other works we must not forget to mention his untiring zeal in the strenuous

[1] Appendix, Note XVI.

efforts he made to forward the great undertaking of forming the road called the 'Queen's Drive' round Arthur's Seat, which was carried out under the supervision of the Commissioners for Woods and Forests. Edinburgh may well be proud of it. It is truly a royal road, with a matchless panorama on a clear day. Another of the city improvements due to Sir Thomas is the substantial road round the back of the Castle. He also promulgated a scheme for reducing the steep hill of the Mound by 'bringing the south end down to the level of Princes Street, and then cutting a Roman arch through the Lawnmarket, and under the houses, so as to pass on a level to George Square,' thus uniting the Old and the New Town. This plan was considered both practical and easy, and had it been expounded sooner might have carried the day.

The public duties which Sir Thomas most unwillingly relinquished as his health began to fail were many and very varied; for besides being Secretary to the Royal Institution for the Encouragement of the Fine Arts, he was Deputy-Lieutenant of the counties of Elgin and Moray, which office he had filled since 1817, and also Deputy-Lieutenant of the county of Haddington. Yet withal he found time to carry on the scientific pursuits of which he was ever fond, his attention being keenly alive to the natural phenomena passing before him, and his pen ever ready to record his impressions, and give them to the public, at the same time 'always in the van in any cause where liberty and human welfare were at stake.'

The article in *Tait's Magazine* for November 1837, which Sir Thomas wrote anonymously, describing the remarkable pageant known as the 'Eglinton Tournament,' called forth a host of comments and critiques in the daily papers, but space will only admit of our transcribing one of these, which we do in order to show the diversity of subjects touched upon by the Baronet's facile pen. The editor of the *Sun*, in the issue of November 2nd, says:—

'We have had many descriptions, serious and comic, some in prose and some in verse, of the "Eglinton Tournament," but none by many degrees so interesting as the sprightly off-hand prose sketch with which *Tait* gaily leads off this month. It is unusually long for a magazine article; but it is so cleverly handled, in so cordial and exciting a spirit, and with such thorough knowledge of effect, that we feel not its length, but are sorry when we come to the end. The writer is a gentleman of accomplished mind and cheerful temperament, ready and willing to be amused; endowed with a salient fancy and a power of giving adequate expression to its lively promptings. The account of the knights' procession to the lists, and their tilting at the barrier of the ladies' gallery, and the thousands of eager spectators, who thronged the grassy slopes that swelled up from the scene of encounter—of the crash and jostling of vehicles when the sports were over, and the hurrying back under umbrellas, and without them, of the myriad pedestrians to the neighbouring town of Irvine—these several details, though hurriedly and boldly dashed off, are in strict accordance with the soberest judgment. From one or two cursory hints let drop towards the close we gather that the article is the production of Sir Thomas Dick Lauder, well known by his agreeable little volume entitled *The Great Morayshire Floods.*'

Notwithstanding all this diversified learning and keen scientific observation, no man living was a more intense lover of the simplest beauties of nature. How charmingly he speaks of Blackford Hill, the schoolboys' haunt close beside the dear old Grange :—

'Blackford Hill!' he exclaims, 'what a place for linnets' nests and primroses in the lovely springtime of the year! How delightful to sit among its furzy knolls with the sun beating hot upon and exhaling the sweet perfume from the yellow flowers,' and 'the sounds of the bee brushing its filmy wings among the flowers of the wild thyme.'

' How pleasing to watch the little golden-crested wrens as they hang on the thorny boughs perking up their little bills, and spreading abroad their golden coronets to receive the sun's bright rays.'

And then the glow-worms in the glen below Borthwick Castle—how daintily he trips among them, telling us how often, 'on a fine, warm summer evening in the month of July, immediately after the sun has left the horizon, every bank and every brake is lighted up with the most beautiful and minute illumination, arising from the immense number of glow-worms that are bred among the thick herbage of the glen. . . . Nothing,' he continues, ' can be more interesting than to watch the progress of these tiny little torch-bearers, but it is impossible for the fanciful mind to regard them without supposing that the gay and merry groups of the fairy-folk are following in their wake.'

Sir Thomas seems to have delighted in fairy lore, for ever and anon, even on his sick couch, we find him telling us stories of haunted castles, benevolent brownies, and the 'nameless little folk' in 'Fairy Dean' or 'Goblin Brook,' with all the charming simplicity of childlike belief. These far-away, out-of-the-world legends seem to have lifted his mirth-loving spirit at times over the jagged rocks of incessant pain. There is not one gloomy thought in all the pages penned during his last, long illness. Each article he wrote is like a new picture taken beside some flowing river or mountain stream ; but to those who knew of his hopeless malady, there is also the underlying current of a deep-toned resignation. When writing of the fields and meadow lands belonging to the Grange Manor, he says : 'One large space is now being laid out in the most beautiful manner with shrubberies and walks as the Great Southern Cemetery, everything being done that refined taste in architecture or gardening can accomplish to remove those dark and chilling associations which have hitherto made us behold with shuddering disgust that grave which ought to be so full of attraction for the weary Christian.'

When Sir Thomas wrote this he knew he was slowly passing on to his own long rest, and the termination of his weary suffering, so bravely borne for eighteen months. 'Never in the full tide of health was he so gentle, affectionate, and serene as while life was ebbing.'

The following extract from an unpublished letter of his most intimate friend Lord Cockburn, to Cosmo Innes, the eminent antiquary, contains a whole volume in itself:—

'I saw Lauder on Sunday; he is obviously dying—but cheerful, gentle, and kind—and making a slow, gradual death, of such pious gaiety and affectionate resignation that Philosophers and Christians might look on it and be instructed. Poor fellow, I wish I could hope. To me his disappearance will be like drawing a cold shade over life's sunniest scenery. H. COCKBURN.

'19th March 1848.'

No wonder Lord Jeffrey told him on one of his visits to the Grange House that he had 'come to take a lesson.'

It was on the 29th of May 1848, in his sixty-fourth year, that Sir Thomas Dick Lauder calmly passed through the shining gates to his mansion in the Golden City, and the outer form of this distinguished Baronet was interred on the following Tuesday in the Grange Cemetery, the spot he had so touchingly described a short time before. The funeral cortège, which consisted of a large hearse preceded by ushers, the family carriage, vacant and closed, and twenty-two mourning and private carriages, left the Grange House at half-past two o'clock, and reached the cemetery by way of the Grange Loan, the Causeway-side, and up the Grange Road to the new entrance.

The spot selected for the burial-ground of the family is situated at the highest part of the cemetery, and was the nearest point to the mansion of the late Baronet at which interments had then been made. The chief mourners were the two sons of Sir Thomas, Sir John Dick Lauder, who succeeded him in the baronetcy of Fountainhall and Grange,[1] and George Dick Lauder, Esq., of Huntly Wood.

Among the gentlemen present were Alexander Mitchell Innes, Esq. of Ayton Castle; T. Mitchell Innes, Esq. of Phantassie; William Mitchell Innes,

[1] Father of the present Baronet, Sir Thomas Dick Lauder, whose mother, Lady Anne Dalrymple, second daughter of the ninth Earl of Stair, is still living. Sir John Dick Lauder died in 1867.

Esq. of Parsonsgreen; Simpson Mitchell Innes, Esq.; George Mitchell Innes, Esq. of Ingliston; Norman Mitchell Innes, Esq.; Gilbert Mitchell Innes, Esq.; C. Craigie Halkett, Esq. of Hallhill; A. Maconochie, Esq. of Meadowbank; Professor Maconochie; Robert Maconochie, Esq., W.S.; Archibald Broun, Esq. of Johnstonburn, Advocate; Warren Hastings Sands, Esq., W.S.; Charles Anderson, Esq.; John Wauchope, Esq. of Edmonstone; Adam Hay, Esq., W.S.; George More Nisbett, Esq. of Cairnhill; Sir Robert Dick-Cunyngham of

THE DICK LAUDER TOMB, GRANGE CEMETERY.

Prestonfield, Bart.; William Dick-Cunyngham, Esq.; North Dalrymple, Esq. of Fordel; Æneas M'Bean, junior, Esq.; Captain Shearman; Mr. Sheriff Gordon; James L'Amy, Esq. of Dunkenny; J. R. L'Amy, Esq., younger of Dunkenny; Lord Fullerton; Lord Cockburn; Lord Jeffrey; Lord Cuninghame; Lord Murray; Right Rev. Bishop Terrot; Rev. Dr. Paul; James Gibson Thomson, Esq.; John Kirkpatrick, Esq.; Professor Miller; Mr. Miller, surgeon; Dr. Moir; James Wilson, Esq. of Woodville, etc.; besides many others, and several hundred spectators who had assembled in the cemetery to witness the funeral.

362 LITERARY WORK OF SIR THOMAS DICK LAUDER

The Royal Institution was closed throughout the day, and a number of the officials followed in the cortége. The whole tenantry on the Fountainhall and Grange estates were also among the company.

The leading papers of the day [1] all bore their testimony to the high moral power and beneficent influence of the late Sir Thomas Dick Lauder, seventh Baronet of Fountainhall, but no truer epitaph could have been penned than the words so tenderly written by his second daughter, Miss Cornelia Dick Lauder, twenty-five years later, in an introductory note to one of his own works, in which she says: 'My father's memory still lives in the hearts of so many who knew him. His genial, kindly, sympathetic nature made him the joy of the home circle and of his intimate friends. . . . He had also a tender heart for the poor, and exerted himself with energy and success in many useful labours of philanthropy.' [2]

[1] *Caledonian Mercury*, *Scottish Press*, the *Witness*, the *North British Mail*, and the *Elgin Courant*.
[2] Introductory note to the new edition of *The Morayshire Floods*, republished in 1873.

CHAPTER XXVIII

OLD STONES, FAMILY RELICS, TRADITIONAL STORIES

'These stones, alas ! these grey stones ; are they all ?
All of the famed and the colossal left
By the corrosive hours.'
EDGAR POE.

N searching for external evidences of antiquity, we naturally look at every old carved stone with a critical eye, feeling much inward satisfaction if we can discover any date that will bear the minutest scrutiny.

Of sculptured stones there are several upon various parts of the exterior of the Grange House. They do not however appear to belong in any way to the original structure as an ecclesiastical grange. As far as we can judge, they mostly all bear the arms of the Lauder family ; and yet the date upon the oldest is 1574, more than a hundred and fifty years before the Lauders of Fountainhall possessed the Grange; therefore it is self-evident they must have been brought there from some former mansion belonging to the various branches of this ancient family —the Lauders of Lauder Tower, Hatton, or the Bass. There is one stone, however, with a monogram and date which would  lead us to suppose that it must have belonged to the Dick family prior to their intermarriage with the Lauders ; and there is good reason to believe that it was intended to commemorate the marriage of William Dick, second Baron of Grange, with his second wife, Dame Charles Leslie of Kinclaven.

We have already mentioned the coat-of-arms over the courtyard, which bears the initials of John Cant and Katherine Creich, with the date 1613.[1]

There is no ambiguity whatever in the substantial evidence of the antiquity of old Sanct Geilie-Grange itself; as the vaulted arches upon which the whole centre of the building rests speak for themselves. They are traditionally called '*the Cloisters*'; which in all probability simply meant the ancient

[1] See illustration, p. 26.

kitchens, as they are still used as the servants' dining-hall. By their solid masonry these six-feet-thick walls tell their own story; and the old sculptured lintel REPOSE ALLEURS 1592,[1] which is still above the original doorway, built up in the foundation wall, unquestionably marks another distinct period after its transition from an ecclesiastical grange to a private manor-house—when not only the ancient serfs, but the whole brotherhood of St. Giles, had gone to ' *Rest Elsewhere.*'

In a shady nook at the foot of the grounds there is an old stone seat, very quaint, very mediæval-looking—to all appearance most appropriately called ' *The Monk's Seat*'—exactly the kind of relic one would expect to find belonging to some old monastery or sixteenth-century garden. So shady is its leafy retreat that the sun rarely glints across the pious motto carved along the back, in very ornamental letters—IN · THE · IS · AL · MY · TRAIST · 1569. It has all the likelihood of having weathered its three centuries and a half. Upon the lower margin of this curiously-shaped seat the beautiful old Scotch legend HE · YT · THOLIS · OVERCVMMIS is clearly legible in characters of a much earlier period. On first looking at this fine old piece of workmanship, our mind naturally wanders back to the olden times, wondering how many of the brethren who used it took fresh courage from its twofold lesson of piety and patience. But alas! romance is not history, and history affirmeth that never monk sat upon this stone seat of Sanct Geilie-Grange. Its pious motto formerly graced the lintel of the house which Robert Gourlay built in 1569 in Old Bank Close. This historical mansion was demolished in 1834 to make way for the building of Melbourne Place at George IV. Bridge, and this sculptured stone then went into the possession of Charles Kirkpatrick Sharpe, Esq. of Hoddam, the well-known antiquarian, from whom it eventually found its way to the manor-house of Grange, to bear part in the adornment of the beautiful grounds of the reconstructed mansion of Sir Thomas Dick Lauder.

According to Sir Daniel Wilson, Robert Gourlay's house 'was built on the site, and partly at least with the *materials, of an old religious house*,' so that this antique lintel may have originally belonged to the Dominican Friars after all, the date being added when the said Robert Gourlay placed it over his own doorway in 1569—for the pious motto in his case could only have been a burlesque, since he put his trust first in *riches*, and secondly in *princes*, leaving very little for the Lord. Nothing could be more appropriate, however, than its present combination with the beautiful Scotch legend, '*He that tholes overcomes*,' which was the original lintel-stone of a religious house of a much earlier date

[1] See illustration, p. 24.

THE ROCKY MT. GRAVES CABIN.

belonging to the Knights-Templars in the Grassmarket—those renowned soldier-priests of the Middle Ages, whose badge was the Agnus Dei and the figure of two knights mounted on one horse,[1] which some old writers consider to denote their poverty, whereas others maintain it was the emblem of their perfect unity and protective power. The shield with the St. Andrew's cross in saltire, which is in the centre of this fine old legend, certainly marks its pre-Reformation origin, these powerful military priests having been suppressed long before the abolition of the monasteries. They are sometimes called the 'Red Cross Knights,' from the colour of the Maltese cross upon their white banners. Some of the finest of the antique houses in Old Edinburgh had belonged to them; and they were bound by the laws of their order to place an iron cross, the badge of their knighthood, upon every building they erected.

OLD STONE—BURGH ARMS.

This cross 'marked them as beyond the Civic Corporation laws,' for they were not allowed to submit to any jurisdiction but that of their own spiritual lords. So masterful had they become in the twelfth and thirteenth centuries that they possessed lands in every county and nearly every parish of Scotland. Their first instalment, like most of the other religious orders, had taken place in the reign of David I. The Templars, however, were cast in a very different mould from the monks, and had no connection with parish churches, though one of their carved lintels has found its way to the Grange of St. Giles.

There is also another old stone which cannot fail to be of historical interest to many, being one of the very few relics of the ancient University of Edinburgh, and a lasting memento of Dr. Robertson as Principal.

It consists of the Burgh Arms, which had graced the portal of the quaint square tower of the original College of King James in 1582, upon the

[1] T. Fuller's *Holy Warre*, Book ii. Cap. xvi.

demolition of which this sculptured stone was removed to the residence of the energetic promoter of the new buildings, and eventually was built into the grand archway leading from the avenue to the mansion at Sanct Geilie-Grange. This stone had been completely hidden for many years, by the wealth and weight of the overhanging ivy, consequently few knew of its existence, until Mr. Gibson, the gardener, unveiled it in 1893, while trimming this over-luxuriant evergreen. The arms are quite decipherable, though considerably weather-worn.

THE PENNY WELL.

Another of these time-honoured folklore relics, so full of past associations, is the 'Penny Well,' in the Grange Loan, which, with its quaint mural tablet and ever-flowing stream, belonged from time immemorial to the old manor-house.

It was one of the most interesting curiosities of the last century, though its real age is quite unknown. Tradition affirms it was one of the holy wells of the convent of Siena, and it has the reputation of having effected many wonderful cures, among those troubled with sore eyes, when its consecrated waters were faithfully applied. It came into the Grange estate, with the gardens and orchard-lands of the Sciennes, in the feuing days of the Cants of Cant's Close, who owned so much of the Sanct Geilie lands, with the House of Grange. They also say Queen Mary drank of its waters. It could not belong to Scottish lore if the tradition did not somehow interweave the name of Mary Stuart. But it is quite possible, and it may be true enough that Scotland's beauteous Queen did partake of the Convent's pure spring; for she had great faith in the efficacy of mineral waters, and she certainly did visit the Sisterhood of St. Katherine of Siena.

Judging from the information given many years ago by Mr. M'Kenzie the florist, who lived in the cottage close beside it, the 'Penny Well' has passed through many vicissitudes since its palmy days of universal popularity. One of the peculiarities of this spring was that when all the other fountains and wells seem to have been dried up in the summer seasons of drought, the waters of this well flowed on as bountifully as ever.

When Sir Thomas Dick Lauder came to live at the Grange House he seems to have taken a peculiar interest in this old well, which he found in a very

THE GRANGE GATE TOLL.

dilapidated condition. After supplying a new stone basin for it, and getting it all put into good order, he placed the tablet on the wall.

In Lord Cockburn's day an old widow woman had charge of the spring, which was not then allowed to run to waste. She lived in a cottage on the south side of the Loan, almost opposite to it, and the well soon became quite famous in that district, as she sold the water at a penny a glass to wayfarers, or a 'stoupful' for family use at the same price.

Before the water from the Pentlands was introduced into the city the inhabitants far and near flocked to the 'Penny Well' for their daily supply.

Somewhere about 1870 this never-failing spring suddenly ceased to flow— owing no doubt to the cutting off of the supply by the divergence of the stream in digging the foundations for the numerous villas which sprang up so rapidly in this district as soon as the ground was feued for building.

Then the unfrequented well fell into disrepair again, and in course of time the water tried to force its way back to the old channel, but finding the passage cut off, it made a pond for itself, in the old familiar spot, greatly to the annoyance of Mr. M'Kenzie, as it flowed unceasingly for a whole winter exactly in front of his house. To rectify this state of matters he dug a deep pit at the corner of his garden, and when it was five feet deep, lo! as a reward for his labours, and to the delight of antiquarians, he came upon the original trough of the Holy Well. A detailed notice of this circumstance appeared in the *Scotsman*, in the month of February 1887, which attracted considerable notice from some of our influential citizens. The writer says 'this interesting and unexpected find' was covered with a large flat cover of a hard marly sandstone, which unfortunately was broken in the digging operation. The trough itself is a circular cup, hollowed out of a large square block of sandstone, one side of which was roughly hewn. The stone is 32 inches across, while the diameter of the cup is 28 inches, with a depth in the centre of $10\frac{1}{2}$ inches. The whole of the basin was filled up with a hard fibrous-looking stalactite mass. On this being taken out, a lead perforated 'rose' was found on the top of a lead pipe which was carried through the bottom of the cup, and the end of which has been found cut about a foot on the other side. A circumstance which points to the antiquity of the basin is the curious configuration of an old wall which separates Mr. M'Kenzie's garden ground from that of his neighbour on the west side. There are titles extant, it would seem, which prove that this wall, which is of great thickness, is at least two hundred and fifty years old. The wall runs in a straight line between the two gardens from north to south, but at a distance of a few yards inwards from what is now called the Grange Loan north pavement it suddenly strikes off at a sharp angle to the west. Why it did so was always a matter for speculation to old Mr. M'Kenzie, for had it come straight down to the pavement the 'Penny Well' would have been taken out of his ground. The existence of the basin at the time the wall was built would account for the deflection.

This 'find' created a beneficial sensation in favour of the restoring of this interesting relic to its public functions; but when the pure-looking spring-water that still continued steadily to flow was analysed by Dr. Littlejohn, it was found to have become contaminated with the sewage of a drain-pipe with which it had amalgamated in its days of darkness and neglect. So the original spring was allowed to meander under the ground according to its own natural will. At the same time the sympathies which had been awakened for the old 'Penny Well' were not allowed to die out. Mr. George

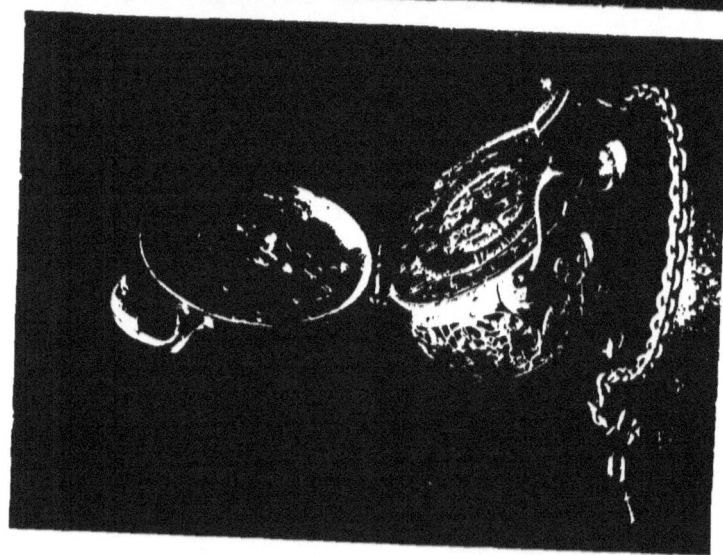

THE 'MEMENTO MORI' WATCH PRESENTED BY QUEEN MARY TO LADY MARY SETON.

Dobie, a public-spirited citizen, forthwith applied to the Lord Provost and the Town Council of Edinburgh for a grant towards its restoration, and thirty pounds being allotted for that purpose, it was accordingly accomplished about six years ago, the town water being substituted for the original spring.

On its completion Mr. Dobie was presented with a very pretty little model of the new 'Penny Well,' as a memento of his efforts on behalf of the restoration of an old public friend, which thirsty travellers can now frequent with perfect safety, its purity constituting its holiness.

Before leaving the Grange Loan we will mention another last century tradition of an old stone in that locality. It was situated at the north-west corner of West Grange, which was for many years the jointure-house of the Grange Manor. Folklore says that this was called the 'Wishing Stone,' and every one who passed it *wishfully* lifted a stone to throw at it. If the missile hit the mark, the wish would be accomplished within the year; if it fell beyond it, the period of waiting would be still more deferred, but if it fell short of it the desire would never be fulfilled.

From old stones with a history we shall now pass on to the more personally historic relics belonging to the Dick Lauder family, some of which are of peculiar interest; such, for example, as the 'Memento Mori' watch, given by Mary, Queen of Scots, to Mary Seton, one of her four Maries, and transmitted to the Lauders by intermarriage.

This mediæval timepiece is in the form of a skull. On the forehead is a figure of Death standing between a palace and a cottage; around is this legend from Horace: 'PALLIDA MORS EQUO PULSAT PEDE PAUPERUM TABERNAS REGUM QUE TURRES' (*Pale Death, with equal and impartial foot, enters the cottage door and palace gate*). On the hind part of the skull is the figure of Time, with another legend, taken from Ovid: 'TEMPUS EDAX RERUM TU QUE INVIDIOSA VETUSTAS' (*Time, the devourer of all things, and thou, envious Old Age*). The upper part of the skull bears representations of Adam and Eve in the Garden of Eden and of the Crucifixion, each with Latin legends, and between these scenes is open work to let out the sound when the watch strikes the hour upon a silver bell, which fills the hollow of the skull, and to receive the works within it when the watch is shut.[1]

Many of our readers will no doubt remember having seen this beautiful piece of mediæval workmanship at the Stuart Exhibition in the Bishop's

---

[1] For the beautiful photograph of this watch, from which our illustration was reproduced, by Messrs. M. and T. Scott, we are indebted to the kindness of George Dick Lauder, Esq., and to Mr. F. Moffat, the photographer.

Palace in Glasgow in 1888, to which it had been loaned by Sir Thomas Dick Lauder, ninth Baronet, who inherited it and the Thistle of Prince Charles from his ancestors of the Seton family.

It is worthy of note that this valuable historical relic was in its beautiful shrine on the chimney-piece in the drawing-room the night on which the burglars were so busy at the Grange House. Fortunately it had not attracted their notice at first, and being interrupted in their nefarious work by Mr. George Lauder (who, having heard an unusual noise, had come downstairs suddenly) they had just time to escape out of the drawing-room window on to the balcony, which had a most convenient flight of steps ready to hand. Between them the men managed, however, to carry off the charter-chest and at least fifty pounds worth of jewelry, but they had not had time to collect the rare old silver plate, which was untouched. We have already given an illustration of this carved chest, which was recovered in a cornfield at Craiglockhart with the hinges wrenched off —the lock having been of such a peculiar make the men could not pick it. Finding more parchment and less coin than they had expected, they cast away the chest after scattering the deeds and documents, some of which were never found.

Among the curious epistles now enshrined within it is one which will be most appropriately mentioned here. It is addressed, 'C 2 Gipsies' Encampment, Stonehenge, Salisbury.' Inside this cover are two pieces of paper, on one of which is written, in a scrawling hand, ' Take care of Hawks—move the Whirlgigs—Spy the House—Douse the glimslash—peppers—plank peep holes. —X. Y. Z.—Edin., 8th Oct. 1836. . . . I amoust forgot to tell you to plank some blowing snuff in Stonehenge—for an occasion.' 'The plot' on the other sheet of paper consists of a rude kind of drawing, such as a small schoolboy might make on his slate. It commences with the vowels all placed in a row backwards, U,O,I,E,A, each letter being designedly ornamented to bear its own significance, beneath which are three rough outlines of faces. On the right and left of the paper are two grotesque creatures, evidently meant for griffins. In the centre is a chess-board and one man seated as if playing, while another is standing directing the moves. Above them hovers a large kite attached by two strings, one held by a small figure below and the other by one above. Some mysterious symbolical signs are scattered here and there over the paper.

This gipsy letter was picked up by a Mr. Graves at the old quarry where Bronte had tried to save the drowning boy. On reading the contents Mr. Graves felt assured it had some secret reference to the Grange House, and consequently, not wishing to risk sending it by a messenger, he wrote a note to Sir Thomas Dick Lauder, telling him that he feared some plan had been formed for robbing his premises, and if he would fix an hour to meet him he would give him the paper containing the plot. This request Sir Thomas most readily complied with, and on closely studying the rude hieroglyphical sketch they both came to the conclusion that the same gang of housebreakers who had only partially succeeded on the 18th of September had resolved to make another attempt in October. But as the letter never reached the parties it was intended for, *forewarned* became *forearmed*, and the precautionary measures adopted were fortunately not called into action.

CARVED SETTLE.

In giving a sketch in Chapter IV. of the little copper coin, which belonged to Sir William Dick of Braid, we forgot to mention that it was picked up when the ground was being levelled at the north side of the Grange House in 1826. It is wonderfully legible considering the hundred and fifty years it had lain hidden in the earth.

Another very interesting family relic is the 'Lang Settle,' already mentioned as formerly standing behind the entrance-door of the Grange House, but which was removed in September 1896 to the residence of Lady Anne Dick Lauder. This elaborate piece of carving originally formed part of the antique bedstead of James Beaton, Archbishop of St. Andrews. Above the centre panel is the word I.E.S.V.S., and on either side, among the ornamental scrolls and emblems, are a cardinal's hat and a bishop's mitre, with the initials

I. B. There is evidently no date upon it, but it is more than probable that this valuable relic came into the family through John Lauder,[1] who was for many years secretary to Cardinal Beaton, the Archbishop's nephew.

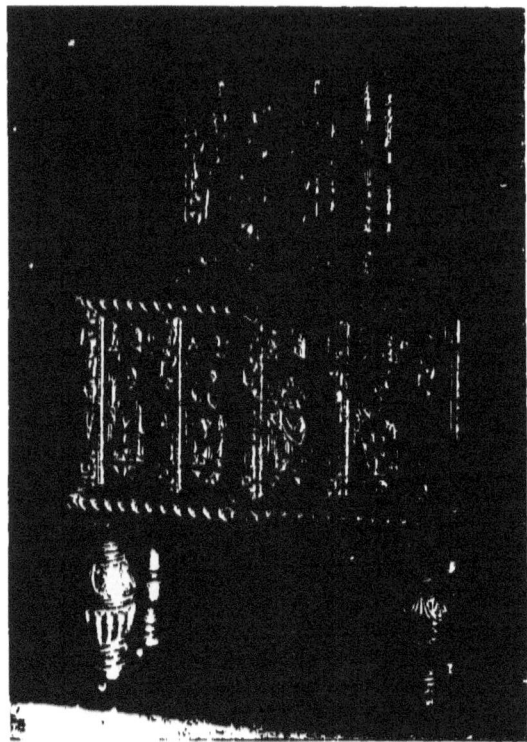

SIR WILLIAM DICK'S CABINET.

Our next illustration, though not ecclesiastically connected, is equally interesting as an ancestral relic, it being the fine old carved cabinet of Sir William Dick of Braid.

In the lower portion of it he is said to have kept the public money, of which he was banker and custodian. This he called 'the world.' In the upper and smaller compartment he kept his private purse, which he called 'a friend.' When any of the frequent tribe of needy suitors appealed to him for financial help or loan he would quietly say, tapping the lower portion, 'I have not a shilling in the *world*, but I will see what a *friend* can do.' We all know

---

[1] The said John Lauder's name frequently occurs, appended to various ecclesiastical documents—to wit, 'The Dispensation for the Marriage of Alexander Hume and Mariota Lauder,' dated 23rd January 1520-21, which is at present in the charter-chest of Sir Hugh Hume Campbell, Bart. This is witnessed by John Lauder, 'secretus'; and also the 'Papal Dispensation to George Ramsay and Elizabeth Hepburn to marie, albeit they be in the fourth degree of consanguinitie one with another,' 1532. This deed is in the charter-chest of Sir Thomas Dick Lauder, but the Pope's seal, formerly attached to the document, was wrenched away by the robbers who broke into the Grange House—its weight and imposing appearance being irresistible.

how much of his private exchequer went to the State, so we can well imagine how often this 'friend' was applied to.

Speaking of cabinets, we have seen several belonging to the Dick Lauder family, some of massive black oak, others rich and daintily carved, while a few of the smaller ones are heirlooms of especial value. But there is one of simple antique form which we would like to mention because of the tender associations that have clung to it from generation to generation. It came into the family through Lady Susan Hamilton of Tyninghame, who was daughter of the fourth Earl of Haddington, and wife of Adam Cockburn of Ormiston. From her it descended to her daughter, Susan Cockburn, who became Lady Inglis of Cramond, who left it to her daughter, Susan Inglis, who married Mr. Craigie of Dunbarnie, by whose daughter, Anne Craigie, it was inherited before she became Mrs. Craigie-Halkett of Lawhill. She bequeathed it to her daughter, Susan Craigie-Halkett, who married Mr. George Cumin of Relugas, whose daughter, Charles Ann Cumin, inherited it after she became Lady Dick Lauder of Fountainhall. At her death she left it to her daughter, Susan Dick Lauder, who bequeathed it to her sister, Miss Cornelia Dick Lauder, in whose possession it is at present, and most carefully treasured for the family associations attached to it.

We now come to the traditional stories which usually hover about old houses like the picturesque ivy which clothes them so deftly: the latter giving a grace and a beauty to the time-honoured stones, and the former an undying interest in their associations with the past.

The historic fact of Sanct Geilie-Grange having been possessed in its earliest days by King David's monks of Holm Cultrane seems to have repeated itself from age to age like some fascinating legend, for we not only find the 'cloisters' within the building but the 'Monk's Walk' without, the high terrace above the avenue being so called; and certainly it might still be deemed sufficiently secluded to warrant its designation by any of the cowled fraternity desiring to revisit it, breviary in hand. By the younger members of Sir Thomas Dick Lauder's family it was known as the 'Quarter-deck' and the 'Cannon Terrace,' from two ancient but very harmless pieces of artillery stationed there.

By some strange coincidence the other side of the boundary wall to the 'Monk's Walk' is called the 'Lover's Loan,' a long narrow lane, which, until some few years ago, had untrimmed, picturesque, old hawthorn bushes as a hedgerow on either side. For many generations past this lane has ever been the direct pathway from the Grange through the Meadows to the Parish Kirk of St. Giles, its egress being through a wicket-gate struck out of the town-wall in 1744. Why or when it received this popular but very anti-monastic appellation we know not, but there is no gainsaying the fact that from time immemorial it has been a favourite trysting-place with gallant swains and bonnie lassies in summer twilight; while just as truly, on the other hand, many a timid maiden has run the whole length of it on some dark winter night, flying as though she had wings to her feet, and all the ghosts of 'the monks of St. Giles' were chasing her. We must confess the present high cemetery-wall, built along one portion of it, has by no means enhanced its cheering effect.

A very pleasant reminiscence of this lane in its leafy days is mentioned by Mr. Thomas Constable in the life of his father with reference to Sir Thomas Dick Lauder, the grandfather of the present baronet. He says—

'I well remember, on more than one occasion after breakfasting at Grange House, that home of love and happiness, when leaving it along with Sir Thomas to return to town, the tribe of suitors, chiefly female, who beset him in the Lover's Loan, and to each of whom he seemed to give a daily and expected dole from the heavy pocket which he was not long in lightening. On my venturing to remonstrate he said, "I only give them pence; if they walk so far for so small a sum they *must be needy*."'

Many scores of beggars must have trudged that lane five hundred years before Sir Thomas's day, but it would be still fewer pence, we trow, they would get from the farming fraternity of Sanct Geilie-Grange.

It has often been asserted that the subterranean passage beneath the Grange House and lands extended in former days from the House to Saint Giles' Kirk. Such a tradition is not difficult to credit, for these underground passages seem to have been of no uncommon occurrence in connection with most of the old keeps built in the thirteenth and fourteenth centuries in Scotland. Most naturally they would be designed either as places of safety wherein to drive their cattle and conceal their goods in times of southern invasion, or as a means of escape.

> 'In time o' need,
> In day of ire,
> In hour o' dreed,
> In night o' fire.'

Since this passage really did exist it is not unreasonable to suppose that it may have been used at times as a place of refuge by the fugitive priests of St. Giles in their hour of need, knowing as they would the secret entrance from it to the turnpike stair that led to the turret above, whereby they could reach the keep in safety; some such incident very probably giving rise among the populace to the traditional story of the old Tower being haunted. But is

THE MONK'S WALK, GRANGE HOUSE.

there any old tower on the face of the earth that is not? And is there any family of note that does not consider the family ghost as much a part of the baronial home as the coat-of-arms above the entrance-door? The traditional ghost of the Grange is said to be a miser who is doomed to roll a barrel of gold coins throughout the oldest part of the building upon periodic occasions. Should any member of the family behold him he or she will become possessed of the treasure. On asking Miss Dick Lauder about this curious old traditional story she related a strange coincidence that happened while the family were still living at the Grange Manor :—

The house being full of visitors a young lady connected by marriage had to sleep in Lady Lauder's boudoir, which adjoined her bedroom so closely that the slightest call might have been heard. These rooms being a whole storey above the ancient part of the building there was no cause whatever for the play of imagination had she even heard of the ghost, which she had not. During the early hours of the night, just after she had fallen asleep, she awoke, hearing a rumbling sound as of something heavy being rolled along the corridor. The noise increased as it approached her room, stopping exactly opposite her door, which she expected to see suddenly opened. But there the sound ceased, and all was quiet for a while. Her fear had just begun to abate when the rumbling recommenced in the distance as before, and slowly advanced with heavy footsteps the whole length of the long passage until it reached the boudoir again. Feeling certain that some one must have got into the house she sprang out of bed and locked the door, and then lay trembling with fear. A third time the rolling sound recommenced, increasing gradually as it came towards the young lady's room, and when the footsteps stopped at her door she almost fainted with fright, and had no power to call out. Strange to say, as she was leaving the Grange House the next morning, and had to travel by one of the early stage-coaches which started in those days from the Grassmarket at six o'clock, she rose and dressed in haste, and what with the bustle of such an early breakfast, and the agitation of a hurried farewell, not a word was said about her nocturnal experience. Before the lady's next visit to the Grange, however, she had found an opportunity of telling her sister the whole story, to whom it was equally unaccountable, neither of them having any knowledge whatever of the traditional ghost.

Shortly after this occurred an old colonel was invited to dine at the Grange House, and in the course of conversation he happened to remark, 'Surely, Sir Thomas, an old manor-house like this must have a ghost?' 'Undoubtedly it has,' replied his daughter, Miss Cornelia, who then related the tradition of the miser as it had been given to them on their arrival from Relugas to the Grange by Mrs. Stark, third daughter of Sir Alexander Cuningham-Dick of Prestonfield. The two sisters being both at table they looked at each other in astonishment, but the younger lady turned so pale, that on being asked what was the matter with her she frankly told of the strange noises she had heard, and of the effect it had had on her nerves.

As far as we know, no other member of the family has ever been troubled by the ghost of the 'haunted tower,' though many strangers who have slept in the house from time to time, with no previous knowledge of this tradition, have also passed through a somewhat similar experience, but to them the sound was more like heavy luggage being dragged about. In almost every case it betokened hasty removal, and on one very vivid occasion it certainly was the precursor to the unexpected death of the head of the household, but not a member of the family.

That mysterious noises do occur in very old houses we are all aware, but a little courageous investigation soon clears up matters, and unquestionably we may affirm that very frequently rats alone are responsible for the weird-like sounds and creepy sensations often attributed to ghostly visitants. But it is quite another matter when the ghost does really appear; and if few are brave enough to face a ghost unflinchingly, there are still fewer in our day who can positively *deny* that apparitions do appear, for there is hardly a family circle of any extent but has a ghost story to relate when circumstances call it forth. We cannot always believe our ears, but '*seeing is believing*' they say The following little incident at least proves the truth of the old adage :—

On one occasion, during the lifetime of Sir Thomas, the young people at the Grange were suddenly roused by a noise in the middle of the night. Thinking some one had broken into the house again, and fearing to disturb their mother, Miss Dick Lauder and her younger sister rose and crept tremblingly down to the library, from whence they thought the sound issued. To their amazement they beheld a man seated at the fireplace with his feet stretched out as if to warm them at the extinct ashes. His back being towards them they had time to note that he was wrapped in Sir Thomas Dick Lauder's own dressing-gown, and his slippers also were on his feet. In their alarm they shrunk back into a recess, not daring to move or whisper. Presently the man rose, and silently taking off the dressing-gown he folded it neatly and laid it on a chair, then, in a strangely noiseless manner, he proceeded to pass out of the library through the dining-room; but in doing so he had to brush closely past the two young ladies in the recess, who, with utter amazement, not only perceived that his eyes were shut, and that he was simply clad in his nightgear, but also that it was their own butler, who had taken the liberty of walking in his sleep.

Before closing this chapter we must not forget to mention again that among the traditional stories there is one which asserts that a little room high up in the old square tower was occupied by Mary Stuart. It is difficult, however, to conceive how it could have been possible for Mary, Queen of Scots, to have slept a single night at Sanct Geilie-Grange when we consider that during the whole of her *personal* reign in Scotland, *i.e.* between the years of 1561 and 1567, the Grange House, having ceased to be ecclesiastically connected with St. Giles, was simply a burgher's home. Much more truly might it have been said that Mary Stuart stayed at the Convent of St. Katherine of Siena, for there is no want of evidence that Queen Mary was deeply interested in the fate of the gentle sisters of the Sciennes (two of whom were of the Seton family), whose distress she no doubt personally witnessed, since she 'compelled the magistrates to allow the destitute nuns a subsistence out of those very funds with which their own predecessors had endowed the convent'; but that she had any intercourse with the Grange of St. Giles, either to lodge there as a visitor, or even as a refugee from her rebellious nobles, seems altogether improbable. Had it in those days been the residence of the loyal Setons, the Dicks, or the Lauders, the story would have needed little corroboration. As it is, we can only try to explain how such a tradition could have arisen.

After the battle of Carberry Hill, on the 15th June 1567, Queen Mary surrendered herself to Sir William Kirkcaldy of *Grange* upon the strength of his promise that she should be treated by the Lords with all due respect, and on being conducted to Edinburgh she was shut up for twenty-two hours in the *Provost's House*. Now it so happened that Kirkcaldy of Grange was Provost of Edinburgh in 1569—though not in 1567—and the similarity in the name of his family estate in Fife, with the approximate date, is quite sufficient foundation for a *traditional* story a hundred years later, when the lands of Sciennes and the House of Grange had both passed into the hands of the Setons by intermarriage. It is quite possible also that the story only came to the Grange with the Setons; for it is a well-known fact that George, seventh Lord Seton, did most loyally shelter Queen Mary in his old castle-keep at Niddry after her escape from Lochleven, which story would no doubt be recounted two centuries later, when the Setons were entertaining her descendant, Prince Charles Stuart, at the Grange; after which, like all hearsay stories, the main facts would remain, but the details would be filled in *ad libitum*, and thus this romantic episode would become domiciled with the name of Seton at the Grange without any reference to its possibility. The tradition, we are assured, finds no credence in the family of Sir Thomas Dick Lauder ; nor yet that of the finding of a skeleton built into the wall of the library at the Grange House, when it was being reconstructed, which event also actually transpired at Niddry Castle. Were our story of the Grange of St. Giles a romantic fiction, how gladly would we avail ourselves of this tradition, which would indeed have been a coincidence ' passing strange,' that the first inhabitants of the old monastic farm of Sanct Geilic-Grange should have been the monks of King David's abbey of Holm-Cultrane, and the last tenant ere it vanished *as such* to rise in its grander form should be an incarcerated brother, whose very ashes crumbled into air as the light of an architectural reformation gleamed upon them. That such things did take place many an old ruin has testified, but not the Grange of St. Giles, which we now leave with regret, silent and tenantless, after being the glad home of many generations, and for more than thirty years an educational centre of Edina's romantic city.

' The glory of a building is not in its stones, nor in its gold. Its glory is in its age, and in that deep sense of voicefulness, of stern watching, or mysterious sympathy—even of approval or condemnation—which we feel in the walls that have been long washed by the passing waves of humanity.'—RUSKIN.

' Far down into the distant past I gaze
With anxious, eager, soul-inquiring eyes :
So haply from the dim and shadowy maze
One long deep-buried truth may answering rise ;
Clad in no modern transcendental guise,
But issuing from the whilome dark profound,
The charter-house of Nature's mysteries ;
In simple garb, with soft and silvery sound,
Awaking echoing truths to earth's remotest bound.'

THE HAUNTED TOWER.

CONCLUSION

AVING brought our record of the Lauders of Lauder and Bass up to the point of union with the Dicks of Orkney and Grange, and from thence to the seventh Baronet, Sir Thomas Dick Lauder of Fountainhall and Grange, we desire ere closing the volume simply to append a lineal chart of the Baronet's descendants without infringing in any way on the sacred privacy of the personal history of the individual members, many of whom are still living.

Sir Thomas Dick Lauder, seventh Baronet of Fountainhall, succeeded his father, Sir Andrew Lauder Dick, in 1820. In 1808 he had married Charles Anne, only child and heiress of George Cumin, Esq., of Relugas, by his wife, Susanna Judith Craigie-Halkett, eldest daughter of Colonel Craigie-Halkett of Hall Hill, county Fife. Of their children the first three daughters died young; then followed—

I. John, born in 1813; lieutenant and adjutant, cavalry, Bundelkund Legion, India; married on the 22nd May 1845, at Cleland, Lanarkshire, by the Rev. William Francis Sandys, M.A., vicar of St. Mary's, Beverley, and domestic chaplain to Lord Belhaven, to Anne, second daughter of North Dalrymple, Esq., of Fordel, afterwards ninth Earl of Stair.

II. George, born in 1820, whose patrimonial estate was Huntly Wood; married on the 28th January 1850, at Leamington Priors, by the Rev. J. J. Campbell, vicar of Great Tew, Oxon., to Antoinette Amelia Barclay, eldest daughter of the late James Macpherson, Esq.; died on the 23rd of the following month, February 1850, at Great Tew Vicarage, aged thirty. His widowed bride was married again at Greenhill House, by the Right Rev. Bishop Terrot, to Gilbert Mitchell Innes, youngest son of William Mitchell Innes, Esq., of Ayton, in 1851.

III. Susanna, eldest surviving daughter; died in 1872.

IV. Cornelia, the present Miss Dick Lauder.

V. Charlotte Gordon; married on the 23rd September 1840 to Alexander Mitchell Innes, Esq., eldest son and heir of William Mitchell Innes of Ayton Castle; died before her father, 1845.

CONCLUSION

VI. Isabella ; died on the 20th of February 1846.

VII. Julia Jane ; married on the 20th January 1841 to Thomas Shairp Mitchell Innes, Esq., of Phantassie, East Lothian, second son of William Mitchell Innes, Esq., of Ayton Castle. Mr. Thomas died on the 18th March 1892.

VIII. Maddalena ; married in 1848 to Colonel W. J. Wilson, police magistrate, Madras.

IX. Beatrice Ambrosia ; married in July 1870 to George Ramsay, Esq., who died on the 11th September 1887.

Sir John Dick Lauder succeeded his father, Sir Thomas, as eighth Baronet of Fountainhall and Grange in 1848 ; having married Lady Anne Dalrymple, daughter of the ninth Earl of Stair, in 1845, by whom he had—

I. Thomas North, the present Baronet.

II. John Edward Arthur (the Grange, Agra, Patnas, Ceylon), born 28th July 1848 ; married on the 14th October 1873 Rose, only surviving daughter of C. H. Caldecott, Esq., of Fort Jackson, King Williamstown, South Africa, whose daughters are Zella Evelyn, Norma Anne, and Margaret Maud Elizabeth.

III. George William Dalrymple (Punjab, India), born 4th Sept. 1852 ; married in 1882 Jane Emily Clifford, daughter of W. P. Woodward, Esq., and has one son, John North Dalrymple, born in 1883.

IV. Stair (Canada), born 4th November 1853 ; married on the 2nd December 1878 Eleanor Alma, youngest daughter of George Gordon Browne Leith, Esq., of the Hermitage, Ancaster, Canada, and grand-daughter of Major-General Sir George Leith, Bart., K.C.B.

Sir John Dick Lauder had also three daughters—

I. Margaret Louisa ; married on the 29th of October to Captain Arthur Charles Pole, 13th Hussars, who died at Lucknow on 14th December 1879.

II. Charlotte Anne ; married, 1st March 1875, to Lieut.-Colonel John Fletcher Hathorn, of Castle Wigg, county Wigton, who died 1888 ; and secondly, to Francis Sommerville Head, Esq., on the 16th of April 1891.

III. Catherine Seton ; married on the 2nd August 1871 to Stewart James Charles Duckell, Esq., of Russellstown Park, county Carlow.

The present Baronet, Sir Thomas North Dick Lauder, late lieutenant 10th Rifles, succeeded his father, Sir John Dick Lauder, as ninth Baronet of Fountainhall and Grange in 1867.

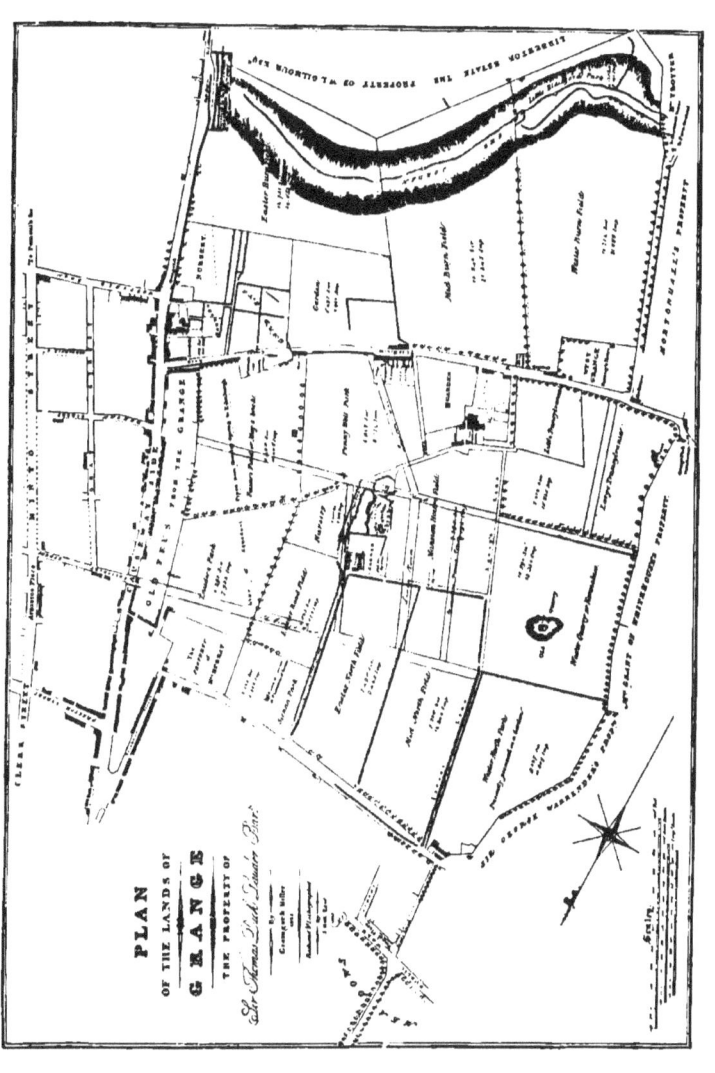

APPENDIX

APPENDIX

NOTE 1

LIST OF ALDERMEN AND PROVOSTS OF THE CITY OF EDINBURGH, whose names are on record, from the year 1296 to the Union of Scotland and England in 1707.[1]

Aldermen.

1296. William de Dedyk.
1362. William Cuppilde.
1373. Adam Forrester.

Provosts.

1377. John de Quhitness.
1377. Adam Forrester.
1425. William Liberton.
1427. William Levinton.
1429. William Liberton.
1434. Sir Henry Preston of Craigmillar.
1439. Thomas Cranston.
1447. Patrick Cockburn.
1451. Thomas de Cranston.
1457. Alexander Naper.
1462. Andrew Ker.
1467. Robert Mure of Polhellie.
1470. John Naper.
1477. James Crichton of Ruthven.
1481. William Bertraham.
1482. Patrick Baron of Spittlefield.
1484. John Naper.
1491. Richard Lawson.
1492. John Murray of Tulchadam.
1494. Walter Bertraham.
1501. Alexander Lauder.
1504. Richard Lawson of Hieriggs.
1508. Alexander Lauder.
1511. Sir Alexander Lauder.
1513. Archibald Douglas, Earl of Angus.
1514. Archibald, Lord Hume, Great Chamberlain of Scotland.
1515. Patrick Hamilton of Kincavel.
1516. David Melvine.
1517. Archibald Douglas.
1520. Robert Logan of Coatfield.
1522. Allan Stewart.
1524. Francis Ruthwell.
—— Robert, Lord Maxwell.
—— Sir John Murray of Tuchadam.
—— Sir Thomas Tod.
—— Adam Otterburn.
1534. James Lawson.
1536. Simon Preston.
1543. William Craik.
1550. Sir Andrew Ker of Little Dane.
1553. Archibald Douglas of Kilspindy.
1557. Lord Seaton.
1558. Thomas MacCalzean of Clifton Hall.
1559. Archibald Douglas of Kilspindy.
1561. Thomas MacCalzean of Clifton Hall.
1562. Archibald Douglas of Kilspindy.
1565. Sir Simon Preston of Craigmillar.
1569. The Laird of Grange.
1570. James Macgill.
1573. Lord Lindsay.
1576. George Douglas of Parkhead.
1578. Archibald Stewart.
1579. Alexander Clark of Balbirney.
1584. James, Earl of Anan.
1586. William Little.
1587. John Arnot.
1591. William Little.
1592. Nicoll Edward.
1593. Alexander Hume of North Berwick.
1597. Henry Nisbet.
1598. Alexander, Lord Fyvie, President of the Session.
1606. Alexander, Earl of Dunfermline.

[1] *Annals of Edinburgh.*—Appendix.

384   APPENDIX

1608. Sir John Arnott, Knight of Bersick.
1616. Sir William Nisbet of Deane, Knight.
1619. Alexander Clark.
1620. David Aikenhead.
1622. Sir William Nisbet of Deane, Knight.
1623. Alexander Clark of Stentoun.
1626. David Aikenhead.
1630. Alexander Clark.
1634. David Aikenhead.
1637. Sir John Hay.
1638. Sir William Dick.
1640. Sir Alexander Clark, Knight.
1643. Sir John Smith, Knight.
1646. Sir Archibald Tod, Knight.
1648. Sir James Stewart, Knight.
1650. A Committee of Englishmen.
1651. Archibald Tod.
1654. Archibald Tod and Andrew Ramsay.
1655. Sir Andrew Ramsay, Knight.
1658. Sir James Stewart, Knight.
1660. Sir Robert Murray, Knight.
1662. Sir Andrew Ramsay, Knight.

1673. Sir Andrew Ramsay and James Currie.
1674. James Currie.
1675. James Currie and Sir William Binning.
1676. Sir William Binning, Knight.
1677. Francis Kinloch.
1679. Sir James Dick, Knight.
1681. Sir James Fleming, Knight.
1683. Sir George Drummond, Knight.
1685. Sir Thomas Kennedy, Knight.
1687. Magnus Prince.
1689. Sir John Hall, Knight.
1690. Sir John Hall and Archibald Muir.
1691. Archibald Muir.
1692. Sir John Hall, Knight.
1694. Sir Robert Chiesly, Knight.
1696. Sir Archibald Muir, Knight.
1698. George Home.
1699. Sir George Home, Knight.
1700. Sir Patrick Johnston, Knight.
1702. Sir Heugh Cunningham, Knight.
1704. Sir Patrick Johnston, Knight.
1707. Sir Samuel M'Clellan, Knight.

NOTE II

INVENTORY OF THE RELICS AND SACRED UTENSILS OF THE CHURCH OF ST. GILES

THE arm of St. Giles, a relic, enshrined in silver, weighing five pounds three ounces and a half.
Item. A silver chalice, or communion cup, weighing twenty-three ounces.
Item. The great eucharist with golden weike and stones.
Item. Two cruets of twenty-five ounces.
Item. A golden bell with a heart of four ounces and a half.
Item. A golden unicorn.
Item. A golden pix to keep the host.
Item. A small golden heart with two pearls.
Item. A diamond ring.
Item. A silver chalice, patine and spoon, of thirty-two ounces and a half.
Item. A communion table-cloth of gold brocade.
Item. St. Giles' coat, with a little piece of red velvet which hung at his feet.
Item. A round silver eucharist.
Item. Two silver censors, of three pounds fifteen ounces.
Item. A silver ship for incense.
Item. A large silver cross, with its base, weighing sixteen pounds thirteen ounces and a half.
Item. A triangular silver lamp.
Item. Two silver candlesticks of seven pounds three ounces.

APPENDIX

Item. Other two candlesticks of eight pounds thirteen ounces.
Item. A silver chalice, gilt, of twenty ounces and a half.
Item. A silver chalice and cross, seventy five ounces.
Various priestly robes, and other vestments of gold brocade—crimson velvet embroidered with gold, and green damask—[1]
These things were all sold, and the money used for making the necessary repairs upon the church, for the installation of John Knox. The surplus then became a part of the funds of the Corporation.

NOTE III

THE first baronial Charter under the great Seal granted by King Charles to William Dick, dated 2nd August 1631, was that of Braid Manor, and the lands of Braid, which are herein comprehended. 'Apud Halyruid hous.—2 Aug. Rex. etc.[2] King Charles . . . with consent, etc., grants de novo to the said William Dick of Sanctgelegrange, merchant burgess of Edinburghe—and Elizabeth Moresoun his spouse, the lands and barony of Braid comprehending the Mains of Braid, called Nether Braid, with the Manor place, with the pendicles called Egypt (occupied by James Yule) and East Briggis (occupied by Nicolas Hodge and Johne Sympsoun) the lands of Over-Braid with the two corn mills of Braid, and Mill-lands—etc. —the lands of Blackfuird, alias Champunyie, the lands of East-hill of Braid, the lands of Greenbank, alias Over-Plewlands (formerly belonging in property to Sir Robert Fairlie of Braid Knight) the lands of Nether Plewlands with fourteen acres arable, to the West of the Market Road, with the pendicle called West Briggis and Smiddigrein (formerly belonging to the said Sir Robert in tenandry and to Patrick Eleis son and heir of the late James Eleis, son of the late Patrick Eleis senior, merchant burgess of Edinburgh in propriety) with the Manor place, Mills, fishings, etc.,— in the County of Edinburgh, which the said Sir Robert and Lady Margareta Dalmahoy his spouse with the consent of Alexander Fairlie their eldest son and heir apparent resigned by instruments taken in the hands of Robert Pringill notary public —and which the King incorporated into one free Barony of Braid, ordaining the place of Braid to be the principal Messuage.

PROVISO—That the said Elizabeth renounce the lands of Sanctgelegrange, with the Manor place, the lands and acres of the South Borrowmuir of Edinburgh (acquired from John Cant of Sanctgelegrange—and Katherine Creich his spouse) the heirs male, successors and assignees of the said William Dick at the time of the renunciation of said lands and teinds, giving security to the said Elizabeth for an annual rent of two thousand merks from the said lands and teinds during her life, and this with the foresaid barony to be in full satisfaction to her of all terce.

To be held by the said William and Elizabeth in conjunct fee, and to the lawful heirs male of the said William Dick and his Assignees whomsoever.

NOTE IV

WILL OF THOMAS BANNATYNE

Testament testamentar of THOMAS BANNATYNE, merchant burgess of Edinburgh, who died on 11th July 1635, given up by himself on 4th November 1633, so far as relates to nomination of executors, etc., and by Jonet Makmath, his relict spouse, in so far as relates to his goods, etc., as only Executrix.

In his inventory of goods are sugar, confeits, and sweetmeats, paper in whole reams and

[1] Coun. Reg. V. S. p. 29. 45. 76.
[2] 1843—Registrum Magni Sigilii Regum Scotorum 16.0-1633, Register House, Edinburgh.

broken, two gross of 'cairts' (cards) and other small wares. He had 5000 merks in ready money, and his furniture, silver work, and abuliaments are estimated at 1000 merks.

Sum of inventory, £4200.

There were debts due to him by William, Lord Sinclair of Berridale, and others, amounting to £4600.

Inventory and debts, £8800.

There was due by him to Samuel Small, confect maker, citizen of London, for merchant wares conforme to account, £31, 11s. 7d. sterling = in Scots to £378, 19s. 0d., which has been paid since his death.

Deducting this debt, remains of free gear, £8421, 1s. 0d. Divided into two parts. Deceased's part is £4210, 10s. 6d.

Legacie and Latter Will.

I, Thomas Bannatyne, merchant burgess of Edinburgh, calling to mynd the internitie of mans lyff in this transitorie world, nathing being moir certane to mortall man then death, bot the tyme quhen, the maner how, and the plaice quhair, to be altogidder uncertane, have thairfoir, in consideratioun thairof and for diverse guid and godlie respectis moving me now at the pleasour of my mercifull and gracious God, being perfite in bodie and mynd thocht guid to mak my latter will and testament as followes. And first, according to my exemple of my gracious and rich redemer at his last hore in the handis of my gracious God, I resigne and give up my saull and spirit, being surelie persuadit throw the merites and richteousnes of my blissed Lord and onlie Saviour Chryst Jesus, that at the separatioun of this my saull and spirit frome this mortell bodie, it sall with his heavenlie angellis (my guaird heir upone earth) be convoyit to that heavenlie mansioun, our duelling plaice, quhilk my blissed God and Saviour, quha diet for my sinnes and raise agane for my richteousnes, hes provydit and hes provydit and prepairit for me thair to praise and glorifie him eternellie. And as to my bodie, I desire the samyn to be bureid in the ordinar buriall plaice of Edinburgh, thair to be bureid with the bodies of the faithfull, and to remane quhill the day of the generall resurrectioun at quhilk my trust in the mercie of my God is that saull and bodie being reunited togidder sall in the meritis of my blissed Saviour inherite lyfe everlasting. And as concerning my wardlie effaires I be thir presentes for the love and singular affectioun I have and beires to Jonet Makmath, my loving spous, makes nominatis and constitutes be thir presentes the said Jonet Makmath my onlie executrice haill and universall intrometrice with my haill guidis, geir debtis and sowmes of money perteaning and belonging to me the tyme of my deceis quhen at the pleasour of God the samyn sall fall out. Lykas I be thir presentes leaves giftis and dispones the saymn giudis, geir, debtis, sowmes of money and utheris quhatsumever perteaning and belonging to me the tyme forsaid to the said Jonet Makmath my spous, with power and full libertie to hir to intromet thairwith, use and dispone thairupone as hir awjn propir guidis and geir, debtis and sowmes of moncy at hir pleasour, schoe alwayes paying furth of the first and reddiest thairof to the persones respective efter following the debtis and legacies efter specifeit, viz., the sowme of threttie ane pundis, xij^s vij^d usuall and lawfull money of Ingland addebtit be me to Samuell Small, confeitmaker, citiner of Londoun, for merchand waires conforme to the compt thairof. Item. Paying to the persones underwrittin my legatouris, first to Isobell Makmath, my sister in law, ane thowsand merkis; item to Sara Makmath, also my sister in law, twa thowsand merkis money; item to Mareone Makmath, also my sister in law, ane thowsand merkis; item to James Bannatyne, merchand, my wyffes uncle, twa thowsands merkis, the yeirlie annuel rent quhairof to perteane to himselff during his lyftyme, and efter his deceis the principall sowme to be devydit amongs his fowr barnes, viz., ilk ane of thame fyve hundreth thairof. Item to Mr. William Bannatyne, reidar at Crawmont v^c merkis; Item to Thomas Bannatyne in Leswaid, viij^c merkis; item to John Bannatyne, George Bannatyne, and Isobell Bannatyne, thrie lawfull barnes to Johne

APPENDIX

Bannatyne, Writter, to ilk ane of thame j^m merkis, quhilkis thrie thowsand merkis amongst thame thric. Item, to the biging of ane new kirk in Edinburgh as ane help to that guid work, iiij^m merkis; item, to the puire of the hospitall, j^m merkis; item, to the poore of Edinburgh, j^m merkis; item, to Mr. Archibald Skeldie, ij^c merkis; item, to Mr. George Lichtbodie, uther twa hundreth merkis; to Thomas Bannatyne, master of fence, ij^c merkis; item, to James Charles in Leith, the annuell rent of the principall sowme of j^c lib. conforme to the Act of Parliament, and efter his deceis the hundreth pundis of principall sowme to perteane and belong to his doughter; item, to John Charles in Mussilburcht xl merkis; item, to John Finlasoun, my kinsman, j^c merkis; item, to Thomas Braidfute, my godsone, ij^c merkis; item, to Thomas Johnstoun, my uther godsone, sone to David Johnstoun, uther ij^c merks money, and last I leave to Pawll Bannatyne of Spittells, fyve hundreth merkis; and this my latter will and testament I mak manifest and knowne to all and quhatsumever. In witnes quhairof I have subscrivit thir presentis with my hand, being writtin at my speciall directioun by John Bannatyne, writter, at Edinburgh, the fowrt day of November the yeir of God 1633 yeiris, before thir witnesses, Sir William Nisbitt of Deane, knycht, Sir Lues Stewart, knycht, Advocat before the Lordis of Sessioun, Robert Davidsoun, merchand, and Johne Bannatyne, writter. And finallie I leave to Thomas Johnstoun, sone to David Johnstoun, merchand burges of Edinburgh ij^c merkis money, abowe writtin allennarlie (Sic subscribitur) Thomas Bannatyne, Sr Villiam Nisbit, witnes, L. Stewart, witnes, Ro^t Davidsone, witnes, J. Bannatyne, witnes.'

Confirmed 28th October 1635.[1]

Marion Macmath.

Testament dative of Mareon M'Math daughter to the deceased Hectour M'Math merchant burgess of Edinburgh, who died on May 1636. Given up by Jonet Issobell and Sara M'Mathes, her lawful sisters and executors dative on 1637.

There was due to her by Sir John Sinclare of Stevinstone, knight, £533, 6s. 8d. in his hands as her 'partage and bairns pairt' of gear; and also due by him as upliftit by him the legacy of £666, 13s. 4d. left her by Thomas Bannatyne.

Sum j^m ij^c lib. No division. Quota £40

Confirmed 10th June 1637.[2]

Hectour M'Math.

Testament dative of Hectour M'Math, son to the deceased Hector M'Math, merchan burgess of Edinburgh, who died on 25th January 1637, given up by William Dik, younger, merchant burgess of Edinburgh as Executor dative.

He had only a mare worth £60 and the abulgiaments of his body = £200. In all £260.

Quota £9, 15s.

Confirmed 14th, May 1638.[3]

Sara Macmath.

Testament dative of Sara M'Math, lawful daughter to the deceased Edward (Hectour, M'Math, merchant burgess of Edinburgh, who died on January 1638, given up by Jonet Makmath, her sister, spouse to William Dik, younger, merchant burgess of Edinburgh, and by Isobell Makmath, also her sister, spouse to James Loche, merchant burgess of Edinburgh only executors dative to her.

Her estate consisted of—

Ready money, £621; Abulzaments and ornaments of her body, £133, 6s. 8d.

Sum, £256, 6s. 8d.

[1] Commissariot of Edinburgh, *Register of Testaments*, vol. 7. [2] *Ibid.* vol. 58. [3] *Ibid.* vol. 58.

APPENDIX

The debts due to her amount to £168; one of her debtors being Alexander M'Math of Dalpe.
Sum of estate, £424, 6s. 8d.   No division.   Quota £15, 15. od.
Confirmed 1st January 1639.[1]

NOTE V

COPY ESTIMATE OF SIR WILLIAM DICK'S ESTATE as made out by his fourth son, Mr. Alexander Dick.

August the 1st, 1642.

	MERKS SCOTS
The Lands of North Berwick, etc.,	240,000
,, ,, Braid and Briggs,	110,000
,, ,, Grainge,	80,000
,, ,, Heugh pr. Wadset,	63,000
,, ,, Edinbr. Leith & Kings Works,	66,000
Herring Works in Dunbar & Ld. Areskines Wadset,	60,000
Shipping,	70,000
Orkney & Shetland,	400,000
Earl of Nithsdale pr. Infeftments,	100,000
Marquis of Huntly pr. oblidgement,	90,000
Coal & Salt Works,	150,000
Bygone Rests of Customs and Imposts,	350,000
Rests of Earl Marishall Bargenie & Soap Work,	30,000
Rests by the Tennants of Braid, North Berwick & Grange,	100,000
Rests by Bonds of lent money,	150,000
Rests by Victual Bonds,	150,000
Roll Debts for Commodities,	60,000
Edinbrugh & Leith Society,	60,000
Victual with said Society & Girnell at Leith,	40,000
In France,	40,000
Owing by the Publick,	790,000
Desperate Debts besides the above,	800,000
Total,	3,999,000

Total in sterling money, £222,166, 13s. 4d.

NOTE VI

COPIA OF SCOTLAND'S LETTER TO THE HOUSE OF COMMONS

Concerning Sir William Dick.

1 May 1644.

Right honorable,

About a year since or thereby, we recommended to you to pay Sir William Dick of Braid the last forty thousand pounds sterling of the Brotherly Assistance, due at Midsummer 1642, assigned by us to the said Sir William for satisfaction of several great sums advanced by him in the Publick Cause. Whereof (as we are informed) he has only received Five thousand six hundred pounds, and there rests Thirty-four thousand four hundred pounds, and has forborn to urge the payment thereof, hithertils in regard of your more pressing affairs: But now as the great prejudice the said Sir William suffers in his affairs by

[1] Commissariot of Edinburgh, *Register of Testaments*, vol. 59.

APPENDIX 389

want of this sum, has moved him in his great necessity to implore our intercession with you for his satisfaction, so we calling to minde the seasonable advancement of great sums made by the said Sir William to us in time of our troubles, his readiness according to his power in everything to further the Publick Cause, and the great straits we are put to by want of these ordinary supplies we did truly receive from him (and which for want of the moneys aforesaid he is now disabled to make). Do therefore most earnestly recommend the said Sir William and the Bearer hereof, Robert Inglis, Merchant, his Commissioner, requesting that the said sum of Thirty-four thousand four hundred pounds sterling, with interest since Midsummer 1642, may be paid (hilsoon possibly can be) to the said Sir William or Mr. Inglis in his name, which will be most acceptable to the States here, and very much oblige
         Your assured Friends,
                 Loudon Cancellarius, J. P. D.
Edinburgh,
1 May 1664.

COPIA OF SCOTLAND'S LETTER TO SIR WILLIAM DICK

                       12th Dec. 1645.
Assured Friend,
We do acknowledge your Advancements and Service to your Country and us in our streights and difficulties, to have been timeous, comfortable and useful for our assistance and the opposition of the Enemies of the Covenant and good Cause: And we do the more highly value and prize the same for that cheerfulness and alacrity which singularly you did always manifest therein, which did make you to engage not only your own Means and Estate but to use your best credit with others for our supply, beyond all men of your Condition, whereby the kingdom hath found your ready help in its greatest necessities; For the which we finde our selves bound in Honour and Conscience, to see you timeously relieved and satisfied: And albeit your frequent supplications formerly presented to us and our Orders issued thereupon have not produced the intended effect for your satisfaction: yet we have so much taken to heart your deep Engagements, That we are resolved to take such a solid and real course for your payment, and put such a mark of your merited Reward upon you to be recorded to posterity, as may give you just content, and convince those of foolish Rashness who have so mis-termed your Advancements, being resolved as we do hereby assure, That before dissolving of this Session of Parliament, we shall use all possible means for obtaining money, and giving you real satisfaction; which we think is the best way to stop the mouths of your unfriends, and to give you self-encouragement: All which are justly deserved by you, and really intended to you by
         Your affectionate Friends
         Crauford Lindsay, J. P. D. Parl.—
St. Andrews,
12th December 1645.
    To our assured Friend, Sir William Dick of Braid, Knight.

RECOMMENDATION BY THE ASSEMBLY OF THE CHURCH OF SCOTLAND, to the Parliament and Commitee of State in that Nation, concerning Sir William Dick, date the 15th June 1646.

The General Assembly having received, and heard a Petition from Sir William Dick, representing his great sufferings in his Estate and Credit by lending so great sums of money for advancing the Publick-good Cause, in its greatest streights and difficulties, and humbly desiring that the Assembly would interpose their earnest desires to the State in his behalf, for his payment and relief of his Credit, and having found themselves obliged in Conscience to resent his Engagement in and for that Cause ; therefore the General Assembly, from the sense they have of the sufferings of the good cause in his sufferings do humbly represent their most earnest desires to the honourable Committees of Parliament, whom it doth concern, That their Lordships may be pleased to take some speedy course for his real satisfaction and payment of so huge sums, that his name, credit and estate, may be yet saved, the honor of the Kingdom engaged by their Publick Faith and Surety may be preserved, and appoints Masters, Andrew Cant, David Dickson, Robert Murray, Clarkington and Libberton, to present this humble desire in the behalf of the said Sir William, and further to assist the said Sir William before their Lordships, during the time of the sitting of the said Assembly ; And that thereafter any two of the Ministers of Edenburgh whom he shall desire, with any one or two of the Commisioners of the Assembly in Town present the same Desire to the honorable States of Parliament being sitting, or their Committees, as he shall decide necessary.

ANDREW KER, Clerk to the Assembly.

COPIA OF TWO LETTERS from the Scots Commissioners at London, to the Committee of Parliament at Edenburgh, and the Committee of State at Newcastle, date 12 Sept. 1646. Concerning Sir William Dick.

May it please your Lordships—We have received your Letters concerning Sir William Dick, and our care to use all means in our power for his relief with both Houses of Parliament, it is sufficiently known to us, that his affection in laying out his whole Estate for the Publick, and exposing his credit at home and abroad to evident hazard and danger, cannot be paralleled by any other : And we are fully sensible that his growing burthens are now become insupportable, and so much the more that all the ways and means hitherto taken for his relief have proved ineffectual. Whereby his Creditors so often frustrated, are ready to take some desperate course for their own satisfaction, which certainly will tend to his utter undoing, and bring him and his Family to ruine, to the great discouragement of all others to undertake for the Publick : These considerations do so far prevail with us, and the sad estate to which he is now reduced, for his forward Zeal and Publick Affection, maketh so deep an impression on us, as there is no means that can be devised, nor lawful ways essayed for his relief which we shall most willingly undertake—And therefore shall contribute our best endeavours with the Houses of Parliament that he may have some speedy supply out of his right to the brotherly Assistance : But because we find ourselves obliged in honour, justice, and charity not to make him depend upon us altogether ; We therefore bring of the like favourable minde with you, to his sore sufferings for the Publick, do request as far as may be you will commiserate the very sad condition of his Affairs here and at home, it being without all controversie that his sufferings in that Kinde are far beyond any other in this Kingdom.

We rest, your Lordships most humble servants,

LOUDON, LAUDERDAIL, SIR CHARLES
ERSKINE, SIR ARCHIBALD JOHNSON,
MR. ROBERT BARKELEY.

A SHORT STATE OF THE DEBTS DUE BY ENGLAND AND SCOTLAND to the deceased Sir William Dick, and of the securities he hath thereupon.

By good and seasonable services done to England by Sea, and otherways, there is due to the deceased Sir William, at Candlemas last past 2 February 165$\frac{8}{9}$ of Principal and Interest, (all payments being deducted, and besides great charges and expenses, losses, damages, and ruine in Credit and Estate, by so many disappointments these twelve years past) the sum of 36803l. 5s. 9d.

For this sum he hath security upon the friendly Assistance due by Ordinance of Parliament, the 24th June 1642, upon the Chamber of London by Receipt of the 400,000l. Bill past by King and Parliament in 1641. Secondly upon the Customs, And thirdly by Ordinance of Parliament upon Goldsmiths-Hall : By Receipt of Papists and Delinquents Estates, Sale or Composition thereof (now turned into the Exchequer) and still Standing charged upon that Hall, with some scores of Orders following thereupon, all confirming the original Ordinance for his payment; albeit as yet nothing paid thereupon ; but 1000l.

6 August 1653.—By good service done to Scotland, the time of their greatest streits and difficulties and in relation to their union with England, and assistance to their sufferings, there is due to the said Sir William Dick at Candlemas last 165$\frac{3}{4}$ of Principal and Interest (all payments being deducted, and besides great charges and expenses, losses, damages, and ruine in Credit and Estate, by so many disappointments these sixteen years past) the sum of 28,131l.

For this sum he hath several Bonds conform to the Fundamental Law of that Land.

Secondly—The Loan-Moneys in the Shires of Southerland, Cathnes, Orkney and Yettland.

Thirdly—An Order for 11,000l. out of all other Loans, with an Order for a Loan upon those who had gotten payment of their first Loan and the payment thereof to be made to the said Sir William.

Fourthly—Two months Sess and Excise of that Nation after December 1647, and January 1648—Scots stile.

Fifthly—2000l. Sterling Monethly out of the Sess and Excise, thereafter when the army in Ireland should be supplied by England.

Sixthly—The third part of the fines and Forfeitures in that Nation ; and of all these five last Securities nothing performed.

Seventhly—The Excise of all Wines from 1 Novemb, 1649 to 1 Novemb. 1651, but interrupted by the Army from England.

And lastly the half of the Excise of all Wines and Strong-Waters, after 1 Nov. 1651, till he should be compleatly paid, but interrupted also by the Army from England.

Debt due by England, 36,803l. 5s. 9d.
Debt due by Scotland, 28,131l. 0s. 0d.

Sum-total, 64,934l. 5s. 9d.

COPIA OF SCOTLAND'S LETTER TO THE PARLIAMENT OF ENGLAND, CONCERNING SIR WILLIAM DICK. *Date* 21 *Nov.* 1648

Honored Sir,—The Sincerity and Affection of Sir William Dick (a person who with much cheerfulness hath laid out his Estates for the Publick Good very largely, and hazarded all his Fortune in Maintenance of the Cause) and his zealous opposition to the Engagement against England hath moved us at this time to appear in his behalf, and to desire in most serious manner, That seeing it hath pleased the honorable House by their Ordinance of January 13, 1646 (English stile), to appoint him to be paid the Sum of Nineteen thousand Eighteen pounds, Twelve Shillings, Four pence, Sterling, out of the last Two hundred thousand pounds for the Arrears of our Army that was in England : Your Honors in regard of his very extraordinary Engagements not only for this Kingdom but also for the Kingdom of England, will now Ordain some speedy and effectual course to be taken for the payment thereof according to the said Ordinance : We are so confident that your Honors will have a speciall regard to his Con-

stant Affection (even in times of the greatest defection) and his Engagements for both Kingdoms, that we will relye upon your Care to preserve his Credit, and inable him to continue his Service for the good of the Publique : and your Favor and Encouragement to be shewed him herein, shall be esteemed as done to Your affectionate Friends and Servants.
Edinburgh, November 21, 1648.

         Signed by Warrant, and in the Name of the Committee of Estates.
Indorsed:—For the Honorable William Lenthall, Esq., Speaker of the Honorable House of Commons of the Parliament of England, to be communicated by him to the said House.

$$\begin{array}{r} £\ 19{,}018\ 12\ 4 \\ 200{,}000 \\ \hline £219{,}018\ 12\ 4\ \text{Sterlg.} \end{array}$$

NOTE VII

THE BURIAL-PLACE OF SIR WILLIAM DICK OF BRAID, Knight, Provost of Edinburgh.

THE first Record dated October 28, 1640, says :—'The Provost, Baillies, &c.—grants license of ane buriell-place to William Dick, lait Provost, and in such a part of the Grayfrier-Churche-yaird as the Dene of Gild &c. sall designe unto him.'[1] The next Record, dated 1664, June 15, 'Appoynts William Reid, Auld Dene of Gild, and Johne Milne Deakin, to designe a boundis in the Grayfrier-Churche-yaird of this burgh, to be a buriell-place for the familie of the deceist Sir William Dick, sometyme Provost of this burghe, of sixteen fute of length from the wall east and west, and fourteen fute of breidth south and north, *quhar the said deceist Sir William Dick his corpse ar buried*, and that without any raills or timber or other enclosure to be set about the boundis.'[2] Another Record, four years later, is very conclusive :—'1668, Janry. 10—Anent the petitioun given in by Sir Andrew Dick of Craighouse, for himself and remanent familie of the late Sir William Dick of Braid, his father, making mention that when the said Sir William had oftymes borne publick office of the highest dignity in the city, and was ever of constant affection and respect to the welfair thairof, weall knowen to all the Councell and inhabitants, and that in Anno 1640 he had been at the charge of the drying a piece of ground in the Greyfrier-yeard, where he is now buried himself with his wife, and most part of his childrein and grandchildrein. And therefor craved the said ground might be appoynted and destinated for a proper buriall-place for the familie of the said Sir William Dick, exclusive of all uther inhabitants, and uther whatsumever ; in all tyme cumeing with power to set merths and merchstanes in the length and breadth of the same, as it is now designed and measured by the twa baillies George Reid and John Fullerton, by commission to that effect.

Thairfor the Lord Provost, Baillies, and Communit Councell, upon consideration of the premisses, do hereby most cheirfullie and willinglie grant the desire of the said petition, and dothe separate for ever the forsaid place, and ground in the Greyfrier yeard sua visited and measured in lenth and breadth by the twa baillies George Reed and John Fullerton, as the proper place of the said Sir William Dick of Braid, and his familie descending of him—with power to the said Sir Andrew Dick of Craighouse as the only son now alive of the said Sir William his father, or any uther his representatives to sett merths and merchstanes in lenth and breadth about the said place, at sight of any one of the baillies forsaids, and to erect tombs and uther memorials within the said boundis upon the wall—and lay through stones upon the ground joyning to the saids tombe or memoriall, and to bury their deid their—discharging hereby all uther persons or inhabitants whatsumever to enter their deid within said bounds and place in any tyme cuming for ever—in prejudice of the families of the said Sir William Dick.'[3]

[1] *Council Records of Edinburgh*, 1606-1726, vol. xv. fol. 163.
[2] *Ibid.* vol. xxiii. fol. 26.   [3] *Ibid.* vol. xxxi. fol. 308.

APPENDIX 393

NOTE VIII

To the High and Honourable Court of Parliament.—[Presented *c.*1661.]

The Lamentable and Sad Petition of the distressed Family and numerous Creditors of the late deceased Sir William Dick, in Scotland, Knight ;

Humbly sheweth :—

THAT the deceased Sir William Dick, with his Children and Friends at home, and beyond Seas, out of Christian zeal to the purity of true Religion ; freed from the vain Inventions of man, and in order to the preservation (if not restauration) of the lawful Liberties of the Israel of God, from the abuse and oppression of corrupt Council, profanity and wickedness about authority : Did exemplarily in the beginning of these late Troubles and Distractions in the Commonwealth, expend his whole Fortune and Estate, and all the Trust which he could command from others, most chearfully and with great Affection ; (without a parallel by any of his Quality in the Three Nations). And most constantly (without the least change of his Principles in pursuance of the ends aforesaid) counting nothing too dear, nor anything too much, in the day of England's Calamity, Scotland's Troubles, and Ireland's Blood ; as may appear by a Letter from the Parliament of Scotland to the Parliament of England, 21 November 1648 (the time of the greatest defection of many), a Copy whereof for Evidence doth hereafter follow.

That for these Incomparable and most Seasonable Disbursements for the Nations (being above Fifty Thousand pounds of Remainder at this present) he had and hath made to him by those who were then in power, all the acknowledgments of good Service and solemn Promises before Heaven and Earth, that the sons of men can make, one to another for thankful and speedy Repairment with Recompence and Reward, as is evident by Letters from the Parliament of Scotland, to the aforesaid Sir William Dick, dated 12 December 1645. And by several other Letters hereafter also following direct from that Parliament and Committee of Estates there to the Parliament of England, and to the Commissioners of Scotland for the time at London, Anno 1644 and 1646. And by a Recommendation of the General Assembly of the Church of Scotland to the Parliament and their Committees in June 1646, etc. And farther he hath made and granted unto him all Securities of Parliaments, Committees of Parliaments, and Councils of State, that Justice or Law can devise for Assurance of Satisfaction : and more particularly upon the Chamber of London, Anno 1641. Upon the Customs of England, in the years 1643 and 1644. Upon the Receipts of Papists and Delinquent's Estates Sale or Composition thereof, 13 Jan. 1646. By the Treasurers at Goldsmith's Hall, and still charged thereupon for the same ; with many scores of Orders and Ordinances of all the Three late Parliaments and their Committees ; and of his Highness Privy Council, in August and September 1654, and June 1655. All confirming and approving for the most part the said Sir William Dick, his original Securities, and ordering his forthwith payment and satisfaction. And lastly, he was secured by the Scots Parliament in the Lease of the Excise of Wines in that Nation, to begin Anno 1651, though since he was interrupted therein by the Army ; so that Humane Faith and Christian Bonds cannot establish to any man a Stronger Right or Security and Assurance thereof.

That notwithstanding all this, and of the aforesaid Sir William Dick his expense and painful Solicitation by Agents and Friends, the space of Sixteen years, and of his own personal attendance upon the Three Parliaments, and his Highness Council, from Nov. 1652 until Nov. 1655 in his great Old Age of Seventy and five years, and grey Hairs full of Sorrows and heaviness of Heart, for such deplorable Sufferings in Credit and Estate, by so good Service performed for England, and with cries to Heaven for Justice and Mercy, to his deep Afflictions for well-doing, yet nevertheless, little or nothing was recovered all his time

3 D

APPENDIX

here, but one small sum of One Thousand pounds in August 1653. Insomuch that by reason of this Delay, Floods of Desolation and Distress have overwhelmed him and his Children with their numerous Families and little ones; Their Lands and Houses being extended and possessed by the Creditors in the cruel execution of the Law; Their Chattels and Goods, yea, their Garments, the covering of their Nakedness, and the Coverlet in which they should sleep, being publickly distrained and seized upon for these Debts and Disbursements engaged in by them to promote the Publick Service. Neither is this all, One wo is past, and behold two woes come after this; Ah! the Old Man himself was once and again disgracefully cast into prison for small Debts contracted for necessary livelihood, during his attendance for Satisfaction. And in the end through heart-break, by so long disappointment, and in the sight of so great miseries upon himself, family, and so fair an Estate and precious Credit and Trust he formerly had, died in Westminster, the 19th December 1655, in great misery and want, and without the Benefit of a decent Funeral; after Six months petitioning for some little money towards the same.

And to compleat the third Wo and perfection of Sorrowful Afflictions his children are cast at this day and lying in Prisons these twenty moneths past for Publick Debts in great sufferings of their Persons, Credit and Calling, and weariness of Life, longing for Death more than for Treasures. And where they and their numerous Families, with their desolate wives and little ones, had already perished for Want of Bread, if some little supply of his Highness goodness had not been lately appointed them: By which means the Old Mans Memory and Posterity is almost rooted out from under Heaven with great Disgrace and Shame, and this for Righteousness sake, to the no small scandal of Reformed Religion, the dishonor of the Commonwealth, the violation of the present Government; the discouragement of the Godly in sight of such neglect towards the welaffected in the Land. And to the great Triumph and proud insulting of the wicked and malignant Enemy, who do rage and swell in their *Shimei*-like revilings, and tauntily in their seeming compassion to your Petitioners Miseries (yet insolently in their real Malice), accuse the Commonwealth of forgetfulness of their first and faithful old Servants, who have forsaken all and followed them through the fire and water of all Streights and Difficulties. And even in the Esteem and Judgment of these Enemies, should in these peacable Harvest times by the Commonwealth, of their Friends and Servants former painful and expensive Labors, have satisfaction of their just Debts and sufferings in time past, and some Subsistences, especially considering the large and solemn Promises made in the Declarations of both Kingdoms, Anno 1643. That such as should approve themselves faithfull to the Parliament, and should continue constant in their course of doing or suffering unto the End, should according to their Merits be taken into Publick notice and consideration, their Debts and Losses repaid, and themselves honored and rewarded. And that no man who hath been eminent in action, or had suffered any notable loss for the Publick, should be neglected or slighted, but one way or other should be thankfully remembered to his own honor, and the good of his Posterity. And also remembering that, besides all this, it is provided and promised by the Nine and thirtieth Article of the present government that Publick Debts shall be confirmed and assuredly Paid.

The lamentable Premisses considered, and that your Honors are now again met by singular Divine Providence as the Light and Eyes of the Lord's People, as the hiding place from the Wind, the refuge from the Tempest, the Rivers of Water in a Wilderness, the shadow of a great Rock in a wearied Land—and as the Sovereign Physitians of the languishing Diseases of the Body Politick, and healers of the Breaches of the Nations, by whom the Messengers may see, and say that the Lord hath established Zion, and that the poor of his people shall trust in it, and by whose wholesome Councils and Conclusions, Righteousness and Peace may kiss each other, Beauty and Bands may be joyned and the hearts of the afflicted may rejoice.

Your Honors distressed Petitioners and prisoners—Do therefore if not for Justice and

APPENDIX 395

Righteousness sake, your general and particular Promises sake, yet humbly pray for Christ's sake, how at last after Sixteen years delay and disappointment of such honourable and solemn Parliamentary Promises and Protestations, Church and State recommendations, and of so many Acts; Orders and Ordinances, as nothing more clear and just, and after so great and deplorable sufferings sustained by them in Person, Credit, Estate and Relations, and in the Death of their broken-hearted Father, in so great and disgraceful Misery and Want (which hath given too much cause to the Enemy to Blaspheme, and caused the Daughters of the Philistines to rejoyce) and as the cry of their scattered poor Families of Fifty Children and Grandchildren, and numerous Creditors (for the most part all Orphans, Widows, and poor People, and welaffected to the Commonwealth) may be dear before you, and tender to your Ears, That a present, speedy, real, effectual course may be taken for their fully Satisfaction of their great Disbursements for the Publick, with such Recompense and Reward as shall stand with your Honors Pleasure and Justice. And to that purpose, That some few Select Persons of this most honorable Court, best known to your Petitioners Fathers good Services and Sufferings, may be presently nominated as a Committee for considering thereupon, and upon the Liberty of their persons from these their wearisome Bonds, and Stocks of cruel and unadvised Creditors for the time to come, until their compleat payment of these Publick Debts due by the Commonwealth : And thereafter to certifie their opinion therein, for your Honors Ordinance of Parliament, to pass and to be issued forth thereupon—By which doing Religion and Righteousness will be well spoken of by the Nations—the honour of the Commonwealth and present Government will receive further glory and praise; the Godly and well-affected party in the Land will rejoyce, the common enemy will be cloathed with Shame, and Iniquity shall stop her mouth. And your honors Petitioners and Prisoners will be restored again from the Grave of such inexpressible sorrows and sufferings, and have matter and occasion all their days to bless the God of their Fathers, which shall put in the hearts of this most honorable Court to execute such Judgment and Justice towards them, And incline Mercy towards them before his Highness and his Councillors, and before all his Highness' Rulers and Officers. And in this Confidence,
Your distressed Petitioners and Prisoners
shall ever humbly pray, etc.

(Presented about 1661.)

[Of date 1702.]—*Unto His Grace Her Majesty's High Commissioner and the Right Honourable Estates of Parliament.*

THE PETITION of William Dick, Heir to the deceast Sir William Dick of Braid, and of William Viscount of Kilsyth, Sir Robert Sibbald of Kipps Dr. of Medicine, John Spotiswood of that Ilk, Advocat, Walter Lockhart of Kirktown, Mr. James Colvil, Advocat, and Mr. Thomas Ackman, Writer to the Signet, for themselves and in name and behalf of the remanent Creditors of the deceast Sir William Dick of Braid and his sons.

Humbly sheweth :—

The deceast Sir William Dick was the Merchant of greatest Riches and Credit, that ever lived in Scotland. He did preceeding the year 1650 Advance and Lend to the English Nation, the Sum of 36,803l. 5s. 9d. Sterl. Money, as appears by a Representation given in by him, to the Parliament of England, *anno* 1651, but neither he, nor his Sons, nor Creditors could obtain payment thereof.

Sir William did betwixt the years 1640 and 1648 Borrow from your Petitioners; Authors and Predecessors, no less than 500,000 Merks, Scots Money, which with more of his own Estate he did Lend to Several of the Nobility and Gentry of this Kingdom, who for their Relief, obtained Acts from the Parliament then in Being, as will appear by the unprinted Acts of Parliament in the Months of January and March 1647. And by these Acts will also appear, that the Nation of Scotland and the Nobility and Gentry thereof, were then owing to the said Sir William Dick the sum of 500,008 Merks Money foresaid: but neither Sir William, his Sons, nor Creditors, could obtain payment of these Sums. For,

The Parliament 1663 did without calling Sir William Dick's Representatives or Creditors, Suspend the Execution of publick Debts (whereof these were reckoned a part) till the next Parliament—and was continued by that Parliament 1669, and by the Parliament 1672, but with this addition, that they gave Sir William Dick's Sons a Protection; But the Parliament 1681 without precedent, did by their 26 Act most amply discharge these Debts upon Condition these Bound for the same, or their Heirs should take the Test imposed by that Parliament. By this Sir William Dick's Representatives and Children were Ruin'd; your Petitioners their Creditors frustrate of our Payment, and many others of the Creditors reduced to great Misery by want of their Just Debts. This being our case we do most humbly offer to the Consideration of the Honourable Estates of Parliament —That seeing England is to take course with their Debts; the Estates of Parliament would interpose on our behalf, with the Parliament of England, for obtaining payment of the Debts due by them to Sir William Dick, and his Representatives and Creditors, it being just they should pay their Debts, and most unjust they should be Bettered by our so great Disadvantages and Losses.

In the next Place, your Petitioners Represent, that since that Act of Parliament 1681 did pass without calling your Petitioners and hearing what they had to object against the same, the said Act ought either to be rescinded or your Petitioners Reponed against the same; that they may have Access, against Sir William Dick's Debtors for the Debt due to him, or that the Honourable Estates of Parliament may fall upon some other Equivalent for satisfying your Petitioners.

May it therefore please your Grace, and the Honourable Estates of Parliament, in consideration of the Premises, either to represent to Her Majesty the circumstances of Sir William Dick's Representatives and Creditors with respect to England to be laid before the Parliaments of England for effectual payment to us of the Sums due by England to Sir William Dick's Representatives and Creditors.

And in the next place that your Grace and Honourable Estates would Rescind the Act of Parliament 1681, Or allow us an equivalent therefore, out of any other suitable Fund, for effectual payment to us of the Debts due by Scotland and the Nobility and Gentry thereof.

And your Petitioners shall ever pray.

Date 1702.

NOTE IX

KIRK-SESSION RECORDS ANENT THE CORSTORPHINE COMMUNION CUPS

1718. June 2. 'The Mod^r informed the Session that he had spoke to the Heritors of the parish anent Communion Cups, and it was agreed among them that Sir James Dick, Heritor of Corstorphine, should buy one at his own charge, having his name and arms on the same, and that the other Heritors, viz., Sir Andrew Myretoun, Saughton, and Ravelstoune should furnish the other Cup, and pay for the same proportionally conform to their several valuations.'

1719. May 31. 'The Mod^r informed the Session that the Heritors had caused make two

APPENDIX

Communion Cups, and that he had received one of them, which Sir Andrew Myretoun, Saughton, and Reavelstoune had payed proportionally for, conform to their respective valuations, but Sir James Dick, Heritor of Corstorphine, who had promised to gift the other, had not yet given it up.'

1721. Oct. 5. The Mod^r reported that Sir Andrew Myretoun of Gogar before his death had appointed his Lady to pay the sum of Ten pounds Sterling to the Kirk Session in order to buy another Communion Cup (notwithstanding he had paid his proportion with the other Heritors for one cup already) in caice Sir James Dick refused to give up the cup he had caused make, but if Sir James gave that cup to the Session, then the said ten pound be employe'd to some pious use about the Church, and that he had lately put her La^{s}p, in remembrance of the same, who said they might have it payed when they pleased, since Sir James had now consented to give the other cup.'

1721. May 17. 'The Mod^r informed the Session that Sir James Dick of Prestonfield had now condescended to give up to the Kirk Session the Communion Cup at this occasion, and desired that the Session might record it in their books, and the particular weight thereof as he should send a note of the same. 20th, the Session agreed to.'

1722. May 17. 'This day there was presented to the Session a Com^n Cup gifted to them by Sir James Dick of Prestonfield with this Inscription— "May 23rd 1722. This silver Cup is given as a free gift by Sir James Dick, baronet, and Heritor and Patron of the Church of Corstorphine, and that for the use and service of the said Church, the weight being thirty ounces seven drop and one half." The Session order this to be insert in their Register.'[1]

NOTE X

CHARTER OF THE ENTAIL OF PRIESTFIELD

(*Registrum Magni Sigilli*, Lib. 96, No. 9.)

'KING George grants to Lady Janet Dick, daughter of the deceased Sir James Dick of Priestfield, Baronet, and spouse of Sir William Cunningham of Caprington, Baronet, in liferent, and to Sir William Dick, now of Priestfield, Baronet (designed in the Bond of Taillie after mentioned William Cunningham, third son of the said Sir William Cunningham and Lady Janet Dick) and his lawful heirs-male in fee; whom failing, to Alexander Cunningham, their fourth son, then to Adam, their fifth son, then to Archibald, their sixth son; whom failing, any other heirs male of the said Sir William and Lady Janet, and their heirs male; according to their births and ages—Whom failing, to the second and younger sons of John Cunningham, eldest lawful son of the said Sir William and Lady Janet, according to their ages and births— Whom failing, to Anna Cunningham, their eldest daughter, then to Margaret, Janet, and Christian, 2nd, 3rd, and 4th daughters, then to any other daughters, and their heirs male as above—Whom failing to the heirs female (without division) of James Cunningham, their second lawful son, and their heirs male—then of the said William Dick and the other sons in succession, then of the said John Cunningham; and then of the heirs female of the said Sir William and Lady Janet, and their heirs male—Whom failing the heirs female without division of the daughters of the said James Cunningham and his younger brothers successively according to their ages and births—Whom all failing, the heirs whomsoever of the said Lady Janet Dick by any other marriage—Whom failing to Helen Sydserf, eldest daughter of Mr. John Sydserf of Collegehead and the deceased Helen Dick his spouse, sister of the said late Sir James Dick, and her lawful heirs male—Whom failing to Alexander Gordon, lawful son of Mr. George Gordon, writer in Edinburgh, and the deceased Janet Dick, sister of the said deceased Sir James Dick, and his heirs male whomsoever—Whom failing, to William Dick, only lawful son now in

[1] *Old Scottish Communion Plate*, by the Rev Thomas Burns, p. 233.

life of the deceased William Dick of Braid, and (Elizabeth) Duncan his spouse, and his heirs whomsoever—Whom failing, the nearest and lawful heirs whomsoever of the deceased Sir James Dick, of the lands of Priestfield, Loch adjoining, lands of Cameron, and Corstorphine, and Whitehouse (under exceptions). [Here follow a great many declarations and provisions.] These lands were possessed by Sir James Dick of Prestonfield and resigned by his procurators on the 29th November inst., in favour of his said daughter, and her heirs. To be held of the Crown for payment annually, for Priestfield of a pair of gloves, and 20s. for the teinds for relief of the heirs and successors of John Lord Holyroodhouse—for the patronage of the Chapel and lands of Cameron one penny—and for Corstorphine, etc., one penny, in name of blench, if asked.' Dated at Edinburgh 29th November 1735.

NOTE XI

CHARTER TO GEORGE LAUDER OF BASS

(Register of the Great Seal, vol. 1593-1608, No. 688.)

AT Holyroodhouse 21st March 1591, King James the Sixth, for himself, and as administrator and tutor of his son Henry, Prince and Steward of Scotland, Duke of Rothesay, Earl of Carrick, Lord of the Isles and of the barony of Renfrew, grants to his familiar councillor, Mr. George Lauder of Bass, in liferent, and to George Lauder, his son and heir apparent, and the lawful heirs male to be procreated of his body, whom failing, to the said Mr. George and his heirs male bearing the arms and surname of Lauder, and assignees whomsoever, heritably, the lands of Beill, otherwise the carucate of Pitcokis on the north side of the water of Beill, the lands of Johniscleuch and Cluttis [? Clintis], with the fortalice, manor place and mills of Beill, tenants, etc., the lands of Poppill called Lauders lands and Haitleis lands otherwise Quhitlawis lands, Newhall, with tenants, etc.; £42 of annual rent from the said land of Newhall, and from the lands of Ballingrug, Hawdene, Hewmurcroce, Wodeheid, and Wodfitt, in the constabulary of Haddington and shire of Edinburgh; the lands of Edgrenetoun (Eddringtoun) with the fishings of Eddirmouth and Coillistaill, with the mills, tenants, etc.; the lands and mill of Mersingtoun, and mill lands thereof, with tenants, etc., in the shire of Berwick; the lands of Wester Spott, Grenedenheid and Nukis, with tenants, etc.; the lands of Petcokkis, both east and west parts thereof, lying on the south side of the water of Beill, with the advocation of the church and prebendary of Petcokkis and of the chaplainry called Burnehousis; and the husband land called Blaklawis in the town and territory of Stentoun: granting likewise to the said Mr. George and Elizabeth Hepburne, spouses, in liferent, and to the said George, younger, and his heirs aforesaid, heritably, the lands of Craig, of Ballugan, with tenants, etc.: granting also to the said Mr. George in liferent, and to the said George, younger, and his above mentioned heirs heritably, the lands called the Wardlands of Tynninghame, Grenespott, Briggis Easter and Wester, Baxterland otherwise Ducat-aiker, with the principal mansion, fortalice, and dovecot of Tynninghame situated upon Wardlaw; the lands called Lochhousis, extending to two husband lands, six acres pertaining to them in the town of Tynninghame (upon part of which the said manor place and others are built), with tenants, etc.; the lands of Scowgall, with tenants, etc.; the lands of Knowis, with the mill, a piece of land called Downykerishill, the fishing on the water of Tyne adjoining the lands of Knowis, four diets of fuel in the muir of the mains of Tunnynhame, three brewery lands in the town of Tunnynghame, with the maltkill, etc., and two husband lands in the Inche, in the barony of Tunnynghame, constabulary of Haddington and shire of Edinburgh ; the lands of Easter Penkaitland, with the mill, and advocation of the chaplainry called . . . . in the parish church of North Berwick, with tenants, etc. ; the lands of Stentoun, of Dewchary in the constabulary of Haddington and shire of Edinburgh, which in addition to Knowis and Blaklawis, Mr. George Knowis, Walter Henrisoun of Dungrene, Writer to His Majesty's Signet, Blaklawis, James Douglas, baker, burgess of Haddington, and Margaret Gibsoun, his spouse, resigned at the Palace of Holyrood in favour of the said Mr. George, and which the King, for the service rendered by the said Mr. George and his predecessors without default, and for payment of a composition, granted of new to the said persons with the liberty of pasturing their cattle and of digging turf and fuel, faill and divot, upon all parts of the east and west common muirs of Lammremure, called the Common muir of the Earl of March, and with the pertinents of Stentoun and Dewcharie, viz., Rammersyde, Mikill-rig, Lichous, with the woods called Pressmannane Akkiesyde and Dodd ; and he incorporated the same excepting the Wardlands and others above enumerated as far as Lochhousis, which remain as part of the barony and regality of Tynninghame) into the free barony of Beill, ordaining the fortalice and Manor Place thereof to be the principal messuage ; and he declared that the lands of Knowis, Inche, and Scowgall shall remain subject to the regality of Tynninghame just as if they had not been comprehended in the said incorporation, and that, if need be, it shall be lawful to the said Mr. George to sell the said lands or an annual rent from the same, and that it shall be lawful to the said Mr. George during his lifetime only to redeem the foresaids from George, younger, by payment or consignation of ten crowns of gold, or of any part of these ten at different times, paying one crown at each time, within the church of St. Giles at Edinburgh, at that place where the tomb of James, Earl of Moray, is erected, upon premonition of eight days, consignation being made in the hands of the treasurer or dean of guild of the burgh of Edinburgh, to be held, the lands of Stentoun and Ducharie, of the Prince and Steward of Scotland, and the rest of the King; Paying for Beill (and so forth as far as Mersingtoun) three pairs of gilt spurs and four pennies of silver in name of blench ; for Stentoun, etc., one penny of silver in name of blench farm ; for Wester Spott, etc., £15, and 10s. of augmentation, with the other feu duties, if any be, and with duplication of the duty on the entry of heirs ; for Petcokkis, £20, and 20s. of augmentation, with the other feu duties (etc., as above) ; for Blaklaws 29s. and 6d. of augmentation, with duplication (etc., as above), in name of feu farm and for the other rights and services due and customary to be paid : Moreover the King has taxed the ward and nonentry of Craig and Ballowgoun at 350 merks, of Easter Pencaitland at 400 merks, of Wairdelandis with the fortalice, etc., at 7½ merks, of Lochhousis at 30 merks, of Grenespot, Briggis Easter and Wester at 7½ merks, of Skowgall at 150 merks, of Knowis at £60, extending in whole to 1000 merks annually (the retoured duties extending to 178 merks or thereby), and the relief of the same to 178 merks, and the marriage duty at 5000 merks. Witnesses as in other charters. (xli. 361.)

NOTE XII

EXTRACTS FROM 'THE LOADSTAR, OR DIRECTORY TO THE NEW WORLD AND TRANSFORMATIONS.'

'THE King's Majesty shall be counselled to follow forth and continue his Revocation, to exact his new Impositions, Taxes, Subsidies, Annuities, and what else may procure him the Hatred of his Subjects.'
'The King's Majesty shall be counselled, by Virtue of his Royal Prerogative, to change the Service of the Church of Scotland, and to transform it into that of England. And the People

of Scotland by those selfsame men who move the King to bring in the English Service Book into the Church of Scotland shall raise the People of Scotland to storm at it, resist and oppose it.'

'Men shall be placed about the King's Majesty who shall not suffer him to have any Knowledge, Intelligence, or Verity of the Grievances of his Subjects.'

'The Prelates, and such of the Churchmen as adhere unto them, shall be in all places most contumeliously abused by the Commons and Rascality.'

'A League and Covenant shall be drawn up between some Gentlemen first, after imitated by some Noblemen, for mutual Defence one of another, and after the like shall be urged upon the People by Way of Religion.'

'The Confession of the Scottish Faith, subscribed by King James and his Household, Anno 1580 (being a Trial of Religion rather than a confession of Faith consisting of Negatives), is a sure Foundation and Introduction to this New League.'

'That all such who will not subscribe this Confession and Introduction to whatever shall be proceeded upon, shall be holden for Papists—Men loving or affecting Old Rites and Superstition.'

'They shall be denied Civil Conversation, and if it be possible not admitted to the Sacrament of the Lord's Supper.'

'The most sly and eloquent Ministers shall essay the universal subscription of this Confession; suppressing still that there is anything intended against the present form of Ecclesiastical Government, but refer all to a General Assembly.'

'The Scottish Commanders in Germany shall be in Readiness, if the King oppose, to come over to the Defence of the Country, and for the Liberty of the Subject.'

'The King shall make a Shew to levy Armies, but shall be kept in England till the Parliament conclude what the Nobles desire.'

'The Ministers shall give a Roll of all their Parishoners able to bear Arms.'

'All shall be sworn to obey what is decreed in General Assembly, and for that to expose their Estate, Persons, and what they hold dearest.'

'The Bishopricks shall be distributed to the Noblemen and Courtiers.'

'To beat down and raze to the ground the Castles and Strong Holds of all Gentlemen and others of the contrary Party, which can but serve for Retreats and Receptacles of Robbers, etc.'

'Because Men are inconstant, and, imagining Danger, may turn Apostates from the good Cause, the Oath of the Union would be renewed by all Noblemen, Barons, Gentlemen, and Burgesses.'

'That Preachers be chosen, the fittest in the Presbyteries, for the Army—not too learned, but Men who have greater Fancy than Judgment, vehement and zealous in their Utterance, and who dare sometimes play the Souldiers to Keep the Army in the Fear of GOD and exhort them to Service, comforting them in Extremities.'

'That all Swearing and Blasphemies be discharged, under grievous Punishment, through the Whole Camp.'

CONSIDERATIONS TO THE PARLIAMENT, *Sept.* 1639

'THAT whatever hath been done by the Clergy, Noblemen, Barons, Gentlemen and Burgesses in Scotland during these late Troubles, shall be for ever holden, estimate, and accounted Good Service to the Crown.'

'That it shall be lawful, in time of Trouble and Necessity, for the Provost of Edinburgh to offer up his prayers in the Cathedral Church by Shot of Pistols, which are more Conform to the Times than Organs.'

'That Bickering upon the Sunday shall be lawful against Coaches in the High Streets, provided there be either Bishop, New Counsellor, or *not Covenanter* in them.'

'That not only Noblemen, Barons, Gentlemen, and Town's Magazine-houses be furnished

APPENDIX

with Arms, but every Burgess' House, every Farmer's and Tenant's, to be ready at all Occasions to arise and defend themselves, and

'That in Time of War, it shall be lawful, for the Weal of the Kingdom, to the Noblemen, Barons, etc., to choose a *Dictator, providing he can neither read nor write.*'

'That if our old Enemies of England invade this Kingdom, it shall be lawful to us to renew our old League again with the Kingdom of France.'

'That Bastardy shall not hereafter derogate from any Privilege of the Kingdom, Honour or Reputation of the Name of the Lords; but whether Lord, Baron, or Gentleman, without the Bar in the Blazoning of his Arms, he shall still, after the great Service of this Time, be repute, holden, and decerned legitimate, neither shall any King claim their lands, possessions, or other Substance thereby.'

'That Buchanan's Chronicle shall be translated into the Vulgar Scottish, and read in the Common Schools; and the Books of Apocrypha being taken away from the Bible, his book *De Jure Regni* be in the Place thereof insert.'

'That if any man be so malicious to call Plundering Robbery, or any breach of the Ten Commandments, he stand Three Days in a white sheet at the Church Doors.'

'That it shall be lawful for the King to establish Bishops; but it shall also be lawful to the chosen People of our good Towns to astonish them or stone them, as common Enemies of the Country, and be rewarded for the same by the Presbyteries.'

'That Desks or Pews in the Paroch Churches of the Country be not granted but to Noblemen, Magistrates, and Gentlemen, holding *in capite* their Lands of the King.'

'That a constant Fashion of Apparel be determined and resolved upon; and not only the Wearers of any other Fashion, but the Artificers, when they shall happen to be found, shall be fined; excepting always the Church Men, who shall have Liberty to wear the old Fashion of Geneva Hats and Apparel.'

'That the Statue of King James, superstitiously erected within the Porch of the Chief Gate of Edinburgh, be taken down, and solemnly buried beside the Body of King James the Fifth in Holyrood-house.'

'That all Tombs, Monuments, in which there are any Images, especially these in the Common Burial Place of Edinburgh, be demolished, as bearing Resemblances of Ancient Idolatry.'

'That all Bells of Steeples, excepting Two or Three (at the most), be taken down and transfounded into Pieces of Ordnance; especially the superstitious Bells of Holyrood-house, and the Old College Church of Aberdeen.'

'That the Organs in the Chappel of Holyrood-house be taken away, or the Chappel with the Organ.'

'That the Old Translation in Verse of the Psalms, which was in the Threescore six year of God, be sung, and none else, it being even approved by our little Children and most ignorant Persons; and all Printers and Booksellers be discharged to print or sell any others.'

'That all Bishops' Houses, Concierges, Abbays, and Nunries, be made Places to entertain Souldiers, and their rents be imployed for the maintenance of Arms, the Prior or Abbot possessing them only for his lifetime, or during a Lease or Tack given by the State.'

'That the Tour of Leith be more strongly fortified, and that walls be raised about the old castle of Restalrig, Pilrig, Broughty, Warriston, Bonintoun, and many waste Houses within the town be pulled down to that effect.'

'That the former year's Provost of Edinburgh shall be still Captain of Leith, and shall have a guard of 24 to defend his Person.'

'That Leith shall have the Privileges of a City of Refuge, or the ancient Places called Sanctuaries, no man daring trouble another or molest any for whatsoever crime, except *Lese Majesty, against the State*, and *not covenanting.*'

'That the Beards of all Judges, as Lords of Session, Commissaries, Sheriffs and

APPENDIX

Bailies, shall be long, except the Provost of Touns and the Chief City, who shall have them short.'

'That all women be discharged wearing of Plaids, excepting in cold weather, and Time of Bickering in the Chief City.'

'That all Purple Robes be discharged, being old Remains of the Idolatrous Government, as well to be worn in Parliament as Session, and every Judge to ride or sit in such a Fashion of Apparel as his Taylor shall think most convenient.'

'That Heraulds, Officers of Arms, and other Messengers, shall not speak at any Market-Cross before they open their mouths.'

'That no Nobleman, Baron, Gentleman or Burgess, send his Children to other countries without Liberty from the Council.'

'That no man wear a *Gregorian* or Periwig unless he have a Testimonial from a Town Clerk that he is either Bald, Sickly or asham'd of white Hairs.'

'That School Masters be placed in the remotest High-Lands to instruct Youth in Civility and the English Language.'

'That no man stand bare-headed in the Presence-Chamber or Parliament House of Scotland, or before any Chair of State, since hereby open Idolatry is committed, and a worship of Lions and Unicorns.'

'That the COVENANT be holden and esteem'd in all Times coming the First Evangel ; and Anathema be pronounced against all contradictors.'

'That the Books of Wallace and King Robert the Bruce be printed over again, against our old Enemies of England, and pensions be given to some learned Rimers to write XII Books of our Expedition and Victory at Dunslaw, or DUNSLAIDOS, Libri 12.'

'That all Chronicles be burnt which are not approved by the Clerk of our General Assembly.'

'That none in Lochaber wear Castor-Hats or Velvet Breeches.'

'That no man Swear the oath of Supremacy, except in England ; yet it shall be lawful for any man to swear it to his wife if he please.'

'That there be neither the Name of Bishop, nor Superintendent in our Kirk, but the Overseers of Ministers, Deacons, and Elders, be named Duniwassels of the Kirk, being a Word far from the Language of the Beast of Rome.'

'That no Man call a Contract a COVENANT, under such Pain as is decreed against the Prophanation of the Sabbath.'

'That no Covenanter in his Travels abroad, or Abode at Home, shall learn to dance, or at least practise Dancing, under the Pain of the Transgression of the 7th Commandment.'

'That it shall be lawful for all Gentlemen-Covenanters to kiss all Gentlewomen at all Assemblies, especially the Night-Conventions, under Pain to be reputed and holden as Cowards amongst the Ladies.

'That there shall be *Cover-feu* Bells rung in all best Towns of Shires, after the Ringing of which no man shall be found upon the Streets, except he justify himself to have been in a Tavern, or at Clandestine Meeting of Holy Sisters, under the Pain of Ten Merks.'

'That all Gardeners, Gentlewomen or others, which have any Fruit-Trees named from Bishops, shall either change their Name, or dig them up by the Roots, in Failure of which not only these Trees, but the whole Orchard may be lawfully plundered.'

'That Coal-Pits, Lime Quarries, within Fourty Foots of the King's Highways, be filled up, and such like pernicious Holes, under Pain of 10 lib. from the Master of the Ground, or in case of Leases, from the Farmer.'

'That Lanterns be hung in the High Streets and passages of the great Towns, from seven till Ten in the Night ; from the First of November to the First of February.'

'That the Church-Race marry only among themselves, Ministers' Sons upon Ministers' Daughters : and it shall be lawful, for the Procreation of this Race, and the number of She-Children, that any Ministers' Son shall take unto him Two Wives.'

'That if a King of Scotland remaining in England, every Five years at least come not to Scotland, the First Five Years he shall lose his Imposts and Taxations; the Second Five Years his Wards and Feu-duties; the Third his whole Properties, and the Demesne of the Crown of Scotland; which shall be kept and religiously laid up to his successor.'

'That if the King shall not approve these our Acts they shall be observed most strictly amongst our selves, without his Approbation; and the Contraveeners punished by consent Publick.'

'That it shall be lawful for Servants to reveal their Masters, Children their Parents, Wives their Husbands, in the Matter of the Breach of these Acts.'

'That an Act of Parliament be made for keeping all the Acts of former Parliaments.'

'That it shall be lawful for the School-Boys in all Towns and Villages, every Seventh Year, once, to take the Schools against their Masters, put them out, and in their Places appoint new Doctors, Under Doctors, Masters, for the space of Twenty Days, in perpetual Remembrance of our Happy and Blessed Relief from the Ecclesiastick and Episcopal Government.'

NOTE XIII

'MEMORANDUM FOR SIR JOHN LAUDER anent the patent—and also for a libell agt. etc. 1690. Holograph of Sir John Lauder, Lord Fountainhall.' (*Signed*) T. D. LAUDER.

'Memorandr. for Sr. John Lauder.'

'To raise a lybell att privy Counsell att the instance of Sr. John Lauder, Mr. William, and Andrew Lauder his brother germain, against Margaret Ramsay, their step-mother, George Ramsay of Idington, her fayther; Doctor Robt. Trotter her brother in law, and their wives; and J. L. husband to said Margaret Ramsay, for their untruths; making mention and complaining, that albeit by the lawes of God, nature and nations that be, and require of a high nature; yet for a wyfe, by herself and her friends, insolently and impudently to abuse and obtend her husband and by presumptuous force and mastery to impose things upon him downright contraire to his honour and inclinations, and, that their defaming and oppressing of His Maiteis leidges, and the sowing discord betwixt parents and children, and their robbing persons of their birthright, and their depriving husbands of their free dissposall of their properties, and the liberty of their persons, are crimes by all laws, divine and human, highly punishable.

'Yet true it is that albeit John Lauder of Fountainhall hath lived to a great age, and born several honourable offices in affairs publick, and gained reputation during the whole tract of his life, and that the complainers his children of the first marriage had never done anything to merit his displeasure nor unworthy in itself, but had carried always dutifully and obediently to him, yet the said Margaret Ramsay his present wyfe has done what in her lay to tarnish and blacken, now in his old age, that honour and reputation he had so justly gathered, by giving him his *delinimentis notabilis* against the Complainers descended of his own bowells, and so farr as she having wearied him by her incessant importunity and ambition for many years, to procure and accept a Knight-baronet's patent, and he never imagining that it was to be taken in any other terms but in favour of himself and the Complainers his own males; yet by the fraudulent assistance of the said George Ramsay, and Doctor Trotter, she caused frame the said patent to descend after her husband's decease to George Lauder her son of the second marriage, a child who, as he can have done nothing as yet to merit it, so has no state wherewith to support such a dignity—all that is provided to the whole children of the marriage being but fifty thousand marks

APPENDIX

—albeit his mother resolves to sacrifice the other little children for aggrandizing him, yet the whole is no competency, as such an honour requires—and so soon as the said John Lauder understood this shocking (conspiracy) of his wife and her friends he did openly declare his dissent to it, and gave the Complainers a Declaration under his hand dishonouring the same, and appointing another patent to be obtained running in the natural channel of his lawful heirs — and then her relations above mentioned, were so ashamed of what they had done, that they declared in presence of many famous witnesses that it was most reasonable it should be altered and swore hands on this, that they should never oppose the same—notwithstanding of all which the said Margaret Ramsay, without any regard to her husband's honour and inclination, so frequently reiterated both by word and writing, and fully resolved to have that patent to descend to her son whatever it should cost—She runs to the house of Mr. Robert Lauder (in whose hands the said patent was put in order to be testified) in the month of May 1688 att eleven o'clock of night, with several other of her accomplices, intending by force to have taken the patent from him, and threatening to get his heart's blood if he didn't deliver it presently—And thus by order of Privy Counsel to prevent these violent courses, it was ordained to be put in the Clerk's hands till the affair was heard—Yet in open affront and contempt of the Counsell's authority she procured a new patent from Court by misrepresenting the Complainer as an enemy to the late King James, and that therefore any honour bestowed upon his fayther ought not to descend to him, and so high did her malice run, that she made ye interruption of the patent to terminat on her four sons, (tho' there was never a patent but it fell to all the sons of the first person, and failing issue of one, always to the other,) and so frighted her husband to comply with her unreasonable and unjust demands, she threatened that she would stab herself if that patent were not taken to her sons, and that she would kill herself if ever she saw any of the Complainers come near the house, and if he did not absolutely discharge them his presence ; most wickedly proposing by this means to effectuate her rapacious designs of ingrossing all her husband's estate and of obtaining contradictorie and dishonourable papers from him, that for peace sake he might declare in favours of her son, and so working upon his tenderness that she might not put violent hands on herself nor resort to those dreadful threats she had uttered in her frantic transports ; and which the Earl of Lauderdale and others had come to the said John Lauder to speak in behalf of the Complainers, and that he had told him that he could not but love his children of the first marriage for they had never disobliged him, and that he was convinced it was most unreasonable to rob them of the primogeniture and cast a blot of infamy on them without any cause—She was so enraged at this fatherly declaration that she tore the clothes off her body and the hood off her head and swore fearful oaths that she would drown herself, and her children ; and frequently abused the Complainers, and defamed and traduced them in all places ; and threatened that she hoped to live to see them all rooted out, they and their posterity off the face of the earth — and her children would succeed to all—and she studied by all the diabolical acts that feminine malice could inspire to alienate the said John Lauder's affection from his children, and to sow discord and division between them, and by dread and terror to fright him from converse with them, tho' that be one of the greatest gratifications of aged parents ; and when she could not get them absolutely debarred from paying that natural respect and duty they owed to their fayther, yet to render the converse and freedom altogether uneffectual, and to make him a close prisoner she constantly intruded herself in the room that she might hear all that past, and block up all information of their trials coming to his ears, and refused to remove when her husband bade her, but most impiously, insolently and impudently followed him to other rooms, when he retired to shun her; depriving him of all that natural liberty and freedom every man ought to enjoy in his own house ; and in all lawful things as he had the power of commanding so it was the duty to oblige

APPENDIX 405

and obey, seeing by the law of God and the Statutes of the land the husband is Lord, Head and Ruler over his house—and it was a subverting of the law of nature in her for to assume the government and power over her husband, and to preclude him from all means of knowing the truth, beseiging disquieting and molesting him perpetually with lies of his dutiful children to that height that it made him oft declare with much sorrow that her marriage made him wearie of his life. Knowing that the surest way to compass her evil design was to debar the Complainers from paying the natural duty to their fayther, and then to misrepresent them and incense and stir him up against them. She and her friends having access at all hours, and dividing themselves so that he should never be without one or other of them as a spy, and consequently they had opportunities in instilling into him what they pleased—and particularly that *all* his Estate was little enough to bestow upon her son who was to succeed him in the title of Knight-Baronet—For, as the laws of all nations hath, for securing husbands against such impious women, declared all donations made by husbands to wives revokable, and which in no case was ever more necessary than here, the said John Lauder being more liable than any man to the wicked and unjust suggestions, he being of a great age, and one who comes not abroad out of his own house, and so is continually obnoxious and lyable to these villanous threats and transgressions. As all men should be left free in the disposal of their own, and the common law hath declared imposing in such cases punishable with the forfeiture and amission of that which was so fraudulently acquired, and made them incapable of any benefit from what they had extorted by such concussion, and without such caution Mankind would not be secured nor the honour and interests of husbands hedged up and protected against the perversions and encroachments of their younger wives. And the Complainers as Children of the first marriage, and creditors, are not to be defrauded by subsequent children, who are less favourable in law than they—especially when the Matrimonial provisions are more than implemented to these younger children. And, George Ramsay the guidsire's design is to get himself and his friends to be the only managers of the affairs, because he has the greatest part of the means in his hands as debitor, that so he may dilapidate and embezzle what he pleases and defraud the Complainers, who will be the only persons who behoved to look to the welfare, standing, and protection of these children, and for recovery and seeking of the means. And, for carrying on this designe the said Mr. Ramsay broke open her husband's Cabinets, and searched his whole papers, and forced him to alter his Testament, and insert only her own friends as tutors to her children—who on the event will find their interests more tenderly assured by the complainers than by her pretended friends, who are truly the direct parties having the name and estate in their hands.

'And, if riots of this nature were in the Court connived at, no man at all as to his goods or Writs would be secure against the insolent rapine of a wyfe having the desire and opportunity to defraud others.

'And, as if all these practises were not sufficient, the said Margaret Ramsay has these many years pilfered and squandered and given away the said John Lauder's means and Estate, for maintaining her father and said Doctor Trotter her brother-in-law, and their families, in bed, board, and in merchants' accounts and clothing, so that he has to spend upwards of 8000 marks per year on his family, tho' it is notoriously known that the same is keepit so privately that she does not bestow the half of it. And, as a further evidence of the conspiracies and Knavery among them to hurt and abuse the said John Lauder, Doctor Trotter (who was employed to procure the aforesaid pretended patent) did make him believe that he could not get it for less than 100 pounds sterling, as he had agreed with Mr. Thomson in the Canongate for 1000 marks ; and falsely and theftously kept 800 marks of it to himself—which theft and complication of breach of trust had many other crimes therein.' [Sidenote on margin :—'And yet he affirmed he had goten from him wholly 1800 marks without—until he was confronted with said Mr. Thomson. M. R. and G. R. have so far im-

APPENDIX

posed on said John Lauder that they caused him to give a bond for 600 marks though the several rents and (gifts) was sufficient to pay for his pretended attendance as a physician.']
'And when Mr. Thomson refused to deliver up the patent till the 1000 marks were paid (which was to be advanced out of the first and readiest of the few Rents owing by Eglintoun to the said John Lauder), they in a most base and dishonourable manner by their reproaching that honour and integrity, with which he has lived all his time—did impound (pawn) his silver plate, whereon his name and arms were graven—with the said Mr. Thomson, without the said John Lauder's Knowledge or privilege—and so little care had this unjust stepmother, and bad wyfe of her husband's and his children's fame, that she did oft pound the said silver work to Widow Cranstoun and others to remain as a pledge for money she borrowed to give to said George Ramsay her father, and Doctor Trotter her brother-in-law—not being ashamed for her base ends to bring her husband's fame and condition in question—whose ingenuity would have abhored the thoughts of such sordid and sneaking methods, tho' she would rather ruin his honour than want money for herself and friends to carry on their unworthy doings. And the Complainers solemnly protest, that nothing could have prevailed with them to have discovered the usage they have met with had it not been notoriously known already, and was it not to assert and vindicate their fayther's honour—and expose the above named persons—who ought and should be severely punished in their persons and goods, to the terror and example of others not to commit the like in time coming.'

At this point there is a pause in the Document, with the following note in French, and the translation, written on the margin :—

* ' *De Souvenir les bracelets faites du cheveux de A. R. de Wigton.*' * ' *That's to say, to remember the Bracelets made of the Hair of Andrew Ramsay of Wigton.*'

The libel Case is then continued in the neat, small German-looking characters of Sir John Lauder's own handwriting—though evidently at a much later date, judging from the colour of the Ink—

'And, to all the former acts of injustice and oppression the said Margaret Ramsay added a still farther, imposing on her said husband, so that he was prevailed on to purchase the lands of Idington from her father, and to take the rights to himself, and give in liferent to George Lauder her eldest son in feu—which same is most unjustly provided to his heirs whatsomever—so that failing of him and the other sons of that marriage these lands might fall and descend to their sisters—and which case has now existed by the *death of all the four sons of that marriage*—and whereof no example can be given that ever a parent provided lands to fall to his daughters, when he had sons in any other marriage. Many parents have preferred their daughters in their Estates, and excluded their own brothers from the procession, but never any parent preferred his daughters to his own sons—but all this was the effect of the influence and imposing—and no ways understood by her husband ; otherways he would never have consented to so unjust and unreasonable a conveyance, especially his daughters being competently provided and married without it. Like as this contrivance was made, and the disposition of the lands of Idington goten from the said John Lauder, he was truly on his deathbed, and never went to Kirk or market hereafter : and so, any conception that the Bailzie was drawn in, nor his acceptance thereof, could never prejudge the said Sir John Lauder's heir, to whose enorme hurt, loss and prejudice the same was ; and therefore ought and should be reduced at his instance, as well as being *infra trat* by imposition in manner aforesaid, as also *ex capite lecti.*'

It is evident from this Addendum that it was written after Bailie Lauder's death, which took place in 1692, having borne his title of Baronet scarcely six years.[1]

[1] Family Writs in Charter Chest.

NOTE XIV

HOLOGRAPH NOTES of SIR JOHN LAUDER, LORD FOUNTAINHALL, from the CHARTER CHEST of SIR THOMAS DICK LAUDER.

NOTE I.—'A note of my relations and branches by Isobell Eleis, my Mother.'

'I find in 1513 in the end of King James the 4th reign (it being unnecessary to mention any before, tho' Eleis' son assured me he could doe it for severall prior generations), one Alexander Elois merchand in Edin^r in his burgesse ticket of that date designed son to Patrick Elois Bailzie of Edin. This Alexander Elois had a son called Patrick after his goodsire, and this Patrick was also a merchand and Bailzie in Edin^r, and the first lands he acquired was Stanopmilnes, then Plewlands, Southsyde and Mortonhall, which he gave to his severall sons, being upwards of twenty thousand pounds sterling in lands and money. He was twice married; his first wife was Marion Inglis, daughter to James Inglis, merchand in Edin^r, and predecessor to the present Laird of Cramond. His 2nd wife was Isobel Seton, daughter to John Seton, son to the Seton of Parbroath in Fyffe. Which Isobel Seton's mother was called Margaret Nisbet, daughter to Adam Nisbet, merchand to King James 5th, and which Margaret Nisbet's mother was Madame Beatrix Ambrosia, daughter to Monsieur Ambroise, an Italian who was Secretary to Queen Mary of Lorraine, our King James 5th's relict.

'The said Adam Nisbet (of whom the Lairds of Dean, Craigintinny, Dirleton, etc., are all descended), having married this Dame Ambrosia one of the Queen Marie of Lorraine's Maids of Honor, and had by her besides other children the aforesaid Margaret Nisbet, which Margaret being married (as beforesaid) to the said John Seton, son to the Laird of Parbroath, was mother to the said Isobel Seton, and which Isobel Seton was married to Patrick Eleis, which Patrick Elois, amongst other children, had Mr. Alexander Eleis, so called after his goodsire, Patrick's father, and to whom he gave the Lands of Mortonhall.

'This Mr. Alexander Eleis of Mortonhall married Elizabeth Edward, daughter to Nicol Edward, Dean of Gild of Edin^r., grandchild to another Nicol Edward, provost of Edin^r., in 1592, being of a most antient descent in that Burgh, and who built these great lodgings in the middle of Niddrie's Wynd, where I have seen the said Nicol Edward's name and arms on the lintell of a Chimney with this Anagram on his name, in french, "Va d'un vol à Christ," "goe with one flyght to Christ."

'Of this marriage between the said Mr. Alexander Eleis and Elizabeth Edward was Isobel Eleis borne, which Isobel Eleis was in 1645 married to John Lauder, merchand in Edin^r., afterwards designed Sir John Lauder of Fountainhall, who was lineally descended of the Lairds of Lauder of that Ilk, of which marriage and parents by God's appointment I am descended and sundry other sons, so, as I have brought forward my Mother's geneallogie, so to trace it back. Our maternal coat-of-arms is Eleis of Mortonhall, which is the same writ Stanopmylne and Southsyde, being a helmet on a spear (as is to be seen in Sir George M'Kenzie's book of Heraldrie, page 66).

'Then my mother's mother is the said Edward's arms, her father, Mr. Alex. Eleis' mother's arms is the said Setons of Parbroath and his mother's goodame is the said Nisbet of Dean and his goodame's mother's arms is the coat armorial of Monsieur Ambroise the Italian Secretary, which we cannot well know without consulting the books published in France and Italy containing the bearings of these nations, and what were the gentilian armes of the Ambrosian Sirname.'

NOTE II.—'A note of the branches of my paternal coat.'

'In regard we had occasion to touch thir branches in the blazoning my father's coat and painting the arms at his funerall, therefor I shall do no more but name them.

'My Father was by descent a cadet of the Lairds of Lauder of that Ilk, so that if he had not taken out his own special coat by the name of Lauder of Newington or Fountainhall, he would have borne Lauder of that Ilk arms with the distinction of a 2nd Brother.

'My Father's Mother was Janet Ramsay, daughter to David Ramsay of the Hillhead; which David was a son of Ramsay of Polton, who was come of Dalhousie, so his 2nd coat was by the name of Ramsay of Polton.

'The said Janet Ramsay's mother was Sinclair of the family of Roslin, so his 3rd coat was Sinclair of Roslin.

'Andrew Lauder (my father's father), his mother was Jean Ballanden, daughter to the Ballandens of Lasswade, who were descended of the Ballandens of Brughton. His 4th bearing is by the name of Ballanden of Brughton.

'And there needs no more than 4 coats; yet to add one more, William Lauder, father to the said Andrew Lauder my goodsire (which William was the Laird of Lauder's son), his mother was Mary Macdougall, daughter to the Laird of Mackairston, so by my grandsire's mother our 5th coat would be Mackairston arms, which Sir G. MacKenzie in his Heraldry, page 3rd, rolls us to be a Lyon collared with a broken crown about his neck in memory of killing the tyrant Notharus by Debalius.'

NOTES from a MS. in the Advocates' Library, by Sir GEORGE M'KENZIE, anent LAUDER and HALTON.

(This paper is also in Lord Fountainhall's handwriting.)
'Collection of the most Remarkable accts. that relate to the families drawn from their own Charters and of the Auchinleck Writs, and from the Chartularies of the Abbacies of Scotland wherein they are Mortifiers or witnesses in Mortifications, and from our Histories, and in which many passages of our Histories are corrected from the Auchinleck Charters, and writts of their family.

'With an account of the Arms and the Reasons of them.' By Sir George M'Kenzie,
MS. Advocates' Library, Lauder.
'Lauder beareth argent an griefflie and sallient sable with wings Displayed, beiked gules. The Chieff was Lauder of Lauder Toure. Bass dispute for it. But they say the eldest Charter of Bass bore Joanin Lauder filio, Q^{do}. Genito de Lauder Toure. Halton is certainly descended of Lauder Toure, but soe ancient that one of his predecessors was at the Holy Wars with David, Brother to K. Wm., and got for his Crest a Saracen's Head and a sword. The chiefe of the name now is the said Lauder of Halton in West Lothian, whose predecessor Sir Allan Lauder of Halton in the days of K. Robt. the Bruce, acquired ye lands of Halton from John Halton of that Ilk, and was confirmed in them by the said King. He married Elizabeth Campbell, daughter to — Campbell of Lochaw, predecessor to the Earl of Argyle, and was killed with the Lord Douglas in Spain as he returned from the Holy Grave.[1]

'These of your Family have been very considerable Barons ever since the time they were heritable Baillies of Lauderdale, till Alexander Lauder of Halton did quit of the office in favour of John Maitland, Lord Thirlestane, Chancellor of Scotland, whose sister he had married.

'Lauder of Halton had no sons, and gave his 2nd daughter and his Estate to Charles Maitland, now Earl of Lauderdale, brother-germain and heir to the Duke of Lauderdale, and sometime Treasurer Deputy and one of the Members of the College of Justice. Which Earl of Lauderdale has disponed the same to Sir John Maitland, alias Lauder, his second son, one of the Senators of the College of Justice, who married Lady (Margaret) Cunninghame' ('only child of Alexander, 10th Earl of Glencairn, and heir of line to that ancient family).'

Dick-Lauder Charter Chest.

[1] This we have proved to be quite a mistake, as Sir Alan received eight charters after that date.

NOTE XV

CATALOGUE OF THE FAMILY PORTRAITS AT THE GRANGE HOUSE

1. Sir William Dick of Braid in his robes as Provost of Edinburgh in 1639.
2. Sir William Dick of Braid, Knight, visited in prison by his wife, Elizabeth Morrison of Prestongrange (and their five sons and daughters). He died in prison 19th Dec. 1655.
3. William Dick, first Baron of Grange.
4. Janet M'Math, wife of William Dick, first Baron of Grange; died 1678.
5. William Dick, second Baron of Grange, son of Janet M'Math; died 1695.
6. Miss Janet Leslie, first wife of William Dick, second Baron of Grange, and daughter of Sir John Leslie of Newton.
7. Sir John Leslie of Newton, one of the Senators of the College of Justice; younger son of Andrew, fourth Earl of Rothes.
8. Miss Charles Leslie, daughter of Robert Leslie of Kinclaven, second wife of William Dick, second Baron of Grange.
9. Hon. Catherine Basset, married on Robert Leslie, and mother of Miss Charles Leslie, wife of second Baron of Grange.
10. Colonel Leslie, son of the Hon. Robert Leslie of Kinclaven and the Hon. Catherine Basset; lived part of 17th and 18th centuries.
11. William Dick, third Baron of Grange, 1755.
12. Dame Isobel Dick, heiress of Grange, wife of Sir Andrew Lauder of Fountainhall; died 1758.
13. Sir Andrew Lauder, fifth Baronet of Fountainhall, husband of Dame Isobel Dick; died 1769.
14. Sir John Lauder, Lord Fountainhall; died Sept. 1722.
15. Janet Ramsay, first wife of Lord Fountainhall, daughter of Sir Andrew Ramsay of Abbotshall.
16. Sir Andrew Ramsay of Abbotshall, fifteen years Lord Provost of Edinburgh; died 1688.
17. Rev. Andrew Ramsay of Abbotshall, Rector of the University of Edinburgh.
18. James Seaton, first Baron of Pitmedden, elder brother of Lord Pitmedden; died unmarried 1667.
19. Sir Alexander Seton, Lord Pitmedden, father of the wife of William Dick, third Baron of Grange and also of Sir John Lauder of Fountainhall.
20. Elizabeth Seton, eldest daughter of Lord Pitmedden, and wife of Sir Alexander Wedderburn.
21. Margaret Seton, second daughter of Lord Pitmedden, wife of Sir John Lauder of Fountainhall.
22. Anne Seton, third daughter of Lord Pitmedden, and wife of William Dick, third Baron of Grange; received Prince Charles at 'the Grange House' in 1745.
23. Isabel Seton, fourth daughter of Lord Pitmedden, received Prince Charles at 'the Grange House' in 1745; died unmarried at the age of 90.
24. Jane Seton, fifth daughter of Lord Pitmedden, received Prince Charles at the Grange House in 1745.
25. Dame Rachel Dunsmuir, daughter of David Dunsmuir, advocate; married to Sir John Wedderburn, first Baron of Blackness.
26. Matilda Wedderburn, a daughter of Sir J. Wedderburn of Blackness; 15th century.
27. Rachel Wedderburn, only daughter of Sir Alexander Wedderburn, second Baron of Blackness, and Dame Elizabeth Seton, 1777.
28. Sir John Wedderburn, third Baron of Blackness, unmarried; died in 1772.
29. Sir John Cockburn of Ormiston, painted in 1670.

APPENDIX

30. Adam Cockburn of Ormiston ; three times Lord Justice-Clerk.
31. Lady Susan Hamilton, daughter of fourth Earl of Haddington, wife of Adam Cockburn of Ormiston, great-grandmother of Dame Charles Anne Cumin, Lady Dick Lauder.
32. Rev. Patrick Cumin of Relugas, Professor of Divinity in the University of Edinburgh ; grandfather of Dame Charles Anne Cumin, Lady Dick Lauder (in crayon by Coates) ; died 1st April 1776.
33. Sir Thomas Dick Lauder, 7th Baronet of Fountainhall, and his wife, Lady Charles Anne Dick Lauder, by the late W. Nicholson, R.S.A.
34. Mary Cumin, wife of Hon. T. Butler, by Sir P. Lely.
35. Mary Butler, daughter of Hon. T. Butler (by Coates).
36. Renowned General David Leslie, first Lord of Newark, fifth son of Lord Lindores.
37. Jane Yorke, wife of General Leslie, and daughter of Sir John Yorke ; 17th century.
38. Dame Barbara Stewart, mother of Mrs. Lauder of Huntley.

There are also a few historical portraits in the Drawing-room :—
Shakespeare, by Jameson.
Oliver Cromwell, by do.
Sir Walter Raleigh, by do.
Ben Jonson, by do.
Villiers, Duke of Buckingham, by Jansen.
A Burgomaster's Wife, by N. Maes, 1664.
A Musician—name unknown.
Relugas, by Gibb.
Four Allegorical paintings, and some fine old engravings.

NOTE XVI

CATALOGUE OF SIR THOMAS DICK LAUDER'S WORKS

'Lochandhu.' · 3 vols.
'Wolfe of Badenoch.' 2 vols.
'Highland Rambles.' 2 vols.
'Legendary Tales.' 3 vols.
'Morayshire Floods.'
'Gilpin.'
'Sir Wedale Price.'
'Queen's Progress in Scotland, 1842.'
Article on 'The Parallel Roads of Lochaber,' in *Transactions of Royal Society*, vol. ix. Part 1.
Articles in Thomson's *Annals of Philosophy* :—
'Of a Toad found in the Trunk of a Beech Tree.' Vol. vi. No. 31, p. 11, July 1815.
'Account of the Worm which infests the Stickleback.' Vol. vii. No. 38, p. 106, Feby. 1816.
'Account of the Aluminous Chalybeate Spring at Fountainhall.' Vol. vii. No. 43, p. 3, 1816.
'Account of the Aluminous Chalybeate Spring at Fountainhall.' No. 47, p. 341, Nov ; also
'Account of the late Earthquake in Scotland.' P. 364.
'Account of different Currents of Air observed at the same Time.' Vol. x. No. 55, p. 66, July 1817.
'On a Spiral Bar.' Vol. xi. No. 66, p. 438, June 1818.
'On the Fountainhall Chalybeate Spring.' Vol. xii. No. 68, p. 91, August 1818.

APPENDIX

Edinburgh Tales :—
   'Story of Farquharson of Inverey.' Vol. i. p. 403.
   'Donald Lamont.' Vol. ii. p. 70.
Articles in *Tait's Magazine* :—
   'Toryoscopy.' September 1832.
   'The Funeral of Sir Walter Scott, by an Eyewitness.' No. 8, November 1832.
   'Scottish Voters.' November 1832.
   'The Scottish Elections.' September 1837.
   'The Election of Scottish Peers.' October 1837.
   'What ought the Whigs to do?' November 1837.
   'The Eglinton Tournament.' November 1837.
   'Love, Jealousy and Vengeance.' January and February 1846.
   'Visit to Auch Melvich.' January 1847.
   'Scottish Rivers.' From May 1847 to April 1848.
   Afterwards collected into one volume, with preface by Dr. John Brown. Published by his daughter, Miss Cornelia Dick Lauder.
In *Chambers's Journal* :—
   'St. Symphorien de Lay.' Vol. iv. No. 208.
In *Scottish Annual* :—
   'Story of a Trip to Dieppe.' Vol. vi. No. 295.
   'The Little Apothecary.' Vol. vi. No. 306.
   'My Two Lodgings.' Vol. vii. No. 319.
   'Paris. The Bet.' Vol. vii. No. 321.
In *Blackwood's Edinburgh Magazine* :—
   'Anecdotes illustrative of the State of the Highlands after the Rebellion of 1745.' Vol. ii. p. 155, No. 8, November 1817.
   'Remarkable Instance of Second Sight.' Vol. iii. p. 18, No. 13, April 1818.
In *Constable's Magazine* :—
   'Scottish Pictures.' February 1822, p. 210.
Article in *Encyclopædia Britannica* (8th Edit.) :—
   'Ross-shire.'
Articles in Brewster's *Encyclopædia* :—
   'Inverness and Inverness-shire.'
In the *Miscellany of Natural History*, by Sir Thomas Dick Lauder and Captain Thomas Brown :—
   'Biographical Sketch of Baron Cuvier.'
   'The Intellectual and Imitative Faculties of Parrots.'

INDEX

ABBEY of the Holy Rood, 5.
Abbot Alwin, 3.
Abbots of Holyrood, 3.
Abbotsford, 87, 88, 89, 90.
Abercromby, Baron, 346.
Aberdour, 40.
Acrostic sonnet, 45.
Æneas Sylvius, 26, 219, 220.
Aitkyn, Edward, 182.
Albany, Duke of, 15.
Alexander I., 2.
Alexander II., 4.
Allan, Sir William P.R.S.A., 342.
Allan with the Red Jacket, 353.
Amateur theatricals, 330, 331.
Ambrosia, Beatrix, 407.
—— Monsieur, Secretary to Mary of Lorraine, 407.
Anderson, Marion, of Balram, 297.
Angus, Archibald, Earl of, 233, 268.
—— Earl of, 225.
—— Godfrey Umfraville, Earl of, 216.
—— Thomas Stewart, Earl of, 217.
Annabella, 169.
Annan, 164.
Anson, Hon. G. E., 345, 346.
Anster Fair, 212.
Apostle of the Lepers, 11.
—— —— Lothians, 190.
Arbroath, 32.
Argyll, Earl of, 296, 297, 299.
—— Duke of, 127.
Arthur's Seat, 5.
Assembly Hall, 344.
Auchinleck, Laird of, 137.
Auchinreoch, 24.
Augustine monks, 3.
Auldcathie, 167, 183.
Auldhame, 190, 192, 206.
Auld Kirk, Lauder, 168.
—— —— North Berwick, 155, 157, 178.
Ayton Castle, 332, 379.
Aytoun, 231.

BAILIES of the Muir, 12.
Bailieship of Lauderdale, 254, 255, 259.
Baillie, Joanna, 331.
Baird, Principal, 90, 322.

Baliol, Henry, 164.
—— John, 7, 162, 164, 166, 255.
Ballenden, Elizabeth or Jean, of Lasswade, 275, 289, 301, 408.
Balm Well, 68.
Balmain, 269, 279.
Balveny, John, Lord, 229.
Bannatine, Thomas, 48, 67, 68; his Will and Testament, 385, 386, 387, App.
Bannatyne Family, 386, 387.
Barnbougle Castle, 97, 98; Links, 99.
Baronetcy patent, Lauder, 293, 294.
Baronial bailies, 264.
Bass Rock, 151, 153, 155, 159, 180, 185, 189, 190, 195, 197, 198, 199, 200.
—— Burgess, 192.
—— Castle, 189, 191, 193, 194, 254.
—— Chapel, 181, 190.
—— Charter, 152, 160.
—— Lady, 197, 204, 209, 210, 220.
—— Prisons, 199.
—— Tenants, 202.
—— Well, 192.
Battles:—
 Almanza, 59.
 Bannockburn, 256.
 Beaugé, 215, 216, 224.
 Brig o' Dee, 69.
 Carberry Hill, 23, 181, 184, 193, 377.
 Culloden, 81.
 Flodden, 10, 11, 16, 233, 234, 278.
 Halidon Hill, 161, 162.
 Pinkie, 236.
 Prestonpans, 70.
 Sauchie-Burn, 177.
 Stirling Bridge, 155.
 Verneuil, 224.
Bawardies or Bawbardy, 235, 237.
Beaugné, Jean de, 191.
Beardie, 226.
Beaton, Cardinal, 9, 171.
—— James, Archbishop of St. Andrews, 371.
—— Mary, 97.
B il, Beill, or Bele, 177, 182, 183, 184, 185, 198.
Beilmouth, 284.
Bell of St. Giles, 13.
Belle:den, Annabella, 169, 241, 243.

INDEX

Bellenden, Dame Christian, Prioress, 17, 18, 19.
—— Sir Ludovick, 240.
Berwick Castle, 163, 174, 177.
—— Tower, 271.
Birsay, 34, 40.
Bishop's Palace, Cowgate, 171.
—— —— Glasgow, 169, 370.
—— —— Kirkwall, 33.
Black, Adam, publisher, 350-352, 356.
—— Canons, 3.
—— Craig, 5.
—— death, 11.
—— Turnpike, 23.
Blackford, 47, 59.
—— Hill, 11, 359.
Blackfriars' Wynd, 119.
Blew Gownis, 295, 296.
Blind Baron, 239.
—— Harry, 155.
Bloodhounds, 176.
Blyth Barony, 232.
Boethius, Hector, 189, 190, 254.
Bore Stone, 12.
Borssele, Wolfaard Van, 31.
Borthwick, Isobel, 279.
—— Janet, 235.
—— Lord, 183, 235.
—— Margaret, 275, 279.
Borthwicke, Thomas de, 165.
Boswell, James, of Auchinleck, 85, 131, 137, 138, 139, 140, 141, 144, 145, 146, 147.
Bothwell, Adam, Bishop of Orkney, 50.
—— 1st Earl, 16.
—— James Hepburn, Earl of, 34, 196.
—— Patrick, Earl of, 182.
Bousta, or Busta, 41.
Bowling-green, Grange House, 327, 332, 333, 338.
—— Prestonfield, 133.
Boyd, Lord, 101.
Braid estate, 46, 47, 57, 59, 95.
—— Hills, 5, 28, 48.
Breadalbane, Marquis of, 345.
Breda, 244.
Brigantia, 274.
Briggs of Braid, 47.
Brig o' Dee, 69.
Bronte, a dog, 333, 334, 338, 370.
Bronze leafed-shaped swords, 130.
Brougham, Henry, 85.
—— Lord, 85, 339.
Broughty Castle, 69.
Broun, Archibald, of Johnstonburn, 361.
—— of Borrowmuir, 230, 248.
—— Dame Elizabeth, 307.
—— John, Laird of Gorgiemylne, 59, 307.
—— Mariota, 95.
—— Thomas, of Johnstonburn, 307.
Brounisfelde Tower, 6, 9, 110, 230, 238, 248.
Brown, Dr. John, 337, 341.

Browning, John, 324, 325.
Bruce, Christian, 162.
—— Sir George, of Carnock, 39.
—— Nicolas, 39.
—— Robert, 7, 159, 160, 161, 255, 260.
Bruges, 31.
Bruntfield, Adam, 99.
—— Henry, 98.
—— Links, 97, 339.
—— Roger, 98.
—— Stephen, 96-99.
Bruntisfield, 241, 248, 249, 250, 251.
Buccleuch, Duke of, 343, 344.
Buchan, Earl of, 215.
Burgess, 263, 264, 265, 266, 267.
—— Acres, 261.
—— of the Bass, 192.
Burgh Arms, 142, 323, 365, 366.
Burghmuir, 4, 5, 8, 9, 10, 11, 27, 76.
Burglars, 80, 152, 370, 371.
Burial-place of Sir William Dick, in the Greyfriars, Edinburgh, 47, 53, 54, 392.
—— of the Earls of Haddington, 213, 220.
—— of John Knox, 144, 145.
—— of the Lauders, 156, 157, 207, 270, 281, 282, 283, 301, 315, 360, 361.
—— of the Maitlands of Pogbie, 171.
—— of the Setons, 16, 72, 73, 315.
Burnett, Bishop, 246.
Burngrains, or Burngrange, 231, 235, 236, 238, 247, 279.
Burrow Loch, 6.
Burrowage, 263.
Butler, David, Esq., of Pembroke, 130.
Butter, Dame Mary, 130.
Burton, John Hill, 95, 103.

CABINET of Sir William Dick, 372, 373.
—— of Lady Susan Hamilton, 373.
Caithness, Countess of, 15.
Caledonian Mercury, 76.
Calton Hill, 5.
Cambscurrie Castle, 353.
Cameron, 128, 135, 398.
Campbell, Alicia, 166, 167, 169, 222.
—— Sir Colin, of Loch Awe, 166, 222.
—— Helen, 251.
—— Sir Hugh Hume, 7th Baronet of Lauderdale, 251.
Cannon Terrace, 373.
Canongate, 3, 8.
Cant, Adam, Dean of Guild, 21, 111.
—— Alexander, 22.
—— Andrew, 390.
—— Henry, 111, 112.
—— Isabel, Sister of St. Katherine's, 17.
—— James, 22.
—— John, 8, 14, 15, 21, 25, 28.
—— Margaret, 111.

INDEX 415

Cant, Thomas, 21, 22, 23.
—— Walter, 21, 22, 23.
—— —— Bailie of Leith, 22, 23.
Cant's Close, 21, 366.
Carberry Hill, 23, 181, 184, 193, 377.
Carkettill, Agnes, 8, 15.
Carlisle, 164.
Carmichael, John, of Meadowflat, 97.
—— Sir John, 215, 216, 217.
—— Marie, 97, 99.
Cartmore, 36.
Carrick, Earl of, 7.
—— John of, 166.
—— Nigel of, 166.
Castle of Bass. *See* Bass.
—— Guard, 266.
—— of the Maidens, 6.
Catalogue of Sir Thomas Dick Lauder's Works, 410, 411.
Cathedral of St. Giles, 29.
—— of St. Halvard, 36.
—— of St. Magnus, 32.
Chalmeris, William, 29.
Chalmers, George, 254.
Chalybeate spring at Fountainhall, 313, 410.
Chambaudie, 36.
Chambers, Robert, 96.
Chapel of St. Anthony, 5, 76.
—— of St. John the Baptist, 13, 14, 15, 21.
—— of St. Roque, 11, 12, 13.
Charles Cruikshanks, 321, 322.
Charles I., 37, 39, 197.
—— II., 40.
—— Edward, Prince, came to Scotland, 70; at the Grange House, 74, 377; gives the Thistle to Miss Jean Seton, 74; receives the Dicks of Grange to breakfast at Holyrood, 75; his manifestoes in the *Caledonian Mercury*, 76; takes possession of Holyrood, 76, 77; his letter to George Gordon, 78; signs discharge of land-tax upon Sir Andrew Lauder, 80; escapes to France, 81; at Duddingston and Priestfield, 131.
Charter-chest, Dick Lauder, 28, 77, 79, 80, 370.
Charteris, Henry, Principal of the College, 117.
Charters of Bass, 152, 181, 242.
—— of Bele, or Beil, 177, 178, 198.
—— of Blyth, 232, 233.
—— of Braid Barony, 47, 385, App.
—— of Brountisfield, 230, 231, 238, 239, 249.
—— of Burghmuir, 27, 28.
—— of the Convent of St. Katherine, 14, 15.
—— of Craighouse, 94, 95, 96, 99.
—— of Craiglockhart, 94.
—— of the Earldom of Orkney, 40, 94.
—— of the Grange of St. Giles, 7, 23, 25.
—— of Halton, 222, 223, 230, 237, 239, 241.
—— of Holland House, Orkney, 39, 93.
—— of Holyrood, 3, 4.
—— of Lauder lands, 165, 273.

Charters to Sir Alan de Lawedre, 165, 166, 167, 255.
—— to George Lauder of Bass, including Beill, Popill, Tynninghame, Pencaitland, and Stentoun, etc., 398, 399.
—— of the Morton estate, 40.
—— of North Berwick and Heugh, 107, 108, 109.
—— of Northfield, Orkney, 41.
—— of Pencaitland, 159.
—— of Popill, 154, 183, 196, 198.
—— of Preaching Friars of Dundee, 179, 180.
—— of Priestfield, 110, 111, 112, 126.
—— of the Entail of Priestfield, 397, 398, App.
—— of Quhitlawis and Burngrains, 236, 237, 238.
—— of the Sciennes land, 18, 19, 29.
—— of the succession of the Grange estate, 71.
—— of Tyninghame, 196, 198, 203, 204.
Chepman, Walter, 111.
Chevalier de St. George, 69, 70.
Chisholm, Anna, 28, 29.
Christiana, 36.
Chronicle, Seytoun family, 16.
Clarence, Duke of, 215.
Clearburn House, 134.
Clyntis, 177, 183.
Coal, 26.
Coats-of-Arms:—
—— of Bass junior, 181, 274.
—— of Cant and Creich, 25, 26.
—— of Dick, 64, 65.
—— of Eleis of Mortonhall, 407.
—— of Elphinston, Sir James, 101, 102.
—— of Lauder, 408, App.
—— —— Bishop, 168, 169, 170.
—— —— Dick, 73.
—— —— Hatton, 222, 246.
—— of Mackerston, 274, 408.
Cockburn, Henry Lord, lived at Hope Park, 83; as a boy at the Grange, 85; his description of Dr. Robertson, 87; his opinion of Sir Walter Scott, 89, 90; at Caroline Park, 127; at Halton House, 227; at Relugas, 316; dedication of the Mornayshire Floods, 319; at Bonally, 338; on the hillside at Menstrie, 338, 339; among the Whigs, 340; describes the eclipse, 341, 342; his letter to Cosmo Innes, 360; at Sir Thomas Dick Lauder's funeral, 361.
—— Dame Jean, 240, 241.
—— John, 240.
—— Sir John, of Ormiston, 329.
College of Edinburgh, 117.
—— Wynd, 142, 143, 144.
Colville, Lord, 226.
Communion Cup, Church of Corstorphine, 124, 125, 396, 397.
Congalton, 156, 159, 189.
Conservator, 52.
Constable, Archibald, publisher, 248, 346, 356, 374.
—— Thomas, 346, 374.
Constable of Edinburgh Castle, 9, 18, 222.

Constable of Scotland :—
—— Alane, Lord of Galloway, 255.
—— Charles, Earl of Errol, 256.
—— Gilbert de Haye, 256.
—— Hugh de Morville, 255, 256.
—— James, Earl of Errol, 102.
—— Rowland, Lord of Galloway, 255.
—— William de Morville, 255.
Convent of St. Katherine of Siena, 15, 21, 68, 366, 377.
Copia of Scotland's letters anent Sir William Dick, 388-391.
Corstorphine, 124, 128.
Cospatrick, Earl of Dunbar, 155.
Covenant, 50, 51, 145, 208, 209, 400.
Covington, Lord, 101, 105.
Cowgate, 8.
Cowden-knowes, 253.
Crag, 109 ; le Craig, 178.
Craig, Sir James Gibson, 56, 337, 339.
Craigcrook, 248.
Craighouse, 94-106.
Craiglockhart, 80, 94, 370.
Cramond, 128.
—— Island, 98.
Cranstoun, Alison, 180, 273.
—— John, 275.
Creech, or Creich, Katherine, 25, 28.
Cressingham, Sir Hugh, 155, 156.
Crichton, Chancellor, 173, 224.
Cromarty, 349, 350, 351, 352.
Cromwell, 39, 51, 210, 211.
Culloden Moor, 77, 81.
Cumberland, Duke of, 81.
Cumin, Dame Charles Anne, 308, 379. *See* also Lauder, Lady.
—— George, of Relugas, 302.
—— Dr. Patrick, of Relugas, 308.
Cuningham, Sir John, of Cuninghamhead, 240.
Cuninghame, Lady Susanna, 241.
Cunningham, Allan, 350.
—— Sir Hugh, of Crosshill, 113.
Cunyngham, Dr. Alexander, 101, 129, 130.
—— Sir John, 126.
—— Sir William, of Caprington, 111, 114.
Curfew drum, 262, 263, 265.
Customs on wine, 37.

DALKEITH PALACE, 343, 344.
Dalmahoy, Lady Margaret, 47.
Dalrymple, Lady Anne, 360.
—— North, of Fordel, 361.
Darnley, Lord, 193.
David I., 2, 3, 4, 6, 7, 260.
—— II., 7, 161, 162, 163.
Davidson, Captain, 248.
—— Dr., of Muirhouse, 248.
Dean of Guild, 21, 28.
—— of Restalrig, 182, 183, 184, 185, 186.

Dean of St. Giles, 49.
Dean's Seat, Glasgow Cathedral, 169, 170.
Deans, Davie, 51.
Denholm, Dame Cecil, 101.
Denmark, 36.
Devaux, William, 56.
Devorgilla of Galloway, 162, 255.
Dick, Agnes, wife of John Dick of Loudon, 60.
—— of New York, 59, 60.
—— Alexander, Archdeacon of Glasgow, 32.
—— —— of Heugh, in business with his father, 48 ; signs the Covenant, 50; cautioner, 58 ; fiar of Heugh, 107 ; his wife and family, 109 ; lessee of Craighouse, 99 ; his death, 109.
—— —— of Craighouse and Clermiston, 100, 101.
—— Sir Alexander, of Prestonfield (*alias* Dr. Cunyngham), succeeds his brother in the barony, 128 ; takes his degree as Doctor, 129 ; travels in Italy, 129 ; elected President of the Royal College of Physicians, 129 ; his portrait hung in the Hall, 139; his marriage, 130 ; the death of his wife, 130 ; his second marriage, 130 ; his antiquarian researches, 130 ; enclosure of parks and plantations, 131 ; entertains Dr. Johnson, 130-137 ; his garden, 132 ; the medicinal Chinese rhubarb, 132 ; letter from Sir Alexander to Dr. Johnson, 146 ; his gift of rhubarb, 147 ; his death, 134.
—— Sir Andrew, of Craighouse and Northfield, obtains Charter of the Earldom of Orkney, 40 ; knighted by Charles II., 41, 47, 100 ; signs the Covenant, 50 ; his unnatural conduct to his nephew, 57, 58, 100 ; his family connections, 92 ; his marriage, 93 ; the death of his wife and only son, 93 ; elected Sheriff of Orkney, 93 ; his second marriage, 93 ; acquires the estate of Holland in the Isle of Stronsay, 93 ; loan to the Earl of Morton, 93 ; purchase of Craighouse, 94 ; his sons, 100 ; at the baptism of his niece Janet, 110.
—— Captain Andrew, his parentage, 39, 41 ; appointed Steward Chamberlain of Orkney and Shetland, 41 ; member of Parliament, 41 ; his marriage and property, 41 ; his only son, 41, 60 ; executor-dative on his brother's Will, 60.
—— Andrew, of West Newton, 64.
—— —— of Wormadale, 60, 61.
—— —— 4th Baron of Grange, inherits his mother's estate, 72 ; his correspondence, 73 ; becomes Sir Andrew Lauder-Dick, 6th Bart. of Fountainhall, 73, 305, 307, 310.
—— Anne, daughter of 2nd Baron of Grange, 66.
—— —— daughter of Alexander Dick of Clermiston 101.
—— Lady Anne (*née* Mackenzie), wife of Sir William Dick of Prestonfield, 126, 127, 128.
—— Baronetcy, 47.
—— Charles, of Fracafield, 61, 62.
—— William Hockaday, 63.

INDEX

Dick, Elizabeth, daughter of Sir Andrew of Craighouse, 56, 100.
— George, of Meiklewood, 36.
— Captain George of Craighouse, 100.
— Henry Page, 63, 64.
— Isobel, heiress of Grange, 71, 72, 304.
— James, burgess of Arbroath, 32.
— — fiar of Grange, 71, 72.
— Sir James, of Priestfield, his parentage, 109; his business firm in the Lawnmarket, 110; acquires Priestfield, 112; created a Baronet, 112; elected Provost, 113, 384; his marriage, 113; death of his children, 114; his heiress, 114; receives the Duke of York, 115; Yuletide contest with the students of the College, 118, 119; his house at Priestfield burnt down, 119; narrow escape from drowning, 120, 121; re-elected Provost, 121; in the Law Court about the swans on Duddingston Loch, 122; the wise Provost, 122; cleansing the streets of the city, 123; death of his son and heir, 124; entails his estate, 124; gift of communion cup to Corstorphine, 124, 396, 397; his death, 124.
— Miss Janet, of Clermiston, heirs her brother Patrick, 101; marries her cousin, Dr. Alexander Cunyngham, 101; her two daughters, 130; her death, 130.
— — — daughter of Sir Alexander Dick of Prestonfield, 130.
— Lady Janet, heiress of Prestonfield, 114; her marriage with Sir William Cunyngham, 114, 124; entails the property, 124; retires to Cameron as Dowager Lady Cunyngham, 135.
— John, fiar of Braid, 38, 41, 57, 60; Sheriff-Depute of Orkney, 38, 39; his marriage, 39; his sons, 39; present at the infeftment of Sanct-Geilie Grange, 46; signs the Covenant, 50; his death and burial, 39, 47.
— — 2nd son of John, fiar of Braid, 39; enters a mercantile firm in London, 57, 60; present at the baptism of his cousin, Janet Dick, 110; his testament-dative, 60; his widow, 60.
— Sir John, British Consul at Leghorn, 62; his progenitors and parents, 62, 64; becomes a merchant abroad, 64; his marriage, 64; appointed British Consul by George II., 65; served heir to his ancestor Sir William Dick of Braid, 65.
— Lewis, Captain, R.N., 5th son of Sir William Dick of Braid, 38; chooses a sea-faring life, 38, 50, 64; becomes Commander, 64; his patrimony, and his marriage, 64, 229; his father-in-law, 64; his early death, 64.
— Captain Lewis, eldest son of Sir Andrew Dick of Craighouse, 100.
— Sir Page Keble, 63.
— Robert, of Fracafield, 61.
— Walter, of Wormadale, 60.
— Sir William, of Braid, merchant prince of Edinburgh, 28, 51; his birth, 36; farms the Crown rents in Orkney, 37; advances money to the King, 37; obtains the customs on wine, 37; becomes an eminent banker, 38; his marriage and family, 38; playing golf on the Braid Hills, 28, 46; the purchase of Sanct-Geilie Grange, 28, 29, 30, 46; acquires the Barony of Braid, 46, 47; knighted by King Charles I., 47, 59, 62; a zealous Covenanter, 49, 50; his warehouse in the Luckenbooths, 50, 51; is elected Provost, 50, 56, 384; his estate drawn up, 50, 388; his town residence, 50; his enormous loan to the State, 51; becomes bankrupt, 51; estates mortgaged, takes shelter at the Grange, 51, 52; travels to London to seek redress, 52; cast into prison, 53; visited by his wife and family, 53; dies in the debtors' jail at Westminster, 53; buried at Greyfriars, Edinburgh, 53, 54, 392; Petitions to the State, 54, 388, 389, 391, 393; old pamphlet of his 'Distressed Case,' 55, 56, 57; his coin, 50, 371; his cabinet, 372.
Dick, Major William, son of Charles Dick of Fracafield, entered the East India Company's service, 62; becomes the representative of the family on the death of Sir John Dick of Mount Clare, 62; assumes the Baronetcy, 62; his marriage and death, 62, 63.
— William, heir of Braid, eldest son of John, fiar of Braid, his parentage, 39, 57; his misfortunes and petitions, 57, 58; his marriage and early death, 59.
— — son of William, heir of Braid, petitions Parliament, 59, 393, 396; enters the Foot Guards, 59; bravery at the Battle of Almanza, 59; promoted to be fort-major and deputy-governor of New York, 59; assumes the title of Baronet, acquires land and marries a widow, 59; dies without male heir, 59.
— — of Fracafield, 61.
— — of Wormadale, Commissary clerk of Zetland, 62.
— — 1st Baron of Grange, 3rd son of Sir William Dick of Braid, Knt., signs the Covenant, 50; his marriage, 48, 49; fiar of Sanct-Geilie Grange, 48; dies before his father, 52.
— — 2nd Baron of Grange, enters as heir of his father at the age of sixteen, 52; twice married, 66; served heir to his mother, Janet M'Math, 68, 71.
— — 3rd Baron of Grange, 68; marries Dame Anne Seton of Pitmedden, 69; charter of Grange lands, 69; death of their only son, James, 71, 72.
— Sir William, of Prestonfield (alias Cunyngham), heirs his grandfather, 126; his progenitors, 126; his marriage, 126; his wife's eccentricities, 127; death of Lady Anne, childless, 128; his successor, 129.
— — 4th Bart. of Prestonfield, son of Sir Alexander Dick, 132; Lord Cockburn's description of him, 133; he joins the Grenadier Guards at the age of sixteen, 134; his marriage and his sudden death, 134; his widow and children, 134.

INDEX

Dick Cunyngham, Sir Alexander, 5th Bart. of Prestonfield, 134.
—— —— Sir John, 6th Bart., 134.
—— ——Sir Robert Keith, 7th Bart. of Prestonfield, 3rd son of Sir Alexander Dick, 134; built the circular stables, 135; removed the garden and changed the boundary wall of the policy, 138; succeeded to the Baronetcy of Caprington, 135; his marriage, his sons, and his death, 135.
—— —— Sir William Hanmer, 8th Bart. of Prestonfield, 135.
—— —— Sir Robert Keith Alexander, 9th Bart., passed through the Indian Mutiny, 135.
—— —— Sir William, 10th Bart., appointed to the command of the 2nd Gordon Highlanders, 135; received the Victoria Cross, 136.
—— Lauder and Lauder Dick, 310.
Divie, river, 316, 317, 318, 322, 324.
—— Bridge, 318, 322.
—— Fall, 318, 320.
Dobbin, the Dunphail pony, 323.
Dobie, Mr. George, 369.
Dogs' Cemetery, 333-336.
Dorback Rock, 323, 325.
Dornoch, 299; the forest, 353.
Dougall, John, 25, 27, 29.
Douglas, Archibald, Earl of Angus (Bell the Cat), at Lauder Bridge, 177, 268; Provost of Edinburgh, 233, 383; at Flodden, 233.
—— Sir Archibald, killed at Halidon Hill, 161, 162.
—— —— Commander of the Scottish army at Beaugé and Verneuil, 215, 216, 224.
—— Archibald, of Drumlanrig, 173.
—— —— Earl of Moray, 225, 229.
—— David, a youth, murdered by Chancellor Crichton, 173, 174, 224.
—— of Glenbervie, 15.
—— Hugh, Earl of Ormond, 228, 229.
—— James, Lord, 160, 162; goes to the Holy Land with the heart of Bruce, 165.
—— —— Earl of Marr, 171.
—— —— Earl of, 229.
—— Sir James, a churchman, 224, 225.
—— Jean, Sister at the Sciennes, 17.
—— Johannah, heiress of Garvaldfoot, 134.
—— John, Lord Balveny, 229.
—— Mary, Dowager Countess of Angus, 215, 216, 217.
—— William, Earl of, grants a charter to Alan de Lawedre, 166.
—— —— —— murdered in Edinburgh Castle, 173, 174, 224.
—— —— 8th Earl of, his power and ambition, 223; goes to Rome, travelling through France, 224; receives safe-conduct for himself and his retinue from the king of England, 225; meditates revolt, 225; his revengeful cruelties, 226; his treasonable bond with the Earls of Crawford and Ross, 226; his reception of Sir Patrick Gray, the King's messenger, 226; his murder of Maclellan, 227; requested to attend the king at Stirling Castle, 225; accepts the King's invitation, 227; his reception, 227; his assassination, 228.
Dovalus, 274.
Dovecot at Craighouse, 106.
—— at Fountainhall, 313.
—— at Heugh, North Berwick, 107, 109.
—— at Sanct-Geilie Grange, 28.
—— at Tyninghame, 398, App.
Drake, Dr., 358.
Drummond, Annabella, wife of King Robert III., 169.
—— Castle, 345.
—— Sir William, of Hawthornden, 244, 245.
Drummossie Moor, 77, 81.
Dryburgh, 88, 90, 255.
Drygrange, 253.
Dunbar, Hugh de, 178.
—— Miss, of Boath, 325, 352.
Duncan, Elizabeth, 59, 398.
Dundas, Sir Laurence, Bart. of Kerse, 42.
Dunphail, 316, 317, 320, 322, 323.
Dysart, Earl of, 122.
Dyck, William de, 31, 383.
Dyke, Graafs, 31.

EARLDOM OF ORKNEY, 38, 40, 94.
Earl Grey's Oak, 340.
Earl's Palace, Kirkwall, 33, 35.
Eclipse of the Sun, 341.
Edinburgh Asylum, 95, 104.
—— Castle, 97.
Edrington, 155.
Edward III., 7, 160.
—— Elizabeth or Margaret, 290, 407.
—— Nicol, Dean of Guild, 290, 407.
—— Provost, 290, 383, 407.
Edwinsburgh, 2, 3.
Eglinton, Countess of, 142.
—— Tournament, 358.
Egypt, 47.
Fleis, or Ellis, Alexander, of Mortonhall, 290, 407.
—— —— Isobel, 29, 293, 301, 407.
—— James, 385, 407.
—— Patrick, 385, 407.
El-Gran-Griffon, 43.
Elphinstoun, Sir James, 101.
—— Sir Thomas, of Calderhall, 245.
—— William, 167.
Epitaph on Elphinstoun tomb, 245.
—— of Sir John Lauder, 1st Bart. of Fountainhall, 293.
—— of Robert Lauder, last of the Lauders of Lauder Tower, 281.
—— of Robert Lawedre of Congalton and Bass, 156.
Epitaphs in the Dogs' Cemetery, 336.
Ercildoune, 253.

INDEX 419

Errol, Charles, Earl of, High Constable of Scotland, 256.
—— James Boyd, 13th Earl of, 101, 102.
—— —— Earl of, at the coronation of George III., 102.
Ettrick Forest, 273.

FAIR ISLE, 43.
Fairlie, Alexander, 47, 48.
—— John, 241.
—— Robert, of Braid, 22, 47, 48.
—— William, 27, 249.
Family portraits, 409.
Father Damien, 11.
Faulau, or Fallow, Agnes, 178.
Fiery Cross, 42.
Findhorn, river, 316, 317.
Findlay, Mr. J. R., 234, 247, 248.
Fleming, Sir Malcolm, of Cumbernauld, 173, 174.
—— Mary, 97.
Flodden, 10, 11, 16, 233, 234, 278.
Forbes, Sir William, 101.
Forest of Drumsheugh, 4-6.
—— of Lauder, 273.
Forestare, Archibald, 231.
—— John, of Nudri, 231.
Forman, Andrew, Archbishop of St. Andrews, 203.
Forrest, Alexander, 83.
—— Catherine, 83.
—— James, 83.
—— Sir James, Bart., Provost of Edinburgh, 83, 343, 344.
—— —— of Comiston, 183, 342.
—— John, 83, 84.
Forster, Alexander, 229.
—— Elizabeth, 223.
—— Sir John, of Corstorphine, 223.
Foulis, Sir James, of Colinton, Bart., 64, 229, 241.
Fountainhall, 73, 74, 289, 291, 293, 297, 299, 300, 310, 311, 312, 313, 314.
—— Lord (Sir John Lauder), his indignation about fanatics, 117 ; his opinion of the Duke of Lauderdale, 246, 298, 299 ; his estimate of John Ramsay of Balmain, 269 ; holograph notes of his ancestors, 274, 407, 408 ; his excerpt of the murder of William Lauder, 277 ; his knighthood, 289 ; his marriage, 291, 294, 295 ; denounced by his stepmother, 292 ; sends a memorial to Parliament, 292 ; thwarts the design of his stepmother, 292, 293 ; his parentage, 293 ; his journey to France, 294 ; his studies and his diary, 294 ; counsel for the Earl of Argyll, 296 ; beheld his execution, 297 ; his 'observe' upon the Test Act, 297 ; M.P. for Haddington, 297 ; his wife's death, and his second marriage, 297 ; his title as Senator of the College of Justice, 297 ; refuses a seat on the Bench, 297, 298 ; his voluminous manuscripts, 298 ; the spectre at Roseneath, 299 ; at the trial of Major Weir, the notorious wizard, 299 ; intermarriage of cousins, 300, 304 ; his children, 300 ; the tombs of his ancestors, 301 ; his death, and burial at Greyfriars, 301 ; his town residence, and story of his grandchildren, 302.
Fracafield, 60.
Friars of Dundee, 178-180, 273.
Fulling-mill at Lauder, 166.

GALLOWAY, ALLAN, Lord of, 255.
—— Rowland, Lord of, 255.
Garden, Grange House, 85.
—— Halton House, 246.
—— Pitmedden, 79.
—— Prestonfield, 132, 133.
—— Royston, 127.
Geddes, Jenny, 49.
George III., 102.
Gilmerton, 26.
Gipsy letter, 370.
Glasgow Bridge, 169.
—— Cathedral, 169, 170.
Glencairn, James, Earl of, 241.
Gloucester, man-of-war wrecked, 121.
Goldsmith, Oliver, 141.
Golf, 28, 46.
Gordon of Cluny, 48, 102.
—— George, of Beldorney, 77, 78, 79, 80.
—— Sir George, of Haddo., 121.
—— George, of Woodhead, 110.
—— Mary, 80.
Gourlay, Robert, 364.
Grange Avenue, 336
—— Cemetery, 359-361.
—— House, 1, 10, 13 ; home of the Cants, 22, 23, 24, 25 ; purchased by Sir William Dick, 28, 31, 46 ; his son William's patrimony, 48 ; its 'guardian angel,' 49, 51, 52, 53 ; political rendezvous, 49 ; bridal home, 66 ; heritors, 68 ; Charter of Succession, 71 ; heiress of Grange, 72 ; home of the Setons, 17, 72, 73, 377 ; Prince Charles Stuart entertained there, 74, 75, 76 ; burglary, 80, 152, 153 ; vacated, 83 ; leased to Mr. John Forrest, 83; Dr. Robertson, tenant, 84 ; Lord Cockburn and Lord Brougham there as boys, 85 ; Sir Walter Scott and the Griffins, 87 ; traditional story of him, 88 ; commencement of the reconstruction, 319 ; Sanct-Geilie Grange as a baronial residence, 327-338 ; the eclipse of the Sun seen from the Tower, 341, 342 ; burning of Greyfriars Church, 347 ; Hugh Miller's visit, 351, 352, 353; meeting between Hugh Miller and Mr. Adam Black, publisher, 352 ; funeral of Sir Thomas Dick Lauder, 7th Bart., 360 ; sculptured stones, 363 ; ghost story, 374, 375 ; Queen Mary tradition, 377 ; story of the skeleton, 378.
—— of St. Giles, 2, 7, 8, 9, 12, 13, 21, 327, 339, 377, 378.
—— lands, 8, 9, 22.
—— Loan, or Loan, 28, 75, 360, 366, 368.

INDEX

Grange portraits, 329, 409, 410.
Grant, Francis J., Carrick Pursuivant of Arms, 62.
Granton Castle, 127.
Grassmarket, 8, 304, 365, 375.
Graves, Mr., 370.
Gray, Sir Patrick, 226, 227, 228.
Greenbank, 47.
Greenwich, Baroness, 128.
Grene, Meldoun, 234.
Grey, Earl, 339, 340.
Greyfriars Church steeple blown up, 301 ; Church destroyed by fire, 347, 348.
—— Churchyard, burial-place of the plague-stricken, 12 ; burial-place of Sir William Dick, 53 ; tomb of Janet M'Math, 67 ; Lauder tomb, 301, 310, 315 ; signing of the Covenant, 50, 145.
Griffins, 73, 87, 170, 173.

HADDINGTON, 297.
—— 1st Earl of, 112, 198, 210.
—— Thomas, 6th Earl of, 218, 220.
—— Right Hon. Earl of, 220, 221.
Hailes, Lord, 278.
Haitlie, Elizabeth, 207.
Halkett, Craigie, 309, 373, 379.
Halton estate, 167, 222, 223, 229, 230, 252.
—— House besieged by the Douglases, 228 ; forfeited, 229 ; bestowed by King James on his Queen, Mary of Guelderland, 230 ; restored to Sir George Lauder, 230 ; description of it, 246, 247.
—— Lord (Charles Maitland), 245, 246.
—— John de, 167, 222.
Hamilton, Archibald, burgess, 29.
—— Sir Alexander, 112.
—— Duke of, 122.
—— Sir James, of Crawford, Knt., 17.
—— —— of Priestfield, 198.
—— Sir Thomas, of Orchardfield, 111, 112.
—— —— 1st Earl of Haddington, 112, 198, 210.
—— —— of Priestfield, 112.
Hammihill, 42.
Hanmer, Harriet, 135.
—— Thomas, of Stapleton, 135.
Harehope, 7, 24.
Haunted Tower, 332, 374-376.
Hay, Elizabeth, 82, 193.
—— Isobel, 178.
—— James, Lord Boyd, 13th Earl of Errol, 101.
—— John, 12th Baron of Yester, 178.
—— Margaret, 183.
—— Lady Mary, 102.
—— William, Lord of Yester, 21, 183.
'Heart of Midlothian,' 51, 55, 144, 303.
Hebergare (Hospital), 3.
Henderson, Agnes, 234.
Henrison, Josina, 15.
Henry, of Brade, 48.
Henryson, William, 39.
Hepburn, James, of Keith, 77.

Hepburn, Jane, 182.
—— Janet, 16.
—— Isobel, 106, 197, 204.
—— Patrick, 16.
—— Sir Patrick, of Wauchton, 196, 204.
Hereditary bailieships of Lauder, 153, 254, 259, 264, 270, 275, 277.
Heriot, George, goldsmith, 28.
Heriot's Hospital, 297, 347.
Hermitage, St. Anthony's, 5.
—— of St. John, 14.
Herries, Sir John, 226.
—— Sister Elizabeth, 17.
Hetherington, William, of Birkenhead, 135.
—— Sarah Mary, 135.
Heugh, North Berwick, 59, 107, 108, 109.
High School Wynd, 119.
Holinshed, 181, 190, 254, 278.
Holland, 31, 32.
—— manor-place, Orkney, 39, 44, 93.
Holme Abbey, 7.
—— Cultrane, 2, 7, 235, 378.
Holograph notes of Lord Fountainhall, 274, 407, 408.
Holy Isle, 7.
—— Well, 219, 220.
Holyrood Abbey, 3.
—— Palace, 75-78, 344.
Home, Alexander, 108.
—— Sir Alexander, 9th Baron, 271.
—— —— —— 10th Baron, 271.
—— Earl of, 275.
—— Sir George, 108, 109.
—— Sir John, 108, 109.
—— Lord, 278.
—— Magdalene, 275.
—— Sir Patrick, 108, 109.
Hope, Sir Archibald, of Rankeillor, 101.
—— of Craighall, Ceres, 101, 127.
—— Margaret, 101.
Hopetoun, Earls of, 247.
—— Lord, 121.
Hoppringle, James, 272.
Hot-trode, 176.
Howman Manor, 167.
Hoy, 40.
Humby, 78.
Hunter, Rev. John, of Lerwick, 61.
Huntingdon, Earl of, 153.
Hutcheon, Isabel, 96.
Hutoun, Janet, 25.

IBBOK of Norton, 166.
Indenture, 179.
Inglis, James, 407, App.
Innes, Cosmo, 169, 360.
—— Miss Jean, of Stow, 302, 305-307.
—— Mitchell, Alexander, of Ayton Castle, 332, 345, 360, 379.

INDEX 421

Innes, Mitchell, George, of Ingleston, 361.
—— —— Gilbert, 361, 379.
—— —— Thomas, of Phantassie, 360, 379.
—— —— William, of Ayton Castle, 379.
—— —— William, of Parson's Green, 361.
Inscriptions : Birsay Castle, 34.
—— Craighouse, 95, 106.
—— Dean's Seat, Glasgow Cathedral, 170.
—— Grange lintel, 24.
—— Kirk-of-Field, 142.
—— Monk's Seat, 364.
—— Scalloway Castle, 35.
—— St. Leonard's, 285.
Inventory, sacred utensils of St. Giles, 20, 384.

JAMES I. as Prince of Scotland takes refuge on the Bass, 189 ; his imprisonment in England, 189 ; his liberation, 173, 189.
—— II., 174, 226-229.
—— III., at Lauder, 177; appoints Sir Robert Lauder Keeper of Berwick Castle, 174 ; on the Burghmuir, 11; grants Novodamus to Lauder Burgh, 261 ; his death at Beaton's Mill, Sauchie, 177, 278.
—— IV., at St. Roque's Chapel, 10 ; confirms the Charter of St. John's, 15 ; encamped on Burghmuir, 12 ; dies at Flodden, 234.
—— V., 178.
—— VI., 25, 96, 117, 118, 195.
—— Duke of York, the King's Commissioner, 115, 116; his Duchess, 116 ; his daughter, Princess Anne, 117 ; his narrow escape from drowning, 121 ; an exiled King, 70.
Jarls of Orkney, 33.
Jedburgh, 164.
Jeffrey, Lord, 247, 248, 337, 339, 340, 360, 361.
Jenny, the Highland pony, 307.
Johnson, Dr. Samuel, introduction to Dr. Robertson, 85 ; at Prestonfield, 131, 132 ; his popularity, 137; his uncouth manners, 138 ; his arrival in James's Court, 139; Boswell meets him at the White Horse Close, 140; his first interview with him in Temple Lane, 139 ; his love of tea, 140 ; a reputed 'bear,' 141 ; his story of the Countess of Eglinton, 142; his remarks on John Knox, 144 ; in Greyfriars and the Canongate, 145; his veneration for second-sight, 146; letter from Sir Alexander Dick, 146, 147; his death, 148.
Jordaens, 328.
Jougs at Fountainhall, 313.
—— at Pencaitland, 313.
—— at Tyninghame, 205, 219.
Justiciary of the Lothians, 161, 163, 164.

KATHERINE OF SIENA, 18.
Kelliechrist, 353, 354.
Ker, Ralph, Bailie of Lauder, 280.
Kerkettill, Agnes, 15, 21.

Kerr, Sir Andrew, of Faudonside, 48.
Kildrummie, 162.
Kincaid, Alexander, 18.
—— David, 18.
—— Henry, 18, 23, 24, 27, 28, 29.
—— Sir James, of Craighouse, 96.
—— John, 18.
—— —— of Craighouse, 96.
King's Burgh, 263, 264.
—— Peace, 266.
Kinninmonth, Elizabeth, 36.
Kinross, 40.
Kirkcaldy, Sir William, of Grange, 377.
Kirk-of-Field, 118.
—— of St. Giles, 2, 6.
Kirkwall, 32, 35.
Knight-Templars, 365.
Knox, John, 20, 48, 144, 148.
—— Martha, 48.
Kol, 33.
Kyle, Lord, 7.
Kyncades of Campsie, 18.

LADIES' WELL, 68, 313.
Laing, David, 243, 357.
Laird of Auchinleck, 137.
—— of Carolside, 284, 285.
—— of Colmestoun, 30.
—— of Congalton, 156, 159.
—— of Cramond, 407.
—— of Gorgiemylne, 307.
—— of Halton, 223.
—— of Lauder, 274, 275.
—— of Leswaid, 289.
—— of Ochiltree, 48.
Lamberton, William, Bishop of St. Andrews, 151, 152, 153.
Lammermoors, 171, 253.
Lang Settle, 371.
Lasswade, 275, 277, 279, 289, 408.
Lauder Aisle in St. Giles' Cathedral, 232.
—— Branches, 284.
—— Bridge, 177, 268.
—— Burgh, 77, 253, 258, 259, 263.
—— Common, 260, 261.
—— Fort, 168, 255, 256, 279, 280.
—— Kirk, 168, 177.
—— Mills, 255, 267, 272, 273.
Lauderdale, 153, 246, 253, 254, 268.
—— Duchess of, 122, 299.
—— Duke of, 122, 245, 246, 258, 298, 299.
—— Earls of, 252, 255, 258.
LAVEDRE, LAWEDRE, LAWDER, or LAUDER :—
Lawedre, Adrien, 203.
Lawder, Alan, of Bass, 224, 225.
—— Alexander, of Burngrange, 231.
Lavedre, Alexander de, of Popill, 154.
Lawedre, Sir Alan de, of Halton, 9, 165-169, 173, 222, 255.

INDEX

Lauder, Alexander, Bishop of Dunkeld, 168, 171.
— Alexander, of Blyth, Provost, 233, 278.
— — Chaplain at Whittinghame, 207.
— Sir Alexander, 2nd Laird of Halton, 223.
— — — 5th Laird of Halton, Provost, 233.
— — — 10th Laird of Halton, 47, 238, 239, 240, 241, 242, 243.
— Alexander, fiar of Halton, 241, 242.
— — of Over-Gogar, 8th Laird of Halton, died at Pinkie, 235, 236.
— Andrew, of Melvin-Mylne, Lasswade, 277, 287, 301.
— — 3rd son of Bailie Lauder of Newington, 291.
— Archibald, Lord of Idington, 293.
— Arthur, of Seuney, 182, 186.
— Barbara, daughter of Sir William Lauder of Halton, 240.
— Beatrice, granddaughter of Sir Robert Lauder of Bass, 167.
— Colin, brother of Lord Fountainhall, 291.
— David, Esq. of Huntly Wood, 300, 302.
Lawder, David, of Popill, 154.
Lauder, Sir Edward, 173, 174.
— Elizabeth, wife of David Preston, 11th Baron of Craigmillar, 183.
— Elizabeth, Countess of Lauderdale, 245, 246.
— — wife of John Cuninghame of Woodhead, 293.
— — wife of Thomas Redpath, 279.
— — heiress of Swynset, 167.
— George, Bishop of Argyll, 171.
— — Rector of Auldeathy, 183.
— — Laird of Bass, 182.
— — last Laird of Bass, 180, 195, 196, 197, 198, 204, 209, 211.
— Sir George, 1st Baron of Halton, 223.
— — — Knt., of Quhitslaid, 230, 233.
— George, son of Sir John Lauder, 1st Bart. of Fountainhall, 291, 292.
— Col. George, the soldier-poet, son of Sir Alexander Lauder of Halton, 243, 244, 245.
— Gilbert of Balbardies, 239.
— — of Bawbardy, 235, 237, 238.
— — Vicar of Twynam, 231, 232.
— Helen, wife of George Ogilvy, 4th Lord Banff, 300, 305.
— Helene, wife of Michael Scott, 235.
— Henry, Lord St. Germains, 178, 179.
— James, of Burngrains, 276, 279.
— — Dean of Restalrig, 182, 183, 184, 185, 186, 187.
— — son of Sir William Lauder of Halton, 240.
— — of Muircleuch, 239.
— Jean, Lady Calderhall, 245.
— — wife of Dr. Patrick Cumin of Relugas, 302.
— Miss Jean, of Fountainhall, 73, 305, 306, 307.

Lavedre, Johannes, of Popill, 154.
— John de, 154.
Lauder, John, son of Sir Robert Lauder of Bass, 167.
— Sir John, 4th Laird of Halton, 64, 229.
— — Archdean of Tweedda'e, Secretary to Cardinal Beaton, 181, 190, 372.
— — of Beill, 182, 187.
— — Bailie of Tyninghame, 206, 208.
— — of Burngrange, 172.
— John, minister of Tyninghame, 206, 207, 208, 209.
— Ludovick, 24.
— Margaret, daughter of Alexander Lauder, 187.
— — wife of Edward Aitkyn, 182.
— — second wife of Sir Alexander Hume, 4th Baron of Polwarth, 179.
— — wife of Sir Alexander Seton of Pitmedden, 69.
— Mistress Margaret, alias Maggie Lauder, 211, 212.
— Mariota, or Marion, heiress of Howman, 167.
— — wife of Alexander Home, 9th Baron, 271.
— — wife of Sir Alexander Home, 10th Baron, 272.
— — wife of Thomas Otterburn of Reidhall, 182.
— — wife of David Lauder, 154.
— Moreis, burgess of Dunbar, 185.
— Oliver Lauder, of Lauder Tower, 272.
— Patrick, of Gervat, 182, 187.
— Richard, 11th Laird of Halton, 242, 243, 245.
Lavedre, Robertus de, 1st Baron, 153, 253, 273.
— Robert de, 5th Baron, the Crusader, 154.
Lawedre, Sir Robert, Laird of Congalton and Bass, 155, 156.
Lawdre, Sir Robert de, of Bass, companion of Sir William Wallace, 151; assignee of Lamberton Charter, 152, 153, 159, 160, 161.
— Sir Robert de, of Bass, Chancellor and Governor of Berwick, 161.
Lawedre, Sir Robert de, of Bass, Justiciary, 163.
Lauder, Sir Robert, of Bass, 167.
— — of Quarrelwood and Bass, defender of Urquhart Castle, 162.
— Robert, junr., taken prisoner at Jedburgh, 164.
Lawedre, Sir Robert de, of Lauder and Bass, Lord Justice of Scotland, 168, 178.
Lawder, Sir Robert, of Bass, Governor of Berwick Castle, called by King James 'our loveit of the Bass,' 177, 178, 189.
— — — Younger, Laird of Edrington, son of 'our loveit of the Bass,' 174; intrusted with an instalment of Princess Cicely's dowry portion, 174, 175, 176, 177.
— — of Bass, granter of the indenture to the preaching friars of Dundee, 178, 179, 180; supporter of Mary of Guise as Queen Regent, 180.
— — Laird of Bass, with Queen Mary on Carberry Hill, 181, 182, 183, 184, 185, 186, 187; last feudal Baron of Bass, 188.

INDEX

Lawder, Robert, of Burngrange, 255.
—— —— Bishop of Dunblane, 171.
—— —— Canon of Glasgow, 171.
—— —— of Gunsgrene, 209.
—— —— of that Ilk, 275, 276, 279, 289.
—— —— —— last laird of Lauder Tower, 280, 281, 282, 283.
—— ——, jun., of Lauder Tower, 280, 281.
—— —— of Muircleuch, 272.
—— —— heir of Popill, 183.
—— Sir Robert, Knt., of Popill, 182, 183.
—— Robert, portioner of Tyningham, 207, 209.
—— —— minister of Whitekirk, 206, 207.
—— Susanna, daughter of Sir William of Halton, 240.
—— Thomas, Bishop of Dunkeld, 171, 172.
—— —— Master of Soltra, 171, 172.
—— - Walter, 203.
—— William, Bishop of Glasgow, 168, 169, 170, 171, 223.
—— Sir William, 3rd Laird of Halton, 223, 229, 230.
—— —— 7th Laird of Halton, 234, 235, 236.
—— —— 9th Laird of Halton, 236, 237, 238, 239, 240.
—— William, Lord Lauder, 193, 273, 274, 275.
—— Dr. William, Preston, 291.
Lauder Dick and Dick Lauder, 310.

LAUDER BARONETS OF FOUNTAINHALL:—
—— Sir John, Bailie of Newington, 1st Bart. of Fountainhall, 279, 289-93, 298-301.
—— —— 2nd Bart. *See* Fountainhall, Lord.
—— —— 3rd Bart., 303, 304.
—— Sir Alexander, 4th Bart. of Fountainhall, 303.
—— Sir Andrew, 5th Bart. of Fountainhall, 303, 304, 305.
—— —— —— 6th Bart., third son of Isabel Dick, heiress of Grange, 72, 73; Sir Andrew Lauder of Fountainhall inherits his mother's estate, and becomes Sir Andrew Lauder-Dick, 305, 307, 308, 309, 310.
Lauder, Sir Thomas Dick, 7th Bart. of Fountainhall and Grange, 50, 52, 53, 54, 87, 302, 310, 379; at Sir Walter Scott's funeral, 89, 90; at the mineral spring, 312; at Relugas, 316; sketching with the Rev. John Thomson of Duddingston, 318, 338; the Morayshire Floods, 321; literary work, 331; the Reform Bill, 339; voyage round the coast of Scotland, 342; the Royal Progress, 342, 345, 346; correspondence with Hugh Miller, 325, 349, 350, 351; false report of his death, 352; his legendary works, 353, 354; scientific paper on the Parallel Roads of Glen Roy, 355; Secretary of the Board of Manufactures, 357; Eglinton tournament, 358; his love of fairy-lore, 359; city improvements, 358; Deputy Lieutenant, 358; pious resignation and death, 360; funeral, 360, 361; epitaph, 362.
—— Sir John Dick, 8th Bart. of Fountainhall and Grange, 360, 379, 380.
—— Sir Thomas, North Dick, 9th Bart., 53, 370, 380.

Lauder, Lady Charles Anne Dick (LADY LAUDER), wife of 7th Baronet, 308, 325, 329, 341, 345, 346, 353.
—— Lady Anne Dick, 360, 371, 379.
—— Miss Beatrice Dick, 88, 89, 380.
—— Catherine Seton Dick, 380.
—— Charlotte Anne Dick, 380.
—— ——Gordon Dick, 379.
—— Miss Cornelia Dick, 317, 319, 320, 321, 322, 324, 330, 331, 334, 338, 345, 356, 362, 373, 376, 379.
—— George Dalrymple Dick, 369, 380.
—— —— Dick, of Huntly, 331, 360, 370, 379.
—— Isabella Dick, 345, 380.
—— John Edward Arthur Dick, 380.
—— Julia Jane Dick, 380.
—— Maddalena Dick, 345, 380.
—— Margaret Louisa Dick, 380.
—— Stair Dick, 380.
—— Susanna Dick, 373, 379.
Leader Haughs, 253.
—— river, 253, 258, 268.
Leprosy, 265.
Lerwick, 41, 43.
Leslie, Miss Charles, 2nd wife of William Dick, and Baron of Grange, 65, 409.
—— Janet, first wife of William Dick of Grange, 48.
—— Jean, wife of Sir Andrew Dick of Craighouse, 37, 94, 100.
—— Sir John, of Newton, 66, 93, 409.
—— Robert, of Kinclaven, 66.
Libel case, 403, 404, 405, 406.
Liberton, 2, 28.
Lindisfarne, 7.
Lindsay, Rev. David, 36.
—— Sir David, 18, 26, 215.
Little, William, Provost, 17, 383.
Loadstar Directory, 399-403.
Lochiel, 71, 81.
Loch Leven, 40, 149.
Lockhart, Alexander, Lord Covington, 101.
—— Rebecca, 101, 105.
Logan, James, 23.
Loudon, Lord High Chancellor, 52, 389, 390.
Lowis, Alexander, 99.
—— Ninian, 99.
Luckenbooths, 50, 51.
Lundie, Sir Richard, 155.

MACBETH, 153.
M'Dougall, Anne, of Mackerstoun, 279, 281.
—— Mary, 274, 275, 408.
—— Sir William, of Mackerston, 280.
Mackenzie, Anne, Lady Dick of Prestonfield, 126-8.
—— Sir George, King's Advocate, 116, 126, 246.
—— Sir James, of Royston, 127.
Mackelligan, William, 326.
Maclellan, tutor of Bomby, 226, 227.
M'Math, Isabella, 386, 387.
— — Janet, Lady Grange, 48, 59, 66-8, 385, 386.

M'Math, Hector, 387.
—— Marion, 386, 387.
—— Sara, 336, 387.
Maggie Lauder, 211, 212.
Maidment, James, 2, 15.
Maitland, Chancellor, 258.
—— Charles, Lord Halton, 3rd Earl of Lauderdale, 245, 246, 252, 256, 258, 408.
—— James, of Auchinchamper, 280, 281.
—— John, Archbishop of St. Andrews, 203.
—— Sir John, of Thirlestane, 238, 239.
—— John, Duke of Lauderdale, 122, 245, 246, 298, 299.
—— Marie, 239, 240, 241, 252.
—— Sir Richard, of Lethington, the 'Blind Baron,' 239, 252, 273.
—— Sir William, of Lethington, Queen Mary's Secretary, 258.
Malcolm Canmore, 3, 153, 171, 254, 260.
Malmo, 34.
Mar, Earl of, 96.
Market Cross, Lauder, 262.
—— —— Ormiston, 310.
—— —— Pencaitland, 314.
Mary of Guelder, 224.
—— of Guise and Lorraine, 180, 191, 231, 274, 407.
—— Stuart, 131, 366, 377.
Maxwell, Sir John, of Pollok, 300.
—— Lady, 302.
—— Margaret, wife of David Lauder, of Huntly Wood, 300, 302.
Meadows, The, 6, 340.
Medina, Duke de, 144.
Melrose Abbey, 235.
Melville, Andrew, 204.
Menteith, Sir John, 156, 160.
Mercat Cross of Edinburgh, 81, 112, 118, 295, 297.
Merchiston Castle, 6, 9, 12.
Mersintoun, 177, 196.
Miller, Hugh, 325; becomes acquainted with Sir Thomas Dick Lauder, 325; describes the fire at Old Greyfriars, 347; letters from Cromarty, 349-354.
Mineral springs, 312,
Modena, Mary d'Este de, 116.
Monastery of the Holy Cross, 3.
—— of Tyninghame, 217, 220.
Monboddo, Lord, 142.
Money transference, 176.
Monk's seat, 333, 344.
Monk's Walk, 373.
Mons Meg, 115, 228.
Moor, Loch, 19.
Moray, James, Earl of, 34.
—— Regent, 33, 193, 194, 399.
Morayshire Floods, 320-325.
Moresoun, Elizabeth, 28, 38, 47, 53.
—— John, 24, 38.

Morrison, Henry, 38.
—— Sir John, of Dairsie, 39.
Morton, Earl of (Earl of Orkney), 93.
—— Earl of, and Regent Moray, 193, 194.
—— Robert, 8th Earl of, 39, 40.
—— William, 7th Earl, 39, 40.
—— —— 9th Earl, 39.
Morvill, or Moorvill, Hugh de, 254, 255, 272.
Moorvill, William, Constable of Scotland, 255.
Mowbray, Sir Robert, of Barnbougle, 97.
Muircleuch, 239, 259, 285.
Murray, John, Secretary to Prince Charles, 78, 80.
—— Sir Robert, 112.
Myreton, Sir Andrew, of Gogar, 396, 397.

NAIRNE, FRANCISCA, 41.
Napier, or Naper, family, 9.
—— Alexander, of Lauriston, 30.
—— Sir Alexander, of Merchiston, Master of the Mint, 23.
—— Sir Archibald, 29, 37.
—— Elizabeth, sub-prioress, 17.
—— Janet, 269.
—— John, of Chamboudie, 30.
—— Sir John, of Merchiston, 23, 29.
—— Margaret, wife of James Stewart of Rosyth, 30.
—— William, of Wrychteshouses, Constable of Edinburgh Castle, 9.
—— —— 4th Baron of Merchiston, 222.
Newbotle, 94, 95.
Niddry, 229, 377, 378.
Nisbet of Dean, 29, 407.
—— of Dirleton, 290.
Nor' Loch, 4, 6, 302.
Norrie, James, panel painter, 105.
North Berwick, 107, 108, 109, 182.
—— Bridge, 306.
—— field, 41.
—— Ronaldshay, 36,
Norton, 166, 230, 231, 237, 241.
Nunnery of St. Katherine, 15, 16.

OATH of a knight, 159.
Ogilvy, George, 4th Lord Banff, 300.
—— Helen, wife of Sir Robert Lauder of Bielmouth, 300.
—— Lady Mary Hamilton, 300.
Old stones, 363, 365.
Order of the Star of France, 216.
Orkney, 32, 33, 34, 40.
—— Dukedom of, 34.
—— Earl of, 34, 37.
—— Earldom of, 38.
—— Sheriff of, 94.
Ormiston, 310.
Ormond, Hugh, Earl of, 229.
Oronsay, 36.
Otterburn, Thomas, of Reidhall, 182.
Over-Braid, 48.

INDEX 425

Over-Gogar, 235, 237, 241.
—— Grange, 52.
—— Redstoune, 230.
—— Sanct-Geilie-Grange, 68.
Oxenfoord Castle, 340.

PAPAL Bull, 4; seal, 372.
Parallel Roads of Glenroy, 355, 356.
Parish Church of St. Giles, 2, 6.
Parliament Square, 144.
Paterson, Andrew, of Dunmore, 113.
—— Dame Anne, 113, 120, 132.
—— Janet, 231, 232.
Pavilion, 340.
Peaston Burn, 289.
Poebles, 32, 230.
Pencaitland, 159, 310, 314, 315.
Penny Well, 366, 367.
Phantassie, 360, 379.
Phantom lady, 99.
Picardy, 229, 249.
Pit and gallows, 3, 153.
Pitcairn, 96.
Pitmedden, 69, 70.
Pius II., 26.
Playfair, W. H., architect, 322, 327.
Plewlands, 47.
Pluscarden Priory, 354.
Pontage, 267.
Pope Benedict XIII., 169.
Pope's effigy, 119.
Popill, 154, 155, 196.
Porteous, Captain, 304.
—— George, herald painter, 101, 105.
Portraits, Grange House, 409.
Preston, David, 11th Baron of Craigmillar, 183.
Prestonfield Manor, 126, 130, 131, 135.
Prestongrange, 38.
Prestoun, Margaret, 23, 24.
—— Sir Simon, of Craigmillar, Provost, 23, 38, 383.
Priestfield, 2, 7.
Prince Albert, 342, 343, 344, 345, 346.
Prince Charlie. *See* Charles Edward.
Princess Anne, afterwards Queen of England, 117.
—— Cicely, 174, 177.
—— Johanna, 161.
—— Margaret of Norway, 34.
Pringill, Robert, W.S., 29.
Pringle, Catherine, 95.
—— David, 272.
—— family, 312.
Prisons of the Bass, 199, 292.
Provost of St. Magnus, 32.
Provosts, 9, 19, 38, 233, 383, App.

QUARRELWOOD, 162, 164.
Queen Caroline, 127.
—— Margaret, 2.

Queen Mary, 32, 97, 131, 178, 181, 193, 195, 366, 377.
—— Mary's watch, 369.
—— Victoria, 342, 343, 344, 345, 346.
Queen's Drive, 358.
Quhitslaid (Whitslaid), 230.
Quhytlawis (Whitlaw), 238.
Quiraing, 356.

RAE, BISHOP, 169.
—— Cristane, 23.
—— John, 23.
Raith, 336.
Ramsay, Sir Andrew, of Abbotshall, 198, 270, 294, 295, 296.
—— of Balmain, 268, 269, 270.
—— David, of Hillhead, 277, 278.
—— George, of Iddington, 290, 291, 292.
—— Janet, wife of Lord Fountainhall, 291, 294, 297, 304.
—— Janet, of Polton, 277, 289, 301.
—— Margaret, 3rd wife of Baillie Lauder, 290, 291, 292, 293, 300, 403, 404, 405, 406.
—— Sir John, 96.
Randolph, Thomas, Earl of Moray, 159-161, 329.
Ratho, 166, 168, 241.
Rattle, 336.
Ravensbee, 25.
Ravenscraig Castle, 34.
Redpath, Thomas, of that Ilk, 279.
Reform Bill, 339, 349.
—— Jubilee, 339.
Regality, grant of, 264.
Reid, Robert, Bishop of Orkney, 33.
Relics of St. Giles, 384, 385, App.
Relugas, 302, 308, 309, 316, 317, 318, 319, 320, 322, 324, 325, 326.
Renfrew, Baron of, 165, 166.
Restalrig, 183, 185.
Rhymer, Thomas the, 253.
Ricardistoun, 7, 8.
Riccio, David, 230.
Riding the marches, 261.
Rigg of Riggsland, 249.
Robert II., 7, 167.
—— III., 189.
—— Bruce, 7, 159, 160, 161, 255, 260.
Robertson, Dr. William, Principal of the University, 84; greets Dr. Johnson, 85; resides at the Grange House, 85; Lord Cockburn's description of him, 86; his Disquisition, 351; his death, 87, 351; his tomb, 87.
——, Rev. William, 84.
Rob the Ranter, 212.
Rocheid, Helen, 109.
—— Sir James, of Inverleith, Bart., 109.
Rognvald, Jarl, 33, 34.
Ronaldshay, 36.
Rose noble, 185, 260.
Rosebery, Archibald, Earl of, 340.

Ross, Andrew, Chamberlain, 61.
—— Hugh, Earl of Orkney, 161.
Rosythe, 30, 36.
Rothes, Andrew, 4th Earl of, 66, 93.
Roxburgh Castle, 229.
Roxburghe, Duchess of, 314.
—— Lord, 121.
Royal Levee, 344.
—— Progress, 342, 345, 346.
—— Squadron, 342.
—— Standard, 12.
Royston, 127.
Ruthven, Lady, of Winton Castle, 314.

SANCT-GEILL (Giles or Egidius), 2, 20.
—— Geilie Grange (Gelygrange), 2, 4, 5, 8, 13, 18, 19, 21, 46, 92, 304, 327, 331.
Scalloway Castle, 35.
Sciennes, 18, 23.
Scots Sea, 268.
Scott, Alexander, poet, 237.
—— Gen. John, of Balcomie, 102.
—— Michael, 235.
—— —— the Wizard Baron of Balwearie, 235.
—— Patrick, 235.
—— of Rossie, 101.
—— of Scotstarvit, 248.
—— Sir Walter, 55, 87, 88, 89, 90, 91, 257, 353.
—— Sir William, of Balwery, 235.
—— William, of Dalkeith, 277.
Seton, Sir Alexander de, 163.
—— —— —— of Pitmedden, 69, 300, 303, 409.
—— Dame Anne, 69, 71, 72, 74, 304, 409.
—— Chapel, 16, 72, 73.
—— Chronicle, 16.
—— Lady Elizabeth, 69, 409.
—— George, Lord, 315.
—— —— 3rd Lord, 16.
—— —— 4th Lord, 17.
—— —— 5th Lord, 16.
—— —— 6th Lord, 17.
—— —— 7th Lord, 377.
—— Lady Janet, 16, 18.
—— Isobel, 72, 74, 328, 409.
—— Jean, 72, 74, 409.
—— Sir John, of Pitmedden, 69.
—— Katherine, 16, 17.
—— Margaret, 300, 303, 304, 409.
—— Mary, 17, 97.
—— Palace, 16.
Setons of Parbroath, 290, 407.
Scytoun, Catherine, 17.
—— Lady Isabella, 242.
Sharpe, Charles Kirkpatrick, of Hoddam, 18, 364.
Sheriff of Berwickshire, 271, 275.
—— Depute of Orkney, 38, 39, 94.
Shetland, 37.
Sibbald, Sir Robert, 246.
Sienn, modes of spelling, 19.

Simon Roy, 317.
Sinclair, Adam, 7th Laird of Brew, 48.
—— of Roslyn, 15.
Sinclare, Maister Johne, 299.
Sisters of the Convent of St. Katherine, 17, 18, 29, 377.
Skorrie, 41.
Slaines Castle, 102.
Slough Dogs, 176.
Smith, George, of Relugas, 326.
Solan geese, 191, 192, 195, 202.
Solangoosifera Act, 193.
Soltra, or Soutra, 171, 172.
South Ronaldshay, 40.
Speirs, Margaret, 290.
Spence, Elizabeth, 99.
—— John, 99.
St. Ann's Yards, 339.
—— Baldred, 181, 189, 190, 191, 217.
—— Baldred's Church at Tyninghame, 205, 207, 217, 218, 219, 221.
—— Clair, Henry, 2nd Earl of Orkney, 189.
—— Clair, William, 34.
—— Giles, 20.
—— James's Court, 126, 139.
—— John's Chapel, 13, 14, 15.
—— John's of Corstorphine, 5.
—— Katherine of Siena, 15, 18.
—— Leonard's, 255, 285.
—— Leonard's Crags, 5.
—— Magnus, 32, 33, 34.
—— Mary's in the Fields, 118.
—— Ronald, 33.
—— Roque, 9, 10, 11, 13.
Stair, Earl of, 340, 379.
Stevinsoun, Andrew, 27.
—— John, 27.
Stewart, James, of Rosythe, 30.
—— Sir John, of Traquair, 193.
—— Master Ludovick, advocate, 29.
—— Margaret, 36.
—— Margaret, 2nd wife of John Knox, 48.
—— Patrick, Earl of Orkney, 33, 35.
—— Robert, Earl of Orkney, 34, 35, 37, 40.
Stirling Bridge, 156.
—— Elizabeth, of Keir, 29.
Stocks, 313, 314.
'Stoney Sunday,' 49.
Stow, 259, 262.
Studites, 14.
Subterranean passage, Craighouse, 95; Grange House, 374.
Sully, Sire de, 160.
Swans, 122.
Swynset, 167.
Sycamore tree, 128.
Sydserf, Helen, 297.
Sydserf, John, of Collegehead, 110, 397.
Sylvius, Æneas, 26.

INDEX 427

Tait's Magazine, 331, 358.
Tantallon Castle, 99, 165, 210, 216.
Tarlxt, Viscount, 127.
Taylor, John, the Water Poet, 192.
Taymouth Castle, 345.
Tea, 117.
Templar Stone, 221.
Temple Hall, 289.
Test Oath, 296, 297.
Thirlestane Castle, 165, 245, 257, 258, 280, 281.
—— John, Lord, 242, 280.
—— Mains, 232.
Thistle, Prince Charlie's, 74.
Thomson, Alexander, of Duddingston, 24.
—— Thomas, of Duddingston, 29.
—— Rev. John, Scottish landscape-painter, Duddingston, 318, 338.
Thrieve Castle, 226, 228.
Tolbooth, Edinburgh, 119.
—— Lauder, 261, 262, 275, 276, 277.
Toll, 267.
Tower-Garden, 254, 282.
Tranent, 77.
Trotter, Doctor, 291.
—— of Mortonhall, 200.
Tyndall, Professor, 355, 356.
Tyninghame Church. See St. Baldred's
—— Manor, 196, 203, 204, 210.
—— Manse, 206, 207, 209.
—— Records, 207, 208, 209, 211.
—— Village, 205, 212, 219, 220, 221.

UDDERT, Alexander, Dean of Guild, 28.
Udiesland, 41.
Udny, 69.
Umfraville, Godfrey, 216.
Unicorn, seal, 234.
Upper Keith, 78.
Urquhart Castle, 162, 163, 165.
Uthward. See Edward.

VAUGHAN, Robert, 55, 56.
—— William, 56.
Vere, Lord of, 31.
Via Vaccarum, 8.
Vicar of St. Giles, 2, 9.
Victoria Cross, 136.
—— Hall, 344.
Viking Jarls, 33.
Vipont, Alan, 162.
Vitrified fort, 318.

WADDELL, Rev. Hately, 206, 217, 219.
Wallace, Sir William, 126, 151, 155, 156, 169.
Wallas, 40.
Ward Hill, 43.
Wardlaw, Andrew, of Warynstoun, 7.
—— Sir Andrew, Knt., of Torrie, 7.

Wardlaw, Gilbert de, 7.
—— James, of Ricardtoun, 8, 110.
—— Walter, Bishop of St. Andrews, 189.
—— —— —— Glasgow, 7.
Warrender, George, of Lochend, 249, 250.
—— Sir George, 6th Bart. of Bruntisfield, 249, 251.
—— Right Hon. Sir George, M.P., 250.
—— Hugh, 250.
—— Miss Margaret, 249.
Warriestoun, 18, 19.
Watch-dogs, 265.
Webster, Dr., 145.
Wedderburn, Sir Alexander, of Blackness, 69, 245.
—— —— poet, 245.
—— Sir David, Bart., 248.
—— Sir John, 71, 81, 409.
Weir, Grizel, 299.
—— Major, Wizard of the West Bow, 299
Wester Common Moor, 27, 28.
—— Duddingston, 24.
West Grange, 369.
—— Newton, 64.
White Hart, 5.
—— Horse Close, 140.
Whitehouse Loan, 85.
Whitekirk, 206, 211, 220.
Whitlaw, 262.
Whittinghame, 154, 207.
Whytslaid, or Whitslaid, 165, 279.
William the Lion, 260, 267.
Will of the West Port, 260, 275, 277, 289.
Wilson, Sir Daniel, 6, 232, 233, 364.
—— Mr. James, 342.
—— Professor (Christopher North), 342, 350.
Windmills, 36.
Wine customs, 37.
Winton Castle, 314, 315.
—— Earl of, 121.
Wishart, George, martyr, 181, 190.
—— of Pitarrow, 194.
Wishing Stone, 369.
—— Well, 313.
Witchcraft, 299, 300.
Witness newspaper, 334, 362.
Wolfaard Van Borselle, 31.
Woodhall, 310.
Wormadale, 61.
Wormistoun, 166, 230, 234.
Wrychtishouses, 9.

YARMOUTH, 121.
Yester, Lady, 21.
York, Duke of, 115, 116, 117, 120, 121.
Young, Elizabeth, 283, 284.

ZETLAND, 34.
—— lordships of, 40.

www.ingramcontent.com/pod-product-compliance
Lightning Source LLC
Chambersburg PA
CBHW021419300426
44114CB00010B/566